ASP.NET MVC
with Entity Framework
and CSS

Lee Naylor

Apress®

ASP.NET MVC with Entity Framework and CSS

Lee Naylor
Newton-le-Willows, Merseyside
United Kingdom

ISBN-13 (pbk): 978-1-4842-2136-5   ISBN-13 (electronic): 978-1-4842-2137-2
DOI 10.1007/978-1-4842-2137-2

Library of Congress Control Number: 2016952810

Managing Director: Welmoed Spahr
Lead Editor: Celestin Suresh John
Development Editor: Laura Berendson
Technical Reviewer: Fabio Ferracchiati
Editorial Board: Steve Anglin, Pramila Balan, Laura Berendson, Aaron Black, Louise Corrigan, Jonathan Gennick, Robert Hutchinson, Celestin Suresh John, Nikhil Karkal, James Markham, Susan McDermott, Matthew Moodie, Natalie Pao, Gwenan Spearing
Coordinating Editor: Nancy Chen
Copy Editor: Kezia Endsley
Compositor: SPi Global
Indexer: SPi Global
Artist: SPi Global

Distributed to the book trade worldwide by Springer Science+Business Media New York, 233 Spring Street, 6th Floor, New York, NY 10013. Phone 1-800-SPRINGER, fax (201) 348-4505, e-mail orders-ny@springer-sbm.com, or visit www.springer.com. Apress Media, LLC is a California LLC and the sole member (owner) is Springer Science + Business Media Finance Inc (SSBM Finance Inc). SSBM Finance Inc is a **Delaware** corporation.

For information on translations, please e-mail rights@apress.com, or visit www.apress.com.

Apress and friends of ED books may be purchased in bulk for academic, corporate, or promotional use. eBook versions and licenses are also available for most titles. For more information, reference our Special Bulk Sales–eBook Licensing web page at www.apress.com/bulk-sales.

Any source code or other supplementary materials referenced by the author in this text are available to readers at www.apress.com. For detailed information about how to locate your book's source code, go to www.apress.com/source-code/. Readers can also access source code at SpringerLink in the Supplementary Material section for each chapter.

I would like to dedicate this book to two special women in my life; my late mother Pauline, who sadly passed away while I was drafting the first few chapters, and my wife, Michelle. To Mum, thanks for always being there for me and I miss you every day, and to Michelle, thanks for all your support during difficult times, for giving me our wonderful son Peter, and for finding my best friend, our dog Chocky.

Contents at a Glance

Contents

About the Author

Lee Naylor is a software engineer from Manchester in the United Kingdom with expertise in programming and Agile project management. He spends his free time with his family, playing football (soccer) and golf.

About the Technical Reviewer

Fabio Claudio Ferracchiati is a senior consultant and a senior analyst/developer using Microsoft technologies. He works at BluArancio S.p.A (www.bluarancio.com) as a senior analyst/developer and Microsoft dynamics CRM specialist. He is a Microsoft Certified Solution Developer for .NET, a Microsoft Certified Application Developer for .NET, a Microsoft Certified Professional, and a prolific author and technical reviewer. Over the past 10 years, he's written articles for Italian and international magazines and co-authored more than 10 books on a variety of computer topics.

Acknowledgments

I want to thank everyone I've worked with at Apress for their help in taking an idea and turning it into a reality. In particular, I want to thank Nancy Chen for keeping everything moving along, and to former Apress employee James DeWolf, for taking me on in the first place.

I'd like to thank my wife (again) for all her support and putting up with my lack of time and my day-dreaming about how to code something when she's trying to have a real-life conversation with me about nappies.

Introduction

I decided to write this book for people who learn by doing. I've read several software books over the years where you can read the whole book and learn many things but never quite put the full pieces of the jigsaw together. This book aims to allow the user to follow a step-by-step guide to learn how to use ASP.NET MVC with Entity Framework, while sticking to all the main topics you will encounter in everyday work scenarios, without focusing on academic details that very few people will ever use. I've tried to keep things relatively close to real life in the book, which is why I chose to make a baby store, but the examples can be applied to almost any type of shopping web site or indeed any web site driven by a database. I've also included a redesign of the site, including several popular CSS topics to recognize the fact that these days web developers need to be competent in front-end development too.

The book starts with an introduction to Microsoft ASP.NET MVC and then quickly progresses into showing you how to create a database driven web site, and from this how to enhance the site and use some of Entity Framework's more advanced features. I'll show you how to work with related tables and data, how to create and update a database schema, and how to populate data from your code.

I also cover how to use Microsoft Identity to add some user authentication and authorization to the site along with roles, and how to manage both of these. You'll also learn how to deploy to Azure to allow your site run over the Internet.

The latter part of the book focuses on restyling the web site using CSS, with an introduction to jQuery thrown in, with the goal of this section being to get you up and running from basic to advanced CSS as quickly as possible.

The book mainly covers using ASP.NET MVC 5 with Entity Framework 6, which are the most widely used versions at the time of writing; however, it also includes an introduction to ASP.NET core and shows you how to create a basic web site and database.

The full source code for the examples shown in the book is available for download from `http://www.apress.com`.

CHAPTER 1

▓ ▓ ▓

Building a Basic MVC Web Site

In this first chapter, you'll learn how to quickly get up and running with Microsoft ASP.NET MVC by building a simple web site using scaffolding.

Before we jump right in and start coding, I'll provide some simple background information on ASP.NET MVC and Entity Framework and go over the details of how to set up a development environment.

MVC and ASP.NET MVC

This book covers Microsoft's version of MVC, namely ASP.NET MVC. At the time of writing the production version of ASP.NET MVC is 5 and this is what has been used in the examples in this book. There is also a chapter covering ASP.NET Core 1.0 MVC (MVC 6).

MVC stands for Model-View-Controller and is a recognized design pattern for developing software applications. ASP.NET MVC based applications are made up of:

- **Models**—These are classes that model the data of the application. They are often referred to as POCOs which stands for Plain Old CLR Objects. These classes are also used to model and enforce any business logic such as shopping basket logic, as you will see later.

- **Views**—These are templated files that generate HTML to be sent to the web browser. A view typically deals with displaying data from a model. Views should not contain any business logic, although they can contain logic for making decisions on what HTML to generate.

- **Controllers**—These are classes that process incoming requests, obtain data model data, and typically return this data to a view for displaying as HTML. Controllers may contain logic for filtering data based on information sent by the request. For example, the code in the controller can be used to generate queries based on parameters passed into a method by a request.

The examples in this book will help broaden your understanding of the definitions for models, views, and controllers and where appropriate to use more advanced concepts such as view models.

MVC has its origins from the Smalltalk (a precursor to Java) project from the late 70s and since then has been adapted and used in several technologies. The main principles behind MVC are to build applications that are architected with distinct layers, testable, and maintainable. One of the features of MVC is that is lends itself to unit testing thanks to the separation between models, views, and controllers. Unit testing is not covered in this book but for a comprehensive overview of using unit testing within ASP.NET MVC applications I recommend that you read Adam Freeman's *PRO ASP.NET MVC* book series.

Electronic supplementary material The online version of this chapter (doi:10.1007/978-1-4842-2137-2_1) contains supplementary material, which is available to authorized users.

© Lee Naylor 2016

L. Naylor, *ASP.NET MVC with Entity Framework and CSS*, DOI 10.1007/978-1-4842-2137-2_1

Entity Framework and Code First

Entity Framework (EF) is an object relational mapping (ORM) framework produced by Microsoft as part of the .NET framework. Throughout this book, Entity Framework is used in a Code First approach enabling developers to write classes and relationships between them in code in order to model and build a database without writing any SQL. The current available version of EF is 6 and this is what is used for the code in the book; however, there is also a chapter on using EF 7 with MVC 6 (part of ASP.NET Core 1.0). All the examples in this book use SQL Server but Entity Framework can also be used with other relational databases such as Oracle.

Using Code First with an Existing Database

As mentioned, Code First is an approach to using Entity Framework where the model is first developed in code classes. This is an ideal approach for new projects where no database exists; however, from EF 6.1 upward, Code First can also be used with existing databases by generating classes based on the existing database. This topic is covered in depth later in the book.

Software Required for Web Site Development

The software required for this book is Visual Studio 2015 Community Edition. This is available to download for free from Microsoft. It contains virtually all the features of the Visual Studio 2015 paid editions and was used to develop all the software shown in this book. A web browser is also required, and the examples in this book were all developed and tested using Google Chrome as the primary browser, due to the fact that it offers excellent developer tools. I also recommend using a Windows PC to run Visual Studio on with at least 4GB of RAM.

Visual Studio 2015 Community edition is available to download from `https://www.visualstudio.com/en-us/downloads/download-visual-studio-vs.aspx`.

■ **Note**   When you install Visual Studio 2015 Community SQL LocalDB should automatically be included in your installation; however, on Windows 10 this does not appear to be the case and it may be necessary to install LocalDB separately. SQL Server Express can be downloaded from `https://www.microsoft.com/en-US/download/details.aspx?id=42299`.

Creating the Project

The first thing we need to do when creating a web site using ASP.NET MVC and Entity Framework is to create a new project in Visual Studio. Start by selecting File ➤ New ➤ Project from the Visual Studio menu bar. Then from the New Project window, ensure you select Installed ➤ Templates ➤ Visual C# ➤ Web and then select the ASP.NET Web Application type of project, as shown in Figure 1-1. Choose .NET Framework 4.6.1 as the version of .NET.

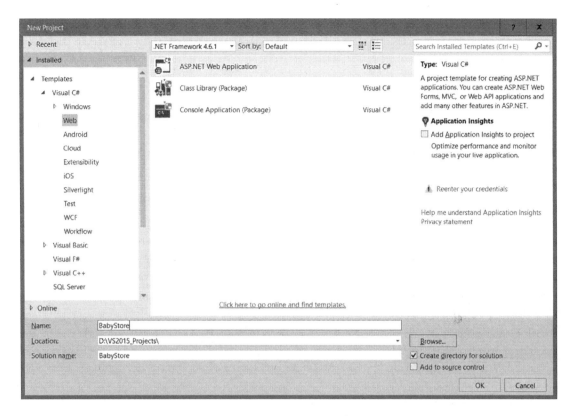

Figure 1-1. *Choosing the ASP ➤ NET Web Application type*

Name the project BabyStore and click OK to continue. You will see another window, as shown in Figure 1-2. In this window, select MVC from the ASP.NET 4.6.1 Templates and ensure the authentication is set to Individual User Accounts.

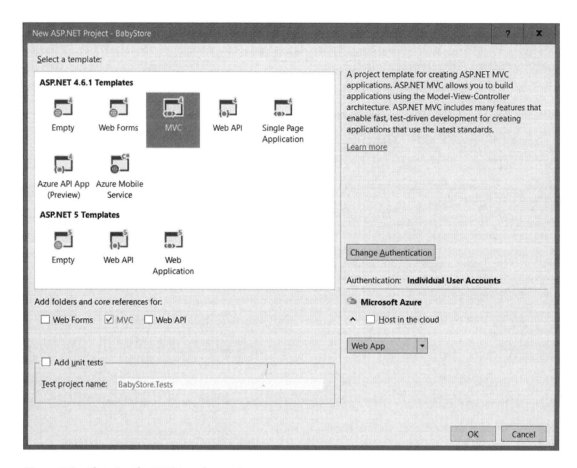

Figure 1-2. *Choosing the MVC template option*

Click OK to create the project. Once the project is created, you should see a page with large text entitled "Your ASP.NET Application". Close this file as we won't be using it. Look at the Solution Explorer window to the right of Visual Studio. Visual Studio uses a process known as *scaffolding* to generate a basic MVC project automatically. We will use this as a starting point to develop our project.

In Solution Explorer, expand the Controllers, Models, and Views folders, as shown in Figure 1-3. The models created are used later in the project for authentication. In this chapter, we will examine the HomeController class and some of its associated views.

Figure 1-3. Solution Explorer with expanded Controllers, Models, and Views folders

Viewing the Web Site

From the Visual Studio menu, choose Debug ➤ Start Without Debugging and the web site will open in the browser you have assigned Visual Studio to use, as shown in Figure 1-4. To change the browser, choose a different browser from the drop-down list in the second line of the Visual Studio menu bar.

■ **Note**   The web site will run on a random port number assigned by Visual Studio. The URL will appear in a form `http://localhost:port/Controller/View/additionalparameters`. When the web site starts up, it does not show the Controller or View in the URL, and in this case it defaults to use the Index View called by the Home Controller's `Index` method.

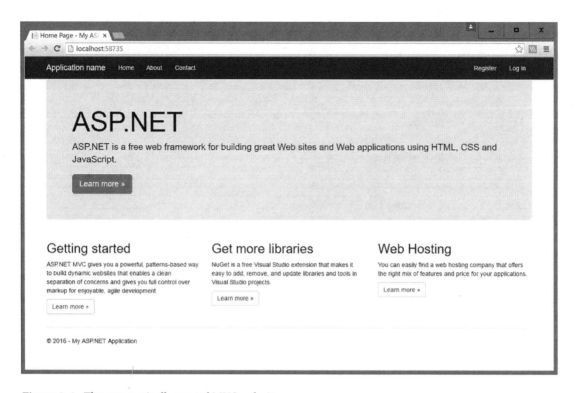

Figure 1-4. *The automatically created MVC web site*

How the Home Page Works

The home page in Figure 1-4 is shown because the web site made a request to the URL /Home/Index. Although this is not shown in the web browser's address bar, it's used by default when the application launches. If you add /Home/Index to the end of the URL, the page displayed will not change.

The URL tells the MVC web application that a request has been made to the Index action method of the Home Controller. The method is found in the HomeController.cs file, as shown in the following code listing. This method contains a simple line of code return View() and this tells the web site to open the corresponding view file. In this case, the corresponding view file is found under Views\Home\Index.cshtml. By convention, this is how ASP.NET MVC projects work with the default view for a controller method found in the Views\ControllerName\MethodName.cshtml path. It is of course possible to make a method open a different view and we will see how to do this later in the book. The contents of the file Controllers\ HomeController.cs including the Index method is as follows:

```
using System;
using System.Collections.Generic;
using System.Linq;
using System.Web;
using System.Web.Mvc;

namespace BabyStore.Controllers
{
    public class HomeController : Controller
    {
        public ActionResult Index()
```

```
    {
        return View();
    }

    public ActionResult About()
    {
        ViewBag.Message = "Your application description page.";

        return View();
    }

    public ActionResult Contact()
    {
        ViewBag.Message = "Your contact page.";

        return View();
    }
    }
}
```

The Views\Home\Index.cshtml file contains the HTML corresponding to the text shown in the home page. In this file you will see several HTML elements with classes assigned to them. The classes are Bootstrap CSS classes and they control the layout of the home page. I will cover some of the ways to style Bootstrap later in the book plus a comprehensive review of how to restyle the web site completely without Bootstrap.

The About and Contact Pages and ViewBag

Ignoring the links for Register and Login, there are links to two other pages in the web site menu: About and Contact. These links target the URLs /Home/About and /Home/Contact.

These two pages follow the same convention as before, meaning that the About and Contact methods of the HomeController.cs are called and they load the views found in Views\Home\About.cshtml and Views\ Home\Contact.cshtml, respectively.

If you examine the two methods for About and Contact in the previous code listing, you will see that there are some additional lines of code that make use of the ViewBag.

The About method includes the code ViewBag.Message = "Your application description page."; and the Contact method includes ViewBag.Message = "Your contact page."; both of which are then displayed in the respective views.

For example, if you look at the code for the About.cshtml file, it contains the code <h3>@ViewBag. Message</h3>, which the view uses to display the contents of the ViewBag's Message property. When this is displayed by a web browser, the page renders showing the string "Your application description page", as shown in Figure 1-5.

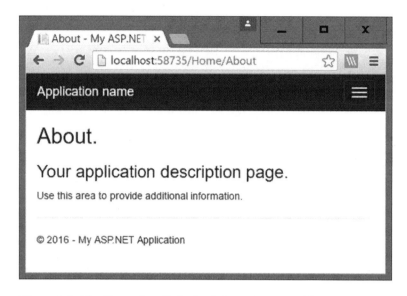

Figure 1-5. *The About view displaying information passed from the controller via the ViewBag*

ViewBag is a dynamic object and is one way of passing data to a view. It is not recommended for passing several pieces of data into a view because of its dynamic nature. ViewBag is not strongly typed, meaning that it can contain any random data and, therefore, when you're using it in coding a view, there is no IntelliSense available. The recommended practice is to use a strongly typed view model to pass several pieces of data to a view at once. I cover this in Chapter 3.

Routing: How the Web Site Knows Which Controllers and Methods to Request

ASP.NET MVC uses ASP.NET routing to control how the application translates URLs. It also controls which controllers and methods the incoming HTTP requests target and hence which views to display. To explain how this works we'll examine the default route that was set up when we created the application.

Open the file RouteConfig.cs file, which is located in the App_Start folder. The code contained in this file defines rules that the application uses to target the correct controller and method depending on the URL entered into the web browser. The code listing is as follows:

```
using System;
using System.Collections.Generic;
using System.Linq;
using System.Web;
using System.Web.Mvc;
using System.Web.Routing;

namespace BabyStore
{
    public class RouteConfig
    {
        public static void RegisterRoutes(RouteCollection routes)
        {
            routes.IgnoreRoute("{resource}.axd/{*pathInfo}");
```

```
        routes.MapRoute(
            name: "Default",
            url: "{controller}/{action}/{id}",
            defaults: new { controller = "Home", action = "Index", id =
                UrlParameter.Optional }
        );
    }
  }
}
```

The code that we are interested in is the routes.MapRoute method. This defines a route named "Default" as per line 17. The code url: "{controller}/{action}/{id}" instructs the site to expect the controller name first, followed by the action (which matches up with the method name in the controller), and then a third segment of the URL called id. We'll cover the id segment shortly but first we'll focus on the controller and action segments.

The third entry named defaults tells the application what to target when there is no controller or action specified in the URL. This default entry tells the application to target the Index method of the Home Controller, which in turn calls the Views\Home\Index.cshtml page. This is why this page loads when the site is run with any additional parameters in the URL.

Using the Optional URL ID Parameter

To complete this very simple overview of the default routing setup, we'll alter the site to use the optional ID parameter.

Alter the About method of the Controllers\HomeController.cs file so that it reads as follows:

```
public ActionResult About(string id)
{
    ViewBag.Message = "Your application description page. You entered the ID " + id;

    return View();
}
```

Here we are telling the method to process a parameter passed into it called id. This corresponds with the name of the optional third parameter in the default route. The ASP.NET MVC model binding system is used to automatically map the ID parameter from the URL into the id parameter in the About method. We will cover model binding in more detail later.

Now start the web site without debugging and navigate to the About page. Now add an ID onto the end of the URL such as http://localhost:58735/Home/About/7.

This will then process 7 as the value of the ID parameter and pass this to the About method, which then adds this to the ViewBag for display in the view. The result should be as shown in Figure 1-6.

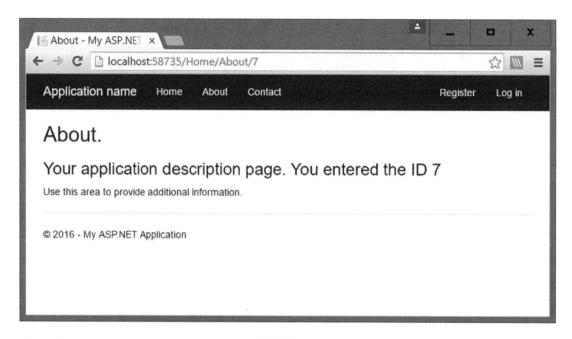

Figure 1-6. *Applying and processing an optional ID URL parameter*

ASP.NET MVC also automatically matches any parameters in the HTTP request to a method parameter if they have the same name. The matching is case insensitive. For example, entering the URL http://localhost:58735/Home/About?id=7 will return the same result as previously, because the id parameter in the query string is automatically mapped to the id parameter in the About method. This is covered in more detail in Chapter 2.

The Purpose of the Layout Page

You will have noticed that when we navigate to different pages, the web site shows the same heading and navigation menu. This is achieved by using a layout page. The layout page used is contained in the file Views\Shared_Layout.cshtml as follows:

```
<!DOCTYPE html>
<html>
<head>
    <meta charset="utf-8" />
    <meta name="viewport" content="width=device-width, initial-scale=1.0">
    <title>@ViewBag.Title - My ASP.NET Application</title>
    @Styles.Render("~/Content/css")
    @Scripts.Render("~/bundles/modernizr")

</head>
<body>
    <div class="navbar navbar-inverse navbar-fixed-top">
        <div class="container">
            <div class="navbar-header">
                <button type="button" class="navbar-toggle" data-toggle="collapse" data-
```

```
                target=".navbar-collapse">
                <span class="icon-bar"></span>
                <span class="icon-bar"></span>
                <span class="icon-bar"></span>
            </button>
            @Html.ActionLink("Application name", "Index", "Home", new { area = "" }, new {
                @class = "navbar-brand" })
        </div>
        <div class="navbar-collapse collapse">
            <ul class="nav navbar-nav">
                <li>@Html.ActionLink("Home", "Index", "Home")</li>
                <li>@Html.ActionLink("About", "About", "Home")</li>
                <li>@Html.ActionLink("Contact", "Contact", "Home")</li>
            </ul>
            @Html.Partial("_LoginPartial")
        </div>
    </div>
</div>
<div class="container body-content">
    @RenderBody()
    <hr />
    <footer>
        <p>&copy; @DateTime.Now.Year - My ASP.NET Application</p>
    </footer>
</div>

@Scripts.Render("~/bundles/jquery")
@Scripts.Render("~/bundles/bootstrap")
@RenderSection("scripts", required: false)
</body>
</html>
```

If you open this file, you will see that it contains HTML elements containing the site navigation. The @ RenderBody() code in the file is responsible for displaying the content of the view being requested.

The web site knows to use the Views\Shared_Layout.cshtml file as the main layout page because of the contents of the Views_ViewStart.cshtml. The MVC framework treats this file as if it belongs to each view and therefore effectively adds its contents to the start of every view. The following code listing shows the content of the _ViewStart.cshtml file, which specifies the layout page to use.

```
@{
    Layout = "~/Views/Shared/_Layout.cshtml";
}
```

■ **Tip** If you want a view not to use the layout page specified in the _ViewStart.cshtml file, add the entry @ { Layout = null; } to the top of the file.

Summary

In this chapter, I gave a very brief overview of ASP.NET MVC and Entity Framework, showed you how to create the project we will use throughout this book, and explained the basics of the web site, including controllers, views, ViewBag, and routing. I've kept this chapter brief since the rest of the book will explain these concepts further and allow you to quickly develop a data driven web site. You'll notice that this chapter does not contain any explanation of models. This is what we will cover in the next chapter, by diving straight in and adding some products and categories to our new baby store site.

CHAPTER 2

■ ■ ■

Creating Views, Controllers, and a Database from Model Classes

In this chapter we will jump right into the project and add some basic model classes for products and categories. We will use these to create a database using Entity Framework Code First. I'll show you how to set up a database context class, specify a connection string, create a database from your code, and add new views and controllers to manage and display the product and category data.

■ **Note**   If you want to follow along with the code in this chapter, you must either have completed Chapter 1 or downloaded Chapter 1's source code from www.apress.com as a starting point.

Adding the Model Classes

Entity Framework Code First allows the creation of a database from classes. To start this chapter we will create two new model classes to represent products and categories. We are going to add a zero or one-to-many relationship between categories and products, where a category may have many products and a product can belong to none or one category.

Right-click the Models folder and choose Add ➤ Class from the menu. Create a new class called Product and add the following code to the class:

```
namespace BabyStore.Models
{
    public class Product
    {
        public int ID { get; set; }
        public string Name { get; set; }
        public string Description { get; set; }
        public decimal Price { get; set; }
        public int? CategoryID { get; set; }
        public virtual Category Category { get; set; }
    }
}
```

Remove all the unnecessary using statements from the top of the file.

© Lee Naylor 2016
L. Naylor, *ASP.NET MVC with Entity Framework and CSS*, DOI 10.1007/978-1-4842-2137-2_2

■ **Tip**   To remove unnecessary using statements, hover over the `using` statements, click on the light bulb that appears, and choose the Remove Unnecessary Usings option.

This file contains the following properties:

- `ID`—Used to represent the ***primary key*** for products in the database.

- `Name`—The name of the product.

- `Description`—A textual description of the product.

- `Price`—Represents the price of the product.

- `CategoryID`—Represents the ID of the category that the product is assigned to. It will be set up as a ***foreign key*** in the database. We have allowed this to be empty by setting the type to `int?` to model the fact that a product does not need to belong to a category. This is crucial to avoid the scenario where, upon deletion of a category, all products in that category are also deleted. By default, Entity Framework enables cascade deletes for on-nullable foreign keys, meaning that if the CategoryID was not nullable, then all the products associated with a category would be deleted when the category was deleted.

- `Category`—A ***navigation property***. Navigation properties contain other entities that relate to this entity so in this case this property will contain the category entity that the product belongs to. If a navigation property can hold multiple entities, it must be defined as a list type. Typically the type used is `ICollection`. Navigation properties are normally defined as virtual so that they can be used in certain functionality such as with Lazy Loading.

■ **Tip**   You can auto-generate properties in a class in Visual Studio by typing `prop` and then pressing Tab.

Next, complete the model classes by adding a new class named `Category` to the `models` folder and then adding the following code to this new class:

```
using System.Collections.Generic;

namespace BabyStore.Models
{
    public class Category
    {
        public int ID { get; set; }
        public string Name { get; set; }
        public virtual ICollection<Product> Products { get; set; }
    }
}
```

Remove all the unnecessary `using` statements from the top of the file. The `Category` class contains the following properties:

- `ID`—The primary key

- `Name`—The name of the category

- Products—A navigational property that will contain all the product entities belonging to a category

Adding a Database Context

The database context is the main class that coordinates Entity Framework functionality for a data model.

Create a new folder in the project named DAL by right-clicking the project (BabyStore) in Solution Explorer. Click Add then New Folder. Now add a new class named StoreContext.cs to the new DAL folder. Update the code in the StoreContext class as follows:

```
using BabyStore.Models;
using System.Data.Entity;

namespace BabyStore.DAL
{
    public class StoreContext:DbContext
    {
        public DbSet<Product> Products { get; set; }
        public DbSet<Category> Categories { get; set; }
    }
}
```

The context class derives from the class System.Data.Entity.DbContext and there is typically one database context class per database, although in more complex projects it is possible to have more. Each DbSet property in the class is known as an Entity Set and each typically corresponds to a table in the database; for example the Products property corresponds to the Products table in our database. The code DbSet<Product> tells Entity Framework to use the Product class to represent a row in the Products table.

Specifying a Connection String

Now we have a database context and some model classes, so we need to tell Entity Framework how to connect to the database. Add a new entry to the connectionStrings section of the main Web.Config file as follows:

```
<connectionStrings>
    <add name="DefaultConnection" connectionString="Data Source=(LocalDb)\MSSQLLocalDB;AttachDbFilename=|DataDirectory|\aspnet-BabyStore-20160203031215.mdf;Initial Catalog=aspnet-BabyStore-20160203031215;Integrated Security=True"
        providerName="System.Data.SqlClient" />
    <add name="StoreContext" connectionString="Data Source=(LocalDB)\MSSQLLocalDB;AttachDbFilename=|DataDirectory|\BabyStore.mdf;Initial Catalog=BabyStore;Integrated Security=True"
providerName="System.Data.SqlClient" />
    </connectionStrings>
```

This new entry tells Entity Framework to connect to a database called BabyStore.mdf in the App_Data folder of our project. I've chosen to store the database here so that it can be copied with the project. AttachDbFilename=|DataDirectory|\BabyStore.mdf; specifies to create the database in the App_Data folder.

An alternative would be to specify the connectionString entry as Data Source=(LocalDB)\MSSQLLocalDB;Initial Catalog=BabyStore.mdf;Integrated Security=True, which would then create the database under the user's folder (normally C:\Users\User on Windows).

The other existing connectionString entry is used for the database that was created automatically at the beginning of the project when we chose the authentication option Individual User Accounts. We will cover the use of this later in the book.

It's also worth noting that you don't need to define a connection string in web.config. If you don't do so, then Entity Framework will use a default one based on the context class.

■ **Note**   Make sure you update the Web.config file in the root of the project and not the one in the Views folder.

Adding Controllers and Views

Now we need to add some controllers and views in order to display and manage our product and category data.

Adding a Category Controller and Views

1. Build the solution by clicking Build ➤ Build Solution from the Visual Studio menu.

2. Right-click the Controllers folder and choose Add ➤ Controller.

3. In the Add Scaffold window, choose the MVC 5 Controller with views option, using Entity Framework (see Figure 2-1).

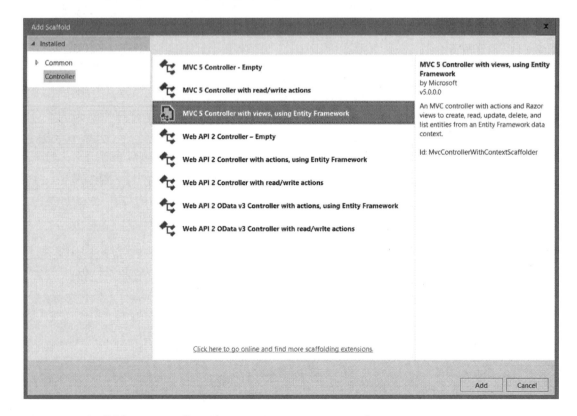

Figure 2-1. *Scaffolding a controller with views using Entity Framework*

4. Click Add and then, in the Add Controller window, choose the following options:

- Model class: Category

- Data Context class: StoreContext

- Ensure that Generate Views, Reference Script Libraries, and Use a Layout Page are all checked

- Leave the controller name set to CategoriesController (see Figure 2-2 for full details)

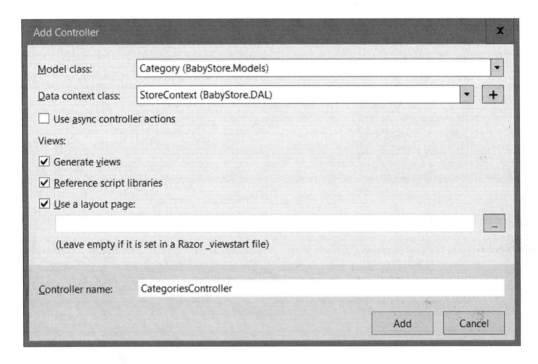

Figure 2-2. *Options for adding a new category controller*

5. Click Add and a new CategoriesController class will be created in the Controllers folder. Corresponding views will also be created in the Views\Categories folder.

Examining the CategoriesController Class and Methods

The newly scaffolded CategoriesController.cs file contains several methods for performing CRUD (Create, Read, Update, and Delete) operations on categories.

The code private StoreContext db = new StoreContext(); instantiates a new context object for use by the controller. This is then used throughout the lifetime of the controller and disposed of by the Dispose method at the end of the controller code.

The new CategoriesController contains the following methods.

The Index method is used to return a list of all the categories to the Views\Categories\Index.cshtml view:

```
// GET: Categories
public ActionResult Index()
{
    return View(db.Categories.ToList());
}
```

The Details method finds a single category from the database based on the id parameter. As you saw in Chapter 1, the id parameter is passed in via the URL using the routing system.

```
// GET: Categories/Details/5
public ActionResult Details(int? id)
{
    if (id == null)
    {
        return new HttpStatusCodeResult(HttpStatusCode.BadRequest);
    }
    Category category = db.Categories.Find(id);
    if (category == null)
    {
        return HttpNotFound();
    }
    return View(category);
}
```

The GET version of the Create method simply returns the Create view. This may seem a little strange at first but what it means is that this returns a view showing a blank HTML form for creating a new category.

```
// GET: Categories/Create
public ActionResult Create()
{
    return View();
}
```

There is another version of the Create method that's used for HTTP POST requests. This method is called when the user submits the form rendered by the Create view. It takes a category as a parameter and adds it to the database. If it's successful it returns the web site to the Index view; otherwise, it reloads the Create view.

```
// POST: Categories/Create
// To protect from overposting attacks, please enable the specific properties you want
to bind to, for
// more details see http://go.microsoft.com/fwlink/?LinkId=317598.
[HttpPost]
[ValidateAntiForgeryToken]
public ActionResult Create([Bind(Include = "ID,Name")] Category category)
{
    if (ModelState.IsValid)
    {
        db.Categories.Add(category);
```

```
        db.SaveChanges();
        return RedirectToAction("Index");
    }

    return View(category);
}
```

Because this method is an HTTP POST, it contains some extra code:

- The [HttpPost] attribute tells the controller that when it receives a POST request for the Create action, it should use this method rather than the other create method.

- [ValidateAntiForgeryToken] ensures that the token passed by the HTML form, thus validating the request . The purpose of this is to ensure that the request actually came from the form it is expected to come from in order to prevent cross-site request forgeries. In simple terms, a cross-site request forgery is a request from a form on another web site to your web site with malicious intentions.

- The parameters ([Bind(Include = "ID,Name")] Category category) tell the method to include only the ID and the Name properties when adding a new category. The Bind attribute is used to protect against overposting attacks by creating a list of safe properties to update; however, as we will discuss later, it does not work as expected and so it is safer to use a different method for editing or creating where some values may be blank. As an example of overposting, consider a scenario where the price is submitted as part of the request when a user submits an order for a product. An overposting attack would attempt to alter this price data by changing the submitted request data in an attempt to buy the product cheaper.

The GET version of the Edit method contains code identical to the Details method. The method finds a category by ID and then returns this to the view. The view is then responsible for displaying the category in a format that allows it to be edited.

```
// GET: Categories/Edit/5
public ActionResult Edit(int? id)
{
    if (id == null)
    {
        return new HttpStatusCodeResult(HttpStatusCode.BadRequest);
    }
    Category category = db.Categories.Find(id);
    if (category == null)
    {
        return HttpNotFound();
    }
    return View(category);
}
```

The POST version of the Edit method is very similar to the POST version of the Create method. It contains an extra line of code to check that the entity has been modified before attempting to save it to the database and, if it's successful, the Index view is returned or else the Edit view is redisplayed:

```
// POST: Categories/Edit/5
// To protect from overposting attacks, please enable the specific properties you want to
bind to, for
```

```
// more details see http://go.microsoft.com/fwlink/?LinkId=317598.
[HttpPost]
[ValidateAntiForgeryToken]
public ActionResult Edit([Bind(Include = "ID,Name")] Category category)
{
    if (ModelState.IsValid)
    {
        db.Entry(category).State = EntityState.Modified;
        db.SaveChanges();
        return RedirectToAction("Index");
    }
    return View(category);
}
```

There are also two versions of the Delete method. ASP.NET MVC scaffolding takes the approach of displaying the entity details to the users and asking them to confirm the deletion before using a form to actually submit the deletion request. The GET version of the Delete method is shown here. You will notice this is very similar to the Details method in that it finds a category by ID and returns it to the view:

```
// GET: Categories/Delete/5
public ActionResult Delete(int? id)
{
    if (id == null)
    {
        return new HttpStatusCodeResult(HttpStatusCode.BadRequest);
    }
    Category category = db.Categories.Find(id);
    if (category == null)
    {
        return HttpNotFound();
    }
    return View(category);
}
```

The POST version of the Delete method performs an anti-forgery check. It then finds the category by ID, removes it, and saves the database changes.

```
// POST: Categories/Delete/5
[HttpPost, ActionName("Delete")]
[ValidateAntiForgeryToken]
public ActionResult DeleteConfirmed(int id)
{
    Category category = db.Categories.Find(id);
    db.Categories.Remove(category);
    db.SaveChanges();
    return RedirectToAction("Index");
}
```

This auto-generated Delete method does not work correctly due to the fact that the product entity contains a foreign key referencing the category entity. See Chapter 4 for how to correct this issue.

▓ **Note** There are several reasons why ASP.NET takes this approach to disallow a GET request to update the database and several comments and debates about the different reasons about the security of doing so; however, one of the key reasons for not doing it is that a search engine spider will crawl public hyperlinks in your web site and potentially be able to delete all the records if there is an unauthenticated link to delete records. Later we will add security to editing categories so that this becomes a moot point.

Examining the Category Views

The views associated with Categories are found in the folder \Views\Categories. There is one view per CRUD action (Details, Create, Edit, and Delete) and an Index view currently used to show a list of all categories.

The Categories Index View

The auto-generated Categories\Views\Index.cshtml view file is as follows:

```
@model IEnumerable<BabyStore.Models.Category>

@{
    ViewBag.Title = "Index";
}

<h2>Index</h2>

<p>
    @Html.ActionLink("Create New", "Create")
</p>
<table class="table">
    <tr>
        <th>
            @Html.DisplayNameFor(model => model.Name)
        </th>
        <th></th>
    </tr>

@foreach (var item in Model) {
    <tr>
        <td>
            @Html.DisplayFor(modelItem => item.Name)
        </td>
        <td>
            @Html.ActionLink("Edit", "Edit", new { id=item.ID }) |
            @Html.ActionLink("Details", "Details", new { id=item.ID }) |
            @Html.ActionLink("Delete", "Delete", new { id=item.ID })
        </td>
    </tr>
}

</table>
```

Here is a breakdown of the code in this view:

- `@model IEnumerable<BabyStore.Models.Category>` is the model that the view is based on. The `Index` method of the `CategoriesController` class passes a list of categories to the Index view. In this case, the view needs to display a list of categories to the user so the model is specified as a collection of categories that implements the `IEnumerable` interface (the List type implements this).

- The title of the page is set by this code:

```
@{
    ViewBag.Title = "Index";
}
```

- `@Html.ActionLink("Create New", "Create")` creates a hyperlink to the Create view with the link text set to `"Create New"`. This is an example of an HTML helper and these are used through ASP.NET MVC to render various data-driven HTML elements.

- `@Html.DisplayNameFor(model => model.Name)` displays the `Name` of the specified field in the model. In this case, it displays the name of the Category field, which is currently `"Name"`.

- The code then loops through each of the categories contained in the model and displays the value contained in the `Name` field, followed by three links to edit, show the details of, or delete each category (see Figure 2-3). The third parameter in each ActionLink provides the `id` of the category to show in the view opened by the link:

```
@foreach (var item in Model) {
    <tr>
        <td>
            @Html.DisplayFor(modelItem => item.Name)
        </td>
        <td>
            @Html.ActionLink("Edit", "Edit", new { id=item.ID }) |
            @Html.ActionLink("Details", "Details", new { id=item.ID }) |
            @Html.ActionLink("Delete", "Delete", new { id=item.ID })
        </td>
    </tr>
}
```

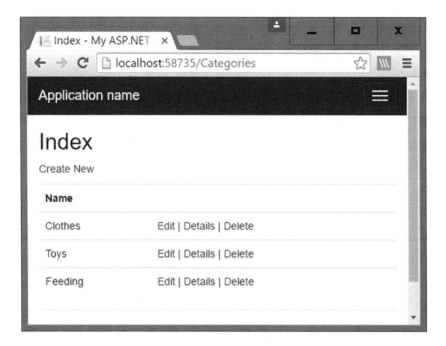

Figure 2-3. The HTML page generated by the Categories Index view (including the sample data)

Category Details View

The code generated by the scaffolding process for the Views\Categories\Details.cshtml view file is as follows:

```
@model BabyStore.Models.Category

@{
    ViewBag.Title = "Details";
}

<h2>Details</h2>

<div>
    <h4>Category</h4>
    <hr />
    <dl class="dl-horizontal">
        <dt>
            @Html.DisplayNameFor(model => model.Name)
        </dt>

        <dd>
            @Html.DisplayFor(model => model.Name)
        </dd>

    </dl>
```

```
</div>
<p>
    @Html.ActionLink("Edit", "Edit", new { id = Model.ID }) |
    @Html.ActionLink("Back to List", "Index")
</p>
```

The code is simpler than the Index view, as it displays only a single entity. The model is now a single category rather than a collection as specified by the first line of the file.

```
@model BabyStore.Models.Category.
```

The same HTML display helpers are used as in the Index view, but this time there is no need for a loop, as there is only a single entity, as shown in Figure 2-4.

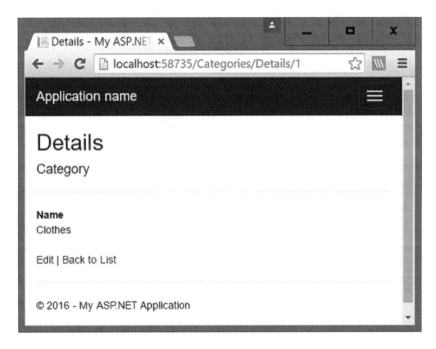

Figure 2-4. *The HTML page generated by the Category Details view*

The Category Create View

The Create view displays a blank HTML form to allow the creation of a category. This view implements a lot of new features not included in the Index and Details views in order to generate an HTML form. The form is submitted as a POST request and processed by the POST version of the Create method. The auto-generated code for this view is as follows:

```
@model BabyStore.Models.Category

@{
    ViewBag.Title = "Create";
}
```

```
<h2>Create</h2>

@using (Html.BeginForm())
{
    @Html.AntiForgeryToken()

    <div class="form-horizontal">
        <h4>Category</h4>
        <hr />
        @Html.ValidationSummary(true, "", new { @class = "text-danger" })
        <div class="form-group">
            @Html.LabelFor(model => model.Name, htmlAttributes: new { @class = "control-label
            col-md-2" })
            <div class="col-md-10">
                @Html.EditorFor(model => model.Name, new { htmlAttributes = new { @class =
                form-control" } })
                @Html.ValidationMessageFor(model => model.Name, "", new { @class = "text-
                danger" })
            </div>
        </div>

        <div class="form-group">
            <div class="col-md-offset-2 col-md-10">
                <input type="submit" value="Create" class="btn btn-default" />
            </div>
        </div>
    </div>
}


<div>
    @Html.ActionLink("Back to List", "Index")
</div>

@section Scripts {
    @Scripts.Render("~/bundles/jqueryval")
}
```

Figure 2-5 shows the fully generated HTML page. Here are the key points from the code shown above:

- The first new feature used is the code @Using(Html.BeginForm()), which tells the view to wrap everything inside this using statement in an HTML form.

- @Html.AntiForgeryToken() then generates an anti-forgery token, which is checked for a match by the POST version of the Create method (using the [ValidateAntiForgeryToken] attribute).

- @Html.ValidationSummary(true, "", new { @class = "text-danger" }) is a helper that will display an error summary if for any reason the form is not valid. The first parameter tells the summary to exclude any property errors and the third parameter, new { @class = "text-danger" }, is used to style the error message with the text-danger Bootstrap CSS class (this is bold red text; more on Bootstrap and CSS is included later in the book).

- @Html.LabelFor(model => model.Name, htmlAttributes: new { @class = "control-label col-md-2" }) creates a new HTML label element associated with the following HTML input control for the Name property of the category.

- @Html.EditorFor(model => model.Name, new { htmlAttributes = new { @ class = "form-control" } }) is an HTML helper method that attempts to display the correct HTML input element for the data type of the specified property. For this example, the property is Name, so the EditorFor method tries to display the correct type of HTML element to allow the user to edit a string. In this case, it produces a text box HTML element inside the HTML form so the user can enter the name of a category.

- The final new piece of HTML helper in this view is @Html.ValidationMessageFor (model => model.Name, "", new { @class = "text-danger" }). This adds a specific validation message for the property if the user enters an incorrect value based on the validation rules set in the application. At the moment, there are no rules set, but I will show you in Chapter 4 how to set these.

- There is an additional section in this view not seen in the Index and Details view files. It is used to include the JavaScript files required for validation (more on this in Chapter 4):

```
@section Scripts {
        @Scripts.Render("~/bundles/jqueryval")
}
```

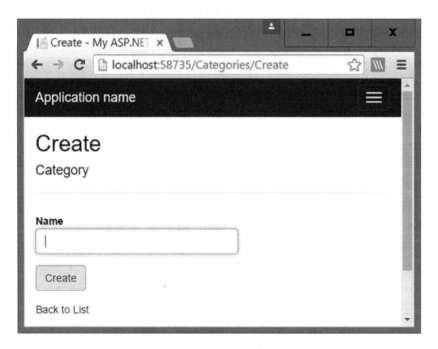

Figure 2-5. *The HTML page generated by the Categories Create view. This page contains an HTML form in order to submit the details of the new category*

The Category Edit View

The Edit view displays an HTML form to allow the editing of the category passed to it by the GET version of the Edit method in the CategoriesController class. This view is very similar to the Create view. The auto-generated code for this view is as follows:

```
@model BabyStore.Models.Category

@{
    ViewBag.Title = "Edit";
}

<h2>Edit</h2>

@using (Html.BeginForm())
{
    @Html.AntiForgeryToken()

    <div class="form-horizontal">
        <h4>Category</h4>
        <hr />
        @Html.ValidationSummary(true, "", new { @class = "text-danger" })
        @Html.HiddenFor(model => model.ID)

        <div class="form-group">
            @Html.LabelFor(model => model.Name, htmlAttributes: new { @class = "control-label
            col-md-2" })
            <div class="col-md-10">
                @Html.EditorFor(model => model.Name, new { htmlAttributes = new { @class =
                    "form-control" } })
                @Html.ValidationMessageFor(model => model.Name, "", new { @class = "text-
                    danger" })
            </div>
        </div>

        <div class="form-group">
            <div class="col-md-offset-2 col-md-10">
                <input type="submit" value="Save" class="btn btn-default" />
            </div>
        </div>
    </div>
}

<div>
    @Html.ActionLink("Back to List", "Index")
</div>

@section Scripts {
    @Scripts.Render("~/bundles/jqueryval")
}
```

27

Figure 2-6 shows the fully generated HTML edit page. The only new HTML helper is @Html.HiddenFor (model => model.ID). This creates a hidden HTML input element containing the ID of the category. This is used in the Bind element of the POST version of the Edit method in the CategoriesController class: public ActionResult Edit([Bind(Include = "**ID**,Name")] Category category).

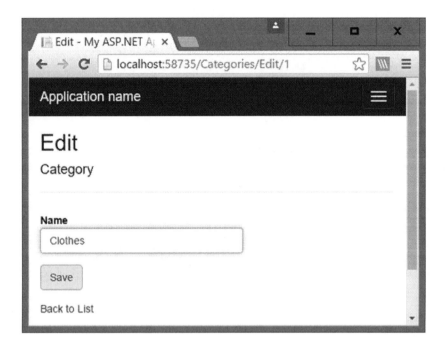

Figure 2-6. *The HTML page generated by the Category Edit page. The Name input box is prepopulated with the category's current name*

The Category Delete View

The Delete view is similar to the Details view but also contains an HTML form to submit to the POST version of the Delete method in the CategoriesController class. It does not introduce any new features in addition to those already covered in the examination of the other views. The auto-generated code is as follows and the HTML it generates is shown in Figure 2-7:

```
@model BabyStore.Models.Category

@{
    ViewBag.Title = "Delete";
}

<h2>Delete</h2>

<h3>Are you sure you want to delete this?</h3>
<div>
    <h4>Category</h4>
    <hr />
    <dl class="dl-horizontal">
```

```
    <dt>
        @Html.DisplayNameFor(model => model.Name)
    </dt>

    <dd>
        @Html.DisplayFor(model => model.Name)
    </dd>

</dl>

@using (Html.BeginForm()) {
    @Html.AntiForgeryToken()

    <div class="form-actions no-color">
        <input type="submit" value="Delete" class="btn btn-default" /> |
        @Html.ActionLink("Back to List", "Index")
    </div>
}
</div>
```

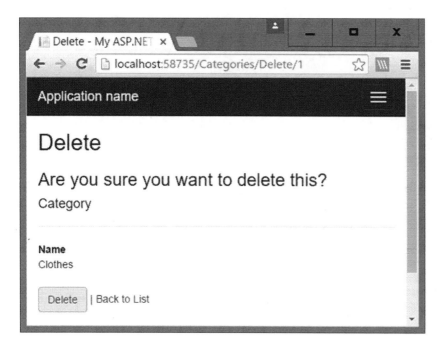

Figure 2-7. *The HTML page generated by the Category Delete view*

Adding a Product Controller and Views

1. Right-click the Controllers folder and choose Add ➤ Controller.

2. In the Add Scaffold window, choose the MVC 5 Controller with views option, using Entity Framework (see Figure 2-1).

3. Click Add. Then in the Add Controller window, choose the following options:

- Model class: Product

- Data Context class: StoreContext

- Ensure that Generate Views, Reference Script Libraries, and Use a Layout Page are checked

- Leave the Controller name set to ProductsController (see Figure 2-8 for full details)

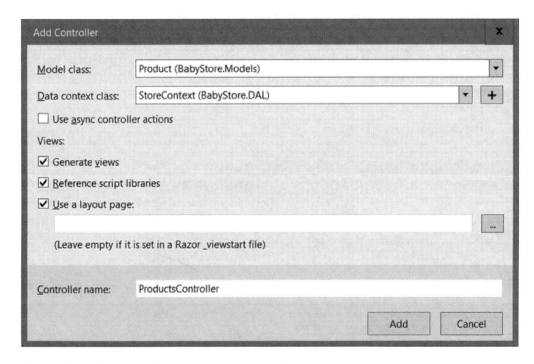

Figure 2-8. *Options for adding a new product controller*

4. Click Add and a new ProductsController class will be created in the Controllers folder. Corresponding views will also be created in the Views\Products folder.

Examining the Product Controller and Views

The ProductsController class and the associated views are very similar to the CategoriesController class and I am not going to cover them in great detail; however, there is one significant new piece of functionality to cover. The application needs to provide a way to associate a product with a category and it does this by rendering an HTML select element so that the users can pick a category from a list when creating or editing a product.

In the controller, the new code responsible for this is found in both versions of the Edit methods, as well as in the POST version of the Create method:

```
ViewBag.CategoryID = new SelectList(db.Categories, "ID", "Name", product.CategoryID);
```

In the GET version of the Create method, the following similar code is used:

```
ViewBag.CategoryID = new SelectList(db.Categories, "ID", "Name");
```

This code assigns an item to a ViewBag property named CategoryID. The item is a SelectList object consisting of all the categories in the database, with each entry in the list using the Name property as the text and the ID field as the value. The optional fourth parameter determines the preselected item in the select list. As an example, if the fourth argument product.CategoryID is set to 2, then the Toys category will be preselected in the drop-down list when it appears in the view. Figure 2-9 shows how this appears in a view.

The views display an HTML select element by using the following HTML Helper: @Html. DropDownList("CategoryID", null, htmlAttributes: new { @class = "form-control" }).

This code generates an HTML element based on the ViewBag.CategoryID property and assigns the CSS class form control to it. If the string specified in the first argument matches a ViewBag property name, it is automatically used rather than having to specify a reference to the ViewBag in the DropDownList helper method.

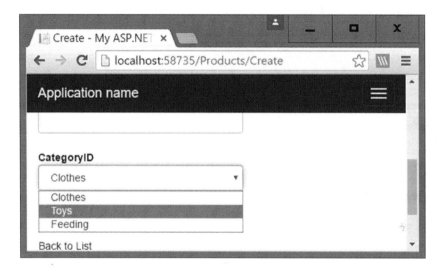

Figure 2-9. *A select list with the Toys element preselected by using the product.CategoryID parameter*

Using the New Product and Category Views

We can't expect users to navigate to our new views by entering the URL manually in the web browser, so we need to update the main site navigation bar as follows:

1. Open the Views\Shared_Layout.cshtml file.

2. Below the line of code <li>@Html.ActionLink("Contact", "Contact", "Home")</li>, add the following code to add links to the Categories and Products index pages:

    ```
    <li>@Html.ActionLink("Shop by Category", "Index", "Categories")</li>
    <li>@Html.ActionLink("View all our Products", "Index", "Products")</li>
    ```

3. Click on the Debug menu and choose Start Without Debugging. The web site will launch. Click on the Shop by Category link, When you click the link, two things happen:

- The Categories Index view appears. It does not contain any data since we have no data in the database (see Figure 2-10).

- The BabyStore database is created by Entity Framework based on our new model classes using Code First. To view the database, open SQL Server Object Explorer in Visual Studio. If SQL Server Object Explorer is not visible, click on View ➤ SQL Server Object Explorer from the main menu.

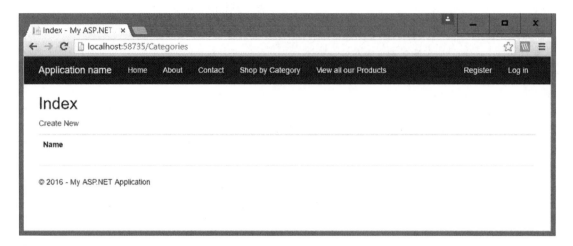

Figure 2-10. *The Categories Index page containing no data*

Examining the Newly Created BabyStore Database

To view the new columns in the database, expand the following chain within Server Object Explorer: SQLServer>(localdb)\MSSQLLocalDB>Databases>BabyStore>Tables>dbo.Categories>Columns. Also expand dbo.Products>Columns, as per Figure 2-11.

The columns listed in the database match the properties in our model classes. The table names have been pluralized by default. The Categories table contains the columns ID and Name. The Products table contains the columns ID, Name, Description, Price, and a foreign key CategoryID. The data types of the columns match the types specified in each model class.

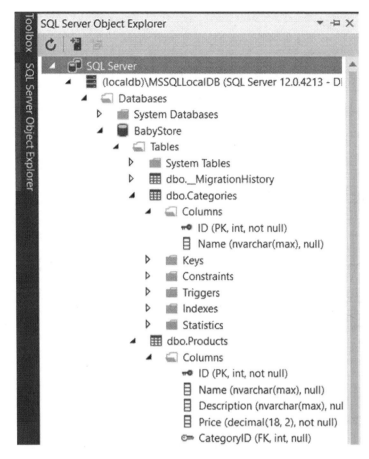

Figure 2-11. *The initial BabyStore database in SQL Server Object Explorer, expanded to show the columns of the Categories and Products tables and the data types of each column*

To see more details of each table, view the design of each table by right-clicking on the table and choosing View Designer from the menu. Using the designer, you can see more details about each column including foreign keys. In Figure 2-12 you can see the design of the Products table and in the T-SQL section with the Foreign Key Constraint for CategoryID highlighted on line 8. This shows that the foreign key references the ID column in the Categories table.

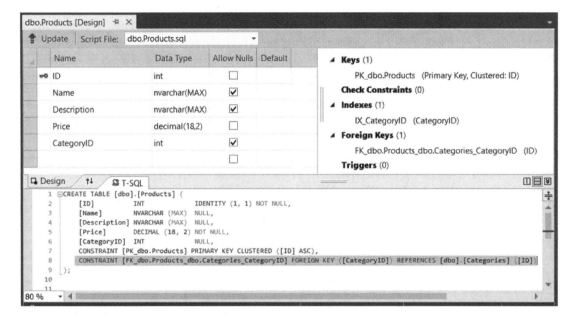

Figure 2-12. *Design of the Products table with the Foreign Key constraint highlighted*

Adding Some Data Using the Views

Add some new data to test the new views by clicking on the Create New link in the Categories Index page. Add three new categories named Clothes, Toys, and Feeding using the Create page. When you have finished this, the Categories Index page should look like Figure 2-13.

The new categories have been added to the database because when a user clicks the Create button on the Category Create page, the POST version of the Create method in the CategoriesController class is called to save the new category to the database.

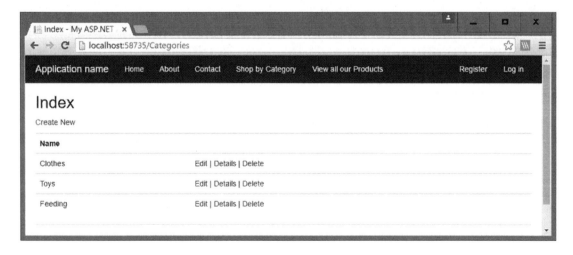

Figure 2-13. *Categories Index page with three test categories*

Next add some product data by first clicking on the View All Our Products link and then clicking the Create New Link. Add the products shown in Table 2-1.

Table 2-1. *Test Products to Add to the Web Site*

Name	Description	Price	Category
Red sleep suit	For sleeping or general wear	5	Clothes
Blue vest	An underlayer for wearing below other clothing	3	Clothes
Red fluffy dog	Makes a squeaking noise	2	Toys
Three-pack of no leak bottles	For a cleaner feeding time	25	Feeding

Each time the Create button is clicked on the Products Create page, the POST version of the Create method in the ProductsController class is called to save the data to the database.

Once completed, the Products Index page should appear in the web site, as shown in Figure 2-14. The data is also now saved to the database, as shown in Figure 2-15. The data can be viewed by right-clicking on the dbo.Products table in SQL Server Object Explorer and choosing View Data from the menu.

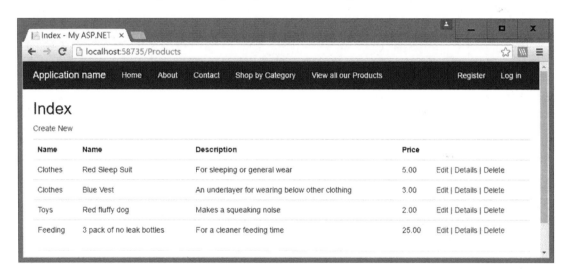

Figure 2-14. *The Products Index page with product data*

Figure 2-15. *Viewing the data in the Products table in the database*

35

■ **Note**   Some of the default headings and labels used in the auto-generated views are not very user-friendly so I have updated them in the screenshots that follow. If you want to update them yourself, refer to the source code for Chapter 2, which can be downloaded from Apress.com. I haven't included the code updates in the book, as they are very repetitive and trivial.

Changing the Way the Category and Product Name Properties are Displayed Using DataAnnotations

The Products Index page contains two columns named Name as per Figure 2-16. This is because the view uses the code @Html.DisplayNameFor(model => model.Category.Name) to display the Name property of the category and then also following this, displays the Name property of the product. This also causes confusion in the Product Details page where the same issue is present.

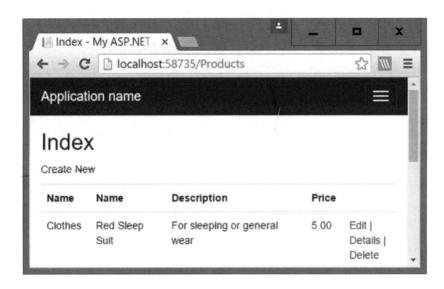

Figure 2-16. *Two Name headings in the Products Index page*

To fix this issue, we can use a feature of ASP.NET called DataAnnotations to add a display name attribute to the Name properties of the Category and Product model classes.

Modify the Models\Category.cs file with the changes highlighted in bold:

```
using System.Collections.Generic;
using System.ComponentModel.DataAnnotations;

namespace BabyStore.Models
{
    public class Category
    {
        public int ID { get; set; }
        [Display(Name = "Category Name")]
```

```
        public string Name { get; set; }
        public virtual ICollection<Product> Products { get; set; }
    }
}
```

The entry [Display(Name = "Category Name")] tells the MVC framework to display Category Name rather than Name when displaying a label for the name of the property.

Make similar changes to the Models\Product.cs file as follows:

```
using System.ComponentModel.DataAnnotations;

namespace BabyStore.Models
{
    public class Product
    {
        public int ID { get; set; }
        [Display(Name = "Product Name")]
        public string Name { get; set; }
        public string Description { get; set; }
        public decimal Price { get; set; }
        public int? CategoryID { get; set; }
        public virtual Category Category { get; set; }
    }
}
```

Build the solution and run it by choosing Debug ➤ Start Without Debugging from the menu. Click the View All Our Products link to open the Products Index page and you will see that the double Name headings now appear as Category Name and Product Name, as shown in Figure 2-17.

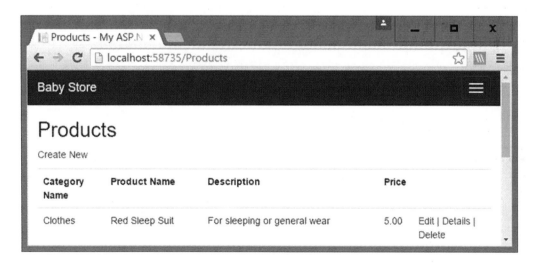

Figure 2-17. Products Index page displaying data annotation display names

Applying DataAnnotations to the class allows us to keep the code that controls the display name of a property in a single place and makes the code easier to maintain. We could have altered the name in the views but this would have involved modifying two files rather than one and been more difficult to maintain, plus every future view we create that used the property would need to be updated.

Splitting DataAnnotations into Another File Using MetaDataType

Some developers prefer the model classes as clean as possible, therefore preferring not to add DataAnnotations to them. This is achieved by using a MetaDataType class as follows.

Add a new class to the Models folder called ProductMetaData.cs and update the contents of the file to the following code:

```
using System.ComponentModel.DataAnnotations;

namespace BabyStore.Models
{
    [MetadataType(typeof(ProductMetaData))]
    public partial class Product
    {
    }

    public class ProductMetaData
    {
        [Display(Name = "Product Name")]
        public string Name;
    }
}
```

This declares the Product class as now being a partial class, meaning it is split across multiple files. The DataAnnotation [MetadataType(typeof(ProductMetaData))] is used to tell .NET to apply metadata to the Product class from the ProductMetaData class.

Modify the Product class back to its original state but declare it as a partial class so that it can be used in conjunction with the other class declaration in the ProductMetaData.cs file.

```
namespace BabyStore.Models
{
    public partial class Product
    {
        public int ID { get; set; }
        public string Name { get; set; }
        public string Description { get; set; }
        public decimal Price { get; set; }
        public int? CategoryID { get; set; }
        public virtual Category Category { get; set; }
    }
}
```

The results of this code are exactly the same as in Figure 2-17; however, using this code, the Product class was not altered except to declare it as partial. This can be a useful strategy when working with classes that have been automatically created that you do not want to alter, for example, when using Entity Framework Database First. I don't cover Entity Framework Database First in this book, but I do cover an alternative scenario to allow you to create classes from an existing database using Code First.

A Simple Query: Sorting Categories Alphabetically

Categories in the Categories Index page are currently sorted by the ID property so we'll change this to sort them alphabetically by the Name property.

This is a simple change to make. Open the Controllers\CategoriesController.cs file and update the Index method as follows:

```
// GET: Categories public ActionResult Index()
{
    return View(db.Categories.OrderBy(c => c.Name).ToList());
}
```

Click Debug ➤ Start Without Debugging to run the web site and click on the Shop by Category link. The categories are now sorted in alphabetical order by the category name, as shown in Figure 2-18.

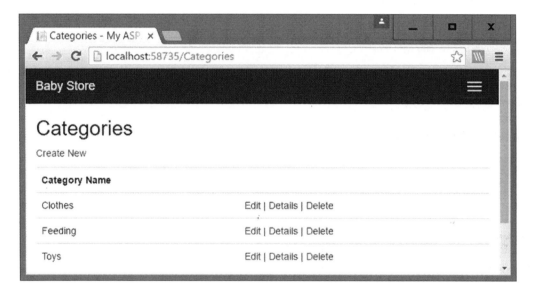

Figure 2-18. *Categories sorted by name in alphabetical order*

This code uses LINQ method syntax to specify which column to order by. A lambda expression is used to specify the Name column. This code then returns an ordered list of categories to the view for display. LINQ stands for Language-Integrated Query and it is a query language built into the .NET framework. Using LINQ method syntax means that queries are built using a dot notation to quickly chain methods together. An alternative to method syntax is query syntax and I give an example of this in Chapter 3 when writing a more complex query. Method syntax is more SQL-like in its appearance and can be easier to understand for more complex queries; however, for shorter queries it can appear more long-winded.

Lambda expressions are anonymous functions that can be used to create delegates. In simple terms, they enable you to create an expression where the value on the left side of the lambda operator (=>) is the input parameter and the value on the right is the expression to be evaluated and returned. Considering the lambda expression we have entered above, it takes a category as an input and returns the Name property. Therefore, in plain English, it says to order by the category's Name property.

I don't cover LINQ or lambda expressions in detail in this book. I suggest if you want to learn more about them that you read the excellent *Pro C#* books by Andrew Troelsen.

Filtering Products by Category: Searching Related Entities Using Navigational Properties and Include

You've seen how to create a very basic web site showing two lists of different entities. Now we are going to add some useful functionality and get these lists to interact. We'll do this using a chosen value from the list of categories to filter the list of products. To do this, we'll need to make the following changes to the code:

- Update the Index method in the ProductsController so that it receives a parameter representing a chosen category and returns a list of products that belong to that category.

- Transform the list shown in the Category Index Page to a list of hyperlinks that target the ProductsController Index method rather than a list of text items.

First change the ProductsController Index method as follows:

```
public ActionResult Index(string category)
{
        var products = db.Products.Include(p => p.Category);

        if (!String.IsNullOrEmpty(category))
        {
            products = products.Where(p => p.Category.Name == category);
        }
        return View(products.ToList());
}
```

This code adds a new string parameter named category to the method. An if statement has been added to check if the new category string is empty. If the category string is not empty, the products are filtered by using the navigational property Category in the Product class using this code: products = products.Where(p => p.Category.Name == category);.

The use of the Include method in the following code line is an example what is known as *eager loading:*

```
var products = db.Products.Include(p => p.Category);
```

It tells Entity Framework to perform a single query and retrieve all the products and also all the related categories. Eager loading typically results in an SQL join query that retrieves all the required data at once. You could omit the Include method and Entity Framework would use lazy loading, which would involve multiple queries rather than a single join query.

There are performance implications to choosing which method of loading to use. Eager loading results in one round trip to the database, but on occasion may result in complex join statements that are slow to process. However, lazy loading results in several round trips to the database. Here eager loading is used since the join statement will be relatively simple and we want to load the related categories in order to search over them.

The products variable is filtered using the Where operator to match products when the Name property of the product's Category property matches the category parameter passed into the method. This may seem a little like overkill and you may be wondering why I didn't just use the CategoryID property and pass in a number rather than a string. The answer to this lies in the fact that using a category name is much more meaningful in a URL when using routing. We will cover this later in the book.

This is an excellent example of why navigational properties are so useful and powerful. By using a navigational property in my Product class, I am able to search two related entities using minimal code. If I wanted to match products by category name, but did not use navigational properties, I would have to enter the realm of loading category entities via the ProductsController which by convention is only meant to manage products.

To demonstrate the new method in action, start the web site without debugging and navigate to the Product Index page. Now append `?category=clothes` onto the end of the URL. The list of products should now be filtered to items matching those in Figure 2-19.

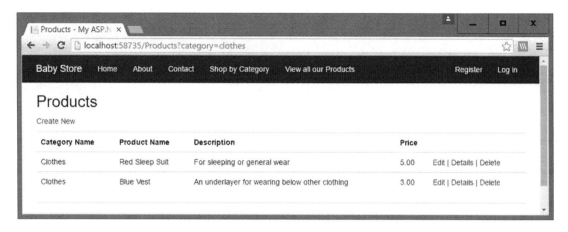

Figure 2-19. *Products filtered to the clothes category by using the URL address bar*

Any parameters in the query string part of the URL after ? are automatically matched to parameters in the method being targeted. So in this case, the `?category=clothes` part of the URL is used in the `ProductsController` Index method as a parameter named `category` with a value of `clothes`.

■ **Caution**   A common error often made by programmers new to using Entity Framework is using `ToList()` in the wrong place. During a method, LINQ is often used for building queries and that is precisely what is does; it simply builds up a query, it does not execute the query! The query is only executed when `ToList()` is called. Novice programmers often use `ToList()` at the beginning of their method. The consequences of this are that more records (usually all) will be retrieved from the database than are required, often with an adverse effect on performance. All these records are then held in memory and processed as an in-memory list, which is usually undesirable and can slow the web site down dramatically. Alternatively, do not even call `ToList()` and the query will only be executed when the view loads. This topic is known as *deferred execution* due to the fact that the execution of the query is deferred until after `ToList()` is called.

To finish the functionality for filtering products by category, we need to change the list of categories in the Categories Index page into a list of hyperlinks that target the `ProductsController` Index method.

In order to change the categories to hyperlinks, modify the `Views\Categories\Index.cshtml` file by updating the line of code `@Html.DisplayFor(modelItem => item.Name)` to:

```
@Html.ActionLink(item.Name, "Index", "Products", new { category = item.Name }, null)
```

This code uses the HTML ActionLink helper to generate a hyperlink with the link text being the category's name targeting the Index method of the `ProductsController`. The fourth parameter is `routeValue` and if `category` is set as an expected route value, its value will be set to the category name; otherwise, the string `category=categoryname` will be appended to the URL's query string in the same manner as we entered manually to demonstrate the product filtering was working.

The result of this change is that the Category Index Page now contains hyperlinks that pass the name of the category to the Index method of the ProductsController, as shown in Figure 2-20.

Clicking on each of the links will now open the Products Index page with the list of products displayed limited to the category the user clicked on in the web browser.

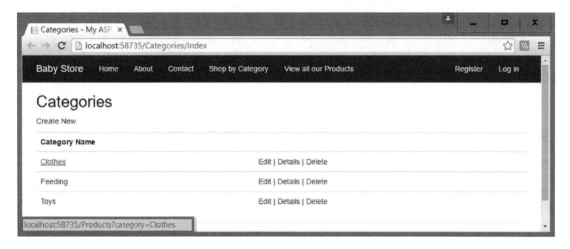

Figure 2-20. The Categories Index page with hyperlink to filter products. The URL format generated by the clothes link is highlighted in red

Summary

In this chapter, I've covered how to create model classes and create a database from them. I've also covered how to enter a connection string to specify where the database is created and how to create a database context class. This class and our model classes were then used to create controllers and views and we also created and populated the database.

Once the database was created, I showed you how to examine it and then how to modify the views to correct any issues with scaffolding. Following on from this, the final part of the chapter covered how to filter products by category, thus making use of navigational properties and how to target a different action or method from a view.

CHAPTER 3

Searching, Advanced Filtering, and View Models

This chapter will enhance the site functionality by adding a feature to search for products and add a more advanced select control using a view model to pass complex data to the view instead of using ViewBag.

> **Note** If you want to follow along with the code in this chapter, you must either have completed Chapter 2 or download Chapter 2's sour code from www.apress.com as a starting point.

Adding Product Search

To perform a search for products, I'm going to add some functionality to search through product names, descriptions, and categories so that the user has a better chance of finding relevant results.

The category search is included so that if, for example, a user searches for "clothes" rather than a specific item of clothing, then all clothes will be returned. If we did not search the category field then it's likely that the user wouldn't find anything because it's unlikely that many clothing products actually contain the word "clothes" in the name or the description fields.

I'll use the LINQ to Entities Contains method to search for matches in the product properties.

Updating the Controller for Product Searching

To add product search, modify the Index method of the Controllers\ProductsController.cs file as shown here:

```
public ActionResult Index(string category, string search)
{
    var products = db.Products.Include(p => p.Category);

    if (!String.IsNullOrEmpty(category))
    {
        products = products.Where(p => p.Category.Name == category);
    }
```

© Lee Naylor 2016

L. Naylor, *ASP.NET MVC with Entity Framework and CSS*, DOI 10.1007/978-1-4842-2137-2_3

```
    if (!String.IsNullOrEmpty(search))
    {
        products = products.Where(p => p.Name.Contains(search) ||
        p.Description.Contains(search) ||
        p.Category.Name.Contains(search));
    }
    return View(products.ToList());
}
```

First, a search parameter is added to the method and then if search is not null or empty, the products query is modified to filter on the value of search using this code:

```
if (!String.IsNullOrEmpty(search))
{
        products = products.Where(p => p.Name.Contains(search) ||
        p.Description.Contains(search) ||
        p.Category.Name.Contains(search));
}
```

Translated into plain English, this code says "find the products where either the product name field contains search, the product description contains search, or the product's category name contains search". The code again makes use of a lambda expression but this expression is more complex and uses the logical OR operator ||. Note that there is still only one operator required on the left of the => lambda operator despite there being multiple alternatives in the code statement to the right of =>. When the query is run against the database, the Contains method is translated to SQL LIKE and is case-insensitive.

Testing Product Search

Test the new search functionality by starting the application without debugging and clicking on View All Our Products to open the Products Index page. Manually append ?search=red to the end of the URL so that it now reads as /Products?search=red. You should now get matching products as shown in Figure 3-1.

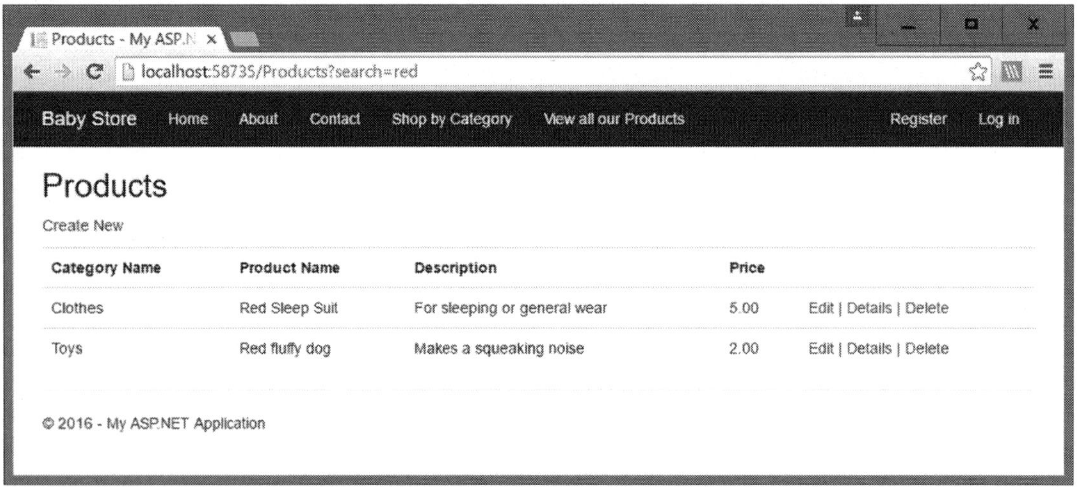

Figure 3-1. *Searching products manually for "red" via the URL*

To test that searching within category names works properly, modify the URL to /Products?search=clothes. The query will now match products that either contain the word clothes in the title or description or that belong to the clothes category, as shown in Figure 3-2.

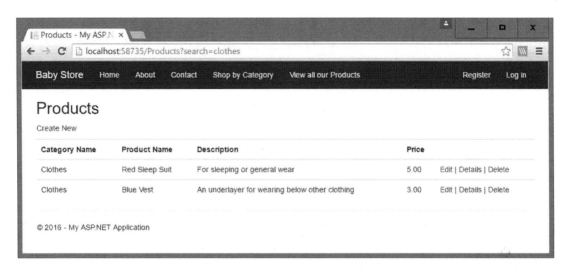

Figure 3-2. *Searching for products in the clothes category by altering the URL*

Adding a Search Box to the Main Site Navigation Bar

We can't expect users to manually type searches into the URL, so we need to add a search box to the site. I'll place this in the main navigation bar of the site so that it is always visible to users to enable them to find products from any page.

As covered in Chapter 1, the main navigation bar is part of the site layout page and therefore it is contained in the Views\Shared_Layout.cshtml file.

First of all, delete the About and Contact links from the site. We will not be using them in this example and they take up space. To do this, delete the following code from the Views\Shared_Layout.cshtml file:

```
<li>@Html.ActionLink("About", "About", "Home")</li>
<li>@Html.ActionLink("Contact", "Contact", "Home")</li>
```

To add a search box, edit the div with the class navbar-collapse collapse in the Views\Shared_Layout.cshmtl file, as highlighted in the following code listing:

```
<!DOCTYPE html>
<html>
<head>
    <meta charset="utf-8" />
    <meta name="viewport" content="width=device-width, initial-scale=1.0">
    <title>@ViewBag.Title - My ASP.NET Application</title>
    @Styles.Render("~/Content/css")
    @Scripts.Render("~/bundles/modernizr")

</head>
<body>
```

```
<div class="navbar navbar-inverse navbar-fixed-top">
    <div class="container">
        <div class="navbar-header">
            <button type="button" class="navbar-toggle" data-toggle="collapse" data-
                target=".navbar-collapse">
                <span class="icon-bar"></span>
                <span class="icon-bar"></span>
                <span class="icon-bar"></span>
            </button>
            @Html.ActionLink("Baby Store", "Index", "Home", new { area = "" }, new {
                @class = "navbar-brand" })
        </div>
        <div class="navbar-collapse collapse">
            <ul class="nav navbar-nav">
                <li>@Html.ActionLink("Contact", "Contact", "Home")</li>
                <li>@Html.ActionLink("Shop by Category", "Index", "Categories")</li>
                <li>@Html.ActionLink("View all our Products", "Index", "Products")</li>
            </ul>
            @using (Html.BeginForm("Index", "Products", FormMethod.Get, new { @class =
                "navbar-form navbar-left" }))
            {
            <div class="form-group">
                @Html.TextBox("Search", null, new { @class = "form-control", @placeholder
                    = "Search Products" })
            </div>
            <button type="submit" class="btn btn-default">Submit</button>
            }
                @Html.Partial("_LoginPartial")
        </div>
    </div>
</div>
<div class="container body-content">
    @RenderBody()
    <hr />
    <footer>
        <p>&copy; @DateTime.Now.Year - My ASP.NET Application</p>
    </footer>
</div>

@Scripts.Render("~/bundles/jquery")
@Scripts.Render("~/bundles/bootstrap")
@RenderSection("scripts", required: false)
</body>
</html>
```

Here an HTML form has been created to target the Index method of the ProductsController and everything is styled using Bootstrap. The form is similar to those we have already seen in the various Create and Edit views, but this form uses an overloaded version of the BeginForm HTML helper to specify to use GET rather than POST when submitting the form: @using (Html.BeginForm("Index", "Products", **FormMethod.Get**, new { @class = "navbar-form navbar-left" })).

The form uses GET rather than POST so that the search term can be seen in the URL. Therefore, users can copy it and share it with others by using other means such as e-mail or social media. By convention, GET requests are used when making database queries that do not alter the data in the database.

One additional thing covered in this code but not seen before is the use of an HTML5 placeholder attribute, which is used to display the text "Search Products" in the search box to indicate what it is used for when the page is first loaded. This is done by passing an additional item into the htmlAttributes parameter object in the line of code: @Html.TextBox("Search", null, new { @class = "form-control", @placeholder = "Search Products" }). The name of the textbox is specified as Search and this is mapped to the Search parameter by the MVC Framework. Figure 3-3 shows the resulting navigation bar, complete with the search box including placeholder text.

Figure 3-3. Navigation bar complete with search box

Perform some searches using the search box. The results should be identical to manually entering the search term into the URL.

How to Style Using Bootstrap

Bootstrap is an HTML, CSS, JavaScript framework originally built at Twitter. It's used by default in ASP.NET projects where scaffolding is used and has been used throughout our project so far for styling the web site's appearance. There's a whole raft of information about Bootstrap available online, so I'm not going to cover it in any great detail, but whenever I introduce something new, I will explain how and why I've styled it as I have.

So how did I know how to style the search box? Well, the answer lies in the web site http://www. bootswatch.com made by Thomas Park. This web site features several free themes for Bootstrap and it offers HTML previews for many elements. If you click on the Preview button on one of the themes and then scroll down the page and hover over an element, a <> symbol appears at the top-right corner of the element, as shown in Figure 3-4. If you click this symbol, an HTML preview appears, as shown in Figure 3-5.

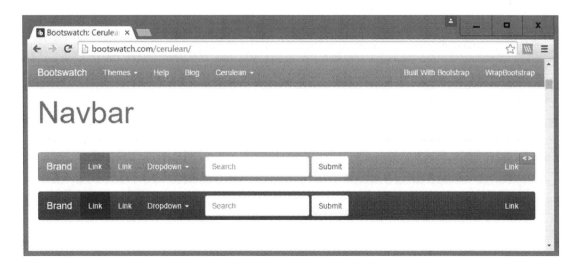

Figure 3-4. The preview <> symbol in the top-right corner of an element on bootswatch.com

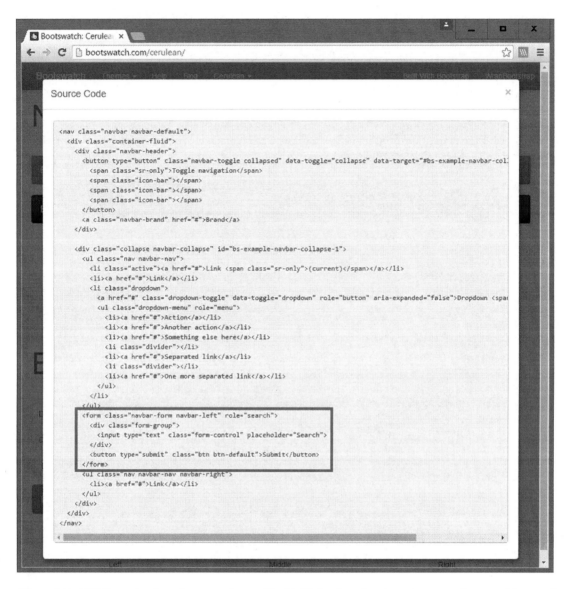

Figure 3-5. HTML preview from bootswatch.com. The highlighted section shows how to style a search box and form inside the navbar class

Filtering the Search Results by Category Using ViewBag

Next, we will add a feature so that the user can filter search results down to a particular category. In this example, we will use ViewBag to display a select control with categories in the search results page. We'll relate the select control to any search term entered by the user so that it only shows categories relevant to the products returned by a search and does not allow a user to select an empty category.

Updating the ProductsController Index Method to Filter by Category

Modify the Index method of the Controllers\ProductsController.cs file as follows in order to store the current search in the ViewBag and generate a list of distinct categories to be stored in the ViewBag as a SelectList.

```
public ActionResult Index(string category, string search)
{
    var products = db.Products.Include(p => p.Category);

    if (!String.IsNullOrEmpty(category))
    {
        products = products.Where(p => p.Category.Name == category);
    }

    if (!String.IsNullOrEmpty(search))
    {
        products = products.Where(p => p.Name.Contains(search) ||
        p.Description.Contains(search) ||
        p.Category.Name.Contains(search));
        ViewBag.Search = search;
    }

    var categories = products.OrderBy(p => p.Category.Name).Select(p =>
        p.Category.Name).Distinct();

    ViewBag.Category = new SelectList(categories);

    return View(products.ToList());
}
```

The search is stored in the ViewBag to allow it to be reused when a user clicks on the category filter. If it weren't stored, the search term would be discarded and the products would not be filtered correctly.

The code var categories = products.OrderBy(p => p.Category.Name).Select(p => p.Category. Name).Distinct(); then generates a distinct list of categories ordered alphabetically. The list of categories is not exhaustive; it only contains categories from the products that have been filtered by the search.

Finally, a new SelectList is created from the categories variable and stored in the ViewBag ready for use in the view.

Adding the Filter to the Products Index Page

To make the HTML page generated by the \Products\Index.cshtml file filter by category, we need a new HTML form to submit the category to filter by. Add a new form with an HTML select control by adding the following code to the Views\Products\Index.cshtml file after the CreateNew link.

```
<p>
    @Html.ActionLink("Create New", "Create")
    @using (Html.BeginForm("Index", "Products", FormMethod.Get))
    {
        <label>Filter by category:</label> @Html.DropDownList("Category", "All")
        <input type="submit" value="Filter" />
```

```
        <input type="hidden" name="Search" id="Search" value="@ViewBag.Search" />
    }
</p>
```

This code adds a form that targets the Index method of ProductsController using GET so that the query string contains the values it submits. A select control is generated for the ViewBag.Category property using the code @Html.DropDownList("Category", "All"), where the "All" argument specifies the default value for the select control. A Submit button is added to allow the user to submit the form and perform filtering. A hidden HTML element is also included to hold the value of the current search term. It's resubmitted so that the search term originally entered by the user is preserved when the products are filtered by category.

Start the web site without debugging. Figure 3-6 shows you how the Products Index page now looks with the category filter in place and a search in place for the word "red". Notice that All is the default value of the filter.

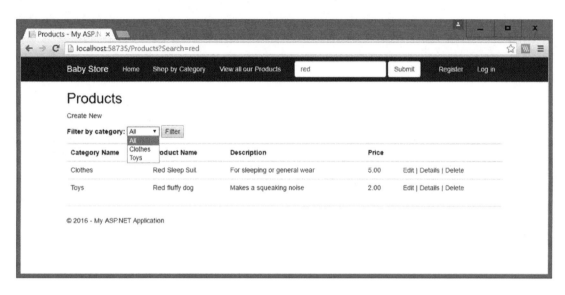

Figure 3-6. *The Products Index page with category filter in place*

Everything looks as though the code is working as expected; however, there is an issue with it. Figure 3-7 shows the search for "red" with the results filtered to the Clothes category.

Figure 3-7. *A search for "red" filtered to the Clothes category*

The issue is that the toys category has disappeared from the list of categories to filter by. It's simple to correct this issue, but it highlights the need to build your queries in the correct order. In order to rectify this issue, modify the Index method of the \Controllers\ProductsController.cs file as follows, so that products are filtered by category after the categories variable has been populated:

```
public ActionResult Index(string category, string search)
{
    var products = db.Products.Include(p => p.Category);

    if (!String.IsNullOrEmpty(search))
    {
        products = products.Where(p => p.Name.Contains(search) ||
        p.Description.Contains(search) ||
        p.Category.Name.Contains(search));
        ViewBag.Search = search;
    }

    var categories = products.OrderBy(p => p.Category.Name).Select(p =>
        p.Category.Name).Distinct();

    if (!String.IsNullOrEmpty(category))
    {
        products = products.Where(p => p.Category.Name == category);
    }

    ViewBag.Category = new SelectList(categories);

    return View(products.ToList());
}
```

Start the web site without debugging. If you now perform a search and filter by category, the category filter will still contain the other matching categories in the filter, as shown in Figure 3-8.

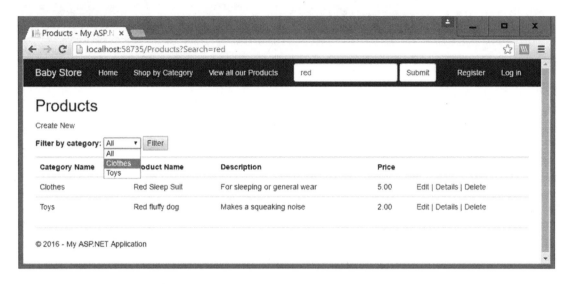

Figure 3-8. *A search for "red" filtered to the Clothes category but now also allows the user to select the Toys category*

Using a View Model for More Complex Filtering

Using the ViewBag to pass data to views works, but once you need to send more and more data, it becomes messy. This is particularly true when coding because due to the dynamic nature of ViewBag, Visual Studio offers no IntelliSense to tell you what properties are available in ViewBag. This can easily lead to coding errors with incorrect names being used.

Rather than using ViewBag, it is better practice to use a view model for the purpose of passing information from a controller to a view. The view is then based on this model rather than being based on a domain model (so far, all of our views have been based on domain models). Some developers take this concept further and base all their views solely on view models. In this book, we'll use a mixture of the view models and domain models.

In this example, I'll show you how to add a count to the category filter control to show how many matching products are in each category. To do this, we require a view model to hold all the information we want to pass to the view.

Creating a View Model

Create a new folder named ViewModels under the BabyStore project and add a new class to it named ProductIndexViewModel. Next, add the following code to the new file:

```
using BabyStore.Models;
using System.Collections.Generic;
using System.Linq;
using System.Web.Mvc;
```

```
namespace BabyStore.ViewModels
{
    public class ProductIndexViewModel
    {
        public IQueryable<Product> Products { get; set; }
        public string Search { get; set; }
        public IEnumerable<CategoryWithCount> CatsWithCount { get; set; }
        public string Category { get; set; }

        public IEnumerable<SelectListItem> CatFilterItems
        {
            get
            {
                var allCats = CatsWithCount.Select(cc => new SelectListItem
                {
                    Value = cc.CategoryName,
                    Text = cc.CatNameWithCount
                });

                return allCats;
            }
        }
    }

    public class CategoryWithCount
    {
        public int ProductCount { get; set; }
        public string CategoryName { get; set; }
        public string CatNameWithCount
        {
            get
            {
                return CategoryName + " (" + ProductCount.ToString() + ")";
            }
        }
    }
}
```

This class file looks more complex than the code we have used so far so I will break it down step-by-step to explain what each property is used for.

First, the file contains two classes, called ProductIndexViewModel and CategoryWithCount. CategoryWithCount is a simple class used to hold a category name and the number of products within that category.

The ProductCount property holds the number of matching products in a category and CategoryName simply holds the name of the category. The CatNameWithCount property then returns both of these properties combined into a string. An example of this property is Clothes(2).

ProductIndexViewModel needs to hold a combination of information that was previously passed to the view using ViewBag and also the model IEnumerable<BabyStore.Models.Product> (since this is the model currently specified at the top of the /Views/Products/Index.cshtml file).

The first property in the class is public IQueryable<Product> Products { get; set; }. This will be used instead of the model currently used in the view.

The second property, called public string Search { get; set; }, will replace ViewBag.Search currently set in the ProductsController class.

The third property, called public IEnumerable<CategoryWithCount> CatsWithCount { get; set; }, will hold all of the CategoryWithCount *items* to be used inside the select control in the view.

The fourth property, Category, will be used as the name of the select control in the view.

Finally, the property public IEnumerable<SelectListItem> CatFilterItems is used to return a list of the type SelectListItem, which will generate a value of the categoryName to be used as the value when the HTML form is submitted and the text displayed in the format of CatNameWithCount.

Updating the ProductsController Index Method to Use the View Model

Update the Index method of the \Controllers\ProductsController.cs file so that it matches the following code. The changes—which use the view model rather than the ViewBag and return categories along with a count of items—are highlighted in bold. First of all, ensure that you add a using statement to the top of the file so that the class can access the ProductIndexViewModel class you just created.

```
using BabyStore.ViewModels;
public ActionResult Index(string category, string search)
{
    //instantiate a new view model
    ProductIndexViewModel viewModel = new ProductIndexViewModel();

    //select the products
    var products = db.Products.Include(p => p.Category);

    //perform the search and save the search string to the viewModel
    if (!String.IsNullOrEmpty(search))
    {
        products = products.Where(p => p.Name.Contains(search) ||
        p.Description.Contains(search) ||
        p.Category.Name.Contains(search));
        viewModel.Search = search;
    }

    //group search results into categories and count how many items in each category
    viewModel.CatsWithCount = from matchingProducts in products
                        where
                        matchingProducts.CategoryID != null
                        group matchingProducts by
                        matchingProducts.Category.Name into
                        catGroup
                        select new CategoryWithCount()
                        {
                            CategoryName = catGroup.Key,
                            ProductCount = catGroup.Count()
                        };

    if (!String.IsNullOrEmpty(category))
    {
```

```
        products = products.Where(p => p.Category.Name == category);
    }

    viewModel.Products = products;
    return View(viewModel);
}
```

The first code change ensures that a new view model is created for use within the method:

```
ProductIndexViewModel viewModel = new ProductIndexViewModel();
```

The code viewModel.Search = search; assigns the search variable to the viewModel instead of to ViewBag.

The third code change is a LINQ statement that populates the CatsWithCount property of viewModel with a list of CategoryWithCount objects. In this example, I used a different form of LINQ than what I used previously due to the complexity of the query. I used a form of LINQ known as query syntax to make the query easier to read.

The statement works by grouping products by category name, where the category ID is not null, using this code:

```
from matchingProducts in products
            where
            matchingProducts.CategoryID != null
            group matchingProducts by matchingProducts.Category.Name into
            catGroup
```

For each group, the category name and the number of products are then assigned to a CategoryWithCount object:

```
select new CategoryWithCount()
{
   CategoryName = catGroup.Key,
   ProductCount = catGroup.Count()
};
```

The final code change assigns the products variable to the Products property of the viewModel instead of passing it to the view and then instead passes the viewModel to the view as follows:

```
viewModel.Products = products;
return View(viewModel);
```

Note that any products not belonging to a category will not be shown in the category filter; however, they can still be searched for.

Modifying the View to Display the New Filter Using the View Model

Next update the \Views\Products\Index.cshtml file so that it uses the new view model to update the way it generates the filter control, retrieves the search string, displays the table headings, and displays the list of products. Make the following changes:

```
@model BabyStore.ViewModels.ProductIndexViewModel
```

```
@{
    ViewBag.Title = "Products";
}

<h2>@ViewBag.Title</h2>

<p>
    @Html.ActionLink("Create New", "Create")
    @using (Html.BeginForm("Index", "Products", FormMethod.Get))
    {
        <label>Filter by category:</label>
        @Html.DropDownListFor(vm => vm.Category, Model.CatFilterItems, "All");
        <input type="submit" value="Filter" />
        <input type="hidden" name="Search" id="Search" value="@Model.Search"
        />
    }
</p>

<table class="table">
    <tr>
        <th>
            @Html.DisplayNameFor(model => model.Category)
        </th>
        <th>
            @Html.DisplayNameFor(model => model.Products.First().Name)
        </th>
        <th>
            @Html.DisplayNameFor(model => model.Products.First().Description)
        </th>
        <th>
            @Html.DisplayNameFor(model => model.Products.First().Price)
        </th>
        <th></th>
    </tr>

@foreach (var item in Model.Products) {
    <tr>
        <td>
            @Html.DisplayFor(modelItem => item.Category.Name)
        </td>
        <td>
            @Html.DisplayFor(modelItem => item.Name)
        </td>
        <td>
            @Html.DisplayFor(modelItem => item.Description)
        </td>
        <td>
            @Html.DisplayFor(modelItem => item.Price)
        </td>
        <td>
            @Html.ActionLink("Edit", "Edit", new { id=item.ID }) |
```

```
            @Html.ActionLink("Details", "Details", new { id=item.ID }) |
            @Html.ActionLink("Delete", "Delete", new { id=item.ID })
        </td>
    </tr>
}
</table>
```

The code changes made to this file are simple but significant. The first change, @model BabyStore. ViewModels.ProductIndexViewModel, simply tells the view to use ProductIndexViewModel as the model on which to base the view. Note that this is now a single class and not an enumeration.

The second change, @Html.DropDownListFor(vm => vm.Category, Model.CatFilterItems, "All");, generates a filter control based on the CatFilterItems property of the view model as per the second parameter. The first parameter, vm => vm.Category, specifies the HTML name of the control and hence what it will appear as in the query string section of the URL when the form is submitted. Since the name of the control is category, our previous code that looks for the category parameter in the URL will continue to work correctly.

The third change ensures that the hidden search control now references the view model instead of the ViewBag:

```
<input type="hidden" name="Search" id="Search" value="@Model.Search"/>
```

We then need to generate the table headings. This is not as straightforward as it appears because the DisplayNameFor HTML helper method does not work with collections and we want to display headings based on the Products property of the view model. The category heading is straightforward since this is a property of the view model, but to display, for example, the name of the description property of the product class, we cannot now use code such as @Html.DisplayNameFor(model => model.Products. Description). Instead, we need to force the helper to use an actual product entity from the products collection by using the First() method as follows:

```
@Html.DisplayNameFor(model => model.Products.First().Description)
```

This code will now generate the table heading based on the description property of the product class. This code will continue to work even when there are no products in the database.

▧ **Tip**   When using the DisplayNameFor HTML helper method with a collection rather than a single object, use the first() method to enable access to the properties you want to display the name for.

The final change to the code, @foreach (var item in Model.Products) {, ensures that we now use the Products property of the view model to display products.

Start the web site without debugging and click on View All Our Products. The Filter by Category control now appears with a count in it, which reflects the number of matching products in each category. Figure 3-9 shows the filter displaying the number of items matching a search for "red".

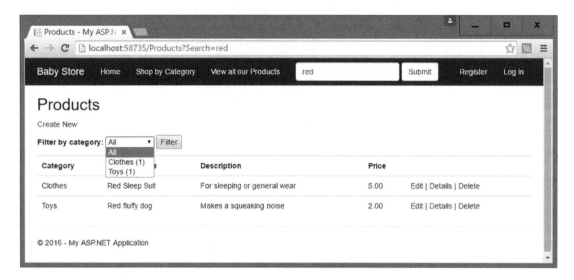

Figure 3-9. *The category filter control, now including a count of matching items in each category*

Summary

In this chapter, I showed you how to add search functionality, including how to add a search box using Bootstrap, and how to find out more about how to style using Bootstrap. I also showed you how to add a filter to the search results using ViewBag and how to add a more complex filter using a view model and use it within a view.

CHAPTER 4

■ ■ ■

More Advanced Data Management

This chapter will cover how to delete categories correctly, how to seed the database with data, how to update the database using Code First Migrations based on code changes, and how to perform data validation with custom error messages.

■ **Note**   If you want to follow along with the code in this chapter, you must either have completed Chapter 3 or download Chapter 3's source code from www.apress.com as a starting point.

Deleting an Entity Used as a Foreign Key

So far we have updated our web site to add some useful search and filter features, and we've been able to add some categories and products to the site. Next we'll consider what happens if we try to delete entities.

First of all, add a new category named Test Category to the web site and then add a new product named Test Product with any description and price and assign it to Test Category. Now try to delete Test Category by using the Categories/Index page and confirming the deletion. The web site will throw an error, as shown in Figure 4-1.

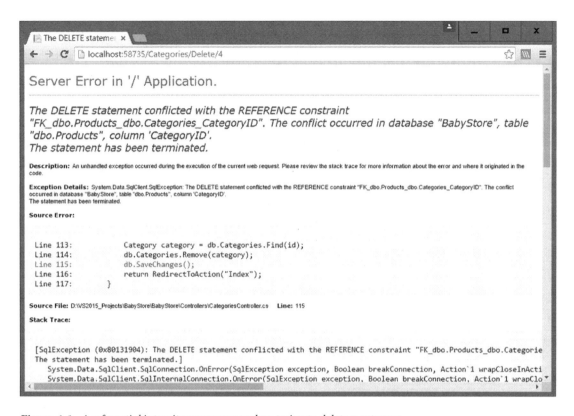

Figure 4-1. *A referential integrity error occurs when trying to delete a category*

This error occurs because the database column `CategoryID` is used as a foreign key in the `Products` table and currently there is no modification of this table when a category is deleted. This means that a product will be left with a foreign key field that contains an ID that no longer refers to a record in the Category table; this causes the error.

To fix this issue, the code created by the scaffolding process needs to be updated so that it sets the foreign key of all the affected products to `null`. Update the `HttpPost` version of the `Delete` method in the file `\Controllers\CategoriesController.cs` with the following changes highlighted in bold:

```
// POST: Categories/Delete/5
[HttpPost, ActionName("Delete")]
[ValidateAntiForgeryToken]
public ActionResult DeleteConfirmed(int id)
{
    Category category = db.Categories.Find(id);

    foreach (var p in category.Products)
    {
        p.CategoryID = null;
    }
```

```
db.Categories.Remove(category);
db.SaveChanges();
return RedirectToAction("Index");
}
```

This code adds a simple foreach loop using the products navigational property of the category entity to set the CategoryID of each product to null. When you now try to delete Test Category, it will be deleted without an error and the CategoryID column of Test Product will be set to null in the database.

Enabling Code First Migrations and Seeding the Database with Data

At present we have been entering data manually into the web site to create products and categories. This is fine for testing a new piece of functionality in a development environment, but what if you want to reliably and easily recreate the same data in other environments? This is where the feature of Entity Framework, known as seeding, comes into play. Seeding is used to programmatically create entries in the database and control the circumstances under which they are entered.

I am going to show you how to seed the database using a feature known as *Code First Migrations*. Migrations are a way of updating the database schema based on code changes made to model classes. We will use migrations throughout the book from now on to update the database schema.

The first thing we're going to update is the database connection string in the web.config file so that a new database is used for testing that the seed data works correctly. Update the StoreContext connectionString property as follows to create a new database named BabyStore2.mdf:

```
<add name="StoreContext" connectionString="Data Source=(LocalDB)\MSSQLLocalDB;AttachDbFile
name=|DataDirectory|\BabyStore2.mdf;Initial Catalog=BabyStore2;Integrated Security=True"
providerName="System.Data.SqlClient" />
```

Although the connectionString is shown over multiple lines in the book, be sure to keep it on a single line in Visual Studio.

Enabling Code First Migrations

Open the Package Manager Console by choosing View ➤ Other Windows in the main menu. This is where all the commands to use migrations are entered. The first thing to do when using migrations is to enable them for the database context you want to update the database schema for. If there is only one context, then the context is optional.

In this chapter, we are interested in the product and category data, so in Package Manager Console, enter the command:

```
Enable-Migrations -ContextTypeName BabyStore.DAL.StoreContext
```

If you have done this correctly, Visual Studio should respond as shown in Figure 4-2.

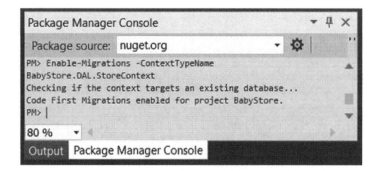

Figure 4-2. *Enabling Code First Migrations*

Enabling migrations also adds a new folder to the project named `Migrations`, which contains a new `Configuration.cs` file that is used to configure migrations. Figure 4-3 shows the new folder and file as they appear in Solution Explorer.

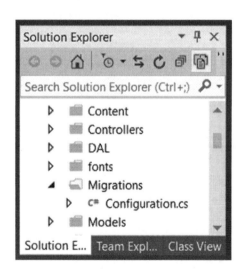

Figure 4-3. *The Migrations folder and Configuration.cs file created when migrations are enabled*

Next add an initial migration called `InitialDatabase` by entering the following command in Package Manager Console:

```
add-migration InitialDatabase
```

This command creates a new file in the `Migrations` folder with a name in the format `<TIMESTAMP>_InitialDatabase.cs`, where `<TIMESTAMP>` represents the time the file was created. The `Up` method creates the database tables and the `Down` method deletes them. Following is the code generated in this new class file. You can see that the `Up` method contains code to recreate the `Categories` and `Products` tables along with the data types and keys.

```
namespace BabyStore.Migrations
{
    using System;
    using System.Data.Entity.Migrations;

    public partial class InitialDatabase : DbMigration
    {
        public override void Up()
        {
            CreateTable(
                "dbo.Categories",
                c => new
                    {
                        ID = c.Int(nullable: false, identity: true),
                        Name = c.String(),
                    })
                .PrimaryKey(t => t.ID);

            CreateTable(
                "dbo.Products",
                c => new
                    {
                        ID = c.Int(nullable: false, identity: true),
                        Name = c.String(),
                        Description = c.String(),
                        Price = c.Decimal(nullable: false, precision: 18, scale: 2),
                        CategoryID = c.Int(),
                    })
                .PrimaryKey(t => t.ID)
                .ForeignKey("dbo.Categories", t => t.CategoryID)
                .Index(t => t.CategoryID);

        }

        public override void Down()
        {
            DropForeignKey("dbo.Products", "CategoryID", "dbo.Categories");
            DropIndex("dbo.Products", new[] { "CategoryID" });
            DropTable("dbo.Products");
            DropTable("dbo.Categories");
        }
    }
}
```

The code in this file will be used shortly to create a new database. Before that, we need to update the Seed() method of the Migrations\Configuration.cs file to add some test data to the database.

Seeding the Database with Test Data

When using Code First Migrations, the Seed method adds test data into a database. Generally, the data is only added when the database is created or when some new data is added to the method. Data is not dropped when the data model changes. When migrating to production, you will need to decide if any data is initially required, rather than using test data, and update the seed method appropriately.

To add some new data for Categories and Products to the database, update the Seed method of the Migrations\Configurations.cs file as follows:

```
namespace BabyStore.Migrations
{
    using Models;
    using System.Collections.Generic;
    using System.Data.Entity.Migrations;
    using System.Linq;

    internal sealed class Configuration :
    DbMigrationsConfiguration<BabyStore.DAL.StoreContext>
    {
        public Configuration()
        {
            AutomaticMigrationsEnabled = false;
        }

        protected override void Seed(BabyStore.DAL.StoreContext context)
        {
            var categories = new List<Category>
            {
                new Category { Name = "Clothes" },
                new Category { Name = "Play and Toys" },
                new Category { Name = "Feeding" },
                new Category { Name = "Medicine" },
                new Category { Name= "Travel" },
                new Category { Name= "Sleeping" }
            };
            categories.ForEach(c => context.Categories.AddOrUpdate(p => p.Name, c));
            context.SaveChanges();

            var products = new List<Product>
            {
                new Product { Name = "Sleep Suit", Description="For sleeping or general wear",
                Price=4.99M, CategoryID=categories.Single( c => c.Name == "Clothes").ID },
                new Product { Name = "Vest", Description="For sleeping or general wear",
                        Price=2.99M, CategoryID=categories.Single( c => c.Name ==
                        "Clothes").ID },
                new Product { Name = "Orange and Yellow Lion", Description="Makes a squeaking
                        noise", Price=1.99M, CategoryID=categories.Single( c => c.Name ==
                        "Play and Toys").ID  },
                new Product { Name = "Blue Rabbit", Description="Baby comforter", Price=2.99M,
                        CategoryID=categories.Single( c => c.Name == "Play and Toys").ID  },
```

```
        new Product { Name = "3 Pack of Bottles", Description="For a leak free
                drink everytime", Price=24.99M, CategoryID=categories.Single( c =>
                c.Name == "Feeding").ID  },
        new Product { Name = "3 Pack of Bibs", Description="Keep your baby dry
                when feeding", Price=8.99M, CategoryID=categories.Single( c => c.Name
                == "Feeding").ID  },
        new Product { Name = "Powdered Baby Milk", Description="Nutritional and
                Tasty", Price=9.99M, CategoryID=categories.Single( c => c.Name ==
                "Feeding").ID  },
        new Product { Name = "Pack of 70 Disposable Nappies", Description="Dry and
                secure nappies with snug fit", Price=19.99M, CategoryID=
                categories.Single( c => c.Name == "Feeding").ID  },
        new Product { Name = "Colic Medicine", Description="For helping with baby
                colic pains", Price=4.99M, CategoryID=categories.Single( c => c.Name
                == "Medicine").ID  },
        new Product { Name = "Reflux Medicine", Description="Helps to prevent milk
                regurgitation and sickness", Price=4.99M, CategoryID=categories.Single(
                c => c.Name == "Medicine").ID  },
        new Product { Name = "Black Pram and Pushchair System", Description="Convert
                from pram to pushchair, with raincover", Price=299.99M, CategoryID=
                categories.Single( c => c.Name == "Travel").ID  },
        new Product { Name = "Car Seat", Description="For safe car travel",
                Price=49.99M, CategoryID= categories.Single( c => c.Name ==
                "Travel").ID  },
        new Product { Name = "Moses Basket", Description="Plastic moses basket",
                Price=75.99M, CategoryID=categories.Single( c => c.Name ==
                "Sleeping").ID  },
        new Product { Name = "Crib", Description="Wooden crib", Price=35.99M,
                CategoryID= categories.Single( c => c.Name == "Sleeping").ID  },
        new Product { Name = "Cot Bed", Description="Converts from cot into bed for
                older children", Price=149.99M, CategoryID=categories.Single( c =>
                c.Name == "Sleeping").ID  },
        new Product { Name = "Circus Crib Bale", Description="Contains sheet, duvet
                and bumper", Price=29.99M, CategoryID=categories.Single( c => c.Name ==
                "Sleeping").ID  },
        new Product { Name = "Loved Crib Bale", Description="Contains sheet,
                duvet and bumper", Price=35.99M, CategoryID=categories.Single( c =>
                c.Name == "Sleeping").ID  }
    };

    products.ForEach(c => context.Products.AddOrUpdate(p => p.Name, c));
    context.SaveChanges();
        }
    }
}
```

This code creates a list of category and product objects and saves them to the database. To explain how this works, we will break down the code used for the categories. First a variable named categories is created and a list of category objects is created and assigned to it using the following code:

```
var categories = new List<Category>
{
    new Category { Name="Clothes" },
    new Category { Name="Play and Toys" },
    new Category { Name="Feeding" },
    new Category { Name="Medicine" },
    new Category { Name="Travel" },
    new Category { Name="Sleeping" }
};
```

The next line of code, categories.ForEach(c => context.Categories.AddOrUpdate(p => p.Name, c));, will add or update a category if there is not one with the same name already in the database. For this example, we made the assumption that the category name will be unique.

The final piece of code—context.SaveChanges();—is called to save the changes to the database. WE call this twice in the file but this is not required; you only need to call it once. However, calling it after saving each entity type allows you to locate the source of the problem if there is an issue writing to the database.

If you do encounter a scenario where you want to add more than one entity with very similar data (for example, two categories with the same name), you can add to the context individually as follows:

```
context.Categories.Add(new Category { Name = "Clothes" });
context.SaveChanges();
context.Categories.Add(new Category { Name = "Clothes" });
context.SaveChanges();
```

Again there is no need to save the changes multiple times, but doing so will help you to track down the source of any error. The code used to add products follows the same pattern as that to add categories, apart from the fact that the category entity is used to generate the CategoryID field using the following code to find a category's ID value based on its name: CategoryID=categories.Single(c => c.Name == "Clothes").ID.

Creating the Database Using the Initial Database Migration

Now we are ready to create the new database with test data from the Seed method. In Package Manager Console, run the command: **update-database**. If this works correctly, you should be informed that the migrations have been applied and that the Seed method has run, as shown in Figure 4-4.

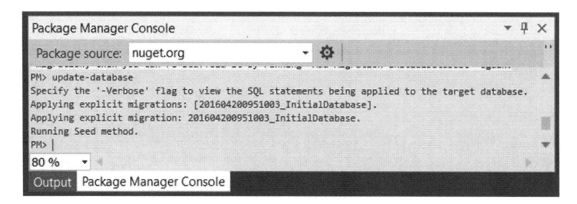

Figure 4-4. Output of running a successful database update using the update-database command

A new database named BabyStore2.mdf should now have been created in the App_Data folder of the project. When the update-database command ran, the Up method of the Migrations\Configuration.cs file was called to create the tables in the database. To view the database, open SQL Server Object Explorer and navigate to the BabyStore2.mdf database. You may have to click the Refresh button for the database to appear if you already have SQL Server Object Explorer open. View the data in the Products table by right-clicking on the table and choosing *View Data* from the menu. Figure 4-5 shows the data from the Products table. This data was generated when the Seed method ran.

dbo.Products [Data]

Max Rows: 1000

ID	Name	Description	Price	CategoryID
1	Sleep Suit	For sleeping or general wear	4.99	1
2	Vest	For sleeping or general wear	2.99	1
3	Orange and Yellow Lion	Makes a squeaking noise	1.99	2
4	Blue Rabbit	Baby comforter	2.99	2
5	3 Pack of Bottles	For a leak free drink everytime	24.99	3
6	3 Pack of Bibs	Keep your baby dry when feeding	8.99	3
7	Powdered Baby Milk	Nutritional and Tasty	9.99	3
8	Pack of 70 Disposable Nappies	Dry and secure nappies with snug fit	19.99	3
9	Colic Medicine	For helping with baby colic pains	4.99	4
10	Reflux Medicine	Helps to prevent milk regurgitation and sickness	4.99	4
11	Black Pram and Pushchair System	Convert from pram to pushchair, with raincover	299.99	5
12	Car Seat	For safe car travel	49.99	5
13	Moses Basket	Plastic moses basket	75.99	6
14	Crib	Wooden crib	35.99	6
15	Cot Bed	Converts from cot into bed for older children	149.99	6
16	Circus Crib Bale	Contains sheet, duvet and bumper	29.99	6
17	Loved Crib Bale	Contains sheet, duvet and bumper	35.99	6
N...	NULL	NULL	NULL	NULL

Figure 4-5. The Products table data created by running the Seed method

■ **Tip**   If you can't see anything in the App_Data folder, click on the Show All Files Button in Solution Explorer.

Start the web site without debugging and you will now see the new categories (see Figure 4-6) and products (see Figure 4-7), as populated by the Seed method.

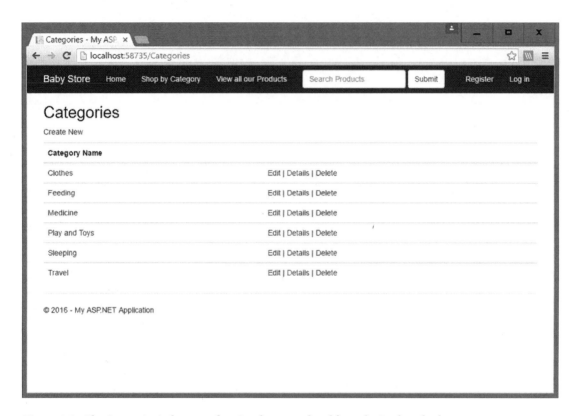

Figure 4-6. *The Categories index page showing data populated from the Seed method*

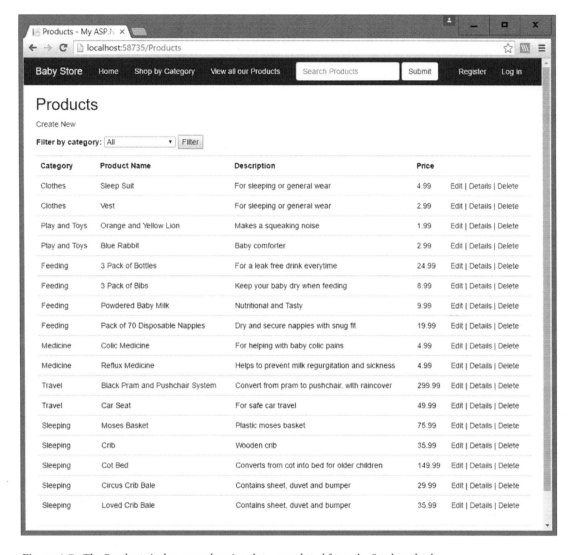

Figure 4-7. *The Products index page showing data populated from the Seed method*

Adding Data Validation and Formatting Constraints to Model Classes

At the moment, the data in the site is not validated on entry or displayed in the relevant formats such as currency. As an example try creating a new category called 23. You are able to do so. A user can also enter a completely blank category name, which causes the application to throw an error when rendering the category index.cshtml page.

Delete the new 23 category you just created. If you did create a category with a blank name, then delete it from the database using SQL Server Object Explorer.

In Chapter 2, I showed you how to use a MetaDataType class to add DataAnnotations to an existing class rather than directly adding them to the class itself. Throughout the rest of the book, we are going to revert to modifying the class itself for the sake of simplicity.

Adding Validation and Formatting to the Category Class

We're going to add some validation and formatting to the categories as follows:

- The name field cannot be blank

- The name field only accepts letters

- The name must be between three and fifty characters in length

In order to achieve this, you must modify the Models\Category.cs file, as highlighted in bold:

```
using System.Collections.Generic;
using System.ComponentModel.DataAnnotations;

namespace BabyStore.Models
{
    public class Category
    {
        public int ID { get; set; }
        [Required]
        [StringLength(50, MinimumLength = 3)]
        [RegularExpression(@"^[A-Z]+[a-zA-Z''-'\s]*$")]
        [Display(Name = "Category Name")]
        public string Name { get; set; }
        public virtual ICollection<Product> Products { get; set; }
    }
}
```

The [Required] attribute marks the property as being required, i.e., it cannot be null or empty, while the [StringLength(50, MinimumLength = 3)] attribute specifies that the string entered into the field must be between 3 and 50 characters in length. The final attribute—[RegularExpression(@"^[A-Z]+[a-zA-Z''-'\s]*$")]—uses a regular expression to specify that the field must only contain letters and spaces and start with an uppercase letter. In simple terms, this expression says the first character must be an uppercase letter followed by a repetition of letter and spaces. I don't cover regular expressions in this book since several tutorials are available online. If you want to translate a regular expression into something more meaningful or view a library of commonly used expressions, try using the site https://regex101.com/.

Next, start the web site without debugging and click on Shop by Category. Figure 4-8 shows the resulting page. Instead of displaying the Categories index page, the web site shows an error message informing you that the model backing StoreContext has changed.

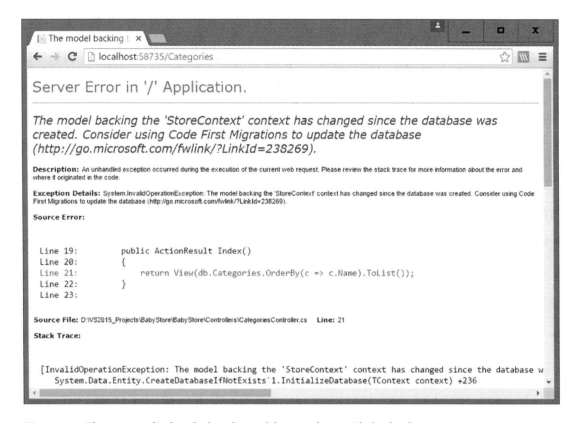

Figure 4-8. *The message displayed when the model is out of sync with the database*

This issue is caused because the Category class now has changes in it that need to be applied to the database. Two of the three attributes we added need to be applied to the database to change the rules for the Name column. This will ensure that the column cannot be null and also apply a maxLength attribute. The regular expression and the minimum length are not applicable to the database.

In order to fix this issue, open Package Manager Console and add a new migration by running the **add-migration CategoryNameValidation** command. A new migration file will be created containing the following code to update the Name column of the Categories table:

```
namespace BabyStore.Migrations
{
    using System;
    using System.Data.Entity.Migrations;

    public partial class CategoryNameValidation : DbMigration
    {
        public override void Up()
        {
            AlterColumn("dbo.Categories", "Name", c => c.String(nullable: false,
            maxLength:
                50));
        }
```

```
        public override void Down()
        {
            AlterColumn("dbo.Categories", "Name", c => c.String());
        }
    }
}
```

To apply these changes to the database, run the **update-database** command in Package Manager Console. The Name column of the Categories table in the database will now be updated, as shown in Figure 4-9. Note that the Allow Nulls box is unchecked and the Data Type is now nvarchar(50).

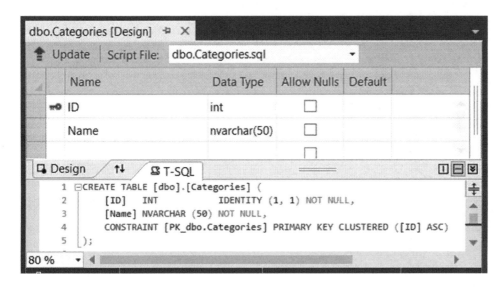

Figure 4-9. *The Categories table and T-SQL script with updated Name column*

Now run the web site again and navigate to the Category Create page by clicking on Shop by Category on the home page. Then click Create New on the Categories index page. Try to create a blank category; the web site will inform you that this is not allowed, as shown in Figure 4-10.

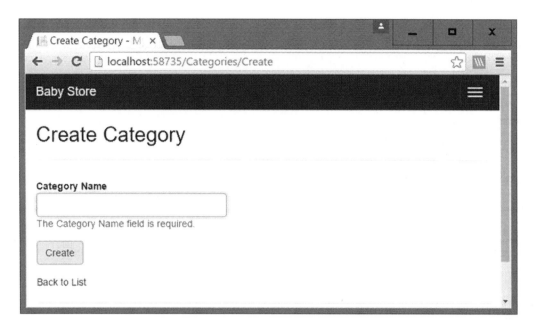

Figure 4-10. Error message now displayed when attempting to create an empty category

Now try to create a category named Clothes 2. Figure 4-11 shows the message the web site displays in response to this.

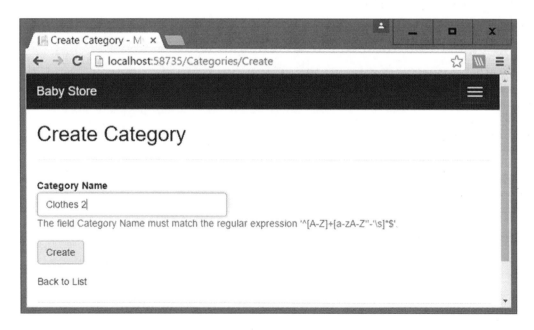

Figure 4-11. The message generated when attempting to put a numeric character in a category name

As you can see, the message displayed in Figure 4-11 is not exactly user friendly. Fortunately, ASP.NET MVC allows us to override the error message text by entering an extra parameter into the attribute. To add some more user friendly error messages for each field, update the \Models\Category.cs file as follows:

```
using System.Collections.Generic;
using System.ComponentModel.DataAnnotations;

namespace BabyStore.Models
{
    public class Category
    {
        public int ID { get; set; }
        [Required(ErrorMessage = "The category name cannot be blank")]
        [StringLength(50, MinimumLength = 3, ErrorMessage = "Please enter a category name
            between 3 and 50 characters in length")]
        [RegularExpression(@"^[A-Z]+[a-zA-Z''-'\s]*$", ErrorMessage = "Please enter a category
        name beginning with a capital letter and made up of letters and spaces only")]
        [Display(Name = "Category Name")]
        public string Name { get; set; }
        public virtual ICollection<Product> Products { get; set; }
    }
}
```

■ **Note**   This error message should be entered on a single line in Visual Studio. They are split here simply for book formatting. Alternatively, if you want to split them over two lines, you must use closing and opening quote with a plus sign: " + ".

Now start the web site without debugging and try creating the Clothes 2 category again. This time, the more meaningful error message is displayed, as shown in Figure 4-12.

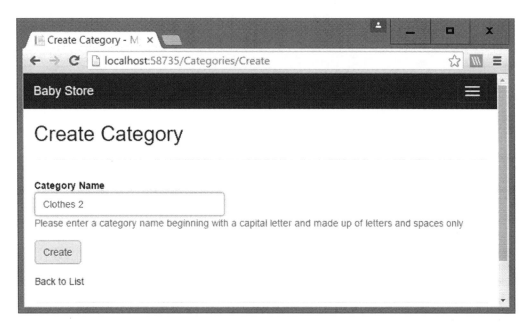

Figure 4-12. *A custom validation error message*

Adding Formatting and Validation to the Product Class

The product class contains properties that require more complex attributes such as formatting as currency and displaying a field over multiple lines. Update the Models\Product.cs file with the following code highlighted in bold:

```
using System.ComponentModel.DataAnnotations;

namespace BabyStore.Models
{
    public partial class Product
    {
        public int ID { get; set; }

        [Required(ErrorMessage = "The product name cannot be blank")]
        [StringLength(50, MinimumLength = 3, ErrorMessage = "Please enter a product name
        between 3 and 50 characters in length")]
        [RegularExpression(@"^[a-zA-Z0-9'-'\s]*$", ErrorMessage = "Please enter a product name
        made up of letters and numbers only")]
        public string Name { get; set; }
```

```
        [Required(ErrorMessage = "The product description cannot be blank")]
        [StringLength(200, MinimumLength = 10, ErrorMessage = "Please enter a product
        description between 10 and 200 characters in length")]
        [RegularExpression(@"^[,;a-zA-Z0-9'-'\s]*$", ErrorMessage = "Please enter a product
        description made up of letters and numbers only")]
        [DataType(DataType.MultilineText)]
        public string Description { get; set; }

        [Required(ErrorMessage = "The price cannot be blank")]
        [Range(0.10, 10000, ErrorMessage = "Please enter a price between 0.10 and 10000.00")]
        [DataType(DataType.Currency)]
        [DisplayFormat(DataFormatString = "{0:c}")]
        public decimal Price { get; set; }

        public int? CategoryID { get; set; }
        public virtual Category Category { get; set; }
    }
}
```

There are some new entries here that we have not seen before. The code [DataType(DataType.MultilineText)] tells the UI to display the input element for the description field as a text area when used in the edit and create views.

[DataType(DataType.Currency)] is used to give a hint to the UI as to what the format should be and it emits HTML5 date attributes to be used by HTML 5 browsers to format input elements. At the moment, web browser implementation of these attributes is unfortunately patchy.

[DisplayFormat(DataFormatString = "{0:c}")] specifies that the price property should be displayed in currency format, i.e., £1,234.56 (with the currency set by the server locale). Generally either of these attributes should work and display the price formatted as currency. We have included them both here for completeness.

Now build the solution and then, in Package Manager Consoler, run the command add-migration ProductValidation followed by update-database to add the range and nullable settings to the database.

Start the web site without debugging and click on View All Our Products. Figure 4-13 shows the list of products with the price field now formatted as currency due to the data annotations we made.

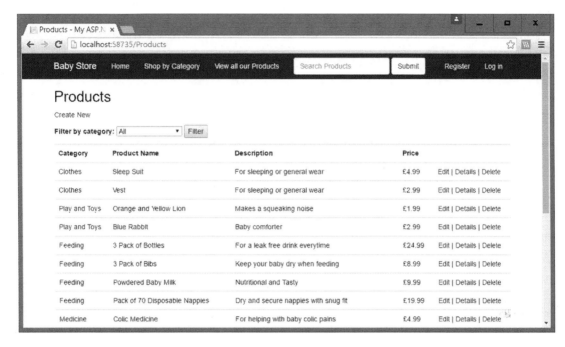

Figure 4-13. *The Products index page with the Price Field now formatted as currency*

■ **Note**   It is possible to use the currency format when editing by using the code [`DisplayFormat(Data`
`FormatString = "{0:c}", ApplyFormatInEditMode = true)`], but I don't recommend that you do this,
because the price when editing will display in the format £9,999.99. When you then try to submit the edit form,
the price will fail validation because £ is not a number.

Click on the Details link and you will see that the price is also now formatted as currency. To see the full
effect of the changes to the product class, we need to try creating and editing a product. Figure 4-14 shows an
attempt to enter some data that does not comply with the rules when creating a new product.

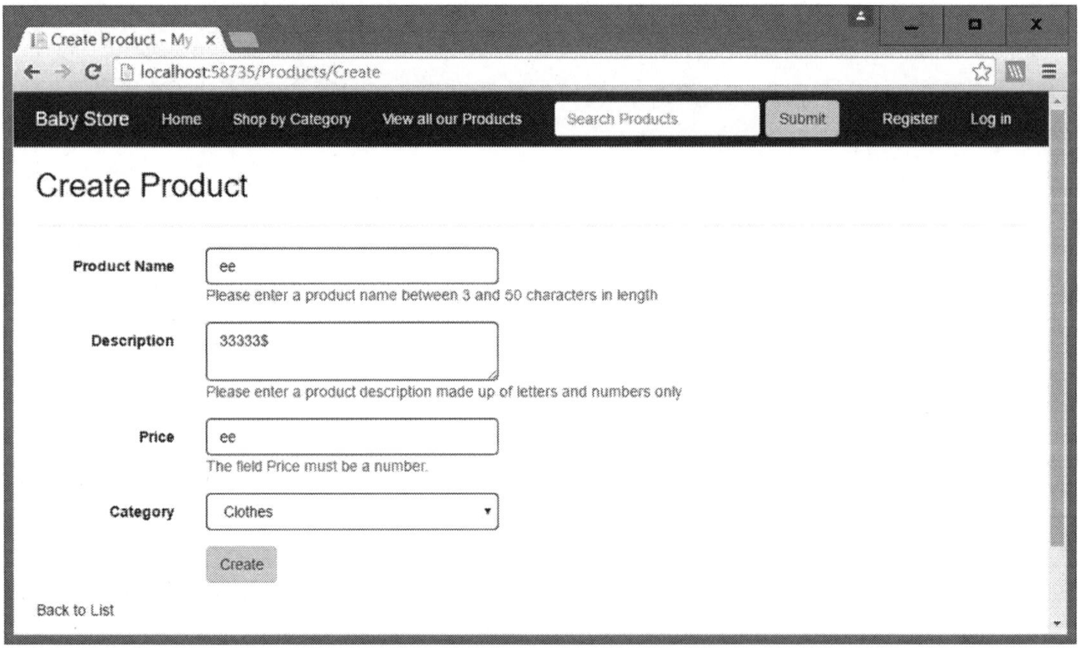

Figure 4-14. *Custom error messages when attempting to create a product with invalid data*

This is a big improvement on our default view and the validation applied to it; however, there are still some issues. The price input still displays a default error message when a number is not entered, which can be fixed in a couple of ways.

One way to fix this is to overwrite the `data-val-number` HTML attribute by modifying the `EditorFor` code for the price field. You do this by passing in a new HTML attribute, as follows:

```
@Html.EditorFor(model => model.Price, new { htmlAttributes = new { @class = "form-control",
data_val_number = "The price must be a number." } })
```

This change must implemented in each view that allows you to edit price, making it more difficult to maintain.

An alternative and more maintainable way to remedy this is to use a regular expression in the product class in the same manner as before, by updating the price property as follows:

```
[Required(ErrorMessage = "The price cannot be blank")]
[Range(0.10, 10000, ErrorMessage = "Please enter a price between 0.10 and 10000.00")]
[DataType(DataType.Currency)]
[DisplayFormat(DataFormatString = "{0:c}")]
[RegularExpression("[0-9]+(\\.[0-9][0-9]?)?", ErrorMessage = "The price must be a number up
to two decimal places")]
public decimal Price { get; set; }
```

This regular expression allows a number optionally followed by a decimal point, plus another one or two numbers. It allows numbers of the following format—1, 1.1, and 1.10—but not 1. without anything following the decimal point. Figure 4-15 shows the validation in action.

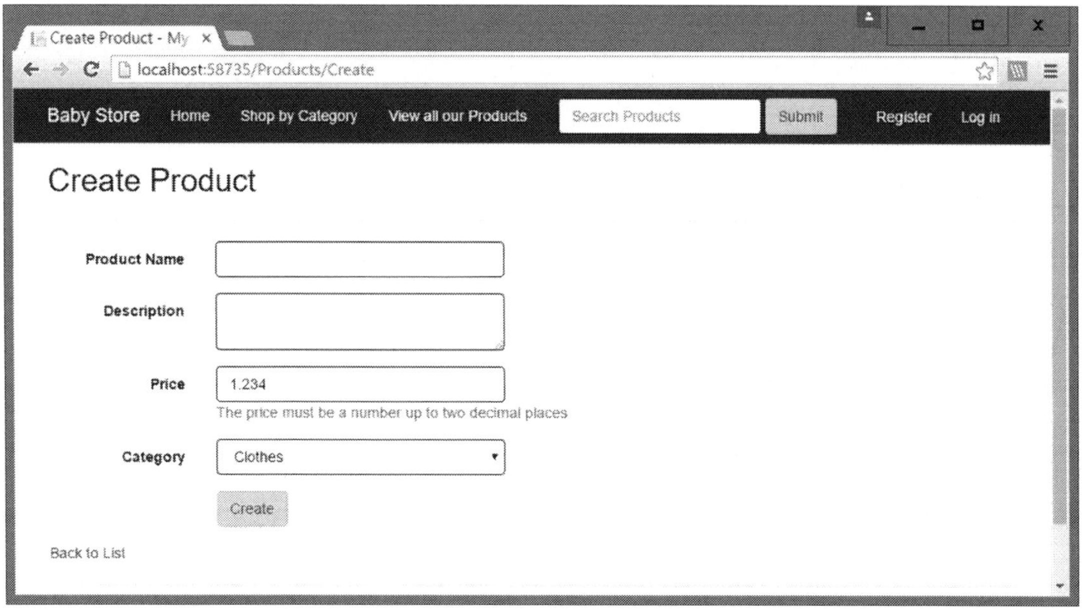

Figure 4-15. *Validation to two decimal places applied to the price field of a product*

How Validation Works

When we first created the project, it was set up with two NuGet packages installed, which are used for the client-side validation: `Microsoft.jQuery.Unobtrusive.Validation` and `jQuery.Validation`. ASP.NET MVC uses jQuery to perform client-side validation whenever the user navigates away from the input field.

The user does not need to submit the form in order to receive validation error messages. Validation is also performed on the server side once the form is submitted since using client-side validation alone is unsafe. Other JavaScript code could be used to bypass the validation.

To see the effect of the server-side validation, remove the following code from the `\Views\Products\Create.cshtml` file:

```
@section Scripts {
    @Scripts.Render("~/bundles/jqueryval")
}
```

This removes the JavaScript files used to perform validation from the view so that only the server side code is used to perform validation. Now run the web site and attempt to create a new product with a blank name, blank description, and a price of 1.234. Click the Create button. The page will respond with the same validation messages as before, but this time they have been thrown by the server, as shown in Figure 4-16.

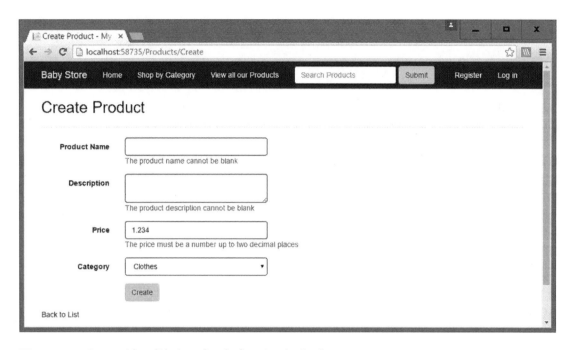

Figure 4-16. *Server-side validation after the form is submitted*

Add the code back in that you removed from the \Views\Products\Create.cshtml file earlier:

```
@section Scripts {
    @Scripts.Render("~/bundles/jqueryval")
}
```

The view files for editing and creating contain lines of code used to display validation messages for each input element and a summary for the whole form. The summary is used for any general error messages for the model that are not specific to an input. The code for the \Views\Products\Create.cshtml file is shown here, with the lines of code responsible for the validation messages highlighted.

```
@model BabyStore.Models.Product

@{
    ViewBag.Title = "Create Product";
}

<h2>@ViewBag.Title</h2>

@using (Html.BeginForm())
{
    @Html.AntiForgeryToken()

    <div class="form-horizontal">
        <hr />
```

```
@Html.ValidationSummary(true, "", new { @class = "text-danger" })
    <div class="form-group">
        @Html.LabelFor(model => model.Name, htmlAttributes: new { @class = "control-label
            col-md-2" })
        <div class="col-md-10">
            @Html.EditorFor(model => model.Name, new { htmlAttributes = new { @class =
                "form-control" } })
            @Html.ValidationMessageFor(model => model.Name, "", new { @class = "text-
                danger" })
        </div>
    </div>

    <div class="form-group">
        @Html.LabelFor(model => model.Description, htmlAttributes: new { @class =
            "control- label col-md-2" })
        <div class="col-md-10">
            @Html.EditorFor(model => model.Description, new { htmlAttributes = new {
                @class = "form-control" } })
            @Html.ValidationMessageFor(model => model.Description, "", new { @class =
                "text-danger" })
        </div>
    </div>

    <div class="form-group">
        @Html.LabelFor(model => model.Price, htmlAttributes: new { @class = "control-label
            col-md-2" })
        <div class="col-md-10">
            @Html.EditorFor(model => model.Price, new { htmlAttributes = new { @class =
                "form-control" } })
            @Html.ValidationMessageFor(model => model.Price, "", new { @class = "text-
                danger" })
        </div>
    </div>

    <div class="form-group">
        @Html.LabelFor(model => model.CategoryID, "Category", htmlAttributes: new { @class
            = "control-label col-md-2" })
        <div class="col-md-10">
            @Html.DropDownList("CategoryID", null, htmlAttributes: new { @class = "form-
                control" })
            @Html.ValidationMessageFor(model => model.CategoryID, "", new { @class =
                "text-danger" })
        </div>
    </div>

    <div class="form-group">
        <div class="col-md-offset-2 col-md-10">
            <input type="submit" value="Create" class="btn btn-default" />
        </div>
    </div>
</div>
}
```

```
<div>
    @Html.ActionLink("Back to List", "Index")
</div>

@section Scripts {
    @Scripts.Render("~/bundles/jqueryval")
}
```

The code @Html.ValidationSummary(true, "", new { @class = "text-danger" }) is responsible for displaying the overall validation summary for the model, while the other lines of code, such as @Html. ValidationMessageFor(model => model.Name, "", new { @class = "text-danger"}), are used to show any validation messages for each individual property (in this case, for the name property). The Bootstrap CSS class text-danger is used to display the messages in red.

Summary

In this chapter, I've shown you how to modify the delete method for an entity with an ID field used as a foreign key in another entity, followed by how to enable Code First Migrations with a view to updating the database schema from your code changes. I then showed you how to seed the database with test data and how to create a new database using migrations. Finally, the chapter covered adding formatting and validation rules to a class, updating the database using migrations, and a high-level discussion of how the validation process works.

CHAPTER 5

Sorting, Paging, and Routing

This chapter focuses on adding, sorting, and paging products and adding support for friendly URLs to use the ASP.NET Routing feature.

Note   If you want to follow along with the code in this chapter, you must either have completed Chapter 4 or download Chapter 4's source code for from www.apress.com as a starting point.

Sorting Products by Price

To demonstrate sorting, I'll show you a simple example to sort products by price, allowing users to order products by price.

First of all, add a new switch statement to the Index method of the Controllers\ProductsController.cs file, as highlighted in the following code, so that the products are reordered by price:

```
// GET: Products
public ActionResult Index(string category, string search, string sortBy)
{
    //instantiate a new view model
    ProductIndexViewModel viewModel = new ProductIndexViewModel();

    //select the products
    var products = db.Products.Include(p => p.Category);

    //perform the search and save the search string to the viewModel
    if (!String.IsNullOrEmpty(search))
    {
        products = products.Where(p => p.Name.Contains(search) ||
        p.Description.Contains(search) ||
        p.Category.Name.Contains(search));
        viewModel.Search = search;
    }
```

© Lee Naylor 2016
L. Naylor, *ASP.NET MVC with Entity Framework and CSS*, DOI 10.1007/978-1-4842-2137-2_5

```
//group search results into categories and count how many items in each category
viewModel.CatsWithCount = from matchingProducts in products
                          where
                          matchingProducts.CategoryID != null
                          group matchingProducts by
                                  matchingProducts.Category.Name into
                          catGroup
                          select new CategoryWithCount()
                          {
                              CategoryName = catGroup.Key,
                              ProductCount = catGroup.Count()
                          };

if (!String.IsNullOrEmpty(category))
{
    products = products.Where(p => p.Category.Name == category);
}

//sort the results
switch (sortBy)
{
    case "price_lowest":
        products = products.OrderBy(p => p.Price);
        break;
    case "price_highest":
        products = products.OrderByDescending(p => p.Price);
        break;
    default:
        break;
}

viewModel.Products = products;
return View(viewModel);
}
```

This new code uses the Entity Framework OrderBy and OrderByDescending methods to sort products by ascending and descending price. Run the application without debugging and manually change the URL to test that sorting works as expected, by using the Products?sortBy=price_lowest and Products?sortBy=price_highest URLs. The products should reorder with the lowest priced item at the top and the highest priced item at the top, respectively. Figure 5-1 shows the products being sorted with the highest price first.

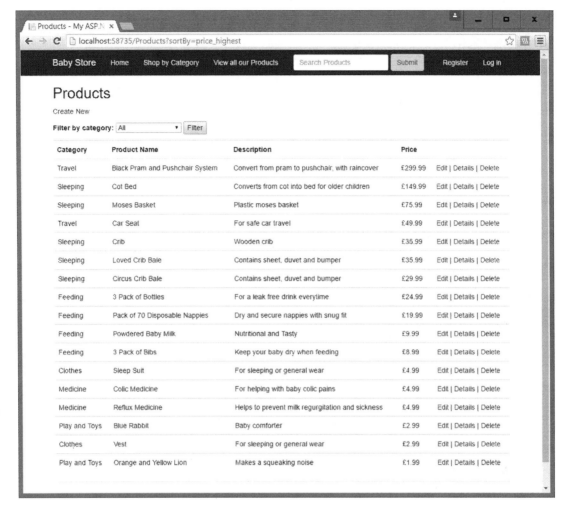

Figure 5-1. *The products list sorted by highest price first*

Adding Sorting to the Products Index View

We now need to add some user interface controls for sorting into the web site to allow users to choose how they want to sort. To demonstrate this, add a select list and populate it with values and text from a dictionary type.

First of all, add the following highlighted SortBy and Sorts properties to the ProductIndexViewModel class in the \ViewModels\ProductIndexViewModel.cs file:

```
using BabyStore.Models;
using System.Collections.Generic;
using System.Linq;
using System.Web.Mvc;
```

```
namespace BabyStore.ViewModels
{
    public class ProductIndexViewModel
    {
        public IQueryable<Product> Products { get; set; }
        public string Search { get; set; }
        public IEnumerable<CategoryWithCount> CatsWithCount { get; set; }
        public string Category { get; set; }
        public string SortBy { get; set; }
        public Dictionary<string, string> Sorts { get; set; }

        public IEnumerable<SelectListItem> CatFilterItems
        {
            get
            {
                var allCats = CatsWithCount.Select(cc => new SelectListItem
                {
                    Value = cc.CategoryName,
                    Text = cc.CatNameWithCount
                });

                return allCats;
            }
        }
    }

    public class CategoryWithCount
    {
        public int ProductCount { get; set; }
        public string CategoryName { get; set; }
        public string CatNameWithCount
        {
            get
            {
                return CategoryName + " (" + ProductCount.ToString() + ")";
            }
        }
    }
}
```

The SortBy property will be used as the name of the select element in the view and the Sorts property will be used to hold the data to populate the select element.

Now we need to populate the Sorts property from the ProductController class. Modify the \Controllers\ProductsController.cs file to add the following line of code to the end of the Index method prior to returning the View:

```
// GET: Products
public ActionResult Index(string category, string search, string sortBy)
{
    //instantiate a new view model
    ProductIndexViewModel viewModel = new ProductIndexViewModel();
```

```csharp
//select the products
var products = db.Products.Include(p => p.Category);

//perform the search and save the search string to the viewModel
if (!String.IsNullOrEmpty(search))
{
    products = products.Where(p => p.Name.Contains(search) ||
    p.Description.Contains(search) ||
    p.Category.Name.Contains(search));
    viewModel.Search = search;
}

//group search results into categories and count how many items in each category
viewModel.CatsWithCount = from matchingProducts in products
                          where
                          matchingProducts.CategoryID != null
                          group matchingProducts by
                          matchingProducts.Category.Name into
                          catGroup
                          select new CategoryWithCount()
                          {
                              CategoryName = catGroup.Key,
                              ProductCount = catGroup.Count()
                          };

if (!String.IsNullOrEmpty(category))
{
    products = products.Where(p => p.Category.Name == category);
}

//sort the results
switch (sortBy)
{
    case "price_lowest":
        products = products.OrderBy(p => p.Price);
        break;
    case "price_highest":
        products = products.OrderByDescending(p => p.Price);
        break;
    default:
        break;
}

viewModel.Products = products;
viewModel.Sorts = new Dictionary<string, string>
{
    {"Price low to high", "price_lowest" },
    {"Price high to low", "price_highest" }
};

return View(viewModel);
}
```

Finally, we need to add the control to the view so that users can make a selection. To achieve this, add the highlighted code to the Views\Products\Index.cshtml file after the filter by category code as follows:

```
@model BabyStore.ViewModels.ProductIndexViewModel

@{
    ViewBag.Title = "Products";
}

<h2>@ViewBag.Title</h2>

<p>
    @Html.ActionLink("Create New", "Create")
    @using (Html.BeginForm("Index", "Products", FormMethod.Get))
    {
        <label>Filter by category:</label>
        @Html.DropDownListFor(vm => vm.Category, Model.CatFilterItems, "All");
        <label>Sort by:</label>
        @Html.DropDownListFor(vm => vm.SortBy, new SelectList(Model.Sorts, "Value", "Key"),
        "Default")
        <input type="submit" value="Filter" />
        <input type="hidden" name="Search" id="Search" value="@Model.Search" />
    }
</p>

<table class="table">
    <tr>
        <th>
            @Html.DisplayNameFor(model => model.Category)
        </th>
        <th>
            @Html.DisplayNameFor(model => model.Products.First().Name)
        </th>
        <th>
            @Html.DisplayNameFor(model => model.Products.First().Description)
        </th>
        <th>
            @Html.DisplayNameFor(model => model.Products.First().Price)
        </th>
        <th></th>
    </tr>

    @foreach (var item in Model.Products)
    {
        <tr>
            <td>
                @Html.DisplayFor(modelItem => item.Category.Name)
            </td>
            <td>
                @Html.DisplayFor(modelItem => item.Name)
            </td>
```

```
            <td>
                @Html.DisplayFor(modelItem => item.Description)
            </td>
            <td>
                @Html.DisplayFor(modelItem => item.Price)
            </td>
            <td>
                @Html.ActionLink("Edit", "Edit", new { id = item.ID }) |
                @Html.ActionLink("Details", "Details", new { id = item.ID }) |
                @Html.ActionLink("Delete", "Delete", new { id = item.ID })
            </td>
        </tr>
    }
</table>
```

This new `select` control uses the `SortBy` property from the view model as its name. It populates itself with the data from the view model's `Sorts` property using the second entry in each line of the dictionary as the value submitted by the control (specified by `"Value"`) and the first entry in each line as the text displayed to the user (specified by `"Key"`), as shown in Figure 5-2.

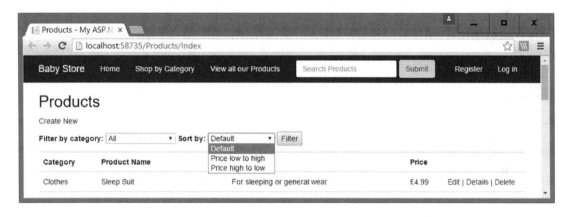

Figure 5-2. *The sort by select control in the Products index page*

Start the site without debugging and click on View All Our Products. Next to the category filter, you will now see a select list allowing the users to select to sort by price, as shown in Figure 5-2. You can use this new control to sort products by price.

Adding Paging

In this section, I will show you a way to add paging to allow users to page through the product search results rather than showing them all in one large list. This code will use the popular NuGet package `PagedList.Mvc`, which is written and maintained by Troy Goode. I have chosen to use this as an introduction to paging because it is easy to set up and use. Later in the book, I will show you how to write your own asynchronous paging code and an HTML helper to display paging controls.

Installing PagedList.Mvc

First of all, we need to install the package. Open the Project menu and then choose Manage NuGet Packages in order to display the NuGet Package Manager window. In this window, select the browse option and then search for pagedlist, as shown in Figure 5-3. Then install the latest version of PagedList.Mvc (currently 4.5.0) by clicking on the Install link. When you install PagedList.Mvc, the PagedList package is also installed.

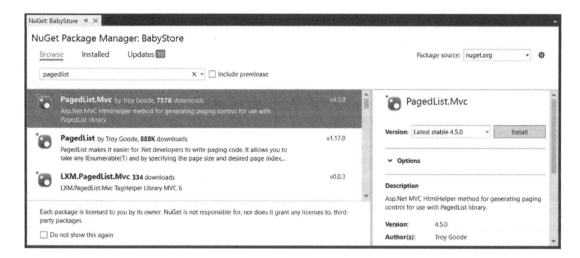

Figure 5-3. *The NuGet Package Manager showing PagedList.Mvc as the top result*

Updating the View Model and Controller for Paging

Once PagedList.Mvc is installed, the first thing that needs to be modified is ProductIndexViewModel, so that the Products property is changed to the type IPagedList. Modify the ViewModels\ProductIndexViewModel.cs file to update the code highlighted here:

```
using BabyStore.Models;
using System.Collections.Generic;
using System.Linq;
using System.Web.Mvc;
using PagedList;

namespace BabyStore.ViewModels
{
    public class ProductIndexViewModel
    {
        public IPagedList<Product> Products { get; set; }
        public string Search { get; set; }
        public IEnumerable<CategoryWithCount> CatsWithCount { get; set; }
        ...rest of code omitted for brevity...
```

We now need to modify the Index method of the ProductsController class so that it returns Products as a PagedList (achieved by using the ToPagedList() method). A default sort order also needs to be set in order to use PagedList. First of all, add the code using PagedList; to the using statements at the top of the file. Then modify the Controllers\ProductsController.cs file, as highlighted, in order to use the new PagedList package.

```
public ActionResult Index(string category, string search, string sortBy, int? page)
{
    //instantiate a new view model
    ProductIndexViewModel viewModel = new ProductIndexViewModel();

    //select the products
    var products = db.Products.Include(p => p.Category);

    //perform the search and save the search string to the viewModel
    if (!String.IsNullOrEmpty(search))
    {
        products = products.Where(p => p.Name.Contains(search) ||
        p.Description.Contains(search) ||
        p.Category.Name.Contains(search));
        viewModel.Search = search;
    }

    //group search results into categories and count how many items in each category
    viewModel.CatsWithCount = from matchingProducts in products
                              where
                              matchingProducts.CategoryID != null
                              group matchingProducts by
    matchingProducts.Category.Name into
                              catGroup
                              select new CategoryWithCount()
                              {
                                  CategoryName = catGroup.Key,
                                  ProductCount = catGroup.Count()
                              };

    if (!String.IsNullOrEmpty(category))
    {
        products = products.Where(p => p.Category.Name == category);
        viewModel.Category = category;
    }

    //sort the results
    switch (sortBy)
    {
        case "price_lowest":
            products = products.OrderBy(p => p.Price);
            break;
        case "price_highest":
            products = products.OrderByDescending(p => p.Price);
            break;
        default:
```

```
                products = products.OrderBy(p => p.Name);
                break;
        }

    const int PageItems = 3;
        int currentPage = (page ?? 1);
        viewModel.Products = products.ToPagedList(currentPage, PageItems);
        viewModel.SortBy = sortBy;
    viewModel.Sorts = new Dictionary<string, string>
    {
        {"Price low to high", "price_lowest" },
        {"Price high to low", "price_highest" }
    };
    return View(viewModel);
}
```

The first change adds the parameter int? page, which is a nullable integer and will represent the current page chosen by the user in the view. When the Products index page is first loaded, the user will not have selected any page, hence this parameter can be null.

We also need to ensure that the current category is saved to the view model so we have added this line of code to ensure that you can page within a category: viewModel.Category = category;.

The code products = products.OrderBy(p => p.Name); is then used to set a default order of products because PagedList requires the list it receives to be sorted.

Next, we specify the number of items to appear on each page by adding a constant using the line of code const int PageItems = 3;. We then declare an integer variable int currentPage = (page ?? 1); to hold the current page number and take the value of the page parameter, or 1, if the page variable is null.

The products property of the view model is then assigned a PagedList of products specifying the current page and the number of items per page using the code viewModel.Products = products. ToPagedList(currentPage, PageItems);.

Finally, the sortBy value is now saved to the view model so that the sort order of the products list is preserved when moving from one page to another by the code: viewModel.SortBy = sortBy;.

Updating the Products Index View for Paging

Having implemented the paging code in our view model and controller, we now need to update the \Views\Products\Index.cshtml file to display a paging control so that the user can move between pages. We'll also add an indication of how many items were found. To achieve this, modify the file to add a new using statement, add an indication of the total number of products found, and display paging links at the bottom of the page, as highlighted in the following code:

```
@model BabyStore.ViewModels.ProductIndexViewModel
@using PagedList.Mvc

@{
    ViewBag.Title = "Products";
}

<h2>@ViewBag.Title</h2>
<p>
    @(String.IsNullOrWhiteSpace(Model.Search) ? "Showing all" : "You search for " +
        Model.Search + " found")  @Model.Products.TotalItemCount products
</p>
```

```
<p>
    @Html.ActionLink("Create New", "Create")
    @using (Html.BeginForm("Index", "Products", FormMethod.Get))
    {
        <label>Filter by category:</label>
        @Html.DropDownListFor(vm => vm.Category, Model.CatFilterItems, "All");
        <label>Sort by:</label>
        @Html.DropDownListFor(vm => vm.SortBy, new SelectList(Model.Sorts, "Value", "Key"),
        "Default")
        <input type="submit" value="Filter" />
        <input type="hidden" name="Search" id="Search" value="@Model.Search" />
    }
</p>

<table class="table">
    <tr>
        <th>
            @Html.DisplayNameFor(model => model.Category)
        </th>
        <th>
            @Html.DisplayNameFor(model => model.Products.First().Name)
        </th>
        <th>
            @Html.DisplayNameFor(model => model.Products.First().Description)
        </th>
        <th>
            @Html.DisplayNameFor(model => model.Products.First().Price)
        </th>
        <th></th>
    </tr>

    @foreach (var item in Model.Products)
    {
        <tr>
            <td>
                @Html.DisplayFor(modelItem => item.Category.Name)
            </td>
            <td>
                @Html.DisplayFor(modelItem => item.Name)
            </td>
            <td>
                @Html.DisplayFor(modelItem => item.Description)
            </td>
            <td>
                @Html.DisplayFor(modelItem => item.Price)
            </td>
```

```
        <td>
            @Html.ActionLink("Edit", "Edit", new { id = item.ID }) |
            @Html.ActionLink("Details", "Details", new { id = item.ID }) |
            @Html.ActionLink("Delete", "Delete", new { id = item.ID })
        </td>
    </tr>
    }
</table>
<div>
    Page @(Model.Products.PageCount < Model.Products.PageNumber ? 0 :
        Model.Products.PageNumber) of @Model.Products.PageCount
    @Html.PagedListPager(Model.Products, page => Url.Action("Index",
        new { category = @Model.Category,
            Search = @Model.Search,
            sortBy = @Model.SortBy,
            page
    }))
</div>
```

The indication of how many products were found is displayed using the code:

```
<p>
    @(String.IsNullOrWhiteSpace(Model.Search) ? "Showing all" : "You search for " +
        Model.Search + " found")  @Model.Products.TotalItemCount products
</p>
```

This code uses the ?: (also known as ternary) operator to check if the search term is null or made up of whitespace. If this is true, the output of the code will be "Showing all xx products" or else if the user has entered a search term, the output will be "Your search for search term found xx products". In effect, this operates as a shorthand if statement. More information on the ?: operator can be found at https://msdn.microsoft.com/en-gb/library/ty67wk28.aspx.

Finally, the paging links are generated by this new code:

```
<div>
    Page @(Model.Products.PageCount < Model.Products.PageNumber ? 0 :
        Model.Products.PageNumber) of @Model.Products.PageCount
    @Html.PagedListPager(Model.Products, page => Url.Action("Index",
        new { category = @Model.Category,Search = @Model.Search,sortBy = @Model.SortBy,
            page
        }))
</div>
```

This code is wrapped in a div tag for presentation purposes. The first code line uses the ?: operator to decide whether or not there are any pages to display. It displays "Page 0 of 0" or "Page x of y" where x is the current page and y the total number of pages.

The next line of code uses the HTML PagedListPager helper that comes as part of the PagedList. Mvc namespace. This helper takes the list of products and produces a hyperlink to each page. Url.Action is used to generate a hyperlink targeting the Index view containing the page parameter. We have added an anonymous type to the helper method in order to pass the current category, search, and sort order to the helper so that each page link contains these in its querystring. This means that the search term, chosen category, and sort order are all preserved when moving from one page to another. Without them, the list of products would be reset to show all the products.

Figure 5-4 shows the effect of this code. A search has been performed for sleeping and the results are filtered to the sleeping category, sorted by price high to low. The user has moved to page 2 of the results.

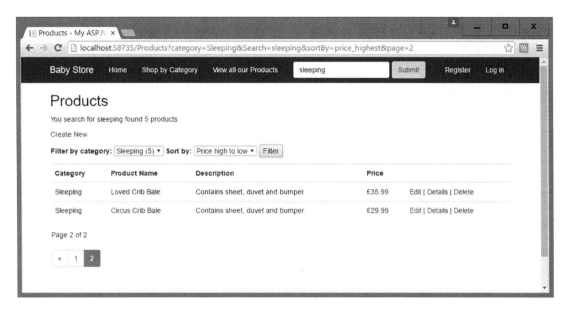

Figure 5-4. *Working paging with search term, sorting, and filtering by categories preserved*

Routing

So far we have been using parameters in the querystring portion of the URL to pass data for categories and paging to the Index action method in the `ProductController` class. These URLs follow the standard format such as `/Products?category=Sleeping&page=2`, and although functional, these URLs can be improved upon by using the ASP.NET Routing feature. It generates URLs in a more "friendly" format that is more meaningful to users and search engines. ASP.NET routing is not specific to MVC and can also be used with Web Forms and Web API; however, the methods used are slightly different when working with Web Forms.

To keep things manageable, we're going to generate routes only for categories and paging. There won't be a route for searching or sorting due to the fact that routing requires a route for each expected combination that can appear and each parameter needs some way of identifying itself. For example, we use the word "page" to prefix each page number in the routes that use it. It is possible to make routing overly complex by trying to add a route for everything. It's also worth noting that any values submitted by the HTML form for filtering by category will still generate URLs in the "old" format because that is how HTML forms work by design.

One of the most important things about routing is that routes have to be added in the order of most specific first, with more general routes further down the list. The routing system searches down the routes until it finds anything that matches the current URL and then it stops. If there is a general route that matches a URL and a more specific route that also matches, but it is defined below the more general route then the more specific route will never be used.

Adding Routes

We are going to take the same approach to adding routes as used by the scaffolding process when the project was created and add them to the \App_Start\RouteConfig.cs file in this format:

```
routes.MapRoute(
    name: "Name",
    url: "Rule",
    defaults: DefaultValues
);
```

The name parameter represents the name of the route and can be left blank; however, we'll be using them in this book to differentiate between routes.

The url parameter contains a rule for matching the route to a URL format. This can contain several formats and arguments, as follows:

- The url parameter is divided into segments, with each segment matching sections of the URL.

- A URL has to have the same number of segments as the url parameter in order to match it, unless either defaults or a wildcard is specified (see the following bullet points for an explanation of each of these).

- Each segment can be:

  - A static element URL, such as "Products". This will simply match the URL /Products and will call the relevant controller and action method.

  - A variable element that is able to match anything. For example, "Products/{category}" will match anything after Products in a URL and assign it to {category} and {category} can then be used in the action method targeted by the route.

  - A combination of static and variable elements that will match anything in the same URL segment matching the format specified. For example, "Products/Page{page}" will match URLs such as Products/Page2 or Products/Page99 and assign the value of the part of the URL following Page to {page}.

  - A catch-all wildcard element, for example "Products/{*everything}, will map everything following the Products section of the URL into the everything variable segment. This is done regardless of whether it contains slashes or not. We won't use wildcard matches in this project.

- Each segment can also be specified as being optional or having a default value if the corresponding element of the URL is blank. A good example of this is the default route specified when the project was created. This route uses the following code to specify default values for the controller and action method to be used. It also defines the id element as being optional:

  ```
  routes.MapRoute(
      name: "Default",
      url: "{controller}/{action}/{id}",
      defaults: new { controller = "Home", action = "Index",
              id = UrlParameter.Optional });
  ```

To start with routes, add a route for allowing URLs in the format /Products/Category (such as /Products/Sleeping to display just the products in the Sleeping category). Add the following highlighted code to the RegisterRoutes method in the \App_Start\RouteConfig.cs file, above the Default route:

```csharp
using System;
using System.Collections.Generic;
using System.Linq;
using System.Web;
using System.Web.Mvc;
using System.Web.Routing;

namespace BabyStore
{
    public class RouteConfig
    {
        public static void RegisterRoutes(RouteCollection routes)
        {
            routes.IgnoreRoute("{resource}.axd/{*pathInfo}");

            routes.MapRoute(
                name: "ProductsbyCategory",
                url: "Products/{category}",
                defaults: new { controller = "Products", action = "Index" }
            );

            routes.MapRoute(
                name: "Default",
                url: "{controller}/{action}/{id}",
                defaults: new { controller = "Home", action = "Index", id =
                                UrlParameter.Optional }
            );
        }
    }
}
```

Start the web site without debugging and click on Shop by Category, then click on Sleeping. The link will now open the /Products/Sleeping URL, as shown in Figure 5-5, due to the new ProductsbyCategory route.

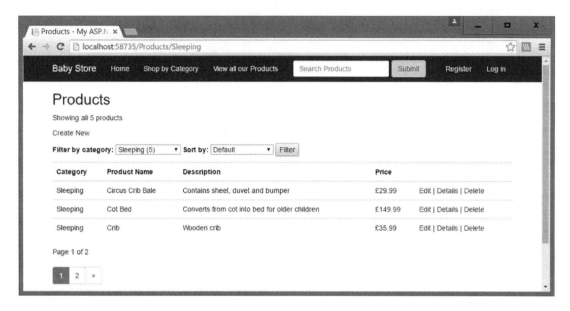

Figure 5-5. *The Products/Category URL in action*

So far so good; everything looks like it's working okay and you can now use the URLs in the format Products/Category. However, there is a problem. Try clicking on the Create New link. The product create page no longer appears and instead a blank list of categories is displayed. The reason for this is that the new route treats everything following Products in the URL as a category. There is no category named Create, so no products are returned, as shown in Figure 5-6.

Figure 5-6. *Broken Create New link*

Now click the back button to go back to the products list with some products displayed. Try clicking on the Edit, Details, and Delete links. They still work! You may be wondering why this is; well, the answer lies in the fact that the working links all have an ID parameter on the end of them. For example, the edit links take the format /Products/Edit/6 and this format matches the original Default route ("{controller}/{action}/{id}") rather than the new ProductsbyCategory route ("Products/{category}").

To fix this issue, we need to add a more specific route for the Products/Create URL. Add a new route the RegisterRoutes method in the App_Start\RouteConfig.cs file above the ProductsbyCategory route, as highlighted:

```
public static void RegisterRoutes(RouteCollection routes)
{
    routes.IgnoreRoute("{resource}.axd/{*pathInfo}");

    routes.MapRoute(
        name: "ProductsCreate",
        url: "Products/Create",
        defaults: new { controller = "Products", action = "Create" }
    );

    routes.MapRoute(
        name: "ProductsbyCategory",
        url: "Products/{category}",
        defaults: new { controller = "Products", action = "Index" }
    );

    routes.MapRoute(
        name: "Default",
        url: "{controller}/{action}/{id}",
        defaults: new { controller = "Home", action = "Index", id = UrlParameter.Optional }
    );
}
```

Start the web site without debugging and click on the Create Product link. It now works again because of the ProductsCreate route. It's very important to add the ProductsCreate route above the ProductsByCategory route; otherwise, it will never be used. If it was below the ProductsByCategory route, the routing system would find a match for the "Products/{category}" URL first and then stop searching for a matching route.

Next we're going to add a route for paging so that the web site can use URLs in the format /Products/Page2. Update the RegisterRoutes method of the App_Start\RouteConfig.cs file to add a new route to the file *above* the ProductsbyCategory route, as follows:

```
public static void RegisterRoutes(RouteCollection routes)
{
    routes.IgnoreRoute("{resource}.axd/{*pathInfo}");

    routes.MapRoute(
        name: "ProductsCreate",
        url: "Products/Create",
        defaults: new { controller = "Products", action = "Create" }
    );
```

```
routes.MapRoute(
    name: "ProductsbyPage",
    url: "Products/Page{page}",
    defaults: new
    { controller = "Products", action = "Index" }
);

routes.MapRoute(
    name: "ProductsbyCategory",
    url: "Products/{category}",
    defaults: new { controller = "Products", action = "Index" }
);

routes.MapRoute(
    name: "Default",
    url: "{controller}/{action}/{id}",
    defaults: new { controller = "Home", action = "Index", id = UrlParameter.Optional }
);
}
```

This new ProductsByPage route will match any URLs with the format Products/PageX, where X is the page number. Again this route must appear before the ProductsbyCategory route; otherwise, it will never get used. Try the new ProductsbyPage route by starting the web site without debugging and clicking View All Our Products. Then click on a page number in the paging control at the bottom of the page. The URL should now appear in the format Products/PageX. For example, Figure 5-7 shows the result of clicking on number 4 in the paging control, which generates the URL Products/Page4.

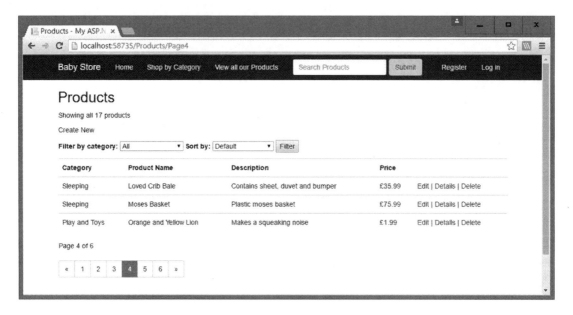

Figure 5-7. *The updated Products/PageX route in action*

So far we have added routes for Products/Category and Product/PageX, but we have nothing for Product/Category/PageX. To add a new route that allows this, add the following code *above* the ProductsByPage route in the RegisterRoutes method of the App_Start\RouteConfig.cs file:

```
public static void RegisterRoutes(RouteCollection routes)
{
    routes.IgnoreRoute("{resource}.axd/{*pathInfo}");

    routes.MapRoute(
        name: "ProductsCreate",
        url: "Products/Create",
        defaults: new { controller = "Products", action = "Create" }
    );

    routes.MapRoute(
        name: "ProductsbyCategorybyPage",
        url: "Products/{category}/Page{page}",
        defaults: new { controller = "Products", action = "Index" }
    );

    routes.MapRoute(
        name: "ProductsbyPage",
        url: "Products/Page{page}",
        defaults: new
        { controller = "Products", action = "Index" }
    );

    routes.MapRoute(
        name: "ProductsbyCategory",
        url: "Products/{category}",
        defaults: new { controller = "Products", action = "Index" }
    );

    routes.MapRoute(
        name: "Default",
        url: "{controller}/{action}/{id}",
        defaults: new { controller = "Home", action = "Index", id = UrlParameter.Optional }
    );
}
```

Start the web site without debugging and click on Shop by Category and then click on Sleeping. Then click on page 2 in the paging control. The URL now generated is Products/Sleeping/Page2 because of the new ProductsbyCategorybyPage route. This is shown in Figure 5-8.

Figure 5-8. *The ProductsbyCategorybyPage route in action*

We now appear to have added all the new routes, but there are still some issues with how the new routes affect the site. To see the first remaining issue, start with the web site filtered as shown in Figure 5-8. Then try to choose another category from the drop-down and clicking the filter button. The results are not filtered and remain on the Sleeping category. This is because the HTML form no longer targets the ProductsController index method correctly. To resolve this issue, we need to add one final route to the /App_Start/RouteConfig.cs file and then configure the HTML form to use it.

First of all, add a new route above the default route in the RegisterRoutes method of the App_Start\RoutesConfig.cs file:

```
public static void RegisterRoutes(RouteCollection routes)
{
    routes.IgnoreRoute("{resource}.axd/{*pathInfo}");

    routes.MapRoute(
        name: "ProductsCreate",
        url: "Products/Create",
        defaults: new { controller = "Products", action = "Create" }
    );

    routes.MapRoute(
        name: "ProductsbyCategorybyPage",
        url: "Products/{category}/Page{page}",
        defaults: new { controller = "Products", action = "Index" }
    );

    routes.MapRoute(
        name: "ProductsbyPage",
        url: "Products/Page{page}",
```

```
        defaults: new
        { controller = "Products", action = "Index" }
    );

    routes.MapRoute(
        name: "ProductsbyCategory",
        url: "Products/{category}",
        defaults: new { controller = "Products", action = "Index" }
    );

    routes.MapRoute(
        name: "ProductsIndex",
        url: "Products",
        defaults: new { controller = "Products", action = "Index" }
    );

    routes.MapRoute(
        name: "Default",
        url: "{controller}/{action}/{id}",
        defaults: new { controller = "Home", action = "Index", id = UrlParameter.Optional }
    );
}
```

This new route is named ProductsIndex and it creates a route that targets the Index action method of the ProductsController class. We've created this to give the web site a way to target this method when using URL links and forms.

Using Routes in Forms

Currently the form that filters by category in the Products index page works incorrectly, as it is still configured to try to target the Index method of the ProductsController class. For example, submitting the form to filter to Feeding after it has previously been set to Sleeping generates the following URL: http://localhost:58735/Products/Sleeping?Category=Feeding&SortBy=&Search=.

This URL contains two category arguments—Sleeping and Feeding—so the web site simply filters by the first one it encounters and the products list remains filtered to the Sleeping category. The Sleeping category must be removed when the form is submitted. In order to fix this issue, the HTML form containing the category filter needs to use the ProductsIndex route, which will enable it to remove all the parameters currently prefixed to the URL and only target the Index action method with the parameters submitted by the form.

To change the form to use the ProductsIndex route, change the following line of code in the Views\Products\Index.cshtml file from:

```
@using (Html.BeginForm("Index", "Products", FormMethod.Get))
```

to:

```
@using (Html.BeginRouteForm("ProductsIndex", FormMethod.Get))
```

Now start the web site without debugging and filter products to page 2 of the Sleeping category, as shown in Figure 5-8. Then change the category to Feeding and click the Filter button. The search result will now be filtered to just the products in the Feeding category.

■ **Note**   HTML forms can only be configured to submit to routes. They will not submit values in the format of routing; for example, the filter form still submits URLs in the format `Products?Category=Feeding&SortBy=&Search=` rather than `Products/Feeding`. This is because the default behavior of HTML forms is to submit URLs in this format, with input elements appended to the `querystring` element of the URL.

The search form also has the same issue as the filter form, so update the search form in the /Views/Shared/_Layout.cshtml file by changing the line:

```
@using (Html.BeginForm("Index", "Products", FormMethod.Get, new { @class = "navbar-form
navbar-left" }))
```

to:

```
@using (Html.BeginRouteForm("ProductsIndex", FormMethod.Get, new { @class = "navbar-form
navbar-left" }))
```

Using a Route in a Hyperlink

The final issue that needs to be resolved is that the View All Our Products link does not show all the products if the user has filtered by category. This is a very similar issue to the one that affected the HTML forms in that the link does not remove any parameters already assigned to the URL. To fix this issue, the outgoing URL link needs to be updated to point to a route rather than an action method. Update the \Views\Shared_Layout.cshtml file to change this line of code:

```
<li>@Html.ActionLink("View all our Products", "Index", "Products")</li>
```

to:

```
<li>@Html.RouteLink("View all our Products", "ProductsIndex")</li>
```

To pass extra parameters via a URL that targets a route, you simply add them into the link as an anonymous object in the same way that HTML attributes are passed. For example, to make a link that targets just the clothing category, you could use this code: `<li>@Html.RouteLink("View all Clothes", "ProductsbyCategory", new { category = "Clothes" })</li>`.

Setting a Project Start URL

Now that we've added some routes, it makes sense to stop Visual Studio from automatically loading the view that you are editing when you start the project. In Visual Studio, open the Project menu and choose BabyStore Properties in order to open the project properties window (or right-click the project in Solution Explorer and choose Properties). Then choose the Web section and set the Start Action to Specific Page, as shown in Figure 5-9. Don't enter a value; simply setting this option will make the project load the home page.

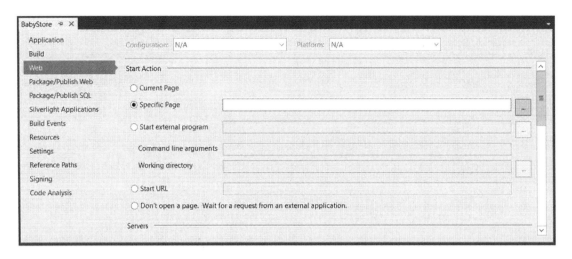

Figure 5-9. *Setting the project start URL to the Specific Page option*

Summary

This chapter started by adding sorting to the search results using Entity Framework and adding a select list to the web page so that users can sort products by price. We then added paging to the Products index page using the PagedList.Mvc package and finally used ASP.NET routing so that the web site now displays friendly URLs for categories and paging.

CHAPTER 6

■ ■ ■

Managing Product Images: Many-to-Many Relationships

This chapter covers how to create a new entity to manage images, how to upload image files using HTML forms and associate them with products using a many-to-many relationship, and how to save images to the filesystem. This chapter also introduces more complex error handling to add custom errors to the model in order to display them back to the user. The product images used in the chapter to seed the database can be found in Chapter's 6 code download available from the Apress web site.

■ **Note**　If you want to follow along with the code in this chapter, you must have completed Chapter 5 or download Chapter 5's source code from `www.apress.com` as a starting point.

Creating Entities to Store Image Filenames

For this project, we're going to store the image files within the web project using the filesystem. The database will contain data relating the filesystem's name of the image with one or more products. To begin modeling image storage, add a new class named `ProductImage` to the `Models` folder as follows:

```
using System.ComponentModel.DataAnnotations;

namespace BabyStore.Models
{
    public class ProductImage
    {
        public int ID { get; set; }
        [Display(Name="File")]
        public string FileName { get; set; }
    }
}
```

You are probably wondering why we added an extra class that basically maps a string to a product rather than simply adding a collection of strings to the `Product` class. This is a common question raised by developers when using Entity Framework. The reason is that Entity Framework cannot model a collection of strings in the database; it requires the collection to be modeled as we have done with the strings stored in a distinct class.

Now update the DAL\StoreContext.cs file to add a new property for ProductImages as follows:

```
using BabyStore.Models;
using System.Data.Entity;

namespace BabyStore.DAL
{
    public class StoreContext:DbContext
    {
        public DbSet<Product> Products { get; set; }
        public DbSet<Category> Categories { get; set; }
        public DbSet<ProductImage> ProductImages { get; set; }
    }
}
```

Next, create a migration to add the new ProductImage entity as a table by entering **add-migration ProductImages** into Package Manager Console and pressing Return. Then run the **update-database** command to update the database and create the new ProductImages table.

Uploading Images

Before we can upload any images, we need somewhere to store them. As stated earlier, we are going to store them on the filesystem rather than the database so create a new folder under the Content folder and name it ProductImages. Under the ProductImages folder, create a new folder named Thumbnails.

The ProductImages folder will hold the uploaded images and the Thumbnails folder will contain smaller images for use in a carousel feature to allow a user to navigate through each product's images.

Defining Reusable Constants

We are going to be referring to these folders in various files throughout the project; therefore, we need a way to store the path of each folder so that we can refer to them easily. To do this, we're going to add a new static class named Constants in the base of the project and add some constants to it for both these file paths. To do this, right-click on the BabyStore project in Solution Explorer and choose Add ➤ Class. Create a new class named Constants. Update the new class with the following code:

```
namespace BabyStore
{
    public static class Constants
    {
        public const string ProductImagePath = "~/Content/ProductImages/";
        public const string ProductThumbnailPath = "~/Content/ProductImages/Thumbnails/";
    }
}
```

We'll now refer to the Constants class when we need to reference the file paths where the images are stored. The class is declared as static so it does not need to be instantiated prior to being used.

Now that we have constants defined globally, add a constant for PageItems (currently defined in the ProductsController class) as highlighted:

```
namespace BabyStore
{
    public static class Constants
    {
        public const string ProductImagePath = "~/Content/ProductImages/";
        public const string ProductThumbnailPath = "~/Content/ProductImages/Thumbnails/";
        public const int PageItems = 3;
    }
}
```

Update the Index method of the ProductsController class to use this new constant by deleting the current PageItems constant from it and using the new constant in its place, as follows:

```
public ActionResult Index(string category, string search, string sortBy, int? page)
{
    //instantiate a new view model
    ProductIndexViewModel viewModel = new ProductIndexViewModel();

    //select the products
    var products = db.Products.Include(p => p.Category);

    //perform the search and save the search string to the viewModel
    if (!String.IsNullOrEmpty(search))
    {
        products = products.Where(p => p.Name.Contains(search) ||
        p.Description.Contains(search) ||
        p.Category.Name.Contains(search));
        viewModel.Search = search;
    }

    //group search results into categories and count how many items in each category
    viewModel.CatsWithCount = from matchingProducts in products
                              where
                              matchingProducts.CategoryID != null
                              group matchingProducts by
                              matchingProducts.Category.Name into
                              catGroup
                              select new CategoryWithCount()
                              {
                                  CategoryName = catGroup.Key,
                                  ProductCount = catGroup.Count()
                              };

    if (!String.IsNullOrEmpty(category))
    {
        products = products.Where(p => p.Category.Name == category);
        viewModel.Category = category;
    }
```

```
//sort the results
switch (sortBy)
{
    case "price_lowest":
        products = products.OrderBy(p => p.Price);
        break;
    case "price_highest":
        products = products.OrderByDescending(p => p.Price);
        break;
    default:
        products = products.OrderBy(p => p.Name);
        break;
}

int currentPage = (page ?? 1);
viewModel.Products = products.ToPagedList(currentPage, Constants.PageItems);
viewModel.SortBy = sortBy;
viewModel.Sorts = new Dictionary<string, string>
{
    {"Price low to high", "price_lowest" },
    {"Price high to low", "price_highest" }
};

return View(viewModel);
}
```

Adding a ProductImage Controller and Views

Next, build the solution and then add a ProductImages controller and its associated views. Do this by right-clicking on the Controllers folder and choosing Add followed by Controller from the menu. Choose the option to add an MVC5 controller with views, using Entity Framework. Click the Add button. Next, add a controller named ProductImagesController, specify the model class as ProductImage, and make the data context class StoreContext. Ensure that all the options for views are checked, as shown in Figure 6-1.

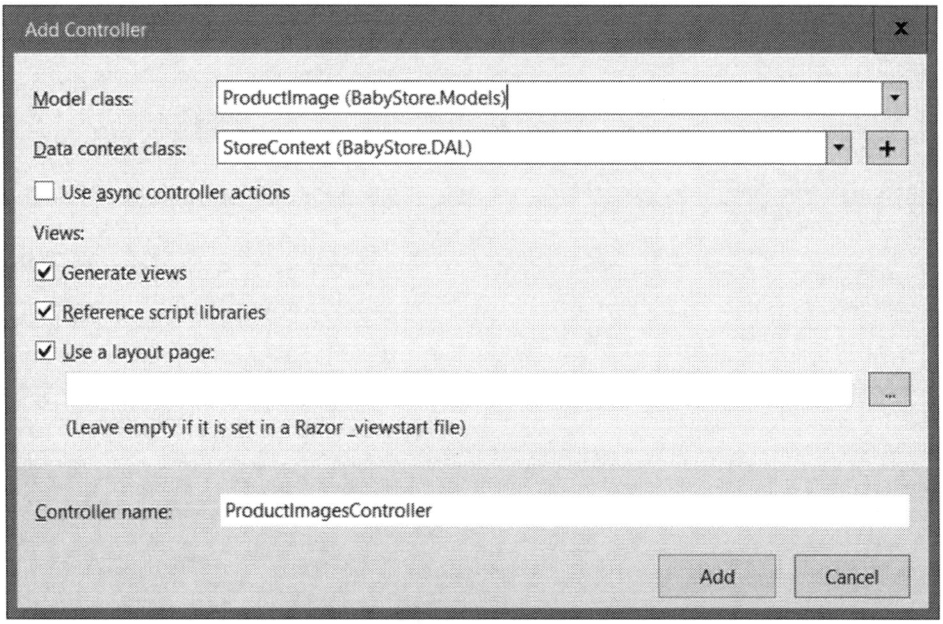

Figure 6-1. *Options for adding a ProductImages controller*

Once it's created, a new `ProductImagesController` class should appear in the `Controllers` folder and the associated CRUD views should appear under the `Views\ProductImages` folder.

The first thing we are going to modify is the `Create` method and the Create view associated with `ProductImages`. If you start the web site and navigate to the `/ProductImages/Create`, you will see a page closely resembling the Category Create page. It allows the user to enter a string, which is not what's required. What is required is a `Create` method and a Create view capable of uploading a file, saving it to disk, and adding the filename to the database.

Updating the ProductImagesController Class for File Uploads

To start with uploading files, we are going to add some methods to the `ProductImagesController` class to validate the file size and format of an upload and resize images to a more appropriate size for displaying in the web site. Normally this code should be split into a distinct reusable class for validating files, but for this demo project, we are going to keep these in the `ProductImagesController` class to make things easier to follow.

Add the following method to the `Controllers/ProductsImagesController.cs` file, below the `Dispose()` method:

```
private bool ValidateFile(HttpPostedFileBase file)
{
    string fileExtension = System.IO.Path.GetExtension(file.FileName).ToLower();
    string[] allowedFileTypes = { ".gif", ".png", ".jpeg", ".jpg" };
    if ((file.ContentLength > 0 && file.ContentLength < 2097152) &&
        allowedFileTypes.Contains(fileExtension))
    {
        return true;
    }
    return false;
}
```

This new method returns a Boolean and takes an input parameter named `file` of the type `HttpPostedFileBase`. The method obtains the extension of the file and checks to see if the file is of the allowed extension types (GIF, PNG, JPEG, and JPG). It also checks if it is between 0 bytes and 2MB in size. If it is, then the method returns true (otherwise, it returns false). One point to note is that rather than loop through the `allowedFileTypes` array, we used the LINQ `contains` operator to shorten the amount of code needed.

Next, add a new method below the `ValidateFile()` method, which will be used to resize images if required and then save them to disk, as follows:

```
private void SaveFileToDisk(HttpPostedFileBase file)
{
    WebImage img = new WebImage(file.InputStream);
    if (img.Width > 190)
    {
        img.Resize(190, img.Height);
    }
    img.Save(Constants.ProductImagePath + file.FileName);
    if (img.Width > 100)
    {
        img.Resize(100, img.Height);
    }
    img.Save(Constants.ProductThumbnailPath + file.FileName);
}
```

To ensure that this code compiles, make sure that you add this `using` statement to the top of the file: `using System.Web.Helpers;`.

The `SaveFileToDisk()` method takes an input parameter file, again of the type `HttpPostedFileBase`. Then it uses the `WebImage` class to resize the image if the width is greater than 190 pixels and save it to the `ProductImages` directory. It then resizes the image down to 100 pixels in width if needed and saves it to the thumbnails directory.

Now that we have the helper methods in place, we need to modify the `Create()` method of the `ProductController` class to upload files when a product is created. First of all, rename both `Create()` methods to `Upload()`. Update the `HttpPost` version of the `Upload()` method, as highlighted in bold:

```
[HttpPost]
[ValidateAntiForgeryToken]
public ActionResult Upload(HttpPostedFileBase file)
{
    //check the user has entered a file
    if (file != null)
    {
        //check if the file is valid
        if (ValidateFile(file))
        {
            try
            {
                SaveFileToDisk(file);
            }
            catch (Exception)
            {
```

```
                ModelState.AddModelError("FileName", "Sorry an error occurred saving the file
                to disk, please try again");
            }
        }
        else
        {
            ModelState.AddModelError("FileName", "The file must be gif, png, jpeg or jpg and
            less than 2MB in size");
        }
    }
    else
    {
        //if the user has not entered a file return an error message
        ModelState.AddModelError("FileName", "Please choose a file");
    }

    if (ModelState.IsValid)
    {
        db.ProductImages.Add(new ProductImage { FileName = file.FileName });
        db.SaveChanges();
        return RedirectToAction("Index");
    }

    return View();
}
```

This first change we have made is to remove the bind section completely because the ID is set by the database and we are going to set the FileName property manually. We've then removed the productImage parameter and added a new input parameter: HttpPostedFileBase[] file. This parameter is a file submitted by the user and will be populated from a file upload control in the view. We're not relying on model binding in this method by performing assignment of data manually, so the method does not require the productImage parameter. Instead, we create a ProductImage object in the method when adding the Product Image to the database in the line of code: db.ProductImages.Add(new ProductImage { FileName = file.FileName });

We've then added an if statement to check the user has actually entered a file. If they have not, then we add an error using ModelState.AddError() to inform them that they need to enter a file as follows:

```
//check the user has entered a file
if (file != null)
{
}
else
{
//if the user has not entered a file return an error message
    ModelState.AddModelError("FileName", "Please choose a file");
}
```

If the user has entered a file, then a check is performed to ensure that a file is "valid," i.e., it is not above 2MB in size and of an allowed format. If it is, the file is then saved to disk using the SaveFileToDisk() method. If the file was not valid, then a model error is added informing the user "The file must be gif, png, jpeg or jpg and less than 2MB in size". All this occurs in the following code:

```
//check if the file is valid
if (ValidateFile(file))
{
    try
    {
        SaveFileToDisk(file);
    }
    catch (Exception)
    {
        ModelState.AddModelError("FileName", "Sorry an error occurred saving the file to disk,
        please try again");
    }
}
else
{
    ModelState.AddModelError("FileName", "The file must be gif, png, jpeg or jpg and less than
    2MB in size");
}
```

Finally, if everything has succeeded and the ModelState is still valid, a new ProductImage is created with the FileName property set to the FileName property of the submitted file and saved to the database. The user is then redirected to the Index view; otherwise, if there were errors in the ModelState, the upload view is returned to the user and displays the errors using the following code:

```
if (ModelState.IsValid)
{
    db.ProductImages.Add(new ProductImage { FileName = file.FileName });
    db.SaveChanges();
    return RedirectToAction("Index");
}
return View();
```

Updating the View

Now that we have updated the controller, we need to update the view file so that it includes a control to submit a form rather than a string. First of all, rename the \Views\ProductImages\Create.cshtml file to Upload.cshtml. Next, modify the file to allow the user to submit a file via an HTML form:

```
@model BabyStore.Models.ProductImage

@{
    ViewBag.Title = "Upload Product Image";
}

<h2>@ViewBag.Title</h2>
```

114

```
@using (Html.BeginForm("Upload", "ProductImages", FormMethod.Post, new { enctype =
"multipart/form-data" }))
{
    @Html.AntiForgeryToken()
    <div class="form-horizontal">
        @Html.ValidationSummary(true, "", new { @class = "text-danger" })
        <div class="form-group">
            @Html.LabelFor(model => model.FileName, htmlAttributes: new { @class = "control-
            label col-md-2" })
            <div class="col-md-10">
                <input type="file" name="file" id="file" class="form-control"/>
                @Html.ValidationMessageFor(model => model.FileName, "", new { @class = "text-
                danger" })
            </div>
        </div>
        <div class="form-group">
            <div class="col-md-offset-2 col-md-10">
                <input type="submit" value="Upload" class="btn btn-default" />
            </div>
        </div>
    </div>
}

<div>
    @Html.ActionLink("Back to List", "Index")
</div>

@section Scripts {
    @Scripts.Render("~/bundles/jqueryval")
}
```

The first changes update the title of the page similar to the way we updated other views in previous chapters. We've then updated the form to have the HTML attribute enctype="multipart/form-data", as this is required for uploading files. This is achieved with the statement @using (Html.BeginForm("Upload", "ProductImages", FormMethod.Post, new { enctype = "multipart/form-data" })).

The next required change is to change the form input to be an HTML file upload control using the code: <input type="file" name="file" id="file" class="form-control" />. The only other change is to change the button text to "Upload". Figure 6-2 shows the resulting HTML page.

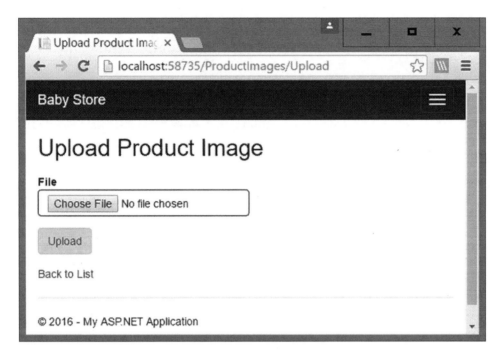

Figure 6-2. *The ProductsImages Upload HTML page with file upload control*

The final changes needed are to add some links to the new view. Modify the \View\Shared_Layout.cshtml file to add a new link to the ProductImages Index page by modifying the unordered list (the <ul> HTML tag) with the nav navbar-nav class as follows:

```
<ul class="nav navbar-nav">
    <li>@Html.ActionLink("Home", "Index", "Home")</li>
    <li>@Html.ActionLink("Shop by Category", "Index", "Categories")</li>
    <li>@Html.RouteLink("View all our Products", "ProductsIndex")</li>
    <li>@Html.ActionLink("Manage Images", "Index", "ProductImages")</li>
</ul>
```

Following this modify the Views\ProductImages\Index.cshtml file to change this line of code in order to create a link to the new Upload view:

```
@Html.ActionLink("Create New", "Create") to @Html.ActionLink("Upload New Image", "Upload")
```

Testing File Uploads

Start the web site and navigate to the ProductImages Upload page, then click Upload without entering a file. The page will display an error message, as shown in Figure 6-3.

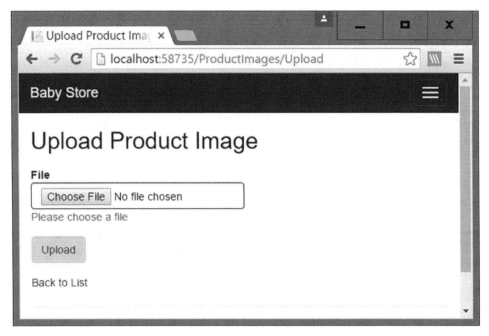

Figure 6-3. *Error message displayed when the user does not choose a file to upload*

Following this test, download the CH06 solution from the Apress web site. Now try to upload the Bitmap01 file from the ProductImages folder of the downloaded solution. The web site should respond with an error message, as shown in Figure 6-4. Next try uploading the LargeImage file. This is a JPG file (of a rather sleepy Labrador) that's over 2MB in size so the web site should respond, as shown in Figure 6-4.

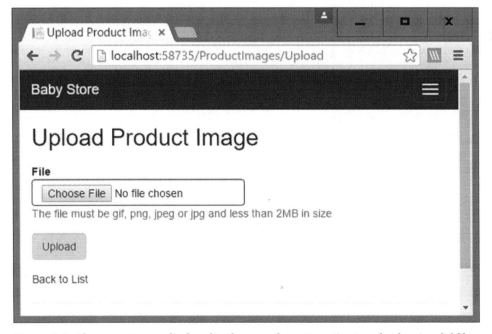

Figure 6-4. *The error message displayed to the user when attempting to upload an invalid file*

Next try to upload the Image01 file; the upload will be allowed. The database table dbo.ProductImages will now contain a record for Image01, as shown in Figure 6-5, and the image will have been resized if required and stored in the Content\ProductImages and Content\ProductImages\Thumbnails folders of the web application. The images should appear under these directories in Solution Explorer, as shown in Figure 6-6. The image will have been resized to 190 pixels wide in the Content\ProductImages folder and to 100 pixels wide in the Thumbnails folder, with the aspect ratio preserved both times.

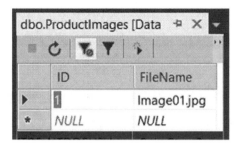

Figure 6-5. *A new entry for Image01.jpg stored in the ProductImages table*

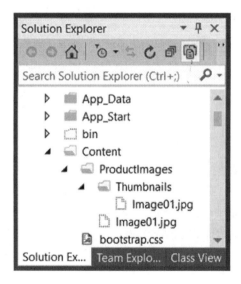

Figure 6-6. *The image Image01.jpg stored in the Content\ProductImages and the Content\ProductImages\Thumbnails directories*

Checking for Unique Records Using Entity Framework

File uploads now work; however, users can upload the same file into the system more than once. Ideally this shouldn't be allowed, so to prevent this from happening, we're going to add a unique constraint that is not a key to the database. To achieve this, we are going to use an index on the FileName field. Update the Models\ProductImage.cs file as follows:

```
using System.ComponentModel.DataAnnotations;
using System.ComponentModel.DataAnnotations.Schema;
```

```
namespace BabyStore.Models
{
    public class ProductImage
    {
        public int ID { get; set; }
        [Display(Name = "File")]
        [StringLength(100)]
        [Index(IsUnique = true)]
        public string FileName { get; set; }
    }
}
```

This code adds a unique constraint and applies a maximum length to the FileName field so that it is no longer set to nvarchar[MAX]. This is required because SQL server applies a maximum size of 900 bytes for index key columns and, without it, the application of the index will fail.

Add a new migration UniqueFileName by typing the following command into Package Manager Console and pressing Return: add-migration UniqueFileName. Next run the update-database command.

The database will now have an index applied to it specifying that the FileName column be unique. This index will prevent duplicate entries in the FileName column and SQL Server will throw an error when an attempt is made to duplicate an entry.

Try to upload the Image01 file again. Figure 6-7 shows how the web site now responds.

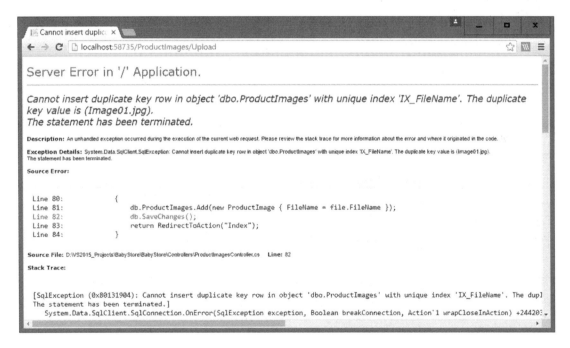

Figure 6-7. *The standard web site error response when trying to add a duplicate record to a unique index column in SQL Server*

To display a more meaningful message to the user, we need to add some error handling so that the web site can respond with an error in the view rather than the standard generated error message. To add error handling, change the HttpPost version of the Upload method in the ProductImagesController class as follows:

```
[HttpPost]
[ValidateAntiForgeryToken]
public ActionResult Upload(HttpPostedFileBase file)
{
    //check the user has entered a file
    if (file != null)
    {
        //check if the file is valid
        if (ValidateFile(file))
        {
            try
            {
                SaveFileToDisk(file);
            }
            catch (Exception)
            {
                ModelState.AddModelError("FileName", "Sorry an error occurred saving the file
                to disk, please try again");
            }
        }
        else
        {
                ModelState.AddModelError("FileName", "The file must be gif, png, jpeg or jpg
                and less than 2MB in size");
        }
    }
    else
    {
        //if the user has not entered a file return an error message
        ModelState.AddModelError("FileName", "Please choose a file");
    }

    if (ModelState.IsValid)
    {
        db.ProductImages.Add(new ProductImage { FileName = file.FileName });
        try
        {
            db.SaveChanges();
        }
        catch (DbUpdateException ex)
        {
            SqlException innerException = ex.InnerException.InnerException as SqlException;
            if (innerException != null && innerException.Number == 2601)
            {
                ModelState.AddModelError("FileName", "The file " + file.FileName +
                    " already exists in the system. Please delete it and try again if you wish
                    to re-add it");
```

```
        }
        else
        {
            ModelState.AddModelError("FileName", "Sorry an error has occurred saving to
                the database, please try again");
        }
        return View();
    }
    return RedirectToAction("Index");
}
return View();
}
```

Also add the following two using statements to the top of the class file so that DbUpdateException and SqlException can be found:

```
using System.Data.SqlClient;
using System.Data.Entity.Infrastructure;
```

This code uses a try catch statement to attempt to save the database changes or catch an exception of the type DBUpdateException. It then checks the InnerException property of the InnerException property of the exception to check if it is exception number 2601 (this is the SQL Exception number for trying to insert a duplicate key when a unique index is in place on a table). If the exception is number 2601, then an error is added to the ModelState to notify the user that the file already exists. If the exception is a different number, a more generic error is thrown. Finally, if there was an exception, the Update view is returned to the user to display the error message.

If we now try to upload the Image01.jpg file, the web site responds as shown in Figure 6-8, rather than throwing a standard error message.

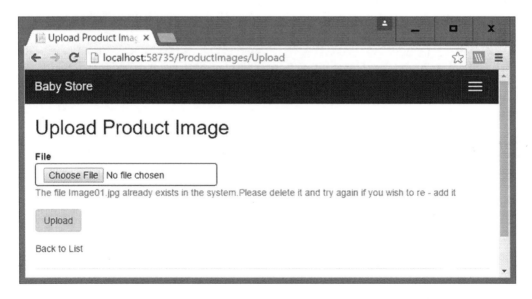

Figure 6-8. *The error message produced by the new try catch statement when trying to upload a duplicate file*

Allowing Multiple File Uploads

The current File Upload system works well, but only allows users to upload one image. A content editor may have to upload many images, so constantly opening the upload page to upload one image at a time will be very time consuming. To help speed this workflow up, we are going to allow users to upload up to 10 files at a time. In order to do this, we need to modify the Upload method in the ProductImagesController class so that it can handle more than one file as an input parameter and then validate these files and upload their filenames to the database. We also need to modify the Views\ProductImages\Upload.cshtml file to allow multiple files to be submitted at once.

The code is more complex than the previous code in the book, so I am going to explain the algorithm in general terms first:

- A user must enter at least one file and cannot upload more than 10 files at a time.

- All the files must be valid (i.e., less than 2MB and of the format GIF, PNG, JPEG, or JPG).

- If any of the files are not valid, then none of the files will be uploaded and an error is returned to the user listing the invalid files.

- If all the files are valid, then each one is saved to disk. If there is a problem saving any of the files, an error is thrown and the user is asked to try again. The code will simply overwrite any existing files and does not attempt to remove any files it has already saved; they will simply be overwritten when the user tries again.

- If all the files are valid and all uploaded okay, then the system will now attempt to save every name to the database.

- If any of the files are duplicates, i.e., they already exist in the database, then they will not be added and an error message will be displayed listing the name of each duplicate file. All the other non-duplicate files will be saved to the database. I am making the code work this way to demonstrate how to manipulate the data store in the database context object. I will explain this later, but in basic terms, the data stored in the context object is not necessarily the same as that stored in the database and can require some local management.

- If any error was thrown, the Upload view is returned. Otherwise, the Index view is returned. In the case where some files were not uploaded due to being duplicates, the Upload view is returned with an indication in the error message that any files that were not duplicates were uploaded.

Updating the ProductImagesController Class for Multiple File Uploads

In order to allow multiple file uploads, we're going to modify the HttpPost version of the Upload method of the ProductImagesController class. To start, clear out the contents of the method and then update the input parameter to be an array of the type HttpPostedFileBase as follows:

```
[HttpPost]
[ValidateAntiForgeryToken]
public ActionResult Upload(HttpPostedFileBase[] files)
{
    return View();
}
```

Next, add a couple of variables to the top of the method to keep track of whether all the files are valid and store the names of any invalid files:

```
[HttpPost]
[ValidateAntiForgeryToken]
public ActionResult Upload(HttpPostedFileBase[] files)
{
    bool allValid = true;
    string inValidFiles = "";
    return View();
}
```

Following these variables, update the code to check if the user has submitted any files. Check the first element of the files variable for a null value and then check that they have not added more than 10 files at a time:

```
[HttpPost]
[ValidateAntiForgeryToken]
public ActionResult Upload(HttpPostedFileBase[] files)
{
    bool allValid = true;
    string inValidFiles = "";
    //check the user has entered a file
    if (files[0] != null)
    {
        //if the user has entered less than ten files
        if (files.Length <= 10)
        {
        }
        //the user has entered more than 10 files
        else
        {
            ModelState.AddModelError("FileName", "Please only upload up to ten files at a
            time");
        }
    }
    else
    {
        //if the user has not entered a file return an error message

        ModelState.AddModelError("FileName", "Please choose a file");
    }
    if (ModelState.IsValid)
    {
    }
    return View();
}
```

Next, if at least one and fewer than 10 files have been added, loop through all the files to check that they are valid by using the following code. If any of the files are not valid, the variable allValid is set to false and the name of the file is appended to the end of the inValidFiles string. If all the files are valid, then loop through the files and save each one to disk. If they are not all valid, add an error to the ModelState including the name of all the invalid files as follows:

```
//if the user has entered less than ten files
if (files.Length <= 10)
{
    //check they are all valid
    foreach (var file in files)
    {
        if (!ValidateFile(file))
        {
            allValid = false;
            inValidFiles += ", " + file.FileName;
        }
    }
    //if they are all valid then try to save them to disk
    if (allValid)
    {
        foreach (var file in files)
        {
            try
            {
                SaveFileToDisk(file);
            }
            catch (Exception)
            {
                ModelState.AddModelError("FileName", "Sorry an error occurred saving the files
                to disk, please try again");
            }
        }
    }
    //else add an error listing out the invalid files
    else
    {
        ModelState.AddModelError("FileName", "All files must be gif, png, jpeg or jpg and less
        than 2MB in size.The following files" + inValidFiles + " are not valid");
    }
}
//the user has entered more than 10 files
else
{
    ModelState.AddModelError("FileName", "Please only upload up to ten files at a time");
}
```

If there were no errors added to the ModelState, the final section of code attempts to add each file to the database. First add the following code to check if the ModelState does not contain any errors and store if there were any errors caused by duplicates or other database-update issues. The code also contains a string for storing the name of any duplicate files:

```
if (ModelState.IsValid)
{
    bool duplicates = false;
    bool otherDbError = false;
    string duplicateFiles = "";
}
```

Next, the code loops through the files and adds each file to the database context and then attempts to save them to the database. Note that we don't use an unnamed anonymous new ProductImage in this code because later in the chapter we need to refer back to the ProductImage that the code attempts to add. If any of the updates fail due to a database error, the error is caught as it was for single file uploads. If the error was caused by an entry already existing in the database, the name of the file is added to the duplicateFiles string and the duplicates Boolean is set to true. Otherwise, we set the Boolean otherDbError to true, indicating something else went wrong. This code is written so that even if saving a file to the database fails, the other files submitted will still be saved to the database.

```
if (ModelState.IsValid)
{
    bool duplicates = false;
    bool otherDbError = false;
    string duplicateFiles = "";

    foreach (var file in files)
    {
        //try and save each file
        var productToAdd = new ProductImage { FileName = file.FileName };
        try
        {
            db.ProductImages.Add(productToAdd);
            db.SaveChanges();
        }
        //if there is an exception check if it is caused by a duplicate file
        catch (DbUpdateException ex)
        {
            SqlException innerException = ex.InnerException.InnerException as SqlException;
            if (innerException != null && innerException.Number == 2601)
            {
                duplicateFiles += ", " + file.FileName;
                duplicates = true;
            }
            else
            {
                otherDbError = true;
            }
        }
    }
}
```

Finally, if either of the two Booleans is set to true, an appropriate error message is added to the ModelState. Where an attempt has been made to add a file that already exists in the database, the list of duplicate files is displayed to the user.

```
if (ModelState.IsValid)
{
    bool duplicates = false;
    bool otherDbError = false;
    string duplicateFiles = "";

    foreach (var file in files)
    {
        //try and save each file
        var productToAdd = new ProductImage { FileName = file.FileName };
        try
        {
            db.ProductImages.Add(productToAdd);
            db.SaveChanges();
        }
        //if there is an exception check if it is caused by a duplicate file
        catch (DbUpdateException ex)
        {
            SqlException innerException = ex.InnerException.InnerException as SqlException;
            if (innerException != null && innerException.Number == 2601)
            {
                duplicateFiles += ", " + file.FileName;
                duplicates = true;
            }
            else
            {
                otherDbError = true;
            }
        }
    }
    //add a list of duplicate files to the error message
    if (duplicates)
    {
        ModelState.AddModelError("FileName", "All files uploaded except the files" +
            duplicateFiles + ", which already exist in the system." + " Please delete them
            and try again if you wish to re-add them");
        return View();
    }
    else if (otherDbError)
    {
        ModelState.AddModelError("FileName", "Sorry an error has occurred saving to the
        database, please try again");
        return View();
    }
    return RedirectToAction("Index");
}
```

The completed HttpPost version of the Upload method should now read as follows:

```
[HttpPost]
[ValidateAntiForgeryToken]
public ActionResult Upload(HttpPostedFileBase[] files)
{
    bool allValid = true;
    string inValidFiles = "";
    //check the user has entered a file
    if (files[0] != null)
    {
        //if the user has entered less than ten files
        if (files.Length <= 10)
        {
            //check they are all valid
            foreach (var file in files)
            {
                if (!ValidateFile(file))
                {
                    allValid = false;
                    inValidFiles += ", " + file.FileName;
                }
            }
            //if they are all valid then try to save them to disk
            if (allValid)
            {
                foreach (var file in files)
                {
                    try
                    {
                        SaveFileToDisk(file);
                    }
                    catch (Exception)
                    {
                        ModelState.AddModelError("FileName", "Sorry an error occurred saving
                        the files to disk, please try again");
                    }
                }
            }
            //else add an error listing out the invalid files
            else
            {
                ModelState.AddModelError("FileName", "All files must be gif, png, jpeg or jpg
                and less than 2MB in size.The following files" + inValidFiles + " are
                not valid");
            }
        }
        //the user has entered more than 10 files
        else
        {
            ModelState.AddModelError("FileName", "Please only upload up to ten files at a
            time");
```

```
        }
    }
    else
    {
        //if the user has not entered a file return an error message
        ModelState.AddModelError("FileName", "Please choose a file");
    }

    if (ModelState.IsValid)
    {
        bool duplicates = false;
        bool otherDbError = false;
        string duplicateFiles = "";
        foreach (var file in files)
        {
            //try and save each file
            var productToAdd = new ProductImage { FileName = file.FileName };
            try
            {
                db.ProductImages.Add(productToAdd);
                db.SaveChanges();
            }
            //if there is an exception check if it is caused by a duplicate file
            catch (DbUpdateException ex)
            {
                SqlException innerException = ex.InnerException.InnerException as
                SqlException;
                if (innerException != null && innerException.Number == 2601)
                {
                    duplicateFiles += ", " + file.FileName;
                    duplicates = true;
                }
                else
                {
                    otherDbError = true;
                }
            }
        }
        //add a list of duplicate files to the error message
        if (duplicates)
        {
            ModelState.AddModelError("FileName", "All files uploaded except the files" +
                duplicateFiles + ", which already exist in the system." +
                " Please delete them and try again if you wish to re-add them");
            return View();
        }
        else if (otherDbError)
        {
            ModelState.AddModelError("FileName", "Sorry an error has occurred saving to the
            database, please try again");
```

```
            return View();
        }
        return RedirectToAction("Index");
    }
    return View();
}
```

Updating the Upload View for Multiple File Uploads

After the large set of changes to the controller, you'll be pleased to hear that updating the view is rather more straightforward. Update the ViewBag.Title so that it now equals "Upload Product Images" and then modify the HTML file input in the Views\ProductImages\Upload.cshtml file as follows:

```
<input type="file" name="files" id="files" multiple="multiple" class="form-control" />
```

The name and ID of the control is changed to files rather than file and the entry multiple="multiple" means that the control will allow a user to select multiple files at once.

Also update the actionLink in the Views\ProductImages\Index.cshtml file so that the text now reads Upload New Images.

Testing Multiple File Uploads

Start the web site without debugging and navigate to the ProductImages/Upload view.

First of all, we're going to test that a user must enter at least one file and cannot upload more than 10 files at a time. Click on the Upload button. The web site should respond with the message "Please choose a file," as shown in Figure 6-3.

Next try uploading more than 10 files at once by attempting to upload the images image01 to image11, from the CH06 solution download, inclusive. The web site should respond as shown in Figure 6-9. Check the database and filesystem to ensure that no files have been uploaded.

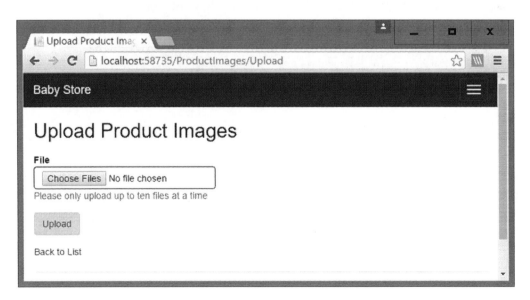

Figure 6-9. *Error message when attempting to upload more than 10 files at once*

The next scenario to test is that if any of the files are not valid, then none of the files is uploaded and an error is returned to the user listing the invalid files. Try uploading the files Image02 and Bitmap01. The web site should respond as shown in Figure 6-10.

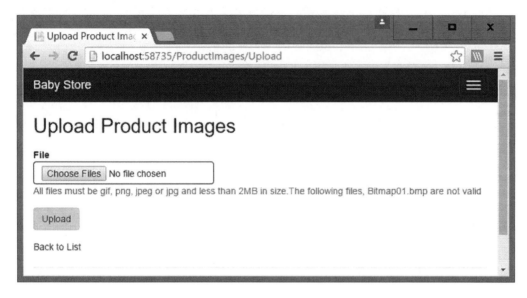

Figure 6-10. *Attempting to upload at least one file with an invalid file type*

Now try uploading the Image02, Image03, and Image04 files. They should upload successfully and the Index view should be shown with the list of uploaded files, as shown in Figure 6-11. The files should appear in the database and in the filesystem, similar to Figures 6-5 and 6-6.

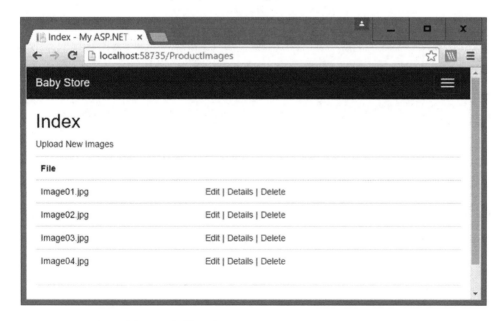

Figure 6-11. *Successful multiple file uploads*

130

Finally, we need to test for duplicate files. Try uploading the Image04 and Image05 files to the database. Image05 should be added, but Image04 should return a message that the image already exists in the system. The result is shown in Figure 6-12.

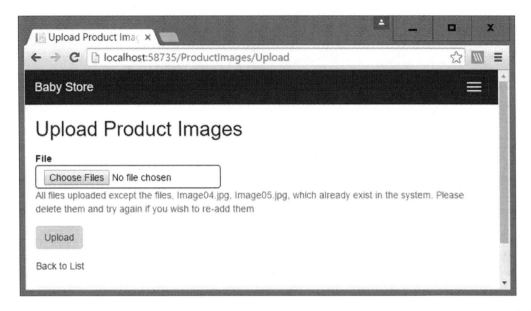

Figure 6-12. *The error message displayed by the web site when one of the files is a duplicate*

Something is wrong because the error message is telling us that both files are duplicates, which we know is not true. This issue occurs because of the way the StoreContext object in the ProductsController class behaves. I will explain why this message occurs and how to prevent it in the following section.

Working with the DbContext Object and Entity States

During the testing of multiple file uploads, an issue was found when one of the files already had a filename record in the database. The issue was that any files that followed the duplicate file were also marked as duplicates, even though they were not. So why does this occur? Well, the answer lies in the code used to add the ProductImage entity to the database and the way that the DbContext object is designed to work. Recall that StoreContext used in the ProductImagesController class derives from DbContext. At the moment, the relevant code contained inside the HttpPost Upload method for detecting duplicate files looks like this:

```
foreach (var file in files)
{
    var productToAdd = new ProductImage { FileName = file.FileName };
    try
    {
        db.ProductImages.Add(productToAdd);
        db.SaveChanges();
    }
    catch (DbUpdateException ex)
    {
        SqlException innerException = ex.InnerException.InnerException as SqlException;
```

```
        if (innerException != null && innerException.Number == 2601)
        {
            duplicateFiles += ", " + file.FileName;
            duplicates = true;
        }
        else
        {
            otherDbError = true;
        }
    }
}
```

To see what is wrong with this code, add a breakpoint to the code on the foreach (var file in files) line.

■ **Tip**   To add a breakpoint in Visual Studio, left-click in the grey margin in the code window and a red dot will appear.

Now start the web site with debugging by clicking on Start Debugging from the Debug menu of Visual Studio. Navigate to the ProductImages/Upload page and try uploading Image04 and Image05 again. When you click the Create button, Visual Studio will open at the breakpoint.

Keep pressing the F10 key to move through the loop once. The code will move into the catch statement. Continue to press F10 until you get to the db.SaveChanges() line again and then pause. Now left-click on ProductImages in the line of code db.ProductImages.Add(productToAdd); and expand the first menu to show the count of items in db.ProductImages. The count is 2. Figure 6-13 shows how to display the count.

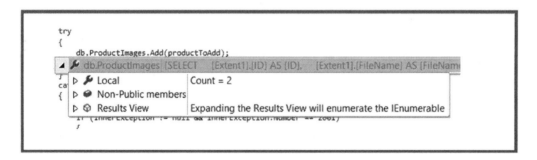

Figure 6-13. *Using debugging to show the count of db.ProductImages*

This means that although Image04 caused an exception to be thrown and was not saved to the database, its entry still exists in the local context instance (in db.ProductImages). Continue to move through the code by pressing F10 and notice that the exception is thrown again, even though the second file is not a duplicate. This is caused by the first duplicate file's entry still existing in the current DbContext instance (db). This is the reason that both filenames are listed in the error message shown in Figure 6-12. Even though adding Image04 to the DbContext (db) threw an exception, it was not removed from db.ProductImages and Entity Framework tracks that has not been saved to the database and so tries to save it again.

To remedy this issue, we have to remove any files that throw an exception from the current DbContext instance (db). There are a couple of options. There is the more brute-force option; to dispose of the context (by calling db.Dispose()) and create a new instance when processing each file. There is an alternative, which is to manipulate the current dbContext instance. This is the option we're going to use to ensure that any files that throw an error do not remain in the DbContext when processing the next iteration of the loop.

To remove an entry from the DbContext, the state of the entity needs to be set to detached. To detach the current file, the following code needs to be used:

```
db.Entry(productToAdd).State = EntityState.Detached;
```

In order to fix the current issue with duplicate files, add this code inside the last catch statement of the Upload method in the Controllers\ProductImagesController.cs file as follows:

```
catch (DbUpdateException ex)
{
    SqlException innerException = ex.InnerException.InnerException as SqlException;
    if (innerException != null && innerException.Number == 2601)
    {
        duplicateFiles += ", " + file.FileName;
        duplicates = true;
        db.Entry(productToAdd).State = EntityState.Detached;
    }
    else
    {
        otherDbError = true;
    }
}
```

Now any files that throw an exception because they already exist in the system will be removed from the DbContext prior to the next file being processed. To see this in action, try adding the two files Image04 and Image05 to the site again, and as shown in Figure 6-14, only the duplicate file Image04.jpg is returned in the error message.

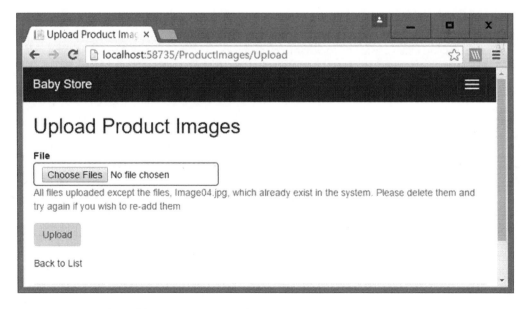

Figure 6-14. *Duplicate file error messages working as expected*

Figure 6-15 shows the Index view confirming that the `Image05.jpg` file was uploaded successfully.

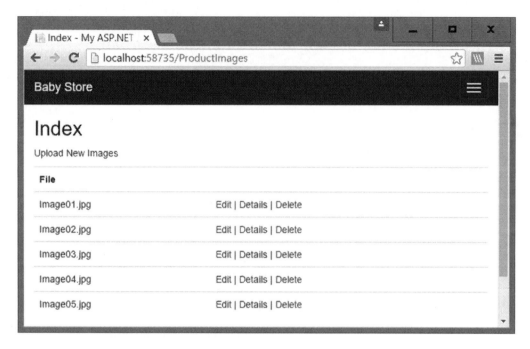

Figure 6-15. *Confirmation that the Image05.jpg file was uploaded even though Image04.jpg already existed in the database*

This scenario only covers entities that have been added to the `DbContext`, but entities may also have been deleted or modified. To reset entity states where the state is currently `EntityState.Deleted` or `EntityState.Modified`, set the state to `EntityState.Unchanged`. For any modified entries, also set the values to `OriginalValues`. For example if we wanted to reset the values for the `ProductToAdd` entry, we could use the code: `db.Entry(productToAdd).CurrentValues.SetValues(db.Entry(productToAdd).OriginalValues);`

Viewing SQL Generated by Entity Framework

There is one more issue to consider with the present code. If we run the web site with debugging and add two valid files, then prior to uploading the second file, the count of `db.ProductImages` is 2, as it was in Figure 6-14. This looks like every time we call `db.SaveChanges()`, we are in fact saving entries for all the previous files too. However, although these entities exist in the context, Entity Framework tracks if an entry in the `DbContext` has already been saved and so does not try to save it again.

You can see the SQL statements generated by Entity Framework by adding this line of code: `db.Database.Log = sql => Trace.WriteLine(sql);` plus adding `using System.Diagnostics;`. The SQL will be written into the Output window in Visual Studio.

As an example to show you this scenario where the db.ProductImages count is 2 but Entity Framework only attempts to save the second file, add the logging line of code to the HttpPost of the Upload method in the ProductImagesController class as follows:

```
[HttpPost]
[ValidateAntiForgeryToken]
public ActionResult Upload(HttpPostedFileBase[] files)
{
    bool allValid = true;
    string inValidFiles = "";
    db.Database.Log = sql => Trace.WriteLine(sql);
    //check the user has entered a file
    if (files[0] != null)
    ...
```

Ensure that you add using System.Diagnostics; to the top of the ProductImagesController class. Add a breakpoint at the line highlighted in bold below and run the web site by choosing Debug then Start Debugging from the menu:

```
if (ModelState.IsValid)
{
    bool duplicates = false;
    bool otherDbError = false;
    string duplicateFiles = "";
    foreach (var file in files)
```

Try uploading the Image06 and Image07 file. When the code hits the breakpoint, run through the code by pressing F10 until you pass db.SaveChanges(). You should see SQL appear in the Output window showing the SQL generated to upload Image06. Now continue to press F10 until you pass the db.SaveChanges() line again. This time, the count of db.ProductImages will be 2 but the generated SQL only attempts to save the second file (Image07), as shown in Figure 6-16.

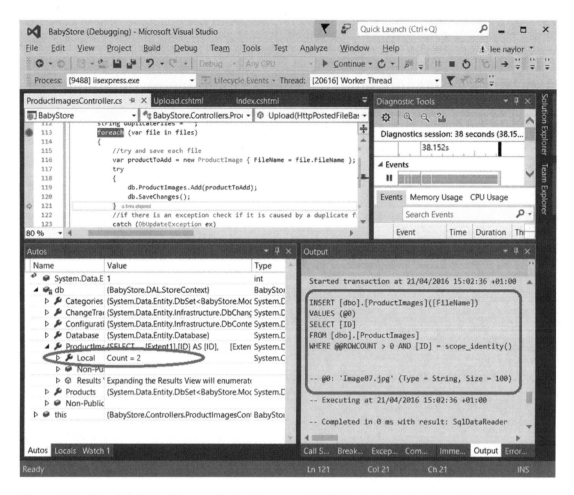

Figure 6-16. *Visual Studio in debug mode showing generated SQL in the Output window. The highlighted areas show that, although the ProductImages count is 2, the SQL generated by Entity Framework only attempts to save the file Image07.jpg*

Performance Considerations When Using db.SaveChanges()

If you are building a system responsible for bulk upload and using Entity Framework, then I do not recommend calling SaveChanges() for each individual record. In the multiple file upload code, I have included the call to SaveChanges() for each item in a loop in order to demonstrate some of the features of Entity Framework and also because the code can deal with only 10 records at a time. In a system that's making bulk uploads, it is much faster to call SaveChanges() once, after all the items have been added to the DbContext.

Dealing with Maximum Request Length Exceeded Errors

If you have attempted to upload any of your own files during this exercise, you may have encountered the rather annoying error screen displayed in Figure 6-17. This error is caused by the web server (IIS) having a maximum limit of 4MB on request lengths. This limit is set with a view to preventing Denial of Service attacks, but it can be overridden.

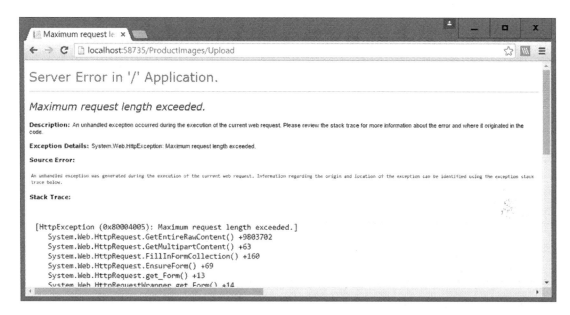

Figure 6-17. *The default maximum upload request length exceeded error screen*

To fix this issue, we are going to do a couple of things:

- Up the limit to 20MB.
- Display a different error page when the error occurs.

Upping the Allowed Maximum Request Size

You change the file size limit in two places in the project's main Web.config file. First of all, edit the <system.web> section as follows, to add the maxRequestLength parameter:

```
<system.web>
  <authentication mode="None" />
  <compilation debug="true" targetFramework="4.6.1" />
  <httpRuntime targetFramework="4.6.1" maxRequestLength="20480" />
</system.web>
```

■ **Note**   The maxRequestLength parameter is set in kilobytes.

Next, update the `<system.webServer>` section of the `Web.config` file to add a new security section containing a `requestLimits` parameter, as follows:

```
<system.webServer>
  <modules>
    <remove name="FormsAuthentication" />
  </modules>
  <security>
    <requestFiltering>
      <requestLimits maxAllowedContentLength="20971520"/>
    </requestFiltering>
  </security>
</system.webServer>
```

■ **Note**   The `maxAllowedContentLength` parameter is set in bytes.

Both of these changes set the value of both parameters to 20MB. The maximum request length allowed will now be 20MB.

Adding a Custom Error Page for Maximum Request Length Exceeded Errors

We are now going to create a custom error page to replace the one shown in Figure 6-17. To do this, we are going to add a new controller to handle requests and a view to display an error page to the users.

Add a new empty controller by right-clicking on the `controllers` folder and choosing Add ➤ Controller from the menu. Then choose the MVC5 Controller - Empty option and click Add. Next name the controller `ErrorController`. A new `ErrorController` class should appear in Visual Studio containing an `Index` method.

Update the new `ErrorController` class as follows to rename the `Index` method:

```
using System.Web.Mvc;

namespace BabyStore.Controllers
{
    public class ErrorController : Controller
    {
        // GET: Error
        public ActionResult FileUploadLimitExceeded()
        {
            return View();
        }
    }
}
```

Next, right-click on the method name (`FileUploadLimitExceeded`) and choose Add View from the popup menu. In the Add View window that appears, name the view `FileUploadLimitExceeded` with an Empty template and also check the Use a Layout Page option, as shown in Figure 6-18.

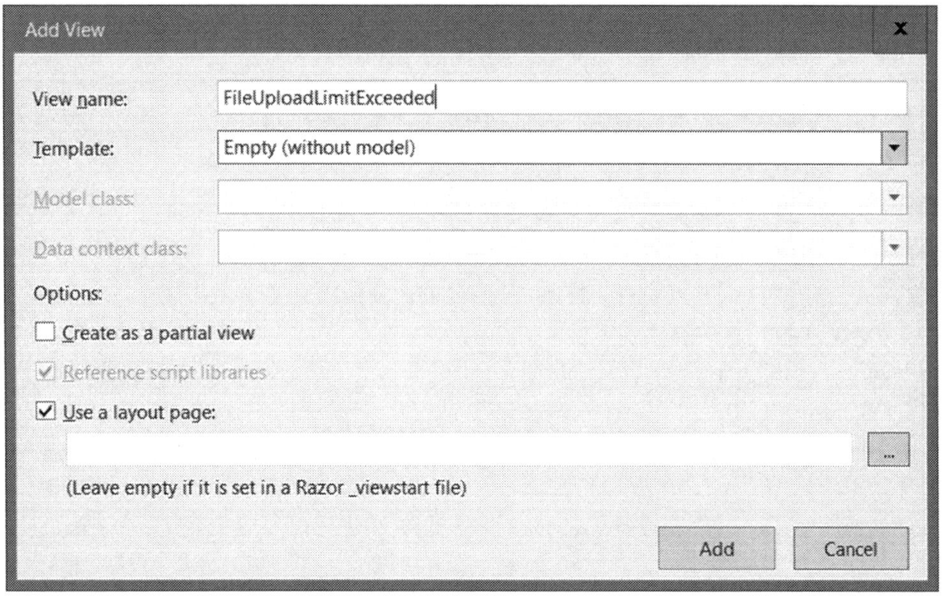

Figure 6-18. *Adding the Error/FileUploadLimitExceeded view*

Click the Add button to add the view and then update the content of the view to:

```
@{
    ViewBag.Title = "File Upload Limit Exceeded";
}
<h2>Sorry. The files you have tried to upload total more than 20MB in size. Please go back
and try uploading them one by one, or saving them into a smaller file size or format.</h2>
```

Next update the main Web.config file to add a new httpErrors section to the <system.webServer> section as follows:

```
<system.webServer>
    <httpErrors errorMode="Custom">
      <remove statusCode="404" subStatusCode="13"/>
      <error statusCode="404" subStatusCode="13" responseMode="Redirect"
             path="/Error/FileUploadLimitExceeded"/>
    </httpErrors>
    ...
```

This change checks for the occurrence of a 404.13 error. If the error occurs, the user is redirected to the new Error/FileUploadLimitExceeded view. 404.13 is the number of the error thrown when the maximum request length allowed is exceeded.

The errorMode parameter can be set to three values: Detailed, DetailedLocalOnly, or Custom. Custom will always display the custom error page, the Detailed value will always display the normal asp.net detailed error message, and DetailedLocalOnly will only display detailed error messages on the local machine. In this case, we are happy to see the custom error message all the time, so we choose Custom.

Now when the users attempt to upload files with a total size of more than 20MB, they will receive the custom error page shown in Figure 6-19.

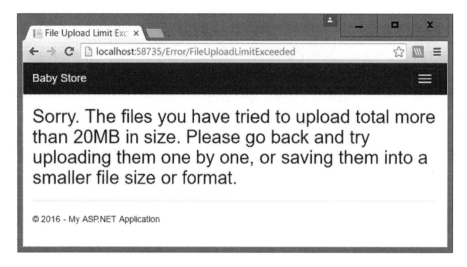

Figure 6-19. *A custom error page displayed in place of the default maximum upload request length exceeded error screen*

Associating Images with a Product

Now that images can be uploaded, the next task is to associate the images with products. We are going to model a relationship where a product can have many images and an image can be associated with many products. In a real production site, this functionality might not be required because an image may only belong to a single product, but we are going to model this for demo purposes as follows:

- An image can be associated with several products and a product can be associated with many images (we're going to place an artificial limit of five images per product by limiting the amount of files that can be chosen in the view).

- Each image will have a number associated with it. This number will specify where the image appears when the images are displayed in a product's details. For example, the first image will be the main default image. We're going to name this field ImageNumber.

Adding a Many-to-Many Relationship with Payload

The relationship between images and products will be modeled as a many-to-many join with payload. This means that we're going to use a join table whereby a record in the table will contain foreign keys for both an image and a product and also a column named ImageNumber containing the number of the image.

Without the ImageNumber column, this would be a relationship known as a many-to-many join without payload, as each record would contain only foreign keys. If we leave out the ImageNumber column, then there will be no way to know what order images should appear in when displayed with a product.

■ **Note**   To model a many-to-many join without payload, you specify a collection of the other entities in each of the affected entities. If you use Code First Migrations, Entity Framework will then add a many-to-many join table automatically without the need to create a code class for the join table.

To model a many-to-many join with payload, you need a new entity. Create a new class named ProductImageMapping in the Models folder and update the contents as follows:

```
namespace BabyStore.Models
{
    public class ProductImageMapping
    {
        public int ID { get; set; }
        public int ImageNumber { get; set; }
        public int ProductID { get; set; }
        public int ProductImageID { get; set; }

        public virtual Product Product { get; set; }
        public virtual ProductImage ProductImage { get; set; }
    }
}
```

This new class contains an ImageNumber property to store the number of each image plus foreign keys and navigational properties, which are in the Product and ProductImage entities.

Next, add the following property containing a collection of ProductImageMappings to the Product class in the Models\Product.cs file:

```
public virtual ICollection<ProductImageMapping> ProductImageMappings { get; set; }
```

Finally, complete the references to this new class by adding the same property to the ProductImage class in the Models\ProductImage.cs file. Ensure that you add the using System.Collections.Generic; statement to each file so that the code compiles. There is now a one-to-many relationship between the ProductImageMapping entity and the Product and ProductImage entities. That means there is effectively a many-to-many relationship between Product and ProductImage.

Next, add a new Code First Migration by running the following command in Package Manager Console: add-migration CreateProductImageMappings. Then run the update-database command.

A new table named ProductImageMappings will now exist in the BabyStore database, as shown in Figure 6-20.

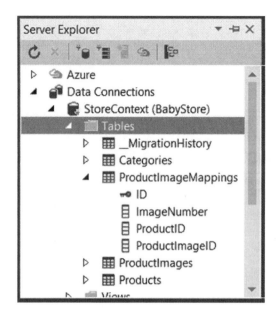

Figure 6-20. *The new ProductImageMappings join table*

Finally, add a new entry to the DAL\StoreContext.cs file for ProductImageMappings as follows:

```
using BabyStore.Models;
using System.Data.Entity;

namespace BabyStore.DAL
{
    public class StoreContext:DbContext
    {
        public DbSet<Product> Products { get; set; }
        public DbSet<Category> Categories { get; set; }
        public DbSet<ProductImage> ProductImages { get; set; }
        public DbSet<ProductImageMapping> ProductImageMappings { get; set; }
    }
}
```

This new property is required in order to delete a ProductImageMapping record directly. We'll use this when updating the HttpPost version of the Edit method in ProductsController.cs later in the chapter.

Adding Images to a New Product

To keep things relatively simple, we are going to use HTML select controls to allow users to pick images to add to a product; there will be five of these per product. In a production system, you may choose a different way to display this; there are several ways to allow users to pick multiple items and order them, but they all have their positives and negatives; hence, I simply chose five lists.

Creating a View Model for Product Creation and Editing

The first thing we are going to do is add a view model rather than relying on the ViewBag to pass data to the view. Add a new class named ProductViewModel to the ViewModels folder. Update the code of this new class as follows:

```
using System.Collections.Generic;
using System.ComponentModel.DataAnnotations;
using System.Web.Mvc;

namespace BabyStore.ViewModels
{
    public class ProductViewModel
    {
        public int ID { get; set; }

        [Required(ErrorMessage = "The product name cannot be blank")]
        [StringLength(50, MinimumLength = 3, ErrorMessage = "Please enter a product name
        between 3 and 50 characters in length")]
        [RegularExpression(@"^[a-zA-Z0-9'-'\s]*$", ErrorMessage = "Please enter a product name
        made up of letters and numbers only")]
        public string Name { get; set; }

        [Required(ErrorMessage = "The product description cannot be blank")]
        [StringLength(200, MinimumLength = 10, ErrorMessage = "Please enter a product
        description between 10 and 200 characters in length")]
        [RegularExpression(@"^[,;a-zA-Z0-9'-'\s]*$", ErrorMessage = "Please enter a product
        description made up of letters and numbers only")]
        [DataType(DataType.MultilineText)]
        public string Description { get; set; }

        [Required(ErrorMessage = "The price cannot be blank")]
        [Range(0.10, 10000, ErrorMessage = "Please enter a price between 0.10 and 10000.00")]
        [DataType(DataType.Currency)]
        [DisplayFormat(DataFormatString = "{0:c}")]
        [RegularExpression("[0-9]+(\\.[0-9][0-9]?)?", ErrorMessage = "The price must be a
        number up to two decimal places")]
        public decimal Price { get; set; }

        [Display(Name ="Category")]
        public int CategoryID { get; set; }
        public SelectList CategoryList { get; set; }
        public List<SelectList> ImageLists { get; set; }
        public string[] ProductImages { get; set; }
    }
}
```

I have chosen the duplication pattern for this view model and duplicated the code from the Products model for several properties and validation. Although duplication involves duplicating code, it allows the two models to act completely independently from one another. This view model differs from the Product class because it contains two properties of the type SelectList that are used to hold a list of categories and images. The properties CategoryID and ProductImages will be used as the name of the SelectLists in the view.

■ **Note** There are various patterns for working with view models and using validation. The main ones are inheritance (where the view model inherits from the original model), composition (where the model is a property of the view model), and duplication (duplicating the code). There is plenty of opinion around what is the best one to use and you should consider the circumstances of your particular project before choosing one.

Specifying a Fixed Number of Images per Product

We're going to allow five images to be associated with a product so implement this by simply adding five lists to the view. Add a new constant to the Constants class by updating the Constants.cs file as follows:

```
namespace BabyStore
{
    public static class Constants
    {
        public const string ProductImagePath = "~/Content/ProductImages/";
        public const string ProductThumbnailPath = "~/Content/ProductImages/Thumbnails/";
        public const int PageItems = 3;
        public const int NumberOfProductImages = 5;
    }
}
```

Updating the ProductsController to Add Images to a New Product

We are now going to update the GET version of the Create method in the Controllers\ProductsController.cs file to use the new view model and add some SelectLists to be used for displaying product images from which the user can choose images. Update the GET version of the Create method as follows:

```
// GET: Products/Create
public ActionResult Create()
{
    ProductViewModel viewModel = new ProductViewModel();
    viewModel.CategoryList = new SelectList(db.Categories, "ID", "Name");
    viewModel.ImageLists = new List<SelectList>();
    for (int i = 0; i < Constants.NumberOfProductImages; i++)
    {
        viewModel.ImageLists.Add(new SelectList(db.ProductImages, "ID", "FileName"));
    }
    return View(viewModel);
}
```

This new code creates a new instance of the ProductViewModel named viewModel and assigns SelectList categories to the CategoryList property. It then creates five SelectLists containing all the product images and adds them to the ImageLists property of the viewModel. We could have just used one SelectList, but I wanted to be able to specify a default value for each SelectList if the binding process fails in the HttpPost version of the Create method, as you will see shortly.

Updating the Product Create View

Before we update the HttpPost version of the Create method, we are going to modify the Product Create view to show you how this view will now look and the changes it requires. Open the Views\Products\ Create.cshtml file and update it as follows. First, modify the model used by the view by updating the top line of the file to:

```
@model BabyStore.ViewModels.ProductViewModel
```

Next, update the code that generates the CategoryID drop-down to change it to use the DropDownListFor helper and assign it to use the CategoryList property of the view model for the data and keep the name as CategoryID. We've also updated the label, as this previously contained a way of defining the label in the view rather than the model:

```
<div class="form-group">
    @Html.LabelFor(model => model.CategoryID, htmlAttributes: new { @class =
    "control-label col-md-2" })
    <div class="col-md-10">
        @Html.DropDownListFor(vm => vm.CategoryID, Model.CategoryList, htmlAttributes: new {
        @class = "form-control" })
        @Html.ValidationMessageFor(model => model.CategoryID, "", new { @class = "text-danger"
        })
    </div>
</div>
```

Finally, add five HTML SELECT elements for selecting a product image by adding the following code after the category code:

```
@for (int i = 0; i < Model.ImageLists.Count; i++)
{
    <div class="form-group">
        <label class="control-label col-md-2">Product Image @(i + 1):</label>
        <div class="col-md-10">
            @Html.DropDownListFor(vm => vm.ProductImages, Model.ImageLists[i], "Choose Image",
            htmlAttributes: new { @class = "form-control" })
            @Html.ValidationMessageFor(model => model.ImageLists, "", new { @class = "text-
            danger" })
        </div>
    </div>
}
```

The revised Views\Products\Create.cshtml file should now read as follows:

```
@model BabyStore.ViewModels.ProductViewModel

@{
    ViewBag.Title = "Create Product";
}

<h2>@ViewBag.Title</h2>
```

```
@using (Html.BeginForm())
{
    @Html.AntiForgeryToken()

    <div class="form-horizontal">
        <hr />
        @Html.ValidationSummary(true, "", new { @class = "text-danger" })
        <div class="form-group">
            @Html.LabelFor(model => model.Name, htmlAttributes: new { @class = "control-label
            col-md-2" })
            <div class="col-md-10">
                @Html.EditorFor(model => model.Name, new { htmlAttributes = new { @class =
                "form-control" } })
                @Html.ValidationMessageFor(model => model.Name, "", new { @class = "text-
                danger" })
            </div>
        </div>

        <div class="form-group">
            @Html.LabelFor(model => model.Description, htmlAttributes: new { @class =
            "control-label col-md-2" })
            <div class="col-md-10">
                @Html.EditorFor(model => model.Description, new { htmlAttributes = new {
                @class = "form-control" } })
                @Html.ValidationMessageFor(model => model.Description, "", new { @class =
                "text-danger" })
            </div>
        </div>

        <div class="form-group">
            @Html.LabelFor(model => model.Price, htmlAttributes: new { @class = "control-label
            col-md-2" })
            <div class="col-md-10">
                @Html.EditorFor(model => model.Price, new { htmlAttributes = new { @class =
                "form-control" } })
                @Html.ValidationMessageFor(model => model.Price, "", new { @class = "text-
                danger" })
            </div>
        </div>

        <div class="form-group">
            @Html.LabelFor(model => model.CategoryID, htmlAttributes: new { @class = "control-
            label col-md-2" })
            <div class="col-md-10">
                @Html.DropDownListFor(vm => vm.CategoryID, Model.CategoryList, htmlAttributes:
                new { @class = "form-control" })
                @Html.ValidationMessageFor(model => model.CategoryID, "", new { @class =
                "text-danger" })
            </div>
        </div>

        @for (int i = 0; i < Model.ImageLists.Count; i++)
        {
```

```
                    <div class="form-group">
                        <label class="control-label col-md-2">Product Image @(i + 1):</label>
                        <div class="col-md-10">
                            @Html.DropDownListFor(vm => vm.ProductImages, Model.ImageLists[i], "Choose
                            Image", htmlAttributes: new { @class = "form-control" })
                            @Html.ValidationMessageFor(model => model.ImageLists, "", new { @class =
                            "text-danger" })
                        </div>
                    </div>
                }

                <div class="form-group">
                    <div class="col-md-offset-2 col-md-10">
                        <input type="submit" value="Create" class="btn btn-default" />
                    </div>
                </div>
            </div>
        </div>
    }

    <div>
        @Html.ActionLink("Back to List", "Index")
    </div>
```

This code displays a drop-down for each member of the ImageLists property of the view model and obtains the data from each individual SelectList element of ImageLists. The result of these changes is shown in Figure 6-21.

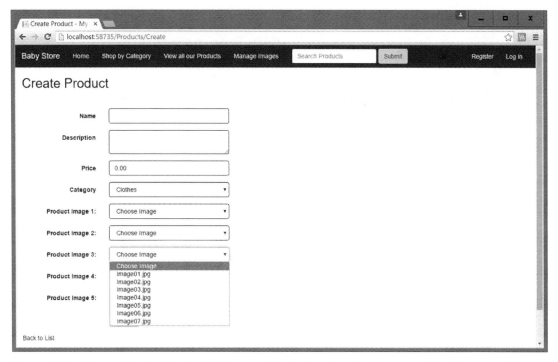

Figure 6-21. *The new Product Create HTML page with the five select list element to allow the users to choose images. The third drop-down list is shown containing the images uploaded earlier in the chapter*

Updating the HttpPost Version of the ProductsController Create Method: Manual Model Binding with a View Model

Now that we have a working view to allow users to input some images for a new product, we need to update the ProductsController HttpPost version of the Create method in order to process the newly submitted product and images. In doing this, we're going to process incoming data from a view model rather than use the default model binding behavior.

The code will address the scenario whereby a user does not make a choice from a drop-down, but then chooses from a following one. If this happens, then the ImageNumber property will be set to the lowest number available. For example, if a user does not make a choice for Product Image 1 but then chooses a file for Product Image 2, the file chosen will become the first image for the product.

We are going to update the method so that it takes a ProductViewModel as an input parameter rather than a product and then manually assigns the data in this view model to a new product. Alter the HttpPost version of the Create method in the Controllers\ProductsController.cs file as follows:

```
[HttpPost]
[ValidateAntiForgeryToken]
public ActionResult Create(ProductViewModel viewModel)
{
    Product product = new Product();
    product.Name = viewModel.Name;
    product.Description = viewModel.Description;
    product.Price = viewModel.Price;
    product.CategoryID = viewModel.CategoryID;
    product.ProductImageMappings = new List<ProductImageMapping>();
    //get a list of selected images without any blanks
    string[] productImages = viewModel.ProductImages.Where(pi =>
        !string.IsNullOrEmpty(pi)).ToArray();
    for (int i = 0; i < productImages.Length; i++)
    {
        product.ProductImageMappings.Add(new ProductImageMapping
        {
            ProductImage = db.ProductImages.Find(int.Parse(productImages[i])),
            ImageNumber = i
        });
    }

    if (ModelState.IsValid)
    {
        db.Products.Add(product);
        db.SaveChanges();
        return RedirectToAction("Index");
    }

    viewModel.CategoryList = new SelectList(db.Categories, "ID", "Name", product.CategoryID);
    viewModel.ImageLists = new List<SelectList>();
    for (int i = 0; i < Constants.NumberOfProductImages; i++)
    {
        viewModel.ImageLists.Add(new SelectList(db.ProductImages, "ID", "FileName",
                viewModel.ProductImages[i]));
    }
    return View(viewModel);
}
```

This code changes the input parameter to a view model using the code: `public ActionResult Create(ProductViewModel viewModel)`. We then create a new `Product` instance named product and assign the data from the simple type properties of the `viewModel` variable into the product's properties using the following code:

```
Product product = new Product();
product.Name = viewModel.Name;
product.Description = viewModel.Description;
product.Price = viewModel.Price;
product.CategoryID = viewModel.CategoryID;
```

■ **Tip** If you have a project with a lot of view models with lots of properties, mapping objects by hand can be a laborious process. There are tools available that will perform these mappings for you, such as AutoMapper.

Next we create a new list of `ProductImageMappings` that will be used to hold any image mappings for the new product with the code: `product.ProductImageMappings = new List<ProductImageMapping>();`.

The `ProductImage` values from the view model are then assigned to a simple string array and any blank entries are removed from the array (to ignore any file controls that the user left blank) using the LINQ query:

```
string[] productImages = viewModel.ProductImages.Where(pi =>
string.IsNullOrEmpty(pi)).ToArray();
```

A `for` loop is then used to add all the entries in the `productImages` array to the image mappings for the product:

```
for (int i = 0; i < productImages.Length; i++)
{
    product.ProductImageMappings.Add(new ProductImageMapping
    {
        ProductImage = db.ProductImages.Find(int.Parse(productImages[i])),
        ImageNumber = i
    });
}
```

This followed the standard code to check if the model is valid, add the product, and submit the changes to the database. There are a couple of things to note about this. The `ModelState` now represents the `viewModel` object so this is what is checked for validity. Also adding the product to the database adds the `productImageMappings` and ensures that all the relevant IDs are generated.

Finally, the code deals with the scenario where the `ModelState` was not valid and generates the `selectList` elements for the view, but this time it also sets the selected elements in each list. This is the reason that we used a collection of `SelectList` objects in the `ProductViewModel` and not a single `SelectList` to contain images. If we used a single `SelectList`, we would not be able to specify the select elements in this section of code.

```
viewModel.CategoryList = new SelectList(db.Categories, "ID", "Name", product.CategoryID);
viewModel.ImageLists = new List<SelectList>();
for (int i = 0; i < Constants.NumberOfProductImages; i++)
{
    viewModel.ImageLists.Add(new SelectList(db.ProductImages, "ID", "FileName",
    viewModel.ProductImages[i]));
}
return View(viewModel);
```

Displaying Images in Product Details

Next we are going to add some code to enable all the images associated with a product to be displayed when viewing a product's details. We are going to display one main image from the Content\ProductImages folder, followed by every image relating to the product from the Content\ProductImages\Thumbnails folder. To achieve this, modify the Views\Products\Details.cshtml file as follows:

```
@model BabyStore.Models.Product

@{
    ViewBag.Title = "Product Details";
}

<h2>@ViewBag.Title</h2>

<div>
    <hr />
    <dl class="dl-horizontal">
        <dt>
            @Html.DisplayNameFor(model => model.Category.Name)
        </dt>

        <dd>
            @Html.DisplayFor(model => model.Category.Name)
        </dd>

        <dt>
            @Html.DisplayNameFor(model => model.Name)
        </dt>

        <dd>
            @Html.DisplayFor(model => model.Name)
        </dd>

        <dt>
            @Html.DisplayNameFor(model => model.Description)
        </dt>

        <dd>
            @Html.DisplayFor(model => model.Description)
        </dd>

        <dt>
            @Html.DisplayNameFor(model => model.Price)
        </dt>

        <dd>
            @Html.DisplayFor(model => model.Price)
        </dd>
```

```
@if (Model.ProductImageMappings!= null && Model.ProductImageMappings.Any())
{
    <dt></dt>
    <dd>
        <img src="@(Url.Content(Constants.ProductImagePath) +
            Model.ProductImageMappings.OrderBy(pim =>
            pim.ImageNumber).ElementAt(0).ProductImage.FileName)"
            style=padding:5px>
    </dd>
    <dt></dt>
    <dd>
        @foreach (var item in Model.ProductImageMappings.OrderBy(pim =>
            pim.ImageNumber))
        {
            <a href="@(Url.Content(Constants.ProductImagePath) +
            item.ProductImage.FileName)"><img
            src="@(Url.Content(Constants.ProductThumbnailPath) +
            item.ProductImage.FileName)" style=padding:5px></a>
        }
    </dd>
}
    </dl>
</div>
<p>
    @Html.ActionLink("Edit", "Edit", new { id = Model.ID }) |
    @Html.ActionLink("Back to List", "Index")
</p>
```

This code first checks that the product has some images associated with it. If it does, it orders the ProductImageMappings by ImageNumber and then displays the first image in the ordered list from the Content/ProductImages web directory. The image display is achieved with this line of code:

```
<img src="@(Url.Content(Constants.ProductImagePath) + Model.ProductImageMappings.OrderBy(pim
=> pim.ImageNumber).ElementAt(0).ProductImage.FileName)" style=padding:5px>
```

This uses Url.Content to display a URL for the ~/Content/ProductImages/ project folder and then generates the filename from the matching ProductImage for the record from the ProductImageMappings table, where the ImageNumber equals 0 and the productID equals the current product.

The code then loops through the matching ProductImageMappings order by ImageNumber and displays a thumbnail image plus a hyperlink for every entry. We added an inline CSS style to add five pixels of padding around every image. We'll remove this later in the book when we restyle the site. The generated hyperlink will open the larger version of each image. We will improve this functionality later in the book by using jQuery to update the main image on the page.

■ **Note** This code is an example of lazy loading because the product images are ordered and fetched on the fly in the view. An alternative to including this code in the view is to include it in the controller and consider having a view model with a collection of strings that is populated in the controller with the filename of each image. For an example of this approach, see the section on bestsellers in Chapter 10, where the main image for each product is found in the controller.

Testing Product Creation with Images

To see the new product creation in action with images, add a new product named Test Creation with Images and place the Image05 to Image03 files in the Product Image 2 to Product Image 5 slots, leaving the Product Image 1 and Product Image 3 slots blank, as shown in Figure 6-22. This will test the scenario where a user leaves an image blank and then enters an image in the next slot.

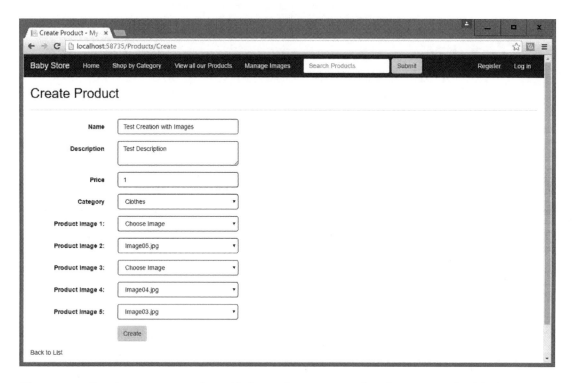

Figure 6-22. *Creating a new test product with the Product Image 1and Product Image 3 slots blank*

Now, when you create the product, the images will be assigned to the product so that Image05 is assigned the ImageNumber 0, Image04 is assigned ImageNumber 1, and Image03 will have ImageNumber 2 assigned to it in the database. Figure 6-23 shows the entries in my ProductImages database table.

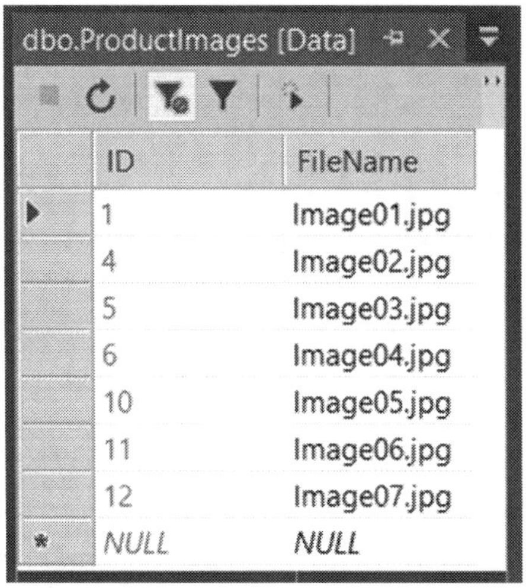

ID	FileName
1	Image01.jpg
4	Image02.jpg
5	Image03.jpg
6	Image04.jpg
10	Image05.jpg
11	Image06.jpg
12	Image07.jpg
NULL	NULL

Figure 6-23. *Current test data in the ProductImages table*

You can see in Figure 6-23 that the IDs for `Image05`, `Image04`, and `Image03` are 10, 6, and 5, respectively. In Figure 6-24, which shows the `ProductImageMappings` table data, you can see that these have been allocated the `ImageNumbers` 0, 1, and 2, respectively, for `ProductID` 18 (the ID of the new `Test Creation with Images` product).

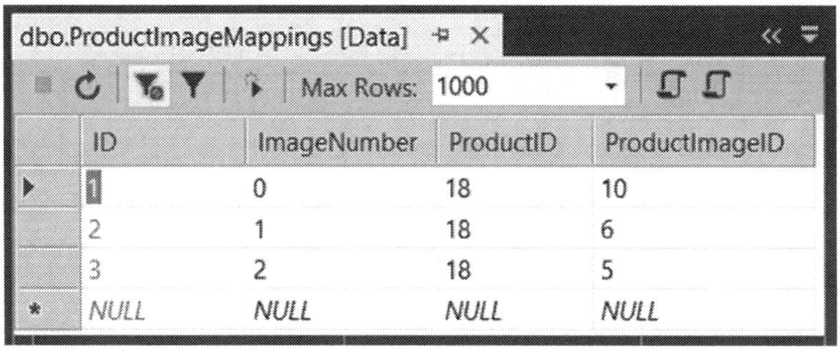

ID	ImageNumber	ProductID	ProductImageID
1	0	18	10
2	1	18	6
3	2	18	5
NULL	NULL	NULL	NULL

Figure 6-24. *The entries in the ProductImageMappings table for the newly created test product*

Now view the details of the `Test Creation with Images` product in the web site. The page should appear as shown in Figure 6-25 and display the product images, starting with `Image05`, followed by `Image04` and `Image03`.

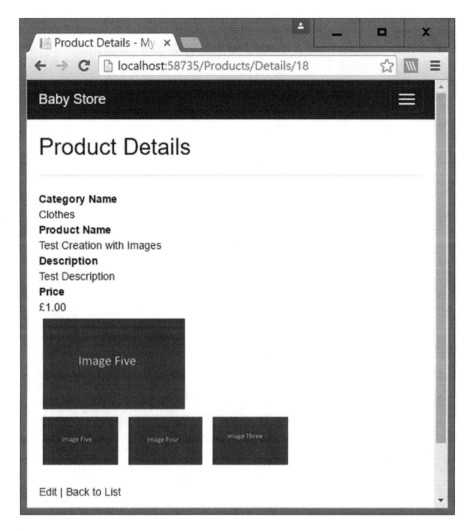

Figure 6-25. *The new test product complete with images. The images take up the first three available image entries for the product*

Displaying Images in Search Results

The other place where we want to display product images is in the search results. We're going to update the Products Index view to display the main image for each product and make this image a hyperlink to the Details page for each product.

To display images in the Products Index view, modify the Views\Products\Index.cshtml file. First modify the table headings to add a blank <th> element and a new column displaying the main image of each product as a hyperlink and then update the product name to be a hyperlink, as highlighted in the following code:

```
@model BabyStore.ViewModels.ProductIndexViewModel
@using PagedList.Mvc
```

```
@{
    ViewBag.Title = "Products";
}

<h2>@ViewBag.Title</h2>
<p>
    @(String.IsNullOrWhiteSpace(Model.Search) ? "Showing all" : "You search for " +
        Model.Search + " found")  @Model.Products.TotalItemCount products
</p>

<p>
    @Html.ActionLink("Create New", "Create")
    @using (Html.BeginRouteForm("ProductsIndex", FormMethod.Get))
    {
        <label>Filter by category:</label>
        @Html.DropDownListFor(vm => vm.Category, Model.CatFilterItems, "All");
        <label>Sort by:</label>
        @Html.DropDownListFor(vm => vm.SortBy, new SelectList(Model.Sorts, "Value", "Key"),
        "Default")
        <input type="submit" value="Filter" />
        <input type="hidden" name="Search" id="Search" value="@Model.Search" />
    }
</p>
<table class="table">
    <tr>
        <th></th>
        <th>
            @Html.DisplayNameFor(model => model.Category)
        </th>
        <th>
            @Html.DisplayNameFor(model => model.Products.First().Name)
        </th>
        <th>
            @Html.DisplayNameFor(model => model.Products.First().Description)
        </th>
        <th>
            @Html.DisplayNameFor(model => model.Products.First().Price)
        </th>
        <th></th>
    </tr>

@foreach (var item in Model.Products) {
    <tr>
        <td>
            @if (item.ProductImageMappings != null && item.ProductImageMappings.Any())
            {
                <a href="@Url.Action("Details", new { id = item.ID})">
                    <img src="@(Url.Content(Constants.ProductImagePath) +
                        item.ProductImageMappings.OrderBy(pim =>
                        pim.ImageNumber).ElementAt(0).ProductImage.FileName)">
                </a>
```

```
                }
            </td>
            <td>
                @Html.DisplayFor(modelItem => item.Category.Name)
            </td>
            <td>
                @Html.DisplayFor(modelItem => item.Name)
            </td>
            <td>
                @Html.DisplayFor(modelItem => item.Description)
            </td>
            <td>
                @Html.DisplayFor(modelItem => item.Price)
            </td>
            <td>
                @Html.ActionLink("Edit", "Edit", new { id=item.ID }) |
                @Html.ActionLink("Details", "Details", new { id=item.ID }) |
                @Html.ActionLink("Delete", "Delete", new { id=item.ID })
            </td>
        </tr>
}

</table>
<div>
    Page @(Model.Products.PageCount < Model.Products.PageNumber ? 0 :
        Model.Products.PageNumber) of @Model.Products.PageCount
    @Html.PagedListPager(Model.Products, page => Url.Action("Index", new { category =
        @Model.Category, Search = @Model.Search, sortBy = @Model.SortBy, page}))
</div>
```

This code first creates a hyperlink to the Products Details view and passes along the product's ID. Next it adds an image tag inside the hyperlink with the source of the image set to the filename of the first image in the ProductImageMapping's (sorted by ImageNumber) property of the product. The code for retrieving the filename is identical to that used in the Product Details view to display the main image. Figure 6-26 displays the updated Products Index view, now showing the first image for the Test Creation with Images product.

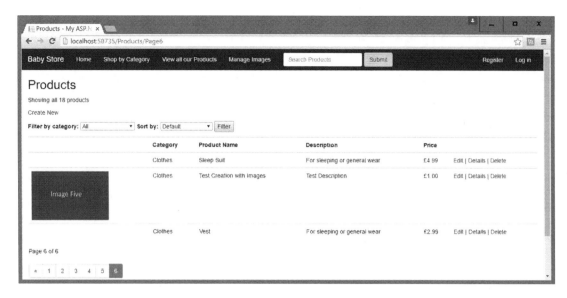

Figure 6-26. *Updated Products Index view displaying images for products*

Editing a Product's Images

To complete this chapter, we are going to cover how to edit the images associated with a product. We're going to allow users to remove an image from a product by simply selecting nothing in a list box or to overwrite an image by choosing another image from the list box. If a user removes an image from a product and there is another image following the removed image, the second image's imageNumber property will be updated to move it higher up in the list of images. For example, if there are two images and the user removes the main image from the product, the second image will become the main image when the changes are saved.

Updating the GET Version of the ProductController's Edit Method

The first thing to do is update the GET version of the Edit method of the ProductController class so that the Edit view can display the current images and controls to allow the users to change them. The Edit view is going to display five HTML SELECT controls as in the Create view, but this time each control will have the images assigned to the product selected by default. To achieve this, we are going to use ProductViewModel again. First update the GET version of the Edit method in the Controllers\ProductsController.cs file, as highlighted here:

```
// GET: Products/Edit/5
public ActionResult Edit(int? id)
{
    if (id == null)
    {
        return new HttpStatusCodeResult(HttpStatusCode.BadRequest);
    }
    Product product = db.Products.Find(id);
    if (product == null)
    {
        return HttpNotFound();
    }
```

```
    ProductViewModel viewModel = new ProductViewModel();
    viewModel.CategoryList = new SelectList(db.Categories, "ID", "Name", product.CategoryID);
    viewModel.ImageLists = new List<SelectList>();

    foreach (var imageMapping in product.ProductImageMappings.OrderBy(pim => pim.ImageNumber))
    {
        viewModel.ImageLists.Add(new SelectList(db.ProductImages, "ID", "FileName",
        imageMapping.ProductImageID));
    }

    for (int i = viewModel.ImageLists.Count; i < Constants.NumberOfProductImages; i++)
    {
        viewModel.ImageLists.Add(new SelectList(db.ProductImages, "ID", "FileName"));
    }

    viewModel.ID = product.ID;
    viewModel.Name = product.Name;
    viewModel.Description = product.Description;
    viewModel.Price = product.Price;

    return View(viewModel);
}
```

This code is similar to the GET version of the Create method, so we are not going to cover it all in detail; however, the main difference between the two methods is the following code that creates the SelectLists:

```
foreach (var imageMapping in product.ProductImageMappings.OrderBy(pim => pim.ImageNumber))
{
    viewModel.ImageLists.Add(new SelectList(db.ProductImages, "ID", "FileName",
    imageMapping.ProductImageID));
}

for (int i = viewModel.ImageLists.Count; i < Constants.NumberOfProductImages; i++)
{
    viewModel.ImageLists.Add(new SelectList(db.ProductImages, "ID", "FileName"));
}
```

The first for loop sorts the ProductImageMappings by ImageNumber and then adds a new SelectList with the selected value set to the current ProductImageID for every entry in the ProductImageMappings for the product. In simple terms, this generates a SelectList for each image currently associated with the product with the current image selected.

Then the second loop checks if there are fewer than five SelectLists. If there were, then more SelectLists are added until five SelectLists have been generated. These additional SelectLists do not have a selected value set. Again, in simple terms, if a product has only two images associated with it, the second loop will add three extra SelectLists with no value selected.

Updating the Product Edit View

The Products Edit view now needs updating to use the view model and display the additional HTML SELECT controls for the images. The Categories drop-down also needs to be updated to use the view model rather than the ViewBag. Update the Views\Products\Edit.cshtml file as follows:

```
@model BabyStore.ViewModels.ProductViewModel

@{
    ViewBag.Title = "Edit Product";
}

<h2>@ViewBag.Title</h2>

@using (Html.BeginForm())
{
    @Html.AntiForgeryToken()

    <div class="form-horizontal">
        <hr />
        @Html.ValidationSummary(true, "", new { @class = "text-danger" })
        @Html.HiddenFor(model => model.ID)

        <div class="form-group">
            @Html.LabelFor(model => model.Name, htmlAttributes: new { @class = "control-label
            col-md-2" })
            <div class="col-md-10">
                @Html.EditorFor(model => model.Name, new { htmlAttributes = new { @class =
                "form-control" } })
                @Html.ValidationMessageFor(model => model.Name, "", new { @class = "text-
                danger"
                  })
            </div>
        </div>

        <div class="form-group">
            @Html.LabelFor(model => model.Description, htmlAttributes: new { @class =
            "control-label col-md-2" })
            <div class="col-md-10">
                @Html.EditorFor(model => model.Description, new { htmlAttributes = new {
                @class= "form-control" } })
                @Html.ValidationMessageFor(model => model.Description, "", new { @class =
                "text-danger" })
            </div>
        </div>

        <div class="form-group">
            @Html.LabelFor(model => model.Price, htmlAttributes: new { @class = "control-label
            col-md-2" })
            <div class="col-md-10">
                @Html.EditorFor(model => model.Price, new { htmlAttributes = new { @class =
```

```
                    "form-control" } })
                @Html.ValidationMessageFor(model => model.Price, "", new { @class = "text-
                    danger" })
            </div>
        </div>

        <div class="form-group">
            @Html.LabelFor(model => model.CategoryID, "Category", htmlAttributes: new { @class
            ="control-label col-md-2" })
            <div class="col-md-10">
                @Html.DropDownListFor(vm => vm.CategoryID, Model.CategoryList, htmlAttributes:
                    new { @class = "form-control" })
                @Html.ValidationMessageFor(model => model.CategoryID, "", new { @class =
                "text-danger" })
            </div>
        </div>
        @for (int i = 0; i < Model.ImageLists.Count; i++)
        {
            <div class="form-group">
                <label class="control-label col-md-2">Product Image @(i + 1):</label>
                <div class="col-md-10">
                    @Html.DropDownListFor(vm => vm.ProductImages, Model.ImageLists[i], "Choose
                    Image", htmlAttributes: new { @class = "form-control" })
                    @Html.ValidationMessageFor(model => model.ImageLists, "", new { @class =
                    "text-danger" })
                </div>
            </div>
        }
        <div class="form-group">
            <div class="col-md-offset-2 col-md-10">
                <input type="submit" value="Save" class="btn btn-default" />
            </div>
        </div>
    </div>
}

<div>
    @Html.ActionLink("Back to List", "Index")
</div>

@section Scripts {
    @Scripts.Render("~/bundles/jqueryval")
}
```

The code changes to this view are identical to those made to the Products create view; the for loop goes through the ImageLists property to display a SelectList for each entry. Figure 6-27 shows the results of the changes to the controller and the view when attempting to edit the Test Creation with Images product. The SELECT lists default to the current images assigned to the product.

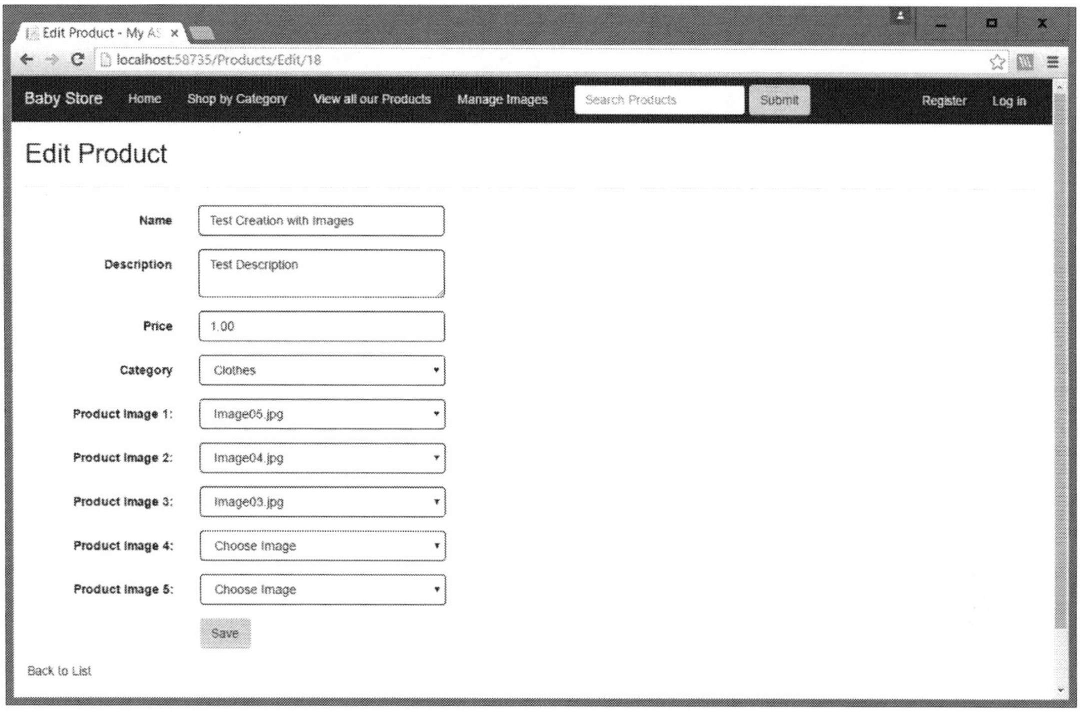

Figure 6-27. *The updated Products Edit view complete with assigned images*

Updating the ProductsController HttpPost Edit Method: Performing Model Binding Using TryUpdateModel

In all the previous methods where model binding occurs, the default code created by the scaffolding process was used; however, this code is actually not recommended for Edit methods by Microsoft because the Bind attribute will clear out any existing data in fields that are not listed in the Include parameter in the method's input parameters. For example, the current Edit method in the Product controller uses the default code as follows:

```
public ActionResult Edit([Bind(Include = "ID,Name,Description,Price,CategoryID")]
Product product)
```

This code attempts the bind the fields ID, Name, Description, Price, and CategoryID to a product based on the model submitted to the method. Microsoft has stated that future versions of MVC will no longer generate Bind attributes for Edit methods.

We could use the view model to manually assign values to fields, but instead I am going to demonstrate how to use TryUpdateModel to whitelist fields that you want to be edited. This is currently the recommended security best practice to prevent overposting. An example of overposting appears in Chapter 2.

To reiterate what I wrote earlier, the code for editing the images associated with a product will follow these rules:

- A user can delete the association between a product and an image by setting the select control to Choose Image.

- If any images are left blank, the images that follow them get a lower image number. For example, if a choice is made to leave Product Image 1 empty but a file has been chosen in the Product Image 2 control, then this file will become the main image. This is the same way creating a product works.

To make the changes to allow editing images associated with a product, start by clearing the contents of the existing Edit method in the ProductsController.cs file and replacing it with the following new code to pass in a ProductViewModel. Then find the product we are going to attempt to update.

```
[HttpPost]
[ValidateAntiForgeryToken]
public ActionResult Edit(ProductViewModel viewModel)
{
    var productToUpdate = db.Products.Include(p => p.ProductImageMappings).Where(p => p.ID ==
    viewModel.ID).Single();
}
```

Next, add a TryUpdateModel statement with a whitelist containing the Name, Description, Price, and CategoryID fields, along with default actions to take if the update fails, as follows:

```
[HttpPost]
[ValidateAntiForgeryToken]
public ActionResult Edit(ProductViewModel viewModel)
{
    var productToUpdate = db.Products.Include(p => p.ProductImageMappings).Where(p => p.ID ==
    viewModel.ID).Single();
    if (TryUpdateModel(productToUpdate, "", new string[] { "Name", "Description", "Price",
        "CategoryID" }))
    {
    }
    return View(viewModel);
}
```

This additional code will try to update the whitelisted fields of the productToUpdate. The data in the whitelist is obtained from the posted form data. The code to return the Edit view back to the user is called only if the TryUpdateModel fails. Note that we have not added any code here to redisplay any values in order to focus the example on the edit process.

Next, add the following highlighted code to add some conditional statements inside the TryUpdateModel. They will check if any images are already assigned, loop through the image selections made by the users, and save any changes to the database:

```
if (TryUpdateModel(productToUpdate, "", new string[] { "Name", "Description", "Price",
    "CategoryID" }))
{
    if (productToUpdate.ProductImageMappings == null)
    {
        productToUpdate.ProductImageMappings = new List<ProductImageMapping>();
    }
    //get a list of selected images without any blanks
```

```
    string[] productImages = viewModel.ProductImages.Where(pi =>
        !string.IsNullOrEmpty(pi)).ToArray();
    for (int i = 0; i < productImages.Length; i++)
    {
    }
    db.SaveChanges();
    return RedirectToAction("Index");
}
```

This additional code will check if any images are currently associated with the product. If they are not, it makes a new list to add to. A new array or string named productImages is created and the file choices picked by the user are assigned to this, with any blank choices removed. Next there is a for loop to loop through all the chosen images. Once they've all been processed, it saves the changes to the database and directs the user back to the Products Index page.

Now inside the for loop, find the image mapping to edit; this is the mapping where the ImageNumber is the same as the current loop iteration. Following this, find the image that the user has chosen and assign it to the image variable.

```
for (int i = 0; i < productImages.Length; i++)
{
    //get the image currently stored
    var imageMappingToEdit = productToUpdate.ProductImageMappings.Where(pim => pim.
    ImageNumber == i).FirstOrDefault();
    //find the new image
    var image = db.ProductImages.Find(int.Parse(productImages[i]));
}
```

Next, add the following highlighted code, which decides whether a new mapping is required or if an existing mapping needs editing.

```
for (int i = 0; i < productImages.Length; i++)
{
    //get the image currently stored
    var imageMappingToEdit = productToUpdate.ProductImageMappings.Where(pim => pim.ImageNumber
    == i).FirstOrDefault();
    //find the new image
    var image = db.ProductImages.Find(int.Parse(productImages[i]));
    //if there is nothing stored then we need to add a new mapping
    if (imageMappingToEdit == null)
    {
    }
    //else it's not a new file so edit the current mapping
    else
    {
    }

}
```

Now modify the code to add a new mapping. This code creates a new `ImageMapping` and assigns the image to it, sets the `ImageNumber` property of the mapping, and assigns the image ID.

```
//if there is nothing stored then we need to add a new mapping
if (imageMappingToEdit == null)
{
    //add image to the imagemappings
    productToUpdate.ProductImageMappings.Add(new ProductImageMapping
    {
        ImageNumber = i,
        ProductImage = image,
        ProductImageID = image.ID
    });
}
```

Next, update the `else` statement to process existing mappings. This code checks if the images are the same or not and, if required, updates the mapping with the new image.

```
else
{
    //if they are not the same
    if (imageMappingToEdit.ProductImageID != int.Parse(productImages[i]))
    {
        //assign image property of the image mapping
        imageMappingToEdit.ProductImage = image;
    }
}
```

This concludes the code for adding or editing file mappings. There is a full listing of the method on the following pages. To complete the method, we need to deal with the scenario whereby a user wants to remove an image from a product. Add the following code to loop through the number of items the user left blank and delete any mappings in those slots. For example, if the user only picked two images for the product, this will loop through the mappings three to five and delete them:

```
[HttpPost]
[ValidateAntiForgeryToken]
public ActionResult Edit(ProductViewModel viewModel)
{
    var productToUpdate = db.Products.Include(p => p.ProductImageMappings).Where(p => p.ID ==
        viewModel.ID).Single();
    if (TryUpdateModel(productToUpdate, "", new string[] { "Name", "Description", "Price",
        "CategoryID" }))
    {
        if (productToUpdate.ProductImageMappings == null)
        {
            productToUpdate.ProductImageMappings = new List<ProductImageMapping>();
        }
        //get a list of selected images without any blanks
        string[] productImages = viewModel.ProductImages.Where(pi =>
            !string.IsNullOrEmpty(pi)).ToArray();
        for (int i = 0; i < productImages.Length; i++)
        {
```

```
            //get the image currently stored
            var imageMappingToEdit = productToUpdate.ProductImageMappings.Where(pim =>
                pim.ImageNumber == i).FirstOrDefault();
            //find the new image
            var image = db.ProductImages.Find(int.Parse(productImages[i]));
            //if there is nothing stored then we need to add a new mapping
            if (imageMappingToEdit == null)
            {
                //add image to the imagemappings
                productToUpdate.ProductImageMappings.Add(new ProductImageMapping
                {
                    ImageNumber = i,
                    ProductImage = image,
                    ProductImageID = image.ID
                });
            }
            //else it's not a new file so edit the current mapping
            else
            {
                //if they are not the same
                if (imageMappingToEdit.ProductImageID != int.Parse(productImages[i]))
                {
                    //assign image property of the image mapping
                    imageMappingToEdit.ProductImage = image;
                }
            }
        }
        //delete any other imagemappings that the user did not include in their
        //selections for the product
        for (int i = productImages.Length; i < Constants.NumberOfProductImages; i++)
        {
            var imageMappingToEdit = productToUpdate.ProductImageMappings.Where(pim =>
                pim.ImageNumber == i).FirstOrDefault();
            //if there is something stored in the mapping
            if (imageMappingToEdit != null)
            {
                //delete the record from the mapping table directly.
                //just calling productToUpdate.ProductImageMappings.Remove(imageMappingToEdit)
                //results in a FK error
                db.ProductImageMappings.Remove(imageMappingToEdit);
            }
        }
        db.SaveChanges();
        return RedirectToAction("Index");
    }
    return View(viewModel);
}
```

Note that this code has to refer to the ProductImageMappings table directly. You cannot delete the
mapping via the product because it will simply try to set the foreign key for the product to null and cause an
exception. The completed method should now appear as in the previous code.

Testing Product Image Editing

To test edit a product's images, start the web site without debugging and open the product Test Creation with Images, as shown in Figure 6-27. Now edit the product's values as follows:

- Change the name to Test Image Editing

- Update the description to Edited Description

- Change the price to 2

- Update the category to Play and Toys

- Remove Image05.jpg and Image04.jpg by changing the value of the select control Product Image 1 and Product Image 2 to Choose Image, respectively

- Update Product Image 4 to Image06.jpg and Product Image 5 to Image07.jpg

Figure 6-28 shows these changes in the Edit page.

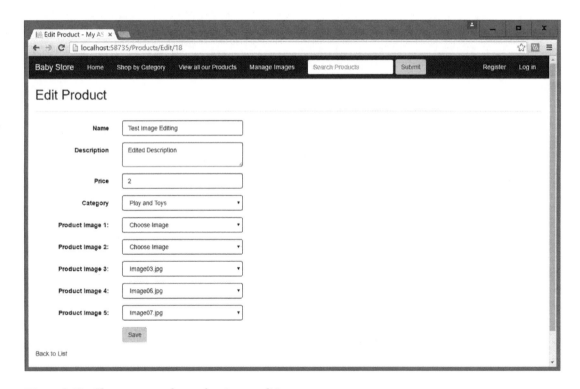

Figure 6-28. *Changes to test the product image editing*

Save the product and then open the Details page. You will see that the values of the product have been updated and that the images have been changed so that Image03 is now the main image, and Image06 and Image07 are now the second and third images, respectively, as shown in Figure 6-29.

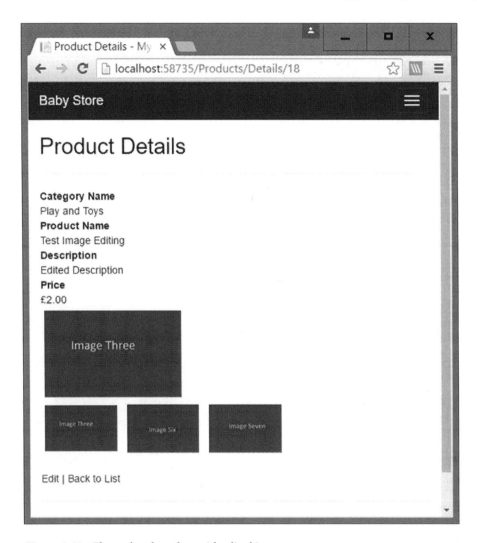

Figure 6-29. *The updated product with edited images*

Deleting Images and Products

We are now going to cover what happens to the ProductImageMappings table when you delete an image or a product. First add some code to the DeletedConfirmed method of the Controllers\ProductImagesController.cs file to delete the file from the filesystem and the database, as highlighted in the following code:

```
// POST: ProductImages/Delete/5
[HttpPost, ActionName("Delete")]
[ValidateAntiForgeryToken]
public ActionResult DeleteConfirmed(int id)
{
    ProductImage productImage = db.ProductImages.Find(id);
    System.IO.File.Delete(Request.MapPath(Constants.ProductImagePath +
    productImage.FileName));
```

```
    System.IO.File.Delete(Request.MapPath(Constants.ProductThumbnailPath +
    productImage.FileName));
    db.ProductImages.Remove(productImage);
    db.SaveChanges();
    return RedirectToAction("Index");
}
```

This code uses the System.IO.File.Delete method to delete the file from Content\ProductImages and Content\ProductImages\Thumbnails. We have to refer to the class System.IO.File directly because the Controller class also contains a property called File. We also used Request.MapPath to ensure that the correct server path is used.

Next add the highlighted code to the Delete method of the Controllers\ProductImagesController.cs file in order to update the ImageNumber property of any other images associated with the same product as the deleted image. This code checks if the ImageNumber is higher than the image being deleted and, if it is, then it lowers the ImageNumber by one so that there are no gaps between images.

```
// POST: ProductImages/Delete/5
[HttpPost, ActionName("Delete")]
[ValidateAntiForgeryToken]
public ActionResult DeleteConfirmed(int id)
{
    ProductImage productImage = db.ProductImages.Find(id);
    //find all the mappings for this image
    var mappings = productImage.ProductImageMappings.Where(pim => pim.ProductImageID == id);
    foreach (var mapping in mappings)
    {
        //find all mappings for any product containing this image
        var mappingsToUpdate = db.ProductImageMappings.Where(pim => pim.ProductID ==
        mapping.ProductID);
        //for each image in each product change its imagenumber to one lower if it is higher
        //than the current image
        foreach (var mappingToUpdate in mappingsToUpdate)
        {
            if (mappingToUpdate.ImageNumber > mapping.ImageNumber)
            {
                mappingToUpdate.ImageNumber--;
            }
        }
    }

    System.IO.File.Delete(Request.MapPath(Constants.ProductImagePath +
    productImage.FileName));
    System.IO.File.Delete(Request.MapPath(Constants.ProductThumbnailPath +
    productImage.FileName));
    db.ProductImages.Remove(productImage);
    db.SaveChanges();
    return RedirectToAction("Index");
}
```

Note that, in this code, we do not delete anything from the ProductImageMappings table directly. The only delete is carried out by the line db.ProductImages.Remove(productImage). When this deletion occurs, it's cascaded into the ProductImageMappings table and the relevant records are then deleted.

Testing Image Deletion

To see image deletion working first, add a new product to the site with the following details:

- Set the name as Test Image Deletion
- Set the description to Test Description
- Set the price as 1
- Set the category to Clothes
- Set the images to Image06, Image03, Image06, and Image07

Figure 6-30 shows this product.

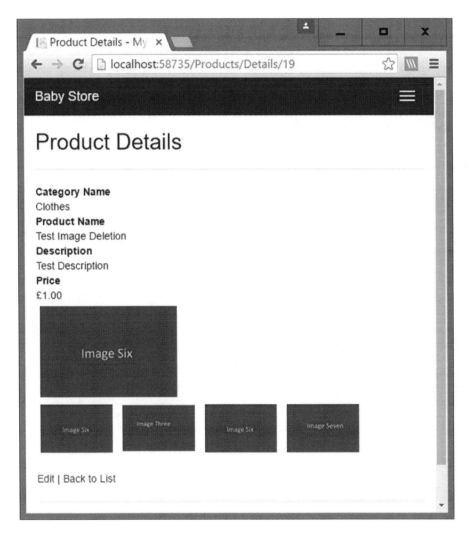

Figure 6-30. *The Test Image Deletion product*

Now click on the Manage Images link and delete the Image06.jpg image. Now open the edit page for the Test Image Deletion and Test Image Editing products. Both products now contain Image03 in the Product Image 1 position and Image07 in the Product Image 2 position. Figure 6-31 shows the updated Test Image Deletion product. The Image06.jpg file has also been deleted from the Content\ProductImages and Content\ProductImages\Thumbnails folders.

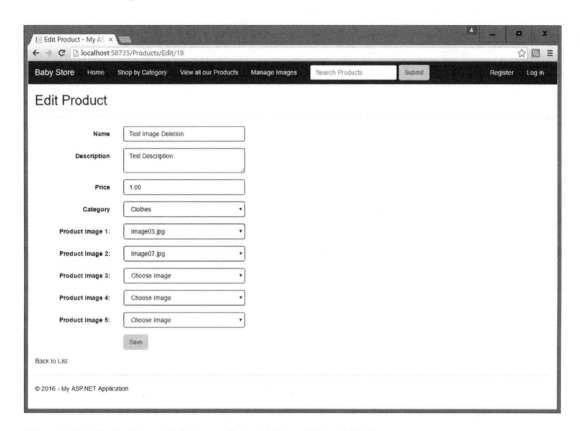

Figure 6-31. *The Test Image Deletion product with Image06.jpg deleted*

To conclude covering deletion for a many-to-many relationship, we're going to delete the Test Image Deletion product. Prior to this deletion, view the data of the ProductImageMappings table via Server Explorer. There should be four entries relating to two ProductIDs. Figure 6-32 shows our version of this table. The ProductID of 19 relates to the Test Image Deletion product.

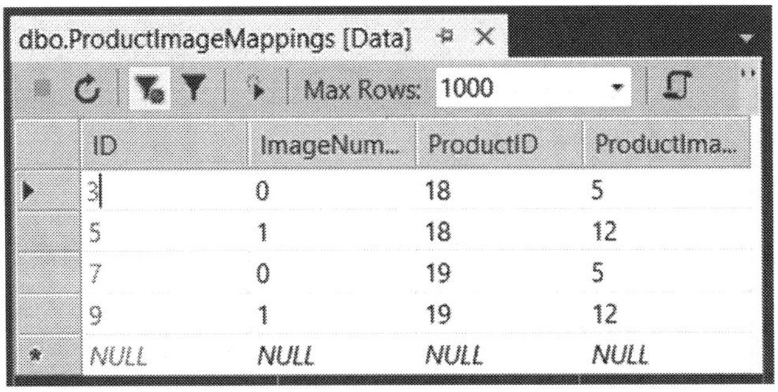

Figure 6-32. *The ProductImageMappings table prior to deleting the "Test Image Deletion" product*

Now in the web site, delete the `Test Image Deletion` product and refresh the data in the `ProductImageMappings` table. All the entries relating to the ProductID (in this example, 19) of the `Test Image Deletion` product are deleted, as shown in Figure 6-33.

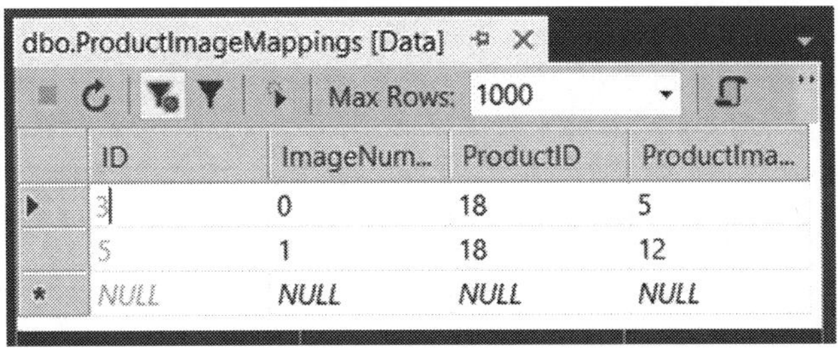

Figure 6-33. *The ProductImageMappings table data after deleting the Test Image Deletion product*

We didn't have to add any extra code to deal with product deletion because when we originally created the `ProductImageMappings` table, it was created with cascade deletes enabled. When a product is deleted, any related rows in the `ProductImageMappings` table are also deleted.

Seeding the Database with Image Data

Now that you can add images and associate them with products, you're going to learn how to seed the database with some test data to add some product images and map these images to products.

Before you attempt to seed the database, ensure that you have added the images from Chapter 6 of the source code available at `Apress.com`. Add the images to your solution as follows:

1. Download the source code to your computer.

2. In Visual Studio with your `BabyStore` solution open, right-click on the `Content\ProductImages` folder in Solution Explorer and choose Add Existing Item.

3. In the Add Existing Item window, navigate to the `Content\ProductImages` folder of the downloaded source code, select all the files, and then click the Add button.

4. Repeat Steps 2 and 3 for the `Content\ProductImages\Thumbnails` folder.

Once you have added the images, add the following code to the end of the Seed method in the Migrations\Configurations.cs file (I recommend you copy and paste this from the downloaded source code as the text is rather long and laborious to type by hand):

```
var images = new List<ProductImage>
{
    new ProductImage { FileName="SleepSuit1.JPG" },
    new ProductImage { FileName="SleepSuit2.JPG" },
    new ProductImage { FileName="Vest1.JPG" },
    new ProductImage { FileName="Vest2.JPG" },
    new ProductImage { FileName="Lion1.JPG" },
    new ProductImage { FileName="Rabbit1.JPG" },
    new ProductImage { FileName="Bottles1.JPG" },
    new ProductImage { FileName="Bottles2.JPG" },
    new ProductImage { FileName="Bottles3.JPG" },
    new ProductImage { FileName="Bibs1.JPG" },
    new ProductImage { FileName="Bibs2.JPG" },
    new ProductImage { FileName="Milk1.JPG" },
    new ProductImage { FileName="Nappies1.JPG" },
    new ProductImage { FileName="Nappies2.JPG" },
    new ProductImage { FileName="Nappies3.JPG" },
    new ProductImage { FileName="ColicMedicine1.JPG" },
    new ProductImage { FileName="Reflux1.JPG" },
    new ProductImage { FileName="Pram1.JPG" },
    new ProductImage { FileName="Pram2.JPG" },
    new ProductImage { FileName="Pram3.JPG" },
    new ProductImage { FileName="CarSeat1.JPG" },
    new ProductImage { FileName="CarSeat2.JPG" },
    new ProductImage { FileName="Moses1.JPG" },
    new ProductImage { FileName="Moses2.JPG" },
    new ProductImage { FileName="Crib1.JPG" },
    new ProductImage { FileName="Crib2.JPG" },
    new ProductImage { FileName="Bed1.JPG" },
    new ProductImage { FileName="Bed2.JPG" },
    new ProductImage { FileName="CircusBale1.JPG" },
    new ProductImage { FileName="CircusBale2.JPG" },
    new ProductImage { FileName="CircusBale3.JPG" },
    new ProductImage { FileName="LovedBale1.JPG" },
};

images.ForEach(c => context.ProductImages.AddOrUpdate(p => p.FileName, c));
context.SaveChanges();
```

This code will add a set of images to the ProductImages table with the FileName column set to the values shown. We assumed the FileName is unique when saving the changes.

Following that code, add the following code to populate the ProductImageMappings table:

```
var imageMappings = new List<ProductImageMapping>
{
    new ProductImageMapping { ProductImageID= images.Single(i => i.FileName ==
        "SleepSuit1.JPG").ID, ProductID = products.Single( c=> c.Name == "Sleep Suit").ID,
        ImageNumber = 0 },
```

```
new ProductImageMapping { ProductImageID= images.Single(i => i.FileName ==
    "SleepSuit2.JPG").ID, ProductID = products.Single( c=> c.Name == "Sleep Suit").ID,
    ImageNumber = 1 },
new ProductImageMapping { ProductImageID= images.Single(i => i.FileName ==
    "Vest1.JPG").ID, ProductID = products.Single( c=> c.Name == "Vest").ID, ImageNumber =
    0 },
new ProductImageMapping { ProductImageID= images.Single(i => i.FileName ==
    "Vest2.JPG").ID,ProductID = products.Single( c=> c.Name == "Vest").ID, ImageNumber = 1
    },
new ProductImageMapping { ProductImageID= images.Single(i => i.FileName ==
    "Lion1.JPG").ID, ProductID = products.Single( c=> c.Name == "Orange and Yellow
    Lion").ID, ImageNumber = 0 },
new ProductImageMapping { ProductImageID= images.Single(i => i.FileName ==
    "Rabbit1.JPG").ID, ProductID = products.Single( c=> c.Name == "Blue Rabbit").ID,
    ImageNumber = 0 },
new ProductImageMapping { ProductImageID= images.Single(i => i.FileName ==
    "Bottles1.JPG").ID, ProductID = products.Single( c=> c.Name == "3 Pack of
    Bottles").ID,ImageNumber = 0 },
new ProductImageMapping { ProductImageID= images.Single(i => i.FileName ==
    "Bottles2.JPG").ID, ProductID = products.Single( c=> c.Name == "3 Pack of
    Bottles").ID,ImageNumber = 1 },
new ProductImageMapping { ProductImageID= images.Single(i => i.FileName ==
    "Bottles3.JPG").ID, ProductID = products.Single( c=> c.Name == "3 Pack of
    Bottles").ID,ImageNumber = 2 },
new ProductImageMapping { ProductImageID= images.Single(i => i.FileName ==
    "Bibs1.JPG").ID, ProductID = products.Single( c=> c.Name == "3 Pack of Bibs").ID,
    ImageNumber = 0 },
new ProductImageMapping { ProductImageID= images.Single(i => i.FileName ==
    "Bibs2.JPG").ID,ProductID = products.Single( c=> c.Name == "3 Pack of Bibs").ID,
    ImageNumber = 1 },
new ProductImageMapping { ProductImageID= images.Single(i => i.FileName ==
    "Milk1.JPG").ID, ProductID = products.Single( c=> c.Name == "Powdered Baby Milk").ID,
    ImageNumber = 0 },
new ProductImageMapping { ProductImageID= images.Single(i => i.FileName ==
    "Nappies1.JPG").ID, ProductID = products.Single( c=> c.Name == "Pack of 70 Disposable
    Nappies").ID, ImageNumber = 0 },
new ProductImageMapping { ProductImageID= images.Single(i => i.FileName ==
    "Nappies2.JPG").ID, ProductID = products.Single( c=> c.Name == "Pack of 70 Disposable
    Nappies").ID, ImageNumber = 1 },
new ProductImageMapping { ProductImageID= images.Single(i => i.FileName ==
    "Nappies3.JPG").ID, ProductID = products.Single( c=> c.Name == "Pack of 70 Disposable
    Nappies").ID, ImageNumber = 2 },
new ProductImageMapping { ProductImageID= images.Single(i => i.FileName ==
    "ColicMedicine1.JPG").ID, ProductID = products.Single( c=> c.Name == "Colic
    Medicine").ID, ImageNumber = 0 },
new ProductImageMapping { ProductImageID= images.Single(i => i.FileName ==
    "Reflux1.JPG").ID, ProductID = products.Single( c=> c.Name == "Reflux Medicine").ID,
    ImageNumber = 0 },
new ProductImageMapping { ProductImageID= images.Single(i => i.FileName ==
    "Pram1.JPG").ID, ProductID = products.Single( c=> c.Name == "Black Pram and Pushchair
    System").ID, ImageNumber = 0 },
```

```
    new ProductImageMapping { ProductImageID= images.Single(i => i.FileName ==
        "Pram2.JPG").ID, ProductID = products.Single( c=> c.Name == "Black Pram and Pushchair
        System").ID,ImageNumber = 1 },
    new ProductImageMapping { ProductImageID= images.Single(i => i.FileName ==
        "Pram3.JPG").ID, ProductID = products.Single( c=> c.Name == "Black Pram and Pushchair
        System").ID,ImageNumber = 2 },
    new ProductImageMapping { ProductImageID= images.Single(i => i.FileName ==
        "CarSeat1.JPG").ID, ProductID = products.Single( c=> c.Name == "Car Seat").ID,
        ImageNumber = 0 },
    new ProductImageMapping { ProductImageID= images.Single(i => i.FileName ==
        "CarSeat2.JPG").ID, ProductID = products.Single( c=> c.Name == "Car Seat").ID,
        ImageNumber = 1 },
    new ProductImageMapping { ProductImageID= images.Single(i => i.FileName ==
        "Moses1.JPG").ID,ProductID = products.Single( c=> c.Name == "Moses Basket").ID,
        ImageNumber = 0 },
    new ProductImageMapping { ProductImageID= images.Single(i => i.FileName ==
        "Moses2.JPG").ID,ProductID = products.Single( c=> c.Name == "Moses Basket").ID,
        ImageNumber = 1 },
    new ProductImageMapping { ProductImageID= images.Single(i => i.FileName ==
        "Crib1.JPG").ID,ProductID = products.Single( c=> c.Name == "Crib").ID, ImageNumber = 0},
    new ProductImageMapping { ProductImageID= images.Single(i => i.FileName ==
        "Crib2.JPG").ID,ProductID = products.Single( c=> c.Name == "Crib").ID, ImageNumber = 1},
    new ProductImageMapping { ProductImageID= images.Single(i => i.FileName == "Bed1.JPG").ID,
        ProductID = products.Single( c=> c.Name == "Cot Bed").ID, ImageNumber = 0 },
    new ProductImageMapping { ProductImageID= images.Single(i => i.FileName == "Bed2.JPG").ID,
        ProductID = products.Single( c=> c.Name == "Cot Bed").ID, ImageNumber = 1 },
    new ProductImageMapping { ProductImageID= images.Single(i => i.FileName ==
        "CircusBale1.JPG").ID, ProductID = products.Single( c=> c.Name == "Circus Crib
        Bale").ID, ImageNumber = 0 },
    new ProductImageMapping { ProductImageID= images.Single(i => i.FileName ==
        "CircusBale2.JPG").ID, ProductID = products.Single( c=> c.Name == "Circus Crib
        Bale").ID, ImageNumber = 1 },
    new ProductImageMapping { ProductImageID= images.Single(i => i.FileName ==
        "CircusBale3.JPG").ID, ProductID = products.Single( c=> c.Name == "Circus Crib
        Bale").ID, ImageNumber = 2 },
    new ProductImageMapping { ProductImageID= images.Single(i => i.FileName ==
        "LovedBale1.JPG").ID, ProductID = products.Single( c=> c.Name == "Loved Crib
        Bale").ID,ImageNumber = 0 },
};

imageMappings.ForEach(c => context.ProductImageMappings.AddOrUpdate(im => im.ProductImageID,c));
context.SaveChanges();
```

There's nothing that you haven't seen before in this code. It adds a set of ProductImageMappings, sets the ProductImageID based on the images added prior to this code, and then sets the ProductID based on the products added earlier in the Seed method.

Next, in order to recreate the database from scratch with no test products from earlier in the chapter, update the `StoreContext` line in the main `Web.Config` file to rename the database as `BabyStore3.mdf` as follows (Ensure that you keep this entry all one on line in the `Web.Config` file.):

```
<add name="StoreContext" connectionString="Data Source=(LocalDB)\MSSQLLocalDB;AttachDbFil
ename=|DataDirectory|\BabyStore3.mdf;Initial Catalog=BabyStore3;Integrated Security=True"
providerName="System.Data.SqlClient" />
```

Next run the `update-database` command in the Package Manager Console window to create the new database and populate it with the new images and image mappings. If this works correctly, you should now be able to view the data in the `ProductImagesMappings` table using Server Explorer, as shown in Figure 6-34.

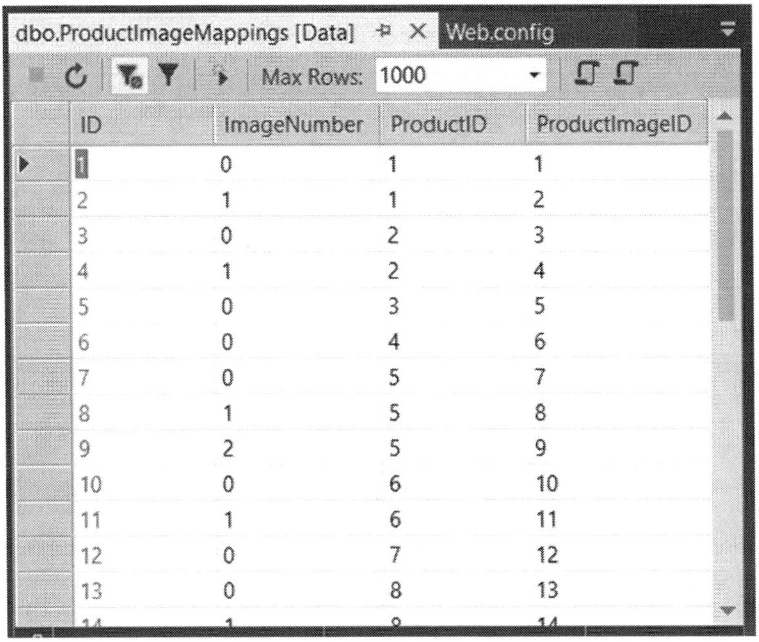

ID	ImageNumber	ProductID	ProductImageID
1	0	1	1
2	1	1	2
3	0	2	3
4	1	2	4
5	0	3	5
6	0	4	6
7	0	5	7
8	1	5	8
9	2	5	9
10	0	6	10
11	1	6	11
12	0	7	12
13	0	8	13

Figure 6-34. *The ProductImageMappings table populated with data from the updated Seed method*

If you get an error message similar to the following, ensure that the spacing in the name of each item is correct in the `imageMappings` variable:

```
System.InvalidOperationException: Sequence contains no matching element
   at System.Linq.Enumerable.Single[TSource](IEnumerable`1 source, Func`2 predicate)
   at BabyStore.Migrations.Configuration.Seed(StoreContext context) in D:\VS2015_Projects\
   BabyStore\BabyStore\Migrations\Configuration.cs:line 92
```

■ **Tip** If you are running through this example for a second time, you may get this error message: Cannot attach the file 'D:\VS2015_Projects\BabyStore\BabyStore\App_Data\BabyStore3.mdf' as database 'BabyStore3'. This occurs because although the MDF file may not physically exist, SQL LocalDb has retained a reference to it. To fix this issue, run the following two commands in the Package Manager Console window: sqllocaldb.exe stop followed by sqllocaldb.exe delete. If you then run update-database, the database will be created.

Next start the web site and navigate to the Products Index page. You will see that each product has images associated with it, as shown in Figure 6-35.

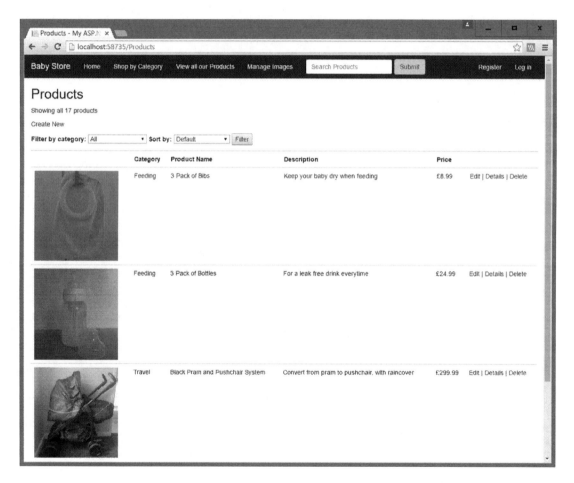

Figure 6-35. Each product now showing an image in the Products Index page

Now open a product. You'll see that it contains the image mappings added in the Seed method. Figure 6-36 shows the images shown when a user opens the Black Pram and Pushchair System product.

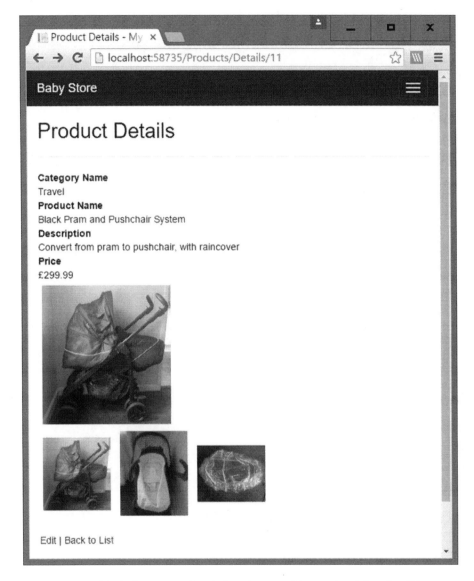

Figure 6-36. *The Black Pram and Pushchair System with associated thumbnail images*

Updating Image Editing, Details, and Index Views

We are not going to allow users to edit or view details of the images, so we're going to remove the code, links, and file associated with doing so. Remove this code as follows:

- In the `Controllers\ProductImagesController.cs` file, delete both of the `Edit` methods and the `Details` method.

- Delete the Edit and Details link from each image in the `ProductImages` Index view by deleting these lines of code: `@Html.ActionLink("Edit", "Edit", new { id=item.ID })` | and `@Html.ActionLink("Details", "Details", new { id=item.ID })` | from the `Views\ProductImages\Index.cshtml` file.

- Finally, delete the `\Views\ProductImages\Edit.cshtml` and `\Views\ProductImages\Details.cshtml` files.

Next, display each image in the `ProductImages` Index view by adding the following highlighted code to the `Views\ProductImages\Index.cshtml` file:

```
@model IEnumerable<BabyStore.Models.ProductImage>

@{
    ViewBag.Title = "Images";
}

<h2>@ViewBag.Title</h2>

<p>
    @Html.ActionLink("Upload New Images", "Upload")
</p>
<table class="table">
    <tr>
        <th>
            @Html.DisplayNameFor(model => model.FileName)
        </th>
        <th></th>
        <th></th>
    </tr>

@foreach (var item in Model) {
    <tr>
        <td>
            @Html.DisplayFor(modelItem => item.FileName)
        </td>
        <td>
            @if (!String.IsNullOrWhiteSpace(item.FileName))
            {
                <img src="@(Url.Content(Constants.ProductImagePath) + item.FileName)">
            }
        </td>
        <td>
            @Html.ActionLink("Delete", "Delete", new { id=item.ID })
        </td>
```

```
    </tr>
}
</table>
```

Figure 6-37 shows how the update `ProductImages` Index page appears following the changes to the view file.

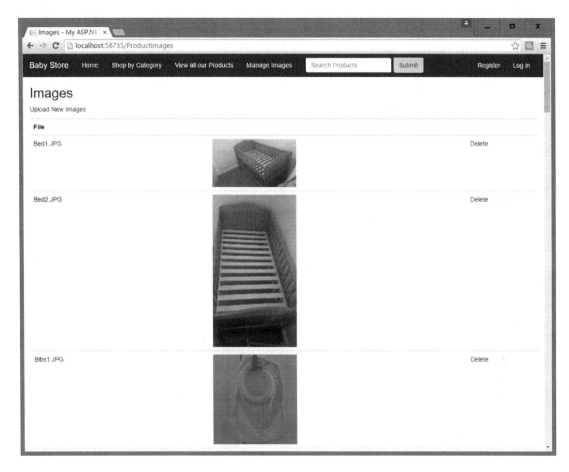

Figure 6-37. *The ProductImages Index page displaying images*

Creating a Partial View for Creating and Editing Products

Earlier in the chapter, we modified the `Views\Products\Create.cshtml` and `Views\Products\Edit.cshtml` files. The code in them is almost identical apart from the fact the Edit view contains a hidden ID element. You've already seen the concept of using a Layout page in Chapter 1, but ASP.NET MVC also allows you to specify partial views to reuse inside other views to help prevent code repetition. To finish this chapter, we're going to create a partial view to contain all the code shared between the Products Create and Products Edit views and then refactor these two views to use the new partial view.

To create the new partial view, right-click on the Views\Shared folder and select Add ➤ View from the menu. Set the view name to _ProductEditCreatePartial, the template the Empty, the Model Class to ProductViewModel(BabyStore.Models), and the data context class to blank (otherwise, Visual Studio will throw an error). Also ensure that the Create as a Partial View and Reference Script Libraries are both checked, as shown in Figure 6-38.

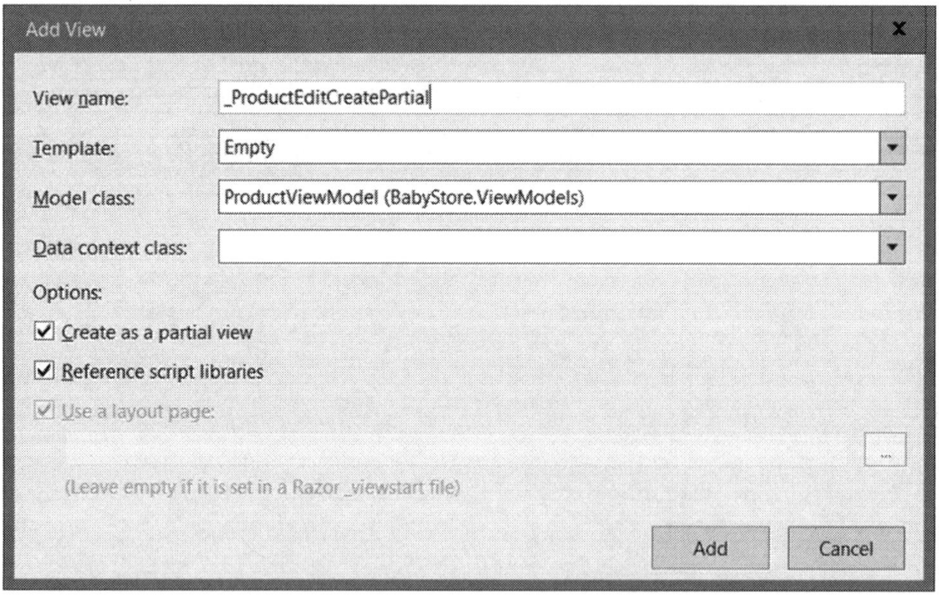

Figure 6-38. *Options for creating the _ProductEditCreatePartial partial view*

■ **Note** It is convention to name a partial view so that it begins with an underscore. We've also followed the convention used by the scaffolding process when it created _LoginPartial.cshtml of ending the name of the partial view Partial. There's no technical reason for these conventions; they are simply used for consistency.

Click the Add button. The new partial view will be created and will contain nothing but the model directive at the top of the file. Update the file as follows so that it contains the code shared between the product's Create and Edit views:

```
@model BabyStore.ViewModels.ProductViewModel

<div class="form-group">
    @Html.LabelFor(model => model.Name, htmlAttributes: new { @class = "control-label col-md-2" })
    <div class="col-md-10">
        @Html.EditorFor(model => model.Name, new { htmlAttributes = new { @class = "form-control" } })
        @Html.ValidationMessageFor(model => model.Name, "", new { @class = "text-danger" })
    </div>
</div>
```

```
<div class="form-group">
    @Html.LabelFor(model => model.Description, htmlAttributes: new { @class = "control-label
    col-md-2" })
    <div class="col-md-10">
        @Html.EditorFor(model => model.Description, new { htmlAttributes = new { @class =
        "form-control" } })
        @Html.ValidationMessageFor(model => model.Description, "", new { @class = "text-
        danger" })
    </div>
</div>

<div class="form-group">
    @Html.LabelFor(model => model.Price, htmlAttributes: new { @class = "control-label col-md-
    2" })
    <div class="col-md-10">
        @Html.EditorFor(model => model.Price, new { htmlAttributes = new { @class = "form-
        control" } })
        @Html.ValidationMessageFor(model => model.Price, "", new { @class = "text-danger" })
    </div>
</div>

<div class="form-group">
    @Html.LabelFor(model => model.CategoryID, htmlAttributes: new { @class = "control-label
        col-md-2" })
    <div class="col-md-10">
        @Html.DropDownListFor(vm => vm.CategoryID, Model.CategoryList, htmlAttributes: new {
        @class = "form-control" })
        @Html.ValidationMessageFor(model => model.CategoryID, "", new { @class = "text-danger"
            })
    </div>
</div>

@for (int i = 0; i < Model.ImageLists.Count; i++)
{
    <div class="form-group">
        <label class="control-label col-md-2">Product Image @(i + 1):</label>
        <div class="col-md-10">
            @Html.DropDownListFor(vm => vm.ProductImages, Model.ImageLists[i], "Choose Image",
                htmlAttributes: new { @class = "form-control" })
            @Html.ValidationMessageFor(model => model.ImageLists, "", new { @class = "text-
            danger" })
        </div>
    </div>
}
```

Next, you need to update the two views so that they use the new partial view. First, modify the Views\
Products\Create.cshtml file as highlighted in the following code:

```
@model BabyStore.ViewModels.ProductViewModel

@{
    ViewBag.Title = "Create Product";
}
```

```
<h2>@ViewBag.Title</h2>

@using (Html.BeginForm())
{
    @Html.AntiForgeryToken()

    <div class="form-horizontal">
        <hr />
        @Html.ValidationSummary(true, "", new { @class = "text-danger" })
        @Html.Partial("_ProductEditCreatePartial", Model)
        <div class="form-group">
            <div class="col-md-offset-2 col-md-10">
                <input type="submit" value="Create" class="btn btn-default" />
            </div>
        </div>
    </div>
}

<div>
    @Html.ActionLink("Back to List", "Index")
</div>

@section Scripts {
    @Scripts.Render("~/bundles/jqueryval")
}
```

Now update the code in the Views\Products\Edit.cshtml file as highlighted in bold:

```
@model BabyStore.ViewModels.ProductViewModel

@{
    ViewBag.Title = "Edit Product";
}

<h2>@ViewBag.Title</h2>

@using (Html.BeginForm())
{
    @Html.AntiForgeryToken()

    <div class="form-horizontal">
        <hr />
        @Html.ValidationSummary(true, "", new { @class = "text-danger" })
        @Html.HiddenFor(model => model.ID)
        @Html.Partial("_ProductEditCreatePartial", Model)
        <div class="form-group">
            <div class="col-md-offset-2 col-md-10">
                <input type="submit" value="Save" class="btn btn-default" />
            </div>
        </div>
    </div>
}
```

```
<div>
    @Html.ActionLink("Back to List", "Index")
</div>

@section Scripts {
    @Scripts.Render("~/bundles/jqueryval")
}
```

If you now start the project without debugging and open the product's Create and Edit views, you will see that they appear and function exactly the same as before.

Although the code created by the Visual Studio scaffolding process is very useful for getting up and running, it can lead to code duplication, especially when there is overlap between views. In real commercial projects, I recommend you use partial views to cut down on this repetition between views and reduce the amount of maintenance required.

Summary

This chapter covered more advanced topics when using Entity Framework and ASP.NET MVC, starting with allowing file uploads and adding project-wide constants. We then showed you how to create a unique constraint, add an error to the ModelState in order to catch a database error, and display a friendly error message back to your users. This was followed by allowing multiple file uploads and how to work with the database context objects and manage the state of an entity. We also covered how to view the SQL generated by Entity Framework and performance considerations when working with bulk data changes. The chapter then moved on to cover how to set a higher upload limit file limit and how to add your own custom error page.

Next we moved on to working with many-to-many relationships with Entity Framework and how to create a many-to-many join table with payload, followed by how to create and then edit the data in many-to-many data relationships. We also covered alternatives to the default method of model binding, including using a view model and using the TryUpdateModel method. I then showed you how to seed the many-to-many relationship with data and closed the chapter by removing the details and update views for images, followed by introducing a partial view for creating and editing products.

■ ■ ■

CHAPTER 7

Authentication and Authorization Using ASP.NET Identity

We now have a web site where users can create, edit, and search for products and manage images. At the moment, though, anyone can just open the site and edit, create, and delete products and images. This chapter shows you how to add some authentication so users can log in and how to add authorization based on roles to determine what tasks users can perform. The code in this chapter uses Microsoft ASP. NET Identity v2 combined with SQL LocalDb. Throughout the code in this chapter, you will see references to OWIN, which stands for Open Web Interface for .NET. The idea behind OWIN is that it acts as a layer of abstraction between a web application and the hosting environment. More information about OWIN is available at `http://owin.org/`.

■ **Note** If you want to follow along with the code in this chapter, you must have completed Chapter 6 or download Chapter 6's source code from `www.apress.com` as a starting point.

To keep the examples as simple as possible and so that you can follow this in your own projects, much of the code is based on the Microsoft sample Identity 2.x code. If you want to view this sample code, open a new empty ASP.NET project and install this package into it. ***Do not install the Microsoft sample identity code into the BabyStore project***. You can find this sample code by choosing Project ➤ Manage NuGet Packages, checking the Include Prerelease box, and then searching for "identity samples" in the NuGet Package Manager window. Figure 7-1 shows the `Microsoft.AspNet.Identity.Sample` package.

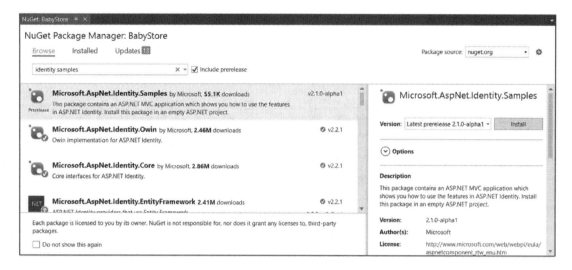

Figure 7-1. *Locating the Microsoft Identity Samples package via NuGet. Never install this package into an existing project. It should only be installed into an empty ASP.NET project as shown in the package description*

Examining the Automatically Created BabyStore Project Identity Code and Database

When we initially created the BabyStore project in Chapter 1, we set the Authentication option to Individual User Accounts. Setting this option meant that the project was created with some Identity code to cater for the basic user registration and management of some user properties. During the project creation a database context was created and a database connection string was added to the Web.Config file. The database context is named ApplicationDbContext and inherits from IdentityDbContext<ApplicationUser>. IdentityDbContext inherits from DbContext. ApplicationDbContext can be found in the Models\IdentityModels.cs file. The default code for the context is shown here.

```
public class ApplicationDbContext : IdentityDbContext<ApplicationUser>
{
    public ApplicationDbContext()
        : base("DefaultConnection", throwIfV1Schema: false)
    {
    }

    public static ApplicationDbContext Create()
    {
        return new ApplicationDbContext();
    }
}
```

This context will use the connection string DefaultConnection to connect to the database to be used for storing Identity details. The Web.Config file contains this connection string. The following code shows the DefaultConnection connectionString as listed in the BabyStore project's Web.Config file:

```
<connectionStrings>
```

```
<add name="DefaultConnection" connectionString="Data Source=(LocalDb)\MSSQLLocalDB;Atta
chDbFilename=|DataDirectory|\aspnet-BabyStore-20160217123618.mdf;Initial Catalog=aspnet-
BabyStore-20160217123618;Integrated Security=True" providerName="System.Data.SqlClient" />
    <add name="StoreContext" connectionString="Data Source=(LocalDB)\MSSQLLocalDB;AttachDbFi
lename=|DataDirectory|\BabyStore3.mdf;Initial Catalog=BabyStore3;Integrated Security=True"
providerName="System.Data.SqlClient" />
</connectionStrings>
```

When a request is made that requires identity (e.g. a user tries to log in), the Identity database is created in the App_Data directory. The database name is generated automatically by Visual Studio; in this case, the database file is aspnet-BabyStore-20160217123618.mdf. Your filename will differ based on the date and time that the connection string is created.

To see the current database state, try to log in to the web site using the username admin@babystore. com and any password. The attempt will fail and you should receive an error from the login page, as shown in Figure 7-2.

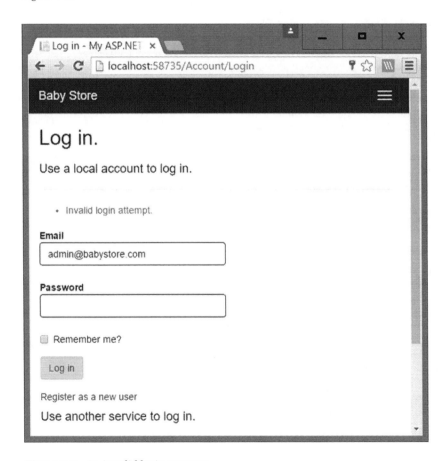

Figure 7-2. *An invalid login attempt*

If you expand the App_Data folder in Visual Studio's Solution Explorer window, you should see the new database file that will be used for identity purposes, as shown in Figure 7-3. If you don't see the new database, try clicking the Refresh button in Solution Explorer.

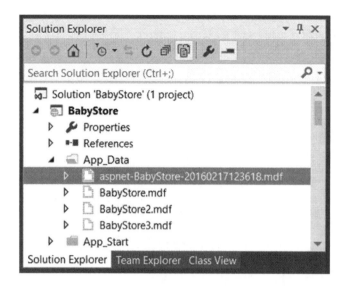

Figure 7-3. The newly created identity database (highlighted) in the App_Data folder

Next, open the database in Server Explorer by right-clicking it and choosing Open from the menu. Note that when the database opens in Server Explorer, it appears under the `DefaultConnection` item rather than `StoreContext`; this is because it uses the `ConnectionString` `DefaultConnection` in `Web.Config`.

The database contains six tables, as shown in Figure 7-4.

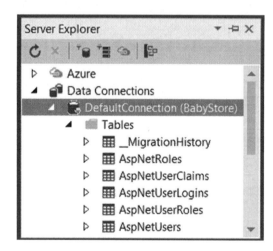

Figure 7-4. The default tables in the Identity database

- `_MigrationHistory` is used by Entity Framework to keep a log of all the migrations relating to the database.

- `AspNetRoles` holds the roles that users can belong to.

- `AspNetUserClaims` holds claims data. A claim is information about a user that can be used as an alternative to a role for authorization purposes.

- AspNetUserLogins is used to hold data about third-party or external logins, for example, users logging in via Google or Facebook.

- AspNetUserRoles is used to map users to roles.

- AspNetUsers holds user data.

In this chapter, we'll work with users and roles and the related tables.

■ **Note**   I don't cover claims or external logins in this book. If you want to learn more about those topics, they are covered in Adam Freeman's *Pro ASP.NET MVC 5 Platform* book.

The current Identity code in the project is quite basic and works only for allowing individual user logins. During the rest of the chapter, we are going to expand this code and the database in order to:

- Create the ability to manage different user roles and users.

- Assign users to roles.

- Create an initial Admin user when the project first runs.

- Add some extra user fields.

Working with Roles

Before looking at users, we are going to work with roles so that when we do come to work with users, we can include code for assigning them to roles during registration, edit the roles they belong to, and display roles in the user details when the administrator views them.

Adding a Role Manager

The first thing required when working with roles is to create a role manager. To start, add the following class inside the BabyStore namespace at the end of the AppStart/IdentityConfig.cs file.

```
public class ApplicationRoleManager : RoleManager<IdentityRole>
{
    public ApplicationRoleManager(IRoleStore<IdentityRole, string> roleStore)
        : base(roleStore)
    {
    }

    public static ApplicationRoleManager Create(IdentityFactoryOptions<ApplicationRoleManager>
        options, IOwinContext context)
    {
        return new ApplicationRoleManager(new
        RoleStore<IdentityRole>(context.Get<ApplicationDbContext>()));
    }
}
```

This code adds a new class named ApplicationRoleManager deriving from the strongly typed class RoleManager<T> for accessing and managing roles. In the code implemented above, RoleManager<IdentityRole> is used. IdentityRole is the class Entity Framework uses for modeling a role and is a simple class consisting of an ID, a name, and a list of users belonging to the role. The Create method returns a new ApplicationRoleManager instance using ApplicationDbContext.

Next, to create a role manager, add the following new line of code to the ConfigureAuth method after the last app.CreateOwinContext call in the App_Start\StartUp.Auth.cs file:

```
app.CreatePerOwinContext<ApplicationRoleManager>(ApplicationRoleManager.Create);
```

This additional code will now create an ApplicationRoleManager instance whenever the application is started. The ConfigureAuth method is called from the project's Startup.cs file and that runs every time the web site starts.

Creating an Admin User and Admin Role Whenever the Identity Database Is Created: Using a Database Initializer

Next we are going to create an Admin user and Admin role to act as an administrator for the web site. Start by adding the following code to the App_Start\IdentityConfig.cs file:

```
// This example shows you how to create a new database if the Model changes
public class ApplicationDbInitializer : DropCreateDatabaseIfModelChanges<ApplicationDbContext>
{
    protected override void Seed(ApplicationDbContext context)
    {
        InitializeIdentityForEF(context);
        base.Seed(context);
    }

    //Create User=admin@mvcbabystore.com with Adm1n@mvcbabystore.com in the Admin role
    public static void InitializeIdentityForEF(ApplicationDbContext db)
    {
        var userManager =
        HttpContext.Current.GetOwinContext().GetUserManager<ApplicationUserManager>();
        var roleManager = HttpContext.Current.GetOwinContext().
        Get<ApplicationRoleManager>();
        const string name = "admin@mvcbabystore.com";
        const string password = "Adm1n@mvcbabystore.com";
        const string roleName = "Admin";

        //Create Role Admin if it does not exist
        var role = roleManager.FindByName(roleName);
        if (role == null)
        {
            role = new IdentityRole(roleName);
            var roleresult = roleManager.Create(role);
        }

        var user = userManager.FindByName(name);
```

```
    if (user == null)
    {
        user = new ApplicationUser
        {
            UserName = name,
            Email = name
        };
        var result = userManager.Create(user, password);
        result = userManager.SetLockoutEnabled(user.Id, false);
    }

    // Add user admin to Role Admin if not already added
    var rolesForUser = userManager.GetRoles(user.Id);
    if (!rolesForUser.Contains(role.Name))
    {
        var result = userManager.AddToRole(user.Id, role.Name);
    }
  }
}
```

■ **Note**   For an alternative way of seeding the database using Code First Migrations, see the opening pages of Chapter 13.

This code adds a new class to initialize the Identity database with an Admin user with the username admin@mvcbabystore.com and the password Adm1n@mvcbabystore.com and assigns them to a new role named Admin. This class demonstrates an alternative way to seed a database with test data as opposed to using migrations. The ApplicationDbInitializer class inherits from DropCreateDatabaseIfModelChang es<T>, meaning that it will take effect only if the database is new or if the model has changed. Alternatives include always dropping and recreating the database using DropCreateDatabaseAlways<T> or the default behavior, which is CreateDatabaseIfNotExists<T>.

The InitializeIdentityForEF method is called by the Seed method and works by first obtaining the application user manager and role manager. Some constants are used to set the admin username and password and the Admin role name. The code then uses the role manager to check if the Admin role exists. If it does not, it creates it by calling the Create method of the role manager. The user manager is then used to search for the Admin user. If it does not exist, it is created using the user manager's Create method. Finally, the code checks to see if the Admin user belongs to any roles. If it does not, it is added to the Admin role.

■ **Note**   I don't recommend hard-coding usernames and plain text passwords into code and have done this only for demonstration purposes. You should never do this in a real commercial project.

Next, we need a way to call the ApplicationDbInitializer class, so add a static constructor to the ApplicationDbContext class in the Models\IdentityModel.cs file, as highlighted:

```
public class ApplicationDbContext : IdentityDbContext<ApplicationUser>
{
    public ApplicationDbContext()
        : base("DefaultConnection", throwIfV1Schema: false)
    {
```

```
    }

    static ApplicationDbContext()
    {
        // Set the database initializer which is run once during application start
        // This seeds the database with admin user credentials and admin role
        Database.SetInitializer<ApplicationDbContext>(new ApplicationDbInitializer());
    }

    public static ApplicationDbContext Create()
    {
        return new ApplicationDbContext();
    }
}
```

Logging In as the Admin User

To be able to log in as the new Admin user, we need to force the database to recreate. To do this, change the DefaultConnection connectionString property in the Web.Config file as follows (make sure it's all on one line in Web.Config):

```
<add name="DefaultConnection" connectionString="Data Source=(LocalDb)\MSSQLLocalDB;AttachD
bFilename=|DataDirectory|\aspnet-BabyStore-Identity.mdf;Initial Catalog=aspnet-BabyStore-
Identity;Integrated Security=True" providerName="System.Data.SqlClient" />
```

Now start the web site without debugging and attempt to log in as the user admin@mvcbabystore.com using the password Adm1n@mvcbabystore.com. You should be logged into the web site as the Admin user, as shown in Figure 7-5.

Figure 7-5. *Logging into the web site as the new Admin user*

The Admin user and role have now been created in the Identity database. To view the user data, expand the DefaultConnection connection in Server Explorer and view the data of the AspNetUsers table. You will see the new admin user data, as shown in Figure 7-6.

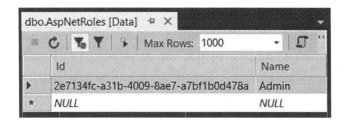

Figure 7-6. *The admin user data in the AspNetUsers table*

Next, view the newly created Admin role by viewing the data of the AspNetRoles table, as shown in Figure 7-7. You will see the auto-generated ID field along with the role name of Admin.

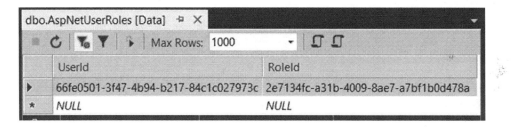

Figure 7-7. *The newly created Admin role in the AspNetRoles database table*

Finally, view the data of the AspNetUserRoles table. This table is used to map users to roles. You should see something similar to Figure 7-8, with a row containing the IDs of the new Admin user and Admin role.

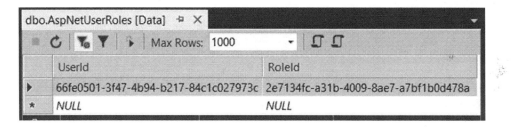

Figure 7-8. *The AspNetUserRoles mapping table showing the mapping between the Admin role and Admin user*

Adding a Roles View Model and RolesAdminController

This first thing we are going to do to allow users to view and manage roles is create a view model for a role. We're going to deviate slightly from the way the Microsoft sample code does this and put this class in its own file. To create the view model, add a new file named AdminViewModel to the ViewModels folder and update the file to add a RoleViewModel class as follows:

```
using System.ComponentModel.DataAnnotations;

namespace BabyStore.ViewModels
{
    public class RoleViewModel
```

```
{
    public string Id { get; set; }
    [Required(AllowEmptyStrings = false)]
    [Display(Name = "Role Name")]
    public string Name { get; set; }
}
}
```

Next, add a controller by right-clicking the Controllers folder and choosing Add ➤ Controller from the menu. In the Add Scaffold window, choose the option MVC5 Controller with read/write actions, as shown in Figure 7-9. This controller will handle all the requests for managing roles.

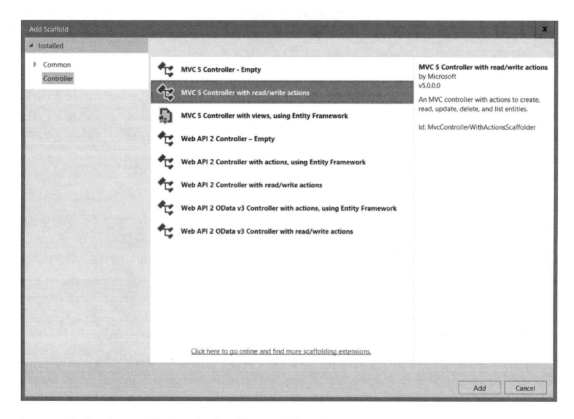

Figure 7-9. *Creating an MVC5 Controller with read/write actions*

Click the Add button and name the controller RolesAdminController. Click the Add button and the RolesAdminController code will appear with basic outline methods for Index, Details, Create, Edit, and Delete.

First of all, add this statement to the top of the Controllers\RolesAdminController.cs file: **using Microsoft.AspNet.Identity.Owin;**.

Now add the following constructors and properties to the RolesAdminController class in order to obtain the RoleManager and UserManager instances for use in the controller:

```
public class RolesAdminController : Controller
{
    public RolesAdminController()
    {
    }

    public RolesAdminController(ApplicationUserManager userManager, ApplicationRoleManager
        roleManager)
    {
        UserManager = userManager;
        RoleManager = roleManager;
    }

    private ApplicationUserManager _userManager;
    public ApplicationUserManager UserManager
    {
        get
        {
            return _userManager ??
                HttpContext.GetOwinContext().GetUserManager<ApplicationUserManager>();
        }
        set
        {
            _userManager = value;
        }
    }

    private ApplicationRoleManager _roleManager;
    public ApplicationRoleManager RoleManager
    {
        get
        {
            return _roleManager ?? HttpContext.GetOwinContext().Get<ApplicationRoleManager>();
        }
        private set
        {
            _roleManager = value;
        }
    }

    // GET: RolesAdmin
    public ActionResult Index()
    {
        return View();
    }
...rest of code omitted for brevity...
```

Displaying All Roles

Now that RoleManager and RolesAdminController are available, we can use them to work with roles. The first change we are going to make to the RolesAdminController methods is to update the Index method to return a list of all the roles in the system. This is very straightforward; you simply update the Index method in the Controllers\RolesAdminController.cs file, as shown here, to return all the roles:

```
public ActionResult Index()
{
    return View(RoleManager.Roles);
}
```

Next, create a view for display the roles by right-clicking on the Index method and create a view named Index with the template set to Empty (without model). Ensure that Use a Layout Page is checked.

Add the following code to the new empty view (Views\RolesAdmin\Index.cshtml) to create a list of roles based on the model IEnumerable<Microsoft.AspNet.Identity.EntityFramework.IdentityRole> with the standard Edit, Details, and Delete links to other views. (Note that to keep this as close as possible to the sample code, we have used the model IEnumerable<Microsoft.AspNet.Identity.EntityFramework. IdentityRole> rather than the RoleViewModel we created earlier).

```
@model IEnumerable<Microsoft.AspNet.Identity.EntityFramework.IdentityRole>

@{
    ViewBag.Title = "Roles";
}

<h2>@ViewBag.Title</h2>

<p>
    @Html.ActionLink("Create New", "Create")
</p>
<table class="table">
    <tr>
        <th>
            @Html.DisplayNameFor(model => model.Name)
        </th>
        <th>
        </th>
    </tr>

    @foreach (var item in Model)
    {
        <tr>
            <td>
                @Html.DisplayFor(modelItem => item.Name)
            </td>
            <td>
```

```
            @Html.ActionLink("Edit", "Edit", new { id = item.Id }) |
            @Html.ActionLink("Details", "Details", new { id = item.Id }) |
            @Html.ActionLink("Delete", "Delete", new { id = item.Id })
        </td>
    </tr>
}
</table>
```

Close your existing browser and ensure that you are logged out of the site. Right-click in the view file and choose the View in Browser option. The new view will display the list of roles (just Admin at the moment), as shown in Figure 7-10.

Figure 7-10. *The RolesAdmin Index page viewed without logging in*

Adding Authorization at a Controller Class Level

At the moment, anybody can anonymously view the roles available in the web site by navigating to the URL / RolesAdmin/Index. To change this so that only an Admin user can see this URL and anything else to do with administering roles, we are going to add some authorization to the RolesAdminController class using an attribute. To enable the authorization, add an Authorize attribute above the class declaration, as highlighted in the following code:

```
[Authorize(Roles = "Admin")]
public class RolesAdminController : Controller
{
...
```

Now build the solution and try opening the Index view again. You will be asked to log in, as shown in Figure 7-11. Log in as the user admin@mvcbabystore.com with the password Adm1n@mvcbabystore.com and you will be redirected to the list of roles. I cover more about redirection after login later in the chapter.

Figure 7-11. Login prompt appearing when user now tries to access the RolesAdmin Index page

Displaying Role Details

Next, to display details for a role, including the users allocated to the role, add the following using statements to the top of the Controllers\RolesAdminController.cs file:

```
using System.Net;
using System.Threading.Tasks;
using BabyStore.Models;
```

Next, update the Details method as follows:

```
public async Task<ActionResult> Details(string id)
{
    if (id == null)
    {
        return new HttpStatusCodeResult(HttpStatusCode.BadRequest);
    }
    var role = await RoleManager.FindByIdAsync(id);
    // Get the list of Users in this Role
    var users = new List<ApplicationUser>();

    // Get the list of Users in this Role
    foreach (var user in UserManager.Users.ToList())
    {
        if (await UserManager.IsInRoleAsync(user.Id, role.Name))
        {
            users.Add(user);
        }
    }

    ViewBag.Users = users;
    ViewBag.UserCount = users.Count();
    return View(role);
}
```

The Details method now becomes an asynchronous method. I cover asynchronous database access later in the book, but what this means in simple terms is that the program can continue with other actions while an asynchronous task is running. In this case, the asynchronous calls are made to the RoleManager. FindByIdAsync and UserManager.IsInRoleAsync methods. These methods are the key to this Details method and are used to find a role by ID (ID is a string), and to determine if a user is in a role based on input parameters of a user's ID and a role name.

The Details method has been updated to take a string named id as an input parameter and attempts to find a role based on this ID. The code then loops through all the users in the application and finds all the ones that are in the role. It then adds the users to the ViewBag, along with the number of users so that this information can be shown in the view. I have kept this code in line with the Microsoft sample code so that you can follow it easily; normally I recommend using a view model, as we have done in other chapters, rather than the ViewBag.

Now add a view by right-clicking on the Details method and choosing Add View from the menu. Add a view named Details with the template set to Empty (without model) and ensure that Use a Layout Page is checked.

Add the following code to the new Views\RolesAdmin\Details.cshtml file:

```
@model Microsoft.AspNet.Identity.EntityFramework.IdentityRole

@{
    ViewBag.Title = "Role Details";
}

<h2>@ViewBag.Title </h2>

<div>
    <hr />
    <dl class="dl-horizontal">
        <dt>
            @Html.DisplayNameFor(model => model.Name)
        </dt>
        <dd>
            @Html.DisplayFor(model => model.Name)
        </dd>
    </dl>
</div>
<h4>List of users in this role</h4>
@if (ViewBag.UserCount == 0)
{
    <hr />
    <p>No users found in this role.</p>
}

<table class="table">

    @foreach (var item in ViewBag.Users)
    {
        <tr>
            <td>
                @item.UserName
            </td>
```

```
        </tr>
    }
</table>
<p>
    @Html.ActionLink("Edit", "Edit", new { id = Model.Id }) |
    @Html.ActionLink("Back to List", "Index")
</p>
```

This view is relatively simple and displays the name of a role along with a list of users belonging to the role.

Start the project without debugging and navigate to the /RolesAdmin/Index URL. Click on the Details link for the Admin role. You will now see the details for the Admin role showing that the user admin@ mvcbabystore.com belongs to the role, as shown in Figure 7-12.

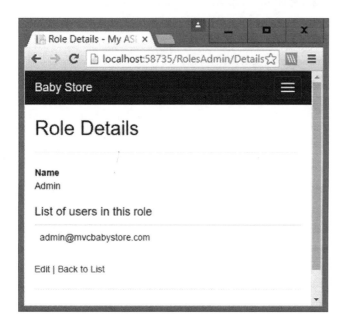

Figure 7-12. *The RolesAdmin Details page*

Creating a Role

We're going to start creating roles by adding a view for the GET version of the Create method in the RolesAdminController class. Right-click on this method in the RolesAdminController class and choose Add View from the menu. Then, in the Add View screen, set the View Name to Create. Set the template to Create and the model to RoleViewModel with Reference Script Libraries and Use a Layout Page both checked, as shown in Figure 7-13. Keep the Data Context Class blank.

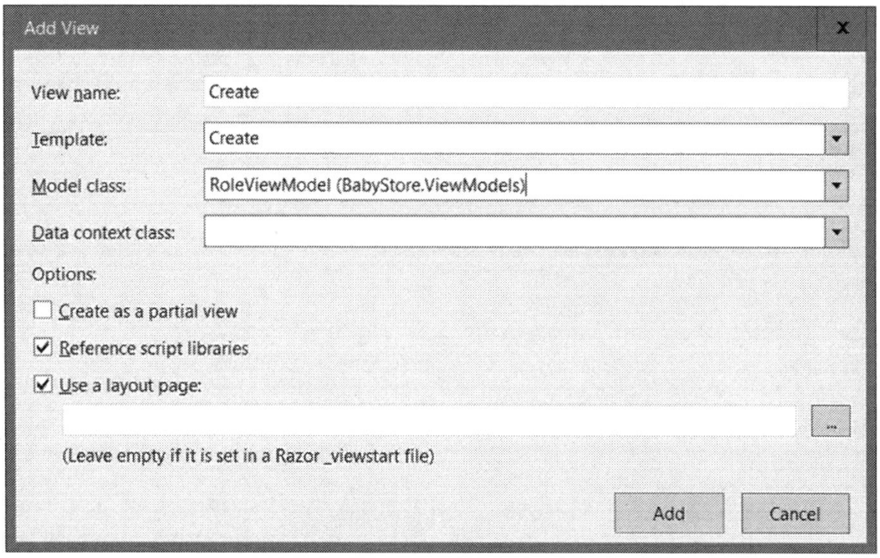

***Figure 7-13.** Adding the RolesAdmin Create view*

When the new view is created, remove the line of code `<h4>RoleViewModel</h4>` and add a new h2 heading as highlighted in the following code:

```
@model BabyStore.ViewModels.RoleViewModel
```

```
@{
    ViewBag.Title = "Create Role";
}
```

```
<h2>@ViewBag.Title</h2>
```

```
@using (Html.BeginForm())
{
    @Html.AntiForgeryToken()

    <div class="form-horizontal">
        <hr />
        @Html.ValidationSummary(true, "", new { @class = "text-danger" })
...following code omitted for brevity
```

To update the `HttpPost` version of the Create method, first add the following using statements to the top of the `Controllers\RolesAdminContoroller.cs` file:

```
using BabyStore.ViewModels;
using Microsoft.AspNet.Identity.EntityFramework;
```

Following this, update the HttpPost version of the Create method as follows:

```
[HttpPost]
public async Task<ActionResult> Create(RoleViewModel roleViewModel)
{
    if (ModelState.IsValid)
    {
        var role = new IdentityRole(roleViewModel.Name);
        var roleresult = await RoleManager.CreateAsync(role);
        if (!roleresult.Succeeded)
        {
            ModelState.AddModelError("", roleresult.Errors.First());
            return View();
        }
        return RedirectToAction("Index");
    }
    return View();
}
```

The key method in this code is the call to the RoleManager.CreateAsync method, which attempts to create a new role based on an IdentityRole object provided as an input parameter. Again, this is an asynchronous method and takes a RoleViewModel as an input parameter. The method checks if roleViewModel's state is valid and if it is then it creates a new IdentityRole type variable and attempts to create this role using the CreateAysnc method of the RoleManager. If this is successful, then the Index action is called, otherwise, the Create view is returned to the user with an error message generated during the creation process.

Test the new Create methods and view by starting the site without debugging and navigating to the URL /RolesAdmin/Create. Create a new view named Users, as shown in Figure 7-14.

Figure 7-14. *Creating a new role named Users*

Click the Create button and the new Users role will be created and displayed in the RolesAdmin Index page, as shown in Figure 7-15.

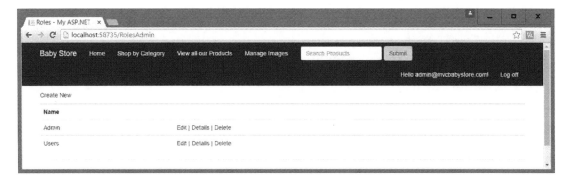

Figure 7-15. *The new Users role displayed in the RolesAdmin Index page*

Fixing the Navigation Bar Style Issues

At the moment, the navigation bar has two issues. The first issue is that the text is split over two lines but more annoyingly this is now overlapping the rest of the content below it, as in Figure 7-15, where the heading "Roles" is not displayed. First, we'll fix the overlapping issue, since sometimes the menu may appear over two lines.

To start, in the Views\Shared_Layout.cshtml file, modify the div with the navbar class assigned to it as follows. Change the css class navbar-fixed-top to navbar-static-top:

```
<body>
    <div class="navbar navbar-inverse navbar-static-top">
        <div class="container">
```

This will make the navbar disappear off the screen when scrolling and pushes the rest of the content down below it so that the "Roles" heading text is now visible on the RolesAdmin Index page, as in Figure 7-16.

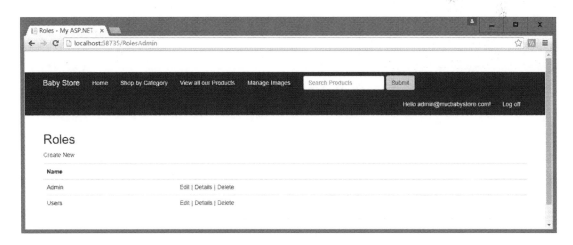

Figure 7-16. *Changing the navigation bar to use the navbar-static-top css class now displays the Roles heading*

Having set the navigation bar to be fixed, there is now another issue that a blank whitespace has appeared above it. To fix this, update the `Content\site.css` file to remove the `padding-top: 50px;` entry from the `css` body class so that it now reads as follows:

```
body {
    padding-bottom: 20px;
}
```

Finally, to make the `nav-bar` wide enough to accept all the text and not wrap over two lines, modify the `Content\bootstrap.css` file to change the `max-width` property value of the container CSS class to 1300px inside the `media-query` for anything over 1200 pixels. This is a bit of a mouthful and I explain what CSS media queries are in part II of the book, but what this change means is that whenever the screen size is at least 1200 pixels, the container class will be set to a maximum of 1300 pixels wide if available. The container class is the CSS class that contains the contents of the navigation bar and hence restricts its width. Update the `Content\bootstrap.css` file as highlighted:

```
@media (min-width: 1200px) {
  .container {
    max-width: 1300px;
  }
}
```

With these two changes in place, the navigation bar now appears as in Figure 7-17, with no whitespace and on one line.

Figure 7-17. *The navigation bar without the whitespace above it and text on one line only*

Editing a Role

Next we'll cover the editing of a role; in this trivial example, it will simply mean editing the role name. First of all, modify the GET version of the Edit method in the `Controllers\RolesAdminController.cs` file as follows:

```
// GET: RolesAdmin/Edit/5
public async Task<ActionResult> Edit(string id)
{
    if (id == null)
    {
```

```
            return new HttpStatusCodeResult(HttpStatusCode.BadRequest);
    }
    var role = await RoleManager.FindByIdAsync(id);
    if (role == null)
    {
        return HttpNotFound();
    }
    RoleViewModel roleModel = new RoleViewModel { Id = role.Id, Name = role.Name };
    return View(roleModel);
}
```

The input parameter type has been changed from int to string so that it can be used in the RoleManager.FindByIdAsync method. IDs used in Identity are long strings rather than integers. The program then searches for the role. If it's found, its data is assigned to a new RoleViewModel object and passed to the view.

Next, add a new Edit view by right-clicking on the Edit method and choosing Add View from the menu. Set the view name to Edit, the template to Edit, the model class to RoleViewModel (BabyStore.ViewModels), and the Data Context Class to blank. Ensure that Reference Script Libraries and Use a Layout Page are checked. Figure 7-18 shows the correct options to set.

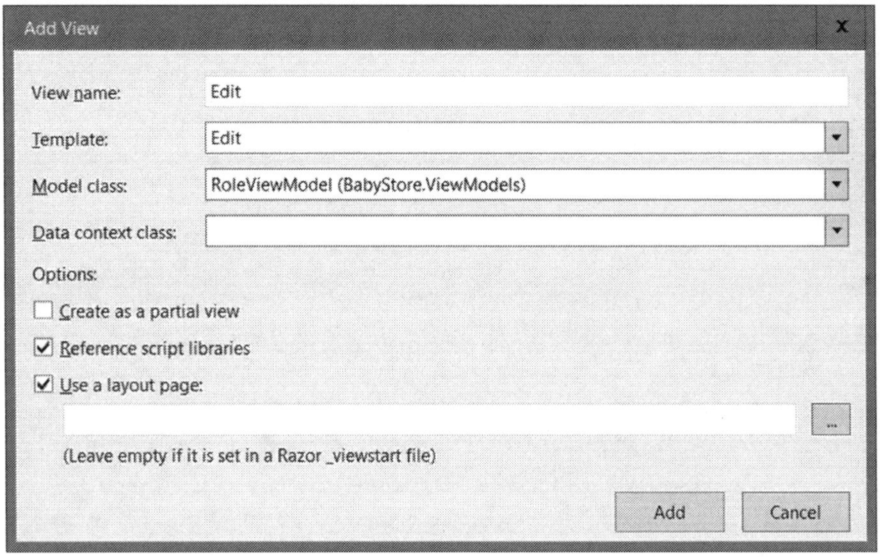

Figure 7-18. Creating the RolesAdmin Edit view

Modify the generated view file to set the ViewBag.Title to Edit Role and use it inside the H2 heading tags. Also remove the <h4> heading as highlighted:

```
@model BabyStore.ViewModels.RoleViewModel

@{
    ViewBag.Title = "Edit Role";
}
```

```
<h2>@ViewBag.Title</h2>

@using (Html.BeginForm())
{
    @Html.AntiForgeryToken()

    <div class="form-horizontal">
        <hr />
        @Html.ValidationSummary(true, "", new { @class = "text-danger" })
        @Html.HiddenFor(model => model.Id)
...rest of code omitted for brevity
```

Next update the HttpPost version of the Edit method in the Controllers\RolesAdminController.cs file as follows:

```
[HttpPost]
[ValidateAntiForgeryToken]
public async Task<ActionResult> Edit(RoleViewModel roleModel)
{
    if (ModelState.IsValid)
    {
        var role = await RoleManager.FindByIdAsync(roleModel.Id);
        role.Name = roleModel.Name;
        await RoleManager.UpdateAsync(role);
        return RedirectToAction("Index");
    }
    return View();
}
```

The key method in this code is the RoleManager.UpdateAsync method, which is used to update a role with any new property values assigned to it. This method takes a RoleViewModel as an input parameter and attempts to update the name of the role using the RoleManager.UpdateAsync method. It returns the user to the index view if everything is successful. Figures 7-19 and 7-20 show the Users group being renamed User.

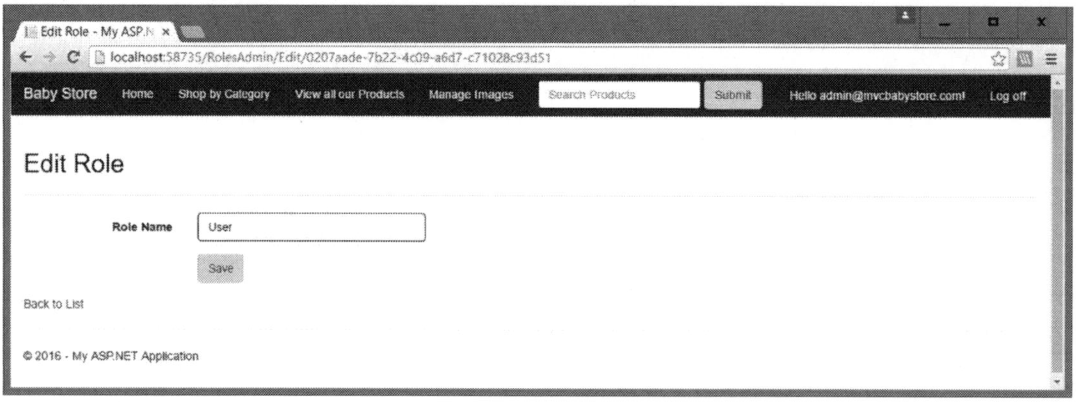

Figure 7-19. *The RolesAdmin Edit view*

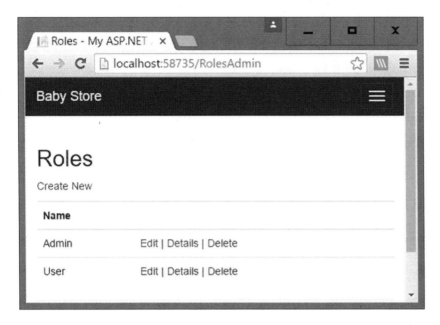

Figure 7-20. *The Users role is renamed User*

Deleting a Role

To enable the deleting of roles, first modify the GET version of the Delete method in the Controllers\
RolesAdminController.cs as file follows:

```
// GET: RolesAdmin/Delete/5
public async Task<ActionResult> Delete(string id)
{
    if (id == null)
    {
        return new HttpStatusCodeResult(HttpStatusCode.BadRequest);
    }
    var role = await RoleManager.FindByIdAsync(id);
    if (role == null)
    {
        return HttpNotFound();
    }
    return View(role);
}
```

This code is very similar to the previous code for the GET version of the Edit method, but does not
populate a view model to return to the view. Instead of using RoleViewModel, the view will be based on the
IdentityRole class.

Add a Delete view by right-clicking on the Delete method and choosing Add View from the menu. Set
the view name to Delete and the template to Empty (without model), with Use a Layout Page checked. In the
generated view file, update the contents as follows:

```
@model Microsoft.AspNet.Identity.EntityFramework.IdentityRole
```

207

```
@{
    ViewBag.Title = "Delete Role";
}


<h2>Delete Role</h2>

<h3>Are you sure you want to delete this Role? </h3>
<p>Deleting this Role will remove all users from this role. It will not delete the users.</p>
<div>
    <hr />
    <dl class="dl-horizontal">
        <dt>
            @Html.DisplayNameFor(model => model.Name)
        </dt>

        <dd>
            @Html.DisplayFor(model => model.Name)
        </dd>
    </dl>
    @using (Html.BeginForm())
    {
        @Html.AntiForgeryToken()

        <div class="form-actions no-color">
            <input type="submit" value="Delete" class="btn btn-default" /> |
            @Html.ActionLink("Back to List", "Index")
        </div>
    }
</div>
```

The view has been modified to display the details of the role passed to the view and is based on the IdentityRole class. Figure 7-21 shows the new delete view for a new role I created named Test Delete:

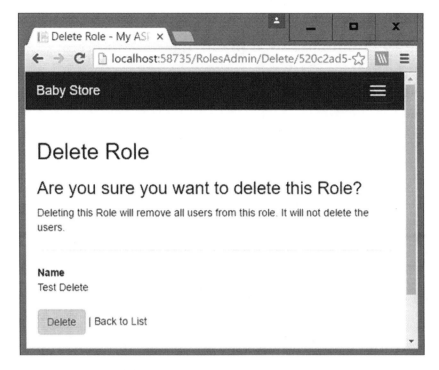

Figure 7-21. *The RolesAdmin Delete view*

To give this view a method to target, update the HttpPost version of the Delete method. First add the following using statement to the top of the Controllers\RolesAdminController.cs file:

```
using Microsoft.AspNet.Identity;
```

Next update the HttpPost version of the Delete method renaming it to DeleteConfirmed and then update it as follows so that it finds a role based on an id and then deletes the role:

```
// POST: RolesAdmin/Delete/5
[HttpPost, ActionName("Delete")]
[ValidateAntiForgeryToken]
public async Task<ActionResult> DeleteConfirmed(string id)
{
    if (ModelState.IsValid)
    {
        if (id == null)
        {
            return new HttpStatusCodeResult(HttpStatusCode.BadRequest);
        }
        var role = await RoleManager.FindByIdAsync(id);
        if (role == null)
        {
            return HttpNotFound();
        }
        IdentityResult result = await RoleManager.DeleteAsync(role);
```

209

```
        if (!result.Succeeded)
        {
            ModelState.AddModelError("", result.Errors.First());
            return View();
        }
        return RedirectToAction("Index");
    }
    return View();
}
```

The key method call in the DeleteConfirmed method is the call to the RoleManager.DeleteAsync method, which takes an IdentityRole object as an input parameter and then attempts to delete the role.

The method has been renamed DeleteConfirmed because if the name was kept as Delete, it would have the same signature as the GET version of the Delete method (public async Task<ActionResult> Delete(string id)) and the compiler would not be able to differentiate between them, resulting in a compilation error. The method has been prefixed with [HttpPost, ActionName("Delete")] so that when a HttpPost request is made to target the Delete action, it actually targets this DeleteConfirmed method.

The method attempts to find a role based on the ID input parameter. Once it's found it attempts to delete it and return the user to the index view. It adds an error to the ModelState and returns the user to the Delete view if it does not succeed.

Adding a Basic Admin Controller and View

At the moment, the web site has no links to the new RolesAdminController or associated views, and it already has a link to allow users to manage images. We are going to create a very simple admin page with links to all the index pages of the different controllers for managing images, roles, and users.

First create an AdminController class by right-clicking on the Controllers folder and choosing Add ➤ Controller from the menu. Then choose to add an MVC5 Controller Empty and name the new controller AdminController.

In the new AdminController.cs file, right-click the Index method and choose Add View from the menu. Set the view name to Index and the template to Empty (without model). Ensure Use a Layout Page is checked.

Update the contents of the new \Views\Admin\Index.cshtml file as follows to add links to the Index pages for ProductImages, RoleAdmin, and UserAdmin:

```
@{
    ViewBag.Title = "Admin";
}

<h2>@ViewBag.Title</h2>
<div class="container">
    <div class="row">
        @Html.ActionLink("Manage Images", "Index", "ProductImages")
    </div>
    <div class="row">
        @Html.ActionLink("Manage Roles", "Index", "RolesAdmin")
    </div>
    <div class="row">
        @Html.ActionLink("Manage Users", "Index", "UsersAdmin")
    </div>
</div>
```

Next, replace the Manage Images link in the `Views\Shared\_Layout.cshtml` file with a link to the new Admin Index page by replacing `<li>@Html.ActionLink("Manage Images", "Index", "ProductImages")</li>` with `<li>@Html.ActionLink("Admin", "Index", "Admin")</li>`.

Start the web site without debugging. In the home page, click the new Admin link in the navigation bar. The new Admin Index page should appear, as shown in Figure 7-22.

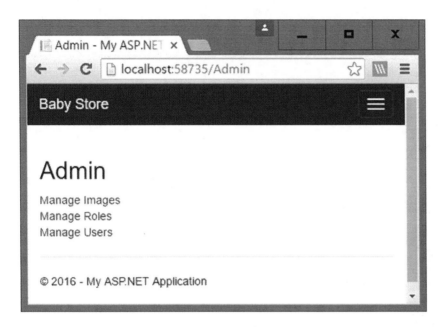

Figure 7-22. *The new Admin Index page with links to Manage Images, Roles, and Users*

Adding Authorization to the Admin Controller and Admin Link

We have already covered adding authorization to a controller earlier in the chapter and will use this again in the `AdminController`. However, first we're going to display the admin link only to the users in the Admin role. To make this change, update the `Views\Shared\_Layout.cshml` file as follows to add a check to see if the user is authenticated and in the admin group before displaying the Admin link:

```
@if (Request.IsAuthenticated && User.IsInRole("Admin"))
{
    <li>@Html.ActionLink("Admin", "Index", "Admin")</li>
}
```

■ **Note** If you need to perform more complex logic in a commercial project to validate a user, I recommend that you perform the logic in your controller classes and then set a Boolean value in your view model where possible. Because we are using pages generated by scaffolding, we've added the logic to check the user's role to the view file directly.

Now if you click on the Logout link in the web site, the Admin link will no longer appear, as shown in Figure 7-23.

Figure 7-23. *The Admin link no longer appears when the user is not logged in*

If you log in as the Admin user admin@mvcbabystore.com with the Adm1n@mvcbabystore.com password, the Admin link should now appear as shown in Figure 7-24.

Figure 7-24. *The Admin link appears in the navigation bar when logged in as the admin@mvcbabystore.com user*

Users can still access the Admin Index page anonymously by simply entering the /Admin URL, so prevent this by modifying the AdminController.cs file as follows. This will add authorization to the AdminController class so it is only available to users in the Admin role:

```
[Authorize(Roles = "Admin")]
public class AdminController : Controller
{
```

When the users try to access the URL /Admin anonymously, they will now be prompted to log in and must do so as a member of the Admin group in order to gain access.

Working with Users

This section covers working with users, including how to add new fields to the existing user class and how to work with two database contexts in one project. It also covers how to manage users as an administrator, user self-registration, viewing and editing personal details, and how users can reset their passwords using ASP.NET Identity. Just as everything to do with working with roles was based on the RoleManager class, working with users is based on the UserManager class.

When we covered working with roles earlier, it was necessary to create a new class named ApplicationRoleManager, which inherited from the RoleManager class. This time, when working with users, we do not need to create an ApplicationUserManager class, because when the project was created, this class was automatically created by setting Authentication to Individual User Accounts. The ApplicationUserManager class can be found in the App_Start\IdentityConfig.cs file.

Adding Extra Properties for a User

If you expand the AspNetUsers database table, you will see the properties (displayed as database columns) currently stored for a user. These columns are generated from the IdentityUser class using Entity Framework. This class is provided by default when using Identity and is part of the Microsoft.AspNet. Identity.EntityFramework namespace. I've listed the contents of this class here so you can see the default properties it specifies for the users:

```
namespace Microsoft.AspNet.Identity.EntityFramework
{

    public class IdentityUser<TKey, TLogin, TRole, TClaim> : IUser<TKey>
        where TLogin : IdentityUserLogin<TKey>
        where TRole : IdentityUserRole<TKey>
        where TClaim : IdentityUserClaim<TKey>
    {

        public IdentityUser();
        public virtual int AccessFailedCount { get; set; }
        public virtual ICollection<TClaim> Claims { get; }
        public virtual string Email { get; set; }
        public virtual bool EmailConfirmed { get; set; }
        public virtual TKey Id { get; set; }
        public virtual bool LockoutEnabled { get; set; }
        public virtual DateTime? LockoutEndDateUtc { get; set; }
        public virtual ICollection<TLogin> Logins { get; }
        public virtual string PasswordHash { get; set; }
        public virtual string PhoneNumber { get; set; }
        public virtual bool PhoneNumberConfirmed { get; set; }
        public virtual ICollection<TRole> Roles { get; }
        public virtual string SecurityStamp { get; set; }
        public virtual bool TwoFactorEnabled { get; set; }
        public virtual string UserName { get; set; }
    }
}
```

We are not going to examine each property in this class in detail. The main reason for listing them is so that you can see what properties are currently defined for a user and crucially *what is not defined*. This class defines that a user will have an e-mail address, a phone number, and a username, but it does not have useful properties that we require for a shopping web site such as a user's actual name, their date of birth, or address.

To add some new user fields, create a new class in the Models folder named Address and edit the contents as follows:

```
using System.ComponentModel.DataAnnotations;

namespace BabyStore.Models
{
    public class Address
    {
        [Required]
        [Display(Name = "Address Line 1")]
        public string AddressLine1 { get; set; }
        [Display(Name = "Address Line 2")]
        public string AddressLine2 { get; set; }
        [Required]
        public string Town { get; set; }
        [Required]
        public string County { get; set; }
        [Required]
        public string Postcode { get; set; }
    }
}
```

We are going to use an address more than once in this project for both users and orders, so it is defined as a distinct class. We've defined all the fields as required apart from the AddressLine2. This class will also be used to demonstrate how Entity Framework works with composition, whereby an object is composed of another object.

To add extra fields to a user, you need to update the ApplicationUser class. In order to add a first name, last name, date of birth, and address for a user, open the Models\IdentityModel.cs file and update the ApplicationUser class as highlighted:

```
public class ApplicationUser : IdentityUser
{
    [Required]
    [Display(Name = "First Name")]
    [StringLength(50)]
    public string FirstName { get; set; }
    [Required]
    [Display(Name = "Last Name")]
    [StringLength(50)]
    public string LastName { get; set; }

    [Required]
    [DataType(DataType.Date)]
    [Display(Name = "Date of birth")]
```

```
[DisplayFormat(DataFormatString = "{0:d}")]
public DateTime DateOfBirth { get; set; }

public Address Address { get; set; }

public async Task<ClaimsIdentity> GenerateUserIdentityAsync(UserManager<ApplicationUser>
manager)
{
    // Note the authenticationType must match the one defined in
            CookieAuthenticationOptions.AuthenticationType
    var userIdentity = await manager.CreateIdentityAsync(this,
            DefaultAuthenticationTypes.ApplicationCookie);
    // Add custom user claims here
    return userIdentity;
}
}
```

Ensure you add **using System;** to the top of the file so that DateTime can be found and add **using System.ComponentModel.DataAnnotations;**. All the properties are required. For the DateOfBirth property, the DataType is set to date, so the time information stored in the field is not displayed. The DisplayFormat attribute is set to use the local server format (in this case, it's the UK format mm/dd/yyyy).

Now that we have updated the ApplicationUser class, we need to apply the model changes to the Identity database. We'll use Code First as we have done throughout the book, but first we have to reconfigure the project so that it can work with migrations for multiple database contexts.

Working with Two Database Contexts: Updating the Identity Database for the New User Properties

In order to enable migrations for the Identity database, we first need to update the existing migration files in the Migrations folder so that we can enable migrations for the ApplicationDbContext. Update the existing files in the Migrations folder as follows:

- Change the name of the Migrations\Configuration.cs file to Migrations\ StoreConfiguration.cs

- Update the class name and constructor in Migrations\StoreConfiguration.cs to StoreConfiguration as highlighted here (You can do this automatically by choosing yes when asked if you want to update all references when changing the class name):

```
internal sealed class StoreConfiguration : DbMigrationsConfiguration<BabyStore.DAL.
StoreContext>
{
    public StoreConfiguration()
    {
        AutomaticMigrationsEnabled = false;
    }
```

- Change the namespace in Migrations\StoreConfiguration.cs to BabyStore. Migrations.StoreConfiguration

- Update the StoreContext connectionString property in the main Web.Config file to change the database name in order to create a new database to verify that migrations still work okay:

```
<add name="StoreContext" connectionString="Data Source=(LocalDB)\MSSQLLocalDB;AttachDbFil
ename=|DataDirectory|\BabyStore4.mdf;Initial Catalog=BabyStore4;Integrated Security=True"
providerName="System.Data.SqlClient" />
```

- Create a new migration by running the following command in Package Manager Console. This will effectively reset the migrations and merge all the previous migrations into one:

```
add-migration twocontextreset -configuration storeconfiguration
```

- You should now see a new migration file with the following code:

```
namespace BabyStore.Migrations.StoreConfiguration
{
    using System;
    using System.Data.Entity.Migrations;

    public partial class twocontextreset : DbMigration
    {
        public override void Up()
        {
            CreateTable(
                "dbo.Categories",
                c => new
                    {
                        ID = c.Int(nullable: false, identity: true),
                        Name = c.String(nullable: false, maxLength: 50),
                    })
                .PrimaryKey(t => t.ID);

            CreateTable(
                "dbo.Products",
                c => new
                    {
                        ID = c.Int(nullable: false, identity: true),
                        Name = c.String(nullable: false, maxLength: 50),
                        Description = c.String(nullable: false, maxLength: 200),
                        Price = c.Decimal(nullable: false, precision: 18, scale: 2),
                        CategoryID = c.Int(),
                    })
                .PrimaryKey(t => t.ID)
                .ForeignKey("dbo.Categories", t => t.CategoryID)
                .Index(t => t.CategoryID);

            CreateTable(
                "dbo.ProductImageMappings",
```

```
            c => new
                {
                    ID = c.Int(nullable: false, identity: true),
                    ImageNumber = c.Int(nullable: false),
                    ProductID = c.Int(nullable: false),
                    ProductImageID = c.Int(nullable: false),
                })
            .PrimaryKey(t => t.ID)
            .ForeignKey("dbo.Products", t => t.ProductID, cascadeDelete: true)
            .ForeignKey("dbo.ProductImages", t => t.ProductImageID, cascadeDelete: true)
            .Index(t => t.ProductID)
            .Index(t => t.ProductImageID);

        CreateTable(
            "dbo.ProductImages",
            c => new
                {
                    ID = c.Int(nullable: false, identity: true),
                    FileName = c.String(maxLength: 100),
                })
            .PrimaryKey(t => t.ID)
            .Index(t => t.FileName, unique: true);

    }

    public override void Down()
    {
        DropForeignKey("dbo.ProductImageMappings", "ProductImageID", "dbo.
        ProductImages");
        DropForeignKey("dbo.ProductImageMappings", "ProductID", "dbo.Products");
        DropForeignKey("dbo.Products", "CategoryID", "dbo.Categories");
        DropIndex("dbo.ProductImages", new[] { "FileName" });
        DropIndex("dbo.ProductImageMappings", new[] { "ProductImageID" });
        DropIndex("dbo.ProductImageMappings", new[] { "ProductID" });
        DropIndex("dbo.Products", new[] { "CategoryID" });
        DropTable("dbo.ProductImages");
        DropTable("dbo.ProductImageMappings");
        DropTable("dbo.Products");
        DropTable("dbo.Categories");
    }
}
}
```

- Run the following command in Package Manager Console in order to create the BabyStore4 database:

```
update-database -configuration storeconfiguration
```

- Now delete the old migration files (apart from the _twocontextreset file) from the Migrations directory.

The `BabyStore4` database will now be set up and ready to use with migrations in the `BabyStore.Migrations.StoreConfiguration.StoreConfiguration` namespace.

■ **Note**   There are several discussions on the web site such as Stack Overflow about how to work with two database contexts using Entity Framework. If you are introducing a new context and decide to change the namespace of your existing context as we have done, it is essential that you create a new migration as we did when creating `twocontextreset`. If you do not do this, everything will *appear* to be fine. However, as soon as you try to recreate your database, your old migrations will no longer be recognized, even if you place your existing migrations into the new namespace, and update the `migrationhistory` table in the database.

To enable migrations for the Identity database, open Package Manager Console and run the command:

```
enable-migrations -ContextTypeName BabyStore.Models.ApplicationDbContext
```

Next, add a new migration by running the following command in Package Manager Console:

```
add-migration update_user_fields -ConfigurationTypeName Configuration
```

Finally, update the database for the new `ApplicationUser` fields by running this command in Package Manager Console:

```
update-database -ConfigurationTypeName Configuration
```

The new fields for First Name, Last Name, and the Address columns should now appear in the `DefaultConnection` in the Server Explorer window. View the data of the `AspNetUsers` table. Figure 7-25 shows how the new columns are appended to the right side of the table.

Figure 7-25. *The new FirstName, LastName, and Address columns in the AspNetUsers database table*

■ **Note**   When creating database fields for a class property composed of another class, Entity Framework creates the column prefixed with the property name. In this case, it has created all the `Address` fields prefixed with `Address`.

Updating the Admin User Creation Code for the New User Fields

Now that we added some extra required fields to the `ApplicationUser` class, we are going to update the code that creates the admin@mvcbabystore.com user. Open the `App_Start\IdentityConfig.cs` file and update the code inside the `InitializeIdentityForEF` method that creates a new `ApplicationUser` as highlighted. This code adds the FirstName, LastName, DateOfBirth, and Address values.

```csharp
//Create User=admin@mvcbabystore.com with Adm1n@mvcbabystore.com in the Admin role
public static void InitializeIdentityForEF(ApplicationDbContext db)
{
    var userManager =
        HttpContext.Current.GetOwinContext().GetUserManager<ApplicationUserManager>();
    var roleManager = HttpContext.Current.GetOwinContext().Get<ApplicationRoleManager>();
    const string name = "admin@mvcbabystore.com";
    const string password = "Adm1n@mvcbabystore.com";
    const string roleName = "Admin";

    //Create Role Admin if it does not exist
    var role = roleManager.FindByName(roleName);
    if (role == null)
    {
        role = new IdentityRole(roleName);
        var roleresult = roleManager.Create(role);
    }

    var user = userManager.FindByName(name);
    if (user == null)
    {
        user = new ApplicationUser
        {
            UserName = name,
            Email = name,
            FirstName = "Admin",
            LastName = "Admin",
            DateOfBirth = new DateTime(2015, 1, 1),
            Address = new Address
            {
                AddressLine1 = "1 Admin Street",
                Town = "Town",
                County = "County",
                Postcode = "PostCode"
            }
        };
        var result = userManager.Create(user, password);
        result = userManager.SetLockoutEnabled(user.Id, false);
    }

    // Add user admin to Role Admin if not already added
    var rolesForUser = userManager.GetRoles(user.Id);
    if (!rolesForUser.Contains(role.Name))
    {
        var result = userManager.AddToRole(user.Id, role.Name);
    }
}
```

Remember that it's important to not hardcode the creation of Admin users inside code in a commercial project. This is done in this project for demonstration purposes only.

Creating a Users Role on Database Creation

Now that we've updated the code to add new data to the Admin user, we are going to recreate the database in order to recreate the Admin user with the new data. Before we do this, however, we are also going to create a new role named Users when the Identity database is created. Modify the InitializeIdentityForEF method in the \App_Start\IdentityConfig.cs file to create a Users role by adding the following highlighted code at the end of the method:

```
//Create User=admin@mvcbabystore.com with Adm1n@mvcbabystore.com in the Admin role
public static void InitializeIdentityForEF(ApplicationDbContext db)
{
    var userManager =
        HttpContext.Current.GetOwinContext().GetUserManager<ApplicationUserManager>();
    var roleManager = HttpContext.Current.GetOwinContext().Get<ApplicationRoleManager>();
    const string name = "admin@mvcbabystore.com";
    const string password = "Adm1n@mvcbabystore.com";
    const string roleName = "Admin";

    //Create Role Admin if it does not exist
    var role = roleManager.FindByName(roleName);
    if (role == null)
    {
        role = new IdentityRole(roleName);
        var roleresult = roleManager.Create(role);
    }

    var user = userManager.FindByName(name);
    if (user == null)
    {
        user = new ApplicationUser
        {
            UserName = name,
            Email = name,
            FirstName = "Admin",
            LastName = "Admin",
            DateOfBirth = new DateTime(2015, 1, 1),
            Address = new Address
            {
                AddressLine1 = "1 Admin Street",
                Town = "Town",
                County = "County",
                Postcode = "PostCode"
            }
        };
        var result = userManager.Create(user, password);
        result = userManager.SetLockoutEnabled(user.Id, false);
    }
```

```
    // Add user admin to Role Admin if not already added
    var rolesForUser = userManager.GetRoles(user.Id);
    if (!rolesForUser.Contains(role.Name))
    {
        var result = userManager.AddToRole(user.Id, role.Name);
    }

    //Create users role
    const string userRoleName = "Users";
    role = roleManager.FindByName(userRoleName);
    if (role == null)
    {
        role = new IdentityRole(userRoleName);
        var roleresult = roleManager.Create(role);
    }
}
```

Next update the connection string for the DefaultConnection entry in the project's main Web.Config file. Update the database name to aspnet-BabyStore-Identity2 as highlighted:

```
<add name="DefaultConnection" connectionString="Data Source=(LocalDb)\MSSQLLocalDB;AttachD
bFilename=|DataDirectory|\aspnet-BabyStore-Identity2.mdf;Initial Catalog=aspnet-BabyStore-
Identity2;Integrated Security=True" providerName="System.Data.SqlClient" />
```

This will create a new database for storing identity information the next time the project is built and any identity code is called.

Next, start the web site without debugging and log in as the Admin user, which is admin@mvcbabystore.com with the Adm1n@mvcbabystore.com password. The Identity database will be recreated and in the AspNetUsers table, the admin@mvcbabystore.com user will now have data in the FirstName, LastName, DateOfBirth, Address_AddressLine1, Address_Town, Address_County, and Address_Postcode fields, as shown in Figure 7-26.

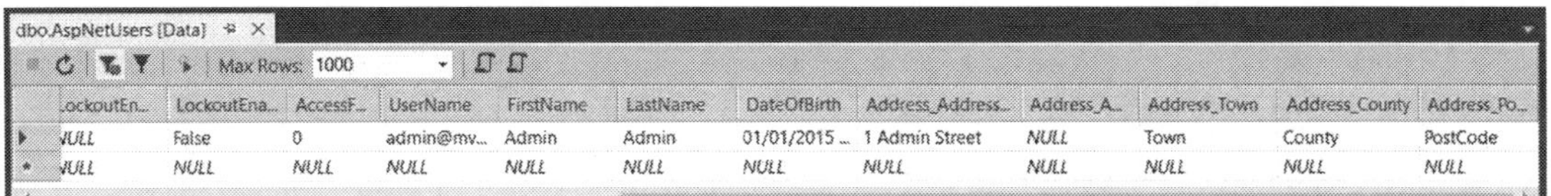

LockoutEn...	LockoutEna...	AccessF...	UserName	FirstName	LastName	DateOfBirth	Address_Address...	Address_A...	Address_Town	Address_County	Address_Po...
NULL	False	0	admin@mv...	Admin	Admin	01/01/2015 ...	1 Admin Street	NULL	Town	County	PostCode
NULL	NULL	NULL	NULL	NULL	NULL	NULL	NULL	NULL	NULL	NULL	NULL

Figure 7-26. *The Admin user now contains the extra data*

In addition to the new user data, the AspNetRoles table will now also contain a Users role, as shown in Figure 7-27.

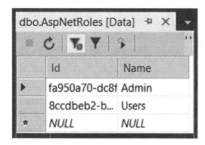

Figure 7-27. *The AspNetRoles table now contains an entry for a Users role*

Adding a UsersAdminController

Now we're going to create a `UsersAdminController`. This controller will handle all the requests from an administrator for managing and viewing user data, in the same way that a `RolesAdminController` was used to handle admin requests for viewing and managing roles.

Add a controller by right-clicking the `Controllers` folder and choosing Add ➤ Controller from the menu. In the Add Scaffold window, choose the option MVC5 Controller with read/write actions, as shown in Figure 7-9.

Click the Add button and name the controller `UsersAdminController`, then click the Add button and the `UsersAdminController` code will appear with basic outline methods for Index, Details, Create, Edit, and Delete.

Next add this statement to the top of the `Controllers\UsersAdminController.cs` file: **using Microsoft.AspNet.Identity.Owin;**.

Then add the following bold line of code above the declaration of the `UsersAdminController` class so that it is limited only to users in the Admin role:

```
[Authorize(Roles = "Admin")]
public class UsersAdminController : Controller
```

Now add the following constructors and properties to the `UsersAdminController` class in order to obtain the `RoleManager` and `UserManager` instances for use in the controller:

```
public class UsersAdminController : Controller
{
    public UsersAdminController()
    {
    }

    public UsersAdminController(ApplicationUserManager userManager, ApplicationRoleManager
        roleManager)
    {
        UserManager = userManager;
        RoleManager = roleManager;
    }

    private ApplicationUserManager _userManager;
    public ApplicationUserManager UserManager
    {
        get
```

```
    {
        return _userManager ??
            HttpContext.GetOwinContext().GetUserManager<ApplicationUserManager>();
    }
    private set
    {
        _userManager = value;
    }
}

private ApplicationRoleManager _roleManager;
public ApplicationRoleManager RoleManager
{
    get
    {
        return _roleManager ?? HttpContext.GetOwinContext().Get<ApplicationRoleManager>();
    }
    private set
    {
        _roleManager = value;
    }
}

// GET: UsersAdmin
public ActionResult Index()
{
    return View();
}
```
...following code omitted for brevity...

Displaying All Users

To display all users, first update the Index method in the UsersAdminController class to return a list of all the users in the system, as shown in the following code.

```
public async Task<ActionResult> Index()
{
    return View(await UserManager.Users.ToListAsync());
}
```

Add the following using statements to the top of the Controllers\UsersAdminController.cs file to ensure that the method compiles:

```
using System.Data.Entity;
using System.Threading.Tasks;
```

The Index method has been updated to be asynchronous, and it obtains the list of users from the UserManager asynchronously. I cover asynchronous database access later in the book.

Next, create a view for displaying the users by right-clicking on the Index method and choosing Add View. Create a view named Index with the template set to Empty (without model). Ensure Use a Layout Page is checked.

Add the following code to the new empty view to create a list of roles based on the model IEnumerable<BabyStore.Models.ApplicationUser>, with the standard Edit, Details, and Delete links to other views:

```
@model IEnumerable<BabyStore.Models.ApplicationUser>

@{
    ViewBag.Title = "Users";
}

<h2>@ViewBag.Title</h2>

<p>
    @Html.ActionLink("Create New", "Create")
</p>
<table class="table">
    <tr>
        <th>
            @Html.DisplayNameFor(model => model.UserName)
        </th>
        <th>
        </th>
    </tr>
    @foreach (var item in Model)
    {
        <tr>
            <td>
                @Html.DisplayFor(modelItem => item.UserName)
            </td>
            <td>
                @Html.ActionLink("Edit", "Edit", new { id = item.Id }) |
                @Html.ActionLink("Details", "Details", new { id = item.Id }) |
                @Html.ActionLink("Delete", "Delete", new { id = item.Id })
            </td>
        </tr>
    }
</table>
```

Right-click on Index.cshtml file and choose View in browser. You will be prompted to log in if you are not already logged in as the Admin user. Log in as the Admin user and you will see the index.cshtml page displaying a list of current web site users, as shown in Figure 7-28. At the moment, only the user admin@ mvcbabystore.com exists, so only that is displayed.

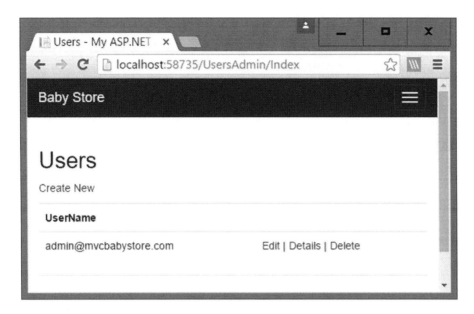

Figure 7-28. *The UserAdmin Index page displaying the current users in the site*

Displaying User Details

To display details for a user, including the roles a user is allocated to, modify the Details method in the Controllers\UsersAdminController.cs file as shown in bold:

```
public async Task<ActionResult> Details(string id)
{
    if (id == null)
    {
        return new HttpStatusCodeResult(HttpStatusCode.BadRequest);
    }
    var user = await UserManager.FindByIdAsync(id);

    ViewBag.RoleNames = await UserManager.GetRolesAsync(user.Id);

    return View(user);
}
```

Add the statement using System.Net; to the top of the file so that the code compiles. The key methods in this code are UserManager.FindByIdAsync(id), which is used to find a user by ID, and UserManager. GetRolesAsync(user.Id), which is used to find the roles that a user is assigned to. The method attempts to find a user by ID and then finds the roles the user is assigned to. The roles are assigned to the ViewBag and the user is then passed to the view to display. We haven't changed this code to use a view model in order to keep it as close as possible to the sample Microsoft code and make it is easier to follow.

Next we need to create the Details view. This view is going to be based on the ApplicationUser class, but creating it is not as straightforward as using the scaffolding process to create a Details view based on the ApplicationUser model. If you try this, the scaffolding process will throw an error with the message "The method or operation is not implemented". Therefore, to create this view, right-click on the method and choose Add View, then create a view named Details with the template set to Empty (without model). Ensure Use a Layout Page is checked.

Modify the new Views\UsersAdmin\Details.cshtml file so that it appears as follows. This code will display the user's personal data, including name, address, e-mail, and date of birth. It also loops through the roles assigned to the ViewBag and lists them. We are not going to attempt to display all the address fields individually; instead, we're going to rely on the HTML helper Html.DisplayFor to display all the fields in an Address object by simply calling @Html.DisplayFor(model => model.Address).

```
@model BabyStore.Models.ApplicationUser

@{
    ViewBag.Title = "User Details";
}

<h2>@ViewBag.Title</h2>

<div>
    <hr />
    <dl class="dl-horizontal">
        <dt>
            @Html.DisplayNameFor(model => model.FirstName)
        </dt>
        <dd>
            @Html.DisplayFor(model => model.FirstName)
        </dd>
        <dt>
            @Html.DisplayNameFor(model => model.LastName)
        </dt>
        <dd>
            @Html.DisplayFor(model => model.LastName)
        </dd>
        <dt>
            @Html.DisplayNameFor(model => model.Email)
        </dt>

        <dd>
            @Html.DisplayFor(model => model.Email)
        </dd>
```

```
        <dt>
            @Html.DisplayNameFor(model => model.DateOfBirth)
        </dt>

        <dd>
            @Html.DisplayFor(model => model.DateOfBirth)
        </dd>
        @Html.DisplayFor(model => model.Address)
    </dl>
</div>
<div class="container">
    <div class="row">
        <h4>Roles this user belongs to:</h4>
    </div>
    @if (ViewBag.RoleNames.Count == 0)
    {
        <hr />
        <p>No roles found for this user</p>
    }

    @foreach (var item in ViewBag.RoleNames)
    {
        <div class="row">
            @item
        </div>
    }
</div>
<p>
    @Html.ActionLink("Edit", "Edit", new { id = Model.Id }) |
    @Html.ActionLink("Back to List", "Index")
</p>
```

Once this code is completed, start the web site and navigate to the UsersAdmin Index page (/UsersAdmin). Click on the Details link of the admin@mvcbabystore.com user. The user's details should appear as shown in Figure 7-29. It shows the name, e-mail, date of birth, address, and role details.

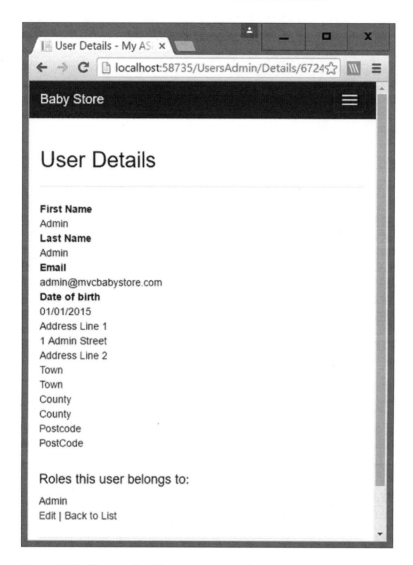

Figure 7-29. *The details of the admin@mvcbabystore.com user viewed via the UsersAdmin Details page*

As you can see, using @Html.DisplayFor(model => model.Address) has shortened the code but displays the data from the user's address differently from the other fields. This is because the HTML helper doesn't have any instruction on how to display the Address model, so uses some default HTML. The effect of this is to attempt to display the address fields inside div elements, whereas the rest of the fields are formatted inside dl, dt, and dd tags as part of a definition list element. The following code snippet shows the generated HTML source for the first few address fields and labels compared with the date of birth field:

```
<dt>
    Date of birth
</dt>

<dd>
    2015-01-01
</dd>
```

```
<div class="display-label">Address Line 1</div>
<div class="display-field">1 Some Street</div>
<div class="display-label">Address Line 2</div>
<div class="display-field"></div>
<div class="display-label">Town</div>
<div class="display-field">Town</div>
```

You can see that date of birth is contained within different HTML tags to the address fields. I'm going to demonstrate how to fix this formatting issue using a feature of ASP.NET MVC known as *display templates*.

Using a Display Template

Display templates are a useful feature of ASP.NET MVC that allow you to specify a template to determine how a particular model will appear when used in the DisplayFor() helper method. We are going to introduce a display template to help display an address object correctly in the UsersAdmin Details view. Taking this approach allows you to reuse the same template every time you want to display an address.

To add a display template, add a new folder under the \Views\Shared folder and name it DisplayTemplates. Next, add an empty view named Address using a Layout page to the new folder so that the \Views\Shared\DisplayTemplates\Address.cshtml file is created. Then update the contents of the file as follows:

```
@model BabyStore.Models.Address

<dt>
    @Html.DisplayNameFor(model => model.AddressLine1)
</dt>

<dd>
    @Html.DisplayFor(model => model.AddressLine1)
</dd>

<dt>
    @Html.DisplayNameFor(model => model.AddressLine2)
</dt>

<dd>
    @Html.DisplayFor(model => model.AddressLine2)
</dd>

<dt>
    @Html.DisplayNameFor(model => model.Town)
</dt>

<dd>
    @Html.DisplayFor(model => model.Town)
</dd>

<dt>
    @Html.DisplayNameFor(model => model.County)
</dt>

<dd>
```

```
    @Html.DisplayFor(model => model.County)
</dd>

<dt>
    @Html.DisplayNameFor(model => model.Postcode)
</dt>

<dd>
    @Html.DisplayFor(model => model.Postcode)
</dd>
```

Start the web site without debugging and then view the details of the admin@mvcbabystore.com user. The address fields should be formatted as part of the definition list and appear consistently with the rest of the page, as shown in Figure 7-30.

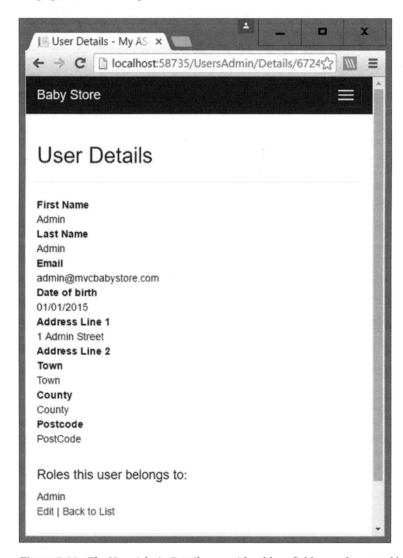

Figure 7-30. *The UsersAdmin Detail page with address fields now formatted by a display template*

Using a display template might seem a bit like overkill at the moment, but it will save code later when dealing with other areas of the site, which also displays addresses such as orders since the same display template can be reused with a single line of code.

Creating a New User as Admin

To create a new user as an Admin user, start by updating the GET version of the Create method in the Controllers\UsersAdminController.cs file to assign the roles available in the database to the ViewBag as follows:

```
// GET: UsersAdmin/Create
public async Task<ActionResult> Create()
{
    //Get the list of Roles
    ViewBag.RoleId = new SelectList(await RoleManager.Roles.ToListAsync(), "Name", "Name");
    return View();
}
```

The SelectList will be used in the view to generate a list of check boxes, with one per role. Again, ViewBag has been used so that the code follows the Microsoft sample as closely as possible.

The view is going to be based on the RegisterViewModel class so this first needs to be updated to include the properties that we added to the ApplicationUser class. Modify the RegisterViewModel class in the Models\AccountViewModels.cs file to add the properties in bold that were previously added to the ApplicationUser class:

```
public class RegisterViewModel
{
    [Required]
    [EmailAddress]
    [Display(Name = "Email")]
    public string Email { get; set; }

    [Required]
    [StringLength(100, ErrorMessage = "The {0} must be at least {2} characters long.",
    MinimumLength = 6)]
    [DataType(DataType.Password)]
    [Display(Name = "Password")]
    public string Password { get; set; }

    [DataType(DataType.Password)]
    [Display(Name = "Confirm password")]
    [Compare("Password", ErrorMessage = "The password and confirmation password do not
    match.")]
    public string ConfirmPassword { get; set; }

    [Required]
    [Display(Name = "First Name")]
    [StringLength(50)]
    public string FirstName { get; set; }
    [Required]
    [Display(Name = "Last Name")]
```

```
    [StringLength(50)]
    public string LastName { get; set; }

    [Required]
    [DataType(DataType.Date)]
    [Display(Name = "Date of birth")]
    [DisplayFormat(DataFormatString = "{0:yyyy-MM-dd}", ApplyFormatInEditMode = true)]
    public DateTime DateOfBirth { get; set; }

    public Address Address { get; set; }
}
```

Ensure you add **using System;** to the top of the file so DateTime can be found. One difference between the files is that we have set the DataFormatString for DateOfBirth differently. This has been set differently because of a bug in Google Chrome that displays date formats incorrectly as the string "dd/mm/yyyy" when editing dates. This leads to an invalid date error when you're editing an existing date.

Next right-click on the Create method in the UsersAdminController class and choose Add View. Add a view called Create using a Create template and the model class RegisterViewModel. Ensure Use a Layout Page and Reference Script Libraries are both checked. Figure 7-31 show the options.

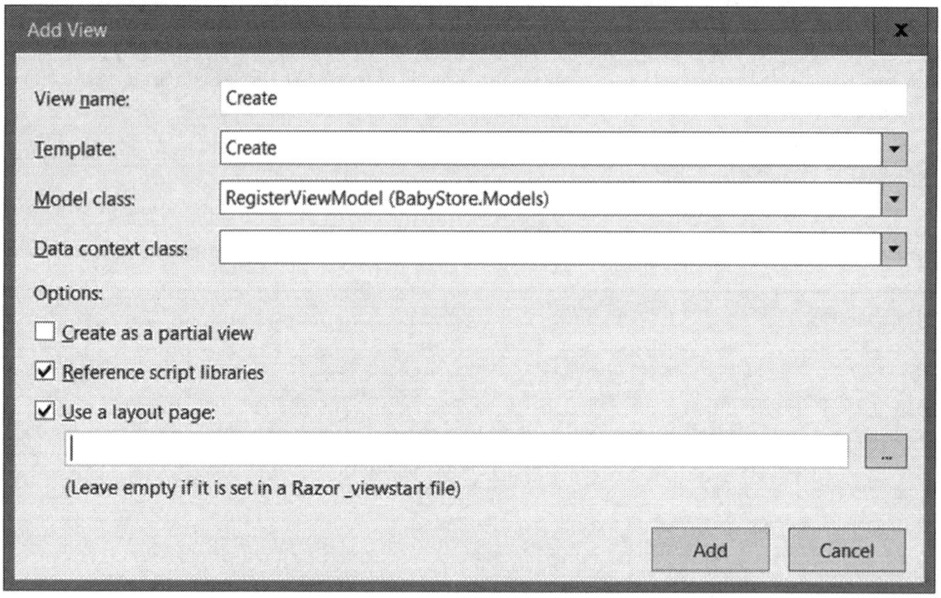

Figure 7-31. *Adding a UsersAdminController Create view*

The scaffolding process runs, but the process does not generate any code in the view for the address property because it is composed of another class. Update the new Views\UsersAdmin\Create.cshtml file to add an HTML EditorFor helper to display editable address fields, generate a set of check boxes for each item in the ViewBag.RoleId property, and update the <h2> heading. Then remove the <h4> heading. These changes are shown in bold in the following code:

```
@model BabyStore.Models.RegisterViewModel

@{
    ViewBag.Title = "Create User";
}

<h2>@ViewBag.Title</h2>

@using (Html.BeginForm())
{
    @Html.AntiForgeryToken()
    <div class="form-horizontal">
    <hr />
        @Html.ValidationSummary(true, "", new { @class = "text-danger" })
        <div class="form-group">
            @Html.LabelFor(model => model.Email, htmlAttributes: new { @class = "control-
            label
                col-md-2" })
            <div class="col-md-10">
                @Html.EditorFor(model => model.Email, new { htmlAttributes = new { @class =
                "form-control" } })
                @Html.ValidationMessageFor(model => model.Email, "", new { @class = "text-
                danger" })
            </div>
        </div>

        <div class="form-group">
            @Html.LabelFor(model => model.Password, htmlAttributes: new { @class = "control-
            label col-md-2" })
            <div class="col-md-10">
                @Html.EditorFor(model => model.Password, new { htmlAttributes = new { @class =
                    "form-control" } })
                @Html.ValidationMessageFor(model => model.Password, "", new { @class =
                "text-
                    danger" })
            </div>
        </div>

        <div class="form-group">
            @Html.LabelFor(model => model.ConfirmPassword, htmlAttributes: new { @class =
                "control-label col-md-2" })
            <div class="col-md-10">
                @Html.EditorFor(model => model.ConfirmPassword, new { htmlAttributes = new {
                    @class = "form-control" } })
                @Html.ValidationMessageFor(model => model.ConfirmPassword, "", new { @class =
                    "text-danger" })
            </div>
        </div>
```

```
    <div class="form-group">
        @Html.LabelFor(model => model.FirstName, htmlAttributes: new { @class =
        "control-
            label col-md-2" })
        <div class="col-md-10">
            @Html.EditorFor(model => model.FirstName, new { htmlAttributes = new { @
            class
="form-control" } })
            @Html.ValidationMessageFor(model => model.FirstName, "", new { @class =
            "text-
                danger" })
        </div>
    </div>


    <div class="form-group">
        @Html.LabelFor(model => model.LastName, htmlAttributes: new { @class = "control-
            label col-md-2" })
        <div class="col-md-10">
            @Html.EditorFor(model => model.LastName, new { htmlAttributes = new { @class =
                "form-control" } })
            @Html.ValidationMessageFor(model => model.LastName, "", new { @class =
            "text-
                danger" })
        </div>
    </div>


    <div class="form-group">
        @Html.LabelFor(model => model.DateOfBirth, htmlAttributes: new { @class =
        "control-label col-md-2" })
        <div class="col-md-10">
            @Html.EditorFor(model => model.DateOfBirth, new { htmlAttributes = new {
            @class = "form-control" } })
            @Html.ValidationMessageFor(model => model.DateOfBirth, "", new { @class =
            "text-danger" })
        </div>
    </div>

    @Html.EditorFor(model => model.Address)

    <div class="form-group">
        <label class="col-md-2 control-label">
            Select User Role
        </label>
        <div class="col-md-10">
            @foreach (var item in (SelectList)ViewBag.RoleId)
            {
                <input type="checkbox" name="SelectedRoles" value="@item.Value"
                  class="checkbox-inline" />
                @Html.Label(item.Value, new { @class = "control-label" })
            }
        </div>
    </div>
```

```
        <div class="form-group">
            <div class="col-md-offset-2 col-md-10">
                <input type="submit" value="Create" class="btn btn-default" />
            </div>
        </div>
    </div>
}

<div>
    @Html.ActionLink("Back to List", "Index")
</div>

@section Scripts {
    @Scripts.Render("~/bundles/jqueryval")
}
```

Right-click the file and click View in Browser from the menu. The UsersAdmin Create HTML page should appear as shown in Figure 7-32, including the check boxes for each role.

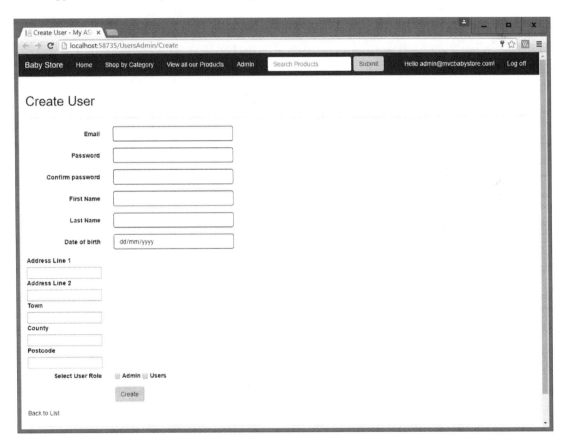

Figure 7-32. The UsersAdmin Create page

There is a similar issue with this page as there was with the Detail page. Using @Html.EditorFor(model => model.Address) has caused the Address fields to use some default HTML tags using the CSS classes editor-label and editor-field. The effect of this is that these fields are formatted differently than the rest of the page. ASP.NET MVC provides a feature similar to display templates called *editor templates,* and it can be used to specify how a model should appear when used with the EditFor() method.

Using an Editor Template

Editor template are a feature of ASP.NET MVC that allow you to specify a template to determine how a particular model will appear when used in the EditorFor() helper method. We're going to introduce an editor template to display an address object correctly in the UsersAdmin Create view. Taking this approach allows you to reuse the same template every time you want to edit an address.

To add an editor template, add a new folder in the \Views\Shared folder and name it EditorTemplates. Next add an empty view using a layout page named Address so that the \Views\Shared\EditorTemplates\ Address.cshtml file is created. Then update the contents of the file as follows:

```
@model BabyStore.Models.Address


<div class="form-group">
    @Html.LabelFor(model => model.AddressLine1, htmlAttributes: new { @class = "control-label
    col-md-2" })
    <div class="col-md-10">
        @Html.EditorFor(model => model.AddressLine1, new { htmlAttributes = new { @class =
        "form-control" } })
        @Html.ValidationMessageFor(model => model.AddressLine1, "", new { @class = "text-
        danger" })
    </div>
</div>

<div class="form-group">
    @Html.LabelFor(model => model.AddressLine2, htmlAttributes: new { @class = "control-label
    col-md-2" })
    <div class="col-md-10">
        @Html.EditorFor(model => model.AddressLine2, new { htmlAttributes = new { @class =
        "form-control" } })
        @Html.ValidationMessageFor(model => model.AddressLine2, "", new { @class = "text-
        danger" })
    </div>
</div>
```

```
<div class="form-group">
    @Html.LabelFor(model => model.Town, htmlAttributes: new { @class = "control-label col-md-
        2" })
    <div class="col-md-10">
        @Html.EditorFor(model => model.Town, new { htmlAttributes = new { @class = "form-
        control" } })
        @Html.ValidationMessageFor(model => model.Town, "", new { @class = "text-danger" })
    </div>
</div>

<div class="form-group">
    @Html.LabelFor(model => model.County, htmlAttributes: new { @class = "control-label col-
    md-2" })
    <div class="col-md-10">
        @Html.EditorFor(model => model.County, new { htmlAttributes = new { @class = "form-
        control" } })
        @Html.ValidationMessageFor(model => model.County, "", new { @class = "text-danger"
})
    </div>
</div>

<div class="form-group">
    @Html.LabelFor(model => model.Postcode, htmlAttributes: new { @class = "control-label col-
    md-2" })
    <div class="col-md-10">
        @Html.EditorFor(model => model.Postcode, new { htmlAttributes = new { @class = "form-
        control" } })
        @Html.ValidationMessageFor(model => model.Postcode, "", new { @class = "text-danger"
        })
    </div>
</div>
```

Start the web site without debugging and then try to create a new user via the admin screen. The address fields should now be formatted like the rest of the page, as shown in Figure 7-33.

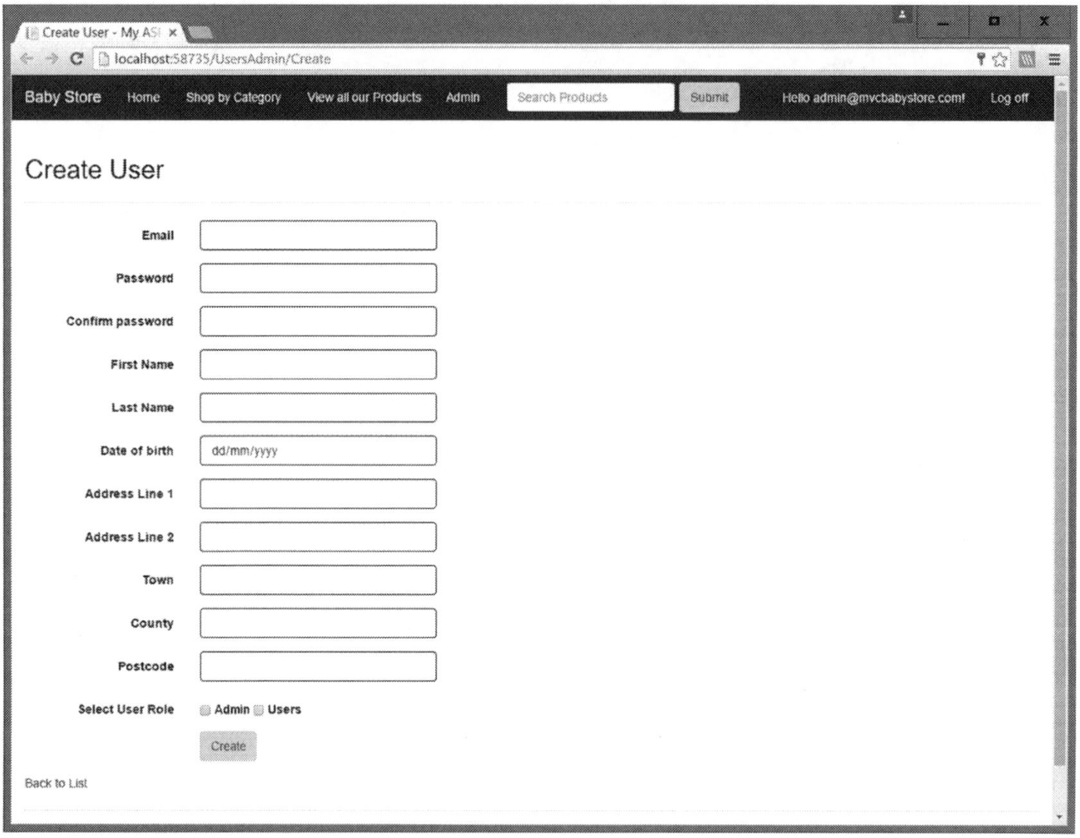

Figure 7-33. The UsersAdmin Create page with address fields now formatted by an Editor Template

Next, the HttpPost version of the Create method in the UsersAdminController.cs file needs to be updated to process the data submitted by HTML form in the create view. Update the method to accept a RegisterViewModel and a collection of strings as input parameters, attempt to create a new user and assign it to the selected roles as follows:

```
// POST: UsersAdmin/Create
[HttpPost]
[ValidateAntiForgeryToken]
public async Task<ActionResult> Create(RegisterViewModel userViewModel, params string[]
    selectedRoles)
{
    if (ModelState.IsValid)
    {
        var user = new ApplicationUser
        {
            UserName = userViewModel.Email,
            Email = userViewModel.Email,
            DateOfBirth = userViewModel.DateOfBirth,
            FirstName = userViewModel.FirstName,
            LastName = userViewModel.LastName,
```

```
            Address = userViewModel.Address
        };
        var adminresult = await UserManager.CreateAsync(user, userViewModel.Password);

        //Add User to the selected Roles
        if (adminresult.Succeeded)
        {
            if (selectedRoles != null)
            {
                var result = await UserManager.AddToRolesAsync(user.Id, selectedRoles);
                if (!result.Succeeded)
                {
                    ModelState.AddModelError("", result.Errors.First());
                    ViewBag.RoleId = new SelectList(await RoleManager.Roles.ToListAsync(),
                        "Name", "Name");
                    return View();
                }
            }
        }
        else
        {
            ModelState.AddModelError("", adminresult.Errors.First());
            ViewBag.RoleId = new SelectList(RoleManager.Roles, "Name", "Name");
            return View();

        }
        return RedirectToAction("Index");
    }
    ViewBag.RoleId = new SelectList(RoleManager.Roles, "Name", "Name");
    return View();
}
```

After updating the method, ensure that you add using BabyStore.Models; to the top of the file. The Create method works by creating a new ApplicationUser based on the data passed in via the userViewModel input parameter, and then attempts to create a user based on this new ApplicationUser. If this succeeds, it adds the user to the roles contained in the selectedRoles input parameter. The key method calls in this method are UserManager.CreateAsync and UserManager.AddToRolesAsync. The UserManager. CreateAsync method attempts to create a user based on an ApplicationUser type and the password property passed into the method as part of the RegisterViewModel and UserManager.AddToRolesAsync adds a user to a number of roles taking a user ID and a collection of strings as input parameters.

Start the web site without debugging, log in as the Admin user, and navigate to the new UsersAdmin Create page. Add a new user to the Users role, with the e-mail address user1@mvcbabystore.com and with the values as shown in Figure 7-34. Set the password field to P@ssw0rd.

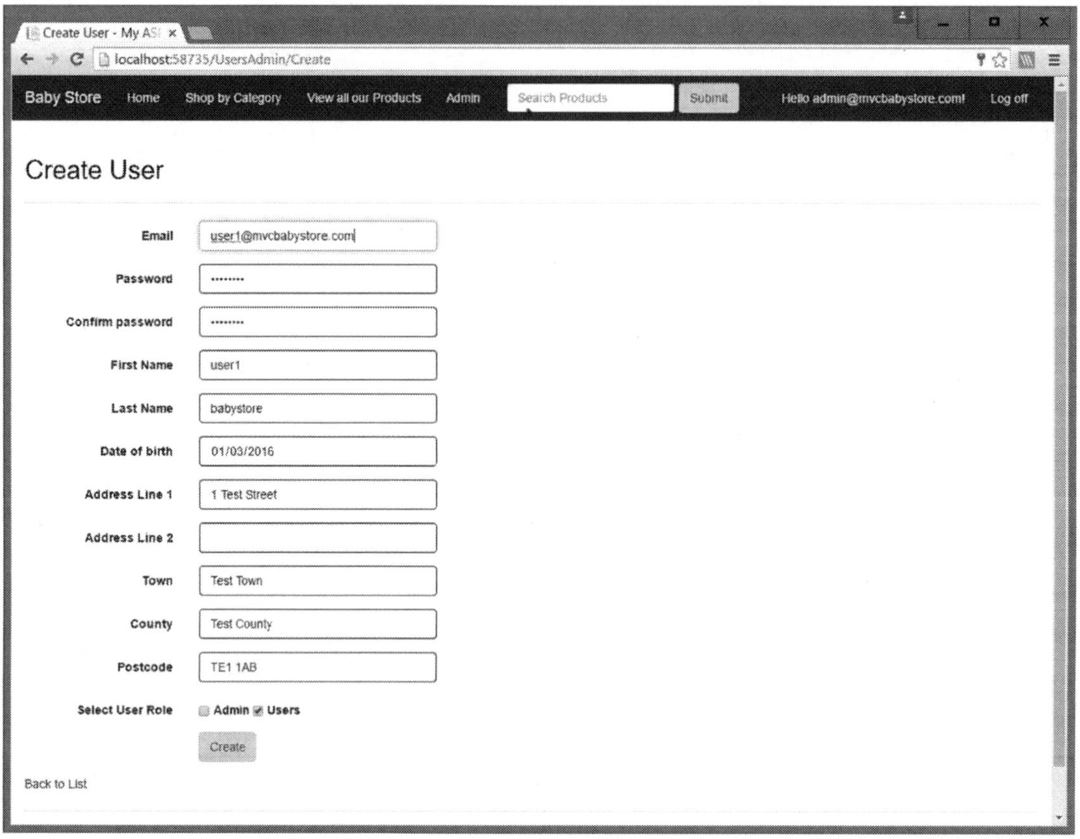

Figure 7-34. *Values to use when creating user1@mvcbabystore.com*

Click the Create button. You should be returned to the Index page with the new user listed with the users, as shown in Figure 7-35.

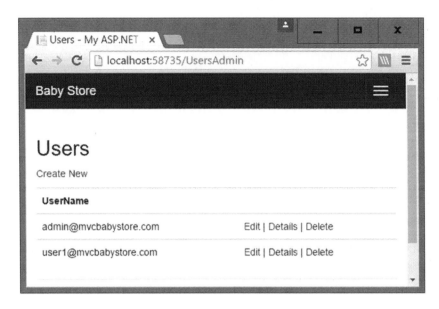

Figure 7-35. *The newly created* user1@mvcbabystore.com *in the UsersAdmin Index page*

Click on the Details link for user1@mvcbabystore.com and you will see the details entered when the user was created, as shown in Figure 7-36.

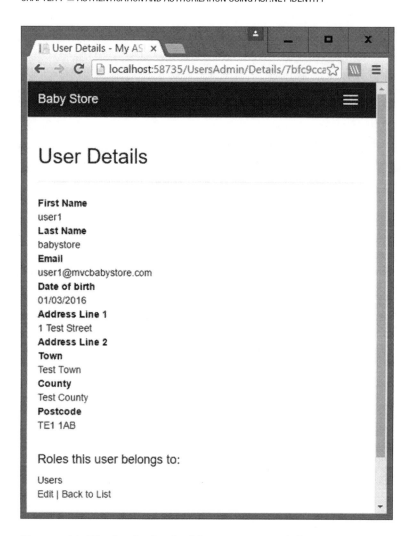

Figure 7-36. Viewing the details of the new user1@mvcbabystore.com user

Editing a User as Admin

To enable the editing of a user, start by adding a new view model class named `EditUserViewModel` to the `ViewModels\AdminViewModel.cs` file, as shown in bold:

```
using BabyStore.Models;
using System;
using System.Collections.Generic;
using System.ComponentModel.DataAnnotations;
using System.Web.Mvc;

namespace BabyStore.ViewModels
{
    public class RoleViewModel
```

```
{
    public string Id { get; set; }
    [Required(AllowEmptyStrings = false)]
    [Display(Name = "Role Name")]
    public string Name { get; set; }
}

public class EditUserViewModel
{
    public string Id { get; set; }

    [Required(AllowEmptyStrings = false)]
    [Display(Name = "Email")]
    [EmailAddress]
    public string Email { get; set; }

    [Required]
    [Display(Name = "First Name")]
    [StringLength(50)]
    public string FirstName { get; set; }

    [Required]
    [Display(Name = "Last Name")]
    [StringLength(50)]
    public string LastName { get; set; }

    [Required]
    [DataType(DataType.Date)]
    [Display(Name = "Date of birth")]
    [DisplayFormat(DataFormatString = "{0:yyyy-MM-dd}", ApplyFormatInEditMode = true)]
    public DateTime DateOfBirth { get; set; }

    public Address Address { get; set; }

    public IEnumerable<SelectListItem> RolesList { get; set; }
}
}
```

This view model will be used in the Edit view. One thing to note is that it does not contain any fields regarding editing a password. Again, we set the DataFormatString for DateOfBirth to {0:yyyy-MM-dd} so that it works correctly in Google Chrome.

Next, update the GET version of the Edit method in Controllers\UsersAdminController.cs file, as shown in bold, so that it finds a user and adds their details to a new instance of EditUserViewModel:

```
// GET: UsersAdmin/Edit/5
public async Task<ActionResult> Edit(string id)
{
    if (id == null)
    {
        return new HttpStatusCodeResult(HttpStatusCode.BadRequest);
    }
```

```
var user = await UserManager.FindByIdAsync(id);
if (user == null)
{
    return HttpNotFound();
}

var userRoles = await UserManager.GetRolesAsync(user.Id);

return View(new EditUserViewModel()
{
    Id = user.Id,
    Email = user.Email,
    DateOfBirth = user.DateOfBirth,
    FirstName = user.FirstName,
    LastName = user.LastName,
    Address = user.Address,
    RolesList = RoleManager.Roles.ToList().Select(x => new SelectListItem()
    {
        Selected = userRoles.Contains(x.Name),
        Text = x.Name,
        Value = x.Name
    })
});
}
```

Ensure that you add the statement using BabyStore.ViewModels; to the top of the file. Next add a view by right-clicking on the Edit method and choosing Add View from the menu. Set the view name to Edit, the template to Edit, and the model class to EditUserViewModel. Then ensure that Reference Script Libraries and User a Layout Page are checked, as shown in Figure 7-37.

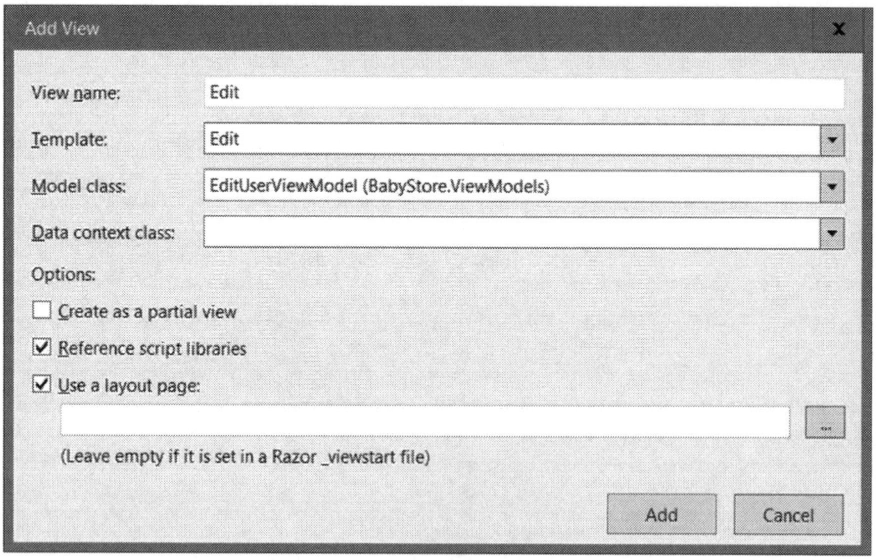

Figure 7-37. *Creating a UsersAdmin Edit view*

In the generated view file, update the headings, add the ability to add an address, and add check boxes for the roles, as shown in bold in the following code:

```
@model EditUserViewModel

@{
    ViewBag.Title = "Edit User";
}


<h2>@ViewBag.Title</h2>

@using (Html.BeginForm())
{
    @Html.AntiForgeryToken()

    <div class="form-horizontal">
        <hr />
        @Html.ValidationSummary(true, "", new { @class = "text-danger" })
        @Html.HiddenFor(model => model.Id)

        <div class="form-group">
            @Html.LabelFor(model => model.Email, htmlAttributes: new { @class = "control-label
            col-md-2" })
            <div class="col-md-10">
                @Html.EditorFor(model => model.Email, new { htmlAttributes = new { @class =
                "form-control" } })
                @Html.ValidationMessageFor(model => model.Email, "", new { @class = "text-
                danger" })
            </div>
        </div>

        <div class="form-group">
            @Html.LabelFor(model => model.FirstName, htmlAttributes: new { @class = "control-
            label col-md-2" })
            <div class="col-md-10">
                @Html.EditorFor(model => model.FirstName, new { htmlAttributes = new { @class
                = "form-control" } })
                @Html.ValidationMessageFor(model => model.FirstName, "", new { @class = "text-
                danger" })
            </div>
        </div>

        <div class="form-group">
            @Html.LabelFor(model => model.LastName, htmlAttributes: new { @class = "control-
            label col-md-2" })
            <div class="col-md-10">
            @Html.EditorFor(model => model.LastName, new { htmlAttributes = new { @class =
            "form-control" } })
```

```
                @Html.ValidationMessageFor(model => model.LastName, "", new { @class = "text-
                danger" })
            </div>
        </div>

        <div class="form-group">
            @Html.LabelFor(model => model.DateOfBirth, htmlAttributes: new { @class =
            "control-label col-md-2" })
            <div class="col-md-10">
                @Html.EditorFor(model => model.DateOfBirth, new { htmlAttributes = new {
                @class = "form-control" } })
                @Html.ValidationMessageFor(model => model.DateOfBirth, "", new { @class =
                "text-danger" })
            </div>
        </div>

        @Html.EditorFor(model => model.Address)

        <div class="form-group">
            @Html.Label("Roles", new { @class = "control-label col-md-2" })
            <span class="col-md-10">
                @foreach (var item in Model.RolesList)
                {
                    <input type="checkbox" name="SelectedRole" value="@item.Value"
                      checked="@item.Selected" class="checkbox-inline" />
                    @Html.Label(item.Value, new { @class = "control-label" })
                }
            </span>
        </div>

        <div class="form-group">
            <div class="col-md-offset-2 col-md-10">
                <input type="submit" value="Save" class="btn btn-default" />
            </div>
        </div>
    </div>
}

<div>
    @Html.ActionLink("Back to List", "Index")
</div>

@section Scripts {
    @Scripts.Render("~/bundles/jqueryval")
}
```

Start the web site without debugging, log in as the Admin user, and navigate to the UsersAdmin Index page. Click the edit link for the user1@mvcbabystore.com user. The new Edit page should appear as shown in Figure 7-38.

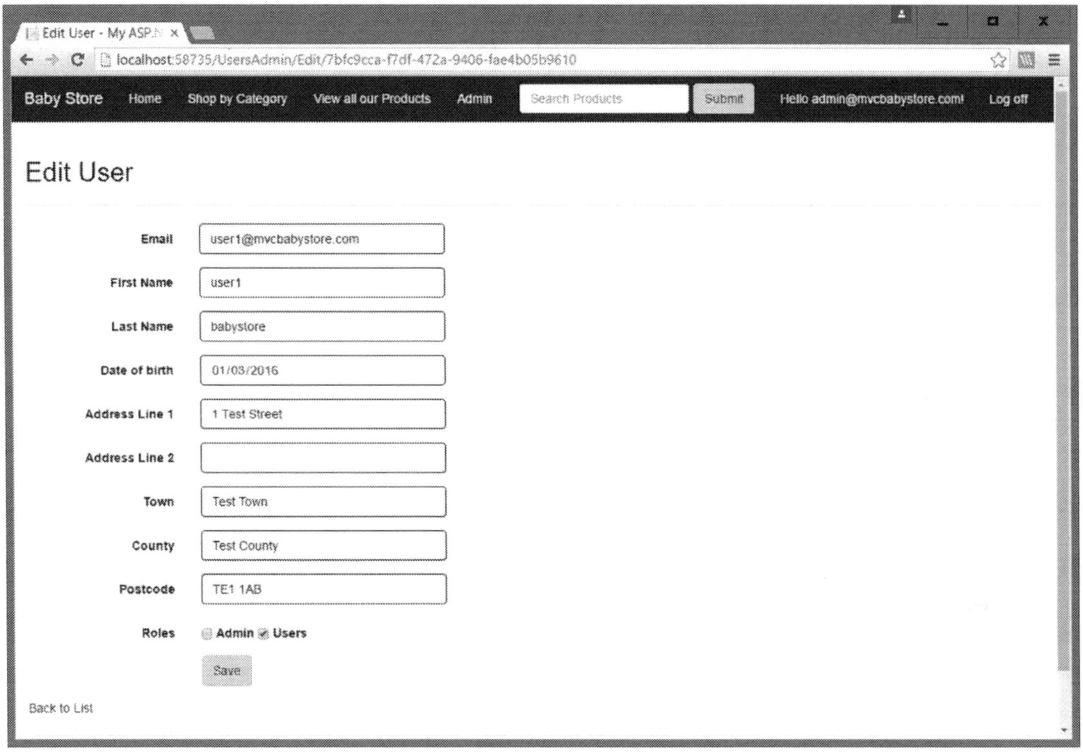

Figure 7-38. *The newly created UsersAdmin Edit page populated with details of user1@mvcbabystore.com*

One additional change we need to make to this view is to make the e-mail read only so it cannot be edited. We won't bind this when updating the user anyway, but we also want to stop the users from thinking they can update it in the view. We could use the `DisplayFor` helper, but it renders the e-mail address as a link and we don't want this. Neither do I like the way that it is aligned if we just use `@Model.Email`, so we're going to use the `readonly` HTML attribute to continue to display the e-mail in a text box and ensure that the users cannot edit it.

Edit the `EditorFor` helper method for the `model.Email` property so that it now reads as follows: `@Html.EditorFor(model => model.Email, new { htmlAttributes = new { @class = "form-control", @readonly = "readonly" } })`. The text box containing the user's e-mail address will now be greyed out.

Next update the `HttpPost` version of the `Edit` method in the `Controllers\UsersAdminController.cs` file so that it takes an `EditUserViewModel` and a collection of strings to represent the selected roles as input parameters and then uses these to update the user's details and roles:

```
// POST: UsersAdmin/Edit/5
[HttpPost]
[ValidateAntiForgeryToken]
public async Task<ActionResult> Edit(EditUserViewModel editUser, params string[]
selectedRole)
{
    if (ModelState.IsValid)
    {
```

```
        var user = await UserManager.FindByIdAsync(editUser.Id);
        if (user == null)
        {
            return HttpNotFound();
        }

        user.DateOfBirth = editUser.DateOfBirth;
        user.FirstName = editUser.FirstName;
        user.LastName = editUser.LastName;
        user.Address = editUser.Address;

        var userRoles = await UserManager.GetRolesAsync(user.Id);

        selectedRole = selectedRole ?? new string[] { };

        var result = await UserManager.AddToRolesAsync(user.Id,
            selectedRole.Except(userRoles).ToArray<string>());

        if (!result.Succeeded)
        {
            ModelState.AddModelError("", result.Errors.First());
            return View();
        }
        result = await UserManager.RemoveFromRolesAsync(user.Id,
            userRoles.Except(selectedRole).ToArray<string>());

        if (!result.Succeeded)
        {
            ModelState.AddModelError("", result.Errors.First());
            return View();
        }
        return RedirectToAction("Index");
    }
    ModelState.AddModelError("", "Something failed.");
    return View();
}
```

This method assigns the properties of the view model submitted from the HTML page (apart from the e-mail address) to the user and then finds the roles that the user belongs to. It then adds the user to any roles in the selectedRole input parameter that they do not already belong to and removes them from any that they do belong to but that are not in selectedRole. The only new method call that has not appeared in the previous methods is UserManager.RemoveFromRolesAsync().

■ **Note**   This code never calls `UserManager.UpdateAsync()`, yet the updated user details are saved. The changes to the rest of the user details are saved during the calls to `UserManager.AddToRolesAsync()` and `UserManager.RemoveFromRolesAsync()`.

Start the web site without debugging and edit user1@mvcbabystore.com by updating the address and date of birth. Add them to the `Admin` group and remove them from the `Users` group, as shown in Figure 7-39.

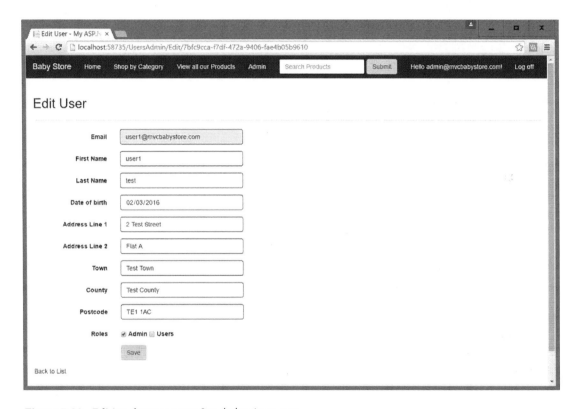

Figure 7-39. *Editing the user user1@mvcbabystore.com*

Click the Save button. The changes will save and you will be redirected to the Index page. Next, view the details for user1@mvcbabystore.com and verify the changes you made, as shown in Figure 7-40.

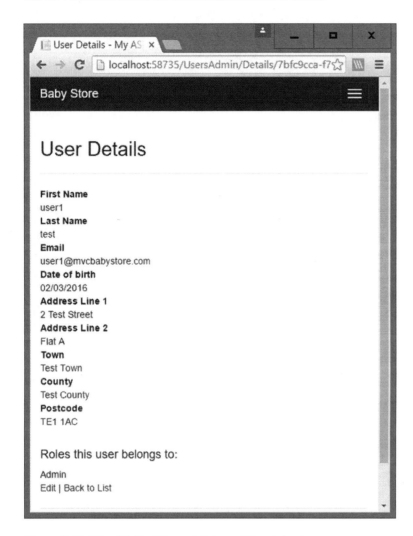

Figure 7-40. *The details of the updated* user1@mvcbabystore.com

Dealing with Deleting Users

I am not going to include code for deleting users in this project because in almost every commercial project I have worked on, deleting users has never been a requirement. Regulatory requirements often specify that user accounts are always kept in the system so that data relating to any user can be found. For example, consider the scenario where a user places several orders in this web site, but the user is then deleted from the system. The company would have no way of knowing who placed the orders.

There are several scenarios for how to manage users who are no longer active or in some cases banned from using the system, including either setting some kind of archive or status field for a user indicating their current status. For example, on gaming web sites it is generally standard of the regulatory requirements that a user can be have many statuses, including registered but awaiting identity verification, approved to play, self-imposed ban, banned from playing by the company, banned from playing by the gaming authorities, and inactive (after a set limit of inactivity), but never deleted. If you do encounter a project where users cannot be deleted, it is also important to apply relevant security and audit trails to the database that holds the user details.

Should you want to delete users via a controller, then you can do this by passing the user as a parameter to the method UserManager.DeleteAsync(user).

If you are following along with the code examples, then remove the code @Html.ActionLink("Delete", "Delete", new { id = item.Id }) from the Views\UsersAdmin\Index.cshtml file and remove the Delete methods from the Controllers\UsersAdminController.cs file.

User Self-Registration

So far we have allowed an Admin user to create users but provided no way for users to register themselves. We'll address this issue by modifying the existing methods and views created when we initially created the project. The controllers that handle user self-management are the Controllers\AccountController.cs and Controllers\ManageController.cs files.

Start by opening the Controllers\AccountController.cs file and modifying the HttpPost version of the Register method so that all the fields in the RegisterViewModel are assigned during the user creation and assign the new user to the Users role, as follows:

```
[HttpPost]
[AllowAnonymous]
[ValidateAntiForgeryToken]
public async Task<ActionResult> Register(RegisterViewModel model)
{
    if (ModelState.IsValid)
    {
        var user = new ApplicationUser {
            UserName = model.Email,
            Email = model.Email,
            DateOfBirth = model.DateOfBirth,
            FirstName = model.FirstName,
            LastName = model.LastName,
            Address = model.Address
        };
        var result = await UserManager.CreateAsync(user, model.Password);
        if (result.Succeeded)
        {
            await UserManager.AddToRoleAsync(user.Id, "Users");
            await SignInManager.SignInAsync(user, isPersistent:false,
            rememberBrowser:false);
                // For more information on how to enable account confirmation and
                password
                //reset please visit http://go.microsoft.com/fwlink/?LinkID=320771
            // Send an email with this link
            // string code = await
                ///UserManager.GenerateEmailConfirmationTokenAsync(user.Id);
            // var callbackUrl = Url.Action("ConfirmEmail", "Account", new { userId =
                //user.Id, code = code }, protocol: Request.Url.Scheme);
            // await UserManager.SendEmailAsync(user.Id, "Confirm your account", "Please
                //confirm your account by clicking <a href=\"" + callbackUrl +
                "\">here</a>");

            return RedirectToAction("Index", "Home");
        }
    }
```

```
        AddErrors(result);
    }

    // If we got this far, something failed, redisplay form
    return View(model);
}
```

■ **Note** The AccountController has authorization applied to it at a class level by using the [Authorize] attribute above the class declaration. However, this is overridden for the Register method, because this needs to be accessed anonymously so users can register, by applying the attribute [AllowAnonymous]. This is applied to both versions of the Register and Login methods.

Next we are going to delete and recreate the Register view file to add the new fields we've added to RegisterViewModel. Delete the Views\Account\Register.cshtml file.

Right-click on the Register method in the AccountController and choose Add View from the menu. Name the view Register using the Create template and set the model class RegisterViewModel. Set the Data Context Class to blank and ensure that Reference Script Libraries and Use a Layout Page are checked, as shown in Figure 7-41.

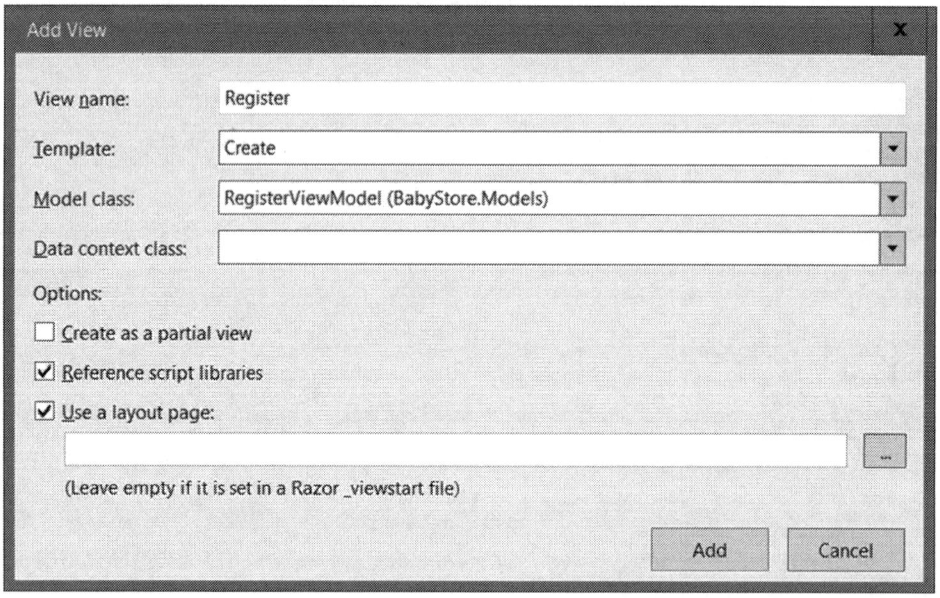

Figure 7-41. Recreating the Account Register view

Update the new file by setting the <h2> heading, removing the <h4> heading, and adding the address fields as follows:

```
@model BabyStore.Models.RegisterViewModel

@{
    ViewBag.Title = "Register";
}
```

```
<h2>@ViewBag.Title</h2>

@using (Html.BeginForm())
{
    @Html.AntiForgeryToken()
    <div class="form-horizontal">
        <hr />
        @Html.ValidationSummary(true, "", new { @class = "text-danger" })
        <div class="form-group">
            @Html.LabelFor(model => model.Email, htmlAttributes: new { @class = "control-label
            col-md-2" })
            <div class="col-md-10">
                @Html.EditorFor(model => model.Email, new { htmlAttributes = new { @class =
                "form-control" } })
                @Html.ValidationMessageFor(model => model.Email, "", new { @class = "text-
                danger" })
            </div>
        </div>

        <div class="form-group">
            @Html.LabelFor(model => model.Password, htmlAttributes: new { @class = "control-
            label col-md-2" })
            <div class="col-md-10">
                @Html.EditorFor(model => model.Password, new { htmlAttributes = new { @class =
                "form-control" } })
                @Html.ValidationMessageFor(model => model.Password, "", new { @class = "text-
                danger" })
            </div>
        </div>

        <div class="form-group">
            @Html.LabelFor(model => model.ConfirmPassword, htmlAttributes: new { @class =
            "control-label col-md-2" })
            <div class="col-md-10">
                @Html.EditorFor(model => model.ConfirmPassword, new { htmlAttributes = new {
                @class = "form-control" } })
                @Html.ValidationMessageFor(model => model.ConfirmPassword, "", new { @class =
                "text-danger" })
            </div>
        </div>

        <div class="form-group">
            @Html.LabelFor(model => model.FirstName, htmlAttributes: new { @class = "control-
            label col-md-2" })
            <div class="col-md-10">
                @Html.EditorFor(model => model.FirstName, new { htmlAttributes = new { @class
                ="form-control" } })
                @Html.ValidationMessageFor(model => model.FirstName, "", new { @class = "text-
                danger" })
            </div>
        </div>
```

```
        <div class="form-group">
            @Html.LabelFor(model => model.LastName, htmlAttributes: new { @class = "control-
            label col-md-2" })
            <div class="col-md-10">
            @Html.EditorFor(model => model.LastName, new { htmlAttributes = new { @class =
            "form-control" } })
                @Html.ValidationMessageFor(model => model.LastName, "", new { @class = "text-
                danger" })
            </div>
        </div>

        <div class="form-group">
            @Html.LabelFor(model => model.DateOfBirth, htmlAttributes: new { @class =
            "control-label col-md-2" })
            <div class="col-md-10">
                @Html.EditorFor(model => model.DateOfBirth, new { htmlAttributes = new {
                @class= "form-control" } })
                @Html.ValidationMessageFor(model => model.DateOfBirth, "", new { @class =
                "text-danger" })
            </div>
        </div>

        @Html.EditorFor(model => model.Address)

        <div class="form-group">
            <div class="col-md-offset-2 col-md-10">
                <input type="submit" value="Create" class="btn btn-default" />
            </div>
        </div>
    </div>
}

<div>
    @Html.ActionLink("Back to List", "Index")
</div>

@section Scripts {
    @Scripts.Render("~/bundles/jqueryval")
}
```

There's a lot of duplication between this code and the code in the Views\UsersAdmin\Create.cshtml file, so we're going to create a partial view to contain the shared code. Right-click on the Views\Shared folder and choose Add View from the menu. Create a new empty view named _CreateRegisterUserPartial based on the model class RegisterViewModel, set the Data Context Class to blank, and ensure that Create as a Partial View is checked, as shown in Figure 7-42.

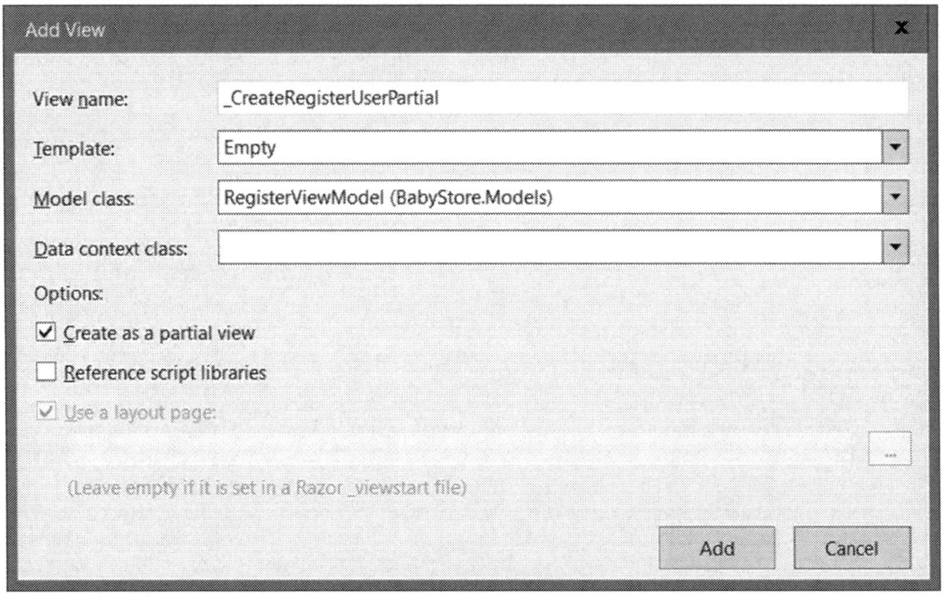

Figure 7-42. *Creating a partial view for user creation and registration*

Update the contents of the new partial view as follows to add the shared fields:

```
@model BabyStore.Models.RegisterViewModel

<hr />
@Html.ValidationSummary(true, "", new { @class = "text-danger" })
<div class="form-group">
    @Html.LabelFor(model => model.Email, htmlAttributes: new { @class = "control-label col-md-
    2"})
    <div class="col-md-10">
        @Html.EditorFor(model => model.Email, new { htmlAttributes = new { @class = "form-
        control" } })
        @Html.ValidationMessageFor(model => model.Email, "", new { @class = "text-danger" })
    </div>
</div>

<div class="form-group">
    @Html.LabelFor(model => model.Password, htmlAttributes: new { @class = "control-label col-
    md-2" })
    <div class="col-md-10">
        @Html.EditorFor(model => model.Password, new { htmlAttributes = new { @class = "form-
        control" } })
        @Html.ValidationMessageFor(model => model.Password, "", new { @class = "text-danger" })
    </div>
</div>
```

255

```
<div class="form-group">
    @Html.LabelFor(model => model.ConfirmPassword, htmlAttributes: new { @class = "control-
    label col-md-2" })
    <div class="col-md-10">
        @Html.EditorFor(model => model.ConfirmPassword, new { htmlAttributes = new { @class =
        "form-control" } })
        @Html.ValidationMessageFor(model => model.ConfirmPassword, "", new { @class = "text-
        danger" })
    </div>
</div>

<div class="form-group">
    @Html.LabelFor(model => model.FirstName, htmlAttributes: new { @class = "control-label
    col-md-2" })
    <div class="col-md-10">
        @Html.EditorFor(model => model.FirstName, new { htmlAttributes = new { @class = "form-
        control" } })
        @Html.ValidationMessageFor(model => model.FirstName, "", new { @class = "text-danger"
            })
    </div>
</div>

<div class="form-group">
    @Html.LabelFor(model => model.LastName, htmlAttributes: new { @class = "control-label col-
    md-2" })
    <div class="col-md-10">
        @Html.EditorFor(model => model.LastName, new { htmlAttributes = new { @class = "form-
        control" } })
        @Html.ValidationMessageFor(model => model.LastName, "", new { @class = "text-danger"
            })
    </div>
</div>

<div class="form-group">
    @Html.LabelFor(model => model.DateOfBirth, htmlAttributes: new { @class = "control-label
    col-md-2" })
    <div class="col-md-10">
        @Html.EditorFor(model => model.DateOfBirth, new { htmlAttributes = new { @class =
        "form-control" } })
        @Html.ValidationMessageFor(model => model.DateOfBirth, "", new { @class = "text-
        danger"})
    </div>
</div>

@Html.EditorFor(model => model.Address)
```

Next update the Views\UsersAdmin\Create.cshtml file to use the new partial view as follows:

```
@model BabyStore.Models.RegisterViewModel
```

```
@{
    ViewBag.Title = "Create User";
}

<h2>@ViewBag.Title</h2>

@using (Html.BeginForm())
{
    @Html.AntiForgeryToken()
    <div class="form-horizontal">
        @Html.Partial("_CreateRegisterUserPartial", Model)
        <div class="form-group">
            <label class="col-md-2 control-label">
                Select User Role
            </label>
            <div class="col-md-10">
                @foreach (var item in (SelectList)ViewBag.RoleId)
                {
                    <input type="checkbox" name="SelectedRoles" value="@item.Value"
                      class="checkbox-inline" />
                    @Html.Label(item.Value, new { @class = "control-label" })
                }
            </div>
        </div>

        <div class="form-group">
            <div class="col-md-offset-2 col-md-10">
                <input type="submit" value="Create" class="btn btn-default" />
            </div>
        </div>
    </div>
}

<div>
    @Html.ActionLink("Back to List", "Index")
</div>

@section Scripts {
    @Scripts.Render("~/bundles/jqueryval")
}
```

Then also update the Views\Account\Register.cshtml file to use the new partial view as follows:

```
@model BabyStore.Models.RegisterViewModel

@{
    ViewBag.Title = "Register";
}
```

```
<h2>@ViewBag.Title</h2>

@using (Html.BeginForm())
{
    @Html.AntiForgeryToken()
    <div class="form-horizontal">
        @Html.Partial("_CreateRegisterUserPartial", Model);
        <div class="form-group">
            <div class="col-md-offset-2 col-md-10">
                <input type="submit" value="Create" class="btn btn-default" />
            </div>
        </div>
    </div>
}

<div>
    @Html.ActionLink("Back to List", "Index")
</div>

@section Scripts {
    @Scripts.Render("~/bundles/jqueryval")
}
```

Start the web site without debugging and ensure that you are logged out. Test the new user self-registration code by clicking on the Register link and registering as a new user with the e-mail address user2@mvcbabystore.com. Use the values shown in Figure 7-43 and set the password fields to P@ssw0rd. When you click the Create button, the user should be created successfully, and you should be logged in as the new user and redirect to the home page.

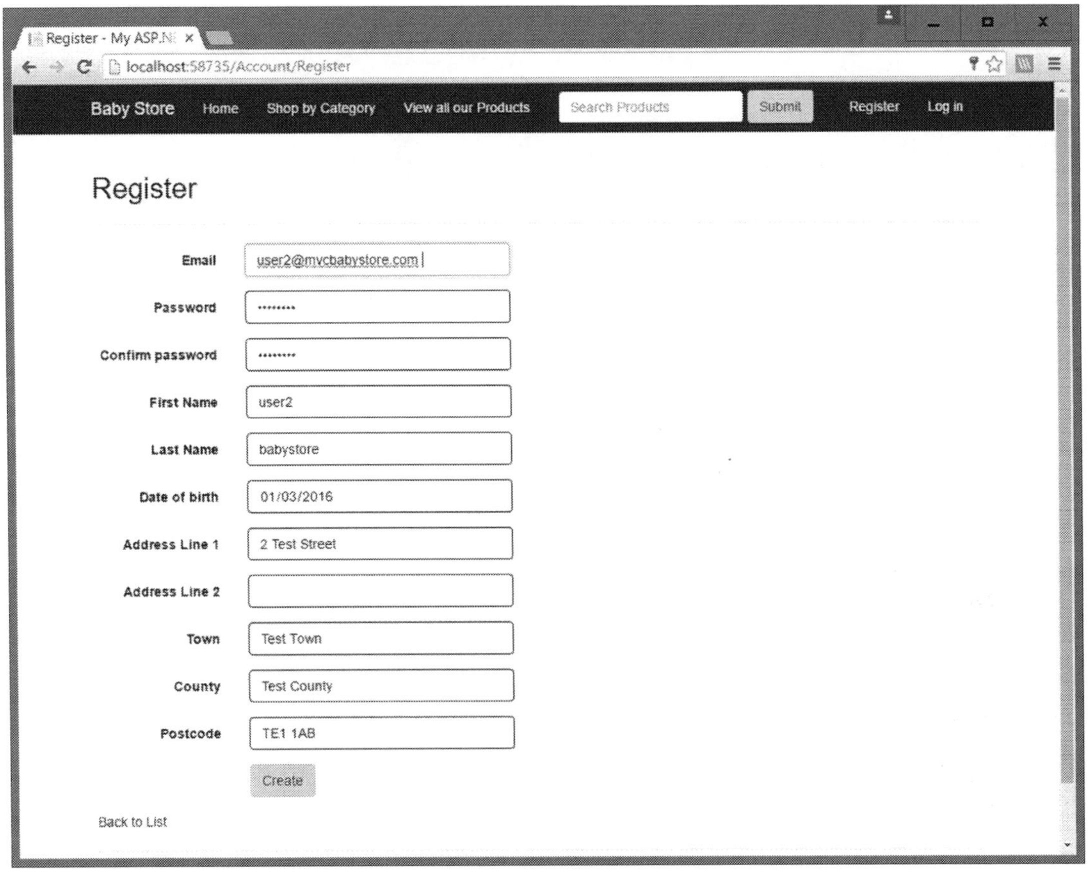

Figure 7-43. *Registering as the new user2@mvcbabystore.com user*

Log out and log back into the web site as the Admin user admin@mvcbabystore.com with the Adm1n@ mvcbabystore.com password. Navigate through the Admin section to view the details of the new user user2@ mvcbabystore.com. You will see that the user belongs to the Users role, as shown in Figure 7-44.

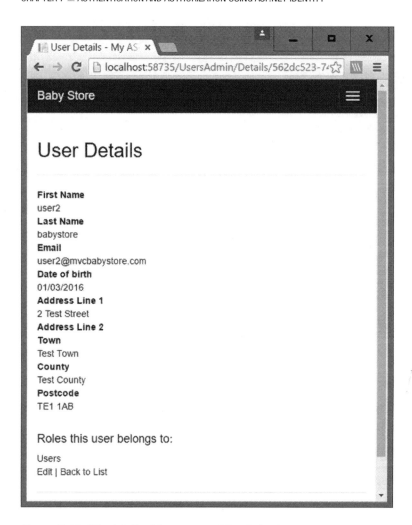

Figure 7-44. The details of the user user2@mvcbabystore.com

Allowing a User to View Personal Details

To allow users to view their personal details, start by modifying the Index method of the Controllers\ManageController.cs file so that it reads as follows:

```
public async Task<ActionResult> Index()
{
    var userId = User.Identity.GetUserId();
    var user = await UserManager.FindByIdAsync(userId);
    return View(user);
}
```

This method uses the User.Identity.GetUserId code to get the current user's ID, ensuring that a user cannot view another user's details.

Next we need to create a new Index view. The current Index view does not contain anything that we want to show to the users, so delete it and add a new view similar to the UsersAdmin Details view.

First, delete the Views\Manage\Index.cshtml file and then right-click on the Index method in the ManageController class and click Add View. Create a new view named Index and set the template to Empty (without model). Ensure that Use a Layout Page is checked and then click the Add button. A new empty Index.cshtml file should be created. We're going to base this view on the ApplicationUser model and, as I mentioned when creating the UsersAdmin Details view, this model does not work with the scaffolding process.

Before we code the view, we're going to add a partial view, because just as there was with the registration process, there is also some overlap between this Index view and the UsersAdmin Details view.

Add a new partial view by right-clicking on the Views\Shared folder and choosing Add View. Set the view name to _UserDetailsPartial and the template to Empty (without model). Then ensure that Create as a Partial View is checked, as shown in Figure 7-45.

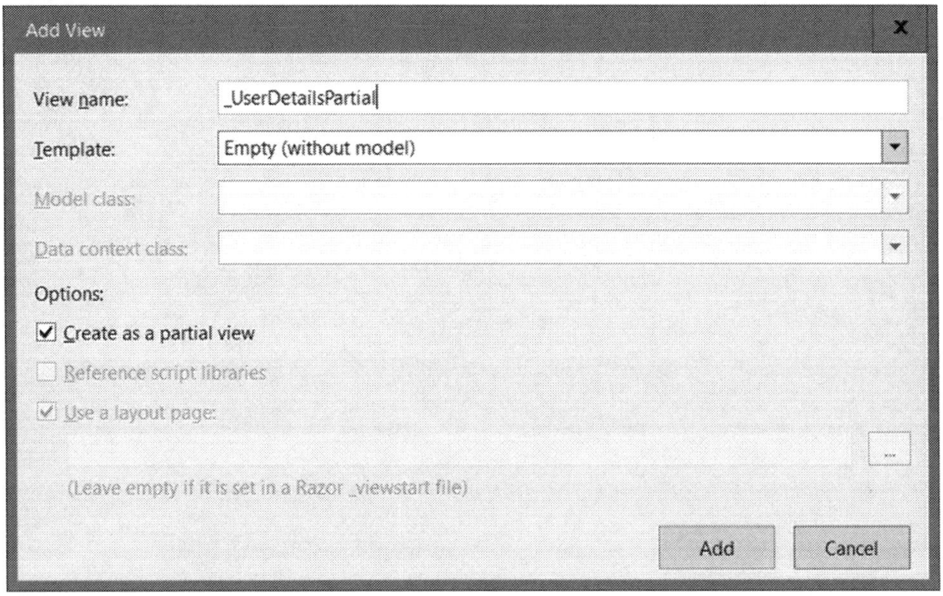

Figure 7-45. *Creating a partial view for user details*

Modify the new _UserDetailsPartial.cshtml file contents as follows to base it on the ApplicationUser class and display common information between the UsersAdmin Details and the Manage Index views:

```
@model BabyStore.Models.ApplicationUser

<dt>
    @Html.DisplayNameFor(model => model.FirstName)
</dt>
<dd>
    @Html.DisplayFor(model => model.FirstName)
</dd>
<dt>
```

```
    @Html.DisplayNameFor(model => model.LastName)
</dt>
<dd>
    @Html.DisplayFor(model => model.LastName)
</dd>
<dt>
    @Html.DisplayNameFor(model => model.Email)
</dt>

<dd>
    @Html.DisplayFor(model => model.Email)
</dd>

<dt>
    @Html.DisplayNameFor(model => model.DateOfBirth)
</dt>

<dd>
    @Html.DisplayFor(model => model.DateOfBirth)
</dd>
@Html.DisplayFor(model => model.Address)
```

Next update the Views\UsersAdmin\Details.cshtml file to use the new partial view:

```
@model BabyStore.Models.ApplicationUser
@{
    ViewBag.Title = "User Details";
}

<h2>@ViewBag.Title</h2>

<div>
    <hr />
    <dl class="dl-horizontal">
        @Html.Partial("_UserDetailsPartial", Model)
    </dl>
</div>
<div class="container">
    <div class="row">
        <h4>Roles this user belongs to:</h4>
    </div>
    @if (ViewBag.RoleNames.Count == 0)
    {
        <hr />
        <p>No roles found for this user</p>
    }

    @foreach (var item in ViewBag.RoleNames)
    {
        <div class="row">
            @item
```

```
            </div>
    }
</div>
<p>
    @Html.ActionLink("Edit", "Edit", new { id = Model.Id }) |
    @Html.ActionLink("Back to List", "Index")
</p>
```

This view will work exactly as before when viewing a user's details via the Admin menu. Next update the new Views\Manage\Index.cshtml file to be modeled on the ApplicationUser class and use the new partial view file as follows:

```
@model BabyStore.Models.ApplicationUser

@{
    ViewBag.Title = "My Details";
}

<h2>@ViewBag.Title</h2>

<div>
    <hr />
    <dl class="dl-horizontal">
        @Html.Partial("_UserDetailsPartial", Model)
        <dt>
            Password
        </dt>
        <dd>
            @Html.ActionLink("Change your password", "ChangePassword")
        </dd>
    </dl>
</div>

<p>
    @Html.ActionLink("Edit", "Edit", new { id = Model.Id })
</p>
```

To see the new Views\Manage\Index.cshtml file being used, start the web site without debugging and log in as the user user2@mvcbabystore.com with the P@ssw0rd password. Next, click on the "Hello user2@ mvcbabystore.com" link. The My Details HTML page generated by the Views\Manage\Index.cshtml file will appear, as shown in Figure 7-46.

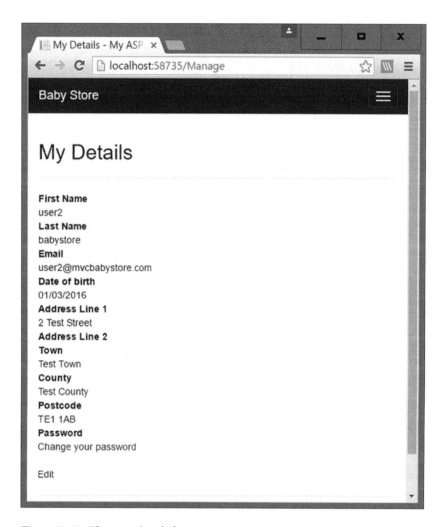

Figure 7-46. The user2@mvcbabystore.com user viewing their personal details

If you log out and then back in as the Admin user admin@mvcbabystore.com with the Adm1n@ mvcbabystore.com password and then navigate through the Admin section to view the details of the new user, you will see that the partial view being used has made no alteration to the HTML generated by the Views\UsersAdmin\Details.cshtml view file. It still appears as in Figure 7-44.

Allowing Users to Edit Personal Details

To complete the section, we're going to cover allowing users to edit their details. This uses a similar process to an administrator editing a user's details.

Start by adding a new Edit method to the Controllers\ManageController.cs file to find the details of the current user, and then return them to the view via a view model. We're going to reuse the view model EditUserViewModel but won't use the ID or RolesList properties. Add the following code to the ManageController class:

```
// GET: /Manage/Edit
public async Task<ActionResult> Edit()
{
    var userId = User.Identity.GetUserId();
    var user = await UserManager.FindByIdAsync(userId);
    var model = new EditUserViewModel
    {
        Email = user.Email,
        DateOfBirth = user.DateOfBirth,
        FirstName = user.FirstName,
        LastName = user.LastName,
        Address = user.Address
    };
    return View(model);
}
```

Ensure that you add the statement using `BabyStore.ViewModels;` to the top of the file. Next, add a new edit view based on an edit template using the `EditUserViewModel` model, and then ensure that Use a Layout Page and Reference Script Libraries are checked. Figure 7-47 shows the options to use for the new view.

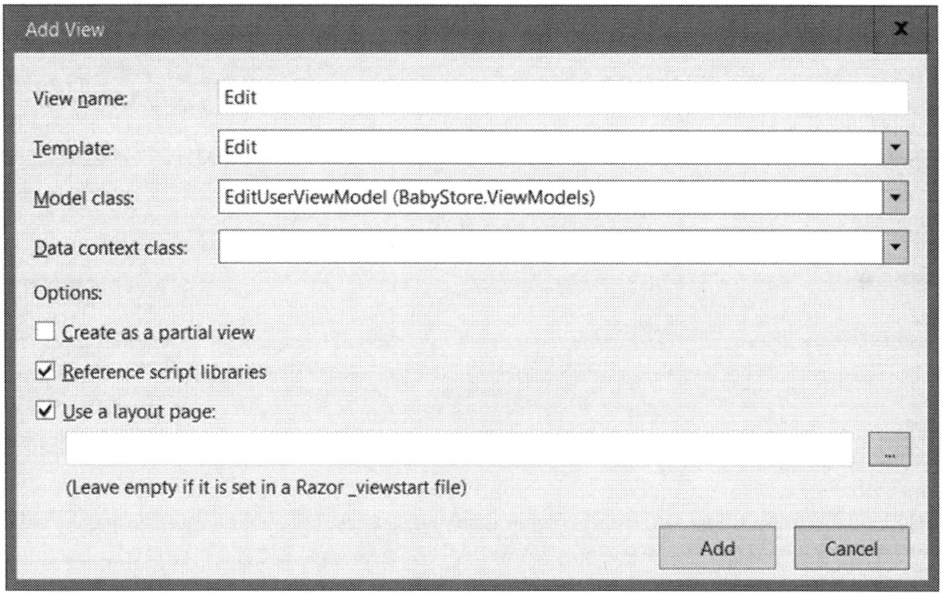

Figure 7-47. *Adding a new Manage Edit view*

As with the previous views we've created for users, we are going to create a partial view to share between this view and the `UsersAdmin` Edit view. Add a new partial view by right-clicking on the `Views\Shared` folder and choosing Add View. Add an empty partial view named `_EditUserPartial` based on the model class `EditUserViewModel`. The options to choose are shown in Figure 7-48.

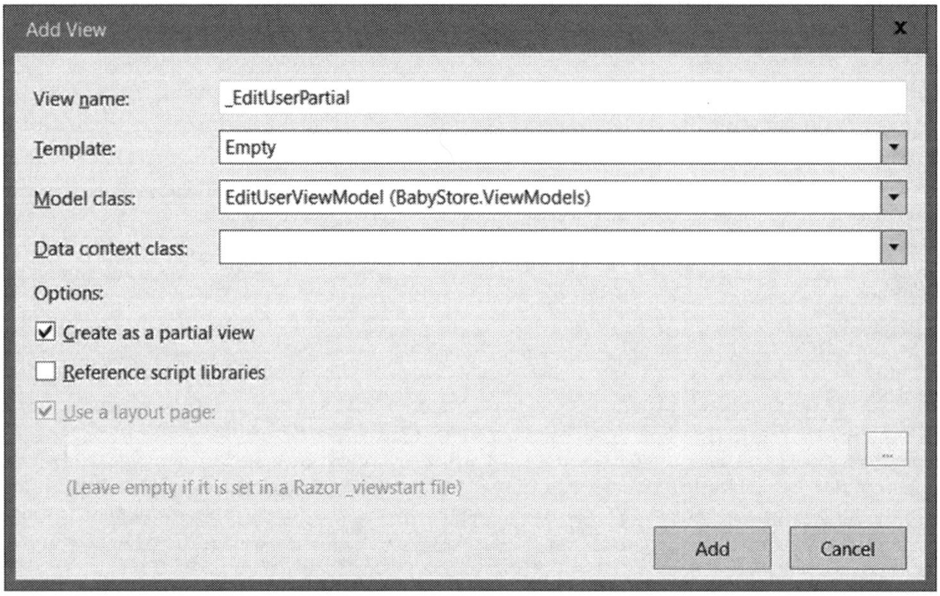

Figure 7-48. Add the _EditUserPartial partial view

Update the contents of the new view so that it contains the HTML common to both Views\Manage\Edit.cshtml and Views\UsersAdmin\Edit.cshtml.

```
@model BabyStore.ViewModels.EditUserViewModel

<hr />
@Html.ValidationSummary(true, "", new { @class = "text-danger" })

<div class="form-group">
    @Html.LabelFor(model => model.Email, htmlAttributes: new { @class = "control-label
    col-md-2"})
    <div class="col-md-10">
        @Html.EditorFor(model => model.Email, new { htmlAttributes = new { @class = "form-
        control", @readonly = "readonly" } })
        @Html.ValidationMessageFor(model => model.Email, "", new { @class = "text-danger" })
    </div>
</div>

<div class="form-group">
    @Html.LabelFor(model => model.FirstName, htmlAttributes: new { @class = "control-label
    col-md-2" })
    <div class="col-md-10">
        @Html.EditorFor(model => model.FirstName, new { htmlAttributes = new { @class = "form-
        control" } })
```

```
        @Html.ValidationMessageFor(model => model.FirstName, "", new { @class = "text-danger"
            })
    </div>
</div>

<div class="form-group">
    @Html.LabelFor(model => model.LastName, htmlAttributes: new { @class = "control-label col-
    md-2" })
    <div class="col-md-10">
        @Html.EditorFor(model => model.LastName, new { htmlAttributes = new { @class = "form-
        control" } })
        @Html.ValidationMessageFor(model => model.LastName, "", new { @class = "text-danger"
            })
    </div>
</div>

<div class="form-group">
    @Html.LabelFor(model => model.DateOfBirth, htmlAttributes: new { @class = "control-label
    col-md-2" })
    <div class="col-md-10">
        @Html.EditorFor(model => model.DateOfBirth, new { htmlAttributes = new { @class =
        "form-control" } })
        @Html.ValidationMessageFor(model => model.DateOfBirth, "", new { @class = "text-
        danger"})
    </div>
</div>

@Html.EditorFor(model => model.Address)
```

Following this, now update the Views\UsersAdmin\Edit.cshtml file to use the new partial view:

```
@model EditUserViewModel

@{
    ViewBag.Title = "Edit User";
}

<h2>@ViewBag.Title</h2>

@using (Html.BeginForm())
{
    @Html.AntiForgeryToken()
    @Html.HiddenFor(model => model.Id)
    <div class="form-horizontal">
        @Html.Partial("_EditUserPartial", Model)
        <div class="form-group">
            @Html.Label("Roles", new { @class = "control-label col-md-2" })
```

```
            <span class=" col-md-10">
                @foreach (var item in Model.RolesList)
                {
                    <input type="checkbox" name="SelectedRole" value="@item.Value"
                      checked="@item.Selected" class="checkbox-inline" />
                    @Html.Label(item.Value, new { @class = "control-label" })
                }
            </span>
        </div>

        <div class="form-group">
            <div class="col-md-offset-2 col-md-10">
                <input type="submit" value="Save" class="btn btn-default" />
            </div>
        </div>
    </div>
}

<div>
    @Html.ActionLink("Back to List", "Index")
</div>

@section Scripts {
    @Scripts.Render("~/bundles/jqueryval")
}
```

Finally, update the new Views\Manage\Edit.cshtml file to use the new partial view and edit the headings as follows.

```
@model BabyStore.ViewModels.EditUserViewModel

@{
    ViewBag.Title = "Edit My Details";
}

<h2>@ViewBag.Title</h2>

@using (Html.BeginForm())
{
    @Html.AntiForgeryToken()

    <div class="form-horizontal">
        @Html.Partial("_EditUserPartial", Model)
        <div class="form-group">
            <div class="col-md-offset-2 col-md-10">
                <input type="submit" value="Save" class="btn btn-default" />
            </div>
        </div>
    </div>
}
```

```
<div>
    @Html.ActionLink("Back to List", "Index")
</div>

@section Scripts {
    @Scripts.Render("~/bundles/jqueryval")
}
```

Start the web site without debugging and log in as user2@mvcbabystore.com with the P@ssw0rd password. View the user's details. Then click the Edit link. The new Edit My Details page generated from the Views\Manage/Edit.cshtml file should appear, as shown in Figure 7-49.

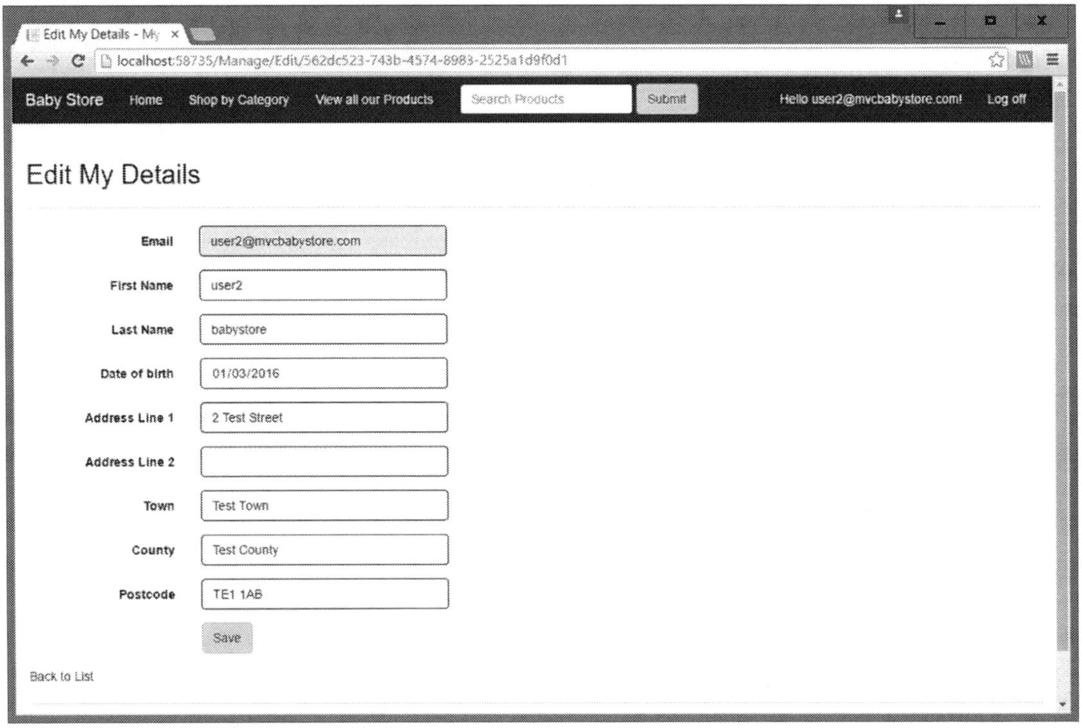

Figure 7-49. *The new User Edit page*

To complete the process of allowing users to edit their details, you need an HttpPost version of the Edit method. This method is not going to take an ID as an input parameter because if it did then a user could edit another user's details by spoofing the details in the HTML form. This is why we did not set the ID property of the EditUserViewModel in the GET version of the Edit method or use it in the Views\Manage\Edit.cshtml file.

To process POST requests, add the following method to the Controllers\ManageController.cs file:

```
// POST: Manage/Edit/
// To protect from overposting attacks, please enable the specific properties you want to bind to, for
// more details see http://go.microsoft.com/fwlink/?LinkId=317598.
[HttpPost, ActionName("Edit")]
```

```
[ValidateAntiForgeryToken]
public async Task<ActionResult> EditPost()
{
    var userId = User.Identity.GetUserId();
    var userToUpdate = await UserManager.FindByIdAsync(userId);
    if (TryUpdateModel(userToUpdate, "", new string[] {
        "FirstName",
        "LastName",
        "DateOfBirth",
        "Address" }))
    {
        await UserManager.UpdateAsync(userToUpdate);
        return RedirectToAction("Index");
    }
    return View();
}
```

The method is named `EditPost` because it has the same signature as the previously created `Edit` method and so needs a different name. It finds the current user and then calls `TryUpdateModel()` to update the `userToUpdate` object. It's then saved to the database by calling the `UserManager.UpdateAsync()` method.

To try the completed editing process, start the web site without debugging and log in as user2@ mvcbabystore.com with the P@ssw0rd password. View the user's details. Then click the Edit link and change the user's address as shown in Figure 7-50.

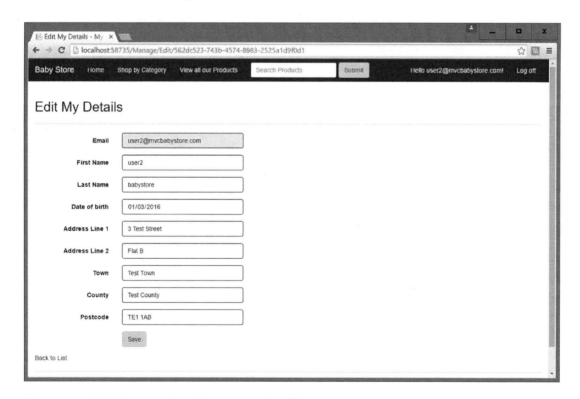

Figure 7-50. *Updating user2@mvcbabystore.com's address*

Click the Save button. You will be returned to the Index page with the updated address displayed as shown in Figure 7-51.

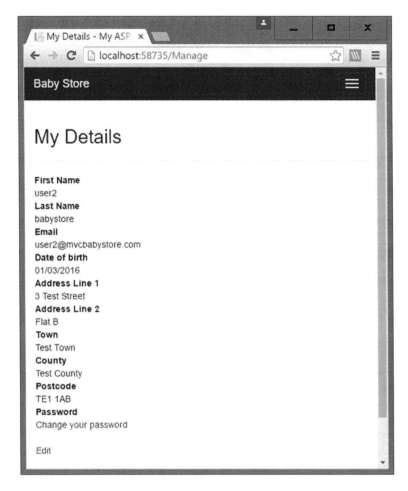

Figure 7-51. *The updated user details of user2@mvcbabystore.com*

Allowing Users to Reset Their Passwords

At the moment the web site has no way for users to reset their passwords. The ASP.NET Identity code that enables users to reset their passwords works on the basis that a user can be e-mailed, but since we're using fictional e-mail addresses, we're going to cut this step out of the code while still explaining how this functionality works.

In a real production system, I recommend that you implement the code to send an external link to the user's e-mail address and then allow them to click on a link back to the reset password page. The code to do this and a link with to a Microsoft tutorial can be found in the ForgotPassword method of the AccountController.

Start by modifying the ResetPassword method in the Controllers\AccountController.cs file as follows. This change comments out the code that checks the value of the variable named code.

```
//
// GET: /Account/ResetPassword
[AllowAnonymous]
public ActionResult ResetPassword(string code)
{
    //return code == null ? View("Error") : View();
    return View();
}
```

If we were sending out e-mails, the code variable would be generated in the HttpPost version of the ForgotPassword function and sent out to the users as an e-mail containing a link to click on. You can view the code to perform this task currently commented out in the ForgotPassword method.

We are now going to generate the code variable at the point where it is used by modifying the HttpPost version of the ResetPassword method as follows:

```
//
// POST: /Account/ResetPassword
[HttpPost]
[AllowAnonymous]
[ValidateAntiForgeryToken]
public async Task<ActionResult> ResetPassword(ResetPasswordViewModel model)
{
    if (!ModelState.IsValid)
    {
        return View(model);
    }
    var user = await UserManager.FindByNameAsync(model.Email);
    if (user == null)
    {
        // Don't reveal that the user does not exist
        return RedirectToAction("ResetPasswordConfirmation", "Account");
    }
    string code = await UserManager.GeneratePasswordResetTokenAsync(user.Id);
    var result = await UserManager.ResetPasswordAsync(user.Id, code, model.Password);
    if (result.Succeeded)
    {
        return RedirectToAction("ResetPasswordConfirmation", "Account");
    }
    AddErrors(result);
    return View();
}
```

■ **Caution**   Because we are doing this for demonstration purposes and have bypassed sending confirmation e-mail, this code will allow you to alter the password for any user that you enter a valid e-mail address for. Therefore, never use this version of code in a real system. With the confirmation email in place, the code variable would be matched up to the e-mail address to ensure that the user is who they claim to be.

Next uncomment the "Forgot your password?" link in the Views/Account/Login.cshtml file and update it to allow the user to access the account ResetPassword view.

```
...previous code omitted for brevity
    <p>
        @Html.ActionLink("Register as a new user", "Register")
    </p>
    <p>
        @Html.ActionLink("Forgot your password?", "ResetPassword")
    </p>
    }
</section>
...following code omitted for brevity
```

Now start the web site without debugging and click on the Log In link. Then click on the Forgot Your Password? link. Use the Reset Password screen to change the password for user2@mvcbabystore.com to P@ ssw0rd1 and save your changes. The password will be changed and you can now use the new password to log in as user2@mvcbabystore.com.

Managing Password Complexity

Throughout this chapter we've been creating users with more complex "strong" passwords. To change the rules for password complexity, update the PasswordValidator code found in the App_Start\ IdentityConfig.cs file. This can be found in the Create method of the ApplicationUserManager class and we've listed the standard code for reference.

```
// Configure validation logic for passwords
manager.PasswordValidator = new PasswordValidator
{
    RequiredLength = 6,
    RequireNonLetterOrDigit = true,
    RequireDigit = true,
    RequireLowercase = true,
    RequireUppercase = true,
};
```

Adding Authorization for Product and Category Administration

We are now going to use the Admin role to manage the availability of the links and for admin features such as creating, deleting, and updating categories and products.

Adding Authorization to Categories

To add authorization to show or hide links for creating, editing, and deleting categories, modify the Views\ Categories\Index.cshtml file as highlighted in bold:

```
@model IEnumerable<BabyStore.Models.Category>
```

```
@{
    ViewBag.Title = "Categories";
}

<h2>@ViewBag.Title</h2>

@if (Request.IsAuthenticated && User.IsInRole("Admin"))
{
    <p>
        @Html.ActionLink("Create New", "Create")
    </p>
}
<table class="table">
    <tr>
        <th>
            @Html.DisplayNameFor(model => model.Name)
        </th>
        <th></th>
    </tr>

@foreach (var item in Model) {
    <tr>
        <td>
            @Html.ActionLink(item.Name, "Index", "Products", new { category = item.Name },
            null)
        </td>
        <td>
            @if (Request.IsAuthenticated && User.IsInRole("Admin"))
            {
                @Html.ActionLink("Edit", "Edit", new { id=item.ID })
                @Html.Raw(" | ")
                @Html.ActionLink("Delete", "Delete", new { id=item.ID })
            }
        </td>
    </tr>
}
</table>
```

In the modified code, checks were added to ensure that the links to create, edit, and delete categories are hidden if a user is not in the Admin role or not logged in, as shown in Figure 7-52. If the user is in the Admin role, then the links will be displayed, as shown in Figure 7-53.

Figure 7-52. *Links for creating, editing, and deleting a category are now hidden unless you're logged in as an Admin*

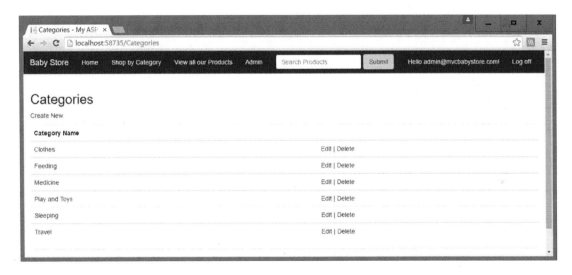

Figure 7-53. *When logged in as admin@mvcbabystore.com the links to create, edit, and delete a category are visible*

At the moment, a "non-admin" user can still manually enter URLs for the edit, delete, and create pages and access them. To prevent access to these methods, we need to modify the Controllers\ CategoriesController.cs file. In order to prevent anyone not in the Admin role from accessing these URLs, add the following line of code prior to the CategoriesController class declaration so it reads as follows:

```
[Authorize(Roles = "Admin")]
public class CategoriesController : Controller
```

Now add the [AllowAnonymous] attribute before the Index method as follows, so that anyone can view the list of categories without logging in:

```
// GET: Categories
[AllowAnonymous]
public ActionResult Index()
{
    return View(db.Categories.OrderBy(c => c.Name).ToList());
}
```

Start the web site without debugging and without logging in. Ensure that you can access the Categories Index page by clicking on the Shop by Category link. Next try to manually enter the following URLs both without logging in and logged in as user2@mvcbabystore.com:

- Categories/Create

- Categories/Edit/1

- Categories/Delete/1

Each time you will be prompted to log in. If you then log in as a user in the Admin role, then you will be able to access these pages.

Finally, delete the Views\Categories\Details.cshtml file and remove the Details method from the Controllers\CategoriesController.cs file, as they are not needed.

Adding Authorization to Products

As we did for categories, we're now going to use the Admin role to manage the availability of the links for the admin features of creating, deleting, and updating products.

To add authorization to show or hide links for creating, editing, and deleting products, modify the Views/Products/Index.cshtml file as follows:

```
@if (Request.IsAuthenticated && User.IsInRole("Admin"))
{
    @Html.ActionLink("Create New", "Create")
}
...
@if (Request.IsAuthenticated && User.IsInRole("Admin"))
{
    @Html.ActionLink("Edit", "Edit", new { id = item.ID })
    @Html.Raw(" | ")
    @Html.ActionLink("Delete", "Delete", new { id = item.ID })
}
```

We've removed the details link since details are now accessed by clicking on the image.

Also for completeness you will need to update the Views\Products\Details.cshtml file to add authorization to the Edit link as follows:

```
<p>
    @if (Request.IsAuthenticated && User.IsInRole("Admin"))
    {
        @Html.ActionLink("Edit", "Edit", new { id = Model.ID })
```

```
        @Html.Raw(" | ")
    }
    @Html.ActionLink("Back to List", "Index")
</p>
```

To prevent users from manually entering the URLs to create, edit, and delete products, add authorization to the `Controllers\ProductsController.cs` file as follows.

Add an authentication attribute to the `ProductsController` class:

```
[Authorize(Roles = "Admin")]
public class ProductsController : Controller
```

Now add the [`AllowAnonymous`] attribute before the `Index` and `Details` methods, as follows, so that anyone can view the list of products or the details of an individual product without logging in:

```
// GET: Products
[AllowAnonymous]
public ActionResult Index(string category, string search, string sortBy, int? page)
{...
```

```
// GET: Products/Details/5
[AllowAnonymous]
public ActionResult Details(int? id)
{
```

Start the web site without debugging and without logging in. Ensure that you can access the Products Index page by clicking on the View All Our Products link. Also click on a product's image to verify you can view the product's details.

Now try to manually enter the following URLs both without logging in and logged in as user2@mvcbabystore.com:

- `Products/Create`

- `Products/Edit/1`

- `Products/Delete/1`

Each time you will be prompted to log in. If you then log in as a user in the Admin role, you will be able to access these pages.

Finally, log in as the admin@mvcbabystore.com user with the Adm1n@mvcbabystore.com password. Click on View All Our Products. You should see links to create, edit, and delete links and should be able to access each of the pages by clicking each link.

▓ **Note** If you need to perform more complex logic to validate a user, I recommend that you try to perform the logic in your controller classes and then set a Boolean value in your view model where possible. Because we are using pages generated by scaffolding, we've added the logic to check the user's role to the view file directly.

Improving Redirection after Logging In or Registration

You might have noticed during this chapter that when you log in to the web site, you are not always redirected to the page you were on. If you are trying to access a page that requires authentication, for example to edit products, and you log in successfully the first time, the redirection works okay. However, under all other circumstances, such as you are just viewing products and log in, or you enter your credentials incorrectly, when you do log in then you are redirected back to the home page.

Redirecting Correctly After an Unsuccessful Then Successful Log In Attempt

To ensure that the URL a user was trying to access is stored even when a user makes an unsuccessful log in attempt, modify the `HttpPost` version of the `Login` method in the `Controllers\AccountController.cs` file to populate the `ViewBag.ReturnUrl` property with the current `returnUrl` parameter as follows:

```
[HttpPost]
[AllowAnonymous]
[ValidateAntiForgeryToken]
public async Task<ActionResult> Login(LoginViewModel model, string returnUrl)
{
    if (!ModelState.IsValid)
    {
        return View(model);
    }

    // This doesn't count login failures towards account lockout
    // To enable password failures to trigger account lockout, change to shouldLockout: true
    var result = await SignInManager.PasswordSignInAsync(model.Email, model.Password,
        model.RememberMe, shouldLockout: false);
    switch (result)
    {
        case SignInStatus.Success:
            return RedirectToLocal(returnUrl);
        case SignInStatus.LockedOut:
            return View("Lockout");
        case SignInStatus.RequiresVerification:
            return RedirectToAction("SendCode", new { ReturnUrl = returnUrl, RememberMe =
                model.RememberMe });
        case SignInStatus.Failure:
        default:
            ModelState.AddModelError("", "Invalid login attempt.");
            ViewBag.ReturnUrl = returnUrl;
            return View(model);
    }
}
```

If you try to access one of the pages that requires authorization, for example to create a product, the `returnUrl` is set and displayed in the browser URL as `/Account/Login?ReturnUrl=%2FProducts%2FCreate`. The view `login.cshtml` uses the `ViewBag.ReturnUrl` value to decide where to redirect the user to. Adding this new line of code ensures that this value is maintained when a user's login attempt fails.

See the effect of this change by attempting to access the /Products/Create URL anonymously and then, on your first login attempt, enter invalid credentials. On the second attempt, enter admin@mvcbabystore. com with the Adm1n@mvcbabystore.com password. You will now be redirected to the Products Create page whereas previously you would have been redirected to the home page.

Always Redirecting to the Previous Page after Log In

By default, the redirectUrl variable is set only if the user was redirected to the login page by ASP.NET Identity; it does not get populated if the user manually opens the login page. This means that if a user is viewing a particular page and then chooses to log in, he is redirected to the home page rather than to the page he was on prior to the login page.

To improve this functionality so that users are always redirected to the page they were on prior to the login page, modify the Log In link generated in the Views\Shared_LoginPartial.cshtml file as highlighted in bold. This link now has the returnURL set as a route value to the current path in the URL by using HttpContext.Current.Request.Url.AbsolutePath.

```
@using Microsoft.AspNet.Identity
@if (Request.IsAuthenticated)
{
    using (Html.BeginForm("LogOff", "Account", FormMethod.Post, new { id = "logoutForm",
        @class = "navbar-right" }))
    {
    @Html.AntiForgeryToken()

    <ul class="nav navbar-nav navbar-right">
        <li>
            @Html.ActionLink("Hello " + User.Identity.GetUserName() + "!", "Index", "Manage",
                routeValues: null, htmlAttributes: new { title = "Manage" })
        </li>
        <li><a href="javascript:document.getElementById('logoutForm').submit()">Log
            off</a></li>
    </ul>
    }
}
else
{
    <ul class="nav navbar-nav navbar-right">
        <li>@Html.ActionLink("Register", "Register", "Account", routeValues: null,
            htmlAttributes: new { id = "registerLink" })</li>
        <li>@Html.ActionLink("Log in", "Login", "Account", new { returnUrl =
            HttpContext.Current.Request.Url.AbsolutePath }, htmlAttributes:
            new { id = "loginLink" })</li>
    </ul>
}
```

Users will now be redirected to the page they were on prior to making a login request. To see this code in action, start the web site without debugging, and click on the Shop by Category link. Then click on the Log In link and log in as user2@mvcbabystore.com with the P@ssw0rd1 password. Once you're logged in, you will be redirected to the Categories Index page rather than the home page.

Always Redirecting to the Previous Page After Registration

One remaining issue is that the registration process redirects the users to the home page once they have registered. To fix this, we need to use a similar process of setting a returnUrl variable in the Register link of the Views\Shared_LoginPartial.cshtml file as follows:

```
@using Microsoft.AspNet.Identity
@if (Request.IsAuthenticated)
{
    using (Html.BeginForm("LogOff", "Account", FormMethod.Post, new { id = "logoutForm",
        @class = "navbar-right" }))
    {
    @Html.AntiForgeryToken()

    <ul class="nav navbar-nav navbar-right">
        <li>
            @Html.ActionLink("Hello " + User.Identity.GetUserName() + "!", "Index", "Manage",
                routeValues: null, htmlAttributes: new { title = "Manage" })
        </li>
        <li><a href="javascript:document.getElementById('logoutForm').submit()">Log
            off</a></li>
    </ul>
    }
}
else
{
    <ul class="nav navbar-nav navbar-right">
        <li>@Html.ActionLink("Register", "Register", "Account", new { returnUrl =
            HttpContext.Current.Request.Url.AbsolutePath },htmlAttributes: new { id =
            "registerLink" })</li>
        <li>@Html.ActionLink("Log in", "Login", "Account", new { returnUrl =
            HttpContext.Current.Request.Url.AbsolutePath }, htmlAttributes:
            new { id = "loginLink" })</li>
    </ul>
}
```

Next modify the GET version of the Register method in the Controllers\AccountController.cs file as follows. This sets the returnUrl in the ViewBag in a similar manner to the Login method:

```
//
// GET: /Account/Register
[AllowAnonymous]
public ActionResult Register(string returnUrl)
{
    ViewBag.ReturnUrl = returnUrl;
    return View();
}
```

Then modify the HttpPost version of the Register method as follows so that it uses a returnUrl variable:

```
//
// POST: /Account/Register
[HttpPost]
[AllowAnonymous]
[ValidateAntiForgeryToken]
public async Task<ActionResult> Register(RegisterViewModel model, string returnUrl)
{
    if (ModelState.IsValid)
    {
        var user = new ApplicationUser {
            UserName = model.Email,
            Email = model.Email,
            DateOfBirth = model.DateOfBirth,
            FirstName = model.FirstName,
            LastName = model.LastName,
            Address = model.Address
        };
        var result = await UserManager.CreateAsync(user, model.Password);
        if (result.Succeeded)
        {
            await UserManager.AddToRoleAsync(user.Id, "Users");
            await SignInManager.SignInAsync(user, isPersistent:false, rememberBrowser:false);

            // For more information on how to enable account confirmation and password reset
            //   please visit http://go.microsoft.com/fwlink/?LinkID=320771
            // Send an email with this link
            // string code = await UserManager.GenerateEmailConfirmationTokenAsync(user.Id);
            // var callbackUrl = Url.Action("ConfirmEmail", "Account", new { userId = user.Id,
            //   code = code }, protocol: Request.Url.Scheme);
            // await UserManager.SendEmailAsync(user.Id, "Confirm your account", "Please
            //   confirm your account by clicking <a href=\"" + callbackUrl + "\">here</a>");

            // redirect the user back to the page they came from if it was local otherwise send
            // them to home page
            return RedirectToLocal(returnUrl);
        }
        ViewBag.ReturnUrl = returnUrl;
        AddErrors(result);
    }

    // If we got this far, something failed, redisplay form
    return View(model);
}
```

Here we've passed in a new parameter named `returnUrl` and then use it to redirect the users to when they registered successfully. We also reset the `ViewBag.ReturnUrl` value if the registration fails so that it can be passed back into the method by the view again on subsequent attempts.

Next, to support the changes to the `Register` method, the `Views\Account\Register.cshtml` file needs to be altered to pass the `ReturnUrl` value into the `HttpPost` version of the `Register` method. To enable this change, update the `Html.BeginForm` method as follows:

```
@model BabyStore.Models.RegisterViewModel

@{
    ViewBag.Title = "Register";
}

<h2>@ViewBag.Title</h2>

@using (Html.BeginForm("Register", "Account", new { ReturnUrl = ViewBag.ReturnUrl },
    FormMethod.Post))
{
    @Html.AntiForgeryToken()

    <div class="form-horizontal">
        @Html.Partial("_CreateRegisterUserPartial", Model)
        <div class="form-group">
            <div class="col-md-offset-2 col-md-10">
                <input type="submit" value="Create" class="btn btn-default" />
            </div>
        </div>
    </div>
}

<div>
    @Html.ActionLink("Back to List", "Index")
</div>

@section Scripts {
    @Scripts.Render("~/bundles/jqueryval")
}
```

Finally, we are going to add some code to deal with the scenario where a user has come from the login page and clicked the Register link. We don't want to redirect the user to the login page after registering; we want to redirect them to the page they were on prior to the login page.

To deal with this scenario, simply change the link to the register page in the `Views/Account/Login.cshtml` file as follows:

```
@Html.ActionLink("Register as a new user", "Register", new { ReturnUrl = ViewBag.ReturnUrl })
```

These code changes enable users to register from any page in the web site and be redirected back to that page once registered.

To see this code in action, start the web site without debugging and click on the Shop by Category link. Then click on the Register link and register a new user called user3@mvcbabystore.com with the P@ssw0rd password. Use the values shown in Figure 7-54.

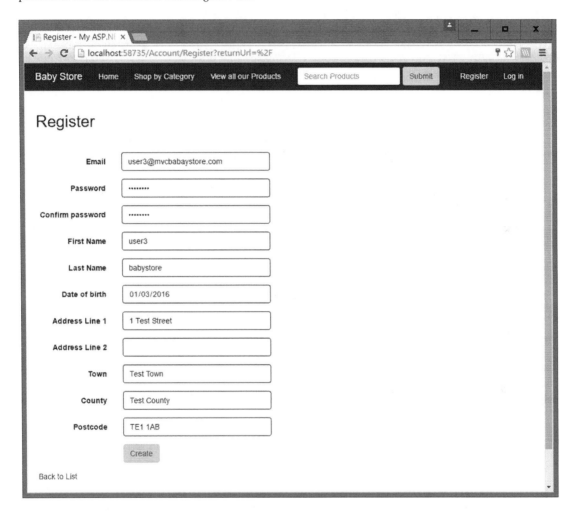

Figure 7-54. *Registering the user3@mvcbabystore.com user*

When you click the Create button, the user will be registered and the web site will redirect you to the Categories Index page rather than to the home page.

Summary

This chapter started by introducing how to work with and manage roles using ASP.NET Identity via ASP.NET MVC. It also covered how to work with the Bootstrap styles to fix some styling issues with the site navigation. You then saw how to create an Admin controller and views to access administrative pages and how to apply authorization to restrict access to the Admin role.

The second half of the chapter covered working with users, including how to work with two database contexts to allow you to store identity data in a separate database and use Code First Migrations on two databases in one project. The chapter also covered how to apply authorization checks to display hyperlinks, and how to use authorization attributes to restrict or allow access to controllers and methods. Finally, the chapter closed by covering how to ensure that the web site always redirects users to the page they were on prior to attempting to log in or register.

CHAPTER 8

■ ■ ■

Creating a Shopping Basket

This chapter covers how to allow users to add products to their shopping basket. We're going to treat a shopping basket as a list of "basket lines" with a basket ID, a product, a quantity, and the time when the entry was added to the basket. The features of the basket will be as follows:

- The basket will allow logged in and anonymous users to add items to their basket and store these baskets in the database.

- For demonstration purposes, we're going to use the session to store a key that will represent the current user. The default session timeout is set to 20 minutes for ASP. NET web applications.

- If the user is anonymous, we'll generate a GUID to represent the user and if the user is logged in, we'll use the username to store basket entries.

- The site will convert the GUID into a userID if a user logs in or registers after adding items to the basket.

- If a logged in user logs out, the site will no longer display the items in the basket since anyone could then see them or edit the basket.

- If a user has previously added items to their basket, the site will display them when they log in.

- The site will not empty a logged in user's basket unless they choose to do so themselves.

■ **Note** If you want to follow along with the code in this chapter, you must either have completed Chapter 7 or download Chapter 7's source code from www.apress.com as a starting point.

Adding a BasketLine Entity

■ **Caution** We use the ASP.NET Session State to store the user's current basket ID; however, in a high-traffic production web site, this is not a viable solution so you will need to consider an alternative. For example, if you are running your site in Azure, one alternative is to use Windows Azure Caching Service.

L. Naylor, *ASP.NET MVC with Entity Framework and CSS*, DOI 10.1007/978-1-4842-2137-2_8

To start creating a basket, we're going to create a BasketLine class containing a basket ID, a product, a quantity, and the time when the entry was added to the basket. The best way to think of this class is that it represents a physical line on the screen in a basket. Add a new class named BasketLine to the models folder of the project as follows:

```
using System;
using System.ComponentModel.DataAnnotations;

namespace BabyStore.Models
{
    public class BasketLine
    {
        public int ID { get; set; }
        public string BasketID { get; set; }
        public int ProductID { get; set; }
        [Range(0,50,ErrorMessage="Please enter a quantity between 0 and 50")]
        public int Quantity { get; set; }
        public DateTime DateCreated { get; set; }
        public virtual Product Product { get; set; }
    }
}
```

This is a simple class with an ID property to act as the key of the BasketLine entry in the database, a BasketID (a GUID or userID) to relate the BasketLine to a basket, a ProductID to relate it to a product, and properties reflecting the quantity of a product and the time the BasketLine was created. We've also added a navigation property to the product referenced by the BasketLine. The Quantity property has a Range attribute that checks that the range entered by a user is between 0 and 50 to prevent users from entering negative or excessive quantities to the basket.

Next, modify the DAL/StoreContext.cs file to add the BasketLines property.

```
using BabyStore.Models;
using System.Data.Entity;

namespace BabyStore.DAL
{
    public class StoreContext:DbContext
    {
        public DbSet<Product> Products { get; set; }
        public DbSet<Category> Categories { get; set; }
        public DbSet<ProductImage> ProductImages { get; set; }
        public DbSet<ProductImageMapping> ProductImageMappings { get; set; }
        public DbSet<BasketLine> BasketLines { get; set; }
    }
}
```

Create a Code First Migration as follows in order to generate the BasketLines table. Run the following commands in Package Manager Console:

```
add-migration AddBasketLine -Configuration StoreConfiguration
```

This will generate a new migration file containing statements to create and drop a BasketLines database table. Now create the new BasketLines table in the database by running the following command in Package Manager Console:

```
update-database -Configuration StoreConfiguration
```

The database will now be updated and contain the new BasketLines table. Verify this by opening Server Explorer in Visual Studio and then opening the StoreContext connection. Then expand the tables node and you should be able to see the new BasketLines table, as shown in Figure 8-1.

Figure 8-1. *Viewing the new BasketLines table in Server Explorer*

Adding Basket Logic

Now that we have a BasketLine class, we're going to create a Basket class to handle the main code for managing the shopping basket. The basket isn't like the other entities in the project in that it doesn't easily map onto CRUD operations or views and is created, updated, and deleted by adding or removing products from it. The main logic required is as follows:

- Get a basket
- Set a session key for a basket
- Add a quantity of a product to a basket
- Update the quantity of one or more products in a basket
- Empty a basket
- Calculate the total cost of a basket
- Get the items in a basket
- Get the overall number of products in a basket
- Migrate the session key for a basket to a username when a user logs in

Start by adding a new class named Basket to the Models folder. Once the class is created, update the class to add a private string property named BasketID, a private constant named BasketSessionKey, and a new StoreContext instance as follows:

```
using BabyStore.DAL;

namespace BabyStore.Models
{
    public class Basket
    {
        private string BasketID { get; set; }
        private const string BasketSessionKey = "BasketID";
        private StoreContext db = new StoreContext();
    }
}
```

Next add the following GetBasketID method to the Basket class, which is used to return a session entry named "BasketID". The session entry is set by the following rules:

If the session item BasketID is not null then return the current entry. If it is null then set the session's BasketID entry to the current user's username if they are logged in; otherwise, create a GUID and set the session's BasketID entry to the GUID.

GUID stands for Globally Unique Identifier and in theory they are always unique. However, if you ran the site for eternity, you would eventually get a duplicate one at some point.

```
using BabyStore.DAL;
using System;
using System.Web;

namespace BabyStore.Models
{
    public class Basket
    {
        private string BasketID { get; set; }
        private const string BasketSessionKey = "BasketID";
        private StoreContext db = new StoreContext();

        private string GetBasketID()
        {
            if (HttpContext.Current.Session[BasketSessionKey] == null)
            {
                if (!string.IsNullOrWhiteSpace(HttpContext.Current.User.Identity.Name))
                {
                    HttpContext.Current.Session[BasketSessionKey] =
                        HttpContext.Current.User.Identity.Name;
                }
                else
                {
                    Guid tempBasketID = Guid.NewGuid();
                    HttpContext.Current.Session[BasketSessionKey] = tempBasketID.ToString();
                }
            }
```

```
            return HttpContext.Current.Session[BasketSessionKey].ToString();
        }
    }
}
```

Ensure you also add the using statements using System.Web; and using System; to the top of the Models\Basket.cs file. Following the GetBasketID method, add a new GetBasket method to the Basket class to create a new Basket instance, get the BasketID using the new GetBasketID method, and return the new Basket as follows:

```
using BabyStore.DAL;
using System;
using System.Web;

namespace BabyStore.Models
{
    public class Basket
    {
        private string BasketID { get; set; }
        private const string BasketSessionKey = "BasketID";
        private StoreContext db = new StoreContext();

        private string GetBasketID()
        {
            if (HttpContext.Current.Session[BasketSessionKey] == null)
            {
                if (!string.IsNullOrWhiteSpace(HttpContext.Current.User.Identity.Name))
                {
                    HttpContext.Current.Session[BasketSessionKey] =
                        HttpContext.Current.User.Identity.Name;
                }
                else
                {
                    Guid tempBasketID = Guid.NewGuid();
                    HttpContext.Current.Session[BasketSessionKey] = tempBasketID.ToString();
                }
            }
            return HttpContext.Current.Session[BasketSessionKey].ToString();
        }

        public static Basket GetBasket()
        {
            Basket basket = new Basket();
            basket.BasketID = basket.GetBasketID();
            return basket;
        }
    }
}
```

Now add a new AddToBasket method to the Basket class, using the productID and quantity parameters to add the specified quantity of the product to the basket.

```
using BabyStore.DAL;
using System;
using System.Linq;
using System.Web;

namespace BabyStore.Models
{
    public class Basket
    {
        private string BasketID { get; set; }
        private const string BasketSessionKey = "BasketID";
        private StoreContext db = new StoreContext();

        private string GetBasketID()
        {
            if (HttpContext.Current.Session[BasketSessionKey] == null)
            {
                if (!string.IsNullOrWhiteSpace(HttpContext.Current.User.Identity.Name))
                {
                    HttpContext.Current.Session[BasketSessionKey] =
                        HttpContext.Current.User.Identity.Name;
                }
                else
                {
                    Guid tempBasketID = Guid.NewGuid();
                    HttpContext.Current.Session[BasketSessionKey] = tempBasketID.ToString();
                }
            }
            return HttpContext.Current.Session[BasketSessionKey].ToString();
        }

        public static Basket GetBasket()
        {
            Basket basket = new Basket();
            basket.BasketID = basket.GetBasketID();
            return basket;
        }

        public void AddToBasket(int productID, int quantity)
        {
            var basketLine = db.BasketLines.FirstOrDefault(b => b.BasketID == BasketID &&
                b.ProductID == productID);
```

```
            if (basketLine == null)
            {
                basketLine = new BasketLine
                {
                    ProductID = productID,
                    BasketID = BasketID,
                    Quantity = quantity,
                    DateCreated = DateTime.Now
                };
                db.BasketLines.Add(basketLine);
            }
            else
            {
                basketLine.Quantity += quantity;
            }
            db.SaveChanges();
        }
    }
}
```

Add the statement using System.Linq; to the top of the file. This method attempts to find the BasketLine record where the BasketID and ProductID match the current basket and the ProductID input parameter. If there is no record found, then a new BasketLine is created because this basket does not contain the required product. Otherwise, the quantity value is updated by the provided quantity.

Next add a method named RemoveLine to the Basket class taking an integer, productID as an input parameter, to search for a BasketLine in the current user's basket containing the productID and deleting it from the database if found:

```
using BabyStore.DAL;
using System;
using System.Linq;
using System.Web;

namespace BabyStore.Models
{
    public class Basket
    {
        private string BasketID { get; set; }
        private const string BasketSessionKey = "BasketID";
        private StoreContext db = new StoreContext();

        private string GetBasketID()
        {
            if (HttpContext.Current.Session[BasketSessionKey] == null)
            {
                if (!string.IsNullOrWhiteSpace(HttpContext.Current.User.Identity.Name))
                {
                    HttpContext.Current.Session[BasketSessionKey] =
                        HttpContext.Current.User.Identity.Name;
                }
```

```
            else
            {
                Guid tempBasketID = Guid.NewGuid();
                HttpContext.Current.Session[BasketSessionKey] = tempBasketID.ToString();
            }
        }
        return HttpContext.Current.Session[BasketSessionKey].ToString();
    }

    public static Basket GetBasket()
    {
        Basket basket = new Basket();
        basket.BasketID = basket.GetBasketID();
        return basket;
    }

    public void AddToBasket(int productID, int quantity)
    {
        var basketLine = db.BasketLines.FirstOrDefault(b => b.BasketID == BasketID &&
            b.ProductID == productID);

        if (basketLine == null)
        {
            basketLine = new BasketLine
            {
                ProductID = productID,
                BasketID = BasketID,
                Quantity = quantity,
                DateCreated = DateTime.Now
            };
            db.BasketLines.Add(basketLine);
        }
        else
        {
            basketLine.Quantity += quantity;
        }
        db.SaveChanges();
    }

    public void RemoveLine(int productID)
    {
        var basketLine = db.BasketLines.FirstOrDefault(b => b.BasketID == BasketID &&
            b.ProductID == productID);
        if (basketLine != null)
        {
            db.BasketLines.Remove(basketLine);
        }
        db.SaveChanges();
    }
}
}
```

CHAPTER 8 ▦ CREATING A SHOPPING BASKET

Next update the Basket class to add a method named UpdateBasket, which takes a list of BasketLines as an input parameter. The method loops through the BasketLines and removes the BasketLine if its quantity is 0, or otherwise it sets the quantity to the input parameter value. This code also checks if the BasketLine is null to cover the case where a session has timed out. Note that if the session has expired, then a new empty basket is generated and returned to the user by the Basket class.

```
using BabyStore.DAL;
using System;
using System.Collections.Generic;
using System.Linq;
using System.Web;

namespace BabyStore.Models
{
    public class Basket
    {
        private string BasketID { get; set; }
        private const string BasketSessionKey = "BasketID";
        private StoreContext db = new StoreContext();

        private string GetBasketID()
        {
            if (HttpContext.Current.Session[BasketSessionKey] == null)
            {
                if (!string.IsNullOrWhiteSpace(HttpContext.Current.User.Identity.Name))
                {
                    HttpContext.Current.Session[BasketSessionKey] =
                        HttpContext.Current.User.Identity.Name;
                }
                else
                {
                    Guid tempBasketID = Guid.NewGuid();
                    HttpContext.Current.Session[BasketSessionKey] = tempBasketID.ToString();
                }
            }
            return HttpContext.Current.Session[BasketSessionKey].ToString();
        }

        public static Basket GetBasket()
        {
            Basket basket = new Basket();
            basket.BasketID = basket.GetBasketID();
            return basket;
        }

        public void AddToBasket(int productID, int quantity)
        {
            var basketLine = db.BasketLines.FirstOrDefault(b => b.BasketID == BasketID &&
                b.ProductID == productID);

            if (basketLine == null)
```

```csharp
        {
            basketLine = new BasketLine
            {
                ProductID = productID,
                BasketID = BasketID,
                Quantity = quantity,
                DateCreated = DateTime.Now
            };
            db.BasketLines.Add(basketLine);
        }
        else
        {
            basketLine.Quantity += quantity;
        }
        db.SaveChanges();
    }

    public void RemoveLine(int productID)
    {
        var basketLine = db.BasketLines.FirstOrDefault(b => b.BasketID == BasketID &&
            b.ProductID == productID);
        if (basketLine != null)
        {
            db.BasketLines.Remove(basketLine);
        }
        db.SaveChanges();
    }

    public void UpdateBasket(List<BasketLine> lines)
    {
        foreach (var line in lines)
        {
            var basketLine = db.BasketLines.FirstOrDefault(b => b.BasketID == BasketID &&
                b.ProductID == line.ProductID);
            if (basketLine != null)
            {
                if (line.Quantity == 0)
                {
                    RemoveLine(line.ProductID);
                }
                else
                {
                    basketLine.Quantity = line.Quantity;
                }
            }
        }
        db.SaveChanges();
    }
  }
}
```

Ensure you add using System.Collections.Generic; to the top of the file. Following this method, add a couple of methods to the Basket class—one named EmptyBasket to allow a user to empty the basket and one named GetBasketLines to return all the BasketLines for the current BasketID, as follows.

```
using BabyStore.DAL;
using System;
using System.Collections.Generic;
using System.Linq;
using System.Web;

namespace BabyStore.Models
{
    public class Basket
    {
        private string BasketID { get; set; }
        private const string BasketSessionKey = "BasketID";
        private StoreContext db = new StoreContext();

        private string GetBasketID()
        {
            if (HttpContext.Current.Session[BasketSessionKey] == null)
            {
                if (!string.IsNullOrWhiteSpace(HttpContext.Current.User.Identity.Name))
                {
                    HttpContext.Current.Session[BasketSessionKey] =
                        HttpContext.Current.User.Identity.Name;
                }
                else
                {
                    Guid tempBasketID = Guid.NewGuid();
                    HttpContext.Current.Session[BasketSessionKey] = tempBasketID.ToString();
                }
            }
            return HttpContext.Current.Session[BasketSessionKey].ToString();
        }

        public static Basket GetBasket()
        {
            Basket basket = new Basket();
            basket.BasketID = basket.GetBasketID();
            return basket;
        }

        public void AddToBasket(int productID, int quantity)
        {
            var basketLine = db.BasketLines.FirstOrDefault(b => b.BasketID == BasketID &&
                b.ProductID == productID);
```

```
    if (basketLine == null)
    {
        basketLine = new BasketLine
        {
            ProductID = productID,
            BasketID = BasketID,
            Quantity = quantity,
            DateCreated = DateTime.Now
        };
        db.BasketLines.Add(basketLine);
    }
    else
    {
        basketLine.Quantity += quantity;
    }
    db.SaveChanges();
}

public void RemoveLine(int productID)
{
    var basketLine = db.BasketLines.FirstOrDefault(b => b.BasketID == BasketID &&
        b.ProductID == productID);
    if (basketLine != null)
    {
        db.BasketLines.Remove(basketLine);
    }
    db.SaveChanges();
}

public void UpdateBasket(List<BasketLine> lines)
{
    foreach (var line in lines)
    {
        var basketLine = db.BasketLines.FirstOrDefault(b => b.BasketID == BasketID &&
            b.ProductID == line.ProductID);
        if (basketLine != null)
        {
            if (line.Quantity == 0)
            {
                RemoveLine(line.ProductID);
            }
            else
            {
                basketLine.Quantity = line.Quantity;
            }
        }
    }
    db.SaveChanges();
}
```

```
        public void EmptyBasket()
        {
            var basketLines = db.BasketLines.Where(b => b.BasketID == BasketID);
            foreach (var basketLine in basketLines)
            {
                db.BasketLines.Remove(basketLine);
            }
            db.SaveChanges();
        }

        public List<BasketLine> GetBasketLines()
        {
            return db.BasketLines.Where(b => b.BasketID == BasketID).ToList();
        }
    }
}
```

Now add two methods to the Basket class to calculate the total cost of the basket and to get the total number of products in the basket. Note that it's important to ensure you include the quantity of each item in your calculations.

```
using BabyStore.DAL;
using System;
using System.Collections.Generic;
using System.Linq;
using System.Web;

namespace BabyStore.Models
{
    public class Basket
    {
        private string BasketID { get; set; }
        private const string BasketSessionKey = "BasketID";
        private StoreContext db = new StoreContext();

        private string GetBasketID()
        {
            if (HttpContext.Current.Session[BasketSessionKey] == null)
            {
                if (!string.IsNullOrWhiteSpace(HttpContext.Current.User.Identity.Name))
                {
                    HttpContext.Current.Session[BasketSessionKey] =
                        HttpContext.Current.User.Identity.Name;
                }
                else
                {
                    Guid tempBasketID = Guid.NewGuid();
                    HttpContext.Current.Session[BasketSessionKey] = tempBasketID.ToString();
                }
            }
            return HttpContext.Current.Session[BasketSessionKey].ToString();
        }
```

```
public static Basket GetBasket()
{
    Basket basket = new Basket();
    basket.BasketID = basket.GetBasketID();
    return basket;
}

public void AddToBasket(int productID, int quantity)
{
    var basketLine = db.BasketLines.FirstOrDefault(b => b.BasketID == BasketID &&
        b.ProductID == productID);

    if (basketLine == null)
    {
        basketLine = new BasketLine
        {
            ProductID = productID,
            BasketID = BasketID,
            Quantity = quantity,
            DateCreated = DateTime.Now
        };
        db.BasketLines.Add(basketLine);
    }
    else
    {
        basketLine.Quantity += quantity;
    }
    db.SaveChanges();
}

public void RemoveLine(int productID)
{
    var basketLine = db.BasketLines.FirstOrDefault(b => b.BasketID == BasketID &&
        b.ProductID == productID);
    if (basketLine != null)
    {
        db.BasketLines.Remove(basketLine);
    }
    db.SaveChanges();
}

public void UpdateBasket(List<BasketLine> lines)
{
    foreach (var line in lines)
    {
        var basketLine = db.BasketLines.FirstOrDefault(b => b.BasketID == BasketID &&
            b.ProductID == line.ProductID);
        if (basketLine != null)
        {
            if (line.Quantity == 0)
            {
```

```
                    RemoveLine(line.ProductID);
                }
                else
                {
                    basketLine.Quantity = line.Quantity;
                }
            }
        }
        db.SaveChanges();
    }

    public void EmptyBasket()
    {
        var basketLines = db.BasketLines.Where(b => b.BasketID == BasketID);
        foreach (var basketLine in basketLines)
        {
            db.BasketLines.Remove(basketLine);
        }
        db.SaveChanges();
    }

    public List<BasketLine> GetBasketLines()
    {
        return db.BasketLines.Where(b => b.BasketID == BasketID).ToList();
    }

    public decimal GetTotalCost()
    {
        decimal basketTotal = decimal.Zero;

        if (GetBasketLines().Count > 0)
        {
            basketTotal = db.BasketLines.Where(b => b.BasketID == BasketID).Sum(b =>
                b.Product.Price * b.Quantity);
        }

        return basketTotal;
    }

    public int GetNumberOfItems()
    {
        int numberOfItems = 0;
        if (GetBasketLines().Count > 0)
        {
            numberOfItems = db.BasketLines.Where(b => b.BasketID == BasketID).Sum(b =>
                b.Quantity);
        }

        return numberOfItems;
    }
  }
}
```

Finally, complete the Basket class by adding a method to change the BasketID of the current Basket instance to the user's username. This method will be used to migrate the BasketID from a GUID to a username, when a user logs in or registers. The code in this method checks to see if a user already has a basket stored. If they do then it calls the AddToBasket method to add the items to the existing basket. This is done to avoid the scenario of getting two lines in the basket for the same product, which can occur if you simply change the BasketID of the BasketLines to the username. Also note that this method calls ToList() to store the baskets in memory. We do this to avoid getting an error relating to having multiple data readers open. Although this can increase memory usage, it will only be a short increase of a small amount and the number of users migrating a basket at the same time is likely to be very low. You should always be careful when using ToList() so as not to load huge lists into memory.

```
using BabyStore.DAL;
using System;
using System.Collections.Generic;
using System.Linq;
using System.Web;

namespace BabyStore.Models
{
    public class Basket
    {
        private string BasketID { get; set; }
        private const string BasketSessionKey = "BasketID";
        private StoreContext db = new StoreContext();

        private string GetBasketID()
        {
            if (HttpContext.Current.Session[BasketSessionKey] == null)
            {
                if (!string.IsNullOrWhiteSpace(HttpContext.Current.User.Identity.Name))
                {
                    HttpContext.Current.Session[BasketSessionKey] =
                        HttpContext.Current.User.Identity.Name;
                }
                else
                {
                    Guid tempBasketID = Guid.NewGuid();
                    HttpContext.Current.Session[BasketSessionKey] = tempBasketID.ToString();
                }
            }
            return HttpContext.Current.Session[BasketSessionKey].ToString();
        }

        public static Basket GetBasket()
        {
            Basket basket = new Basket();
            basket.BasketID = basket.GetBasketID();
            return basket;
        }
```

```
public void AddToBasket(int productID, int quantity)
{
    var basketLine = db.BasketLines.FirstOrDefault(b => b.BasketID == BasketID &&
        b.ProductID == productID);

    if (basketLine == null)
    {
        basketLine = new BasketLine
        {
            ProductID = productID,
            BasketID = BasketID,
            Quantity = quantity,
            DateCreated = DateTime.Now
        };
        db.BasketLines.Add(basketLine);
    }
    else
    {
        basketLine.Quantity += quantity;
    }
    db.SaveChanges();
}

public void RemoveLine(int productID)
{
    var basketLine = db.BasketLines.FirstOrDefault(b => b.BasketID == BasketID &&
        b.ProductID == productID);
    if (basketLine != null)
    {
        db.BasketLines.Remove(basketLine);
    }
    db.SaveChanges();
}

public void UpdateBasket(List<BasketLine> lines)
{
    foreach (var line in lines)
    {
        var basketLine = db.BasketLines.FirstOrDefault(b => b.BasketID == BasketID &&
            b.ProductID == line.ProductID);
        if (basketLine != null)
        {
            if (line.Quantity == 0)
            {
                RemoveLine(line.ProductID);
            }
```

```
                else
                {
                    basketLine.Quantity = line.Quantity;
                }
            }
        }
        db.SaveChanges();
    }

    public void EmptyBasket()
    {
        var basketLines = db.BasketLines.Where(b => b.BasketID == BasketID);
        foreach (var basketLine in basketLines)
        {
            db.BasketLines.Remove(basketLine);
        }
        db.SaveChanges();
    }

    public List<BasketLine> GetBasketLines()
    {
        return db.BasketLines.Where(b => b.BasketID == BasketID).ToList();
    }

    public decimal GetTotalCost()
    {
        decimal basketTotal = decimal.Zero;

        if (GetBasketLines().Count > 0)
        {
            basketTotal = db.BasketLines.Where(b => b.BasketID == BasketID).Sum(b =>
                b.Product.Price * b.Quantity);
        }

        return basketTotal;
    }

    public int GetNumberOfItems()
    {
        int numberOfItems = 0;
        if (GetBasketLines().Count > 0)
        {
            numberOfItems = db.BasketLines.Where(b => b.BasketID == BasketID).Sum(b =>
            b.Quantity);
        }

        return numberOfItems;
    }
```

```
public void MigrateBasket(string userName)
{
    //find the current basket and store it in memory using ToList()
    var basket = db.BasketLines.Where(b => b.BasketID == BasketID).ToList();

    //find if the user already has a basket or not and store it in memory using
    //ToList()
    var usersBasket = db.BasketLines.Where(b => b.BasketID == userName).ToList();

    //if the user has a basket then add the current items to it
    if (usersBasket != null)
    {
        //set the basketID to the username
        string prevID = BasketID;
        BasketID = userName;
        //add the lines in anonymous basket to the user's basket
        foreach (var line in basket)
        {
            AddToBasket(line.ProductID, line.Quantity);
        }
        //delete the lines in the anonymous basket from the database
        BasketID = prevID;
        EmptyBasket();
    }
    else
    {
        //if the user does not have a basket then just migrate this one
        foreach (var basketLine in basket)
        {
            basketLine.BasketID = userName;
        }
        db.SaveChanges();
    }
    HttpContext.Current.Session[BasketSessionKey] = userName;
}
}
```

Adding a Basket View Model

Add a new view model to display the basket contents and total by creating a new class named
BasketViewModel.cs in the ViewModels folder. This class will be used as the model to base the Basket Index
view on and simply contains a list of BasketLines and the total cost of the basket. The DisplayFormat
attribute assigned to the TotalCost property specifies that it should be displayed in the local (server specific)
currency format.

```
using BabyStore.Models;
using System.Collections.Generic;
using System.ComponentModel.DataAnnotations;
```

```
namespace BabyStore.ViewModels
{
    public class BasketViewModel
    {
        public List<BasketLine> BasketLines { get; set; }
        [Display(Name = "Basket Total:")]
        [DisplayFormat(DataFormatString = "{0:c}")]
        public decimal TotalCost { get; set; }
    }
}
```

Adding a Basket Controller

We're now going to create a BasketController class to handle requests for updating the basket. The BasketController class effectively acts as a proxy class, calling the methods of the Basket class and then redirecting to the Index method. The Index method then calls the Index view to redisplay the contents of the basket.

Start by adding an empty MVC5 controller by right-clicking on the Controllers folder and choosing *Add* ➤ *Controller*. Then add an *MVC5 Controller - Empty*. Name the new controller BasketController.

Update the new BasketController class as follows to update the Index method. The updates create a new basket and a BasketViewModel and assign the lines and cost of the basket to it. It then passes the view model to the Index view.

```
using BabyStore.Models;
using BabyStore.ViewModels;
using System.Web.Mvc;

namespace BabyStore.Controllers
{
    public class BasketController : Controller
    {
        // GET: Basket
        public ActionResult Index()
        {
            Basket basket = Basket.GetBasket();
            BasketViewModel viewModel = new BasketViewModel
            {
                BasketLines = basket.GetBasketLines(),
                TotalCost = basket.GetTotalCost()
            };
            return View(viewModel);
        }
    }
}
```

Next update the BasketController class to add a new method named AddToBasket, which first calls the GetBasket method of the Basket class to obtain the current basket and then calls the AddToBasket method, passing in a productID and a quantity to add to the basket. After this, the method redirects to the Index action, resulting in the Index view being displayed with the updates.

```
using BabyStore.Models;
using BabyStore.ViewModels;
using System.Web.Mvc;

namespace BabyStore.Controllers
{
    public class BasketController : Controller
    {
        // GET: Basket
        public ActionResult Index()
        {
            Basket basket = Basket.GetBasket();
            BasketViewModel viewModel = new BasketViewModel
            {
                BasketLines = basket.GetBasketLines(),
                TotalCost = basket.GetTotalCost()
            };
            return View(viewModel);
        }

        [HttpPost]
        [ValidateAntiForgeryToken]
        public ActionResult AddToBasket(int id, int quantity)
        {
            Basket basket = Basket.GetBasket();
            basket.AddToBasket(id, quantity);
            return RedirectToAction("Index");
        }
    }
}
```

Following this, add a new method to the BasketController class named UpdateBasket. This method takes BasketViewModel as an input parameter and then passes its BasketLines property to the UpdateBasket method of the Basket class.

```
using BabyStore.Models;
using BabyStore.ViewModels;
using System.Web.Mvc;

namespace BabyStore.Controllers
{
    public class BasketController : Controller
    {
        // GET: Basket
        public ActionResult Index()
        {
            Basket basket = Basket.GetBasket();
            BasketViewModel viewModel = new BasketViewModel
            {
                BasketLines = basket.GetBasketLines(),
                TotalCost = basket.GetTotalCost()
            };
```

```
        return View(viewModel);
    }

    [HttpPost]
    [ValidateAntiForgeryToken]
    public ActionResult AddToBasket(int id, int quantity)
    {
        Basket basket = Basket.GetBasket();
        basket.AddToBasket(id, quantity);
        return RedirectToAction("Index");
    }

    [HttpPost]
    [ValidateAntiForgeryToken]
    public ActionResult UpdateBasket(BasketViewModel viewModel)
    {
        Basket basket = Basket.GetBasket();
        basket.UpdateBasket(viewModel.BasketLines);
        return RedirectToAction("Index");
    }
  }
}
```

Next add a RemoveLine method. This differs from most of the other methods in the BasketController and pretty much all other the other controller classes in this book because it is an HttpGet version of a method that updates the database. In earlier chapters, I recommended using HttpPost to perform database updates, but here we have a scenario where we're not technically going to be able to use a HTML form to submit a request to remove a line from the basket, so we're going to use HttpGet. You will see in the view file that we generate an HTML form that surrounds all of the lines in the basket and so we cannot then include another HTML form within this larger form because it is not valid HTML. Instead, we'll create a set of hyperlinks to this method. Using HttpGet in this scenario is acceptable because in order to create a basket with items in it, the user first needs to submit an HTML form using POST.

```
using BabyStore.Models;
using BabyStore.ViewModels;
using System.Web.Mvc;

namespace BabyStore.Controllers
{
    public class BasketController : Controller
    {
        // GET: Basket
        public ActionResult Index()
        {
            Basket basket = Basket.GetBasket();
            BasketViewModel viewModel = new BasketViewModel
            {
                BasketLines = basket.GetBasketLines(),
                TotalCost = basket.GetTotalCost()
            };
            return View(viewModel);
        }
```

```
[HttpPost]
[ValidateAntiForgeryToken]
public ActionResult AddToBasket(int id, int quantity)
{
    Basket basket = Basket.GetBasket();
    basket.AddToBasket(id, quantity);
    return RedirectToAction("Index");
}

[HttpPost]
[ValidateAntiForgeryToken]
public ActionResult UpdateBasket(BasketViewModel viewModel)
{
    Basket basket = Basket.GetBasket();
    basket.UpdateBasket(viewModel.BasketLines);
    return RedirectToAction("Index");
}

[HttpGet]
public ActionResult RemoveLine(int id)
{
    Basket basket = Basket.GetBasket();
    basket.RemoveLine(id);
    return RedirectToAction("Index");
}
    }
}
```

Adding a Basket Index View

We now need to add a view to display the basket. We're only going to create one view to display the basket because of the way the basket functions. A basket is effectively created by adding a product to it and updated by adding or removing more products. You add a product via the Product Details page and changing the quantity, removing a product (resulting in removing a BasketLine), and emptying the basket are all done from one page; the Basket Index page.

Prior to adding a new Basket Index view, remove the line of code <li>@Html.ActionLink("Home", "Index", "Home")</li> from the Views\Shared_Layout.cshtml file to remove the home link and make some space in the navigation bar for use later in the chapter.

To add a new Basket Index view, right-click on the Index method in the Controllers\BasketController.cs file and add a new view named Index, using the Details Template option. Set the Model Class to BasketViewModel. Set the Data Context to blank and check the Reference Script Libraries and Use a Layout Page options. Figure 8-2 shows the option to select.

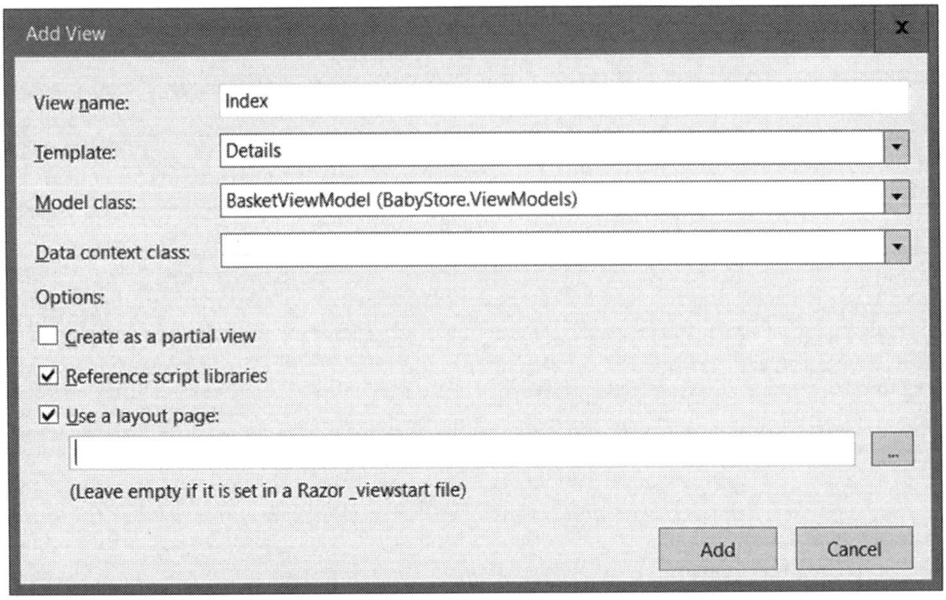

Figure 8-2. *Adding a new Basket Index view*

Update the newly create Views\Basket\Index.cshtml file as follows. This updates the title and the layout to use divs rather than dl, dd, and dt tags:

```
@model BabyStore.ViewModels.BasketViewModel

@{
    ViewBag.Title = "Your Basket";
}

<h2>@ViewBag.Title</h2>

<div>
    <hr />
    <div class="row">
        <div class="col-md-8">
            @Html.DisplayNameFor(model => model.TotalCost)
        </div>
        <div class="col-md-1">
            @Html.DisplayFor(model => model.TotalCost)
        </div>
    </div>
</div>
@section Scripts {
    @Scripts.Render("~/bundles/jqueryval")
}
```

In the code, the div with the CSS class col-md-8 will be eight columns wide and the one with col-md-1 will be one column wide. Right-click in the view file and choose *View in Browser* from the menu to see the new HTML page generated by the Basket Index view file. It should appear as shown in Figure 8-3.

Figure 8-3. *The Basket Index page updated to use divs*

Now add some headings to the view file. They will be used to show headings for each line in the basket as follows:

```
@model BabyStore.ViewModels.BasketViewModel

@{
    ViewBag.Title = "Your Basket";
}

<h2>@ViewBag.Title</h2>

<div>
    <hr />
    <div class="row">
        <div class="col-md-4"><label>Item</label></div>
        <div class="col-md-3"><label>Quantity</label></div>
        <div class="col-md-1"><label>Price</label></div>
        <div class="col-md-1"><label>Subtotal</label></div>
    </div>
    <hr />
    <div class="row">
        <div class="col-md-8">
            @Html.DisplayNameFor(model => model.TotalCost)
        </div>
        <div class="col-md-1">
            @Html.DisplayFor(model => model.TotalCost)
        </div>
    </div>
</div>
```

```
@section Scripts {
    @Scripts.Render("~/bundles/jqueryval")
}
```

The headings will appear in the HTML page, as shown in Figure 8-4.

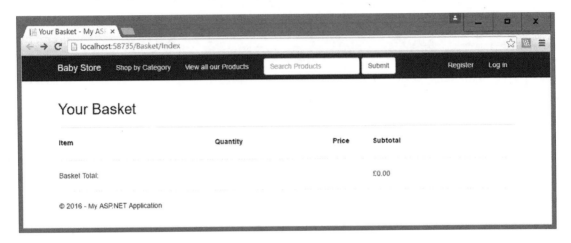

Figure 8-4. *The Basket Index HTML page with added headings*

Now add some code to show each product added to the basket, along with the thumbnail version of its main image as follows:

```
@model BabyStore.ViewModels.BasketViewModel

@{
    ViewBag.Title = "Your Basket";
}

<h2>@ViewBag.Title</h2>

<div>
    <hr />
    <div class="row">
        <div class="col-md-4"><label>Item</label></div>
        <div class="col-md-3"><label>Quantity</label></div>
        <div class="col-md-1"><label>Price</label></div>
        <div class="col-md-1"><label>Subtotal</label></div>
    </div>
    <hr />
    @for (int i = 0; i < Model.BasketLines.Count; i++)
    {
        <div class="row">
            <div class="col-md-4">
                @Html.ActionLink(Model.BasketLines[i].Product.Name, "Details",
                    "Products", new { id = Model.BasketLines[i].ProductID }, null)<br />
                    @if (Model.BasketLines[i].Product.ProductImageMappings != null &&
```

```
                        Model.BasketLines[i].Product.ProductImageMappings.Any())
                    {
                        <a href="@Url.Action("Details", "Products", new { id =
                            Model.BasketLines[i].ProductID })">
                            <img src="@(Url.Content(Constants.ProductThumbnailPath) +
                                Model.BasketLines[i].Product.ProductImageMappings.OrderBy(pim
                                => pim.ImageNumber).ElementAt(0).ProductImage.FileName)">
                        </a>
                    }
                </div>
            </div>
        <hr />
    }
    <div class="row">
        <div class="col-md-8">
            @Html.DisplayNameFor(model => model.TotalCost)
        </div>
        <div class="col-md-1">
            @Html.DisplayFor(model => model.TotalCost)
        </div>
    </div>
</div>
@section Scripts {
    @Scripts.Render("~/bundles/jqueryval")
}
```

This additional code loops through each BasketLine in the view model and displays the name of each product, plus the product's main image as a thumbnail. Both these elements are generated as hyperlinks to the product's details. Note that rather than use a foreach loop, we have used a traditional for loop with a counter. The reason for this is to ensure that the MVC Framework can automatically recognize the values submitted by the form as a BasketViewModel. I will explain this further after the next section.

Allowing a User to Add to Basket

We are going to allow users to add products to their baskets from the Products Details page, so we now need to add an HTML form to this view. The form will target the AddToBasket action method of the BasketController class. In order to generate this form, add the following code to Views\Products\Details.cshtml file as the last element in the <dl> tags just before the closing </dl> element:

```
@model BabyStore.Models.Product

@{
    ViewBag.Title = "Product Details";
}

<h2>@ViewBag.Title</h2>

<div>
    <hr />
    <dl class="dl-horizontal">
```

```
<dt>
    @Html.DisplayNameFor(model => model.Category.Name)
</dt>

<dd>
    @Html.DisplayFor(model => model.Category.Name)
</dd>

<dt>
    @Html.DisplayNameFor(model => model.Name)
</dt>

<dd>
    @Html.DisplayFor(model => model.Name)
</dd>

<dt>
    @Html.DisplayNameFor(model => model.Description)
</dt>

<dd>
    @Html.DisplayFor(model => model.Description)
</dd>

<dt>
    @Html.DisplayNameFor(model => model.Price)
</dt>

<dd>
    @Html.DisplayFor(model => model.Price)
</dd>
@if (Model.ProductImageMappings != null && Model.ProductImageMappings.Any())
{
    <dt></dt>
    <dd>
        <img src="@(Url.Content(Constants.ProductImagePath) +
            Model.ProductImageMappings.OrderBy(pim =>  pim.ImageNumber).
            ElementAt(0).ProductImage.FileName)" style=padding:5px>
    </dd>
    <dt></dt>
    <dd>
        @foreach (var item in Model.ProductImageMappings.OrderBy(pim =>
            pim.ImageNumber))
        {
            <a href="@(Url.Content(Constants.ProductImagePath) +
                item.ProductImage.FileName)">
                <img src="@(Url.Content(Constants.ProductThumbnailPath) +
                    item.ProductImage.FileName)" style=padding:5px>
            </a>
        }
    </dd>
}
```

```
    <dt>
        Quantity:
    </dt>
    <dd>
        @using (Html.BeginForm("AddToBasket", "Basket"))
        {
            @Html.AntiForgeryToken()
            @Html.HiddenFor(model => model.ID)
            @Html.DropDownList("quantity", Enumerable.Range(1, 10).Select(i => new
                SelectListItem { Text = i.ToString(), Value = i.ToString() }))
            <input type="submit" class="btn btn-primary btn-xs" value="Add to Basket">
        }
    </dd>
</dl>
</div>
<p>
    @Html.ActionLink("Edit", "Edit", new { id = Model.ID }) |
    @Html.ActionLink("Back to List", "Index")
</p>
```

This form contains a DropDownList helper that uses a LINQ query to generate an HTML select control showing the values 1 to 10. This control is named "quantity" and the form submits this quantity value along with the product's ID to the AddToBasket method of the BasketController class. I have chosen to add this control directly to the view, but if required you could create a view model and add this new quantity property to it for completeness. To see this in action, start the web site without debugging and click on the *View All Our Products* link from the home page. Then click on the image for the *3 Pack of Bibs* product. You will then see the new form at the bottom of the page, as shown in Figure 8-5.

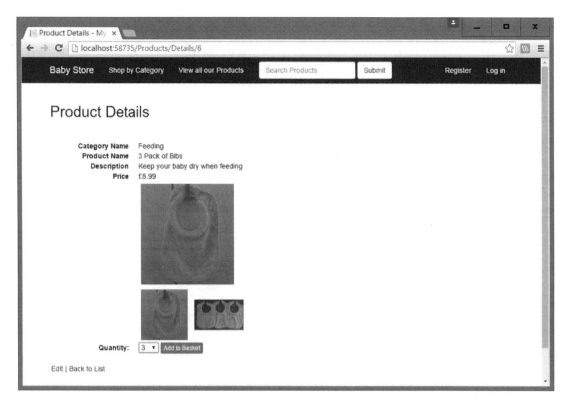

Figure 8-5. *The new "Add to Basket" form displayed in a product's details*

Enter 3 as the quantity and click the *Add to Basket* button. You will be redirected to the Basket Index page, as shown in Figure 8-6, and the basket will now show the product's main image from the thumbnails folder. The basket total will also be displayed, in this case it will be 3 x £8.99, which is £26.97. The process that got you here was that the new form called the AddToBasketMethod of the BasketController with the product's ID and quantity. This in turn called the Basket class and created a new BasketLine entry by calling the AddToBasket method while first generating a new BasketID and storing this in the session.

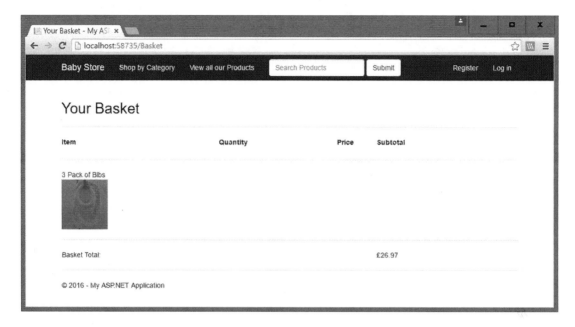

Figure 8-6. *"3 Pack of Bibs" products added to the basket*

To see the effect on the database, open Server Explorer and then expand the StoreContext connection and view the data of the BasketLines table. You should see something similar to Figure 8-7, although DateCreated and BasketID will differ. The BasketID is a GUID generated when first calling the Basket class and this will be stored in the session under the key "BasketID".

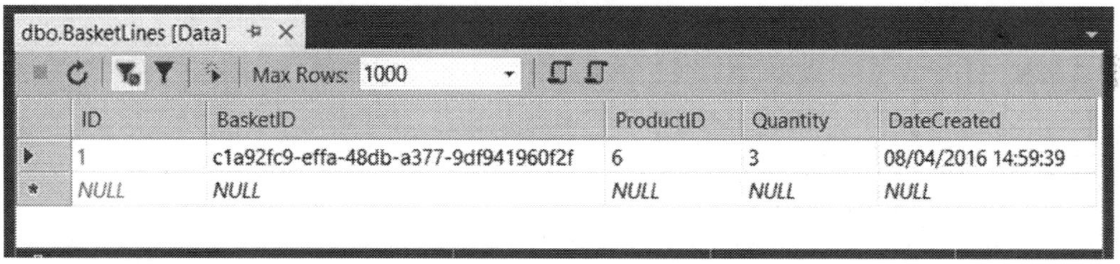

Figure 8-7. *The new BasketLine entry in the BasketLines database table*

Note that if a user adds a previously added item to their basket via the Product Details page, then the quantity of the existing item is simply updated for the additional quantity of items. A new BasketLine is not created.

Updating the Basket: Model Binding to a List or an Array

Now that we have items displayed in the basket, we need a way to be able to update the quantity of items in the basket. The Views\Basket\Index.cshtml file is based on the BasketViewModel and this is the type expected by the UpdateBasket method in the Controllers\BasketController.cs file. This type contains a list of the BasketLine type, and we are going to use an HTML form inside the view to update the quantity of each of these BasketLines. Therefore, we need a way to ensure that a repeating list of BasketLines is correctly bound by the model-binding process.

The model-binding process for list types relies on index numbers to perform binding correctly. Each HTML control must contain an index number. This is the reason that we used a traditional style for loop rather than a foreach loop when displaying the images for each product. With a foreach loop, each HTML control generated for each line would have the same name, so we would have several inputs with the same name for the productID and quantity.

If this sounds a bit confusing, to see this in action, update the Views\Basket\Index.cshtml file as follows to allow the user to update the quantity of each line in the basket. We're also going to fill in the data to display a product's price and the subtotal of the line.

```
@model BabyStore.ViewModels.BasketViewModel

@{
    ViewBag.Title = "Your Basket";
}


<h2>@ViewBag.Title</h2>


<div>
    @using (Html.BeginForm("UpdateBasket", "Basket"))
    {
        @Html.AntiForgeryToken();
        <input class="btn btn-sm btn-success" type="submit" value="Update Basket" />
        <hr />
        <div class="row">
            <div class="col-md-4"><label>Item</label></div>
            <div class="col-md-3"><label>Quantity</label></div>
            <div class="col-md-1"><label>Price</label></div>
            <div class="col-md-1"><label>Subtotal</label></div>
        </div>
        <hr />
        for (int i = 0; i < Model.BasketLines.Count; i++)
        {
        <div class="row">
            <div class="col-md-4">
                @Html.ActionLink(Model.BasketLines[i].Product.Name, "Details",
                    "Products", new { id = Model.BasketLines[i].ProductID }, null)<br />
                    @if (Model.BasketLines[i].Product.ProductImageMappings != null &&
                        Model.BasketLines[i].Product.ProductImageMappings.Any())
                    {
                        <a href="@Url.Action("Details", "Products", new { id =
                            Model.BasketLines[i].ProductID })">
                            <img src="@(Url.Content(Constants.ProductThumbnailPath) +
                                Model.BasketLines[i].Product.ProductImageMappings.OrderBy(pim
                                => pim.ImageNumber).ElementAt(0).ProductImage.FileName)">
                        </a>
                    }
            </div>
```

```
            <div class="col-md-3">
                @Html.HiddenFor(productID => Model.BasketLines[i].ProductID)
                @Html.TextBoxFor(quantity => Model.BasketLines[i].Quantity)
                 <p>@Html.ValidationMessageFor(quantity => Model.BasketLines[i].Quantity,
                     "", new { @class = "text-danger" })</p>
            </div>
            <div class="col-md-1">@Html.DisplayFor(price =>
                Model.BasketLines[i].Product.Price)</div>
            <div class="col-md-1">@((Model.BasketLines[i].Quantity *
                Model.BasketLines[i].Product.Price).ToString("c"))</div>
        </div>
        <hr />
    }
}
<div class="row">
    <div class="col-md-8">
        @Html.DisplayNameFor(model => model.TotalCost)
    </div>
    <div class="col-md-1">
        @Html.DisplayFor(model => model.TotalCost)
    </div>
</div>
</div>
@section Scripts {
    @Scripts.Render("~/bundles/jqueryval")
}
```

The new code adds an HTML form that targets the UpdateBasket method in the BasketController class. We've added this form so it surrounds all the lines of HTML generated by displaying the each BasketLine item in the BasketViewModel and we've added a Submit button at the top of the form labeled "Update Basket". *Ensure you remove the @ character from the beginning of the* for *statement.*

We've also added a hidden input for the ProductId, a text box input for the Quantity. We have used the index number i in these elements. As an example, if we had a basket with two lines in it, when the HTML is generated for each control, it would be generated with the names as follows: BasketLines[0].ProductId, BasketLines[0].Quantity for the first line followed by BasketLines[1].ProductId, BasketLines[1].Quantity for the second line.

When these are now submitted to the UpdateBasket method, it can recognize that each of these controls represents an item in the BasketLines list property of the BasketViewModel.

The input for submitting the quantity is based on the Quantity property of the BasketLine class, which allows a range of 0 to 50, so we have also used the Html.ValidationMessageFor helper to show a validation message if required.

We've also added code to display the price of the product and the subtotal of the current line. We've calculated the subtotal in the view because we are not interested in storing it anywhere. Since this is calculated on the fly, we have also given an example of formatting this in the view as currency by using .ToString("c").

To see how the model binding works in detail, add a break point to the line containing the first bracket after the line of code public ActionResult UpdateBasket(BasketViewModel viewModel) in the Controllers\BasketController.cs file and then start the web site with debugging. This is likely to have destroyed your previous session, so add two Black Pram and Pushchair Systems to the basket. Then add one Blue Rabbit. The basket should now appear as shown in Figure 8-8, with a quantity, price, and subtotal for each line in the basket.

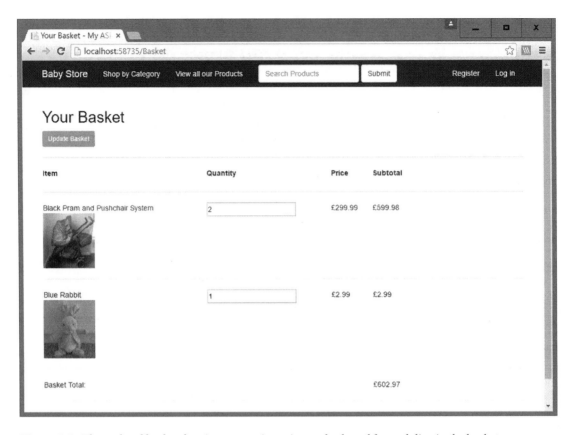

Figure 8-8. *The updated basket showing a quantity, price, and subtotal for each line in the basket*

View the HTML source of the Basket Index page by right-clicking in the browser and choosing *View Source* from the menu. If you look at the source of each of the basket, you will now see the HTML controls generated by using the Index value in the view code. For the pram line, the HTML source code for the ProductId and the Quantity input elements appears as follows, with the element names shown in bold:

```
<input id="BasketLines_0__ProductId" name="BasketLines[0].ProductId" type="hidden"
    value="11" />
<input data-val="true" data-val-number="The field Quantity must be a number." data-val-
    range="Please enter a quantity between 0 and 50" data-val-range-max="50" data-val-range-
    min="0" data-val-required="The Quantity field is required." id="BasketLines_0__Quantity"
    name="BasketLines[0].Quantity" type="text" value="2" />
```

For the rabbit line, the source code appears as:

```
<input id="BasketLines_1__ProductId" name="BasketLines[1].ProductId" type="hidden" value="4"
    />
<input data-val="true" data-val-number="The field Quantity must be a number." data-val-
    range="Please enter a quantity between 0 and 50" data-val-range-max="50" data-val-range-
    min="0" data-val-required="The Quantity field is required." id="BasketLines_1__Quantity"
    name="BasketLines[1].Quantity" type="text" value="1" />
```

Next, update the quantity of the Black Pram and Pushchair System to 3 and click the *Update Basket* button. The breakpoint you added to the `UpdateBasket` method of the `BasketController` class will be hit. Examine the contents of the `viewModel` variable that have been passed to the method by the MVC Framework by hovering over it. You will see that this variable has correctly bound the `ProductId` and `Quantity` for both lines. Figure 8-9 shows the updated quantity value for the first `BasketLine` element (containing the pram) with an updated quantity of 3.

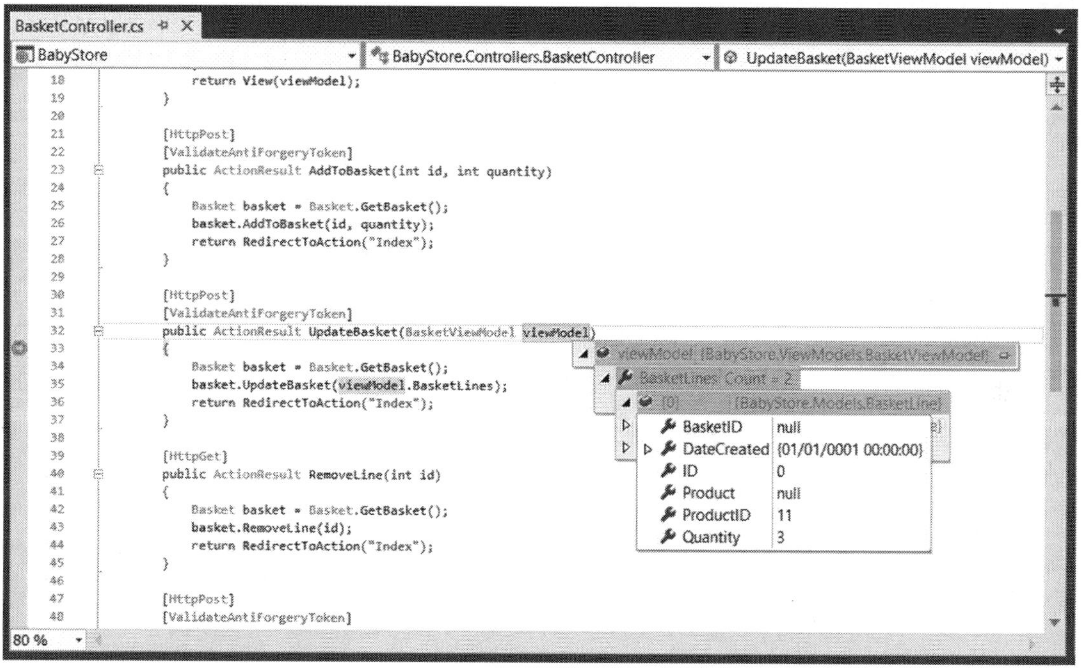

Figure 8-9. *Debugging the UpdateBasket method to show model binding of the viewModel's BasketLine list*

Click the *Continue* button in Visual Studio. The web site will reappear with the basket now updated, as shown in Figure 8-10.

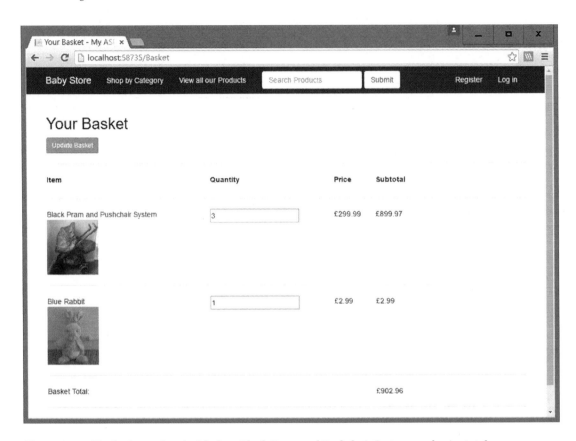

Figure 8-10. *The basket updated with three Black Pram and Pushchair Systems and price totals*

Deleting a Line or Product from the Basket

To complete the functionality in the Basket Index view, update the Views\Basket\Index.cshtml file to add a new link for each BasketLine. This will allow the users to remove a line from the basket by adding the code shown in bold:

```
@model BabyStore.ViewModels.BasketViewModel

@{
    ViewBag.Title = "Your Basket";
}

<h2>@ViewBag.Title</h2>

<div>
    @using (Html.BeginForm("UpdateBasket", "Basket"))
```

```
{
    @Html.AntiForgeryToken();
    <input class="btn btn-sm btn-success" type="submit" value="Update Basket" />
    <hr />
    <div class="row">
        <div class="col-md-4"><label>Item</label></div>
        <div class="col-md-3"><label>Quantity</label></div>
        <div class="col-md-1"><label>Price</label></div>
        <div class="col-md-1"><label>Subtotal</label></div>
    </div>
    <hr />
    for (int i = 0; i < Model.BasketLines.Count; i++)
    {
        <div class="row">
            <div class="col-md-4">
                @Html.ActionLink(Model.BasketLines[i].Product.Name, "Details",
                "Products", new { id = Model.BasketLines[i].ProductID }, null)<br />
                @if (Model.BasketLines[i].Product.ProductImageMappings != null &&
                    Model.BasketLines[i].Product.ProductImageMappings.Any())
                {
                    <a href="@Url.Action("Details", "Products", new { id =
                        Model.BasketLines[i].ProductID })">
                        <img src="@(Url.Content(Constants.ProductThumbnailPath) +
                            Model.BasketLines[i].Product.ProductImageMappings.OrderBy(pim
                            => pim.ImageNumber).ElementAt(0).ProductImage.FileName)">
                    </a>
                }
            </div>
            <div class="col-md-3">
                @Html.HiddenFor(productID => Model.BasketLines[i].ProductID)
                @Html.TextBoxFor(quantity => Model.BasketLines[i].Quantity)
                <p>
                    @Html.ValidationMessageFor(quantity => Model.BasketLines[i].Quantity,
                        "", new { @class = "text-danger" })
                </p>
            </div>
            <div class="col-md-1">
                @Html.DisplayFor(price => Model.BasketLines[i].Product.Price)
            </div>
            <div class="col-md-1">
                @((Model.BasketLines[i].Quantity *
                    Model.BasketLines[i].Product.Price).ToString("c"))
            </div>
            <div class="col-md-1">
                @Html.ActionLink("Remove", "RemoveLine", "Basket", new
                    { id = Model.BasketLines[i].Product.ID }, null)
            </div>
        </div>
        <hr />
    }
}
```

```
    <div class="row">
        <div class="col-md-8">
            @Html.DisplayNameFor(model => model.TotalCost)
        </div>
        <div class="col-md-1">
            @Html.DisplayFor(model => model.TotalCost)
        </div>
    </div>
</div>
@section Scripts {
    @Scripts.Render("~/bundles/jqueryval")
}
```

This new link targets the RemoveLine method of the BasketController class. This link is contained in the HTML form to update the basket and so you will recall this is why the RemoveLine method is an HttpGet method as opposed to HttpPost. Figure 8-11 shows the new *Remove* link as it appears in the Basket Index page.

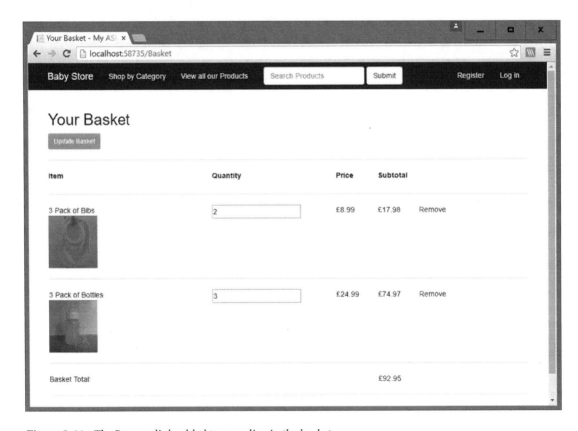

Figure 8-11. *The Remove link added to every line in the basket*

If you remove a line from the basket by using the *Remove* link, it is also deleted from the BasketLines database table. It is also possible to remove a line/product from the basket by setting its quantity to zero and updating the basket.

Finally, add some code to the Views\Basket\Index.cshtml file to check if the basket has any items in it. If it does not, then display a message telling the user their basket is empty. Also add a Continue Shopping link by updating the view as follows:

```
@model BabyStore.ViewModels.BasketViewModel

@{
    ViewBag.Title = "Your Basket";
}

<h2>@ViewBag.Title</h2>
@if (Model.BasketLines.Count() > 0)
{
    <div>
        @using (Html.BeginForm("UpdateBasket", "Basket"))
        {
        ...code omitted for brevity
    </div>
}
else
{
    <p>Your Basket is empty</p>
}
<div>
    @Html.ActionLink("Continue Shopping", "Index", "Products")
</div>
@section Scripts {
    @Scripts.Render("~/bundles/jqueryval")
}
```

Now if a user tries to view an empty basket, they will receive the message shown in Figure 8-12, including a Continue Shopping link.

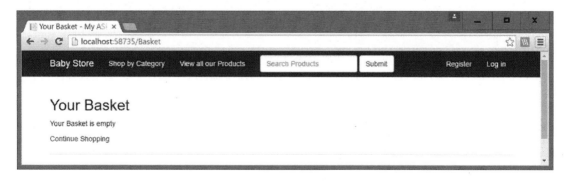

Figure 8-12. *Viewing an empty basket*

Displaying a Basket Summary

We are now going to add a basket summary to the main navigation bar of the web site. This will allow the users to click on it to view their baskets.

Create a new class named BasketSummaryViewModel in the ViewModels folder to include a property to hold the number of items in the basket and the total cost of the basket as follows:

```
using System.ComponentModel.DataAnnotations;

namespace BabyStore.ViewModels
{
    public class BasketSummaryViewModel
    {
        public int NumberOfItems { get; set; }
        [DataType(DataType.Currency)]
        [DisplayFormat(DataFormatString = "{0:c}")]
        public decimal TotalCost { get; set; }
    }
}
```

Next, add a Summary method to the \Controllers\BasketController.cs file to return a PartialViewResult and set the values in an instance of the BasketSummaryViewModel. This happens by calling the GetNumberOfItems and GetTotalCost methods from the Basket instance, as follows:

```
public PartialViewResult Summary()
{
    Basket basket = Basket.GetBasket();
    BasketSummaryViewModel viewModel = new BasketSummaryViewModel
    {
        NumberOfItems = basket.GetNumberOfItems(),
        TotalCost = basket.GetTotalCost()
    };
    return PartialView(viewModel);
}
```

Right-click on the new method and choose Add View. Create a new empty view named Summary with the model class BasketSummaryViewModel.

Open the newly created Views\Basket\Summary.cshtml file and edit it as follows:

```
@model BabyStore.ViewModels.BasketSummaryViewModel

<ul class="nav navbar-nav navbar-right">
    <li>
        @Html.ActionLink("Your basket: " + Model.NumberOfItems + " items(s) " +
            HttpUtility.HtmlDecode(Html.DisplayFor(model => Model.TotalCost).ToString()),
            "Index", "Basket")
    </li>
</ul>
```

This code looks a little awkward with regard to displaying the total value, but this is required to ensure the pound sign is shown correctly. The `Html.DisplayFor` helper is called for the basket's `TotalValue` property, but this then needs to be converted to a string and passed into the `HttpUtility.HtmlDecode` function to get the HTML for the currency symbol to display as £ and not as £.

Finally, add the new basket summary to the main navigation bar by updating the `Views\Shared\_layout.cshtml` file. You do so by adding a new line of code after the line that displays the `loginPartial` view as follows:

```
<!DOCTYPE html>
<html>
<head>
    <meta charset="utf-8" />
    <meta name="viewport" content="width=device-width, initial-scale=1.0">
    <title>@ViewBag.Title - My ASP.NET Application</title>
    @Styles.Render("~/Content/css")
    @Scripts.Render("~/bundles/modernizr")
</head>
<body>
    <div class="navbar navbar-inverse navbar-static-top">
        <div class="container">
            <div class="navbar-header">
                <button type="button" class="navbar-toggle" data-toggle="collapse" data-
                    target=".navbar-collapse">
                    <span class="icon-bar"></span>
                    <span class="icon-bar"></span>
                    <span class="icon-bar"></span>
                </button>
                @Html.ActionLink("Baby Store", "Index", "Home", new { area = "" }, new {
                    @class = "navbar-brand" })
            </div>
            <div class="navbar-collapse collapse">
                <ul class="nav navbar-nav">
                    <li>@Html.ActionLink("Shop by Category", "Index", "Categories")</li>
                    <li>@Html.RouteLink("View all our Products", "ProductsIndex")</li>
                    @if (Request.IsAuthenticated && User.IsInRole("Admin"))
                    {
                        <li>@Html.ActionLink("Admin", "Index", "Admin")</li>
                    }
                </ul>
                @using (Html.BeginRouteForm("ProductsIndex", FormMethod.Get, new { @class =
                    "navbar-form navbar-left" }))
                {
                    <div class="form-group">
                        @Html.TextBox("Search", null, new { @class = "form-control",
                            @placeholder = "Search Products" })
                    </div>
                    <button type="submit" class="btn btn-default">Submit</button>
                }
```

```
                @Html.Partial("_LoginPartial")
                @Html.Action("Summary", "Basket")
            </div>
        </div>
    </div>
    <div class="container body-content">
        @RenderBody()
        <hr />
        <footer>
            <p>&copy; @DateTime.Now.Year - My ASP.NET Application</p>
        </footer>
    </div>

    @Scripts.Render("~/bundles/jquery")
    @Scripts.Render("~/bundles/bootstrap")
    @RenderSection("scripts", required: false)
</body>
</html>
```

Using the Html.Action method has allowed us to call a method from a different controller and include its output in this view. Start the web site without debugging and add items to your basket. You will see the number of items and total cost update in the summary as you add and remove items from the basket. Figure 8-13 shows the new basket summary included in the navigation bar. It reflects the current five items shown in the basket.

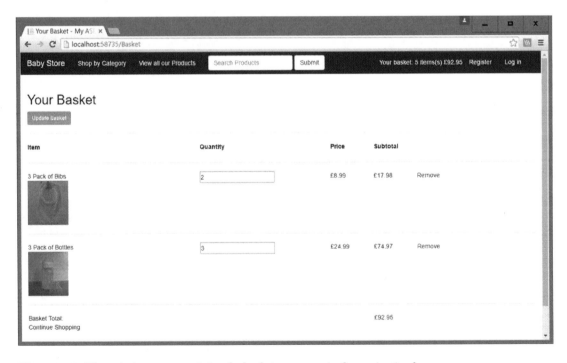

Figure 8-13. *The web site now containing the basket summary in the navigation bar*

The web site doesn't format the navigation bar correctly when the admin user logs in following the addition of the basket summary, so update the `max-width` of the web site to 1500pixels by updating the following in the `Content\bootstrap.css` file:

```
@media (min-width: 1200px) {
  .container {
    max-width: 1500px;
  }
}
```

Migrating a Basket When a User Logs In or Registers

A couple of tasks remain to be dealt with in regard to the basket. We need to migrate the basket to use the current user's username as the `BasketID` whenever a user logs in or a new user registers. This will retain users' baskets even when they log out of the web site.

Migrating the Basket Upon Login

To migrate the basket when a user logs in, we need to modify the `Login` method of `Controllers\AccountController.cs` file. We're going to add code that migrates a user's basket to use their username as the `basketID` rather than a GUID.

We also need to address the scenario whereby a new user logs in without the previous user logging out. We don't want the basket to migrate to the other user. This can occur if a user is redirected to the login page if they try to access an admin page. In this scenario, we do not want to migrate the basket to the admin user; we want it to remain associated with the original user.

Modify the `Login` method of the `AccountController` class with the code shown in bold:

```
// POST: /Account/Login
[HttpPost]
[AllowAnonymous]
[ValidateAntiForgeryToken]
public async Task<ActionResult> Login(LoginViewModel model, string returnUrl)
{

    if (!ModelState.IsValid)
    {
        return View(model);
    }

    //check if a user was previously logged in without logging out. This can occur for example
    //if a logged in user is redirected to an admin page and then an admin user logs in
    bool userWasLoggedIn = false;
    if (!string.IsNullOrWhiteSpace(User.Identity.Name))
    {
        userWasLoggedIn = true;
    }

    // This doesn't count login failures towards account lockout
    // To enable password failures to trigger account lockout, change to shouldLockout: true
    var result = await SignInManager.PasswordSignInAsync(model.Email, model.Password,
        model.RememberMe, shouldLockout: false);
```

```
switch (result)
{
    case SignInStatus.Success:
        //this is needed to ensure the previous user's basket is not carried over
        if (userWasLoggedIn)
        {
            Session.Abandon();
        }
        Basket basket = Basket.GetBasket();
        //if there was no previously logged in user migrate the basket from GUID to the
        //username
        if (!userWasLoggedIn)
        {
            basket.MigrateBasket(model.Email);
        }
        return RedirectToLocal(returnUrl);
    case SignInStatus.LockedOut:
        return View("Lockout");
    case SignInStatus.RequiresVerification:
        return RedirectToAction("SendCode", new { ReturnUrl = returnUrl, RememberMe =
        model.RememberMe });
    case SignInStatus.Failure:
    default:
        ModelState.AddModelError("", "Invalid login attempt.");
        ViewBag.ReturnUrl = returnUrl;
        return View(model);
    }
}
```

To see the effect of this new code, start the web site without debugging add some products to your basket without logging in. Then log in as user2@mvcbabystore.com with the password P@ssw0rd1. The BasketID property for each BasketLine should now have been migrated to user2@mvcbabystore.com. Validate this by using Server Explorer in Visual Studio to view the data of the BasketLines database table (via the StoreContext connection). You should see that the records in the database relating to the current basket have been updated to use user2@mvcbabystore.com as the BasketID. Figure 8-14 shows some sample products we have added to the basket without logging in, after which we logged in as user2@mvcbabystore.com. Figure 8-15 shows the affected records of the database updated to use the username as the BasketID.

Figure 8-14. The basket migrated to user2@mvcbabystore.com

ID	BasketID	ProductID	Quantity	DateCreated
73	0e17cbdf-ad28-4b1a-b11d-86397...	6	1	12/04/2016 15:28:50
76	user2@mvcbabystore.com	6	2	12/04/2016 16:04:24
77	user2@mvcbabystore.com	5	3	12/04/2016 16:04:33

Figure 8-15. The BasketLines database showing the basket records updated to use user2@mvcbabystore.com as the BasketID

If you now log out of the web site, you will see that the basket summary still shows the items in the basket belonging to user2@mvcbabystore.com. To fix this issue, it is necessary to ensure that the session key is updated on logging out. Modify the LogOff method of the AccountController class as follows:

```
//
// POST: /Account/LogOff
[HttpPost]
[ValidateAntiForgeryToken]
public ActionResult LogOff()
{
    AuthenticationManager.SignOut(DefaultAuthenticationTypes.ApplicationCookie);
    Session.Abandon();
    return RedirectToAction("Index", "Home");
}
```

This Session.Abandon method abandons the current session when the user logs out and ensures that any user who follows the previously logged in user cannot see what was previously in the basket.

Migrating the Basket Upon Registration

It is also necessary to migrate the basket to use a user's e-mail address when a new user registers. A new user may have added items to an anonymous basket and in order to make a purchase they must then register. Therefore, after they have registered, we need to ensure they do not lose the contents of their shopping basket. Modify the HttpPost version of Register in the AccountController.cs file so that it contains code for migrating the basket to the new user as follows:

```
// POST: /Account/Register
[HttpPost]
[AllowAnonymous]
[ValidateAntiForgeryToken]
public async Task<ActionResult> Register(RegisterViewModel model, string returnUrl)
{
    if (ModelState.IsValid)
    {
        var user = new ApplicationUser {
            UserName = model.Email,
            Email = model.Email,
            DateOfBirth = model.DateOfBirth,
            FirstName = model.FirstName,
            LastName = model.LastName,
            Address = model.Address
        };
        var result = await UserManager.CreateAsync(user, model.Password);
        if (result.Succeeded)
        {
            await UserManager.AddToRoleAsync(user.Id, "Users");
            await SignInManager.SignInAsync(user, isPersistent:false, rememberBrowser:false);
            Basket basket = Basket.GetBasket();
            basket.MigrateBasket(model.Email);
            // For more information on how to enable account confirmation and password reset
            //    please visit http://go.microsoft.com/fwlink/?LinkID=320771
            // Send an email with this link
            // string code = await UserManager.GenerateEmailConfirmationTokenAsync(user.Id);
            // var callbackUrl = Url.Action("ConfirmEmail", "Account", new { userId = user.Id,
            //    code = code }, protocol: Request.Url.Scheme);
            // await UserManager.SendEmailAsync(user.Id, "Confirm your account", "Please
            // confirm your account by clicking <a href=\"" + callbackUrl + "\">here</a>");
            // redirect the user back to the page they came from if it was local otherwise send
            //    them to home page
            return RedirectToLocal(returnUrl);
        }
        ViewBag.ReturnUrl = returnUrl;
        AddErrors(result);
    }
}
```

```
    // If we got this far, something failed, redisplay form
    return View(model);
}
```

Start the web site without debugging and add some items to the basket. Now register as the new user user5@mvcbabystore.com using the values shown in Figure 8-16 and the password P@ssw0rd.

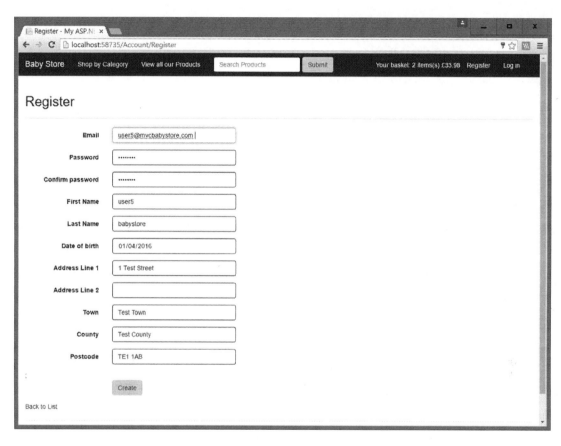

Figure 8-16. *Registering the user user5@mvcbabystore.com*

When you click the Create button, the user will be registered and the `BasketID` in the database table `BasketItems` for the records relating to the basket will be updated to `user5@mvcbabystore.com`, as shown in Figure 8-17.

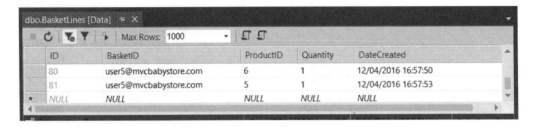

Figure 8-17. *The BasketID field updated for the basket belonging to the newly registered* `user5@mvcbabystore.com`

Summary

In this chapter, you saw how to create a shopping basket and allow a user to anonymously add and remove items from the basket and update the quantity of items in the basket. I showed you how to use ASP.NET MVC model binding to bind to a list in order to update the basket. You also learned how to display a basket summary by using the `Html.Action` helper method to call an action from a different controller and include its output in another view. Finally, you saw how to migrate the basket from using a randomly generated GUID to be associated with a real user when a user logs in or registers.

CHAPTER 9

■ ■ ■

Checkout: Creating and Viewing Orders

This chapter covers working with orders, including creating them via a checkout process, viewing the details of orders as either an administrator or a user, and searching or sorting them. We'll use the display and editor templates for the Address type that we created earlier in the book to simplify some of the view code in this chapter. We don't cover any payment provider integration during this book, but in a real-world system, you would need to add a step to the checkout process to obtain and verify payments prior to confirming an order.

■ **Note** If you want to follow along with the code in this chapter, you must either have completed Chapter 8 or download Chapter 8's source code from `www.apress.com` as a starting point.

Modeling Orders

We are going to model orders in a similar way to the basket, with an order consisting of a list of order lines; however when we modeled a basket, we did not store the basket in the database, whereas we are going to store both order and order lines in the database to model orders. We are going to add a one-to-many relationship between users and orders, where a user can have many orders but an order is placed only by a single user. Add two new classes to the Models folder, in the Order.cs and OrderLine.cs files, as follows:

```
using System;
using System.Collections.Generic;
using System.ComponentModel.DataAnnotations;

namespace BabyStore.Models
{
    public class Order
    {
        [Display(Name = "Order ID")]
        public int OrderID { get; set; }
        [Display(Name = "User")]
        public string UserID { get; set; }
        [Display(Name = "Deliver to")]
        public string DeliveryName { get; set; }
```

```
        [Display(Name = "Delivery Address")]
        public Address DeliveryAddress { get; set; }
        [Display(Name = "Total Price")]
        [DataType(DataType.Currency)]
        [DisplayFormat(DataFormatString = "{0:c}")]
        public decimal TotalPrice { get; set; }
        [Display(Name = "Time of Order")]
        public DateTime DateCreated { get; set; }
        public List<OrderLine> OrderLines { get; set; }
    }
}


using System.ComponentModel.DataAnnotations;

namespace BabyStore.Models
{
    public class OrderLine
    {
        public int ID { get; set; }
        public int OrderID { get; set; }
        public int? ProductID { get; set; }
        public int Quantity { get; set; }
        public string ProductName { get; set; }
        [Display(Name = "Unit Price")]
        [DataType(DataType.Currency)]
        [DisplayFormat(DataFormatString = "{0:c}")]
        public decimal UnitPrice { get; set; }
        public virtual Product Product { get; set; }
        public virtual Order Order { get; set; }
    }
}
```

These two new classes will represent an order and the lines from the basket for the order. We store the
ProductName property in each OrderLines to maintain a record of the product bought even if the actual
product entity is deleted from the database. We also store the unit price in the OrderLines because this
will be the price at the time of the order; in the future, this could change so we'll record this as the order is
placed. The OrderLines will contain two foreign keys via the properties ProductID and OrderID to relate it to
a products and an order. ProductID is nullable because the web site allows products to be deleted, although
in a real system, products would probably be archived rather than deleted.

■ **Note**   Entity Framework 6 does not support cross-database querying, therefore we have not included a
navigational property to the ApplicationUser class in the Order class. Instead, we'll use Entity Framework to
manually relate users to orders. Another possible alternative solution is to create a view in one of the databases
relating one to another, but I have not taken this approach in this book.

Next, update the DAL/StoreContext.cs file as follows to ensure the database context contains a
reference to the new Order and OrderLines classes.

```
using BabyStore.Models;
using System.Data.Entity;

namespace BabyStore.DAL
{
    public class StoreContext:DbContext
    {
        public DbSet<Product> Products { get; set; }
        public DbSet<Category> Categories { get; set; }
        public DbSet<ProductImage> ProductImages { get; set; }
        public DbSet<ProductImageMapping> ProductImageMappings { get; set; }
        public DbSet<BasketLine> BasketLines { get; set; }
        public DbSet<Order> Orders { get; set; }
        public DbSet<OrderLine> OrderLines { get; set; }
    }
}
```

Creating Sample Order Data and Updating the Database

Before we proceed with updating the database for the new Order and OrderLines entities, we're going to add some extra code to the Seed method of the Migrations\StoreConfiguration.cs file to create some sample Order and OrderLines data, as follows:

```
protected override void Seed(BabyStore.DAL.StoreContext context)
{
...previous code omitted for brevity...
    var orders = new List<Order>
    {
        new Order { DeliveryAddress = new Address { AddressLine1="1 Some Street",
            Town="Town1", County="County", Postcode="PostCode" }, TotalPrice=4.99M,
            UserID="admin@example.com", DateCreated=new DateTime(2014, 1, 1) ,
            DeliveryName="Admin" },
        new Order { DeliveryAddress = new Address { AddressLine1="1 Some Street",
            Town="Town1", County="County", Postcode="PostCode" }, TotalPrice=2.99M,
            UserID="admin@example.com", DateCreated=new DateTime(2014, 1, 2) ,
            DeliveryName="Admin" },
        new Order { DeliveryAddress = new Address { AddressLine1="1 Some Street",
            Town="Town1", County="County", Postcode="PostCode" }, TotalPrice=1.99M,
            UserID="admin@example.com", DateCreated=new DateTime(2014, 1, 3) ,
            DeliveryName="Admin" },
        new Order { DeliveryAddress = new Address { AddressLine1="1 Some Street",
            Town="Town1", County="County", Postcode="PostCode" }, TotalPrice=24.99M,
            UserID="admin@example.com", DateCreated=new DateTime(2014, 1, 4) ,
            DeliveryName="Admin" },
        new Order { DeliveryAddress = new Address { AddressLine1="1 Some Street",
            Town="Town1", County="County", Postcode="PostCode" }, TotalPrice=8.99M,
            UserID="admin@example.com", DateCreated=new DateTime(2014, 1, 5) ,
            DeliveryName="Admin" }
    };
```

```
    orders.ForEach(c => context.Orders.AddOrUpdate(o => o.DateCreated, c));
    context.SaveChanges();

    var orderLines = new List<OrderLine>
    {
        new OrderLine { OrderID = 1, ProductID = products.Single( c=> c.Name == "Sleep
            Suit").ID, ProductName="Sleep Suit", Quantity=1, UnitPrice=products.Single( c=>
            c.Name == "Sleep Suit").Price },
        new OrderLine { OrderID = 2, ProductID = products.Single( c=> c.Name == "Vest").ID,
            ProductName="Vest", Quantity=1, UnitPrice=products.Single( c=> c.Name ==
            "Vest").Price },
        new OrderLine { OrderID = 3, ProductID = products.Single( c=> c.Name == "Orange and
            Yellow Lion").ID, ProductName="Orange and Yellow Lion", Quantity=1,
            UnitPrice=products.Single( c=> c.Name == "Orange and Yellow Lion").Price },
        new OrderLine { OrderID = 4, ProductID = products.Single( c=> c.Name == "3 Pack of
            Bottles").ID, ProductName="3 Pack of Bottles", Quantity=1,
            UnitPrice=products.Single( c=> c.Name == "3 Pack of Bottles").Price },
        new OrderLine { OrderID = 5, ProductID = products.Single( c=> c.Name == "3 Pack of
            Bibs").ID, ProductName="3 Pack of Bibs", Quantity=1, UnitPrice=products.Single(
            c=> c.Name == "3 Pack of Bibs").Price }
    };

    orderLines.ForEach(c => context.OrderLines.AddOrUpdate(ol => ol.OrderID, c));
    context.SaveChanges();
}
```

Ensure that you add the statement using System; to the top of the file. Here the DateCreated property is used to distinguish which orders to update and the OrderID property is used to decide which OrderLines to update. These properties are used because the dates are unique and in the past; therefore, the Seed method won't get any conflicts with new orders and we know that the OrderID starts from 1 in sequence and is the easiest way to ensure we don't get any conflicts when updating the OrderLines. Using other properties such as ProductID or UnitPrice will cause an error informing you that more than one item exists in the sequence because the Seed method will find duplicate records if additional orders have been placed by web site users.

Next, open the Package Manager Console and run the following commands to create a new migration named addorders. Update the database to add new tables for Orders and OrderLines:

```
add-migration addorders -Configuration StoreConfiguration
update-database -Configuration StoreConfiguration
```

Open Server Explorer and expand the StoreContext connection. You should be able to see new tables for Orders and OrderLines, as shown in Figure 9-1.

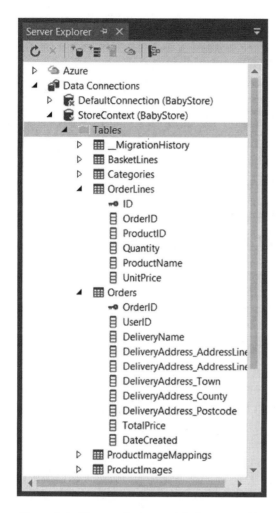

Figure 9-1. *The new Orders and OrderLines tables expanded in Server Explorer*

The `Orders` table contains fields prefixed with `DeliveryAddress` to represent the delivery address fields, because the `Order` class contains a `DeliveryAddress` property composed of the `Address` type.

Next, view the data of both the tables. You should see that the sample data entered by the `Seed` method of the `Migrations\StoreConfiguration.cs` file is now stored in the `OrderLines` and `Orders` tables, as shown in Figure 9-2 and 9-3, respectively.

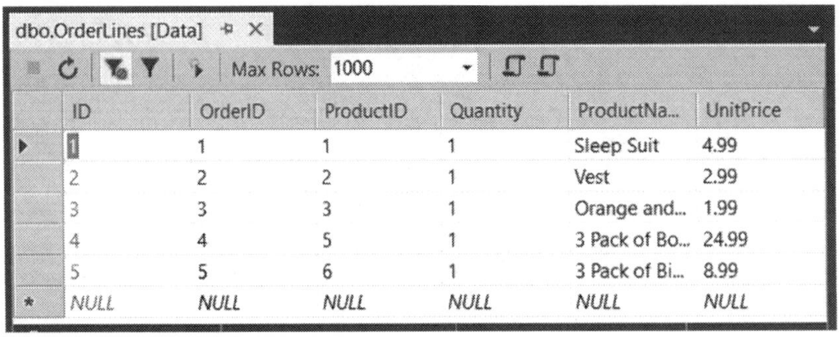

dbo.OrderLines [Data]

ID	OrderID	ProductID	Quantity	ProductNa...	UnitPrice
1	1	1	1	Sleep Suit	4.99
2	2	2	1	Vest	2.99
3	3	3	1	Orange and...	1.99
4	4	5	1	3 Pack of Bo...	24.99
5	5	6	1	3 Pack of Bi...	8.99
NULL	NULL	NULL	NULL	NULL	NULL

Figure 9-2. *The sample data in the OrderLines table*

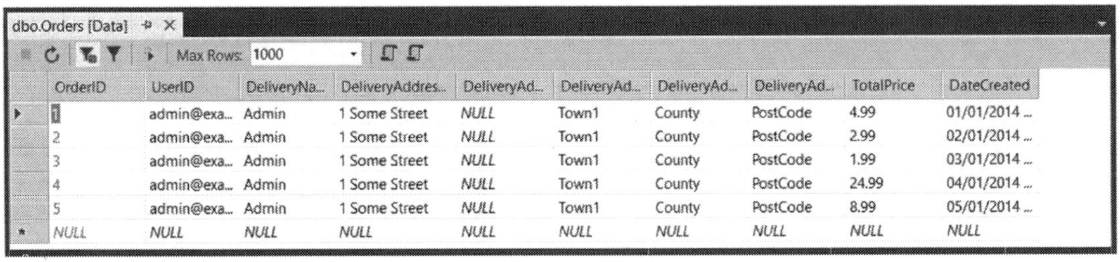

dbo.Orders [Data]

OrderID	UserID	DeliveryNa...	DeliveryAddres...	DeliveryAd...	DeliveryAd...	DeliveryAd...	DeliveryAd...	TotalPrice	DateCreated
1	admin@exa...	Admin	1 Some Street	NULL	Town1	County	PostCode	4.99	01/01/2014 ...
2	admin@exa...	Admin	1 Some Street	NULL	Town1	County	PostCode	2.99	02/01/2014 ...
3	admin@exa...	Admin	1 Some Street	NULL	Town1	County	PostCode	1.99	03/01/2014 ...
4	admin@exa...	Admin	1 Some Street	NULL	Town1	County	PostCode	24.99	04/01/2014 ...
5	admin@exa...	Admin	1 Some Street	NULL	Town1	County	PostCode	8.99	05/01/2014 ...
NULL	NULL	NULL	NULL	NULL	NULL	NULL	NULL	NULL	NULL

Figure 9-3. *The sample data in the Orders table*

Displaying Order Data

Adding an OrdersController Class

In order to start managing the order data, you need to add a new controller called `OrdersController` to the `Controllers` folder. You do this using the scaffolding option MVC5 Controller with Views, Using Entity Framework, based on the `Order` model class and using the `StoreContext` as the data context class and generate views. Figure 9-4 shows the options to choose.

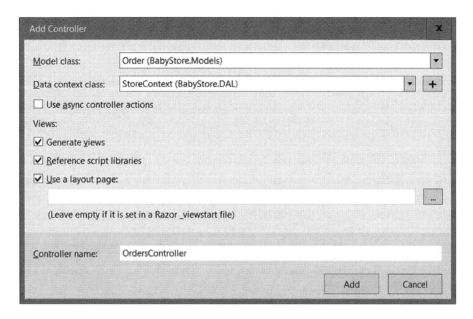

Figure 9-4. *Adding a new OrderController class with views*

In the new controller, delete the `Edit` and `Delete` methods, as they won't be used in this project.

Displaying a List of Orders

To make an order or view orders, it is necessary to be logged in. First, annotate the `OrdersController` class with [`Authorize`] as shown:

```
[Authorize]
public class OrdersController : Controller
{
```

This will ensure that a user must be logged in to use the methods of the `OrdersController` class. Next, to display a list of orders, update the `Index` method as follows in order to control what it shown to the user. When an admin user is logged in, they can see every order, but when a normal user is logged in, then they can only see their own orders:

```
// GET: Orders
public ActionResult Index()
{
    if (User.IsInRole("Admin"))
    {
        return View(db.Orders.ToList());
    }
    else
    {
        return View(db.Orders.Where(o => o.UserID == User.Identity.Name));
    }
}
```

Now modify the auto-generated Views/Orders.Index.cshtml file so that the heading is updated and the OrderID is shown. Ensure that the links to create, edit, and delete orders are removed:

```
@model IEnumerable<BabyStore.Models.Order>

@{
    ViewBag.Title = "Orders";
}

<h2>@ViewBag.Title</h2>

<table class="table">
    <tr>
        <th>
            @Html.DisplayNameFor(model => model.OrderID)
        </th>
        <th>
            @Html.DisplayNameFor(model => model.UserID)
        </th>
        <th>
            @Html.DisplayNameFor(model => model.DeliveryName)
        </th>
        <th>
            @Html.DisplayNameFor(model => model.DeliveryAddress)
        </th>
        <th>
            @Html.DisplayNameFor(model => model.TotalPrice)
        </th>
        <th>
            @Html.DisplayNameFor(model => model.DateCreated)
        </th>
        <th></th>
    </tr>

@foreach (var item in Model) {
    <tr>
        <td>
            @Html.DisplayFor(modelItem => item.OrderID)
        </td>
        <td>
            @Html.DisplayFor(modelItem => item.UserID)
        </td>
        <td>
            @Html.DisplayFor(modelItem => item.DeliveryName)
        </td>
        <td>
            @Html.DisplayFor(modelItem => item.DeliveryAddress)
        </td>
        <td>
            @Html.DisplayFor(modelItem => item.TotalPrice)
        </td>
```

```
        <td>
            @Html.DisplayFor(modelItem => item.DateCreated)
        </td>
        <td>
            @Html.ActionLink("Details", "Details", new { id=item.OrderID })
        </td>
    </tr>
}
</table>
```

■ **Note**   This file uses @Html.DisplayFor(modelItem => item.DeliveryAddress) to display the details of the delivery address for the order. This in turn uses the file Views\Shared\DisplayTemplates\Address.cshtml created earlier in the project.

To see the new Index method of the OrdersController class and the updated Orders index view in action, start the web site without debugging and enter the URL /Orders (e.g., http://localhost:58735/Orders) to access the new Orders index page. You will be prompted to log in because of the [Authorize] attribute added to the OrdersController class, so log in as the user admin@mvcbabystore.com using the password Adm1n@mvcbabystore.com.

You should now see the new Orders index HTML pages showing all the orders in the system (i.e., the ones that we added using the Seed method when updating the database), as shown in Figure 9-5.

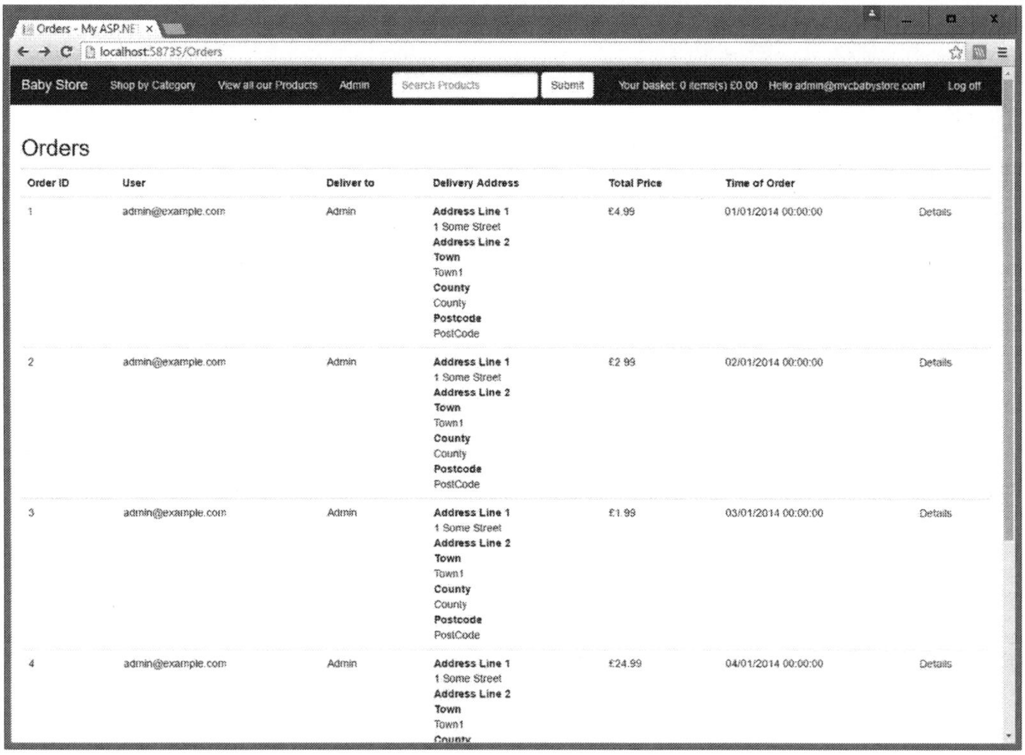

Figure 9-5. *The list of orders in the system as viewed by an admin user*

Now log in as the user user5@mvcbabystore.com using the password P@ssw0rd and access the Orders index page again. This time you will not see any orders because this user has not yet placed any and this user cannot see any of the other orders in the system.

Displaying Order Details

To display the order details, first update the Details method of the OrdersController class. This modification is necessary to ensure that a user cannot view another user's orders. The code will only allow users to view the detail of an order if either they are an admin user or they are the user who the order is for. It also includes the OrderLines property in the order prior to passing it to the view using eager loading:

```
// GET: Orders/Details/5
public ActionResult Details(int? id)
{
    if (id == null)
    {
        return new HttpStatusCodeResult(HttpStatusCode.BadRequest);
    }
    Order order = db.Orders.Include(o => o.OrderLines).Where(o => o.OrderID ==
        id).SingleOrDefault();

    if (order == null)
    {
        return HttpNotFound();
    }

    if (order.UserID == User.Identity.Name || User.IsInRole("Admin"))
    {
        return View(order);
    }
    else
    {
        return new HttpStatusCodeResult(HttpStatusCode.Unauthorized);
    }
}
```

Next, update the Views\Orders\Details.cshtml file to display the OrderLines related to each order, display the order's ID and the total price at the top of the order's details, and then remove the link to edit the order as follows:

```
@model BabyStore.Models.Order

@{
    ViewBag.Title = "Order Details";
}

<h2>@ViewBag.Title</h2>
```

```
<hr />
<div class="row">
    <div class="col-md-8">
        <h4>Items(s)</h4>
    </div>
    <div class="col-md-2">
        <h4>Quantity</h4>
    </div>
    <div class="col-md-2">
        <h4>Unit Price</h4>
    </div>
</div>
@foreach (var item in Model.OrderLines)
{
    <div class="row">
        <div class="col-md-8">@Html.DisplayFor(pn => item.ProductName)</div>
        <div class="col-md-2">@Html.DisplayFor(q => item.Quantity)</div>
        <div class="col-md-2">@Html.DisplayFor(up => item.UnitPrice)</div>
    </div>
}
<hr />
<div>
    <dl class="dl-horizontal">
        <dt>
            @Html.DisplayNameFor(model => model.TotalPrice)
        </dt>

        <dd>
            @Html.DisplayFor(model => model.TotalPrice)
        </dd>

        <dt>
            @Html.DisplayNameFor(model => model.OrderID)
        </dt>

        <dd>
            @Html.DisplayFor(model => model.OrderID)
        </dd>

        <dt>
            @Html.DisplayNameFor(model => model.UserID)
        </dt>

        <dd>
            @Html.DisplayFor(model => model.UserID)
        </dd>

        <dt>
            @Html.DisplayNameFor(model => model.DeliveryName)
        </dt>
```

```
            <dd>
                @Html.DisplayFor(model => model.DeliveryName)
            </dd>

            <dt>
                @Html.DisplayNameFor(model => model.DeliveryAddress)
            </dt>

            <dd>
                @Html.DisplayFor(model => model.DeliveryAddress)
            </dd>

            <dt>
                @Html.DisplayNameFor(model => model.DateCreated)
            </dt>

            <dd>
                @Html.DisplayFor(model => model.DateCreated)
            </dd>

    </dl>
</div>
<p>
    @Html.ActionLink("Back to List", "Index")
</p>
```

Start the web site without debugging, then enter the URL /Orders and log in as the user admin@
mvcbabystore.com using the password Adm1n@mvcbabystore.com. Click on the Details link for the order with
the order ID of 1. You should now see the details of the order, as shown in Figure 9-6.

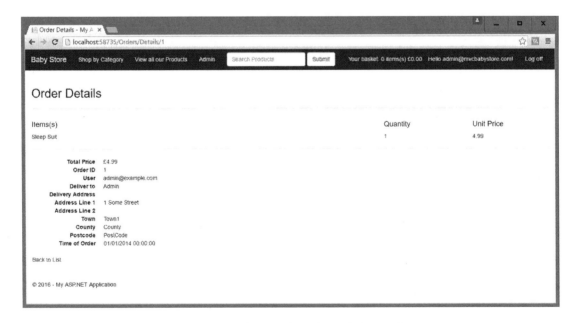

Figure 9-6. *The updated Order Details page showing the order with the ID of 1*

If you now log in as one of the users who is not in the admin role and enter the URL /Orders/Details/1, then you will be prompted to log in. Unless you then log in as an admin user, you will be continuously returned to the login page and will not be able to see the order details.

Placing an Order

We are going to create a simple ordering process that allows users to review their orders prior to submitting them. During this process, users can edit the delivery address details.

Creating an Order for Review

First obtain a user manager in the OrdersController class using the same code you used in previous chapters as shown in bold. We are using this code to access user information when creating first creating an order to be reviewed:

```
using System;
using System.Collections.Generic;
using System.Data;
using System.Data.Entity;
using System.Linq;
using System.Net;
using System.Web;
using System.Web.Mvc;
using BabyStore.DAL;
using BabyStore.Models;
using Microsoft.AspNet.Identity.Owin;

namespace BabyStore.Controllers
{

    [Authorize]
    public class OrdersController : Controller
    {
        private StoreContext db = new StoreContext();

        private ApplicationUserManager _userManager;

        public ApplicationUserManager UserManager
        {
            get
            {
                return _userManager ??
                    HttpContext.GetOwinContext().GetUserManager<ApplicationUserManager>();
            }
            private set
            {
                _userManager = value;
            }
        }
    }
...following code omitted for brevity...
```

Next, rename the GET version of the Create method in the OrdersController class to Review and update it as shown to obtain the current basket details and transfer them to a new Order object.

```
// GET: Orders/Review
public async Task<ActionResult> Review()
{
    Basket basket = Basket.GetBasket();
    Order order = new Order();

    order.UserID = User.Identity.Name;
    ApplicationUser user = await UserManager.FindByNameAsync(order.UserID);
    order.DeliveryName = user.FirstName + " " + user.LastName;
    order.DeliveryAddress = user.Address;
    order.OrderLines = new List<OrderLine>();
    foreach (var basketLine in basket.GetBasketLines())
    {
        OrderLine line = new OrderLine { Product = basketLine.Product, ProductID =
            basketLine.ProductID, ProductName = basketLine.Product.Name, Quantity =
            basketLine.Quantity, UnitPrice = basketLine.Product.Price };
        order.OrderLines.Add(line);
    }
    order.TotalPrice = basket.GetTotalCost();
    return View(order);
}
```

Ensure you add the using statement using System.Threading.Tasks; to the top of the file. We changed the method to be asynchronous in order to use the UserManager's FindByNameAsync method. The method then gets the current basket and creates a new order, then finds the current user and assigns their details to the order, and finally adds all the basketItems to the order. The order is then passed to the view so that that the user can review it and edit it or confirm and submit it.

Displaying an Order for Review

First rename the Views/Orders/Create.cshtml file to Review.cshtml. Next, update the file with the changes shown in bold in the following code:

```
@model BabyStore.Models.Order

@{
    ViewBag.Title = "Review Your Order";
}

<h2>@ViewBag.Title</h2>

@using (Html.BeginForm("Create", "Orders"))
{
    @Html.AntiForgeryToken()
```

```html
<div class="form-horizontal">
    <hr />
    @Html.ValidationSummary(true, "", new { @class = "text-danger" })
    <div class="row">
        <div class="col-md-2"><label>Item</label></div>
        <div class="col-md-2"><label>Quantity</label></div>
        <div class="col-md-2"><label>Unit Price</label></div>
    </div>

    @foreach (var item in Model.OrderLines)
    {
        <div class="row">
            <div class="col-md-2">@Html.DisplayFor(modelItem => item.Product.Name)</div>
            <div class="col-md-2">@Html.DisplayFor(modelItem => item.Quantity)</div>
            <div class="col-md-2">@Html.DisplayFor(modelItem => item.UnitPrice)</div>
        </div>
    }

    <div class="form-group">
        @Html.LabelFor(model => model.TotalPrice, htmlAttributes: new { @class =
        "control-
            label col-md-2" })
        <div class="col-md-10 form-control-static">
            @Html.DisplayFor(model => Model.TotalPrice)
            @Html.HiddenFor(model => Model.TotalPrice)
        </div>
    </div>

    <div class="form-group">
        @Html.LabelFor(model => model.UserID, htmlAttributes: new { @class = "control-
            labelcol-md-2" })
        <div class="col-md-10 form-control-static">
            @Html.DisplayFor(model => Model.UserID)
            @Html.HiddenFor(model => Model.UserID)
        </div>
    </div>

    <div class="form-group">
        @Html.LabelFor(model => model.DeliveryName, htmlAttributes: new { @class =
            "control-label col-md-2" })
        <div class="col-md-10">
            @Html.EditorFor(model => model.DeliveryName, new { htmlAttributes = new {
                @class = "form-control" } })
            @Html.ValidationMessageFor(model => model.DeliveryName, "", new { @class =
                "text-danger" })
        </div>
    </div>
```

```
    @Html.EditorFor(model => model.DeliveryAddress)

    <div class="form-group">
        <div class="col-md-offset-2 col-md-10">
            <input type="submit" value="Create" class="btn btn-default" />
        </div>
    </div>
        </div>
    </div>
}

<div>
    @Html.ActionLink("Edit Basket", "Index", "Basket")
</div>

@section Scripts {
    @Scripts.Render("~/bundles/jqueryval")
}
```

The view has been updated so that it now displays details of each order line and the details of the user, including allowing the delivery name and address to be edited if required. The form has been updated so that it targets the Create action method in the OrdersController class rather than the Review method.

To see how the new code works, we first need a way to allow users to move from the basket to the Orders Review view so add a new button to the \Views\Basket\Index.cshtml file to target the Review method of the OrdersController, as follows:

```
@model BabyStore.ViewModels.BasketViewModel

@{
    ViewBag.Title = "Your Basket";
}

<h2>@ViewBag.Title</h2>
@if (Model.BasketLines.Count() > 0)
{
    <div>
        @using (Html.BeginForm("UpdateBasket", "Basket"))
        {
            @Html.AntiForgeryToken();
            <input class="btn btn-sm btn-success" type="submit" value="Update Basket" />
            <hr />
            <div class="row">
                <div class="col-md-4"><label>Item</label></div>
                <div class="col-md-3"><label>Quantity</label></div>
                <div class="col-md-1"><label>Price</label></div>
                <div class="col-md-1"><label>Subtotal</label></div>
            </div>
            <hr />
            for (int i = 0; i < Model.BasketLines.Count; i++)
            {
```

```
<div class="row">
    <div class="col-md-4">
        @Html.ActionLink(Model.BasketLines[i].Product.Name, "Details",
        "Products",
            new { id = Model.BasketLines[i].ProductID }, null)<br />
        @if (Model.BasketLines[i].Product.ProductImageMappings != null &&
            Model.BasketLines[i].Product.ProductImageMappings.Any())
        {
            <a href="@Url.Action("Details", "Products", new { id =
                Model.BasketLines[i].ProductID })">
                <img src="@(Url.Content(Constants.ProductThumbnailPath) +
                    Model.BasketLines[i].Product.ProductImageMappings.
                    OrderBy(pim
                    => pim.ImageNumber).ElementAt(0).ProductImage.FileName)">
            </a>
        }
    </div>
    <div class="col-md-3">
        @Html.HiddenFor(productID => Model.BasketLines[i].ProductID)
        @Html.TextBoxFor(quantity => Model.BasketLines[i].Quantity)
        <p>
            @Html.ValidationMessageFor(quantity =>
                Model.BasketLines[i].Quantity,"", new { @class = "text-danger" })
        </p>
    </div>
    <div class="col-md-1">
        @Html.DisplayFor(price => Model.BasketLines[i].Product.Price)
    </div>
    <div class="col-md-1">
        @((Model.BasketLines[i].Quantity *
            Model.BasketLines[i].Product.Price).ToString("c"))
    </div>
    <div class="col-md-1">
        @Html.ActionLink("Remove", "RemoveLine", "Basket", new { id =
            Model.BasketLines[i].Product.ID }, null)
    </div>
</div>
<hr />
}
}
<div class="row">
    <div class="col-md-8">
        @Html.DisplayNameFor(model => model.TotalCost)
    </div>
    <div class="col-md-1">
        @Html.DisplayFor(model => model.TotalCost)
    </div>
```

```
        <div class="col-md-1">
            @Html.ActionLink("Order Now", "Review", "Orders", null, new { @class = "btn
                btn-sm btn-success" })
        </div>
    </div>
</div>
}
else
{
    <p>Your Basket is empty</p>
}
<div>
    @Html.ActionLink("Continue Shopping", "Index", "Products")
</div>

@section Scripts {
    @Scripts.Render("~/bundles/jqueryval")
}
```

Now start the web site without debugging and add some items to the basket. Then in the basket, click the new Order Now button, as shown in Figure 9-7.

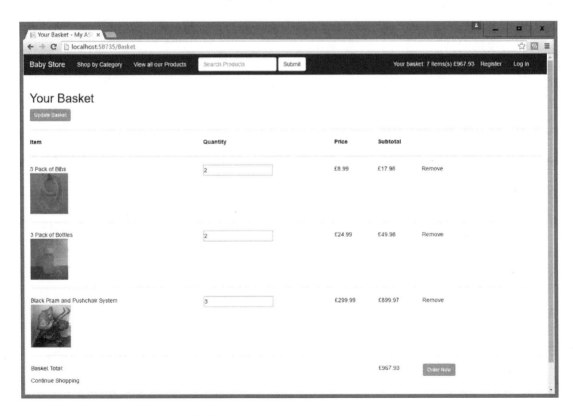

Figure 9-7. *The basket updated with the Order Now button*

After clicking the Order Now button and after logging in, you will be directed to review the order via the Orders Review page generated by the updated Views\Orders\Review.cshtml file, as shown in Figure 9-8. This allows you to edit the delivery details of the order, including the delivery name and the delivery address, plus you can return to the basket to edit its content.

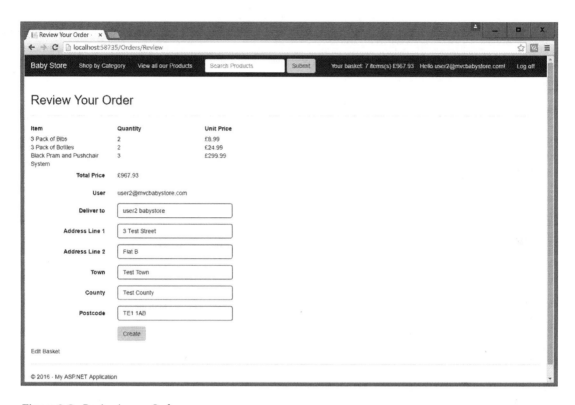

Figure 9-8. *Reviewing an Order*

Saving an Order to the Database

We are going to treat saving an order to the database as a two-step process, allowing the OrdersController class to save the order and then we are going to create the related OrderLines using the Basket class. We have taken this approach because we cannot simply add the Orders and OrderLines to the database using the OrdersController. We use the Basket class to obtain the data for OrderLines via the GetBasketLines method. Attempting to then save OrderLines to the database using Entity Framework in the BasketController results in an error because the BasketLines entity will then be tracked by two contexts.

Add a new method to the Models\Basket.cs file to create a list of OrderLines and then save them to the database as follows:

```
public decimal CreateOrderLines(int orderID)
{
    decimal orderTotal = 0;

    var basketLines = GetBasketLines();
```

```
    foreach (var item in basketLines)
    {
        OrderLine orderLine = new OrderLine
        {
            Product = item.Product,
            ProductID = item.ProductID,
            ProductName = item.Product.Name,
            Quantity = item.Quantity,
            UnitPrice = item.Product.Price,
            OrderID = orderID
        };

        orderTotal += (item.Quantity * item.Product.Price);
        db.OrderLines.Add(orderLine);
    }

    db.SaveChanges();
    EmptyBasket();
    return orderTotal;
}
```

The method takes an integer as an input parameter and this will be the ID of the order associated with the OrderLines to be saved.

Next update the HttpPost version of the Create method in the Controllers\OrdersController.cs file, as shown in the following code to save the order passed from the Review page. The DateCreated property of the order is updated to the current time and the UserID, DeliveryName, and DeliveryAddress are all taken from the Review page. The order is then saved and the CreateOrderLines method of the Basket class is called to save the related OrderLines and set the total price of the order. Once this is saved, the user is redirected to the Details action method, which will lead to them seeing the details of the placed order.

```
// POST: Orders/Create
// To protect from overposting attacks, please enable the specific properties you want to
bind to, for
// more details see http://go.microsoft.com/fwlink/?LinkId=317598.
[HttpPost]
[ValidateAntiForgeryToken]
public ActionResult Create([Bind(Include = "UserID,DeliveryName,DeliveryAddress")] Order
order)
{
    if (ModelState.IsValid)
    {
        order.DateCreated = DateTime.Now;
        db.Orders.Add(order);
        db.SaveChanges();

        //add the orderlines to the database after creating the order
        Basket basket = Basket.GetBasket();
        order.TotalPrice = basket.CreateOrderLines(order.OrderID);
        db.SaveChanges();
        return RedirectToAction("Details", new { id = order.OrderID });
    }
    return RedirectToAction("Review");
}
```

To see this code in action, start the web site without debugging and log in as user2@mvcbabystore. com with the password P@ssw0rd1. Add items to the shopping basket as shown in Figure 9-7 if they are not already in the basket. Click on the *Order Now* button and change the Deliver to Name in the review screen to test user. Click on the Create button. You should now see a new order created and the order details screen returned, as shown in Figure 9-9.

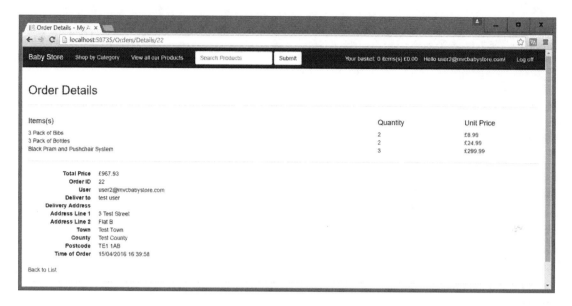

Figure 9-9. *A completed order displayed in the Order Details page*

If you now open the Orders database table via Server Explorer, you will see the new order created, as shown in Figure 9-10.

OrderID	UserID	DeliveryNa...	DeliveryAd...	DeliveryAd...	DeliveryAd...	DeliveryAd...	DeliveryAd...	TotalPrice	DateCreated
1	admin@exa...	Admin	1 Some Stre...	NULL	Town1	County	PostCode	4.99	01/01/2014 00:00:00
2	admin@exa...	Admin	1 Some Stre...	NULL	Town1	County	PostCode	2.99	02/01/2014 00:00:00
3	admin@exa...	Admin	1 Some Stre...	NULL	Town1	County	PostCode	1.99	03/01/2014 00:00:00
4	admin@exa...	Admin	1 Some Stre...	NULL	Town1	County	PostCode	24.99	04/01/2014 00:00:00
5	admin@exa...	Admin	1 Some Stre...	NULL	Town1	County	PostCode	8.99	05/01/2014 00:00:00
22	user2@mvc...	test user	3 Test Street	Flat B	Test Town	Test County	TE1 1AB	967.93	15/04/2016 16:39:58
NULL	NULL	NULL	NULL	NULL	NULL	NULL	NULL	NULL	NULL

Figure 9-10. *The orders database table with the new order highlighted*

The OrderLines table also now contains the lines associated with the order, as shown in Figure 9-11. Note that the OrderID has the same value as the OrderID of the new order; in this example, this is 22.

ID	OrderID	ProductID	Quantity	ProductName	UnitPrice
18	22	6	2	3 Pack of Bibs	8.99
19	22	5	2	3 Pack of Bottles	24.99
20	22	11	3	Black Pram and Pushchair System	299.99
NULL	NULL	NULL	NULL	NULL	NULL

Figure 9-11. *The OrderLines entries related to the new order*

Note that we didn't attempt to perform any complex model binding from the review screen to the Create method of the OrdersController because of the complexity of the model involved. As well as attempting to bind to a set of OrderLines, we would have also had to ensure that the product data was correctly modeled in the Review view and this would have been very complex to undertake. In this scenario, it is much simpler to revisit the database and retrieve the relevant information again.

Updating Product Deletion to Avoid Foreign Key Conflicts

We have a foreign key ProductID in the OrderLines entity referencing the Product entity. When a user deletes a product, we do not want the OrderLines to be deleted, so we created this as a nullable foreign key. To prevent a foreign key violation when a product is deleted, we need to set this foreign key to be null. As an alternative, we could have recorded the product ID but not as a foreign key; however, we've chosen to record the product's name instead in the ProductName property of the OrderLines entity. In a production system, you probably would not allow deletion of products and may simply mark them as no longer available.

To prevent the foreign key violation, update the Controllers\ProductController.cs DeleteConfirmed method as follows:

```
// POST: Products/Delete/5
[HttpPost, ActionName("Delete")]
[ValidateAntiForgeryToken]
public ActionResult DeleteConfirmed(int id)
{
    Product product = db.Products.Find(id);
    db.Products.Remove(product);

    var orderLines = db.OrderLines.Where(ol => ol.ProductID == id);
    foreach (var ol in orderLines)
    {
        ol.ProductID = null;
    }

    db.SaveChanges();
    return RedirectToAction("Index");
}
```

Adding Links to the Orders Index View

At the moment, there is no link to the Order index page. Update the Views\Manage\Index.cshtml file to add a link to the bottom of the page so a user can view their orders as shown in bold:

```
@model BabyStore.Models.ApplicationUser

@{
    ViewBag.Title = "My Details";
}

<h2>@ViewBag.Title</h2>

<div>
    <hr />
    <dl class="dl-horizontal">
        @Html.Partial("_UserDetailsPartial", Model)
        <dt>
            Password
        </dt>
        <dd>
            @Html.ActionLink("Change your password", "ChangePassword")
        </dd>
    </dl>
</div>

<p>
    @Html.ActionLink("Edit", "Edit", new { id = Model.Id })
</p>
<h2>@Html.ActionLink("View my orders", "Index", "Orders")</h2>
```

Next, add a link to the Admin index view file called \Views\Admin\Index so that the admin user can view all orders in the system from this view:

```
@{
    ViewBag.Title = "Admin";
}

<h2>@ViewBag.Title</h2>
<div class="container">
    <div class="row">
        @Html.ActionLink("Manage Images", "Index", "ProductImages")
    </div>
    <div class="row">
        @Html.ActionLink("Manage Roles", "Index", "RolesAdmin")
    </div>
    <div class="row">
        @Html.ActionLink("Manage Users", "Index", "UsersAdmin")
    </div>
```

```
<div class="row">
    @Html.ActionLink("View all Orders", "Index", "Orders")
</div>
</div>
```

Searching and Sorting Orders

So far, we have an orders page where users or admins can view orders, which is a good start. However, we may end up with a site with thousands of orders, so we need to filter and sort the orders. First, we will add a text search feature that will search all the text fields and the ID of an order. We will also include the products of the order in the search so that an order can be located when searching for a product.

Orders Text Searching

To add text search to orders, start by modifying the Index method of the Controllers\OrdersController.cs file as follows:

```
// GET: Orders
public ActionResult Index(string orderSearch)
{
    var orders = db.Orders.OrderBy(o => o.DateCreated).Include(o => o.OrderLines);

    if (!User.IsInRole("Admin"))
    {
        orders = orders.Where(o => o.UserID == User.Identity.Name);
    }

    if (!String.IsNullOrEmpty(orderSearch))
    {
        orders = orders.Where(o => o.OrderID.ToString().Equals(orderSearch) ||
            o.UserID.Contains(orderSearch) || o.DeliveryName.Contains(orderSearch) ||
            o.DeliveryAddress.AddressLine1.Contains(orderSearch) ||
            o.DeliveryAddress.AddressLine2.Contains(orderSearch) ||
            o.DeliveryAddress.Town.Contains(orderSearch) ||
            o.DeliveryAddress.County.Contains(orderSearch) ||
            o.DeliveryAddress.Postcode.Contains(orderSearch) ||
            o.TotalPrice.ToString().Equals(orderSearch) ||
            o.OrderLines.Any(ol => ol.ProductName.Contains(orderSearch)));
    }

    return View(orders);
}
```

We have replaced the entire contents of the method to retrieve all the orders from the database and filter them to the current user if required. We then perform a search over many fields within the order, including the OrderID, DeliveryName, all the DeliveryAddress fields, and the TotalPrice field. Finally we have allowed the user to search within the name of each product within each OrderLines by using the Any operator. We used eager loading at the beginning of the method when obtaining the orders by using the code Include(o => o.OrderLines) in order to allow searching against the OrderLines table.

Now add an HTML form to target this index method by modifying the Views\Orders\Index.cshtml page as follows:

```
@model IEnumerable<BabyStore.Models.Order>

@{
    ViewBag.Title = "Orders";
}

<h2>@ViewBag.Title</h2>
@using (Html.BeginForm("Index", "Orders", FormMethod.Get))
{
    <div class="row form-group">
        <div class="col-md-2">
            <label>Search Orders by ID or Text:</label>
        </div>
        <div class="col-md-3">
            @Html.TextBox("OrderSearch", null, new  {
                @class = "form-control",@placeholder = "Search Orders" })
        </div>
        <button type="submit" class="btn btn-default">Submit</button>
    </div>
}
<table class="table">
    <tr>
        <th>
            @Html.DisplayNameFor(model => model.OrderID)
        </th>
        <th>
            @Html.DisplayNameFor(model => model.UserID)
        </th>
        <th>
            @Html.DisplayNameFor(model => model.DeliveryName)
        </th>
        <th>
            @Html.DisplayNameFor(model => model.DeliveryAddress)
        </th>
        <th>
            @Html.DisplayNameFor(model => model.TotalPrice)
        </th>
        <th>
            @Html.DisplayNameFor(model => model.DateCreated)
        </th>
        <th></th>
    </tr>
```

357

```
@foreach (var item in Model)
{
    <tr>
        <td>
            @Html.DisplayFor(modelItem => item.OrderID)
        </td>
        <td>
            @Html.DisplayFor(modelItem => item.UserID)
        </td>
        <td>
            @Html.DisplayFor(modelItem => item.DeliveryName)
        </td>
        <td>
            @Html.DisplayFor(modelItem => item.DeliveryAddress)
        </td>
        <td>
            @Html.DisplayFor(modelItem => item.TotalPrice)
        </td>
        <td>
            @Html.DisplayFor(modelItem => item.DateCreated)
        </td>
        <td>
            @Html.ActionLink("Details", "Details", new { id = item.OrderID })
        </td>
    </tr>
}
</table>
```

This code generates an HTML form that uses GET to call the Index method of the OrdersController class. The new search form should appear as shown in Figure 9-12.

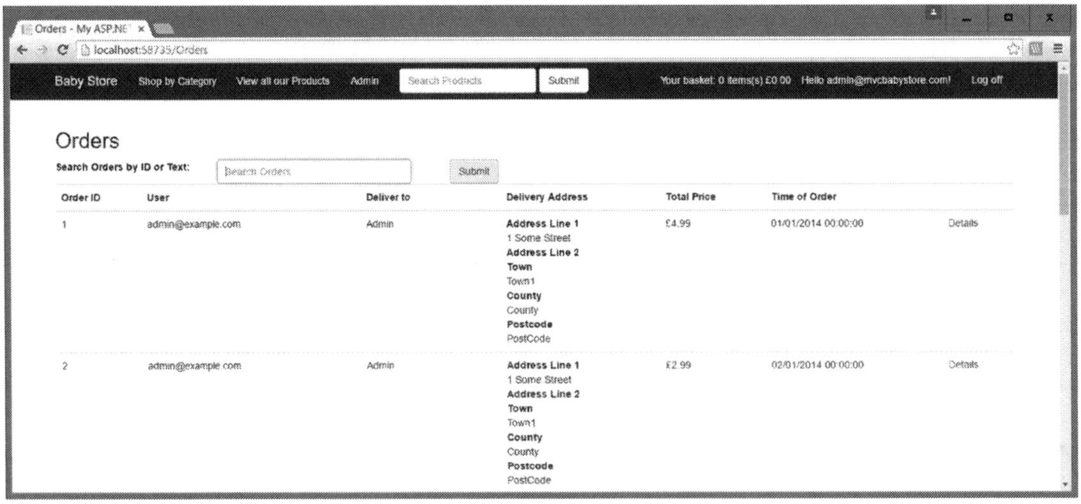

Figure 9-12. *The orders text search form added above the list of orders*

Searching Orders by Date

To add date searching to the Orders page, first modify the Index method of the OrdersController class as follows to add a start and end date between which to search:

```
// GET: Orders
public ActionResult Index(string orderSearch, string startDate, string endDate)
{
    var orders = db.Orders.OrderBy(o => o.DateCreated).Include(o => o.OrderLines);

    if (!User.IsInRole("Admin"))
    {
        orders = orders.Where(o => o.UserID == User.Identity.Name);
    }

    if (!String.IsNullOrEmpty(orderSearch))
    {
        orders = orders.Where(o => o.OrderID.ToString().Equals(orderSearch) ||
            o.UserID.Contains(orderSearch) || o.DeliveryName.Contains(orderSearch) ||
            o.DeliveryAddress.AddressLine1.Contains(orderSearch) ||
            o.DeliveryAddress.AddressLine2.Contains(orderSearch) ||
            o.DeliveryAddress.Town.Contains(orderSearch) ||
            o.DeliveryAddress.County.Contains(orderSearch) ||
            o.DeliveryAddress.Postcode.Contains(orderSearch) ||
            o.TotalPrice.ToString().Equals(orderSearch) ||
            o.OrderLines.Any(ol => ol.ProductName.Contains(orderSearch)));
    }

    DateTime parsedStartDate;
    if (DateTime.TryParse(startDate, out parsedStartDate))
    {
        orders = orders.Where(o => o.DateCreated >= parsedStartDate);
    }

    DateTime parsedEndDate;
    if (DateTime.TryParse(endDate, out parsedEndDate))
    {
        orders = orders.Where(o => o.DateCreated <= parsedEndDate);
    }

    return View(orders);
}
```

The DateTime.TryParseDate method has been used to parse the string passed from the form into a date and then the code searches the CreatedDate property of an order to determine if it is between the two date parameters. Either parameter can be left blank so, for example, you can search for all orders after a particular date. If the string entered was not a date, the search will not be performed.

To add some HTML controls to the form to search by date, add the following code to the Views\Orders\ Index.cshtml file in order to add two date HTML5 date picker controls. The value of each control is also set to the value used in the search by using the code value="@Request.QueryString["StartDate"]" and value="@Request.QueryString["EndDate"]".

```
@model IEnumerable<BabyStore.Models.Order>

@{
    ViewBag.Title = "Orders";
}

<h2>@ViewBag.Title</h2>
@using (Html.BeginForm("Index", "Orders", FormMethod.Get))
{
    <div class="row form-group">
        <div class="col-md-2">
            <label>Search Orders by ID or Text:</label>
        </div>
        <div class="col-md-3">
            @Html.TextBox("OrderSearch", null, new {@class = "form-control",
                @placeholder = "Search Orders" })
        </div>
        <div class="col-md-2">
            <label>Search between dates:</label>
        </div>
        <div class="col-md-2">
            <input type="date" id="StartDate" name="StartDate" class="form-control"
                value="@Request.QueryString["StartDate"]" />
        </div>
        <div class="col-md-2">
            <input type="date" id="EndDate" name="EndDate" class="form-control"
                value="@Request.QueryString["EndDate"]" />
        </div>
        <button type="submit" class="btn btn-default">Submit</button>
    </div>

}
<table class="table">
    <tr>
        <th>
            @Html.DisplayNameFor(model => model.OrderID)
        </th>
        <th>
            @Html.DisplayNameFor(model => model.UserID)
        </th>
        <th>
            @Html.DisplayNameFor(model => model.DeliveryName)
        </th>
        <th>
            @Html.DisplayNameFor(model => model.DeliveryAddress)
        </th>
        <th>
            @Html.DisplayNameFor(model => model.TotalPrice)
        </th>
```

```
        <th>
            @Html.DisplayNameFor(model => model.DateCreated)
        </th>
        <th></th>
    </tr>

    @foreach (var item in Model)
    {
        <tr>
            <td>
                @Html.DisplayFor(modelItem => item.OrderID)
            </td>
            <td>
                @Html.DisplayFor(modelItem => item.UserID)
            </td>
            <td>
                @Html.DisplayFor(modelItem => item.DeliveryName)
            </td>
            <td>
                @Html.DisplayFor(modelItem => item.DeliveryAddress)
            </td>
            <td>
                @Html.DisplayFor(modelItem => item.TotalPrice)
            </td>
            <td>
                @Html.DisplayFor(modelItem => item.DateCreated)
            </td>
            <td>
                @Html.ActionLink("Details", "Details", new { id = item.OrderID })
            </td>
        </tr>
    }
</table>
```

If you view the Orders page using Google Chrome (my browser of choice throughout the book), then you should see the new date inputs, as shown in Figure 9-13, with the ability to pick a date or enter one by hand.

Figure 9-13. *The new date search viewed in Google Chrome*

■ **Note** Google Chrome offers HTML5 support for date picker style controls, but other browser implementations differ. Firefox does not include any kind of date pickers and instead just displays two text boxes, whereas Microsoft Edge (the latest Microsoft browser) offers a scroll style mobile list to allow you to choose a date.

To see the new search in action, perform a search between the dates 02/01/2014 and 03/01/2014. You should see the search results showing to two orders between these dates that we previously entered in the Seed method, as shown in Figure 9-14.

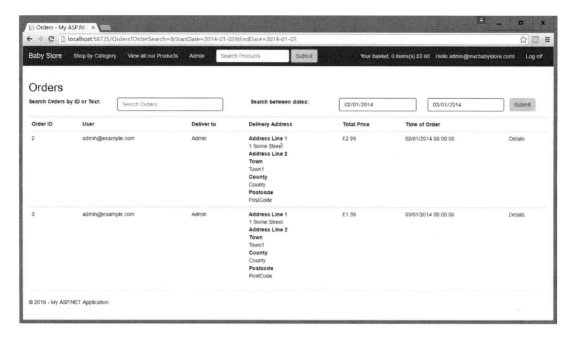

Figure 9-14. *Searching for orders between 02/01/2014 and 03/01/2014*

Sorting Orders

Previously, when sorting on the products index page, we used a view model. This is best practice when modeling additional data in the view that does not belong in the business model for the entity. There is an alternative approach to use the ViewBag object for small amounts of data. We will use this approach in the following code to demonstrate how it can be used. In the orders page we will allow sorting by the user field, total price, and date created (time of order). It doesn't make sense to allow sorting on the other properties since they can be searched for already. Modify the Index method of the OrdersController class as follows to allow sorting to take place:

```
// GET: Orders
public ActionResult Index(string orderSearch, string startDate, string endDate, string
    orderSortOrder)
{
    var orders = db.Orders.OrderBy(o => o.DateCreated).Include(o => o.OrderLines);

    if (!User.IsInRole("Admin"))
    {
        orders = orders.Where(o => o.UserID == User.Identity.Name);
    }
```

```
    if (!String.IsNullOrEmpty(orderSearch))
    {
        orders = orders.Where(o => o.OrderID.ToString().Equals(orderSearch) ||
            o.UserID.Contains(orderSearch) || o.DeliveryName.Contains(orderSearch) ||
            o.DeliveryAddress.AddressLine1.Contains(orderSearch) ||
            o.DeliveryAddress.AddressLine2.Contains(orderSearch) ||
            o.DeliveryAddress.Town.Contains(orderSearch) ||
            o.DeliveryAddress.County.Contains(orderSearch) ||
            o.DeliveryAddress.Postcode.Contains(orderSearch) ||
            o.TotalPrice.ToString().Equals(orderSearch) ||
            o.OrderLines.Any(ol => ol.ProductName.Contains(orderSearch)));
    }

    DateTime parsedStartDate;
    if (DateTime.TryParse(startDate, out parsedStartDate))
    {
        orders = orders.Where(o => o.DateCreated >= parsedStartDate);
    }

    DateTime parsedEndDate;
    if (DateTime.TryParse(endDate, out parsedEndDate))
    {
        orders = orders.Where(o => o.DateCreated <= parsedEndDate);
    }

    ViewBag.DateSort = String.IsNullOrEmpty(orderSortOrder) ? "date" : "";
    ViewBag.UserSort = orderSortOrder == "user" ? "user_desc" : "user";
    ViewBag.PriceSort = orderSortOrder == "price" ? "price_desc" : "price";

    switch (orderSortOrder)
    {
        case "user":
            orders = orders.OrderBy(o => o.UserID);
            break;
        case "user_desc":
            orders = orders.OrderByDescending(o => o.UserID);
            break;
        case "price":
            orders = orders.OrderBy(o => o.TotalPrice);
            break;
        case "price_desc":
            orders = orders.OrderByDescending(o => o.TotalPrice);
            break;
        case "date":
            orders = orders.OrderBy(o => o.DateCreated);
            break;
        default:
            orders = orders.OrderByDescending(o => o.DateCreated);
            break;
    }

    return View(orders);
}
```

In this new code, the ViewBag object is used to store values for the current date sort order, user sort order, and price sort order. By default the normal ascending sort order is used and if this has been chosen by the user then the corresponding descending sort order is used.

The switch statement uses the orderSortOrder parameter to decide which sort order to use. The default sort order when no sorting is chosen by the user is to sort by showing the most recent orders first (date created descending). To add some sorting links, modify the Views\Orders\Index.cshtml file as follows:

```
@model IEnumerable<BabyStore.Models.Order>

@{
    ViewBag.Title = "Orders";
}


<h2>@ViewBag.Title</h2>
@using (Html.BeginForm("Index", "Orders", FormMethod.Get))
{
    <div class="row form-group">
        <div class="col-md-2">
            <label>Search Orders by ID or Text:</label>
        </div>
        <div class="col-md-3">
            @Html.TextBox("OrderSearch", null, new {@class = "form-control",
                @placeholder = "Search Orders" })
        </div>
        <div class="col-md-2">
            <label>Search between dates:</label>
        </div>
        <div class="col-md-2">
            <input type="date" id="StartDate" name="StartDate" class="form-control"
                value="@Request.QueryString["StartDate"]" />
        </div>
        <div class="col-md-2">
            <input type="date" id="EndDate" name="EndDate" class="form-control"
                value="@Request.QueryString["EndDate"]" />
        </div>
        <button type="submit" class="btn btn-default">Submit</button>
    </div>

}
<table class="table">
    <tr>
        <th>
            @Html.DisplayNameFor(model => model.OrderID)
        </th>
        <th>
            @Html.ActionLink("User", "Index", new { orderSortOrder = ViewBag.UserSort })
        </th>
        <th>
            @Html.DisplayNameFor(model => model.DeliveryName)
        </th>
```

```
    <th>
        @Html.DisplayNameFor(model => model.DeliveryAddress)
    </th>
    <th>
        @Html.ActionLink("Total Price", "Index", new { orderSortOrder = ViewBag.
        PriceSort
            })
    </th>
    <th>
        @Html.ActionLink("Time of Order", "Index", new { orderSortOrder = ViewBag.
        DateSort
            })
    </th>
    <th></th>
</tr>

@foreach (var item in Model)
{
    <tr>
        <td>
            @Html.DisplayFor(modelItem => item.OrderID)
        </td>
        <td>
            @Html.DisplayFor(modelItem => item.UserID)
        </td>
        <td>
            @Html.DisplayFor(modelItem => item.DeliveryName)
        </td>
        <td>
            @Html.DisplayFor(modelItem => item.DeliveryAddress)
        </td>
        <td>
            @Html.DisplayFor(modelItem => item.TotalPrice)
        </td>
        <td>
            @Html.DisplayFor(modelItem => item.DateCreated)
        </td>
        <td>
            @Html.ActionLink("Details", "Details", new { id = item.OrderID })
        </td>
    </tr>
    }
</table>
```

If you now start the web site and perform sorting on the Orders index page, the sorting will work as expected; however, if you run a search and then try sorting, the search term will be lost and all the orders will be returned. To fix this, we need to add some code to the Index method of the OrdersController class as follows. This will force the program to remember the search term and any date searches.

```
// GET: Orders
public ActionResult Index(string orderSearch, string startDate, string endDate, string
    orderSortOrder)
{
    var orders = db.Orders.OrderBy(o => o.DateCreated).Include(o => o.OrderLines);

    if (!User.IsInRole("Admin"))
    {
        orders = orders.Where(o => o.UserID == User.Identity.Name);
    }

    if (!String.IsNullOrEmpty(orderSearch))
    {
        orders = orders.Where(o => o.OrderID.ToString().Equals(orderSearch) ||
            o.UserID.Contains(orderSearch) || o.DeliveryName.Contains(orderSearch) ||
            o.DeliveryAddress.AddressLine1.Contains(orderSearch) ||
            o.DeliveryAddress.AddressLine2.Contains(orderSearch) ||
            o.DeliveryAddress.Town.Contains(orderSearch) ||
            o.DeliveryAddress.County.Contains(orderSearch) ||
            o.DeliveryAddress.Postcode.Contains(orderSearch) ||
            o.TotalPrice.ToString().Equals(orderSearch) ||
            o.OrderLines.Any(ol => ol.ProductName.Contains(orderSearch)));
    }

    DateTime parsedStartDate;
    if (DateTime.TryParse(startDate, out parsedStartDate))
    {
        orders = orders.Where(o => o.DateCreated >= parsedStartDate);
    }

    DateTime parsedEndDate;
    if (DateTime.TryParse(endDate, out parsedEndDate))
    {
        orders = orders.Where(o => o.DateCreated <= parsedEndDate);
    }

    ViewBag.DateSort = String.IsNullOrEmpty(orderSortOrder) ? "date" : "";
    ViewBag.UserSort = orderSortOrder == "user" ? "user_desc" : "user";
    ViewBag.PriceSort = orderSortOrder == "price" ? "price_desc" : "price";
    ViewBag.CurrentOrderSearch = orderSearch;
    ViewBag.StartDate = startDate;
    ViewBag.EndDate = endDate;

    switch (orderSortOrder)
    {
        case "user":
            orders = orders.OrderBy(o => o.UserID);
            break;
        case "user_desc":
            orders = orders.OrderByDescending(o => o.UserID);
            break;
```

```
        case "price":
            orders = orders.OrderBy(o => o.TotalPrice);
            break;
        case "price_desc":
            orders = orders.OrderByDescending(o => o.TotalPrice);
            break;
        case "date":
            orders = orders.OrderBy(o => o.DateCreated);
            break;
        default:
            orders = orders.OrderByDescending(o => o.DateCreated);
            break;
    }

    return View(orders);
}
```

Next modify the \Views\Orders\Index.cshtml file to use these additional ViewBag entries and add them to each of the sorting links as follows:

```
@model IEnumerable<BabyStore.Models.Order>

@{
    ViewBag.Title = "Orders";
}

<h2>@ViewBag.Title</h2>
@using (Html.BeginForm("Index", "Orders", FormMethod.Get))
{
    <div class="row form-group">
        <div class="col-md-2">
            <label>Search Orders by ID or Text:</label>
        </div>
        <div class="col-md-3">
            @Html.TextBox("OrderSearch", null, new
    {
        @class = "form-control",
        @placeholder =
            "Search Orders"
    })
        </div>
        <div class="col-md-2">
            <label>Search between dates:</label>
        </div>
        <div class="col-md-2">
            <input type="date" id="StartDate" name="StartDate" class="form-control"
                    value="@Request.QueryString["StartDate"]" />
        </div>
```

```
        <div class="col-md-2">
            <input type="date" id="EndDate" name="EndDate" class="form-control"
                value="@Request.QueryString["EndDate"]" />
        </div>
        <button type="submit" class="btn btn-default">Submit</button>
    </div>

}
<table class="table">
    <tr>
        <th>
            @Html.DisplayNameFor(model => model.OrderID)
        </th>
        <th>
            @Html.ActionLink("User", "Index", new  {orderSortOrder = ViewBag.UserSort,
                orderSearch = ViewBag.CurrentOrderSearch,startdate = ViewBag.StartDate,
                endDate = ViewBag.EndDate })
        </th>
        <th>
            @Html.DisplayNameFor(model => model.DeliveryName)
        </th>
        <th>
            @Html.DisplayNameFor(model => model.DeliveryAddress)
        </th>
        <th>
            @Html.ActionLink("Total Price", "Index", new { orderSortOrder = ViewBag.
            PriceSort, orderSearch = ViewBag.CurrentOrderSearch, startdate = ViewBag.
            StartDate, endDate = ViewBag.EndDate })
        </th>
        <th>
            @Html.ActionLink("Time of Order", "Index", new  {orderSortOrder =
                ViewBag.DateSort,orderSearch = ViewBag.CurrentOrderSearch,
                startdate = ViewBag.StartDate, endDate = ViewBag.EndDate })
        </th>
        <th></th>
    </tr>

    @foreach (var item in Model)
    {
        <tr>
            <td>
                @Html.DisplayFor(modelItem => item.OrderID)
            </td>
            <td>
                @Html.DisplayFor(modelItem => item.UserID)
            </td>
            <td>
                @Html.DisplayFor(modelItem => item.DeliveryName)
            </td>
```

```
        <td>
            @Html.DisplayFor(modelItem => item.DeliveryAddress)
        </td>
        <td>
            @Html.DisplayFor(modelItem => item.TotalPrice)
        </td>
        <td>
            @Html.DisplayFor(modelItem => item.DateCreated)
        </td>
        <td>
            @Html.ActionLink("Details", "Details", new { id = item.OrderID })
        </td>
    </tr>
    }
</table>
```

The search term and any date searches carried out will now be remembered when a user performs a sort of the orders.

Summary

This chapter covered how to model a checkout process by creating an order from a basket. You also saw how to display a list of orders, view order details, and search and sort through orders, including searching by date. We'll build on the code in this chapter in the next chapter when we look at paging through orders.

CHAPTER 10

■ ■ ■

Advanced Scenarios and Common Workarounds

This chapter covers some of the more advanced topics of using ASP.NET MVC with Entity Framework, including how to code asynchronous database access code, how to deal with concurrent database updates where conflicting data edits may occur, and how to manually run SQL queries rather than using those generated by Entity Framework.

■ **Note** If you want to follow along with the code in this chapter, you must either have completed Chapter 9 or download Chapter 9's source code from `www.apress.com` as a starting point.

Asynchronous Database Access

In order to keep this application and book easier to follow, synchronous code has been used in the majority of the examples so far. Synchronous code ties up a thread until its operation has fully completed. A web server has a finite number of threads available and under high load, these may all be in tied up waiting for I/O operations involving the database. Using asynchronous code, these threads are freed up to enable the processing of other requests.

Microsoft's stance on asynchronous code is that it should be used unless you have a reason not to. One key thing to note about using asynchronous database code is that the LINQ queries should be executed within the controller rather than being deferred for calling when the view loads.

A Simple Asynchronous Example: Adding Best Sellers to the Home Page

To demonstrate asynchronous database access, we are going to retrieve the top-selling products from the order data in the database. First of all, we'll create a synchronous version of the code and then update it to be asynchronous.

Create a view model to hold the data to pass to the view. A view model is used because we are going to create a complex query based on the quantity of items sold, and data to the view model about the product, the number of items sold, and the product's images. First, create a new class file called BestSellersViewModel.cs in the ViewModels folder as follows:

```
using BabyStore.Models;

namespace BabyStore.ViewModels
{
    public class BestSellersViewModel
    {
        public Product Product { get; set; }
        public int SalesCount { get; set; }
        public string ProductImage { get; set; }
    }
}
```

Now update the Index method in the Controllers\HomeController.cs file so that it retrieves the top four best-selling products in a synchronous manner and returns them to the view:

```
using BabyStore.DAL;
using BabyStore.ViewModels;
using System.Linq;
using System.Web.Mvc;

namespace BabyStore.Controllers
{
    public class HomeController : Controller
    {
        private StoreContext db = new StoreContext();

        public ActionResult Index()
        {
            var topSellers = (from topProducts in db.OrderLines
                              where (topProducts.ProductID != null)
                              group topProducts by topProducts.Product into topGroup
                              select new BestSellersViewModel
                              {
                                  Product = topGroup.Key,
                                  SalesCount = topGroup.Sum(o => o.Quantity),
                                  ProductImage = topGroup.Key.ProductImageMappings.
                                  OrderBy(pim
                                      =>
                                      pim.ImageNumber).FirstOrDefault().ProductImage.FileName
                              }).OrderByDescending(tg => tg.SalesCount).Take(4);

            return View(topSellers);
        }
...following code omitted for brevity...
```

This code retrieves the top sellers from the database by querying the OrderLines table and selecting the top four products where the sum of the quantities ordered is highest. It also retrieves the main product image so that it can be displayed in the view. Note that this query checks that the ProductID property of OrderLine to ensure that the product still exists in the database. This way, any deleted products are excluded from the best-selling items.

In order to display the best-selling items in the home page, replace the contents of the Views\Home\Index.cshtml file as follows:

```
@model IEnumerable<BabyStore.ViewModels.BestSellersViewModel>
@{
    ViewBag.Title = "Baby Store Home Page";
}

<div class="jumbotron">
    <h1>Welcome to the Baby Store!</h1>
    <h2>Here is a selection of our best selling products</h2>
    <div class="row">
        @foreach (var item in Model)
        {
            <div class="col-md-3">
                @if (item.ProductImage != null)
                {
                    <a href="@Url.Action("Details", "Products", new { id = item.Product.ID
                        })">
                        <img src="@(Url.Content(Constants.ProductImagePath) +
                            item.ProductImage)">
                    </a>
                }
                <p>@Html.ActionLink(item.Product.Name, "Details", "Products", new { id =
                    item.Product.ID }, null)</p>
            </div>
        }
    </div>
    <p>@Html.ActionLink("Shop Now", "Index", "Products", null, new { @class = "btn btn-
primary
        btn-lg" })
    </p>
</div>
```

The view is based on an enumeration of BestSellerViewModels. It loops through the items in the enumeration and displays the name of the product and the main image as links to the product's details. The view also modifies some of the text and adds a Shop Now button, which goes to the Views/Products/Index.cshtml page. Figure 10-1 shows how the best-selling items now appear in the home page.

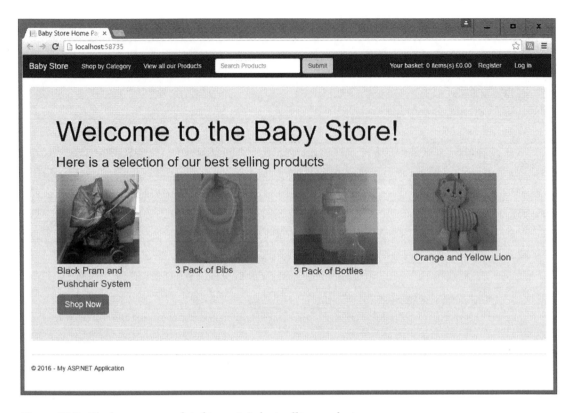

Figure 10-1. *The home page updated to contain best-selling products*

To convert the Index method to become asynchronous, make the changes shown in bold to the Controllers\HomeController.cs file:

```
using BabyStore.DAL;
using BabyStore.ViewModels;
using System.Linq;
using System.Web.Mvc;
using System.Threading.Tasks;
using System.Data.Entity;

namespace BabyStore.Controllers
{
    public class HomeController : Controller
    {
        private StoreContext db = new StoreContext();
```

```
public async Task<ActionResult> Index()
{
    var topSellers = (from topProducts in db.OrderLines
                      where (topProducts.ProductID != null)
                      group topProducts by topProducts.Product into topGroup
                      select new BestSellersViewModel
                      {
                          Product = topGroup.Key,
                          SalesCount = topGroup.Sum(o => o.Quantity),
                          ProductImage = topGroup.Key.ProductImageMappings.
                          OrderBy(pim
                            => pim.ImageNumber).FirstOrDefault().ProductImage.
                          FileName

                      }).OrderByDescending(tg => tg.SalesCount).Take(4);

    return View(await topSellers.ToListAsync());
}
...rest of code omitted for brevity
```

The code has been modified to add some using statements to support the other code changes and then the following four changes were made to the Index method:

- The method was marked as async so that the compiler knows this is now an asynchronous method.

- The return type is now Task<ActionResult>, which represents ongoing work with a return type of ActionResult.

- The await keyword was added to the code that executes the query. In simple terms, this effectively tells the compiler to split the method in two, with the first part starting the code asynchronously and then the second part is called when the operation completes.

- We added a call to ToListAsync() in order to ensure that the query to the database is called asynchronously within the controller. The previous version of this method did not call ToList() and deferred execution to the view.

In this example, we used the ToListAsync() method, but in other methods it may be necessary to use a different command. For example, in a Details method, we would need to change the Find() method to FindAsync().

■ **Tip** You can create asynchronous methods when creating a controller by checking the Use Async Controller Actions option.

Adding Asynchronous Paging

There is one flaw in the project with regard to making it asynchronous. Even if we converted all the controller methods to perform asynchronous database access with eager loading and modified all the views to remove any lazy loading, we currently use the PagedList package in the project and it is not asynchronous. There are some asynchronous paging packages available, but rather than rely on one of them, we are going to build one.

First of all, update the Index method of the Controllers/OrdersController.cs file, as highlighted in bold to make the method asynchronous and return a current page of orders rather than a full set:

```
// GET: Orders
public async Task<ActionResult> Index(string orderSearch, string startDate, string endDate,
    string orderSortOrder, int? page)
{
    var orders = db.Orders.OrderBy(o => o.DateCreated).Include(o => o.OrderLines);

    if (!User.IsInRole("Admin"))
    {
        orders = orders.Where(o => o.UserID == User.Identity.Name);
    }

    if (!String.IsNullOrEmpty(orderSearch))
    {
        orders = orders.Where(o => o.OrderID.ToString().Equals(orderSearch) ||
            o.UserID.Contains(orderSearch) ||
            o.DeliveryName.Contains(orderSearch) ||
            o.DeliveryAddress.AddressLine1.Contains(orderSearch) ||
            o.DeliveryAddress.AddressLine2.Contains(orderSearch) ||
            o.DeliveryAddress.Town.Contains(orderSearch) ||
            o.DeliveryAddress.County.Contains(orderSearch) ||
            o.DeliveryAddress.Postcode.Contains(orderSearch) ||
            o.TotalPrice.ToString().Equals(orderSearch) ||
            o.OrderLines.Any(ol => ol.ProductName.Contains(orderSearch)));
    }

    DateTime parsedStartDate;
    if (DateTime.TryParse(startDate, out parsedStartDate))
    {
        orders = orders.Where(o => o.DateCreated >= parsedStartDate);
    }

    DateTime parsedEndDate;
    if (DateTime.TryParse(endDate, out parsedEndDate))
    {
        orders = orders.Where(o => o.DateCreated <= parsedEndDate);
    }

    ViewBag.DateSort = String.IsNullOrEmpty(orderSortOrder) ? "date" : "";
    ViewBag.UserSort = orderSortOrder == "user" ? "user_desc" : "user";
    ViewBag.PriceSort = orderSortOrder == "price" ? "price_desc" : "price";
    ViewBag.CurrentOrderSearch = orderSearch;
    ViewBag.StartDate = startDate;
    ViewBag.EndDate = endDate;
```

```
switch (orderSortOrder)
{
    case "user":
        orders = orders.OrderBy(o => o.UserID);
        break;
    case "user_desc":
        orders = orders.OrderByDescending(o => o.UserID);
        break;
    case "price":
        orders = orders.OrderBy(o => o.TotalPrice);
        break;
    case "price_desc":
        orders = orders.OrderByDescending(o => o.TotalPrice);
        break;
    case "date":
        orders = orders.OrderBy(o => o.DateCreated);
        break;
    default:
        orders = orders.OrderByDescending(o => o.DateCreated);
        break;
}
int currentPage = (page ?? 1);
var currentPageOfOrders = await orders.Skip((currentPage - 1) *
    Constants.PageItems).Take(Constants.PageItems).ToListAsync();
return View(currentPageOfOrders);
}
```

This code adds an optional input parameter named page and then assigns this to a variable named currentPage. If page is null then the value of currentPage is set to 1. Following this, a new variable is created named currentPageOfOrders and it's assigned the orders to display on the current page. This is computed using the LINQ Skip and Take methods and the PageItems constant (this is currently set to 3). For example, if the user is on the first page, this code skips zero products ((1-1)*3) and then takes the first three products. If the user is on the second page, the code skips the first three products ((2-1)*3) and then takes the next three products, thus giving products 4 to 6 in the results page and so on. ToListAsync() is called to access the database asynchronously and the currentPageOfOrders is passed to the view.

To see how this code affects the orders returned, start the web site without debugging and log in as the user admin@mvcbabystore.com with the password Adm1n@mvcbabystore.com. Now click on View All Orders from the Admin menu and add ?page=2 to the end of the URL. You should now see three orders rather than a list of all the orders and the orders should be the fourth to sixth newest in the system. In our site, these are the orders with IDs 4, 3, and 2, as shown in Figure 10-2.

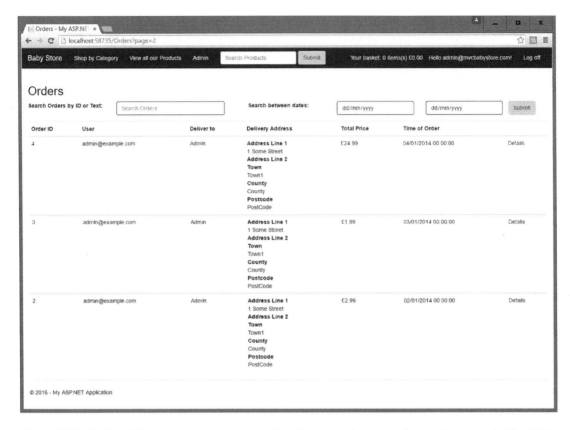

Figure 10-2. *Orders with asynchronous paging working by manually entering ?page=2 to the end of the URL*

Making Asynchronous Paging Reusable with an Extension Method

The new paging code runs as expected and gives us asynchronous paging; however, it is built into the
OrdersController class, which is far from ideal. If we want to use the paging in the ProductsController
class, for example, then we'd have to add a similar query to that class. To avoid this situation, the query can
be moved into a utility class, which can be used anywhere.

To move this code to a utility class, add a new folder named Utilities to the project and then add
a new class named AsyncPaging.cs to the folder. Add the following code to the new file to move the
asynchronous paging code into it. The class and methods are static so they can be accessed without needing
to create a new instance of the class.

```
using System.Collections.Generic;
using System.Linq;
using System.Data.Entity;
using System.Threading.Tasks;
```

```
namespace BabyStore.Utilities
{
    public static class AsyncPaging
    {
        public static async Task<List<T>> ReturnPages<T>(IQueryable<T> inputCollection,
        int pageNumber, int pageSize)
        {
            return await inputCollection.Skip((pageNumber - 1) *
                pageSize).Take(pageSize).ToListAsync();
        }
    }
}
```

Add the following using statement to the Controllers\OrdersController.cs file to allow access
to the new AsyncPaging class: using BabyStore.Utilities; and then update the Index method of the
OrdersController class so that the assignment to currentPageOfOrders uses the new AsyncPaging class as
follows:

```
int currentPage = (page ?? 1);
var currentPageOfOrders = await AsyncPaging.ReturnPages(orders, currentPage,
    Constants.PageItems);
return View(currentPageOfOrders);
```

If you run the web site now, you will see paging working as expected, using the new utility class.
However, the eagle-eyed will have noticed that the PagedList package can use a method directly on the
products variable in the ProductsController class rather than appearing to call a different class; the
code for using PagedList is viewModel.Products = products.ToPagedList(currentPage, Constants.
PageItems);.

This is achieved by using something called an extension method where a new method is added to an
existing type. Because the AsyncPaging class and method are static, we can create an extension method
easily using the existing code. To create an extension method, modify the AsyncPaging.cs file as follows:

```
using System.Collections.Generic;
using System.Linq;
using System.Data.Entity;
using System.Threading.Tasks;

namespace BabyStore.Utilities
{
    public static class AsyncPaging
    {
        public static async Task<List<T>> ReturnPages<T>(this IQueryable<T> inputCollection,
            int pageNumber, int pageSize)
        {
            return await inputCollection.Skip((pageNumber - 1) *
                pageSize).Take(pageSize).ToListAsync();
        }
    }
}
```

Adding the this keyword now allows this method to act as an extension method to the type IQueryable<T>, where <T> is simply a generic placeholder. To use the new extension method, modify the assignment of the currentPageOfOrders variable in the OrdersController class as follows:

```
int currentPage = (page ?? 1);
var currentPageOfOrders = await orders.ReturnPages(currentPage, Constants.PageItems);
return View(currentPageOfOrders);
```

This new code now takes the same format as the code used by the PagedList package in the ProductsController class (products.ToPagedList(currentPage, Constants.PageItems);).

Adding Page Links to the View and Building an Html Helper

Obviously, we cannot expect users to manually type page numbers into the URL so we need to generate some paging links similar to those used in the Products index view. To do this feature, we are going to create an HtmlHelper that can be used to generate links in a view.

In order to display some page links, we need to know a few pieces of data, namely, how many orders to display in a page, which page number is currently displayed, and how many pages there are in total. The total number of pages is calculated from the total number of orders and the page size. We then need to pass this data to the code that generates the paging links.

Since we demonstrated using the ViewBag for displaying orders rather than using a view model, we are going to assign these pieces of data into the ViewBag in the controller. Note that, if you were using a view model in the Views\Orders\Index.cshtml file, then you would assign these values into that view model. To make the paging more reusable and reduce the amount of code, you could instead create a separate view model for holding paging data and assign it as a property of your main view model.

Alter the Index method in the Controllers\OrdersController.cs file to add the current page number and the total number of pages to the ViewBag as follows:

```
// GET: Orders
public async Task<ActionResult> Index(string orderSearch, string startDate, string endDate,
    string orderSortOrder, int? page)
{
    var orders = db.Orders.OrderBy(o => o.DateCreated).Include(o => o.OrderLines);

    if (!User.IsInRole("Admin"))
    {
        orders = orders.Where(o => o.UserID == User.Identity.Name);
    }

    if (!String.IsNullOrEmpty(orderSearch))
    {
        orders = orders.Where(o => o.OrderID.ToString().Equals(orderSearch) ||
            o.UserID.Contains(orderSearch) ||
            o.DeliveryName.Contains(orderSearch) ||
            o.DeliveryAddress.AddressLine1.Contains(orderSearch) ||
            o.DeliveryAddress.AddressLine2.Contains(orderSearch) ||
            o.DeliveryAddress.Town.Contains(orderSearch) ||
            o.DeliveryAddress.County.Contains(orderSearch) ||
            o.DeliveryAddress.Postcode.Contains(orderSearch) ||
            o.TotalPrice.ToString().Equals(orderSearch) ||
            o.OrderLines.Any(ol => ol.ProductName.Contains(orderSearch)));
    }
```

```
DateTime parsedStartDate;
if (DateTime.TryParse(startDate, out parsedStartDate))
{
    orders = orders.Where(o => o.DateCreated >= parsedStartDate);
}

DateTime parsedEndDate;
if (DateTime.TryParse(endDate, out parsedEndDate))
{
    orders = orders.Where(o => o.DateCreated <= parsedEndDate);
}

ViewBag.DateSort = String.IsNullOrEmpty(orderSortOrder) ? "date" : "";
ViewBag.UserSort = orderSortOrder == "user" ? "user_desc" : "user";
ViewBag.PriceSort = orderSortOrder == "price" ? "price_desc" : "price";
ViewBag.CurrentOrderSearch = orderSearch;
ViewBag.StartDate = startDate;
ViewBag.EndDate = endDate;

switch (orderSortOrder)
{
    case "user":
        orders = orders.OrderBy(o => o.UserID);
        break;
    case "user_desc":
        orders = orders.OrderByDescending(o => o.UserID);
        break;
    case "price":
        orders = orders.OrderBy(o => o.TotalPrice);
        break;
    case "price_desc":
        orders = orders.OrderByDescending(o => o.TotalPrice);
        break;
    case "date":
        orders = orders.OrderBy(o => o.DateCreated);
        break;
    default:
        orders = orders.OrderByDescending(o => o.DateCreated);
        break;
}
int currentPage = (page ?? 1);
ViewBag.CurrentPage = currentPage;
ViewBag.TotalPages = (int)Math.Ceiling((decimal)orders.Count() / Constants.PageItems);
var currentPageOfOrders = await orders.ReturnPages(currentPage, Constants.PageItems);
return View(currentPageOfOrders);
}
```

The TotalPages property uses the Math.Ceiling method to round up the decimal value returned by dividing the total number of orders by the number of items in a page; for example, if there are 10 products and the page size is 4 the result will be 2.5, meaning that the total number of pages needed is 3.

Next we are going to create an HTML helper to generate some paging links for use in views. Create a new project folder called HTMLHelpers and add a new class named PagingLinks.cs to it. We're going to use this file to output an HTML unordered list similar to the one generated by the PagedList package.

Modify the file as follows to change the class to be static and create a new static method called GeneratePageLinks. This method is an extension method as we saw earlier with the AsyncPaging class's ReturnPages method. It is an extension of the HtmlHelper type that's used to generate HTML in views. It takes the current page, the total number of pages, and a delegate named pageUrl as input parameters and returns a MvcHtmlString back to the view:

```
using System;
using System.Text;
using System.Web.Mvc;

namespace BabyStore.HTMLHelpers
{
    public static class PagingLinks
    {
        public static MvcHtmlString GeneratePageLinks(this HtmlHelper html, int currentPage,
            int totalPages, Func<int, string> pageUrl)
        {
            StringBuilder linksHtml = new StringBuilder();
            TagBuilder divTag = new TagBuilder("div");
            divTag.InnerHtml = "Page " + currentPage + " of " + totalPages;
            TagBuilder paginationContainer = new TagBuilder("div");
            paginationContainer.AddCssClass("pagination-container");
            TagBuilder ulTag = new TagBuilder("ul");
            ulTag.AddCssClass("pagination");

            paginationContainer.InnerHtml += ulTag.ToString();
            divTag.InnerHtml += paginationContainer.ToString();
            linksHtml.Append(divTag.ToString());
            return MvcHtmlString.Create(linksHtml.ToString());
        }
    }
}
```

This method starts by adding a StringBuilder that is used to add the entire HTML and to return as an MvcHtmlString at the end of the method. It generates a wrapper div and then adds the text "Page X of Y" into the div. A child div with the CSS class attribute of pagination-container is then added inside the first div. Then within this, the method adds an HTML ul tag with a CSS class attribute of "pagination". Throughout this method, the TagBuilder class is used. TagBuilder creates an HTML tag for the string passed into it. This generates HTML as follows:

```
<div>
    Page 1 of 3
        <div class="pagination-container">
            <ul class="pagination">
            </ul>
    </div>
</div>
```

The pageUrl delegate input parameter works by being passed in as a parameter in the view, which creates a URL to the Index view based on the Url.Action method.

We are now going to generate some list items to go into the unordered list. We need to generate the list items as hyperlinks to every page in the total number of pages. To generate an <li> element containing a hyperlink for each page, add the following code to the GeneratePageLinks method in the HTMLHelpers\ PagingLinks.cs file as follows:

```
public static MvcHtmlString GeneratePageLinks(this HtmlHelper html, int currentPage, int
    totalPages, Func<int, string> pageUrl)
{
    StringBuilder linksHtml = new StringBuilder();
    TagBuilder divTag = new TagBuilder("div");
    divTag.InnerHtml = "Page " + currentPage + " of " + totalPages;
    TagBuilder paginationContainer = new TagBuilder("div");
    paginationContainer.AddCssClass("pagination-container");
    TagBuilder ulTag = new TagBuilder("ul");
    ulTag.AddCssClass("pagination");

    for (int i = 1; i <= totalPages; i++)
    {
        TagBuilder liTag = new TagBuilder("li");
        TagBuilder aTag = new TagBuilder("a");
        aTag.InnerHtml = i.ToString();
        if (i == currentPage)
        {
            liTag.AddCssClass("active");
        }
        else
        {
            aTag.MergeAttribute("href", pageUrl(i));
        }
        liTag.InnerHtml += aTag.ToString();
        ulTag.InnerHtml += liTag.ToString();
    }

    paginationContainer.InnerHtml += ulTag.ToString();
    divTag.InnerHtml += paginationContainer.ToString();
    linksHtml.Append(divTag.ToString());
    return MvcHtmlString.Create(linksHtml.ToString());
}
```

This code loops through the total number of pages and creates an <li> HTML tag containing an <a> element. It sets the text of the a element to the number of the page and then checks to see if the page number matches the current page. If it does, then no hyperlink is added. Otherwise, a hyperlink is added using the values passed in via the delegate function from the view (pageUrl) and the number of the page. The <a> tag is then converted into a string and appended to the innerHTML of the <li> tag, which in turn is then appended to the innerHTML of the <ul> tag. Effectively, this makes a list of the following format:

```
<ul>
    <li>
        <a href=link to page i>
    </li>
```

```
    <li>
        <a href=link to page i+1>
    </li>
</ul>
```

In order to generate some arrow links to the previous page, add a conditional statement before the for loop that was just added as follows:

```
public static MvcHtmlString GeneratePageLinks(this HtmlHelper html, int currentPage, int
    totalPages, Func<int, string> pageUrl)
{
    StringBuilder linksHtml = new StringBuilder();
    TagBuilder divTag = new TagBuilder("div");
    divTag.InnerHtml = "Page " + currentPage + " of " + totalPages;
    TagBuilder paginationContainer = new TagBuilder("div");
    paginationContainer.AddCssClass("pagination-container");
    TagBuilder ulTag = new TagBuilder("ul");
    ulTag.AddCssClass("pagination");

    if (currentPage != 1)
    {
        TagBuilder prevPage = new TagBuilder("li");
        TagBuilder prevUrl = new TagBuilder("a");
        prevUrl.InnerHtml = "<";
        prevUrl.MergeAttribute("href", pageUrl(currentPage - 1));
        prevPage.InnerHtml += prevUrl.ToString();
        ulTag.InnerHtml += prevPage.ToString();
    }

    for (int i = 1; i <= totalPages; i++)
    {
        TagBuilder liTag = new TagBuilder("li");
        TagBuilder aTag = new TagBuilder("a");
        aTag.InnerHtml = i.ToString();
        if (i == currentPage)
        {
            liTag.AddCssClass("active");
        }
        else
        {
            aTag.MergeAttribute("href", pageUrl(i));
        }
        liTag.InnerHtml += aTag.ToString();
        ulTag.InnerHtml += liTag.ToString();
    }

    paginationContainer.InnerHtml += ulTag.ToString();
    divTag.InnerHtml += paginationContainer.ToString();
    linksHtml.Append(divTag.ToString());
    return MvcHtmlString.Create(linksHtml.ToString());
}
```

This code checks to see if the users are on the first page. If they are not, it creates a link to the previous page with a < character.

Similarly, to add a link to the next page, you add a conditional statement after the for loop as follows:

```
public static MvcHtmlString GeneratePageLinks(this HtmlHelper html, int currentPage, int
    totalPages, Func<int, string> pageUrl)
{
    StringBuilder linksHtml = new StringBuilder();
    TagBuilder divTag = new TagBuilder("div");
    divTag.InnerHtml = "Page " + currentPage + " of " + totalPages;
    TagBuilder paginationContainer = new TagBuilder("div");
    paginationContainer.AddCssClass("pagination-container");
    TagBuilder ulTag = new TagBuilder("ul");
    ulTag.AddCssClass("pagination");

    if (currentPage != 1)
    {
        TagBuilder prevPage = new TagBuilder("li");
        TagBuilder prevUrl = new TagBuilder("a");
        prevUrl.InnerHtml = "<";
        prevUrl.MergeAttribute("href", pageUrl(currentPage - 1));
        prevPage.InnerHtml += prevUrl.ToString();
        ulTag.InnerHtml += prevPage.ToString();
    }

    for (int i = 1; i <= totalPages; i++)
    {
        TagBuilder liTag = new TagBuilder("li");
        TagBuilder aTag = new TagBuilder("a");
        aTag.InnerHtml = i.ToString();
        if (i == currentPage)
        {
            liTag.AddCssClass("active");
        }
        else
        {
            aTag.MergeAttribute("href", pageUrl(i));
        }
        liTag.InnerHtml += aTag.ToString();
        ulTag.InnerHtml += liTag.ToString();
    }

    if (currentPage != totalPages)
    {
        TagBuilder nextPage = new TagBuilder("li");
        TagBuilder nextUrl = new TagBuilder("a");
        nextUrl.InnerHtml = ">";
        nextUrl.MergeAttribute("href", pageUrl(currentPage + 1));
        nextPage.InnerHtml += nextUrl.ToString();
        ulTag.InnerHtml += nextPage.ToString();
    }
```

```
        paginationContainer.InnerHtml += ulTag.ToString();
        divTag.InnerHtml += paginationContainer.ToString();
        linksHtml.Append(divTag.ToString());
        return MvcHtmlString.Create(linksHtml.ToString());
    }
}
```

This code checks to see if the users are on the last page. If they are not, it creates a link to the next page with a > character. The completed PagingLinks class should now appear as follows:

```
using System;
using System.Text;
using System.Web.Mvc;

namespace BabyStore.HTMLHelpers
{
    public static class PagingLinks
    {
        public static MvcHtmlString GeneratePageLinks(this HtmlHelper html, int currentPage,
            int totalPages, Func<int, string> pageUrl)
        {
            StringBuilder linksHtml = new StringBuilder();
            TagBuilder divTag = new TagBuilder("div");
            divTag.InnerHtml = "Page " + currentPage + " of " + totalPages;
            TagBuilder paginationContainer = new TagBuilder("div");
            paginationContainer.AddCssClass("pagination-container");
            TagBuilder ulTag = new TagBuilder("ul");
            ulTag.AddCssClass("pagination");

            if (currentPage != 1)
            {
                TagBuilder prevPage = new TagBuilder("li");
                TagBuilder prevUrl = new TagBuilder("a");
                prevUrl.InnerHtml = "<";
                prevUrl.MergeAttribute("href", pageUrl(currentPage - 1));
                prevPage.InnerHtml += prevUrl.ToString();
                ulTag.InnerHtml += prevPage.ToString();
            }

            for (int i = 1; i <= totalPages; i++)
            {
                TagBuilder liTag = new TagBuilder("li");
                TagBuilder aTag = new TagBuilder("a");
                aTag.InnerHtml = i.ToString();
                if (i == currentPage)
                {
                    liTag.AddCssClass("active");
                }
```

```
                else
                {
                    aTag.MergeAttribute("href", pageUrl(i));
                }
                liTag.InnerHtml += aTag.ToString();
                ulTag.InnerHtml += liTag.ToString();
            }

            if (currentPage != totalPages)
            {
                TagBuilder nextPage = new TagBuilder("li");
                TagBuilder nextUrl = new TagBuilder("a");
                nextUrl.InnerHtml = ">";
                nextUrl.MergeAttribute("href", pageUrl(currentPage + 1));
                nextPage.InnerHtml += nextUrl.ToString();
                ulTag.InnerHtml += nextPage.ToString();
            }

            paginationContainer.InnerHtml += ulTag.ToString();
            divTag.InnerHtml += paginationContainer.ToString();
            linksHtml.Append(divTag.ToString());
            return MvcHtmlString.Create(linksHtml.ToString());
        }
    }
}
```

Next, to use this new code first, add a line to the `Index` method of the `Controllers/ OrdersController.cs` file to store the current sort order in the `ViewBag` as follows:

```
// GET: Orders
public async Task<ActionResult> Index(string orderSearch, string startDate, string endDate,
string orderSortOrder, int? page)
{
    var orders = db.Orders.OrderBy(o => o.DateCreated).Include(o => o.OrderLines);

    if (!User.IsInRole("Admin"))
    {
        orders = orders.Where(o => o.UserID == User.Identity.Name);
    }

    if (!String.IsNullOrEmpty(orderSearch))
    {
        orders = orders.Where(o => o.OrderID.ToString().Equals(orderSearch) ||
            o.UserID.Contains(orderSearch) ||
            o.DeliveryName.Contains(orderSearch) ||
            o.DeliveryAddress.AddressLine1.Contains(orderSearch) ||
            o.DeliveryAddress.AddressLine2.Contains(orderSearch) ||
            o.DeliveryAddress.Town.Contains(orderSearch) ||
            o.DeliveryAddress.County.Contains(orderSearch) ||
            o.DeliveryAddress.Postcode.Contains(orderSearch) ||
            o.TotalPrice.ToString().Equals(orderSearch) ||
            o.OrderLines.Any(ol => ol.ProductName.Contains(orderSearch)));
    }
```

```csharp
    DateTime parsedStartDate;
    if (DateTime.TryParse(startDate, out parsedStartDate))
    {
        orders = orders.Where(o => o.DateCreated >= parsedStartDate);
    }

    DateTime parsedEndDate;
    if (DateTime.TryParse(endDate, out parsedEndDate))
    {
        orders = orders.Where(o => o.DateCreated <= parsedEndDate);
    }

    ViewBag.DateSort = String.IsNullOrEmpty(orderSortOrder) ? "date" : "";
    ViewBag.UserSort = orderSortOrder == "user" ? "user_desc" : "user";
    ViewBag.PriceSort = orderSortOrder == "price" ? "price_desc" : "price";
    ViewBag.CurrentOrderSearch = orderSearch;
    ViewBag.StartDate = startDate;
    ViewBag.EndDate = endDate;

    switch (orderSortOrder)
    {
        case "user":
            orders = orders.OrderBy(o => o.UserID);
            break;
        case "user_desc":
            orders = orders.OrderByDescending(o => o.UserID);
            break;
        case "price":
            orders = orders.OrderBy(o => o.TotalPrice);
            break;
        case "price_desc":
            orders = orders.OrderByDescending(o => o.TotalPrice);
            break;
        case "date":
            orders = orders.OrderBy(o => o.DateCreated);
            break;
        default:
            orders = orders.OrderByDescending(o => o.DateCreated);
            break;
    }
    int currentPage = (page ?? 1);
    ViewBag.CurrentPage = currentPage;
    ViewBag.TotalPages = (int)Math.Ceiling((decimal)orders.Count() / Constants.PageItems);
    var currentPageOfOrders = await orders.ReturnPages(currentPage, Constants.PageItems);
    ViewBag.CurrentSortOrder = orderSortOrder;
    return View(currentPageOfOrders);
}
```

Finally, update the view file Views\Orders\Index.cshtml as follows to add a using statement for BabyStore.HTMLHelpers. And a new set of paging links to the bottom of the page:

```
@model IEnumerable<BabyStore.Models.Order>
@using BabyStore.HTMLHelpers;


@{
    ViewBag.Title = "Orders";
}


<h2>@ViewBag.Title</h2>
@using (Html.BeginForm("Index", "Orders", FormMethod.Get))
{
    <div class="row form-group">
        <div class="col-md-2">
            <label>Search Orders by ID or Text:</label>
        </div>
        <div class="col-md-3">
            @Html.TextBox("OrderSearch", null, new { @class = "form-control", @placeholder =
                "Search Orders"})
        </div>
        <div class="col-md-2">
            <label>Search between dates:</label>
        </div>
        <div class="col-md-2">
            <input type="date" id="StartDate" name="StartDate" class="form-control"
                value="@Request.QueryString["StartDate"]" />
        </div>
        <div class="col-md-2">
            <input type="date" id="EndDate" name="EndDate" class="form-control"
                value="@Request.QueryString["EndDate"]" />
        </div>
        <button type="submit" class="btn btn-default">Submit</button>
    </div>

}


<table class="table">
    <tr>
        <th>
            @Html.DisplayNameFor(model => model.OrderID)
        </th>
        <th>
            @Html.ActionLink("User", "Index", new { orderSortOrder = ViewBag.UserSort,
                orderSearch = ViewBag.CurrentOrderSearch, startdate = ViewBag.StartDate,
                endDate = ViewBag.EndDate })
        </th>
        <th>
            @Html.DisplayNameFor(model => model.DeliveryName)
        </th>
```

```
        <th>
            @Html.DisplayNameFor(model => model.DeliveryAddress)
        </th>
        <th>
            @Html.ActionLink("Total Price", "Index", new { orderSortOrder = ViewBag.
            PriceSort,
                orderSearch = ViewBag.CurrentOrderSearch,startdate = ViewBag.StartDate,
                endDate = ViewBag.EndDate })
        </th>
        <th>
            @Html.ActionLink("Time of Order", "Index", new { orderSortOrder =
                ViewBag.DateSort, orderSearch = ViewBag.CurrentOrderSearch,startdate =
                ViewBag.StartDate, endDate = ViewBag.EndDate })
        </th>
        <th></th>
    </tr>

    @foreach (var item in Model)
    {
        <tr>
            <td>
                @Html.DisplayFor(modelItem => item.OrderID)
            </td>
            <td>
                @Html.DisplayFor(modelItem => item.UserID)
            </td>
            <td>
                @Html.DisplayFor(modelItem => item.DeliveryName)
            </td>
            <td>
                @Html.DisplayFor(modelItem => item.DeliveryAddress)
            </td>
            <td>
                @Html.DisplayFor(modelItem => item.TotalPrice)
            </td>
            <td>
                @Html.DisplayFor(modelItem => item.DateCreated)
            </td>
            <td>
                @Html.ActionLink("Details", "Details", new { id = item.OrderID })
            </td>
        </tr>
    }

</table>
<div class="paging small-bold-text">
    @Html.GeneratePageLinks((int)ViewBag.CurrentPage, (int)ViewBag.TotalPages, page =>
        Url.Action("Index", new  { page, orderSortOrder = ViewBag.CurrentSortOrder,
            orderSearch = ViewBag.CurrentOrderSearch, startdate = ViewBag.StartDate,
            endDate = ViewBag.EndDate }))
</div>
```

This code uses the new `GeneratePageLinks` extension method and passes in the current page number and the number of the total pages from the `ViewBag`. It also passes in a delegate to return generate a URL to each page number. This includes an anonymous type to pass in the page number, and the current values for text searching, date searching, and sorting so that they are remembered when the user moves between pages.

Start the web site without debugging and view the Orders Index page as admin@mvcbabystore.com. You should now see the new paging controls and be able to move between pages of orders. Figure 10-3 shows the Orders Index page where a user has searched for the term `admin`, between the dates 02/01/2014 and 05/01/2014, while sorting by price and moving to page 2 of the search results.

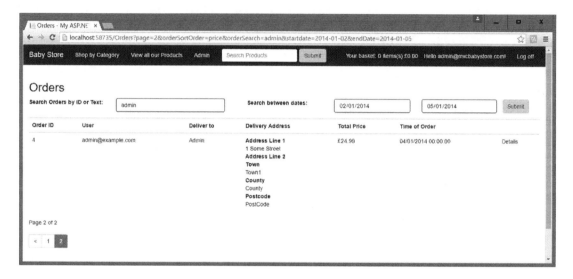

Figure 10-3. *Orders with asynchronous paging*

Dealing with Concurrent Database Updates

This section deals with the scenario in which two different users try to modify a database record at the same time. We cover cases where a record has been edited or deleted and discuss how to inform users that a record has changed since they accessed it and attempted to change it themselves.

Warning Users When the Values They are Editing Have Been Changed by Another User

If two users edit a record at the same time, by default Entity Framework uses a "last wins" scenario where the last person to edit the record has all their values saved into the database. This could cause an issue if there are two people editing the same record in the database at the same time. Changes made by the first user are then overwritten with old values by the second user, assuming they both opened the edit screen prior to any edits being saved.

There are several ways to deal with this scenario; some are more complex than others (such as database locking known as pessimistic concurrency). Entity Framework provides support for optimistic concurrency. This means allowing conflicts to happen but when they do happen the system is aware of them and able to react. The system can react in a number of ways, for example by allowing the "last wins" scenario to occur or recording which user has edited which field and updating only certain fields, or alternatively allowing the first set of edits to occur and then notifying the second user that values have changed since they loaded them. This last alternative is known as "store wins" and I am going to demonstrate a simple example of how to implement this method using the Category entity as an example.

In order to know that a database row has changed, some form of tracking is required. A typical scenario for this using Entity Framework is to use the field RowVersion with a .NET type of byte array that holds sequential data and is updated each time the row is updated in the database.

To track whether a category row has been altered, start by adding a RowVersion property to the Models\Category.cs file, as shown in bold:

```
using System.Collections.Generic;
using System.ComponentModel.DataAnnotations;

namespace BabyStore.Models
{
    public class Category
    {
        public int ID { get; set; }
        [Required(ErrorMessage = "The category name cannot be blank")]
        [StringLength(50, MinimumLength = 3, ErrorMessage = "Please enter a category name
            between 3 and 50 characters in length")]
        [RegularExpression(@"^[A-Z]+[a-zA-Z''-'\s]*$", ErrorMessage = "Please enter a
category
            name beginning with a capital letter and made up of letters and spaces only")]
        [Display(Name = "Category Name")]
        public string Name { get; set; }
        public virtual ICollection<Product> Products { get; set; }
        [Timestamp]
        public byte[] RowVersion { get; set; }
    }
}
```

The TimeStamp attribute specifies that this column is included in the Where part of any Update and Delete commands. Next add a migration for the new field and update the database by running the following commands in the Package Manager Console:

```
add-migration category_rowversion -configuration StoreConfiguration followed by update-
database -configuration StoreConfiguration
```

A new column named RowVersion will now be added to the Categories table in the BabyStore4.mdf database, as shown in Figure 10-4. You can see that although the data type was defined as byte in the model, the data type of the column in the database is defined as RowVersion.

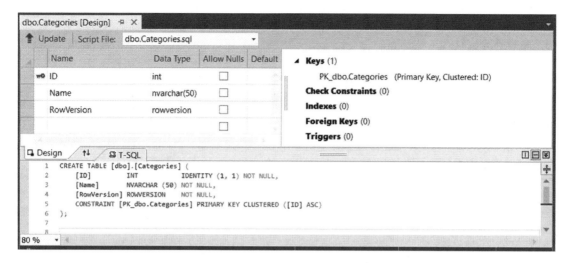

Figure 10-4. *The categories table updated with the RowVersion column*

Next modify the `HttpPost` version of the `Edit` method in the `Controllers\CategoriesController.cs` file as follows in order to check for data conflicts when editing a category:

```
[HttpPost]
[ValidateAntiForgeryToken]
public ActionResult Edit(int? id, byte[] rowVersion)
{
    string[] fieldsToBind = new string[] { "Name", "RowVersion" };

    if (id == null)
    {
        return new HttpStatusCodeResult(HttpStatusCode.BadRequest);
    }

    var categoryToUpdate = db.Categories.Find(id);

    if (categoryToUpdate == null)
    {
        Category deletedCategory = new Category();
        TryUpdateModel(deletedCategory, fieldsToBind);
        ModelState.AddModelError(string.Empty, "Unable to save your changes because the
                category has been deleted by another user.");
        return View(deletedCategory);
    }
```

```
    if (TryUpdateModel(categoryToUpdate, fieldsToBind))
    {
        try
        {
            db.Entry(categoryToUpdate).OriginalValues["RowVersion"] = rowVersion;
            db.SaveChanges();
            return RedirectToAction("Index");
        }
        catch (DbUpdateConcurrencyException ex)
        {
            var exEntry = ex.Entries.Single();
            var currentUIValues = (Category)exEntry.Entity;
            var databaseCategory = exEntry.GetDatabaseValues();

            if (databaseCategory == null)
            {
                ModelState.AddModelError(string.Empty, "Unable to save your changes because
                    the category has been deleted by another user.");
            }
            else
            {
                var databaseCategoryValues = (Category)databaseCategory.ToObject();

                if (databaseCategoryValues.Name != currentUIValues.Name)
                {
                    ModelState.AddModelError("Name", "Current value in database: " +
                        databaseCategoryValues.Name);
                }
                ModelState.AddModelError(string.Empty, "The record has been modified by
                    another user after you loaded the screen. Your changes have not yet been
                    saved. "
                    + "The new values in the database are shown below. If you want to
                    overwrite these values with your changes then click save otherwise go
                    back
                    to the categories page.");
                categoryToUpdate.RowVersion = databaseCategoryValues.RowVersion;
            }
        }
    }

    return View(categoryToUpdate);
}
```

Ensure you add the statement using System.Data.Entity.Infrastructure; to the top of the file so that the DbUpdateConcurrencyException class can be found.

We have changed the signature of the method to take just the ID and RowVersion parameters and then manually build an array of fields to bind to for use with TryUpdateModel. The code then tries to find the category by ID. If it cannot, then a new Category instance is created to display the posted values back to the user, along with an error message informing them that the category has been deleted by another user using this code:

```
var categoryToUpdate = db.Categories.Find(id);

if (categoryToUpdate == null)
{
    Category deletedCategory = new Category();
    TryUpdateModel(deletedCategory, fieldsToBind);
    ModelState.AddModelError(string.Empty, "Unable to save your changes because the category has
        been deleted by another user.");
    return View(deletedCategory);
}
```

Later we will add the RowVersion to the view as a hidden field so that it can be compared to the current RowVersion value in the database. Entity Framework tries to update the matching category by creating an update statement with a where clause that automatically looks for a row that matches the RowVersion passed in by the view. If no matches are found, there is no record with the current version and therefore it must have been altered somehow. When no matches are found, Entity Framework throws a DBUpdateConcurrencyException. This is achieved using the following code:

```
if (TryUpdateModel(categoryToUpdate, fieldsToBind))
{
    try
    {
        db.Entry(categoryToUpdate).OriginalValues["RowVersion"] = rowVersion;
        db.SaveChanges();
        return RedirectToAction("Index");
    }
    catch (DbUpdateConcurrencyException ex)
    {
```

If the exception is thrown then the current values entered by the user are obtained and stored in the currentUIValues variable. The values from the database are then obtained as follows:

```
var exEntry = ex.Entries.Single();
var currentUIValues = (Category)exEntry.Entity;
var databaseCategory = exEntry.GetDatabaseValues();
```

The following code then checks to see if the current database entry is null. This is unlikely to occur since this has already been checked but this code is there in case a deletion happens between finding the category and running db.saveChanges():

```
if (databaseCategory == null)
{
    ModelState.AddModelError(string.Empty, "Unable to save your changes because the category
has been deleted by another user.");
}
```

395

If the database entry is not null, the current database values for the category are obtained and cast into a category object. Then a check is made against each of the fields in the object to see which one is different in the database when compared to those in the values the user can see in the web page. For each field that differs, an error message is created to show what the value is in the database. In this example, we used the Category entity for simplicity and have only compared the Name property since that is the only field that the user can edit. For a product entity, checks could be made against all the fields that can be edited, including Name, Price, Category, etc. The code that performs this check is:

```
else
{
    var databaseCategoryValues = (Category)databaseCategory.ToObject();

    if (databaseCategoryValues.Name != currentUIValues.Name)
    {
        ModelState.AddModelError("Name", "Current value in database: " +
            databaseCategoryValues.Name);
    }
    ModelState.AddModelError(string.Empty, "The record has been modified by another user
    after
        you loaded the screen. Your changes have not yet been saved. "
        + "The new values in the database are shown below. If you want to overwrite these
        values with your changes then click save otherwise go back to the categories
        page.");
```

The last part of the code, categoryToUpdate.RowVersion = databaseCategoryValues.RowVersion;, sets the updates the RowVersion of the categoryToUpdate to the same value in the database so that the user can resubmit the values without getting another conflict. A conflict will now occur only if the values have been re-edited by someone else prior to the current user's next attempt to save the category.

To ensure the new code can work, we need to pass the RowVersion variable back and forth from the view so that the version being edited can be checked against the database. To do this, edit the Views\Categories\Edit.cshtml file as follows to add a hidden HTML field called RowVersion:

```
@model BabyStore.Models.Category


@{
    ViewBag.Title = "Edit Category";
}

<h2>@ViewBag.Title</h2>

@using (Html.BeginForm())
{
    @Html.AntiForgeryToken()
```

```
<div class="form-horizontal">
    <hr />
    @Html.ValidationSummary(true, "", new { @class = "text-danger" })
    @Html.HiddenFor(model => model.ID)
    @Html.HiddenFor(model => model.RowVersion)
    <div class="form-group">
        @Html.LabelFor(model => model.Name, htmlAttributes: new { @class = "control-
        label
            col-md-2" })
        <div class="col-md-10">
            @Html.EditorFor(model => model.Name, new { htmlAttributes = new { @class =
                "form-control" } })
            @Html.ValidationMessageFor(model => model.Name, "", new { @class = "text-
                danger" })
        </div>
    </div>

    <div class="form-group">
        <div class="col-md-offset-2 col-md-10">
            <input type="submit" value="Save" class="btn btn-default" />
        </div>
    </div>
</div>
}

<div>
    @Html.ActionLink("Back to List", "Index")
</div>

@section Scripts {
    @Scripts.Render("~/bundles/jqueryval")
}
```

Now to see how the new code affects the web site, start the web site without debugging and log in to the site as admin@mvcbabystore.com with the password Adm1n@mvcbabystore.com. Open a new browser tab with the web site running in it and you will also be logged in as the admin user.

In one of the tabs, create a new category named Test Concurrency. Next open the Edit page for the category in both tabs and then edit the name to be Test Concurrency Edited in the first tab. Save the changes. Now, in the second tab, attempt to change the name to Test Concurrency Edited Again. You should be informed that the record has been changed in the database after it was loaded with details of the new value in the database, as shown in Figure 10-5.

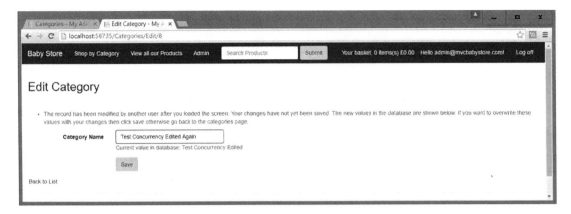

Figure 10-5. *The admin@mvcbabystore.com user being informed that the category has been updated by someone else while they were attempting to edit it*

The user can now abandon the changes or choose to continue and overwrite the changes with their own values by clicking the Save button.

Checking for Conflicts on Deletion

The site also needs to check for conflicts when a user attempts to delete a category. They may decide to delete a category, being unaware that someone has edited it. If this is the case, optimistic concurrency can be used to inform them in the same way as was used for edits. A RowVersion field is again included in the view and used to create a where clause in the delete statement generated by Entity Framework. During the calling of the HttpPost Delete method if the RowVersions do not match and no record is updated, then a DbUpdateConcurrencyException is thrown.

This time, to process the error, a flag is set and passed back to the HttpGet version of the Delete method. Then a check is made to see if the category has been deleted or modified and, depending on the outcome, either an error message is shown to tell the user which field has been modified or the user is redirected back to the Index page as if they have deleted the record themselves.

To enabled checking for concurrency on deletion, modify the GET version of the Delete method in the Controllers\CategoriesController.cs files as follows. This checks if a deletionError flag has been set and, if so, returns the user back to the Index page if the category has been deleted by another user. It displays an error message if its data was changed by adding an appropriate error to the ModelState:

```
// GET: Categories/Delete/5
public ActionResult Delete(int? id, bool? deletionError)
{
    if (id == null)
    {
        return new HttpStatusCodeResult(HttpStatusCode.BadRequest);
    }
    Category category = db.Categories.Find(id);
    if (category == null)
    {
        if (deletionError.GetValueOrDefault())
        {
            return RedirectToAction("Index");
        }
```

```
        return HttpNotFound();
    }

    if (deletionError.GetValueOrDefault())
    {
        ModelState.AddModelError(string.Empty, "The category you attempted to delete has been
            modified by another user after you loaded it. " + "The delete has not been
            performed. The current values in the database are shown above. " + "If you still
            want to delete this record click the Delete button again, otherwise go back to the
            categories page.");
    }

    return View(category);
}
```

Next, update the `HttpPost` `DeleteConfirmed` method as follows by renaming it `Delete` since it no longer uses the same signature as the `HttpGet` version of the `Delete` method.

```
// POST: Categories/Delete/5
[HttpPost]
[ValidateAntiForgeryToken]
public ActionResult Delete(Category category)
{
    try
    {
        db.Entry(category).State = EntityState.Deleted;
        var products = db.Products.Where(p => p.CategoryID == category.ID);

        foreach (var p in products)
        {
            p.CategoryID = null;
        }

        db.SaveChanges();
        return RedirectToAction("Index");
    }
    catch (DbUpdateConcurrencyException)
    {
        return RedirectToAction("Delete", new { deletionError = true, id = category.ID });
    }
}
```

Add the statement using `System.Data.Entity;` to the top of the file, if it is not already included, so that the `EntityState` class can be found. This method has been updated to accept a category rather than just an ID so that it now has access to the `RowVersion` property of the category. If a `DbUpdateConcurrencyException` occurs then the GET version of the `Delete` method is called with the `deletionError` flag set to true.

Finally, the view needs to be updated to display any error message in the model state and to ensure we pass the RowVersion variable back and forth from the view so that the version being edited can be checked against the database:

```
@model BabyStore.Models.Category

@{
    ViewBag.Title = "Delete Category";
}

<h2>@ViewBag.Title</h2>

<h3>Are you sure you want to delete this category?</h3>
<div>
    <hr />
    <dl class="dl-horizontal">
        <dt>
            @Html.DisplayNameFor(model => model.Name)
        </dt>

        <dd>
            @Html.DisplayFor(model => model.Name)
        </dd>
    </dl>

    @using (Html.BeginForm()) {
        @Html.AntiForgeryToken()
        @Html.ValidationSummary(true, "", new { @class = "text-danger" })
        @Html.HiddenFor(model => model.RowVersion)
        <div class="form-actions no-color">
            <input type="submit" value="Delete" class="btn btn-default" /> |
            @Html.ActionLink("Back to List", "Index")
        </div>
    }
</div>
```

To see the code in action, start the web site without debugging and log in as admin@mvcbabystore.com with the password Adm1n@mvcbabystore.com. Then add a new product named test product and assign it to the Test Concurrency Edited Again category. Just assign any valid data to the other fields and leave the images blank. This product is going to be used to show that a product is not disassociated with a category if an attempt to delete the category fails due to a concurrency issue.

Next open another browser tab and, in both tabs, navigate to the Categories Index page. In the first tab, click the delete link for the Test Concurrency Edited Again category to open the delete page. In the other tab, edit the name of the category to be Test Concurrency Delete. Now, in the first tab, press the Delete button and you should see a message in the page informing the user that the category has been edited since it was loaded into the Delete page, as shown in Figure 10-6.

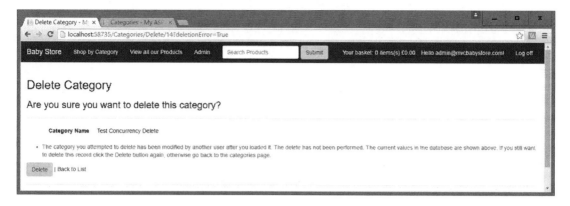

Figure 10-6. *The error message generated when attempting to delete a category that has been edited by another user after opening the Delete page*

If you now move to the second tab and click on the Test Concurrency Delete category from the Categories Index page, you will see that the Test Product is still assigned to the category. Move back to the first tab and click the Delete button again. The Test Concurrency Delete category should now be deleted and the user is returned to the Categories index page. Next, delete Test Product from the site.

Running Raw SQL Queries via Entity Framework

On occasion you may want to run your own SQL query. To do this, you have three options depending on what will be returned from the database:

- DbSet.SqlQuery should be used when an entity is returned by the query

- Database.SqlQuery should be used for queries that return types other than entities

- Database.ExecuteSqlCommand should be used for other non-query commands, such as Updates or Deletes

Queries should be parameterized to prevent SQL injection attacks where input into the web page could be interpreted as SQL. As an example, modify the HttpGet version of the Delete method in Controllers/ CategoriesController.cs as follows to retrieve a category entity by ID:

```
// GET: Categories/Delete/5
public ActionResult Delete(int? id, bool? deletionError)
{
    if (id == null)
    {
        return new HttpStatusCodeResult(HttpStatusCode.BadRequest);
    }
    string query = "SELECT * FROM Categories WHERE ID= @p0";
    Category category = db.Categories.SqlQuery(query, id).SingleOrDefault();
    if (category == null)
    {
...rest of code omitted for brevity...
```

The result of these changes is to run the query to return a category using the ID variable as a parameter in the SQL query. To see the effect of this, start the web site without debugging, log in as an admin user, and open the delete page for a category. The data returned in the view is now provided by the SQL query.

Adding Custom Error Pages to the Site

During the file upload process, we added a custom error controller. It seems to be a common question from developers about how to add custom error pages to ASP.NET MVC web sites, so we are going to briefly cover how to add some pages to cater to 404 and 500 errors.

The web site currently uses standard pages when an error occurs (500) or a page cannot be found (404). To change this, we are going to set up some views and change the web.config file to use these custom views. Modify the main project web.config file system.webServer httpErrors section as follows to add some entries for dealing with 404 and 500 errors:

```
<httpErrors errorMode="Custom" existingResponse="Replace">
  <remove statusCode="404" subStatusCode="13"/>
  <error statusCode="404" subStatusCode="13" responseMode="Redirect"
      path="/Error/FileUploadLimitExceeded"/>
  <remove statusCode="404"/>
  <error statusCode="404" responseMode="ExecuteURL" path="/Error/PageNotFound"/>
  <remove statusCode="500"/>
  <error statusCode="500" responseMode="ExecuteURL" path="/Error/InternalServerError"/>
</httpErrors>
```

Next, add two methods to the Controllers\ErrorController.cs file named PageNotFound and InternalServerError (the same names as in the web.config file above) as follows:

```
using System.Web.Mvc;

namespace BabyStore.Controllers
{
    public class ErrorController : Controller
    {
        // GET: Error
        public ActionResult FileUploadLimitExceeded()
        {
            return View();
        }

        public ActionResult PageNotFound()
        {
            Response.StatusCode = 404;
            return View();
        }
```

```
        public ActionResult InternalServerError()
        {
            Response.StatusCode = 500;
            return View();
        }
    }
}
```

Now, right-click in each method and add two new empty views using a layout page. For the new PageNotFound view, update the contents as follows:

```
@{
    ViewBag.Title = "Page Not Found";
}

<h1>Sorry the requested page cannot be found!</h1>
```

For the InternalServerError view, update the contents to:

```
@{
    ViewBag.Title = "Internal Server Error";
}

<h1>Sorry an error has occurred. Please go back and try again.</h1>
```

To try the new "page not found" page, start the web site without debugging and enter a nonexistent URL such as /ProductsA. You should now receive the custom error page shown in Figure 10-7.

Figure 10-7. The new custom "page not found" page in action

Common Entity Framework Problems and Workarounds

When working with Entity Framework, there are a few issues that you may run into. This section covers those issues with causes and fixes.

Cannot Attach the File Filepath\DatabaseName.mdf as Database "DatabaseName"

Cause

This issue is caused by the database having previously existed and been attached to your SQL Server instance, being deleted and an attempt to recreate it. SQL Server won't allow you to attach to it because it maintains a reference to the old database.

Workaround

This can be fixed by attempting to detach and delete the database via SQL Server Object Explorer, but an easier fix is to open Package Manager Console and run the following two commands: `sqllocaldb.exe stop` followed by `sqllocaldb.exe delete`. If you then recreate the database, for example by running the `update-database` command in Package Manager Console, the database should now work as expected.

Code First Migrations Become Out of Order or No Longer Run Correctly

Cause

This issue tends to be caused by something you have done unintentionally, meaning that the binary model that backs Code First Migrations become out of sync with the actual physical code and migration files. For example, if you work with two database contexts and do not reset the migrations when you add the second context, you will find that everything looks to be working okay but when you delete the database and try to recreate it by running all the migrations, only the migrations you added after adding the second context will run and you will encounter an error in Package Manager Console similar to "unable to create table x due to foreign key violation y".

Workaround

If this scenario happens, your best option is to reset your migrations. To reset the migrations, perform the following actions:

1. Update the `StoreContext connectionString` in your `Web.Config` file to target a new empty database; for example have a number following the database version and increment it by 1.

2. Open Windows Explorer and make a backup copy of the `Migrations` folder from your project. Copy this to another location in case you need to restore it.

3. In Visual Studio, delete all the migration files relating to the affected context.

4. Create a new migration called `Reset` by typing the following command into the package manager console: `add-migration Reset -configuration "NameOfConfigrationClass"`.

5. Run the `update-database -configuration "NameOfConfigrationClass"` command in Package Manager Console and the new database will be created to reflect your current code base. You can now continue to add any new migrations from here.

You Want to Roll Back a Migration

Cause

You've updated the database based on some code you want to remove and you want to remove your changes from the database.

Workaround

You have a couple of options. Either create a new migration for your current code state or, if you have a migration that you want to roll back to exactly then, you can do this by running the `Update-Database -TargetMigration:"NameOfMigration"` command. You can also use ordinal values to target the number of a migration, e.g., `update-database -target:1`.

Summary

This chapter covered some of the more advanced topics you may encounter when using ASP.NET MVC with Entity Framework, starting with how to perform asynchronous database access. The chapter then built on this to add a new paging feature using asynchronous database access. We then covered how to work with concurrent database edits and deletes, followed by a simple example of how to manually execute your own SQL using Entity Framework. The chapter finished by adding some custom error pages and discussing some common issues you may encounter when working with Entity Framework.

CHAPTER 11

Using Entity Framework Code First with an Existing Database

So far all examples in the book have been based on a project started from scratch with a new database; however, in reality this kind of greenfield project is rare. Entity Framework v6.1 onwards now has a feature that supports using a Code First approach with an existing database.

■ **Note** There are no prerequisites for completing this chapter. It does not require any source code downloads or any of the previous chapters to have been completed.

Create a Database to Use with Code First

To create a database, there are various approaches you can take with Visual Studio. I'll show you how to create one using the SQL Server Object Explorer in Visual Studio. You'll create a simple database with products and categories similar to the one used at the beginning of the book so that you can easily follow along.

First, close any existing solutions that you have open in Visual Studio, and then open the SQL Server Object Explorer from the View menu. Next, open your local version of SQL Server (named (localdb)\MSSQLLocalDB) and locate the database folder. Right-click this folder and choose Add New Database, as shown in Figure 11-1.

L. Naylor, *ASP.NET MVC with Entity Framework and CSS*, DOI 10.1007/978-1-4842-2137-2_11

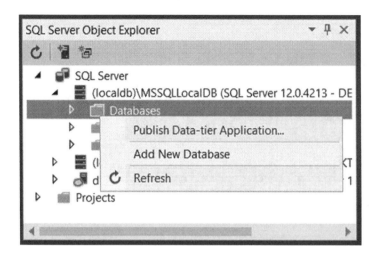

Figure 11-1. *Adding a new database via SQL Server Object Explorer*

In the Create Database window, add a new database named `CodeFirstFromExistingDB` and leave the location as the default. This will store the database under your current user folder in Windows.

Locate the new database in SQL Server Object Explorer and right-click on the Tables folder. Choose Add New Table, as shown in Figure 11-2.

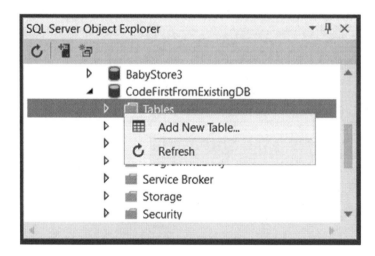

Figure 11-2. *Adding a new table to the CodeFirstFromExistingDB Database*

The design window will now appear in Visual Studio. In the T-SQL pane, change the name of the Table from Table to Categories by updating the first line of the script as follows: CREATE TABLE [dbo]. [Categories]. In the main design pane, add a new Column called Name with a Data Type of nvarchar(50) and uncheck the Allow Nulls column, as shown in Figure 11-3.

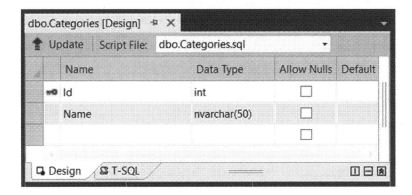

Figure 11-3. *Adding a new Name column to the Categories table*

Finally, we want the primary key to be auto-generated so right-click on the ID column, choose the Properties option from the menu, and change the (Is Identity) property to true in the Properties window (this is normally found in the bottom-right corner of Visual Studio), as shown in Figure 11-4.

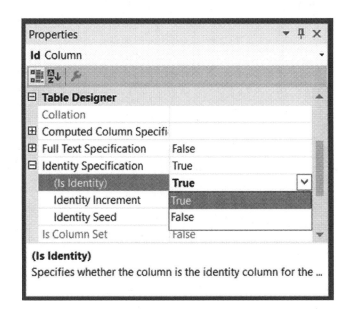

Figure 11-4. *Updating the Is Identity property of the ID column to true*

Click on the Update button at the top-left of the screen. In the Preview Database Updates screen, click the Update Database button. The Data Tools Operations window should appear at the bottom of Visual Studio and inform you that the update completed successfully.

Next create a Products table by choosing Add New Table and performing the following changes:

- ID with Is Identity set to true

- Add a column called Name of data type nvarchar(50) with Allow Nulls unchecked

- Set the table name to Products in the T-SQL pane

- Set a foreign key field named CategoryID, which references the ID column of the categories table by doing the following:

  - Add a new column named CategoryID

  - Set the data type to int

  - Leave Allow Nulls checked

  - Right-click on the Foreign Keys item in the Design window and add a new foreign key named FK_Products_Categories (as shown in Figure 11-5). This will then add a new line to the T-SQL pane containing the new Foreign Key constraint. Alter this to reference the ID column of the categories table as follows:

```
CONSTRAINT [FK_Products_Categories] FOREIGN KEY ([CategoryID]) REFERENCES [Categories]([Id])
```

Figure 11-5. *Adding a new foreign key to the Products table*

When you have made these changes, the design window should appear as shown in Figure 11-6.

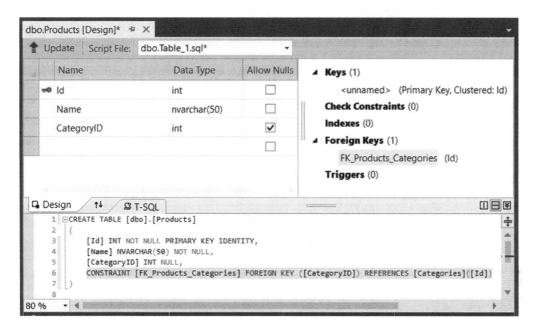

Figure 11-6. *The complete set of changes required to create the Products table*

Update the database; your changes should save successfully. You can now add some data to the database. First of all, add some categories by right-clicking the dbo.Categories table in SQL Server Object Explorer and choosing View Data. In the Data window, add three new categories named Toys, Sleeping, and Feeding. Use the Tab key to move between cells, as shown in Figure 11-7.

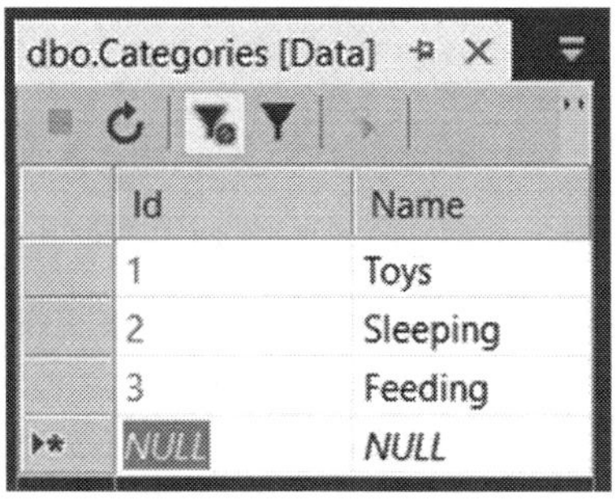

Id	Name
1	Toys
2	Sleeping
3	Feeding
NULL	NULL

dbo.Categories [Data]

Figure 11-7. *Adding data to the Categories table*

Next, add the following data to the Products table:

- Ball with CategoryID of 1

- Rattle with CategoryID of 1

- Sleep Suit with CategoryID of 2

- Milk with CategoryID of 3

- Puree with CategoryID of 3

When you're done, you should now have data in the Products table, as shown in Figure 11-8.

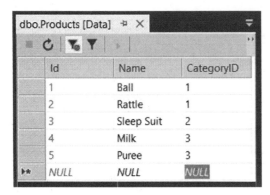

Figure 11-8. *Adding data to the Products table*

We now have a very simple database with products and categories. Finally, right-click on the database and copy the Connection String property so it can be used later.

Setting Up a New Project and Generating a Code First Data Model from the Database

Now we're going to create a new project to use with the CodeFirstFromExistingDB database. Create a new ASP.NET web application called CodeFirstExistingDB with the options shown in Figure 11-9.

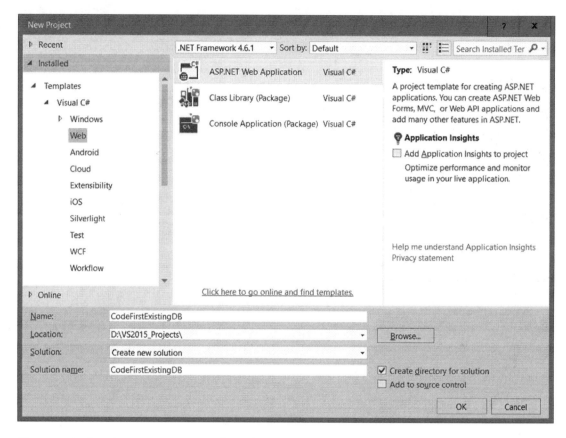

Figure 11-9. *Creating a new ASP.NET web application project named CodeFirstExistingDB*

Click the OK button. In the next window, choose the ASP.NET 4.6.1 MVC Template with the Authentication type set to Individual User Accounts just to be consistent with the main BabyStore project. Figure 11-10 shows the options to select. Click the OK button to create the new project.

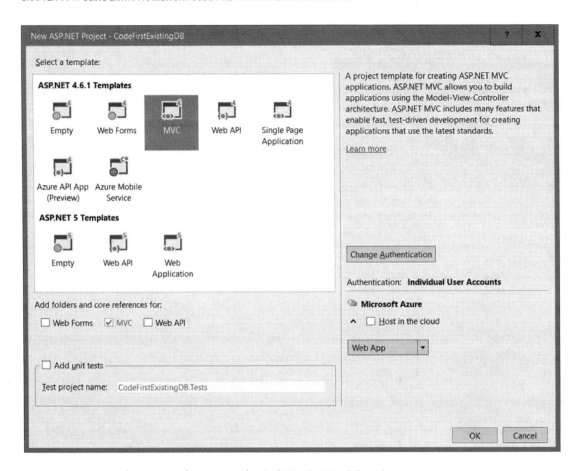

Figure 11-10. *Template options for creating the CodeFirstExistingDB project*

Once the new project is created, right-click on the project in Solution Explorer and choose to add a new item. Choose to add an ADO.NET Entity Data Model and name it StoreContext, as shown in Figure 11-11.

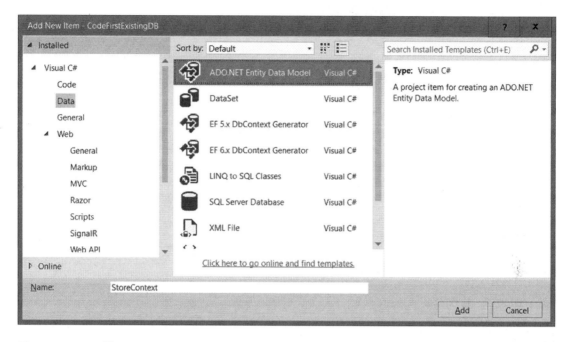

Figure 11-11. *Adding a new ADO.NET entity data model*

Click the Add button and then, in the Entity Data Model Wizard window, choose the Code First from Database option, as shown in Figure 11-12.

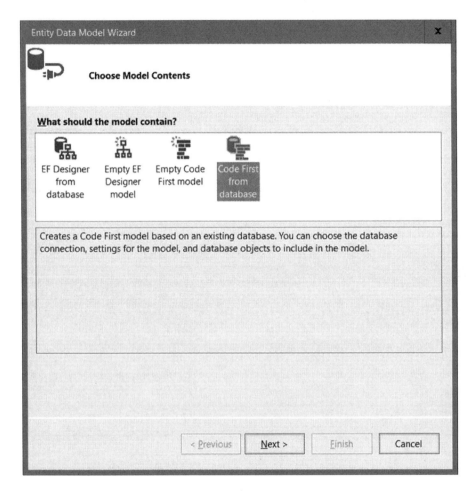

Figure 11-12. *Choosing the Code First from Database model contents*

Click the New Connection button. Now, in the Connection Properties window, set the server name to your local SQL server instance (likely to be (localdb)\MSSQLLocalDB but you can verify this as it will be the first part of the connection string you copied earlier). Then, in the Connect to a Database section, choose the Select option or enter a database name and choose the CodeFirstFromExistingDB database from the list of available databases. Figure 11-13 shows the options to choose.

Figure 11-13. *Choosing the connection properties for the data model*

Next click the OK button. Then, from the Entity Data Model Wizard, accept the new options and click the Next button. Finally, in the Choose Your Database Objects and Settings pane, choose both database tables and check the Pluralize or Singularize Generated Object Names checkbox, as shown in Figure 11-14.

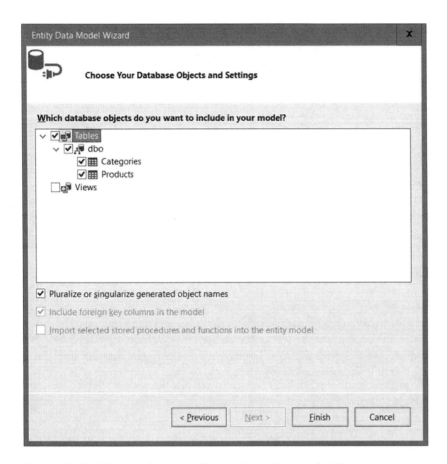

Figure 11-14. *Choosing the options for database objects and settings*

Click the Finish button. Visual Studio will now auto-generate the relevant code, as shown here. The new StoreContext class should appear in the main Visual Studio pane, as follows:

```
namespace CodeFirstExistingDB
{
    using System;
    using System.Data.Entity;
    using System.ComponentModel.DataAnnotations.Schema;
    using System.Linq;

    public partial class StoreContext : DbContext
    {
        public StoreContext()
            : base("name=StoreContext")
        {
        }

        public virtual DbSet<Category> Categories { get; set; }
        public virtual DbSet<Product> Products { get; set; }
```

```
        protected override void OnModelCreating(DbModelBuilder modelBuilder)
        {
        }
    }
}
```

The context class contains two DBSet entries, one for Categories and one for Products similar to the ones we created manually when modeling the BabyStore application. The OnModelCreating method is used for anything that cannot be modeled using attributes. In this example, everything can be covered by using attributes, so this is blank.

The project now also contains two new class files—one for Category and one for Products—representing the Product and Category entities and mapping to the Products and Categories database tables. These classes are contained in the root of the project rather than in the models folder. You can move them into the models folder and change their namespaces if desired.

The auto-generated Category class is as follows:

```
namespace CodeFirstExistingDB
{
    using System;
    using System.Collections.Generic;
    using System.ComponentModel.DataAnnotations;
    using System.ComponentModel.DataAnnotations.Schema;
    using System.Data.Entity.Spatial;

    public partial class Category
    {
        [System.Diagnostics.CodeAnalysis.SuppressMessage("Microsoft.Usage",
                "CA2214:DoNotCallOverridableMethodsInConstructors")]
        public Category()
        {
            Products = new HashSet<Product>();
        }

        public int Id { get; set; }

        [Required]
        [StringLength(50)]
        public string Name { get; set; }

        [System.Diagnostics.CodeAnalysis.SuppressMessage("Microsoft.Usage",
                "CA2227:CollectionPropertiesShouldBeReadOnly")]
        public virtual ICollection<Product> Products { get; set; }
    }
}
```

The class contains properties for each database field and is similar to the one we created by hand when beginning the BabyStore project. It also contains an extra creation of a hashset in an auto-generated constructor and some attributes relating the diagnostic code analysis, which is outside the scope of this book. It also adds attributes to the Name field to control the field length and the fact that the field is required.

The generated Product class is as follows:

```
namespace CodeFirstExistingDB
{
    using System;
    using System.Collections.Generic;
    using System.ComponentModel.DataAnnotations;
    using System.ComponentModel.DataAnnotations.Schema;
    using System.Data.Entity.Spatial;

    public partial class Product
    {
        public int Id { get; set; }

        [Required]
        [StringLength(50)]
        public string Name { get; set; }

        public int? CategoryID { get; set; }

        public virtual Category Category { get; set; }
    }
}
```

This class contains properties for each database field and a virtual property representing the relationship to the category entity. We now have a data model representing the database, which we can use with Entity Framework Code First in the same way as the BabyStore project.

Setting Up a Controller and Views to View the Data

To prove that everything works as expected, we'll set up a new controller and some views by using scaffolding. Build the solution and then right-click on the Controllers folder and choose Add Controller. Then add a new MVC 5 Controller with views, using Entity Framework. Set the Model class as Product and the Data context class as StoreContext. Check the Generate Views, Reference Script Libraries, and Use a Layout Page options, as shown in Figure 11-15. Then click the Add button.

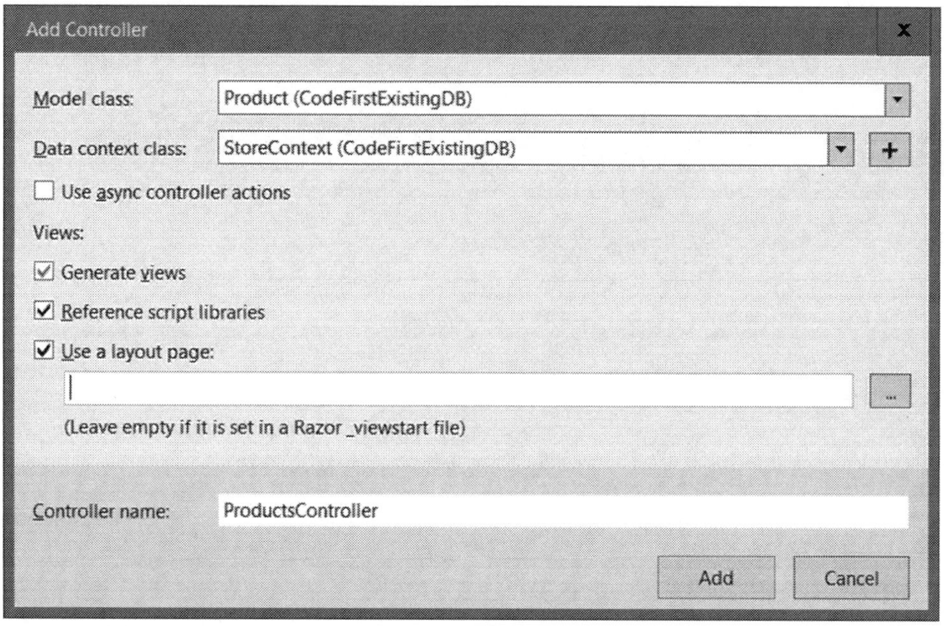

Figure 11-15. *Adding a ProductsController class with views*

Visual Studio will now create a `ProductsController` class with Index and CRUD methods. It will also create a set of views under the `Views/Products` folder. To view the data in your web site, right-click on the `Views/Products/Index.cshtml` file and choose View in Browser. The index page should open as shown in Figure 11-16. It shows the products from the `CodeFirstFromExistingDB` database.

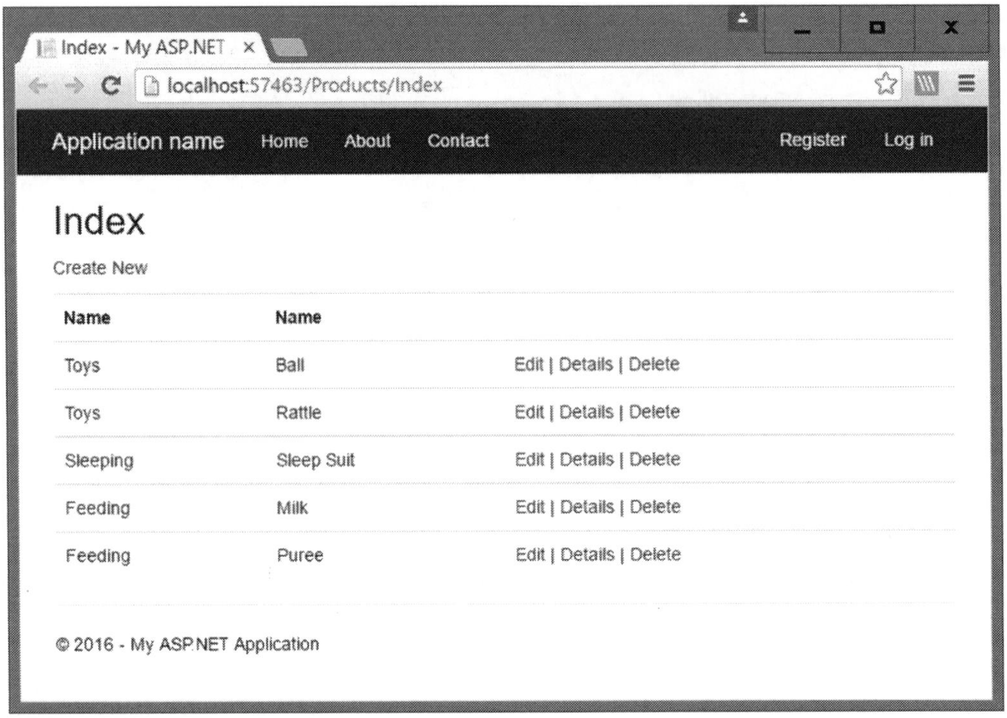

Figure 11-16. *The Products Index page showing data from the Products table of the CodeFirstFromExistingDB database*

Updating the Existing Database Using Code First Migrations

There is going to come a point where you will want to update your existing database model from your code. We've seen earlier in the book that the way to do this is to use migrations; however, using Code First with an existing database requires a little extra care to work correctly.

First of all, you must enable migrations for the project. In Package Manager Console, type the following command (we need to specify the context to use because we included authentication in the project and this uses its own context by default):

```
Enable-Migrations -ContextTypeName CodeFirstExistingDB.StoreContext
```

This will create a `Migrations` folder and add a `Configuration.cs` file to it. Next we want to create our migrations to run. This is where you need to add an extra step for an existing database. If we create a migration now, it will attempt to add all our entities to the database. This will not work because the products and categories tables already exist in the database, so we need to create an initial blank migration and then later we will be able to add a migration for any new changes. To create an initial blank migration for the database, type the following command into Package Manager Console:

```
Add-Migration InitialCreate -IgnoreChanges
```

The key part of this command is the `-IgnoreChanges` flag, which ensures that a migration is created that effectively does nothing. Running it will add an entry to the `migrations` table in the database, thus creating a snapshot of its original schema.

Next, run the update-database command in order to update the existing database with the initial migration. A new migrations table will now have been created in the CodeFirstFromExistingDB database.

Following this, add a new property named Description to the Product class, with a maximum allowed length of 50 characters, as follows:

```
namespace CodeFirstExistingDB
{
    using System;
    using System.Collections.Generic;
    using System.ComponentModel.DataAnnotations;
    using System.ComponentModel.DataAnnotations.Schema;
    using System.Data.Entity.Spatial;

    public partial class Product
    {
        public int Id { get; set; }

        [Required]
        [StringLength(50)]
        public string Name { get; set; }

        [StringLength(50)]
        public string Description { get; set; }

        public int? CategoryID { get; set; }

        public virtual Category Category { get; set; }
    }
}
```

Now add a new migration for the product Description field so you can add it as a new column to the Products table. You do this by typing the following command in the Package Manager Console:

```
Add-Migration add_product_description
```

A new code file will be produced in the Migrations folder that will include code to add a description column to the Products table as follows:

```
namespace CodeFirstExistingDB.Migrations
{
    using System;
    using System.Data.Entity.Migrations;

    public partial class add_product_description : DbMigration
    {
        public override void Up()
        {
            AddColumn("dbo.Products", "Description", c => c.String(maxLength: 50));
        }
```

```
    public override void Down()
    {
        DropColumn("dbo.Products", "Description");
    }
    }
}
```

Now run the update-database command in Package Manager Console to update the database. The new description column will be added to the Products table, as shown in Figure 11-17.

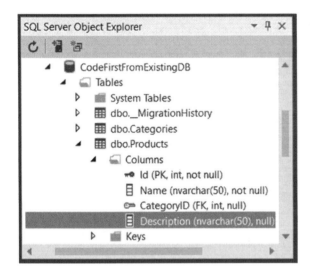

Figure 11-17. *The new Description column in the Products table of the CodeFirstFromExistingDB database*

Now add some test data to the database. View the data of the Products table via SQL Server Object Explorer and enter some descriptions, as shown in Figure 11-18.

Id	Name	CategoryID	Description
1	Ball	1	Round
2	Rattle	1	Noisy
3	Sleep Suit	2	Comfortable
4	Milk	3	Tasty
5	Puree	3	Messy
NULL	NULL	NULL	NULL

Figure 11-18. *Adding test data to the Description column of the Products table*

Next, modify the Views\Products\Index.cshtml file to add a Description field, as highlighted in the following code:

```
@model IEnumerable<CodeFirstExistingDB.Product>

@{
    ViewBag.Title = "Index";
}

<h2>Index</h2>

<p>
    @Html.ActionLink("Create New", "Create")
</p>
<table class="table">
    <tr>
        <th>
            @Html.DisplayNameFor(model => model.Category.Name)
        </th>
        <th>
            @Html.DisplayNameFor(model => model.Name)
        </th>
        <th>
            @Html.DisplayNameFor(model => model.Description)
        </th>
        <th></th>
    </tr>

@foreach (var item in Model) {
    <tr>
        <td>
            @Html.DisplayFor(modelItem => item.Category.Name)
        </td>
        <td>
            @Html.DisplayFor(modelItem => item.Name)
        </td>
        <td>
            @Html.DisplayFor(modelItem => item.Description)
        </td>
        <td>
            @Html.ActionLink("Edit", "Edit", new { id=item.Id }) |
            @Html.ActionLink("Details", "Details", new { id=item.Id }) |
            @Html.ActionLink("Delete", "Delete", new { id=item.Id })
        </td>
    </tr>
}

</table>
```

Now, right-click on the view and choose View in Browser. You should now see the new Description field with the test data, as shown in Figure 11-19.

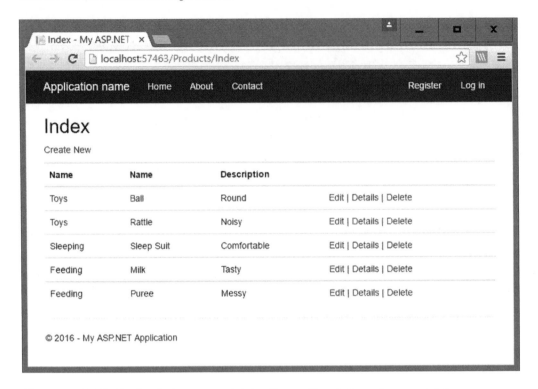

***Figure 11-19.** The Product index page containing the new Description column and data*

You can now work with your existing database as if you had created it using Code First and continue to update it using Code First as required.

Summary

This chapter started by showing you how to manually create a database with data via Visual Studio and then how to create a project containing classes based on this database. We then covered how to work with Code First Migrations in an existing database and update the database based on code changes.

■ ■ ■

CHAPTER 12

Introduction to ASP.NET Core v1.0 (MVC6 and EF 7)

At the time of writing this book, Microsoft was working on the next version of .NET, known as .NET Core v1.0. This contains some significant changes to .NET, with the biggest aim to make it more platform independent. Due to the size of the changes, the release is going to be named ASP.NET Core v1.0. Originally it was going to be known as ASP.NET v5 and ASP.NET MVC included in this release was going to be MVC v6. Entity Framework was going to be known as v7; however, everything is now included under the single umbrella of ASP.NET Core v1.0.

As we write this, the available version of ASP.NET Core is v1.0. One of the most significant changes to ASP.NET MVC Core is an update to the way HTML tags are generated in scaffolded views, using a new feature known as *tag helpers*.

■ **Note**   To complete this chapter, you must have installed Visual Studio 2015 Update 3 in order to access ASP.NET Core v1.0. The chapter does not require any source code downloads or any of the previous chapters to have been completed.

Creating an ASP.NET Core v1.0 MVC Project

The following is an example of working with MVC6 and ASP.NET Core v1.0 to build a simple Baby Store web site. It will show products and categories and use two database contexts—one for the store data and one for authentication—as in the MVC5 project earlier in the book.

Start by creating a new ASP.NET Core web application using .NET Framework 4.6.1 in Visual Studio and name it BabyStoreCore, as shown in Figure 12-1.

© Lee Naylor 2016
L. Naylor, *ASP.NET MVC with Entity Framework and CSS*, DOI 10.1007/978-1-4842-2137-2_12

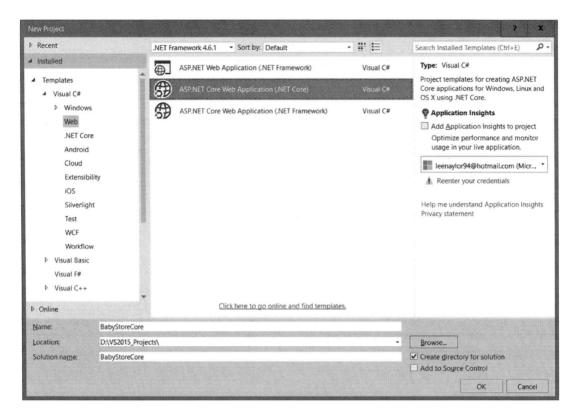

Figure 12-1. *Creating the BabyStoreCore ASP.NET core web application*

In the next window, choose a Web Application template type and leave the authentication set to the Individual User Accounts, as shown in Figure 12-2.

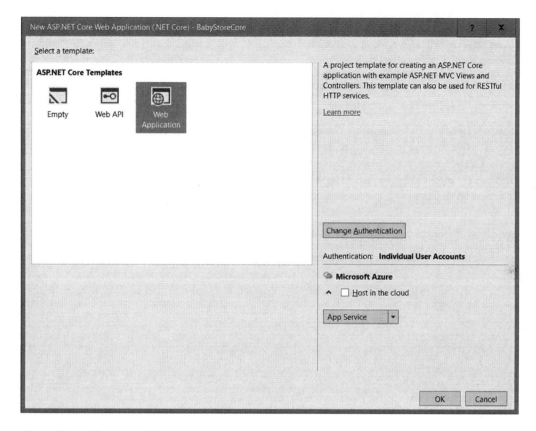

Figure 12-2. *Choosing a Web Application template*

When you click the OK a button, a new solution will be created. The solution contains a different structure than MVC5 projects and now contains two top-level folders—one named Solution Items and one name src. The Solution Items folder will contain a global.json file containing some simple information about the solution in JSON format, containing entries for projects and SDK.

The BabyStoreCore project is located in the src folder and already contains several folders that you will be familiar with from the MVC5 projects. Note that we did not specify we were creating an MVC project when we chose the template type, yet an MVC project was created. This is due to the fact that Microsoft is aiming to move web development away from Web Forms and aims only to support MVC projects in .NET Core.

Adding Product and Category Models

Add a new class named `Category` to the `Models` folder and update the content to add properties to represent the ID, Name, and a navigational property as an `ICollection` of `Products`.

```
using System.Collections.Generic;

namespace BabyStoreCore.Models
{
    public class Category
    {
        public int Id { get; set; }
        public string Name { get; set; }

        public virtual ICollection<Product> Products { get; set; }
    }
}
```

Now add a new `Product` class to the `Models` folder and update the content to add an ID, Name, Description, and Price. Then add a `CategoryID` and navigational property to a `Category` as follows:

```
using System.ComponentModel.DataAnnotations;

namespace BabyStoreCore.Models
{
    public class Product
    {
        public int ID { get; set; }
        public string Name { get; set; }
        public string Description { get; set; }
        [DisplayFormat(DataFormatString = "{0:c}")]
        public decimal Price { get; set; }
        public int? CategoryID { get; set; }

        public virtual Category Category { get; set; }
    }
}
```

These classes work the same as the other simple classes used in the `Models` folder during the MVC5 projects and model a zero-to-many relationship between a category and products (a category can have several products and a product can belong to none or one category).

Adding a Database Context

We're going to follow the pattern we used for MVC5 projects and create a separate database context class for the store data rather than use the existing user database. This time though we're going to add the file to the Models folder rather than create a DAL folder. Add a database context class called StoreContext to the Models folder as follows. The class derives from DbContext and contains properties to represent each table in the database. Note that DbContext is now part of the Microsoft.EntityFrameworkCore namespace rather than Microsoft.Data.Entity:

```
using Microsoft.EntityFrameworkCore;

namespace BabyStoreCore.Models
{
    public class StoreContext : DbContext
    {
        public StoreContext(DbContextOptions<StoreContext> options) : base(options) { }

        public DbSet<Category> Categories { get; set; }
        public DbSet<Product> Products { get; set; }
    }
}
```

The class contains a constructor method, which takes an input parameter named options of the type DbContextOptions<StoreContext>, which is passed to the constructor of the base class (DbContext). This ensures the context is created with a set of options, such as which provider to use (in this case SQL Server). The options are specified in the Startup.cs file, as you will see later.

Seeding the Database with Test Data

Data seeding is done differently in ASP.NET Core (EF7 and MVC6) than with previous versions. To seed the database with some test data, you add a new class named SeedData to the Models folder, as follows:

```
using Microsoft.Extensions.DependencyInjection;
using System;
using System.Linq;

namespace BabyStoreCore.Models
{
    public class SeedData
    {
        public static void Initialize(IServiceProvider serviceProvider)
        {
            var context = serviceProvider.GetService<StoreContext>();

            if (context.Database == null)
            {
                throw new Exception("DB is null");
            }
```

```
        if (context.Products.Any())
        {
            return;   // DB has been seeded
        }

        var feeding = context.Categories.Add(new Category { Name = "Feeding" }).Entity;
        var sleeping = context.Categories.Add(new Category { Name = "Sleeping" }).Entity;

        context.Products.AddRange(
            new Product
            {
                Name = "Milk",
                Description = "Tasty anti-reflux milk",
                Price = 9.99M,
                Category = feeding
            },
            new Product
            {
                Name = "SleepSuit",
                Description = "Comfortable sleep wear",
                Price = 3.99M,
                Category = sleeping
            }
        );

        context.SaveChanges();
    }
  }
}
```

The SeedData contains a method named Initialize and later in the text we will add a call to this method when the application starts up via the Startup.cs file. This method takes an input parameter of the type IServiceProvider named serviceProvider. ASP.NET Core MVC works based on the concept of services, where a service is a feature accessible to the project. This method attempts to obtain the StoreContext service, so we'll need to add this to the services available to the project. We will cover this shortly. The code then checks to determine if the database is null or has been seeded already. If has not been seeded, the new test data is created and added using the Context object in a similar way to the rest of the book (see Chapter 4 for an explanation on seeding with MVC5 and EF6).

Configuring the Connection String for the Database

For ASP.NET Core projects, configuration is no longer performed in a Web.Config file; it is instead done via JSON in the appsettings.json file. To add a new connection string for the StoreContext and to create a database named BabyStoreCore_v1, add the following bold entry to the appsettings.json file:

```
{
  "ConnectionStrings": {
    "DefaultConnection": "Server=(localdb)\\mssqllocaldb;Database=aspnet-BabyStoreCore-4a7d214c-3ec1-4ee6-8ffb-a34de98bdc02;Trusted_Connection=True;MultipleActiveResultSets=true",
    "StoreConnection": "Server=(localdb)\\mssqllocaldb;Database=BabyStoreCore_v1;Trusted_Connection=True;MultipleActiveResultSets=true"
  },
```

```
  "Logging": {
    "IncludeScopes": false,
    "LogLevel": {
      "Default": "Debug",
      "System": "Information",
      "Microsoft": "Information"
    }
  }
}
```

This will create the database under your user folder in Windows in the folder C:\Users\<UserName>, where <UserName> is the Windows account you are logged into.

Configuring the Project to Use the SeedData Class and StoreContext

We now need to configure the application to use the SeedData class, the StoreContext class, and the new connection string. Edit StartUp.cs to add the following to the ConfigureServices method so it can use the new StoreConnection connection string and StoreContext class:

```
// This method gets called by the runtime. Use this method to add services to the container.
public void ConfigureServices(IServiceCollection services)
{
    // Add framework services.
    services.AddDbContext<ApplicationDbContext>(options =>
        options.UseSqlServer(Configuration.GetConnectionString("DefaultConnection")));

    services.AddDbContext<StoreContext>(options =>
        options.UseSqlServer(Configuration.GetConnectionString("StoreConnection")));

    services.AddIdentity<ApplicationUser, IdentityRole>()
        .AddEntityFrameworkStores<ApplicationDbContext>()
        .AddDefaultTokenProviders();

    services.AddMvc();

    // Add application services.
    services.AddTransient<IEmailSender, AuthMessageSender>();
    services.AddTransient<ISmsSender, AuthMessageSender>();
}
```

Next, you'll update the Configure() method to add a call to the Initialize method of the SeedData class. Add this line of code to the end of the method:

```
SeedData.Initialize(app.ApplicationServices);
```

Using Migrations to Create the Database

First, you must build the solution. Migrations in ASP.NET MVC Core no longer run in the Package Manager Console. They instead run in the command window. To create and populate the database, run the following steps:

1. Open a command prompt and navigate to the ...\BabyStoreCore\src\ BabyStoreCore directory.

2. Run the dotnet ef migrations add Initial -c StoreContext command. This adds a migration called Initial to the project using the StoreContext context file, which will target the database that stores products and categories rather than the database that stores users and roles.

   - A new file named <timestamp>_Initial.cs will now have been created under the Migrations folder, where <timestamp> is a numeric representation of the time the file was created. This folder also includes a file named StoreContextModelSnapshot.cs
     which, as its name suggests, contains a snapshot of the models backing the StoreContext file. This allows Entity Framework to differentiate against the current model and it then uses this to scaffold the operations in order to bring the database in line with the current models.

3. Create the database by running the dotnet ef database update -c StoreContext command. This will probably take a few seconds to run and is completed when the Done message appears in the command window. The database will now be visible in SQL Server Object Explorer; however, it will not contain any data.

4. To populate the database, start the project without debugging. The Category and Product tables will now be populated with the data from the SeedData class.

Adding Controllers and Views

We're now going to add two controller classes for Products and Categories to get a simple site up and running with the new data. Right-click on the Controllers folder and choose the Add ➤ Controller option. In the Add Scaffold window, choose the MVC Controller with Views, Using Entity Framework option, as shown in Figure 12-3.

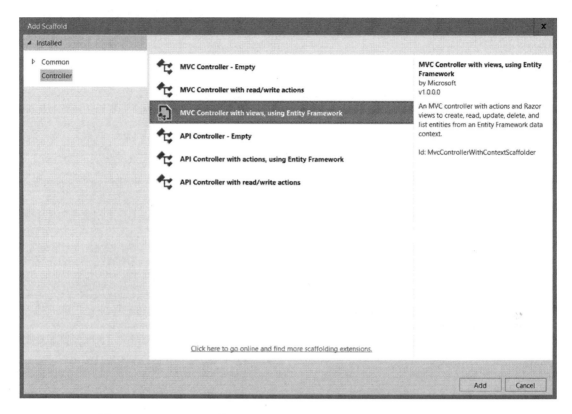

Figure 12-3. *Adding a new MVC controller with views, using Entity Framework*

Click the Add button. Then, in the Add Controller window, add a new controller named CategoriesController with the Model class set to Category, the Data context class set to StoreContext, and all the options for in the views section checked, as shown in Figure 12-4.

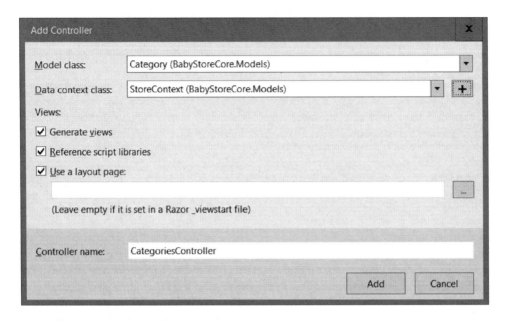

Figure 12-4. *Adding the CategoriesController*

Click the Add button to create the new CategoriesController. The controller class will be created with the scaffolded methods for Index, Details, Create, Edit, and Delete, similar to those found in MVC5; **however, all the methods that query the database are asynchronous by default in ASP.NET Core.** One point to note is that the class no longer creates an instance of StoreContext in the controller itself; instead, it is passed in via the constructor as follows:

```
public class CategoriesController : Controller
{
    private readonly StoreContext _context;

    public CategoriesController(StoreContext context)
    {
        _context = context;
    }
```

ASP.NET Core is geared toward supporting dependency injection to avoid hard-coding dependencies in the code. This is an example of where the generated code no longer hard-codes an instance of the object it requires; instead, it is passed into the class (also known as "injection"). The line of code

```
services.AddDbContext<StoreContext>(options =>
    options.UseSqlServer(Configuration.GetConnectionString("StoreConnection")));
```

that was added to the StartUp.cs file earlier ensures that whenever the project requires an instance of the type StoreContext it will use the StoreContext class. The AddDbContext method deals with creating the instance of StoreContext.

Repeat the process of adding a controller and add a new ProductsController using the Model Class Product and the Data context class StoreContext. Then generate the views. You should now have a ProductsController and a CategoriesController and the views folder should contain Products and Categories folders containing the related views for each method in the respective controllers.

Viewing the Data in the Web Site

First add some new hyperlinks to the Products and Categories controller in the Views\Shared\Layout.cshtml file:

```
<div class="navbar-collapse collapse">
    <ul class="nav navbar-nav">
        <li><a asp-controller="Home" asp-action="Index">Home</a></li>
        <li><a asp-controller="Home" asp-action="About">About</a></li>
        <li><a asp-controller="Home" asp-action="Contact">Contact</a></li>
        <li><a asp-controller="Categories" asp-action="Index">Categories</a></li>
        <li><a asp-controller="Products" asp-action="Index">Products</a></li>
    </ul>
    @await Html.PartialAsync("_LoginPartial")
</div>
```

Note that rather the using the HTML.ActionLink helper, MVC6 now supports a new concept known as tag helpers; the links to the products and categories controllers use the new Anchor Tag Helper. There are many tag helpers available and their aim is to make the markup of the views resemble HTML as much as possible while simplifying the code needed to generate HTML elements. For example, the new way of generating a hyperlink is neater than using the HTML ActionLink helper.

Start the application without debugging. In the home page, click on each of the new links you just added. They should display the category and product data, as shown in Figures 12-5 and 12-6, respectively.

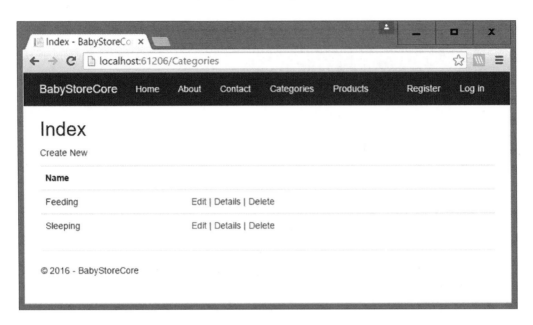

Figure 12-5. Viewing category data

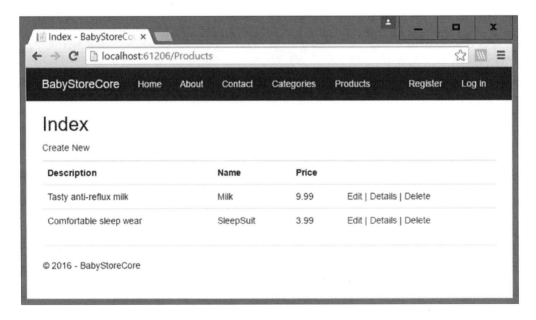

Figure 12-6. Viewing product data

───

■ **Note** At the time of this writing, ASP.NET MVC does not contain tag helpers for displaying model fields. If you open `Views\Products\Details.cshtml`, you will see that the code used to display each of the product's field still uses the MVC5-style HTML helpers.

───

Correcting Bugs with the Scaffolding Generated Code

With the web site running, open the Products Index page and click on the Create New link. You will receive the error "NullReferenceException: `Object reference not set to an instance of an object`". This bug is caused by issues with the scaffolded code in the `Create` and `Edit` methods in the `ProductsController` class.

Update both `Create` methods in the `\Controllers\ProductsController.cs` file to change the data generated in each method so that the `SelectList` element generates the text element of each item in the list. This is generated from the `Name` property of a `Category`. Update the GET version of the `Create` method as follows:

```
// GET: Products/Create
public IActionResult Create()
{
    ViewData["CategoryID"] = new SelectList(_context.Categories, "Id", "Name");
    return View();
}
```

Now update the `HttpPost` version of the `Create` method as follows, in order to cover the creation of the `SelectList` when the model is not valid:

```
// POST: Products/Create
// To protect from overposting attacks, please enable the specific properties you want to
bind to, for
// more details see http://go.microsoft.com/fwlink/?LinkId=317598.
[HttpPost]
[ValidateAntiForgeryToken]
public async Task<IActionResult> Create([Bind("ID,CategoryID,Description,Name,Price")] Product
    product)
{
    if (ModelState.IsValid)
    {
        _context.Add(product);
        await _context.SaveChangesAsync();
        return RedirectToAction("Index");
    }
    ViewData["CategoryID"] = new SelectList(_context.Categories, "Id", "Name",
        product.CategoryID);
    return View(product);
}
```

Make the same changes to the `SelectList` code in the two versions of the `Edit` methods, since they also suffer from the same issue.

Summary

This has been a brief introduction to using MVC in ASP.NET Core. We covered creating a project, a basic model, and the database context. I then showed you how to seed the database with test data and update the project configuration for the new database connection string and use the new database context and seeding method. Finally, we covered adding some simple controllers and views using the scaffolding process.

CHAPTER 13

Deploying to Azure

Azure is Microsoft's cloud hosting solution. This chapter shows how to deploy the web site to Azure and have it run over the Web. Azure is available for a free trial period and so can be used by anyone for a limited period of time. Alternatively, if you have registered your copy of Visual Studio and have a Microsoft account, you should be eligible for the Developer Program Benefit and receive a free 12-month trial with $25 a month credit. There are a few ways to deploy to the cloud from Visual Studio; for example, Visual Studio will offer to host your solution in the cloud as soon as you log into it with a Microsoft account; however, in this example I'm going to provide a more detailed example using the Azure Portal to set up servers prior to deploying to them.

■ **Note** To complete this chapter, you must either have completed Chapter 10 or download Chapter 10's source code from www.apress.com as a starting point.

Preparing to Deploy to Azure

Changing from Using a Database Initializer to using a Code First Migrations Seed Method

The starting point for this chapter is the BabyStore solution from Chapter 10. We need to make some changes to the code in order to deploy to Azure. At the moment, the project uses a database initializer to set up the users and roles in the user database. Database initializers do not work on Azure due to the fact that they seek to potentially drop the database and this is not allowed. Instead Azure uses Code First Migrations to update the database.

In order to allow the code for creating an admin user and creating admin and user roles to be able to run on Azure, we're going to port it to run inside the Seed method of the Configuration class located in the Migrations\Configuration.cs file. This method runs whenever the database is updated via Code First Migrations and is allowed to run on Azure, making it an ideal place to seed the user and role data.

Open the Migrations\Configuration.cs file and modify the Seed method to create a new userStore, userManager, roleStore, and roleManager, as follows:

```
namespace BabyStore.Migrations
{
    using Microsoft.AspNet.Identity;
    using Microsoft.AspNet.Identity.EntityFramework;
    using Models;
    using System;
```

```
using System.Data.Entity;
using System.Data.Entity.Migrations;
using System.Linq;

internal sealed class Configuration :
    DbMigrationsConfiguration<BabyStore.Models.ApplicationDbContext>
{
    public Configuration()
    {
        AutomaticMigrationsEnabled = false;
        ContextKey = "BabyStore.Models.ApplicationDbContext";
    }

    protected override void Seed(BabyStore.Models.ApplicationDbContext context)
    {
        var userStore = new UserStore<ApplicationUser>(context);
        var userManager = new UserManager<ApplicationUser>(userStore);
        var roleStore = new RoleStore<IdentityRole>(context);
        var roleManager = new RoleManager<IdentityRole>(roleStore);

    }
}
}
```

The creation of these store and the manager variables is similar to the code found in the App_Start\
IdentityConfig.cs file for the classes ApplicationUserManager and ApplicationRoleManager; however,
the code inside the Seed method does not use IOwinContext.

Next, cut the code from the InitializeIdentityForEF method of the ApplicationDBInitializer
class in the App_Start\IdentityConfig.cs file (making the method body empty) and paste it into the Seed
method of the Migrations\Configuration.cs file to update it, as follows:

```
protected override void Seed(BabyStore.Models.ApplicationDbContext context)
{
    var userStore = new UserStore<ApplicationUser>(context);
    var userManager = new UserManager<ApplicationUser>(userStore);
    var roleStore = new RoleStore<IdentityRole>(context);
    var roleManager = new RoleManager<IdentityRole>(roleStore);

    const string name = "admin@mvcbabystore.com";
    const string password = "Adm1n@mvcbabystore.com";
    const string roleName = "Admin";

    //Create Role Admin if it does not exist
    var role = roleManager.FindByName(roleName);
    if (role == null)
    {
        role = new IdentityRole(roleName);
        var roleresult = roleManager.Create(role);
    }
```

```
    var user = userManager.FindByName(name);
    if (user == null)
    {
        user = new ApplicationUser
        {
            UserName = name,
            Email = name,
            FirstName = "Admin",
            LastName = "Admin",
            DateOfBirth = new DateTime(2015, 1, 1),
            Address = new Address
            {
                AddressLine1 = "1 Some Street",
                Town = "Town",
                County = "County",
                Postcode = "PostCode"
            }
        };
        var result = userManager.Create(user, password);
        result = userManager.SetLockoutEnabled(user.Id, false);
    }

    // Add user admin to Role Admin if not already added
    var rolesForUser = userManager.GetRoles(user.Id);
    if (!rolesForUser.Contains(role.Name))
    {
        var result = userManager.AddToRole(user.Id, role.Name);
    }

    //Create users role
    const string userRoleName = "Users";
    role = roleManager.FindByName(userRoleName);
    if (role == null)
    {
        role = new IdentityRole(userRoleName);
        var roleresult = roleManager.Create(role);
    }
}
```

Next, we need to test that this code works. The simplest way to do this is to create a new database for holding user and role data. Update the DefaultConnection connectionString entry in the main Web. config file as follows (ensure you keep the entry all on one line):

```
<add name="DefaultConnection" connectionString="Data Source=(LocalDb)\MSSQLLocalDB;AttachD
bFilename=|DataDirectory|\aspnet-BabyStore-Identity3.mdf;Initial Catalog=aspnet-BabyStore-
Identity3;Integrated Security=True" providerName="System.Data.SqlClient" />
```

Now start the web site without debugging and attempt to log in (the login attempt will fail). This should create the new v3 of the Identity database. Figure 13-1 shows how the new database should appear in Solution Explorer.

Figure 13-1. *The new aspnet-BabyStore-Identity3 database shown in Solution Explorer*

Right-click the database in Solution Explorer and select Open from the menu. This will open the database in Server Explorer. If you view the data in the AspNetUsers and AspNetRoles tables, you will see that they are empty. Run the update-database -configuration configuration command in Package Manager Console and the Seed method will run. Open the tables again and they will now contain data, plus you will now be able to log in as the user admin@mvcbabystore.com.

If you want to continue testing locally with the test users created in previous chapters, revert the connectionString entry back to its previous state so it reads as follows. This will ensure that any users or roles you created manually are still available for use:

```
<add name="DefaultConnection" connectionString="Data Source=(LocalDb)\MSSQLLocalDB;AttachD
bFilename=|DataDirectory|\aspnet-BabyStore-Identity2.mdf;Initial Catalog=aspnet-BabyStore-
Identity2;Integrated Security=True" providerName="System.Data.SqlClient" />
```

Setting Up Azure

To set up Azure, either register for a free trial or take advantage of the Microsoft Developer Program Benefit, which grants 12 months' access to Azure with $25 credit each month. Once registered, log into the Azure Portal web site and add a new Web APP + SQL from the Marketplace. (Choose the New + option then click on See All followed by Web + Mobile.) You should see the screen shown in Figure 13-2.

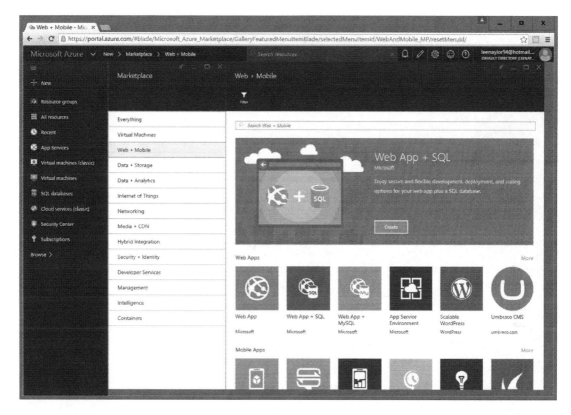

Figure 13-2. *Using the Azure marketplace to add a Web App + SQL*

Choose to add Web App + SQL and you will be prompted to fill in some details for your app. Fill in your app name to give the site a URL to run on. For example, I used MVCBabyStore.azurewebsites.net for this example web site URL. You won't be able to choose this name, since it is used for this demo, so enter your own app name.

Next, add a New Resource Group Name (BabyStore is used here) and optionally add a new App Service plan to run the server nearer to your geographical location. I'm adding a new plan to run in North Europe, as it is closer to our location. Figure 13-3 shows the setup options for this example.

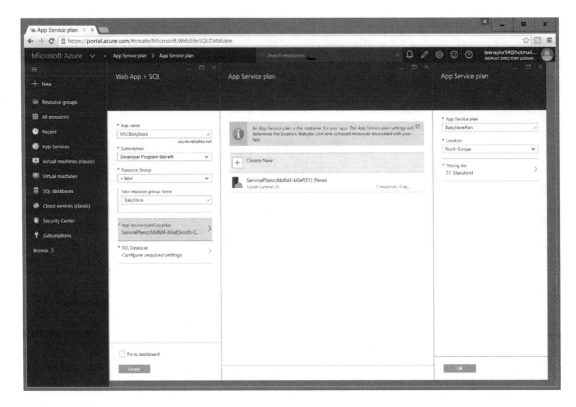

Figure 13-3. *Setting options for the app name, a resource group, and a new app service plan*

If you have entered a new app service plan, click on the OK button to confirm it, and then click on the
SQL Database section to configure the database. First, name the database `aspnet-BabyStore-Identity`, and
then configure the Target server options. Enter an appropriate server name and add an admin user with a
suitable password. Choose a location for you database, ideally the same location as your web server. Ensure
that Allow Azure services to Access Server is checked and accept the default collation for the database server.
Figure 13-4 shows these options.

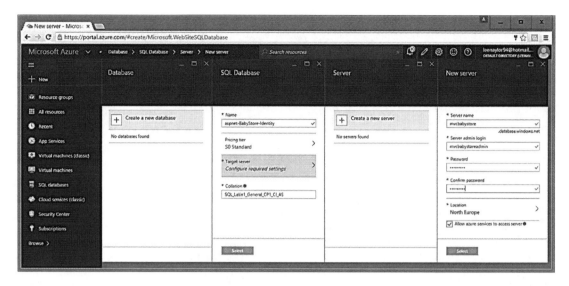

Figure 13-4. *Configuring the database server*

Next click the Select and Create buttons to create the new Web App + SQL application. Azure will run through a deployment process, which will take a few minutes to complete. When this is completed, you should be able to click on the All Resources link in the dashboard. Your newly created resources should be visible, similar to those shown in Figure 13-5.

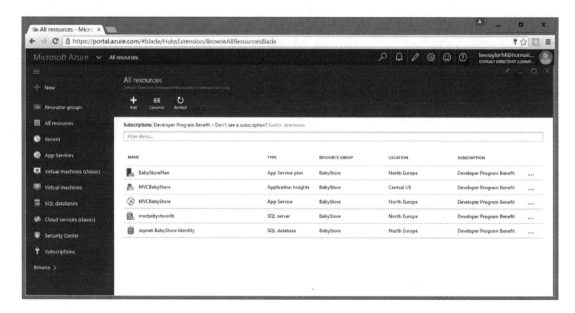

Figure 13-5. *Viewing the new resources*

To recap, this has now created a web server where the web site will run plus a database server to hold the user and role data. We also need to add a database to hold the store data. To add a new database, click SQL Databases from the side menu and click the Add + button. A section of the screen will open to allow you to create a new database. Add a new database named BabyStore, keeping the subscription set to whatever your current subscription is. Keep the Resource group set to BabyStore. Select the source as a blank database and ensure the server is set to your database server name. Keep the collation and pricing tier set to their default values. Figure 13-6 shows the options to choose. Click the Create button; Azure will run a deployment process to create the database.

Figure 13-6. *Adding a database for store data*

If you click the SQL databases item from the side menu, you should see the new database listed along with the aspnet-BabyStore-Identity database, as shown in Figure 13-7.

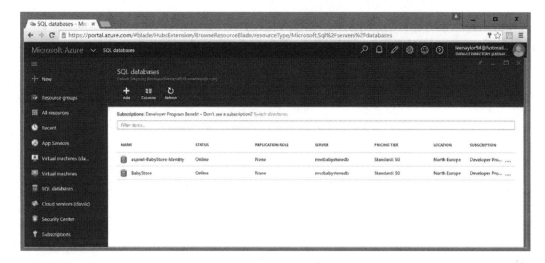

Figure 13-7. *Confirmation that the new BabyStore database has been created*

Deploying to Azure from Visual Studio

Open the current BabyStore solution in Visual Studio and ensure that you have signed into Visual Studio using the Microsoft Account you used for your Azure subscription. Next, click on the Tools menu and choose the Connect to Microsoft Azure Subscription option. You should be promoted to enter an e-mail address, so enter the e-mail address you used for your Azure account. Verify you are connected by opening Server Explorer and the Azure node. You should be able to see the new BabyStore App Service and the BabyStore and aspnet-BabyStore-Identity databases, as shown in Figure 13-8.

Figure 13-8. *Viewing the Azure connection via Server Explorer*

449

To publish the solution to Azure, click on Build from the main Visual Studio menu and the click the Publish BabyStore option. Select Microsoft Azure App Service from the Publish Web window. The Microsoft Azure Web Apps window will appear. Select the MVCBabyStore item, as shown in Figure 13-9, and then click OK.

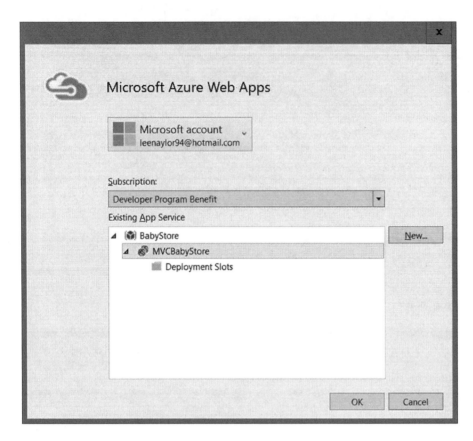

Figure 13-9. *Selecting the MVCBabyStore app to deploy to*

The Publish Web window will appear; choose the Web Deploy method and keep all the other default options. Then click the Validate Connection button. You should get a green checkmark, as shown in Figure 13-10, indicating that the connection was successful.

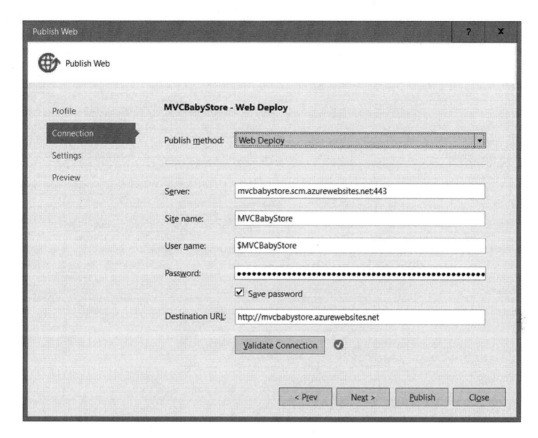

Figure 13-10. *Validating the connection in the Publish Web window*

Now click the Next button. The Settings section of the Publish Web window will appear, as shown in Figure 13-11. Change the Configuration to Debug so that we can use remote debugging later in the chapter.

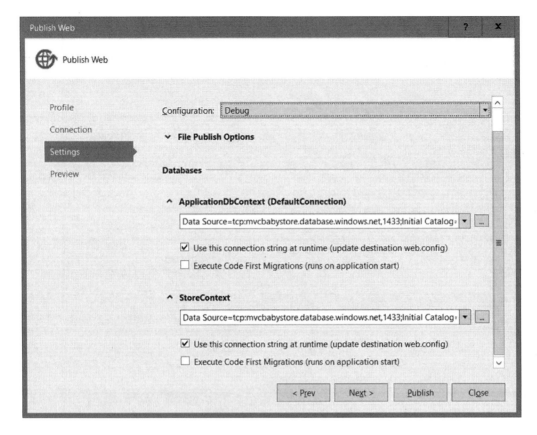

Figure 13-11. *Configuring the Publish Web Settings options*

Configuring Database Publishing

In the Publish Web Settings options, the Databases options contain entries for determining which database each database context in the BabyStore solution should target. In this deployment, ApplicationDBContext needs to target the aspnet-BabyStore-Identity database and StoreContext should target the BabyStore database. If you inspect the connection string for the both connections, you will see that they both contain the text Initial Catalog=aspnet-BabyStore-Identity, meaning that both contexts are targeting the aspnet-BabyStore-Identity database.

To make StoreContext target the BabyStore database, you could just modify the connection string manually; however, we're going to do this using Visual Studio in order to demonstrate a common issue when deploying the Azure. Click the ... button next to the StoreContext connection string in the Publish Web window. The Destination Connection String window will appear, as shown in Figure 13-12.

Dialog window titled "Destination Connection String"

Enter information to connect to the selected data source or click "Change" to choose a different data source and/or provider.

Data source:

Microsoft SQL Server (SqlClient)   [Change...]

Server name:

tcp:mvcbabystoredb.database.windows.net,1433 ▾   [Refresh]

Log on to the server

○ Use Windows Authentication
◉ Use SQL Server Authentication

User name: mvcbabystoreadmin@mvcbabystoredb.databas

Password: ●●●●●●●●●

☐ Save my password

Connect to a database

◉ Select or enter a database name:
aspnet-BabyStore-Identity ▾

○ Attach a database file:

[Browse...]

Logical name:

[Advanced...]

[Test Connection]   [OK]   [Cancel]

Figure 13-12. *The Destination Connection String window*

Now attempt to change the target database name by clicking on the drop-down list containing aspnet-BabyStore-Identity. Visual Studio will attempt to display a list of databases from the remote Azure database server, but it will fail with the error message shown in Figure 13-13.

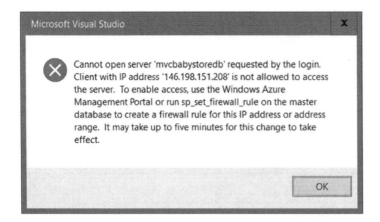

Figure 13-13. *Firewall error message when attempting to connect to the mvcbabystoredb server*

This error is caused because your PC does not have access to the remote database server. To enable this access, open the Azure Portal in a web browser and view All Resources, then click on the database server entry (our server is named mvcbabystoredb). Next click on Show Firewall Settings, which will open the Firewall section on the right of the screen. Finally, click on the Add Client IP link at the top right of the screen to grant your local IP address access to the database server. Figure 13-14 shows the Azure Portal with the options activated.

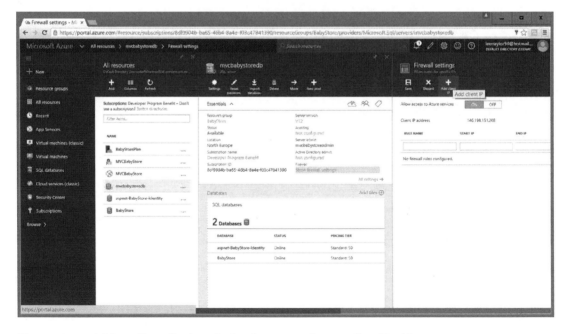

Figure 13-14. *Adding a firewall rule to the database server for your client IP address*

A new firewall rule should appear similar to the one shown in Figure 13-15. Once it has appeared, click the Save button to add the new rule.

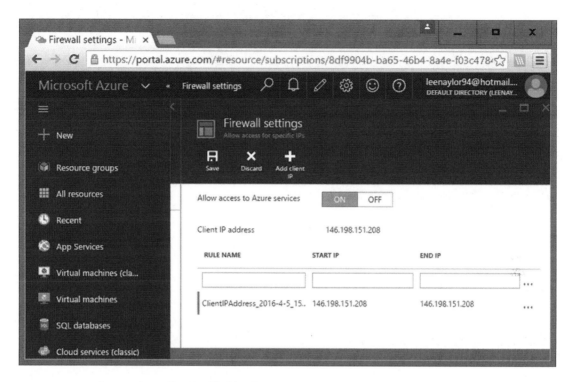

Figure 13-15. *The new firewall rule added for the client IP address*

Now go back to Visual Studio and open the Destination Connection String window for the StoreContext again, and then click on the aspnet-BabyStore-Identity database entry to change it to a different database. You should now see three databases shown in Figure 13-16. Select the BabyStore database and click the Test Connection button. The test should be successful. Assuming it is, click the OK button.

Figure 13-16. *The updated firewall rule now allows selection of a database in Visual Studio*

In the Publish Web window, ensure that you check the Execute Code First Migrations option for both database contexts, as shown in Figure 13-17.

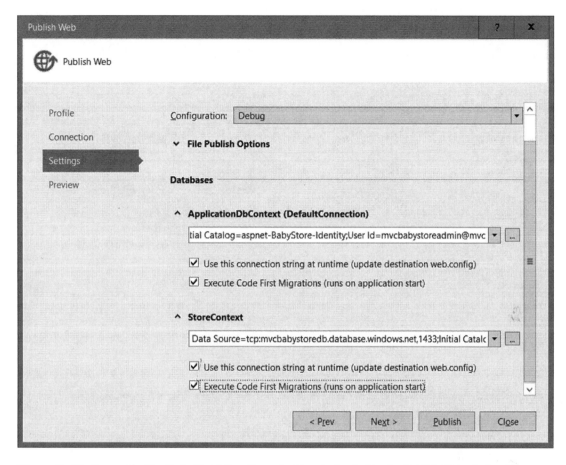

Figure 13-17. Ensure the Use Code First Migrations checkbox is checked in the Publish Web window

Next, click the Publish button to publish the web site and databases to Azure. The output window of Visual Studio will show the progress of the publish; it will probably take a few minutes to complete. When the deployment completes, the web site should open automatically in your default web browser. Figure 13-18 shows the resulting site successfully published and running under the `http://mvcbabystore.azurewebsites.net/` URL.

Figure 13-18. *The site successfully published to Azure*

■ **Caution** Azure is sensitive to the order the databases are added to the web app when you first create it via the Azure portal. Be aware of this if you deploy a site with two connection strings and one of them is named defaultConnection. If we had created the BabyStore database first when creating the web app via the portal, then Azure would have created an entry in the app named defaultConnection with the value set to the BabyStore database rather than the Identity database. This would mean that the app would then have tried to connect to the BabyStore database whenever it tried to use defaultConnection so the web site would error when trying to look up a user.

If you do encounter this scenario, it is easily fixed by opening the Web App ➤ Settings ➤ Application Settings section in the Azure portal. Under the Connection Strings section, change the value of the defaultConnection to point at the same database as the defaultConnection entry in your local solution.

Redeploying Code Changes to Azure

The site is now up and running in Azure, but the currency is set to dollars, yet locally in my development environment, this was always set to British Pounds due to our server locale. If you want to change the currency and locale, configure your application via the Web.Config file by adding a globalization entry to the system.web section, as highlighted in bold:

```
<system.web>
  <authentication mode="None" />
  <compilation debug="true" targetFramework="4.6.1" />
  <httpRuntime targetFramework="4.6.1" maxRequestLength="20480" />
```

```
<globalization uiCulture="en-GB" culture="en-GB"/>
 <customErrors mode="Off"/>
</system.web>
```

Next make a very small change to the Views\Shared\Layout.cshtml file to change the copyright section as follows:

```
<div class="container body-content">
    @RenderBody()
    <hr />
    <footer>
        <p>&copy; @DateTime.Now.Year - MVC Baby Store</p>
    </footer>
</div>
```

We now have a very simple code change and a config change to redeploy to Azure. To deploy them, click on Publish BabyStore from the Build menu and click the Publish button in the Publish Web window. You should see that this deployment is much quicker because only the files that have changed are deployed. The web site should open with the changes in a matter of seconds rather than minutes.

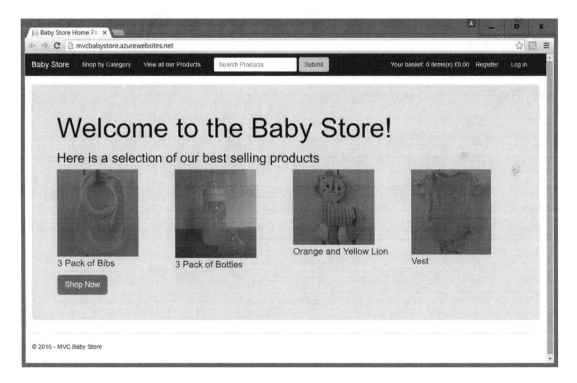

Figure 13-19. The redeployed web site with updated currency and copyright

Remote Debugging an Azure Web Application

To allow your application to be remotely debugged in Azure, you must set the configuration option to Debug when deploying the solution. If you recall, this was already set during the deployment of the BabyStore solution so remote debugging could be demonstrated.

To start remote debugging, ensure you are logged into Azure via Visual Studio (if not, it will prompt you to log in). Then expand the Azure node in Server Explorer until you see your web app. Then right-click the web app (in this example, it's named MVCBabyStore) and choose Attach Debugger from the menu, as shown in Figure 13-20.

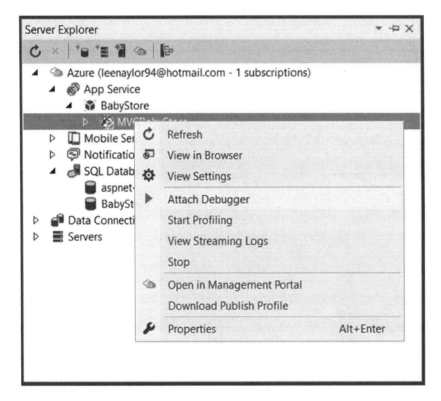

Figure 13-20. *Attaching a debugger to an Azure web app from Visual Studio*

The web site should now start up and if you now add a breakpoint in Visual Studio, you will be able to debug the remote code within Visual Studio as if it were running locally. This is a very useful when the remote code starts behaving differently than your local server due to environment issues (for example, this is how I figured out what was wrong with using a Database Initializer on Azure). Figures 13-21 and 13-22 show the web site http://mvcbabystore.azurewebsites.net/ being debugged on a local PC.

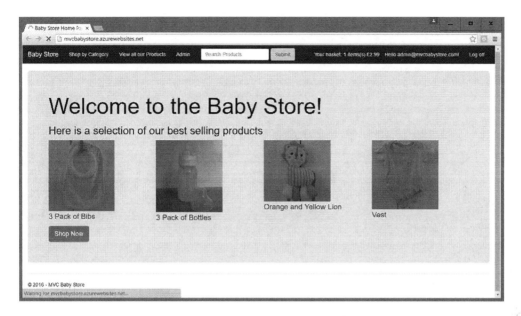

Figure 13-21. *The Azure web site in a waiting state (note the bottom information bar and the circular arrow in the top-left corner of the window)*

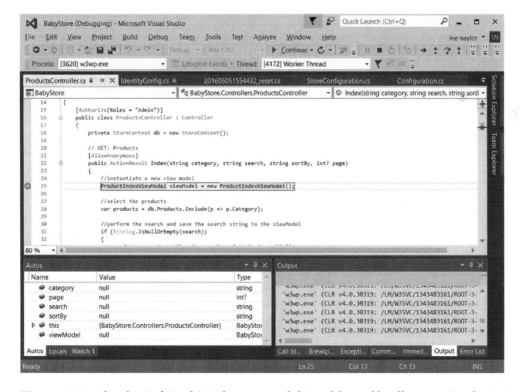

Figure 13-22. *A breakpoint being hit in the remote code being debugged locally, preventing the Azure web site from continuing*

Viewing and Editing an Azure Database with Visual Studio

To view and edit a remote database in Visual Studio, first ensure that you have added a firewall rule to the database server, as demonstrated earlier in this chapter.

Next, locate the database you want to view or edit in Server Explorer and right-click it. Choose Open in SQL Server Object Explorer, as shown in Figure 13-23.

Figure 13-23. *Opening a remote Azure database in SQL Server Object Explorer*

You can now work with the remote database as if it were running locally, adding or deleting tables or data, for example. These changes will take effect in the Azure database. Figure 13-24 shows a new product named Remote Product that we have added to the Products table of the remote BabyStore database.

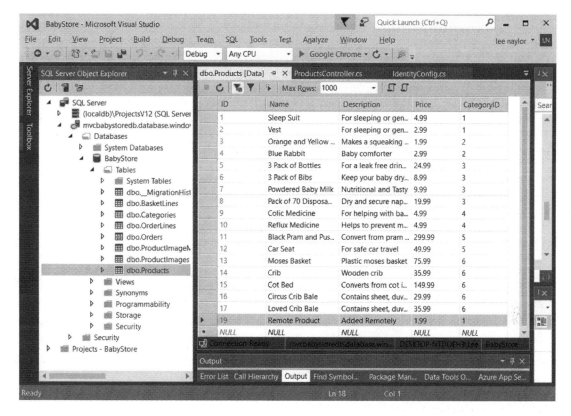

Figure 13-24. *Adding a new product to the remote Azure BabyStore database via Visual Studio*

The remote database will now be updated with the new product data. This can now be viewed through the Azure web site, as shown in Figure 13-25.

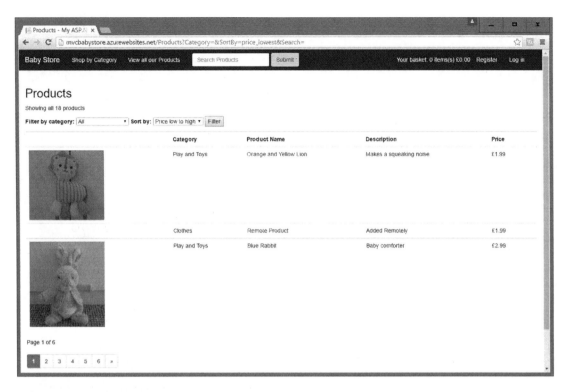

Figure 13-25. *The new Remote Product can now be viewed via the Azure web site, appearing second in the products list when sorted by price*

Connection Resiliency When Using Azure

Azure is a cloud-based platform, and by its very nature (such as throttling of a shared platform for performance reasons or network issues), it is more prone to connection issues than a set of servers running on the same LAN. These issues are known as *transient connection errors*. To help combat this issue, Entity Framework 6 onwards includes a feature known as *connection resiliency*. It allows Entity Framework to automatically retry any commands that fail due to connection issues.

When working with Azure, you can implement an execution strategy known as SqlAzureExecutionStrategy, which inherits from DbExecutionStrategy, and when working with SqlAzure, will retry any exceptions that are likely to be transient.

To configure Entity Framework to use this execution strategy, you need to add a class that derives from the DbConfiguration class, and within the class, set the execution strategy. For example, in the BabyStore project, you could do this by adding a new class named StoreDbConfiguration.cs to the DAL folder:

```
using System;
using System.Data.Entity;
using System.Data.Entity.SqlServer;
```

```
namespace BabyStore.DAL
{
    public class StoreDbConfiguration : DbConfiguration
    {
        public StoreDbConfiguration()
        {
            SetExecutionStrategy("System.Data.SqlClient",
                () => new SqlAzureExecutionStrategy(5, TimeSpan.FromSeconds(30)));
        }
    }
}
```

This code will set the execution strategy to retry a maximum of five times with a 30-second delay between each retry. Entity Framework will automatically run any code it finds in a class that derives from DbConfiguration. Note that the parameters passed into SqlAzureExecutionStrategy are optional.

When working with a commercial project in Azure, you should also consider wrapping your database access code inside try catch statements to deal with anything other than transient errors. You would set the catch part of the statement to catch RetryLimitExceededException; the actual exception will be wrapped inside this type.

Summary

This chapter covered deploying an application to Microsoft's cloud-based hosting platform Azure. I started the chapter by showing you how to prepare for deploying to Azure and by changing the reliance on a database initializer for creating an admin user and instead seeding this data via Code First Migrations.

I then covered how to set up Azure to host a web site and a couple of databases, followed by how to configure and deploy your application via Visual Studio, including making code redeployments. The chapter then moved on to cover how to perform remote code debugging and remote database alterations using Visual Studio, wrapping up with a brief description on dealing with connection issues when using Azure. Azure is a large topic in itself and this chapter has just scratched the surface, but hopefully it will give you confidence to play around with Azure and become more familiar with it.

CHAPTER 14

■ ■ ■

Restyling the Web Site: An Introduction

Over the course of the next few chapters, we're going to introduce how to use Cascading Style Sheets (CSS), in order to change the look and feel of the web site. We are going to stick to formatting the site using plain old CSS rather than using any tools, for example SASS, which is a preprocessor that allows you to write CSS in a more object oriented manner and manages files in smaller chunks. We will also briefly introduce the frontend scripting language JavaScript in the form of the ever-popular jQuery library.

■ **Note** To complete this chapter, you must either have completed Chapter 10 or Chapter 13, if you intend to deploy your restyled site to Azure. Alternatively, download Chapter 13's source code from `www.apress.com` as a starting point.

I included this section in the book because the world of web development is evolving to something where developers need to have a more rounded skill set. In the past someone may just have been a backend developer, but there is now a developing trend of employers looking for "full-stack" developers so I've included CSS as an introduction to working on frontend development. The current version of CSS is known as CSS3 and you will often see CSS referred to by both these names.

■ **Note** Throughout the examples on CSS, I keep the HTML as close as possible to its current state, therefore, at times we will use similar features to those used in the standard Bootstrap CSS, such as grid layouts. Whenever I do this, I include a detailed explanation of how the code works. The reason for doing this is so that the standard Bootstrap styles can be interchanged with the book's stylesheets without having to recode the site. You may see that, from time to time, I add some new CSS classes, but these are specific to our CSS and do not affect the Bootstrap layout.

L. Naylor, *ASP.NET MVC with Entity Framework and CSS*, DOI 10.1007/978-1-4842-2137-2_14

CSS: The Basics

We're going to start by covering the basics of CSS, such as the composition of a style and stylesheets, followed by a brief introduction to selectors and the concept of the box model, which lies at the heart of CSS. I've tried to condense the very main points of CSS into a few pages to bring you up to speed quickly. I'll expand on this section by giving more practical examples throughout the remainder of the book.

Styles

A *style* is a rule that tells a web browser how to format an element of a web page. You have already seen some Bootstrap styles being altered in previous chapters. A style is composed of a *selector* and one or more *declarations*. These declarations make up what is known as a *declaration block* and each declaration consists of a *property* and a *value*.

Consider the following style that we have updated previously in the book when correcting a Bootstrap issue:

```
body { padding-bottom: 20px; }
```

In this style, body is the *selector*, the *declaration block* is the code between the {} brackets, and padding-bottom: 20px is a *declaration*. Within this declaration, padding-bottom is the *property* and 20px is the *value*.

This style effectively says to the browser for the HTML body element set the padding-bottom property to 20 pixels. I'll explain padding when we cover the box model, but this simple style basically adds a space of 20 pixels below the body element.

Stylesheets

A stylesheet is simply a collection of CSS styles. Stylesheets are either internal or external; internal stylesheets are located between opening and closing HTML <style> tags in a page's <head> section, whereas external stylesheets are written in their own distinct files, external to the HTML of a web page. You have already seen some stylesheets during the previous chapters when making alterations to the default Bootstrap styles.

Styles can also be added outside of stylesheets to individual elements, known as inline styles. For example, in the Views\Products\Details.cshtml file, we've applied an inline style to add some padding around each image by adding a style entry as follows:

```
<img src="@(Url.Content(Constants.ProductThumbnailPath) + item.ProductImage.FileName)"
style=padding:5px>
```

Despite the fact that we used this inline style for simplicity, I recommend that you avoid inline styles and stick to using stylesheets whenever you can.

Selectors

Selectors fall into two categories—those that are used to match HTML types or elements, for example p matches all paragraph <p> elements, and those used to match classes or IDs, which are assigned to HTML elements.

Throughout the book, the HTML has included CSS classes; for example, <dl class="dl-horizontal">, in which case the CSS selector .dl-horizontal is used to match it. If this HTML had been written as <dl id="dl-horizontal">, then the selector to match it would be written as #dl-horizontal.

■ **Tip** IDs are best used sparingly if at all; it is likely to be much more efficient and productive in the long run to stick to using classes or HTML elements for styles so that they can be easily reused.

Group Selectors

To apply a style to more than one element at a time, you need to use a group selector. This is used by listing a number of selector that you want to match in a comma-separated list. For example, let's say you wanted to match all HTML <p> elements and the dl-horizontal class to apply the same style to them. You could use a group selector such as:

```
p, .dl-horizontal { color : #000000 }
```

■ **Tip** If you wanted to style everything, rather than listing every element, you can use the universal asterisk selector *.

Descendant Selectors

Descendant selectors match one tag within another. They can be applied to HTML tags or classes or IDs just as the group selector can be. Consider the example where we have this HTML:

```
<div class="news">
    <span>
        Some Text
    </span>
</div>
```

To style the span elements only within the news class, you can use a descendant selector, such as .news span { color : #000000 }.

You can also use the > character in between entries in a selector to find only direct descendants, e.g., div > p will find only the p tags that are direct descendants of a div tag.

Sibling Selectors

Sibling selectors are used to select elements that are next to one another. The most commonly used sibling selector is the adjacent sibling selector; for example, to select every paragraph following each <h1> tag, use the h1+p selector.

Inheritance

Inheritance refers to the way CSS applies a style that's applied to a parent element to all its child elements. A good example of this is using the body selector to apply a standard font to everything within the body of a page. For example, if you use the body { font-family: Arial; } style, then the Arial font will be applied to everything within the body tag. You do not have to specify the same font for every element, therefore saving time.

Cascading

Cascading is the set of rules to decide which style properties get applied to an element. It is responsible for what to do when CSS properties conflict. Style conflicts can happen when the same property is inherited from multiple ancestors, and when one or more styles apply to the same element.

Styles are defined in four ways—from the browser, from internal or external stylesheets, and from inline styles. The following list shows the priority of these when it comes to deciding what wins when a style conflict occurs:

1. Inline style

2. Internal stylesheet

3. External stylesheet

4. Browser default

When it comes to determining which style wins in the same stylesheet, the general priority list is as follows:

1. `#id`

2. `.class`

3. `Element`

In addition to this, a more specific style will override a more generic declaration. For example, the `.myclass ul li` style would override the style `li`. W3C provides the following definition of how to calculate a selector's specificity based on four values—a, b, c, and d—where a has the highest priority and d the lowest (the higher the value of each value, the higher the priority of the style or selector):

- To calculate a, add 1 if the style is an inline style (hence inline styles always win)

- To calculate b, count the number of ID attributes in the selector

- To calculate c, count the number of other classes and pseudo-classes in the selector

- To calculate d, count the number of element names and pseudo-elements in the selector

Concatenating the four numbers a-b-c-d gives the specificity. All this sounds a bit complicated, so W3C provides the following example calculations:

```
*                 {} /* a=0 b=0 c=0 d=0 -> specificity = 0,0,0,0 */
li                {} /* a=0 b=0 c=0 d=1 -> specificity = 0,0,0,1 */
li:first-line     {} /* a=0 b=0 c=0 d=2 -> specificity = 0,0,0,2 */
ul li             {} /* a=0 b=0 c=0 d=2 -> specificity = 0,0,0,2 */
ul ol+li          {} /* a=0 b=0 c=0 d=3 -> specificity = 0,0,0,3 */
h1 + *[rel=up]    {} /* a=0 b=0 c=1 d=1 -> specificity = 0,0,1,1 */
ul ol li.red      {} /* a=0 b=0 c=1 d=3 -> specificity = 0,0,1,3 */
li.red.level      {} /* a=0 b=0 c=2 d=1 -> specificity = 0,0,2,1 */
#x34y             {} /* a=0 b=1 c=0 d=0 -> specificity = 0,1,0,0 */
style=""             /* a=1 b=0 c=0 d=0 -> specificity = 1,0,0,0 */
```

There are a couple of other crucial rules well worth remembering even if you don't remember anything else about cascading:

- If two styles have an equal specificity, the last declared wins (i.e., the last entry in the stylesheet).

- If you declare a style using !important then it will override any other rule (except if there is another !important rule that follows it for the same selector, in which case that will win). An example of using !important might be:

```
p { font-style: italic ! important }
```

If you want to read more to understand how cascading works to resolve conflicts, the official documentation can be found at https://www.w3.org/TR/css3-cascade/. Don't worry if this all seems a bit laborious, as there are several practical examples of cascading in the following chapters.

The Box Model

CSS formatting is based around the concept of the "box model," which in simple terms, means every element displayed in an HTML page is treated as being contained within a box. The box can have borders, margins, padding, and colors applied to it.

Borders

The border, as the name suggests, represents the edge of the box. It can be formatted to have a color, a thickness, and a style such as solid or dashed. Borders can be formatted by using the following shorthand format: border: 1px solid red;. This would create a red solid border on each side of the element that's one pixel thick. Each border can also be formatted individually, for example using the styles:

```
border: 1px solid red;
border-bottom: 2px dashed blue;
```

This would format the bottom border differently than all the other borders. Note that in this example the order of the styles is crucial. If they were swapped, the bottom border would take the same format as all the other borders due to the cascade rule that if there are two conflicting styles of the same priority then the last entry wins.

Each border also has three individual properties—for example, border-right-width, border-right-style, and border-right-color—which can be used to override a single property for a single border.

Margins

The margins represent the space around the outside of a box. Margins can be used to increase the space between elements. A negative margin can also be used to reduce the space or overlap elements if required. Four properties control margins—margin-top, margin-right, margin-bottom, and margin-left. You can use pixels, ems, or percentages to define the size of margins such as margin-top: 5px; margin-bottom: 2em; margin-left: 20%;. This would set the top margin to five pixels, the bottom margin to twice the font size of the element, and the left margin to 20% of the element that contains the element being styled. When using percentages for margin sizes, extra care is needed to test the effect on the margins when the screen is resized.

You can also use a shorthand format to format margins; for example, `margin: 0 10px 10px 20px;` would format an element with a top margin of 0, a right margin of 10 pixels, a bottom margin of 10 pixels, and a left margin of 20 pixels. Use the word TRouBLe to remember the order of the shorthand format.

If you want to set all the margins to the same value, you can simply provide one value. To set the top and bottom margins the same and the left and right margins the same, you can use two values, the first being the top and bottom margin value.

Padding

Padding represents the gap between the content of the box and the border. Padding can be used to increase the size of an element. Padding and margins are sometimes confused. It is best the think of padding occurring inside the border, while margins occur outside the border. Padding styles are formatted in a similar manner to margins; for example, `padding: 5px 10px 5px 10px;` would create a space of five pixels between the top and bottom of the element and its contents, plus a space of 10 pixels between the right and left edges and the content.

Inline and Block Display

There are two kinds of "boxes," *inline* and *block*, and they correspond to inline and block-level tags, respectively. A block-level tag creates a line break before and after it. Examples of the block-level tag are `<div>` and `<p>`. Inline tags run in line with surrounding content and do not have any line breaks before or after them. Examples of inline tags are `<span>` and `<strong>`. Inline and block elements behave differently when it comes to margins and padding in that you cannot increase the height of an inline element using margins or padding.

If you want to change the behavior of an element, you can do so by using the `display` property and setting it to `block`, `inline`, or `inline-block`. An example of when you may want to use this would be to change a list to display items next to one another rather than a vertical list by using `display: inline;`.

Using `display: inline-block` places an element in line with other elements but also adds margins padding to the top and bottom of the element.

Putting It Together: Visualizing the Box Model

If all this sounds a little confusing, help is at hand. Modern day browsers provide excellent support for viewing borders, padding, and margins by using the developer tools that now come bundled with each browser.

To see how all these basics mentioned so far in this chapter work, add a new HTML page in the root of the `BabyStore` project and name it `SimpleExample.html`. Now add a couple of `div` elements with some text and an internal stylesheet to style these as follows:

```
<!DOCTYPE html>
<html>
<head>
    <title></title>
        <meta charset="utf-8" />
    <style>
        body{
            color:white;
        }
```

```
    .styled {
        padding: 10px;
        margin: 20px;
        background-color: red;
        border: solid 4px black;
    }
    div{
        background-color: blue;
    }
    </style>
</head>
<body>
    <div class="styled">
        This is some content
    </div>
    <div>This is some more content</div>
</body>
</html>
```

Right-click inside the file and choose View in Browser. Your browser should open and you will see a page similar to the one displayed in Figure 14-1 (the width and height may vary depending on your window size, but all the elements should appear the same).

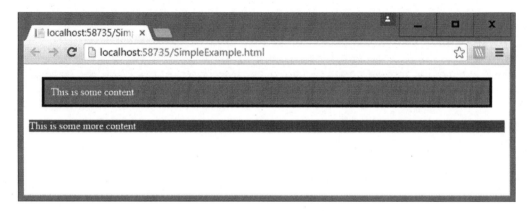

Figure 14-1. *The SimpleExample page*

This page is very simple but there are several things going on with it. First of all, it has an example of inheritance. Both divs have inherited their text color from the body style.

Secondly, it has an example of another cascading rule, the more specific style wins. In this case, although we included the formatting of divs after the formatted styled class, the div with the styled class assigned to it is not blue. This is because it has a specific class assigned to it and this takes precedence over the basic div style.

Finally, and most importantly, it has a simple example of the box model in action. The top div is formatted with margins, a border, and padding.

Viewing the Box Model

We're going to use Google Chrome to view the box model of the first div element to explain how the style affects it. Google Chrome provides excellent developer support for working with CSS, hence I have chosen to use it throughout the book. To see the box model of the first div, right-click on it in Chrome and choose Inspect from the menu. This will open the Developer Tools pane of Chrome and the div will be highlighted in the HTML source code. It will also be highlighted on the page, showing that its size is actually larger than the red area. Figure 14-2 shows how this now appears.

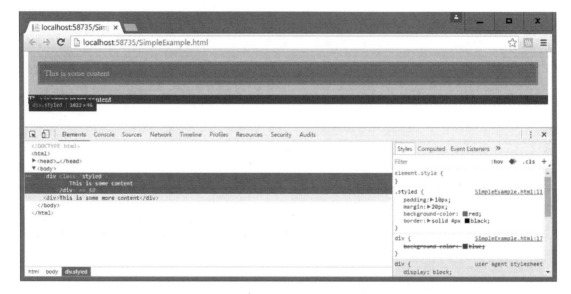

Figure 14-2. *Inspecting an HTML element using Google Chrome developer tools*

Rest assured that the margins, border, padding, and main content of the element are all highlighted in different colors (this can't be seen in the print format). To view the box model of the div, click on the Computed tab in the bottom-right side of the screen. The box model should now be visible, as shown in Figure 14-3.

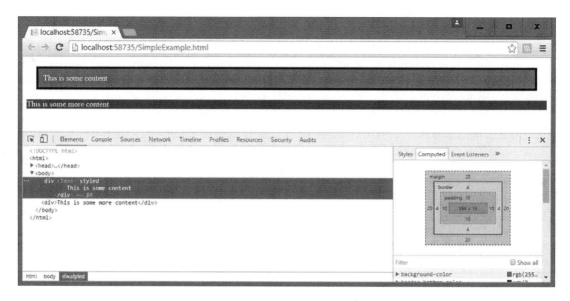

Figure 14-3. Using the Computed tab to view the box model for the first div

You can now see exactly how the styles have affected the div. They have added a space of 20 pixels outside the border, the border is four pixels wide, and the padding has effectively "filled out" the element, adding 10 pixels of space around the text. Figure 14-4 shows a blown-up version of the box model for clarity.

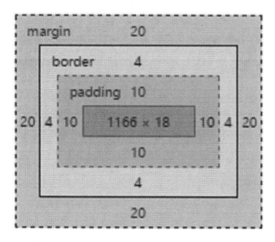

Figure 14-4. The box model as generated by Google Chrome for the div with the styled class applied to it

Understanding the box model is extremely powerful and useful. Without it, you are effectively flying blind when writing CSS. If you ever find yourself getting stuck and moving things around the page hoping it fits correctly, stop and go back to the basics of the box model. Use the built-in browser developer tools (usually accessed by pressing F12) to help you.

Updating the BabyStore Site to Use Your Own Stylesheet

We are now going to make practical changes to the existing BabyStore site developed in the previous chapters. Start by opening the BabyStore solution and examining the Views\Shared_Layout.cshtml file. In this file, you will find the references to the CSS currently used by the web site, which is loaded into the site as a bundle. Bundles are used by ASP.NET to treat several related files as a single unit and optimize the delivery of item such as stylesheets and scripts. The line that loads the CSS bundle is highlighted in bold:

```
<!DOCTYPE html>
<html>
<head>
    <meta charset="utf-8" />
    <meta name="viewport" content="width=device-width, initial-scale=1.0">
    <title>@ViewBag.Title - My ASP.NET Application</title>
    @Styles.Render("~/Content/css")
    @Scripts.Render("~/bundles/modernizr")
</head>
<body>
...following code omitted for brevity...
```

The code that defines what goes into each bundle is contained in the App_Start\BundleConfig. cs file. Open this file and inspect the code. Bundles are added via the RegisterBundles method. This method currently adds five bundles of two types: ScriptBundle and StyleBundle. The code that creates the stylesheet bundle is:

```
bundles.Add(new StyleBundle("~/Content/css").Include(
                "~/Content/bootstrap.css",
                "~/Content/site.css"));
```

Next add you own new site sheet to the Content folder by right-clicking on the folder and choosing Add then Style Sheet from the popup menu. Add a new stylesheet named store.css. Next, update the styles bundle in the App_Start\BundleConfig.cs file as follows:

```
using System.Web;
using System.Web.Optimization;

namespace BabyStore
{
    public class BundleConfig
    {
        // For more information on bundling, visit http://go.microsoft.com/
        fwlink/?LinkId=301862
        public static void RegisterBundles(BundleCollection bundles)
        {
            bundles.Add(new ScriptBundle("~/bundles/jquery").Include(
                    "~/Scripts/jquery-{version}.js"));
```

```
        bundles.Add(new ScriptBundle("~/bundles/jqueryval").Include(
                    "~/Scripts/jquery.validate*"));

        // Use the development version of Modernizr to develop with and learn from.
        Then,
            when you're
        // ready for production, use the build tool at http://modernizr.com to pick only
        the
            tests you need.
        bundles.Add(new ScriptBundle("~/bundles/modernizr").Include(
                    "~/Scripts/modernizr-*"));

        bundles.Add(new ScriptBundle("~/bundles/bootstrap").Include(
                    "~/Scripts/bootstrap.js",
                    "~/Scripts/respond.js"));

        bundles.Add(new StyleBundle("~/Content/css").Include(
                    "~/Content/store.css"));
    }
  }
}
```

Start the web site without debugging and you should now see the web site displayed with just the browser's default formatting applied to it. Figure 14-5 shows how the site now appears in Google Chrome, with the new store.css file being used. Some of the links are purple to reflect that they have been visited.

Figure 14-5. The web site using the default browser formatting

Using a CSS Reset

The aim of removing all the Bootstrap styling from the web site is to get the site to a base point where it can be restyled by adding some new custom styles. However, although all the styles have been removed, this "base point" has not yet been reached. Each web browser shows a web site without styles differently due to the fact that each browser adds its own styles to standard HTML in order to make it more readable, even though this is not an HTML standard. Each of these browser-added styles may be implemented differently from browser to browser. In order to overcome these differences, it has become popular to use something known as a *CSS reset*.

A CSS reset is a set of styles that attempts to reset all the browser applied styles in order to ensure you start from a level playing field no matter which browser you're using. To create a CSS reset, add a new stylesheet to the Content folder and name it reset.css. We are not going to write a CSS reset; instead we are going to employ one of the freely available online ones. We are going to use the CSS reset available from Eric Meyer's web site. This is available to download at http://meyerweb.com/eric/tools/css/reset/index. html.

Update the contents of the Content\reset.css file with the following styles:

```
/* http://meyerweb.com/eric/tools/css/reset/
   v2.0 | 20110126
   License: none (public domain)
*/

html, body, div, span, applet, object, iframe,
h1, h2, h3, h4, h5, h6, p, blockquote, pre,
a, abbr, acronym, address, big, cite, code,
del, dfn, em, img, ins, kbd, q, s, samp,
small, strike, strong, sub, sup, tt, var,
b, u, i, center,
dl, dt, dd, ol, ul, li,
fieldset, form, label, legend,
table, caption, tbody, tfoot, thead, tr, th, td,
article, aside, canvas, details, embed,
figure, figcaption, footer, header, hgroup,
menu, nav, output, ruby, section, summary,
time, mark, audio, video {
        margin: 0;
        padding: 0;
        border: 0;
        font-size: 100%;
        font: inherit;
        vertical-align: baseline;
}
/* HTML5 display-role reset for older browsers */
article, aside, details, figcaption, figure,
footer, header, hgroup, menu, nav, section {
        display: block;
}
body {
        line-height: 1;
}
```

```
ol, ul {
        list-style: none;
}
blockquote, q {
        quotes: none;
}
blockquote:before, blockquote:after,
q:before, q:after {
        content: '';
        content: none;
}
table {
        border-collapse: collapse;
        border-spacing: 0;
}
```

In basic terms, these styles set all the spacing, margin, padding, and fonts to be consistent across all browsers. Now update the StyleBundle in the App_Start\BundleConfig.cs file in order to add the new reset.css file to it as follows:

```
bundles.Add(new StyleBundle("~/Content/css").Include(
            "~/Content/store.css",
            "~/Content/reset.css"));
```

If you now start the web site without debugging, you will see that all the spacing has been removed and the site appears even more basic than before, as shown in Figure 14-6.

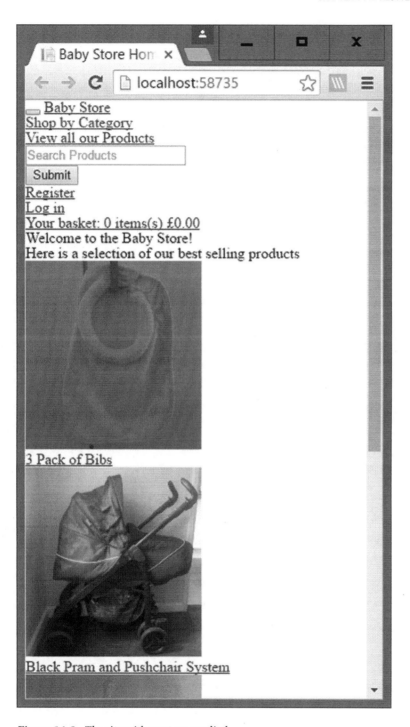

Figure 14-6. *The site with reset.css applied*

Adding Basic Formatting

First of all, we're going to add some basic formatting to the body tag in order to update the maximum width of the web site, add a margin, and set a default font family and a color. Update the body entry in the store. css file with the following styles:

```
body {
    background-color: white;
    max-width: 1024px;
    margin: 0 auto;
    font-size: 12px;
    font-family: Arial, Helvetica, sans-serif;
    color: rgb(14, 117, 204);
}
```

The background-color style ensures that the background of the body is always white, and then max-width specifies the maximum allowed width of the body. The margin style specifies two values—0 and auto. This is a shorthand use of the margin style and it specifies that the top and bottom margins are set to 0, while the left and right margins are set to an automatic width. This allows the left and right margins to take up any remaining available space in the browser window once the body has taken up 1024 pixels. The font-size is set to a default of 12 pixels and the font-family style is set to use three fonts where the preferred font is Arial, followed by Helvetica with the fall back font specified as sans serif. The default text color is set to blue using the color style.

At the moment, these changes only make very subtle alterations to the web site. The most visible are the changes in the text color (note this does not affect hyperlinks) and the fact that if you make the browser window wider, the margin size will change. Figure 14-7 shows the site with these new styles applied.

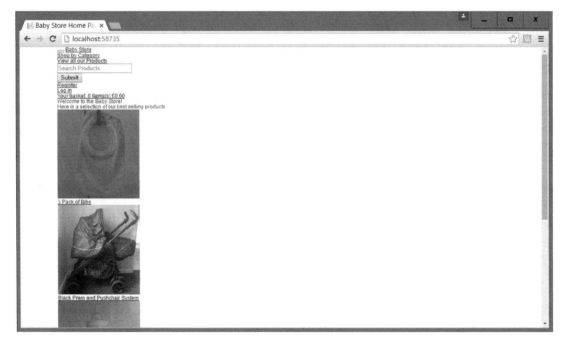

Figure 14-7. *The web site with the basic body styles applied to it. Note that the space on the left generated by setting the margin to auto. The text above the first image has also changed color*

Fading In Each Page

We are now going to jump straight into a more advanced topic of CSS3, animations. With the introduction of CSS3, it became possible to add animations to your site, and many different possibilities exist. However, it's best to use animations sparingly. We are going to use a simple animation to fade in a page every time it loads. To do this, we need to create an animation and then add a style to the element we want to apply it to.

Start by creating an animation named `fadeIn`, which you do by adding the following code to the `store.css` file:

```
@keyframes fadeIn {
    from { opacity: 0; }
    to { opacity: 1; }
}
```

This code specifies that the animation should move from opacity 0 (not visible) to opacity 1 (fully visible). Following this animation, add a new style to apply the animation to the `html` element; this will apply it to the whole page.

```
html {
    animation: fadeIn 2s;
}
```

If you now view the web site in Chrome, you should see that each page slowly appears into view over a two-second period.

■ **Note** In order to keep the example simple, we are going to focus just on the latest version of Google Chrome in terms of cross-browser compatibility. This code also works in the latest versions of Microsoft Edge and Firefox. To support other versions of browsers, it is necessary to update the animation properties with vendor-specific prefixes. To cover as many browsers as possible. this code could be updated as follows for support of older versions of Internet Explorer, Chrome, Firefox, and Opera:

```
@keyframes fadeIn {
    from { opacity: 0; }
    to { opacity: 1; }
}

/* Firefox < 16 */
@-moz-keyframes fadein {
    from { opacity: 0; }
    to   { opacity: 1; }
}

/* Safari, Chrome and Opera > 12.1 */
@-webkit-keyframes fadein {
    from { opacity: 0; }
    to   { opacity: 1; }
}
```

```
/* Internet Explorer */
@-ms-keyframes fadein {
    from { opacity: 0; }
    to   { opacity: 1; }
}

/* Opera < 12.1 */
@-o-keyframes fadein {
    from { opacity: 0; }
    to   { opacity: 1; }
}

html {
    animation: fadeIn 2s;
    -webkit-animation: fadein 2s; /* Safari, Chrome and Opera > 12.1 */
    -moz-animation: fadein 2s; /* Firefox < 16 */
    -ms-animation: fadein 2s; /* Internet Explorer */
    -o-animation: fadein 2s; /* Opera < 12.1 */
}
```

Summary

This chapter gave a basic introduction to using CSS to style a web site. It covered the basics that CSS is based on, including selectors, inheritance, and the box model. The chapter then moved on to restyling the BabyStore web site produced in earlier chapters, adding some new stylesheets to a .NET bundle and using a CSS reset to set a starting point for the restyle. We then covered how to add some basic styles to the web site and add advanced animation to fade in every page.

CHAPTER 15

Styling the Home Page

The chapter introduces some additional features of CSS, including using line-height and border-radius to add rounding effects, as well as controlling font-weight and font sizes. Next we'll show you how to make use of float to display elements vertically next to one another and how to use the clear property to end floating, as well as how to style links to appear like a button, and how to hide an element from the page.

■ **Note** To complete this chapter, you must either have completed Chapter 14 or download the source code for Chapter 14 from www.apress.com as a starting point.

Styling the Footer

We're going to start this chapter by introducing a few CSS concepts. We'll add a new style for the footer to make it a deepskyblue color with rounded corners and white text rather than the standard blue added to the body in the previous chapter.

To start restyling the footer, add a new footer style to the Content\store.css file as follows:

```
footer {
    margin-bottom: 20px;
    background-color:deepskyblue;
    color: white;
}
```

This will add a blue background to the footer and set the text to white. The margin-bottom property adds a space under the footer so that you can more easily see the footer in the figures. The footer will now appear as shown in Figure 15-1.

Figure 15-1. The footer with a sky blue background and white text

Using Line Height to Vertically Align Text

Now set the height of the footer to 30 pixels by updating the style as follows:

```
footer {
    margin-bottom: 20px;
    background-color:deepskyblue;
    color: white;1
    height: 30px;
}
```

The footer now appears taller and takes up more room; however, the text is now aligned to the top edge of the footer, as shown in Figure 15-2.

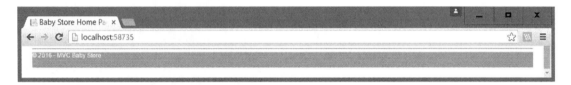

Figure 15-2. *The footer set to 30 pixels high with the text aligned to the top edge*

We want the text to be aligned vertically in the center of the footer rather than along the top edge. To achieve this, add a line-height property and set the value to 30 pixels so it is the same height as the footer. Note that this approach works only with text that is a single line in height.

```
footer {
    margin-bottom: 20px;
    background-color:deepskyblue;
    color: white;
    height: 30px;
    line-height: 30px;
}
```

The text will now be vertically aligned in the center of the footer, as shown in Figure 15-3.

Figure 15-3. *The footer text now aligned in the center*

We also don't want the text aligned to the left edge, so we're going to add a bit of padding to the footer so you can see the effect of this. It will extend the height of the footer, although the width will not change because the footer cannot break out of the containing body element. Update the footer style as follows to add five pixels of padding:

```
footer {
    margin-bottom: 20px;
    background-color:deepskyblue;
    color: white;
    height: 30px;
    line-height: 30px;
    padding: 5px;
}
```

This is a prime example of the padding adding space around the text inside an element and making the element larger. It does not add space around the element. Figure 15-4 shows how the footer now appears.

Figure 15-4. *The footer with padding applied; the text has now moved away from the left edge*

Rounding Corners

To complete the footer, we are going to introduce a new property named `border-radius`. This is used to make square corners appear rounded. Each corner can be styled individually using the appropriately named property, e.g., `border-top-left-radius`, but in this example, we are going to keep things simple and style all the corners the same. Update the `footer` style to add a `border-radius` property as follows:

```
footer {
    margin-bottom: 20px;
    background-color:deepskyblue;
    color: white;
    height: 30px;
    line-height: 30px;
    padding: 5px;
    border-radius: 5px;
}
```

You can change the value for the `border-radius` property in order to make the corners more or less rounded. You can see the effect of adding `border-radius` to the footer in Figure 15-5.

Figure 15-5. *The footer with rounded corners*

Styling the Home Page Headings by Using Font Weights and em Values for Font-Size

We're now going to style the headings in the page, i.e., the text "Welcome to the Baby Store" and "Here is a selection of our best selling products". These are generated using the <h1> and <h2> HTML tags so we are going to add some styles for those. We are going to style both of them the same to demonstrate applying the same style to multiple elements using a group selector. Add the following style to the stylesheet to restyle the h1 and h2 elements:

```
h1, h2 {
    color: hotpink;
    font-size:2em;
    font-weight: bold;
}
```

This will add change the h1 and h2 elements to use a pink color. Using em measurements for the font-size property will make the font-size twice the size of the font applied to the body element. The body element has the font-size set to 12px, so the h1 and h2 elements will have their sizes set to 24px. The font-weight has been set to bold in order to make the letters bold, but this property's values can also be set using numeric values in increments of 100, from 100 to 900 (bold is equivalent to 700). The updated headings will now appear as shown in Figure 15-6.

Figure 15-6. *The updated H1 and H2 styles*

Introducing Float for Displaying Images Next to One Another

The float property can be used to position elements side by side and create columns on a web page. Setting the float property on an element moves it outside of the normal flow of the page. For example, it can be used to place divs side by side rather than stacked on top of each other, as you will now see.

The HTML that is used for displaying product images in the home page is as follows:

```
<div class="row">
    <div class="col-md-3">
        <a href="/Products/Details/6">
            <img src="/Content/ProductImages/Bibs1.JPG">
        </a>
        <p>
            <a href="/Products/Details/6">3 Pack of Bibs</a>
        </p>
    </div>
    <div class="col-md-3">
        <a href="/Products/Details/11">
            <img src="/Content/ProductImages/Pram1.JPG">
        </a>
        <p>
            <a href="/Products/Details/11">Black Pram and Pushchair System</a>
        </p>
    </div>
    <div class="col-md-3">
        <a href="/Products/Details/5">
            <img src="/Content/ProductImages/Bottles1.JPG">
        </a>
        <p>
            <a href="/Products/Details/5">3 Pack of Bottles</a>
        </p>
    </div>
    <div class="col-md-3">
        <a href="/Products/Details/3">
            <img src="/Content/ProductImages/Lion1.JPG">
        </a>
        <p>
            <a href="/Products/Details/3">Orange and Yellow Lion</a>
        </p>
    </div>
</div>
```

Each image is wrapped inside a div with a CSS class of col-md-3 applied to it. Therefore, you need to make these divs appear in a horizontal line rather than vertically stacking them. In order to make this happen, add a new entry to the Content\store.css file as follows:

```
.col-md-3 {
    float: left;
}
```

This now floats each `div` with the class of `col-md-3` to the left of whatever follows it. It sounds good and we now have the images next to one another; however, things are not quite that simple, as shown in Figure 15-7.

Figure 15-7. *The effect of adding float: left to the col-md-3 class*

■ **Note**   CSS now supports an alternative to working with floats, known as Flexbox. Flexbox provides a set of properties that lets you lay out items in a row without floating them or using the `inline-block` value. Items inside a flex container adjust their widths automatically, similar to using floated page elements with percentage values. You can learn more about Flexbox at `http://www.w3schools.com/css/css3_flexbox.asp`.

Using Clear After a Floated Element

The Shop Now link and the footer are now out of place because the last `col-md-3` `div` has floated to the left of everything that follows it. In order to fix this, we need a way to tell everything that follows the container of the floated elements to return to the normal page flow, rather than just following the floated elements. To achieve this, we are going to use code based on something known as the Micro Clearfix, created by Nicolas Gallagher. Add the following to the `store.css` file in order to stop everything after the `row` `div` from being floated:

```
.row:after {
  content: " ";
  display: table;
  clear: both;
}
```

Everything following the `row` `div` now returns to the normal flow of the page and the footer returns to its original position, as shown in Figure 15-8.

Figure 15-8. *The effect of the Micro Clearfix on the home page*

This code works by using the `:after` pseudo-class to apply the style to anything that appears after the `row` class. It sets the content immediately following the `row` element to a space and then uses the `clear: both` declaration to force the content to drop below any left or right floated elements. `Clear` is very useful when dealing with floats and can be used in isolation rather than as part of the Micro Clearfix code; for example, if we just wanted to clear the footer element we could use the style `footer { clear: both }`. However, by using a pseudo-class, we are able to ensure anything after a row always gets cleared.

■ **Tip** *Pseudo-classes* are used for something that is not a tag but can be easily identified. There are several pseudo-classes that are related to styling links, which we will cover later, but other pseudo-classes that exist, including `:hover`, `:before`, `:after`, and `::selection`. All of these have fairly self-explanatory names apart from `::selection`, which is applied to text that users have selected by dragging their mouse over.

Styling the Images

The first thing we are going to do with the images is space them out a little. From the previous code listing, you can see that each image is contained inside a `div` with the class `col-md-3`, which is a column class the Bootstrap uses as part of its grid layout system. The standard bootstrap grid system consists of twelve columns and later we will replicate this in a simplified manner. However, the reason I am mentioning this here is this has implications for how wide the `col-md-3` style should be.

To work out the width of the `col-md-3` style, you divide the number of the column style, in this case 3, by the number of columns, i.e., 12 as a percentage. So in this case the `col-md-3` style needs to have a width of 25%. To reflect this, update `.col-md-3` in the `Content\store.css` file to add a new `width` property as follows:

```
.col-md-3 {
    float: left;
    width: 25%;
}
```

This will now space out the image elements, as shown in Figure 15-9.

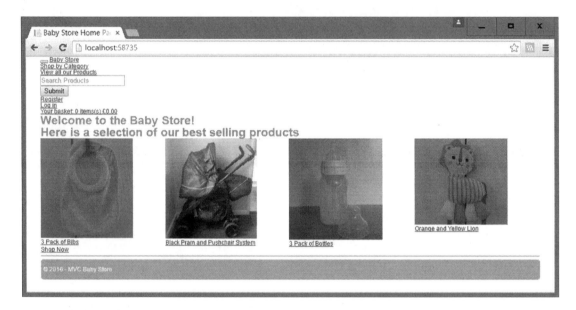

Figure 15-9. *The images now with space in between them*

Add a small bottom margin to the `h1` and `h2` styles to add some space above the images, as follows:

```
h1, h2 {
    color: hotpink;
    font-size:2em;
    font-weight: bold;
    margin-bottom: 5px;
}
```

Next, we are going to add a `deepskyblue` border around the images with slightly rounded corners to make them stand out more. Update the `store.css` file to add a new style for the `img` tag as follows:

```
img {
    border: 3px solid deepskyblue;
    border-radius: 3px;
}
```

The effect of these two changes is shown in Figure 15-10.

Figure 15-10. *Images with rounded borders*

Basic Link Styling

Next, we need to do something with the links to each product. Currently they are pretty small (because the font-size is inherited from the body style) and they appear in different colors once the link has been visited. We are going to update the links so they are larger and appear differently when hovered or visited.

First, we create a new style entry in the store.css file. We'll create a style that targets a class named large-bold-text. We have created this class so it can be reused in pages where we want to show some large text not rendered by the h1 or h2 tags.

```
.large-bold-text {
    font-size: 1.5em;
    font-weight: 700;
}
```

Now update the Views\Home\Index.cshtml file in order to add this class to each link generated for the product's name. Add the HTML attribute shown in bold:

```
@foreach (var item in Model)
{
    <div class="col-md-3">
        @if (item.ProductImage != null)
        {
            <a href="@Url.Action("Details", "Products", new { id = item.Product.ID })">
                <img src="@(Url.Content(Constants.ProductImagePath) + item.ProductImage)">
            </a>
        }
```

493

```
        <p>
            @Html.ActionLink(item.Product.Name, "Details", "Products", new { id =
                item.Product.ID }, new { @class = "large-bold-text" })
        </p>
    </div>
}
```

This will make the links to each product 1.5 times larger and bold, as shown in Figure 15-11.

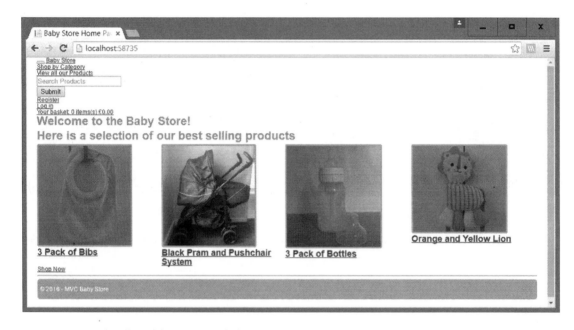

Figure 15-11. *The effect of the new large-bold-text class on the links to each product*

Now we're going to show you how to update all the links so that they are the same color as the other text in the page, plus we're only going to show the underline when a user hovers over the links. When they hover, we're going to change the color of the link to hotpink.

First, in order to change the color of each hyperlink to be the same whether visited or not and to remove the underline, add the following style to store.css:

```
a, a:visited {
    color: rgb(14, 117, 204);
    text-decoration: none;
}
```

Next, to change the color upon hovering and to make the underline reappear, add the following style to store.css:

```
a:hover {
    color: hotpink;
    text-decoration: underline;
}
```

494

Figure 15-12 shows the effect of these changes on the links to products. Each link is now blue, except for the link to the pram, which is pink and underlined, because it is being hovered over.

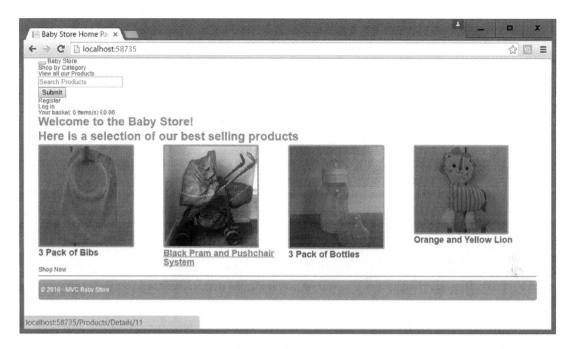

Figure 15-12. *The restyled links*

Styling a Hyperlink to Look Like a Button

We are now going to style the Shop Now link so it looks and behaves like a button. The HTML for this link looks like this: `<a **class="btn btn-primary btn-lg"** href="/Products">Shop Now</a>` so we are going to use the CSS classes btn, btn-primary, and btn-lg to format it. We are going to treat the CSS styles as follows:

- a.btn will represent any link that is a button
- a.btn-primary will be represent a color (in this case, green)
- a.btn-lg will determine the size of the button

Add two new styles to store.css to change the color of any hyperlink that is of the class a.btn-primary as follows:

```
a.btn-primary { background-color: lawngreen; }

a.btn-primary:hover { background-color: green; }
```

This will add a light green background to the Shop Now link. When you hover over the link, the background will become darker. Now add some sizing to the link by adding a style for `a.btn-lg` as follows:

```
a.btn-lg{
    padding: 10px 16px;
    font-size:1.5em;
}
```

Figures 15-13 and 15-14 show the current default state of the Shop Now link and when hovered over. As you can see, there are still a number of issues. It does not look like a button yet and the text is not a suitable color and changes color to pink when hovered over. These are both due to inheriting from the a style created earlier, plus the link now overlaps the `hr` element below it.

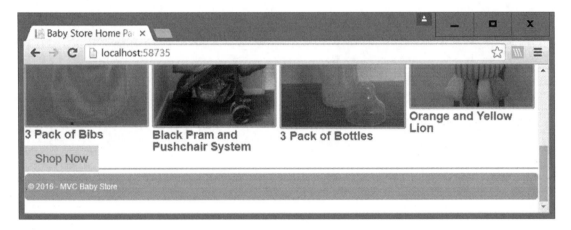

Figure 15-13. *The Shop Now link's current default format*

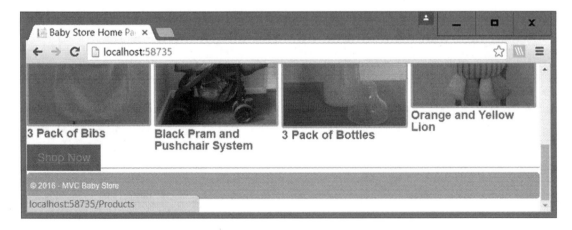

Figure 15-14. *Hovering over the Shop Now link turns the text pink*

To stop the link from overlapping the hr element, add a new style to store.css in order to add a bottom margin to the jumbotron class (the jumbotron class surrounds the content of the home page), as follows:

```
.jumbotron{ margin-bottom: 20px; }
```

Next add a new style for a.btn as follows to create some rounded corners, ensure the text is always white, and that no underline appears:

```
a.btn {
    border-radius: 5px;
    color: #ffffff;
    text-decoration: none;
}
```

You can see in Figure 15-15 that this link now appears much more button like; however, it has a flat appearance.

Figure 15-15. *The updated Shop Now link when hovered over*

To give the button a more raised look, add the following border properties. These create a two-pixel wide border, which is outset with a button style effect:

```
a.btn {
    border-radius: 5px;
    color: #ffffff;
    text-decoration: none;
    border: 2px outset buttonface;
}
```

The Shop Now link should now appear much more button-like, as shown in Figure 15-16.

Figure 15-16. *The Shop Now link with a button-like appearance*

■ **Note**   You're probably wondering why we just didn't nest a button element within an `<a>` tag instead of using CSS to style this. Well, `<a><button></button></a>` is not valid HTML in the HTML5 specification.

Removing an Element from the Page Flow Using CSS

We are going to wrap up this chapter by getting rid of the `hr` element (the line between the Shop Now link and the footer) using CSS. To completely remove this from the flow of the page, add the following style to `store.css`:

```
hr{
    display:none;
}
```

The completed page should appear as shown in Figure 15-17, with the line between the Shop Now link and footer removed.

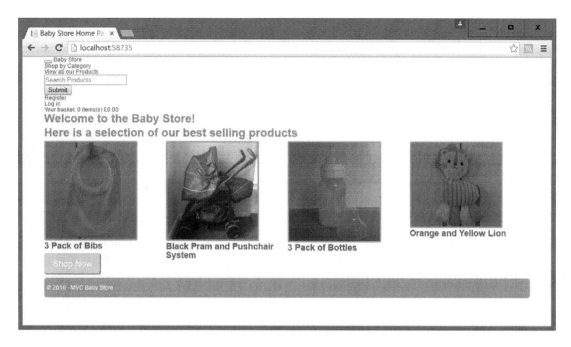

Figure 15-17. The updated home page with the line generated by the hr tag removed

---

■ **Note** Using `display:none` removes the `hr` tag from the flow of the page. It now takes up zero space, but crucially it is still there in the HTML document object model (DOM), which means that it can still be manipulated. It is also possible to hide elements using `visibility:hidden`, and in this case, the element still takes up space in the page but does not appear.

Summary

This chapter covered several different CSS topics and restyled the home page of the site. We started by restyling the footer using `height`, `line-height`, and `padding` to position text within an element, plus we used `border-radius` to make the corners appeared rounded. We then restyled the heading tags followed by introducing working with floats to position elements next to one another, and discussed how to use clearing to reset the flow of the page.

We then moved onto styling the appearance of the images in the page and how to add basic styling to hyperlinks, finishing the chapter with an example of how to style a hyperlink as a button and how to completely hide an element using CSS.

CHAPTER 16

■ ■ ■

Styling Forms, Grid Layouts, and Tables

This chapter focuses on restyling the other main pages of the site, starting with the Categories index page. It covers how to style forms, how to make a simple grid layout, and several common pitfalls and useful features of CSS, such as box-sizing, inheritance, and styling tables.

■ **Note**   To complete this chapter, you must either have completed Chapter 15 or download Chapter 15's source code from www.apress.com as a starting point.

Styling the Categories Index Page

We are going to add some simple updates to the page that shows the categories available in the web site. Figure 16-1 shows the current layout of this page (when logged in as an admin user). It is built using a table.

© Lee Naylor 2016
L. Naylor, *ASP.NET MVC with Entity Framework and CSS*, DOI 10.1007/978-1-4842-2137-2_16

Figure 16-1. *The default layout of the Categories index page*

Adding Space Between Table Cells

The first thing we are going to change is space out the text in the page, so add a new style to the Content\store.css file in order to add some padding to each cell in the table that lists the categories:

```
td { padding: 5px; }
```

The effect of this new class is shown in Figure 16-2.

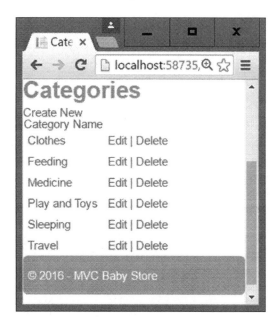

Figure 16-2. *The categories list now spread out*

Styling the Links

We want the admin links to have a different font-weight than the normal category links. To achieve this, we are going to use the existing large-bold-text class to style these links, but we are also going to make the category links the same size but not bold. Add the following class to store.css:

```
.large-text { font-size: 1.5em; }
```

Now to use this new style and style the other links to create, edit, and delete categories, modify the Views\Categories\Index.cshtml file as follows to apply the large-text and large-text-bold classes. Also remove the code that generates the first line of the table that outputs the text "Category Name":

```
<h2>@ViewBag.Title</h2>

@if (Request.IsAuthenticated && User.IsInRole("Admin"))
{
    <p class="large-bold-text">
        @Html.ActionLink("Create New", "Create")
    </p>
}
<table class="table">
    @foreach (var item in Model)
    {
        <tr>
            <td class="large-text">
```

503

```
            @Html.ActionLink(item.Name, "Index", "Products", new { category = item.Name },
            null)
        </td>
        <td class="large-bold-text">
            @if (Request.IsAuthenticated && User.IsInRole("Admin"))
            {
                @Html.ActionLink("Edit", "Edit", new { id = item.ID })
                @Html.Raw(" | ")
                @Html.ActionLink("Delete", "Delete", new { id = item.ID })
            }
        </td>
    </tr>
}
</table>
```

Figure 16-3 shows how the updated page now appears to an admin user and Figure 16-4 shows how it appears to a normal user.

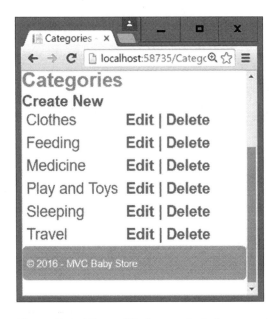

Figure 16-3. *The modified categories index page when logged in as an admin user*

Figure 16-4. *The appearance of the categories index page to a non-admin user*

Styling the Category Edit Form

If you now click on the one of the edit links to edit a category, the Category Edit page will appear in its current default format, as shown in Figure 16-5.

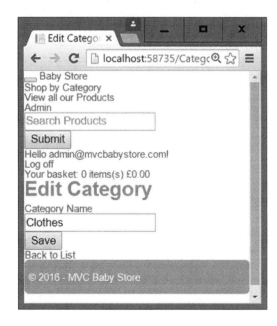

Figure 16-5. *The default category edit page format*

This page differs from the other pages we have seen so far in that it contains an HTML form. Any changes we make to this page will be reflected in all the other HTML forms throughout the site. Before we start to restyle this page, view the source of the page by right-clicking on the page and choosing *View Page Source*, or by right-clicking on the Category Name text and choosing *Inspect*. Depending on which option you choose, you will either see the full source of the page or the developer tools section will open with one of the panes displaying the HTML source immediately surrounding the label element. The relevant HTML that makes up the form is as follows (I've highlighted the relevant classes that need to be targeted by the CSS):

```
<div class="form-horizontal">
    <hr>
    <input data-val="true" data-val-number="The field ID must be a number." data-val-
        required="The ID field is required." id="ID" name="ID" type="hidden" value="1">
    <input id="RowVersion" name="RowVersion" type="hidden" value="AAAAAAAAB9c=">
    <div class="form-group">
        <label class="control-label col-md-2" for="Name">Category Name</label>
        <div class="col-md-10">
            <input class="form-control text-box single-line" data-val="true" data-val-
                length="Please enter a category name between 3 and 50 characters in length"
                data-val-length-max="50" data-val-length-min="3" data-val-regex="Please
                enter a category name beginning with a capital letter and made up of letters
                and spaces only" data-val-regex-pattern="^[A-Z]+[a-zA-Z''-'\s]*$" data-val-
                required="The category name cannot be blank" id="Name" name="Name"
                type="text" value="Clothes">
            <span class="field-validation-valid text-danger" data-valmsg-for="Name"
            data-valmsg-replace="true"></span>
        </div>
    </div>
    <div class="form-group">
        <div class="col-md-offset-2 col-md-10">
            <input type="submit" value="Save" class="btn btn-default">
        </div>
    </div>
</div>
```

Adding Vertical Space Using Margins

First off, we are going to add some spacing between the text box and the Save button. Each of these is contained inside a div with the class form-group assigned. To add some space between them, add the following style to the Content\store.css file to add a bottom margin to the form-group class:

```
.form-group{ margin-bottom: 10px; }
```

The *Back to List* link at the bottom of the form is also touching the footer, which looks a little out of place, so add a top margin to the footer as follows:

```
footer {
    margin-bottom: 20px;
    background-color:deepskyblue;
    color: white;
    height: 30px;
    line-height: 30px;
```

```
    padding:5px;
    border-radius:5px;
    margin-top:10px;
}
```

The effect of these changes is to add some vertical spacing to the form, as shown in Figure 16-6. Note that the changes have also affected the search box and button in the navigation bar. We will override these later in the book when styling this section of the site.

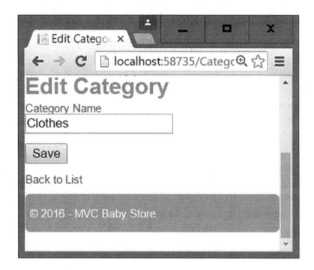

Figure 16-6. *The form with vertical spacing added to it*

Adding a Grid Layout

In the previous chapter, we added a style for the col-md-3 class, assigning it a width property with a value of 25% and floating to the left of following content. This form contains two other column classes so it's now a good point to add some styles for the other possible column classes used in the site. As mentioned in the previous chapter, Bootstrap uses a 12-column grid layout so we are going to add styles for a simple grid system.

■ **Note**   Bootstrap actually contains different sizes of columns (extra small, small, medium, and large relating to the classes col-xs, col-sm, col-md, and col-lg); however, in this example, we are just going to set some styles for the col-md classes.

To start, add some width styles for each available column width by adding the following to the store.css file:

```
.col-md-1 { width: 8.333333333333332%; }
.col-md-2 { width: 16.666666666666664%; }
.col-md-3 { width: 25%; }
.col-md-4 { width: 33.33333333333333%; }
.col-md-5 { width: 41.66666666666667%; }
```

```
.col-md-6 { width: 50%; }
.col-md-7 { width: 58.333333333333336%; }
.col-md-8 { width: 66.66666666666666%; }
.col-md-9 { width: 75%; }
.col-md-10 { width: 83.33333333333334%; }
.col-md-11 { width: 91.66666666666666%; }
.col-md-12 { width: 100%; }
```

Each percentage is worked out by dividing the total number of columns (12) by the number included in the style, e.g., col-md-2 has a width of 2/12. Note that these are the same widths as you will find in the Bootstrap.css file.

In order to make the column styles appear as columns, they need to be floated to the left, so add the following style to accomplish this:

```
.col-md-1,
.col-md-2,
.col-md-3,
.col-md-4,
.col-md-5,
.col-md-6,
.col-md-7,
.col-md-8,
.col-md-9,
.col-md-10,
.col-md-11 {
float: left;
}
```

Next, remove the original style that was previously added for col-md-3, as it is now redundant.

This has now assigned a width to the elements in the form and floated the Category Name text to the left of the text box. You can see the effect of these changes in Figure 16-7.

Figure 16-7. *The form with styles added for all column widths. The Category Name text and the input box now float next to one another.*

There is an issue with the form in that the Back to List link is now out of position on a wide screen. To fix this, we need to apply the same fix as in Chapter 15 to apply a clear after the form-group class (this contains the Save button). Update the existing style that fixes this issue in store.css as follows:

```
.row:after, .form-group:after {
  content: " ";
  display: table;
  clear: both;
}
```

Styling Labels and Text Boxes

Make the label element bold in appearance, with a margin of five pixels above it to align it better with the element it refers to and set the display to inline-block so that the margin-top property can take effect by adding the following style:

```
label {
    font-weight: bold;
    margin-top: 5px;
    display: inline-block;
}
```

Next, update the text box to appear with blue text and a blue border with rounded corners by adding the following style:

```
.form-control {
    width: 100%;
    max-width: 250px;
    border-radius: 3px;
    border: solid deepskyblue;
    color: rgb(14, 117, 204);
}
```

The width settings for the form-control class are different from those used before and the width property is set to 100% to allow the element with this class applied. However, the max-width property limits the element to a maximum of 250 pixels.

The page will now appear as shown in Figure 16-8. The float issue has been fixed, plus the label is bold, the text box now has a rounded deepskyblue border and the text *Category Name* is vertically aligned with it.

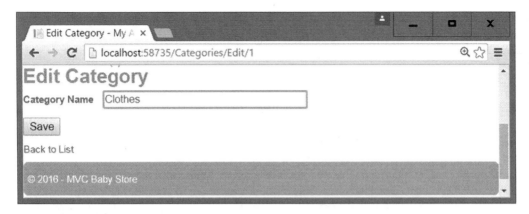

Figure 16-8. *The effect of the updated label and text box styles*

Revisiting the Grid System: Adding Blank Columns Using Margins

Previously, we added a very basic column system and we are now going to add some styles to address the scenario where we want to add an empty column to the left of another column.

Currently the *Save* button is located to the left of the page; we are going to show you how to relocate it to be underneath the text box. The HTML that renders the button is as follows:

```
<div class="col-md-offset-2 col-md-10">
    <input type="submit" value="Save" class="btn btn-default">
</div>
```

In the Bootstrap CSS, the class col-md-offset-2 is used to add a blank column to the left of the button. In order to replicate this, add the following style to the store.css file:

```
.col-md-offset-2 {
    margin-left: 16.666666666666664%;
}
```

This will now move the button over to the right by the equivalent of two column widths and add a left margin, as shown in Figure 16-9.

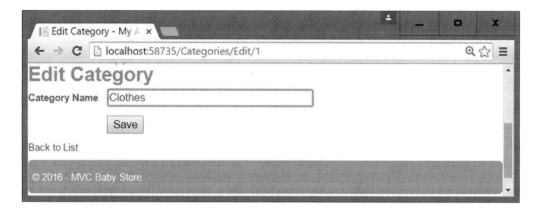

Figure 16-9. *Utilizing a margin to add the effect of an empty column*

For completeness, update store.css to add more offset styles to each column width as follows:

```
.col-md-offset-0 { margin-left: 0; }
.col-md-offset-1 { margin-left: 8.333333333333332%; }
.col-md-offset-2 { margin-left: 16.666666666666664%; }
.col-md-offset-3 { margin-left: 25%; }
.col-md-offset-4 { margin-left: 33.33333333333333%; }
.col-md-offset-5 { margin-left: 41.66666666666667%; }
.col-md-offset-6 { margin-left: 50%; }
.col-md-offset-7 { margin-left: 58.333333333333336%; }
.col-md-offset-8 { margin-left: 66.66666666666666%; }
.col-md-offset-9 { margin-left: 75%; }
.col-md-offset-10 { margin-left: 83.33333333333334%; }
.col-md-offset-11 { margin-left: 91.66666666666666%; }
```

To complete this page, we are going to update the button so it behaves the same as the Shop Now button on the home page.

Styling Buttons

In the previous chapter, we added some styles to allow a hyperlink to have the appearance of a button. Now we are going to reuse these styles to add the same appearance as any normal button input with the classes btn and default-btn. To update the button used in the form, update the styles relating to a.btn and a.btn-primary as follows:

```
a.btn, .btn {
    border-radius: 5px;
    color: #ffffff;
    text-decoration: none;
    border: 2px outset buttonface;
}
```

```
a.btn-primary, .btn-default, .btn-primary { background-color: lawngreen;}

a.btn-primary:hover, .btn-default:hover, .btn-primary:hover { background-color: green; }

a.btn-lg{
    padding: 10px 16px;
    font-size:1.5em;
}
```

These styles now apply to normal buttons styled with the classes `.btn` and `.btn-default`. The form will now be updated, as shown in Figure 16-10 with an updated Save button. The search button in the navigation bar has also been restyled.

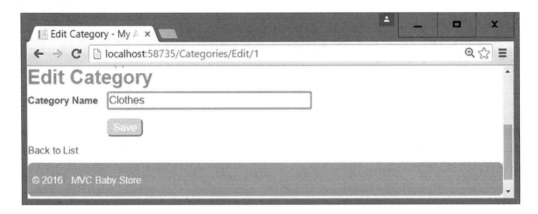

Figure 16-10. *The restyled Save button*

Styling the Cursor

The form looks pretty good now, but we want to make the cursor behave consistently when using actual buttons or links that appear as buttons. When a user hovers over a link, the cursor changes to a hand and I am going to show you how to replicate this when a user hovers over any button in the site. This is relatively straightforward but I've made a point of giving it a small section in the book because it is not obvious that you can change it. To change the cursor style to a hand whenever a user hovers over any submit button (not just one with the `a.btn` or `.btn` class applied), add the following style to the stylesheet:

```
input[type=submit]:hover {
    cursor: pointer;
}
```

Styling Error Messages

The form looks pretty complete now, but there is still one element that we want to restyle; the error messages that appear when the form fails validation. Figure 16-11 shows the Category Edit page with an error message.

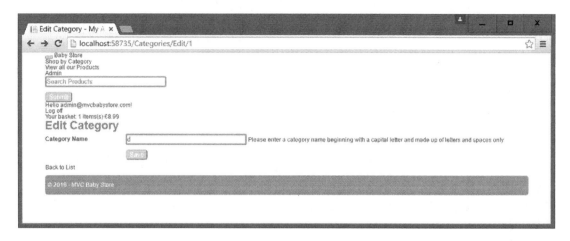

Figure 16-11. *The default formatting of an error message*

We are going to restyle the error messages to be bold, red, and also appear underneath the text box rather than next to it. The HTML that generates the text box and the error message is as follows, I've highlighted the relevant classes we are going to style in bold:

```
<div class="col-md-10">
    <input class="form-control text-box single-line input-validation-error" data-val="true"
        data-val-length="Please enter a category name between 3 and 50 characters in length"
        data-val-length-max="50" data-val-length-min="3" data-val-regex="Please enter a
        category name beginning with a capital letter and made up of letters and spaces only"
        data-val-regex-pattern="^[A-Z]+[a-zA-Z''-'\s]*$" data-val-required="The category name
        cannot be blank" id="Name" name="Name" type="text" value="Clothes">
    <span class="text-danger field-validation-error" data-valmsg-for="Name" data-valmsg-
    replace="true">
        <span for="Name" class="">Please enter a category name beginning with a capital letter
        and made up of letters and spaces only</span>
    </span>
</div>
```

First, add a simple style to store.css for the text-danger class to format it as red with bold text, as follows:

```
.text-danger {
    color: red;
    font-weight: bold;
}
```

If you view the web page, it should now be updated with the error message in bold red text. Next, we are going to shift the error message underneath the text box by using the display property.

513

Changing the Flow of the Page Using the Display Property

In the introduction to CSS, we mentioned the inline and block elements. Block elements add a line break after, them while inline elements flow in line with each other. At the moment, both the text box and the span that follows it are inline elements. We are going to change the behavior of the form-control class so that a line break is added after the text box, therefore forcing the error message to appear below it. To achieve this, update the form-control style as follows:

```
.form-control {
    width: 250px;
    border-radius: 3px;
    border: solid deepskyblue;
    color: rgb(14, 117, 204);
    display: block;
}
```

The error message will now appear on a new line, as shown in Figure 16-12.

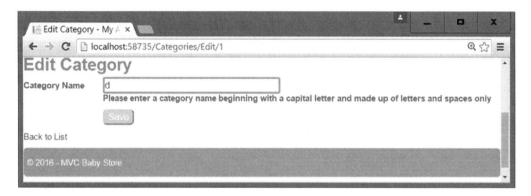

Figure 16-12. *The restyled error message appearing on a new line*

This form looks good, so let's check the effect on the other HTML forms of the site.

Styling the Other Forms in the Site

You might be wondering why we dedicated so much time restyling a small HTML form; well the answer is that by doing so we have also restyled all the other forms in the site. Figure 16-13 shows the form for creating a product. It has been restyled by all the styles we've added; however, it has a couple of things that were not apparent when editing a category. Some of the fonts don't look consistent, and the alignment when a form has more than one line does not look ideal. Later, we will right-align the labels and ensure that all the elements where a user enters text or choose an option are the same width.

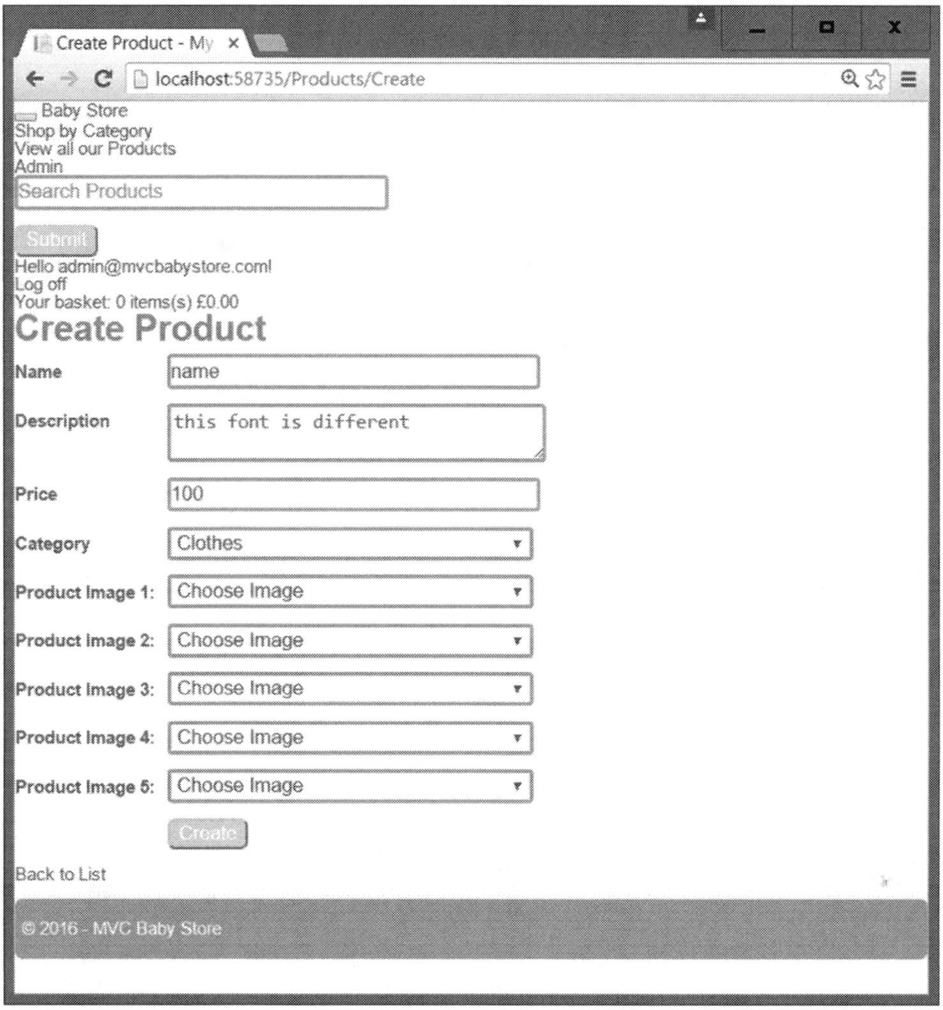

Figure 16-13. *The current format of the Products Create page*

Forcing Inheritance

The textarea element for entering the description has a different font to the rest of the page. In fact, this brings up an interesting feature of CSS in that the font used in all form elements, apart from the labels, all differ from the body font. Each of the form elements actually uses an Arial font with 13.3333px size, which is set by the browser's default stylesheet. It just happens that I chose a font and font-size that made this look as though everything was being inherited correctly. To see what I mean, change the body style so that the font size is set to 20px as follows:

```
body {
    background-color: white;
    max-width: 1024px;
    margin: 0 auto;
    font-size: 20px;
```

515

```
    font-family: Arial, Helvetica, sans-serif;
    color: rgb(14, 117, 204);
}
```

Figure 16-14 shows the updated page highlighting the fact that the fonts in the text box, text area, select lists, and Submit button have all stayed the same and are different from the body.

Figure 16-14. *The form element font is not the same as the body*

To force these elements to all be the same font size and font weight as the body tag, use the `inherit` keyword by adding the following style to the `store.css` file:

```
input, textarea, select, button {
    font-family: inherit;
    font-size: inherit;
}
```

This now forces the text boxes, the text area, the select lists, and the Create button to inherit the fonts from the body tag. Note that the text boxes and Create button are styled by the input selector. Figure 16-15 shows the effect of forcing inheritance for these elements; all the controls in the form now use the same font style and size.

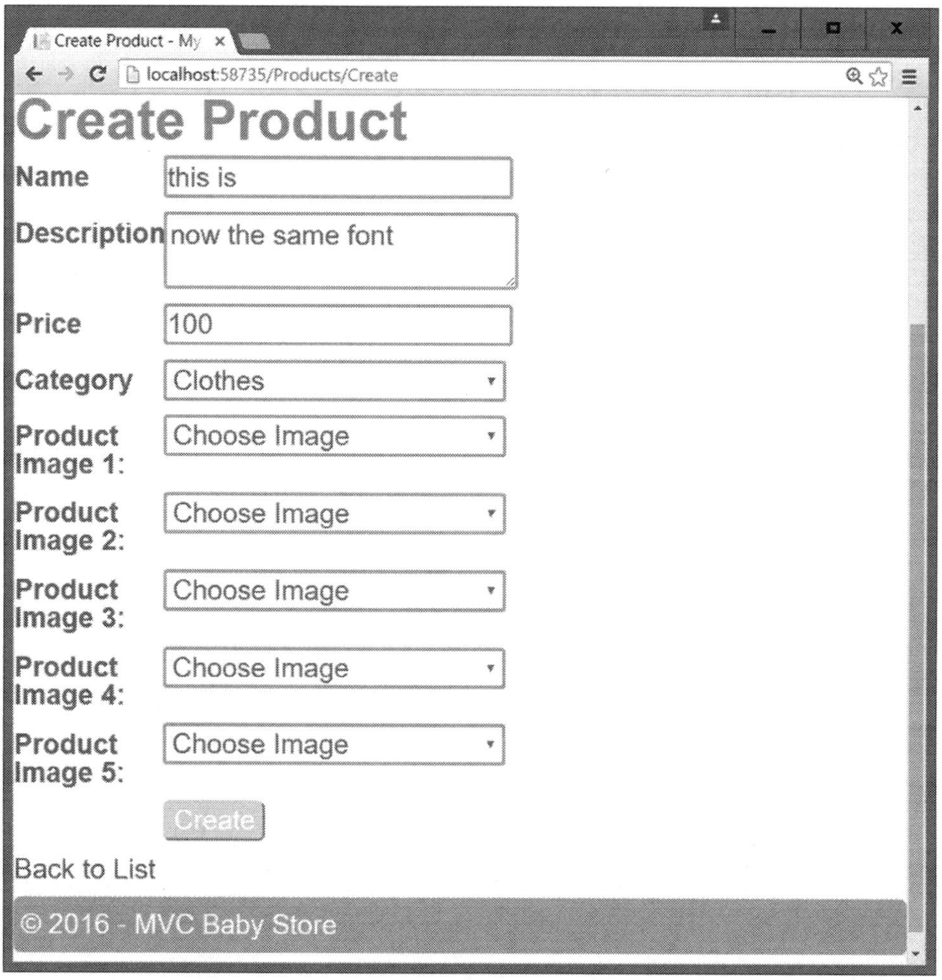

Figure 16-15. *The form elements now inherit the same font as the other elements contained inside the body tag*

Change the font-size of the body style back to 12px:

```
body {
    background-color: white;
    max-width: 1024px;
    margin: 0 auto;
    font-size: 12px;
    font-family: Arial, Helvetica, sans-serif;
    color: rgb(14, 117, 204);
}
```

517

Aligning Text

There are a couple of alignment issues I mentioned earlier—the labels don't read very well when left aligned, so we are going to right align them next to each element they relate to, plus the text boxes, text area, and select controls all have the different widths. First of all, to right-align any labels that are used in a form, add a style that targets the control-label class as follows:

```
.control-label {
    text-align: right;
}
```

The form now appears as shown in Figure 16-16.

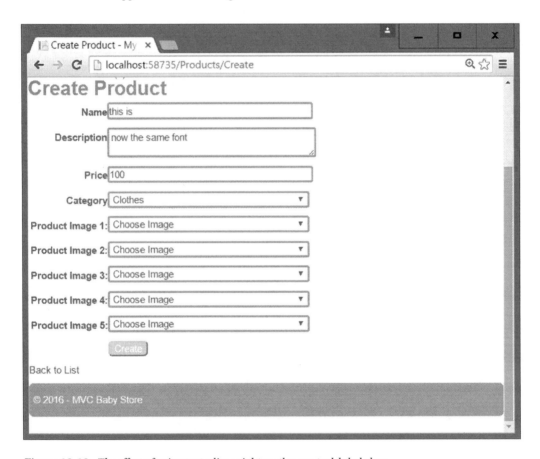

Figure 16-16. *The effect of using text-align: right on the .control-label class*

You can see that the text is right-aligned as expected but that it is tight against each control. To add some spacing, we are going to add some padding to the right of the column styles because it's likely that this may affect other items of text contained in columns throughout the site. Add the following entry to the style that floats the columns:

```
.col-md-1,
.col-md-2,
.col-md-3,
.col-md-4,
.col-md-5,
.col-md-6,
.col-md-7,
.col-md-8,
.col-md-9,
.col-md-10,
.col-md-11 {
float: left;
padding-right: 5px;
}
```

This looks like it should work fine but it does not, as shown in Figure 16-17.

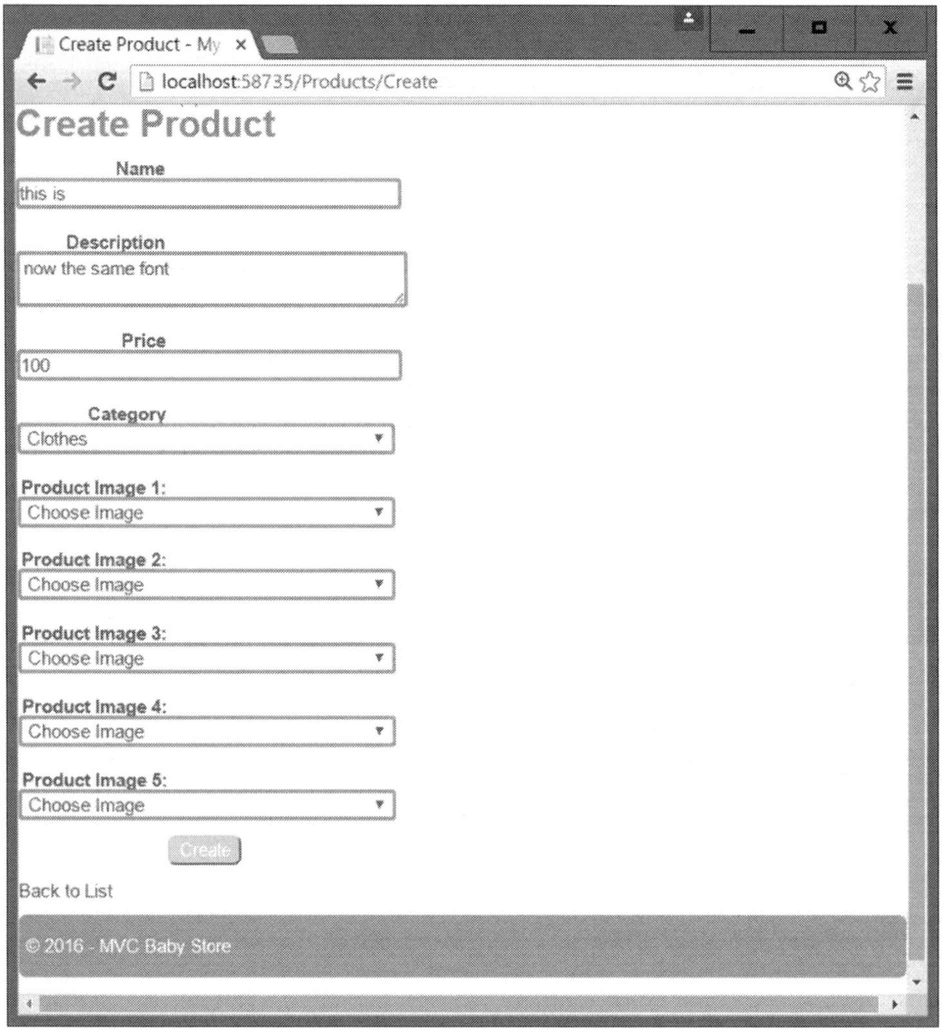

Figure 16-17. Applying a padding to the column styles makes the form move out of alignment

Box-Sizing

This issue is caused by the way the browser calculates widths. By default, it calculates widths as the width of the element plus any padding or margins, so in effect it is now trying to create a col-md-2 element that is 16.666666666666664% of the page, plus five pixels in width. Remember the HTML for the label plus the code is as follows:

```
<div class="form-group">
    <label class="control-label col-md-2" for="Name">Name</label>
    <div class="col-md-10">
        <input class="form-control text-box single-line" data-val="true" data-val-
            length="Please enter a product name between 3 and 50 characters in length" data-
            val-length-max="50" data-val-length-min="3" data-val-regex="Please enter a product
```

```
      name made up of letters and numbers only" data-val-regex-pattern="^[a-zA-Z0-9'-
      '\s]*$" data-val-required="The product name cannot be blank" id="Name" name="Name"
      type="text" value="">
    <span class="field-validation-valid text-danger" data-valmsg-for="Name" data-valmsg-
      replace="true"></span>
  </div>
</div>
```

So based on this HTML, the browser is trying to place a label with a class of col-md-2 next to a div with a class of col-md-2. To the browser this now says to display something that is 16.666666666666664% of the page plus five pixels in width next to something that is 83.33333333333334% of the width of the page. That means the browser is trying to display something that is 100% of the page width plus fixe pixels, which it simply cannot do. So the two elements now appear on different lines. For proof of this, change the width of the col-md-10 class as follows:

```
.col-md-10 { width: 75%; }
```

The page now appears as shown in Figure 16-18, with everything aligned correctly.

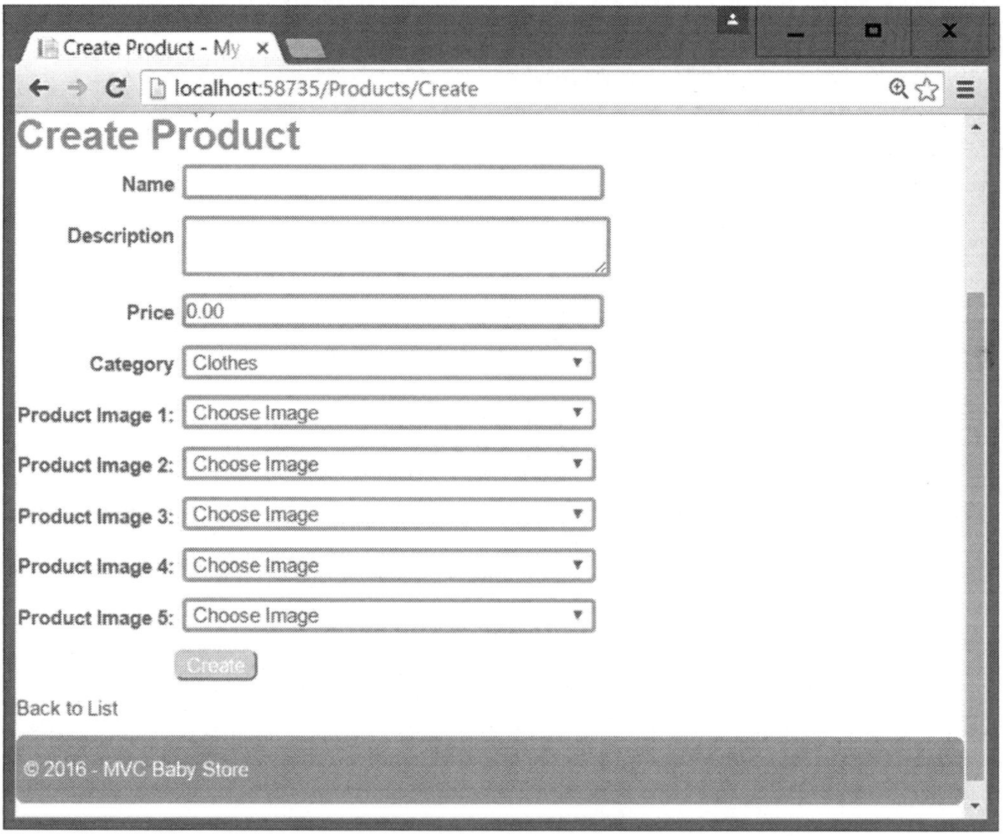

Figure 16-18. *The effect of shortening the width of col-md-10*

Following this, reset the `col-md-10` styles width back to its original value as follows:

```
.col-md-10 { width: 83.33333333333334%; }
```

Clearly, we can't start altering the widths in the stylesheet for each column depending on what padding we use in other columns, so to fix this issue we need to use a CSS property known as `box-sizing`. There are three options for the value of the `box-sizing` property as follows:

- `Content-box` is the default way browsers calculate width and height. The browser adds the border widths and padding thicknesses to the values set for the width and height properties to calculate an element's full width and height.

- `Padding-box` includes the padding as part of the height and width. For example, if you give an element 10 pixels of padding and set the width of the element to 50 pixels, the browser will consider the padding part of the 50 pixels and the content area would only be 30 pixels in width (i.e., 50-10-10). `Padding-box` is a legacy setting and is hardly ever used; it has been removed from the latest CSS specification, although it is currently supported in Firefox.

- `Border-box` includes the padding and the border thickness as part of the width and height values. This setting solves the problem of using percentage values for widths combined with padding. For example, with `box-sizing` set to `border-box`, when you set an element's width to 30%, that element will take up 30 percent of the available width even if you add padding and borders.

To solve the issue in Figure 16-17, we are going to set the `box-sizing` property to `border-box`. This is a setting that it is often included as a wildcard setting and applied to everything. Because this is such a useful setting, we are going to add it to the `Content\reset.css` file. Update this file to add the following entry:

```
* {
  -webkit-box-sizing: border-box;
  -moz-box-sizing: border-box;
  box-sizing: border-box;
}
```

This now ensures that the padding is included in the width of each column element and the Product Create page now appears as shown in Figure 16-19. Note that it has been necessary to include some browser-specific versions of the `box-sizing` property in order to support Chrome and Firefox.

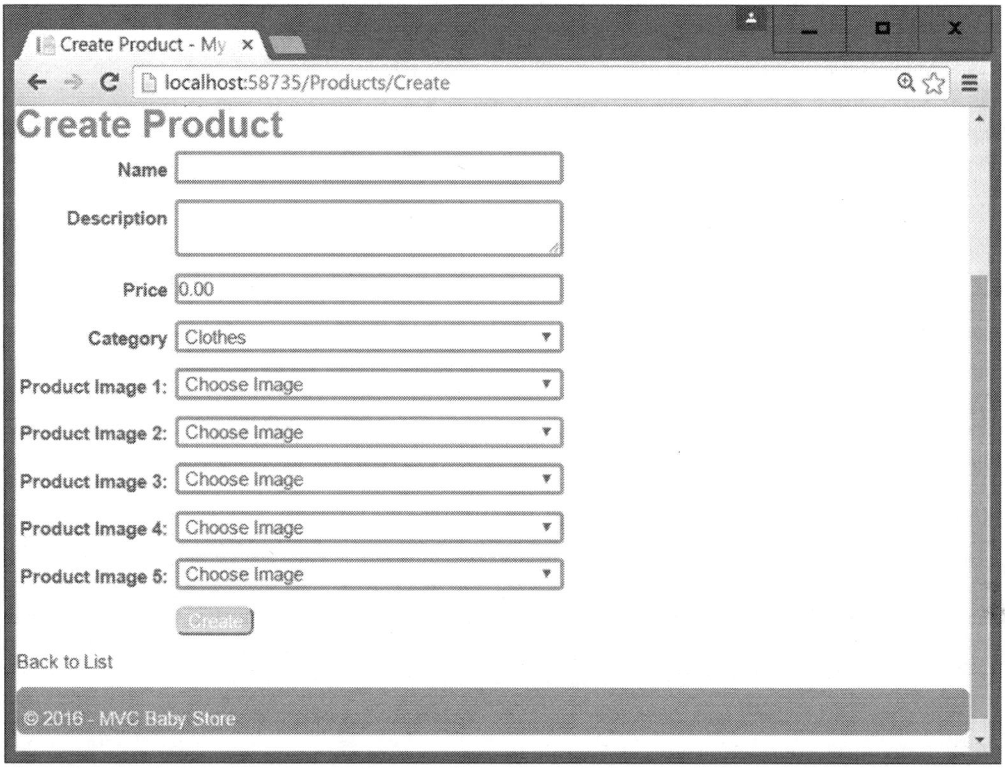

Figure 16-19. *Using box-sizing: border-box allows padding to be used to add spacing between the label and text boxes*

Using Line-Height with Box-Sizing:Border-Box

Setting the box-sizing to border-box has caused one issue. If you inspect Figure 16-19, you will see that the text in the footer is no longer vertically aligned. Ensure that if you are using the line-height property with border-box, that you account for the correct available height of the content area, rather than the whole element. By applying border-box to everything in the page, we have reduced the height of the footer by 10 pixels because it currently has padding: 5px; assigned to it; therefore, reset the line-height from 30 pixels to 20 pixels to realign the footer text correctly:

```
footer {
    margin-bottom: 20px;
    background-color: deepskyblue;
    color: white;
    height: 30px;
    line-height: 20px;
    padding:5px;
    border-radius:5px;
    margin-top:10px;
}
```

Vertically Aligning Something with Another Element Containing Text

If you now log out of the site and click on the *Log In* link, you will see the page shown in Figure 16-20.

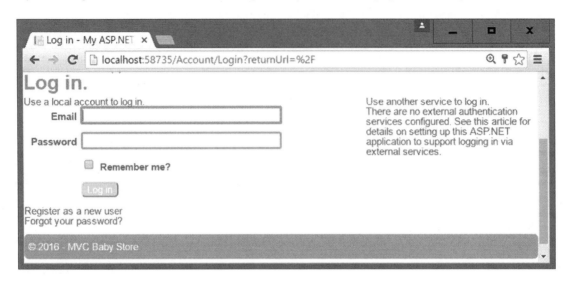

Figure 16-20. *The log in page*

There are a couple of issues with this page, the H4 heading needs tidying up a bit to make the font larger and to add some space between the *Use a Local Account to Log In* text and the E-mail label and text box. Add a simple style to `store.css` to fix this as follows:

```
h4{
    font-size: 1.5em;
    margin-bottom: 5px;
}
```

There is one other issue on the page that you may not have spotted. The checkbox next to the *Remember Me?* link is not vertically aligned with the text. To vertically align these two elements, you might think that you would try to vertically align the text with the checkbox; however, in CSS this works the other way round. You must align the checkbox correctly. To vertically align the checkbox, add the following style to the `store.css` file:

```
input[type=checkbox] {
    vertical-align: middle;
}
```

This will vertically align the checkbox with the text next to it; the effect of these two changes is shown in Figure 16-21.

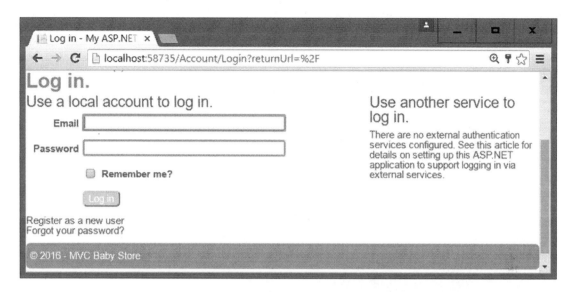

Figure 16-21. *The updated H4 heading and the vertically aligned checkbox*

■ **Note** This is a very trivial example, but vertical align is a very useful property and can be used in several scenarios, including aligning images or the contents of table cells, for instance.

Styling Definition Lists

Many of the pages that display details, including the user details or product deletion pages, are based around using the dl element. At present, with all the styles relating to this removed, this displays as shown in Figure 16-22, which shows the Product Details page.

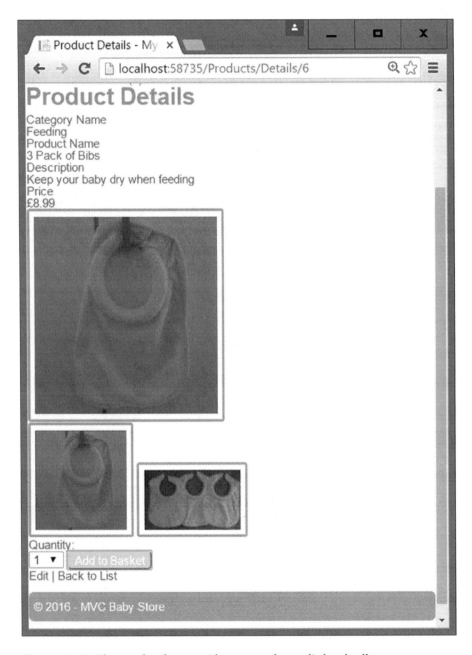

Figure 16-22. *The user details page without any styles applied to the dl tag*

The text for displaying the product name, category description, and price is generated by using the dl tag in the same form as the following:

```
<dl class="dl-horizontal">
    <dt>
        Category Name
    </dt>

    <dd>
        Feeding
    </dd>

    <dt>
        Product Name
    </dt>

    <dd>
        3 Pack of Bibs
    </dd>

    <dt>
        Description
    </dt>

    <dd>
        Keep your baby dry when feeding
    </dd>
... following code omitted...
```

To style the dl tag and its child dt and dd tags, add the following styles to the store.css file:

```
dl {
    width: 100%;
    overflow: hidden;
}

dt {
    float: left;
    /* adjust the width; make sure the total of both is 100% */
    width: 50%;
    /*clear left ensure that if there is an empty dd then the elements do not wrap*/
    clear:left;
    font-weight:bold;
}

dd {
    float: left;
    /* adjust the width; make sure the total of both is 100% */
    width: 50%;
}

dt,dd { line-height:20px; }
```

First of all, this code hides any overflow. This has the effect of ensuring that any content that follows the dl tag is displayed correctly.

The dt tag is floated to the left in order to make it appear to the left of the dd tag. The clear:left element ensures that the dt tag always appears on a new line.

The dd tag is also floated left and set to 50% of the total width of the dl tag. Finally, the line height is set to add space between each line. The result of these changes is shown in Figure 16-23.

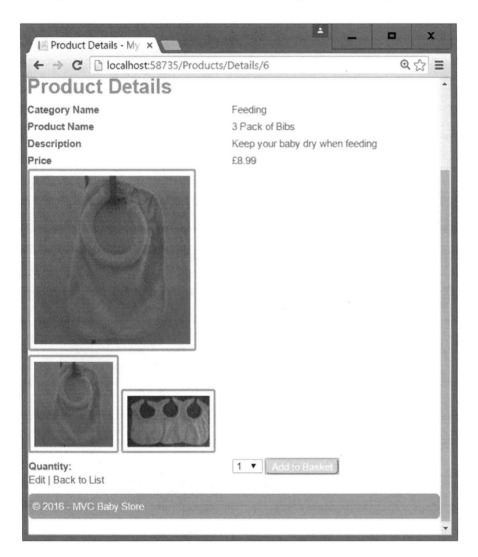

Figure 16-23. *The category name, product name, description, and price are now laid out side by side, thanks to the new dl, dd, and dt styles*

To bring the Product Details page in line with the style of the other pages, remove the entries style=padding:5px from the Views\Products\Details.cshtml file. Update the line of code the generates the quantity drop-down list to @Html.DropDownList("quantity", Enumerable.Range(1, 10).Select(i => new SelectListItem { Text = i.ToString(), Value = i.ToString() }), **new { @class = "form-control" })**.

Styling Tables

Some of the pages in the site contain tables and at the moment these use the browser's default formatting apart from having a padding of 5px, which was applied earlier to each cell. If you log in as admin@ mvcbabystore.com using the Adm1n@mvcbabystore.com password and view the current orders in the site, the Orders Index page appears as shown in Figure 16-24 (I've applied a class of control-label to the labels in the form and a class of col-md-1 to the Submit button).

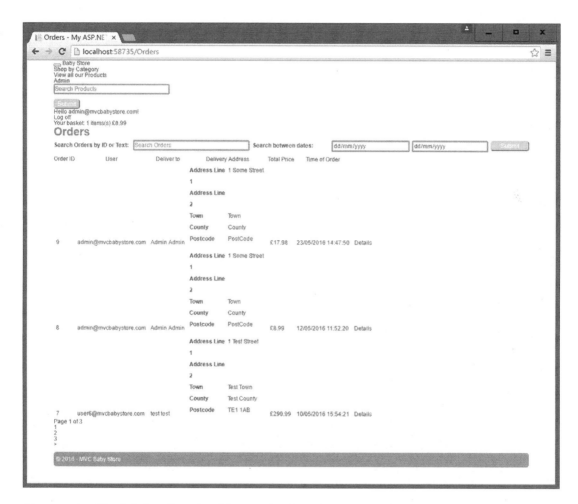

Figure 16-24. *The default styling of a table. Note that the Delivery Address column has some styling because it contains a dl tag*

The table is quite squashed up, so add a style to stretch it to the full width of the page as follows:

```
table{ width: 100%; }
```

Now add a style to change the headings to bold and align them to the left of the cell rather than being center-aligned. Add a 5px padding to bring the heading text in line with the td elements as follows:

```
th {
    font-weight: bold;
    text-align: left;
    padding: 5px;
}
```

The table should now take up the full width of the body with bold headings, as shown in Figure 16-25.

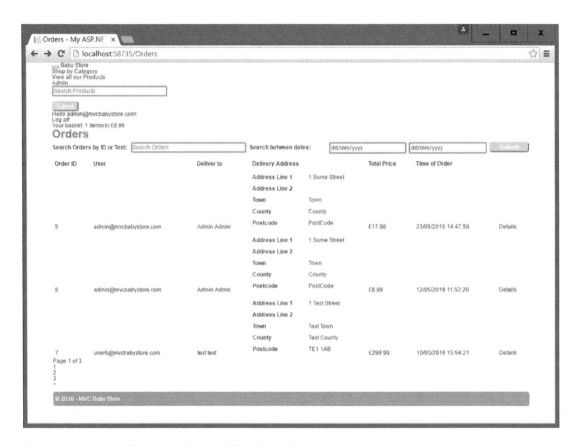

Figure 16-25. *The table with updated width and headings*

The table is still quite cluttered and muddled looking, so we are going to add a few more styles to spruce it up. First of all, update the td style so that the content of each row is aligned to the top of the cell by using the vertical-align property we introduced earlier in the chapter. Then add a border to the bottom of the table headings by updating the th style as follows:

```
th {
    font-weight: bold;
    text-align: left;
    padding: 5px;
    border-bottom:1px solid;
}

td {
    padding: 5px;
    vertical-align: top;
}
```

The table now looks more structured, as shown in Figure 16-26.

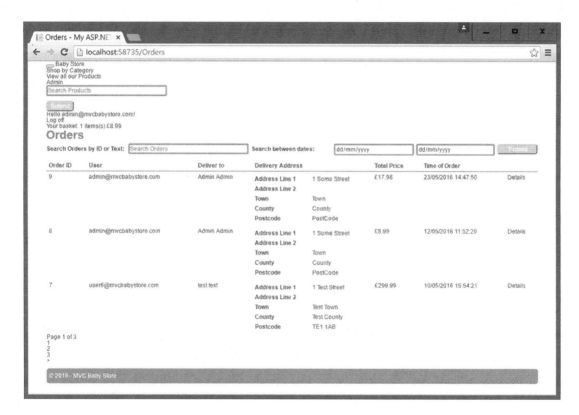

Figure 16-26. *The table with top-aligned text and a border under the table headings*

These styles have also affected several of the other pages in the site, for example, the Products Index page, and we are going to leave the generic styles applied to tables as they are at this point. We now want to change the orders table further, in order to underline any links (to make it more obvious that a user can sort by some of the columns and also add a border between each row of the table). Add a couple of new styles to store.css as follows to target a new class named order-table:

```
.orders-table td {
    border-bottom: 1px solid;
}

.orders-table a {
    text-decoration: underline;
}
```

Finally, update the table element in the Views\Orders\Index.cshtml file so that it uses this new order-table class as follows: <table class="table **orders-table**">. The hyperlinks in the orders-table will now be underlined, overriding the style applied to all a elements due to the fact it is more specific. With these changes in place, the Orders Index table now appears as shown in Figure 16-27.

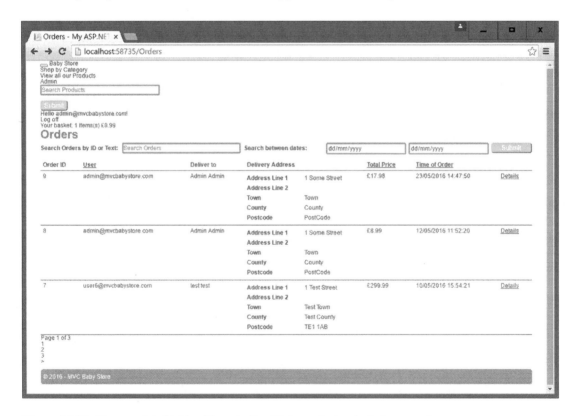

Figure 16-27. *The completed table with underlined links and a border between each row*

Adding the borders has made it obvious that the text "Page 1 of 3" is very close to the bottom of the table. To remedy this, add some space by adding a bottom-margin property to the table style as follows:

```
table{
    width: 100%;
    margin-bottom: 5px;
}
```

Styling the Paging Links

Next we are going to style the paging links at the bottom of the Orders Index page shown in Figure 16-27. This will also style the links in the Products Index page. The HTML that generates the paging links for the first three pages is as follows, with the relevant classes highlighted in bold:

```
<div class="pagination-container">
    <ul class="pagination">
        <li class="active">
            <a>1</a>
        </li>
        <li>
            <a href="/Orders?page=2">2</a>
        </li>
        <li>
            <a href="/Orders?page=3">3</a>
        </li>
        <li>
            <a href="/Orders?page=2">></a>
        </li>
    </ul>
</div>
```

To begin restyling the paging links, add a new style to the store.css file to add some top and bottom margins to the pagination class as follows:

```
.pagination {
    margin: 20px 0;
}
```

This adds whitespace above and below the page links. Now we are going to change the way the list generated inside the <ul> tags is displayed. By default, list elements (built using the <ul> or <ol> HTML tags) are displayed vertically on top of one another. This behavior can be overridden with CSS to make the elements of the list appear side by side in a row. To achieve this, it is necessary to use the display property and set the value to inline. To use this to reformat the paging links, add the following style to the store.css file in order to make the links appear side by side with some spacing between them:

```
.pagination li {
    display: inline;
    margin-right:2px;
}
```

This should now make the list of paging links appear side by side, as shown in Figure 16-28.

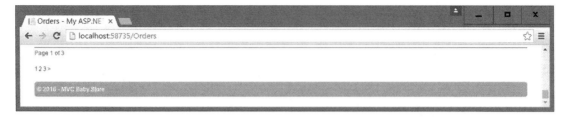

Figure 16-28. *The paging links displayed in line with each other rather than stacked vertically*

The links are now laid out next to one another, but they do not really stand out. To make them look more like paging controls, add the following style. This style targets any links that are descendants of both the .pagination class and the li element:

```
.pagination li a {
    padding: 6px 12px;
    border: 3px solid deepskyblue;
    border-radius: 3px;
    font-weight: bold;
}
```

The padding makes the links look squarer in appearance, and a rounded three pixel deepskyblue border is added. Finally, the font is set as bold so the text stands out. The effect of this style is shown in Figure 16-29.

Figure 16-29. *The links styled with padding to make them squarer, plus a rounded border*

The links now look a lot better but there is still no indication of which page a user is on. To display an indication of this, we need to target the active class and add a style for it to make it appear differently than the other links. Add the following style to change the look of the links that have the active class applied to them, making them have a deepskyblue background and white text, plus they are not underlined.

```
.active a {
  background-color: deepskyblue;
  color:#ffffff;
  text-decoration:none;
}
```

Figure 16-30. *The completed restyled paging links including indication of which page the user is on*

A Sibling Selector Example: Styling the Create New Links

The site looks good now, but one thing we want to do is to style all the *Create New* links to be the same, with large bold text. Rather than go through the web site and alter the HTML, we can use CSS selectors to target the links without adding a class to them. An inspection of these links shows that they always occur after a <h2> tag and they either immediately follow the <h2> tag or they are contained inside a <p> tag that follows the <h2> tag. To target both of these styles, we can use the sibling selector combined with a child selector.

First of all, to target any links that immediately follow a <h2> tag, add the following style:

```
h2 + a{
    font-size: 1.5em;
    font-weight: bold;
}
```

This style will resize any of the *Create New* links that appear directly after a <h2> tag such as the one in the Products Index page. The pages such as the RolesAdmin Index page are not restyled because their *Create New* link is contained inside a <p> tag that directly follows an <h2> tag. To target these links, update the new style as follows:

```
h2 + a, h2 + p > a{
    font-size: 1.5em;
    font-weight: bold;
}
```

The style now also targets any links that are direct children of a <p> tag that follows a <h2> tag. Figure 16-31 shows this style in use. In this figure, we have right clicked on the link and chosen the Inspect option. The bottom-right side pane shows the h2 + p > a selector shown in black, which indicates that it is the selector in use.

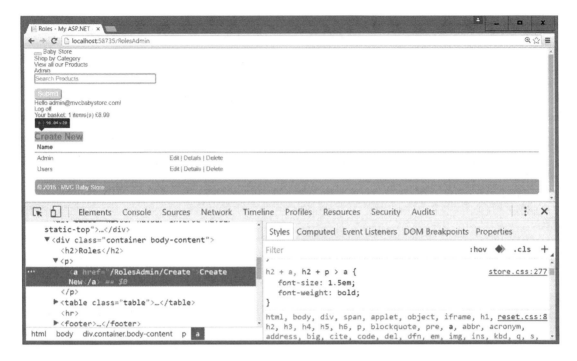

Figure 16-31. *The h2 + p > a being used to style the Create New link in the RolesAdmin Index page*

■ **Note**   I have not included the full restyling of each page in this chapter due to the fact that some of it is repetitive and you would not learn anything new from doing it, such as formatting the form on the Products Index page. However, the code for formatting each page can be found in the source code for this chapter available for download at `www.apress.com`.

Summary

This chapter covered several useful features of CSS to style the rest of the pages in the site, including styling forms, using a grid layout, box-sizing, and styling definition lists and tables. In the next chapter, we'll move onto the remaining element of the site that needs restyling: the navigation bar.

CHAPTER 17

■ ■ ■

Advanced CSS

This chapter focuses on restyling the navigation bar using more advanced features of CSS using positioning and animations. It also introduces the popular JavaScript library jQuery, to change the main product image when a thumbnail is clicked on in the Product Details page.

■ **Note**   To complete this chapter, you must either have completed Chapter 16 or download Chapter 16's source code from www.apress.com as a starting point. Also note that several of the figures dealing with the navigation bar are zoomed in by using the browser zoom feature. The fonts will appear smaller in reality.

Styling the Navigation Bar

So far, we have not added any specific styles to the navigation bar. It is currently a vertical list with the search box and button styled by the styles we have added in the previous chapters, as shown in Figure 17-1.

Figure 17-1.   The initial state of the navigation bar

As with previous chapters, we are going to stick with the default HTML generated by the MVC Framework for use with Bootstrap and base the styles around this. The HTML that generates the navigation bar is as follows; I've highlighted the CSS classes we'll be using, as there are quite a few of them used in generating the navigation bar. Don't worry though, I will break down all the techniques we use step by step so that you can see how each change affects the bar:

```html
<div class="navbar navbar-inverse navbar-static-top">
    <div class="container">
        <div class="navbar-header">
            <button type="button" class="navbar-toggle" data-toggle="collapse" data-
                target=".navbar-collapse">
                <span class="icon-bar"></span>
                <span class="icon-bar"></span>
                <span class="icon-bar"></span>
            </button>
            <a class="navbar-brand" href="/">MVC Baby Store</a>
        </div>
        <div class="navbar-collapse collapse">
            <ul class="nav navbar-nav">
                <li><a href="/Categories">Shop by Category</a></li>
                <li><a href="/Products">View all our Products</a></li>
            </ul>
            <form action="/Products" class="navbar-form navbar-left" method="get">
                <div class="form-group">
                    <input class="form-control" id="Search" name="Search"
                        placeholder="Search Products" type="text" value="" />
                </div>
                <button type="submit" class="btn btn-default">Submit</button>
            </form>
            <ul class="nav navbar-nav navbar-right">
                <li>
                    <a href="/Account/Register?returnUrl=%2F" id="registerLink">Register</a>
                </li>
                <li>
                    <a href="/Account/Login?returnUrl=%2F" id="loginLink">Log in</a>
                </li>
            </ul>
            <ul class="nav navbar-nav navbar-right">
                <li>
                    <a href="/Basket">Your basket: 0 items(s) &#163;0.00</a>
                </li>
            </ul>
        </div>
    </div>
</div>
```

The first style to add will style the whole navigation bar to give it a background and the rounded corners similar to the footer. Add this style to the store.css file:

```
.navbar{
    background-color: deepskyblue;
    border-radius: 5px;
    margin-top: 110px;
    margin-bottom: 10px;
    padding: 0px 5px;
}
```

This will change the background color of the navigation bar and round the corners using the border-radius property. Two margins are added to the top and bottom of the bar. Some space is added between the text and the left and right edges of the bar. The navigation bar should now appear as shown in Figure 17-2.

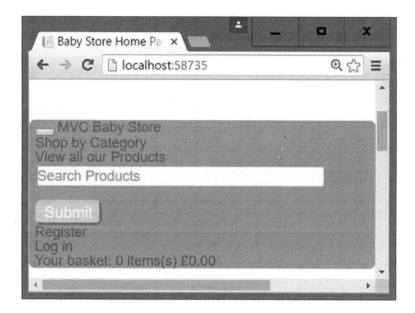

Figure 17-2. *The updated navigation bar with blue background, rounded corners, and margins to the top and bottom*

Transforming the Navigation Bar Content to Display Horizontally

We are now going to change the navigation bar to display content horizontally. This requires a combination of techniques we have used previously because the content is made up of a mixture of divs and list elements. To start displaying the items in a line, we are going to float the main containing div elements. Add the following styles to store.css, which will make the elements with the classes navbar-header, nav, and navbar-left float alongside each other.

```
.navbar-header {
    float: left;
}
```

```
.nav {
    float:left;
}

.navbar-left {
    float: left;
}
```

These style look fine and should make the elements in the nav bar float next to one another; however, there is an unexpected consequence, in that the main navbar div loses all its height and the content is pushed outside, as shown in Figure 17-3.

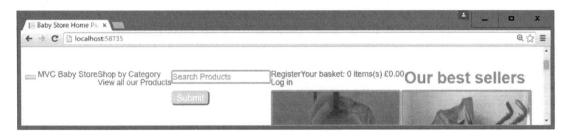

Figure 17-3. *The navbar div has disappeared from view and the content flowed outside it*

This issue occurs because all the children of the main navbar div are floated. This often causes a big headache for web designers and developers, but there a few simple ways to fix this. You can either apply the Micro Clearfix after the containing element or use the overflow property. We are going to use the Micro Clearfix because later in the chapter we use CSS positioning and using the overflow property is not a good combination with positioning as it causes a scroll bar to appear in the navigation bar. Modify store.css to change the current style that implements the Clearfix as follows. Add a new style to the end of the file to change the color of the links to white:

```
.row:after, .form-group:after, .navbar:after {
  content: " ";
  display: table;
  clear: both;
}

.navbar a{
    color: white;
}
```

The navigation bar should now appear as shown in Figure 17-4, with all the content contained inside it and floated next to one another.

Figure 17-4. *The navigation bar now displays with the divs floated*

The navigation bar now looks better but some of the items are still stacked on top of one another. To correct this, we need to add some more styles to lay out the list elements horizontally. Add the following style to make the list elements within the nav class and the form-group class within the navbar-form class display as inline blocks:

```
.nav li, .navbar-form .form-group {
    display: inline-block;
}
```

This should now make the lists used for Shop by Category and Shop by Product and the Register Log in links appear side by side, plus the button should now appear next to the search box, as shown in Figure 17-5.

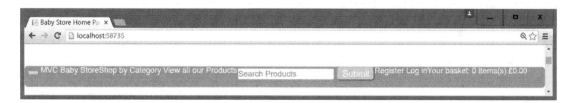

Figure 17-5. *The navigation bar with all elements horizontally aligned*

The elements of the navigation bar are still very squashed together, so add a new style to space out the list elements as follows:

```
.nav li {
    padding: 5px;
}
```

Also update the .navbar-heading style as follows to add the same five-pixel padding:

```
.navbar-header {
    float: left;
    padding: 5px;
}
```

541

Finally, we don't want to display the button with the class `navbar-toggle`, so set its `display` property to none by adding a new style as follows:

```
.navbar-toggle {
    display: none;
}
```

We should now have a nice basic navigation bar, as shown in Figure 17-6.

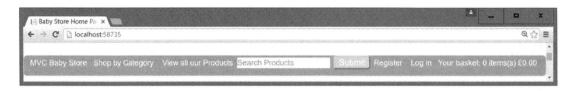

Figure 17-6. *The navigation bar, with everything aligned horizontally*

Moving Elements Using Positioning

We are now going to spruce up the navigation bar and use the large margin we added above it earlier in the chapter. To start with, we are going to move the search box and button using CSS so it appears in the margin above the rest of the bar. To achieve this, we are going to use a CSS feature known as positioning, which allows an element to change position. Elements can be positioned using relative or absolute positioning or a combination of the both to position a child element relative to its parent.

- Absolute positioning sets a fixed position of an element in the page; it is completely removed from the flow of the page.

- Relative positioning is used to move an element relative to its normal position in the page flow. When you use relative positioning, the space taken up by the element will remain in the page flow. Elements positioned using this technique tend not to move smoothly as the page resizes, and instead jump around the page.

- Fixed positioning locks an element into a fixed position so that even if the user scrolls, the element always stays in the same position in the screen.

- By declaring a parent element as relative and a child element as absolute, it is possible to position the child element relative to its parent. When you use this method of positioning, the space occupied by the repositioned element is removed from the page flow. Element positioned using this technique move smoothly as the page resizes.

We are going to use a combination of relative and absolute positioning in this example to position a child element relative to its parent.

To recap, the HTML that generates the search form is as follows:

```
<div class="navbar-collapse collapse">
    <ul class="nav navbar-nav">
        <li><a href="/Categories">Shop by Category</a></li>
        <li><a href="/Products">View all our Products</a></li>
    </ul>
```

```
<form action="/Products" class="navbar-form navbar-left" method="get">
    <div class="form-group">
        <input class="form-control" id="Search" name="Search"
            placeholder="Search Products" type="text" value="" />
    </div>
    <button type="submit" class="btn btn-default">Submit</button>
</form>
```

The parent element in this case is the div with the class navbar-collapse and the child element that we are going to reposition is the navbar-form element. Add the following two new styles to store.css and move the search box relative to the div that contains it:

```
.navbar-collapse {
    position: relative;
}

.navbar-form {
    position: absolute;
    bottom: 40px;
    left: 30%;
}
```

This will move the search box and button up and out of the navigation bar, as shown in Figure 17-7.

Figure 17-7. *The search box and button repositioned using CSS positioning*

Declaring the div with the navbar-collapse class as having a relative position allows any child elements to be positioned relative to it. Absolute positioning is then used in the navbar-form class to position it in relation to the navbar-collapse element. This is a rather confusing naming convention but it is how CSS works. The space occupied by the search box and button is now removed from the navigation bar. If we had used position: relative in the navbar-form element then the space in the navigation bar would remain. The bottom property moves the element 40 pixels upward and the left property moves it 30% of the page in from the left.

Make the search box and button larger by adding the following styles to store.css:

```
.navbar .form-control {
    padding: 5px;
    width: 250px;
}
```

```
.navbar-form button {
    padding: 5px 20px;
    font-size:1.2em;
}
```

Now use the relative and absolute positioning technique again to move the MVC BabyStore link with the class navbar-brand out of the div with the class navbar-header as follows. First, update the .navbar-header style to set its position to relative:

```
.navbar-header {
    float: left;
    padding: 5px;
    position: relative;
}
```

Then add a new style to store.css to reposition the navbar-brand link:

```
a.navbar-brand {
    color: hotpink;
    position: absolute;
    bottom: 10px;
}
```

In this style, we have used a.navbar-brand rather than navbar-brand in order to override the color of the .navbar a style created earlier. The MVC BabyStore text is now repositioned as shown in Figure 17-8.

Figure 17-8. *The repositioned and recolored MVC BabyStore link*

Styling Text

We are now going to restyle the MVC BabyStore text to make it appear more like a branding logo using some more advanced CSS effects, starting with adding some extra styles to the text itself. To start this, first update the a.navbar-brand style to make the font larger and bolder and also remove the underline when a user hovers over the link as follows:

```
a.navbar-brand {
    color: hotpink;
    position: absolute;
    bottom: 10px;
    font-size: 2.5em;
```

```
    font-weight: bold;
    text-decoration: none;
}
```

Adding a Shadow to Text

CSS features a text-shadow property that can be used to add shadow around text. This property has four attributes for horizontal and vertical offset; a value for the amount of blur applied to the text; and a color value that sets the color of the shadow. If the blur is set to 0, a very sharp shadow appears whereas setting the blur to a value such as 10px creates a light blurred shadow. We are going to add a medium grey shadow to the bottom and right of the text; in order to add this, update the a.navbar-brand style as follows:

```
a.navbar-brand {
    color: hotpink;
    position: absolute;
    bottom: 10px;
    font-size: 2.5em;
    font-weight: bold;
    text-decoration: none;
    text-shadow: 3px 3px 5px rgba(0,0,0,0.5);
}
```

The resulting text shadow applied to the MVC BabyStore text is shown in Figure 17-9.

Figure 17-9. The effect of applying text-shadow to the MVC Baby Store link (zoomed in)

Styling Letters and Lines of Text Using CSS

CSS features a couple of pseudo-selectors that allow you to style the first letter or first line of text. These are the first-letter and first-line selectors. Note that in order for these to work, there must be more than one letter or line of text; otherwise they have no effect. To make the first line of the MVC BabyStore deepskyblue and further increase the font size, add the following style to store.css:

```
a.navbar-brand:first-line{
    color: deepskyblue;
    font-size: 1.8em;
}
```

This will restyle part of the MVC BabyStore text, as shown in Figure 17-10.

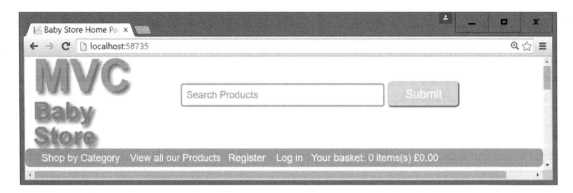

Figure 17-10. *Using the first-line pseudo-selector*

Next, add a width and height to the `a.navbar-brand` style to force the text onto two lines rather than three as follows:

```
a.navbar-brand {
    color: hotpink;
    position: absolute;
    bottom: 10px;
    font-size: 2.5em;
    font-weight: bold;
    text-decoration: none;
    text-shadow: 3px 3px 5px rgba(0,0,0,0.5);
    height: 86px;
    width: 250px;
}
```

This should now nicely format the MVC BabyStore text, as shown in Figure 17-11. Note that we have set a specific width and height so that we can use this later, in particular, the space this leaves to the right of the text.

Figure 17-11. *The effect on the MVC BabyStore text by setting a width and height*

Finally, to complete styling the MVC BabyStore text, we are going to add some spacing between the letters. Rather than having to add spans around each letter and then add margins, CSS has a helpful `letter-spacing` attribute that can be used to accomplish this task. To add some space between the letters of the MVC BabyStore text, update the `a.navbar-brand` style as follows:

```
a.navbar-brand {
    color: hotpink;
    position: absolute;
    bottom: 10px;
    font-size: 2.5em;
    font-weight: bold;
    text-decoration: none;
    text-shadow: 3px 3px 5px rgba(0,0,0,0.5);
    height: 86px;
    width: 250px;
    letter-spacing: 5px;
}
```

Figure 17-12 shows the updated text with spaces between each letter.

Figure 17-12. *The effect of setting the letter-spacing attribute value for the MVC BabyStore text*

Adding Images Using CSS

Throughout the book we have used the HTML `<img>` tag to display images; however, images can also be displayed using CSS. To add an image to something, you can use the CSS property `background-image` to set the image you want to display.

> ■ **Note** In this example, we are going to use the image file `baby_logo.jpg`. This can be downloaded from the Chapter 17 source code available on `apress.com`. The file is located in the folder `BabyStore\Content`.

To set the background image of the MVC BabyStore text to the `baby_logo.jpg` file, update the `a.navbar-brand` style with a `background-image` value as follows:

```
a.navbar-brand {
    color: hotpink;
    position: absolute;
    bottom: 10px;
```

```
    font-size: 2.5em;
    font-weight: bold;
    text-decoration: none;
    text-shadow: 3px 3px 5px rgba(0,0,0,0.5);
    height: 86px;
    width: 250px;
    letter-spacing: 5px;
    background-image: url(baby_logo.jpg);
}
```

This sets the image, but does not quite have the effect we require, as shown in Figure 17-13.

Figure 17-13. *Setting a background image*

By default, the background image will be repeated and fill the whole width of the element it is added to. We only want one version of the image to display; this can be achieved by using the CSS background-repeat property and setting the value to no-repeat. Add the following attribute to the a.navbar-brand style:

```
a.navbar-brand {
    color: hotpink;
    position: absolute;
    bottom: 10px;
    font-size: 2.5em;
    font-weight: bold;
    text-decoration: none;
    text-shadow: 3px 3px 5px rgba(0,0,0,0.5);
    height: 86px;
    width: 250px;
    letter-spacing: 5px;
    background-image: url(baby_logo.jpg);
    background-repeat: no-repeat;
}
```

This now displays one image only, but it is hidden behind the text as shown in Figure 17-14.

Figure 17-14. *Using background-repeat to only display a single image*

■ **Note**   The `background-repeat` also takes other values, in particular the values `repeat-x` and `repeat-y` can be used to only display a repeating image horizontally or vertically, respectively.

Positioning a Background Image

At the moment, the baby image is obscured behind the MVC BabyStore text, making both elements difficult to see. CSS allows you to position background elements by using the `background-position` property. This takes the horizontal and vertical values and accepts both general values (i.e., left, right, top, and bottom) and/or pixel values. For example, you could set something to display in the top left by setting the `background-position: left top`. In this case, we want to display the image to the right of the `a.navbar-brand` in the empty space, so add the following to the `a.navbar-brand` style in `store.css`:

```
a.navbar-brand {
    color: hotpink;
    position: absolute;
    bottom: 10px;
    font-size: 2.5em;
    font-weight: bold;
    text-decoration: none;
    text-shadow: 3px 3px 5px rgba(0,0,0,0.5);
    height: 86px;
    width: 250px;
    letter-spacing: 5px;
    background-image: url(baby_logo.jpg);
    background-repeat: no-repeat;
    background-position: right;
}
```

The updated image and text is shown in Figure 17-15.

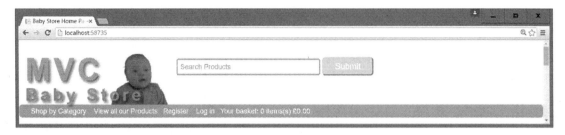

Figure 17-15. *The baby logo right-aligned*

Floating Elements to the Right

Earlier in the chapter when we positioned the search box and search button, it had the effect of removing the space in the navigation bar that was occupied by these elements. We want to reposition to *Register Log In* and *Your Basket* elements to the right of the navigation bar. To achieve this, we're going to use the float property again, but this time we are going to set the value to *right*. This will float the elements to the right of anything that follows them that is not cleared. Earlier we added style that added a Clearfix after the navigation bar so applying a float right to these elements will have the effect of reversing the order of them and moving them to the right of the navigation bar.

The HTML for the elements we want to move to the right is as follows:

```
<ul class="nav navbar-nav navbar-right">
    <li>
        <a href="/Account/Register?returnUrl=%2F" id="registerLink">Register</a>
    </li>
    <li>
        <a href="/Account/Login?returnUrl=%2F" id="loginLink">Log in</a>
    </li>
</ul>
<ul class="nav navbar-nav navbar-right">
    <li>
        <a href="/Basket">Your basket: 0 items(s) &#163;0.00</a>
    </li>
 </ul>
```

As you can see, they both have the Bootstrap class `navbar-right` applied to them. So we will add a style to `store.css` that targets this class to float the elements to the right as follows:

```
.navbar-right{
    float: right;
}
```

This will reverse the order of the element because it will float the first `<ul>` element to the right of the second `<ul>` element, as shown in Figure 17-16.

Figure 17-16. *The Register, Log In, and Basket summary links floated to the right. Note that the Register and Log In links now appear after the basket summary*

▓ **Tip** Be careful when using `float:right` and ensure that the order of your HTML is structured correctly so that when it appears onscreen, it is in the order you require.

Adding Animation to Links Using Scaling

I am now going to demonstrate some more advanced CSS to style the links in the navigation bar. First of all, add a new style entry to the `store.css` file to target the hyperlinks that are contained in the list elements of the navigation bar:

```
.nav li a{
    display: inline-block;
    background-color: rgb(14, 117, 204);
    border-radius: 2px;
    padding: 5px 10px;
    border: 1px solid rgb(14, 117, 204);
    max-width: 210px;
     -moz-box-shadow: inset 0px 1px 0px rgba(255,255,255,0.7);
    -webkit-box-shadow: inset 0px 1px 0px rgba(255,255,255,0.7);
    box-shadow: inset 0px 1px 0px rgba(255,255,255,0.7);
}
```

There aren't any new properties used in this style apart from `box-shadow`, which acts in a similar fashion to the `text-shadow` property used earlier. Also note that setting the display to `inline-block` ensures that the links remain inside the navigation bar. This style changes the links displayed inside the navigation bar to look like rounded blue buttons with a shiny top edge, as shown in Figure 17-17.

Figure 17-17. *The restyled navigation links*

Now add animation to the links when a user hovers over them:

```
.nav li a:hover {
    background-color: hotpink;
    border: 1px solid hotpink;
    transform: scale(1.1);
    text-decoration:none;
}
```

This style changes the background color and the border color to change the button to pink but it also uses the CSS transform property to scale the size of the link up by 10% with the code transform: scale(1.1);. Figure 17-18 shows how the links now appear when you hover over them.

Figure 17-18. *The effect View All Our Products link with color changed and scale applied on hover*

The links now change, but the process is rather quick and jerky. To slow the transformation down, modify the .nav li a style to add a transition property with the ease-in set to quarter of a second. This has the effect of fading in the change. Ease-in and ease-out can be used with a transform to slow the transformation down as desired.

```
.nav li a{
    display: inline-block;
    background-color: rgb(14, 117, 204);
    border-radius: 2px;
    padding: 5px 10px;
    border: 1px solid rgb(14, 117, 204);
    max-width: 210px;
    -moz-box-shadow: inset 0px 1px 0px rgba(255,255,255,0.7);
```

```
    -webkit-box-shadow: inset 0px 1px 0px rgba(255,255,255,0.7);
    box-shadow: inset 0px 1px 0px rgba(255,255,255,0.7);
     -webkit-transition: ease-in .25s;
    transition: ease-in .25s;
}
```

The vendor-specific -webkit-transition property is required in order to make this work in Google Chrome.

Introducing jQuery

I am now going to show you how to use the popular JavaScript library jQuery in order to allow users to click on a thumbnail image in the Product Details page and update the main image with the enlarged version of the thumbnail. The project already has jQuery included in the Scripts folder, as it is used to perform client-side validation. The current version installed in the source code that accompanies the book is version 1.10.2, and at the time of writing the latest version available is either 1.12.4 or 2.2.4. Rather confusingly, there are two branches of jQuery available for download—the difference is that v2.x does not support Internet Explorer 6, 7, or 8.

How the Project References jQuery

Generally, Visual Studio will include jQuery in an MVC project, but if you ever need to download it into a project, then to use it you simply need to ensure it is included in each page that uses it by adding a reference to it in your HTML. To add a reference to jQuery (or indeed to any JavaScript file), you add a script element. For example, in the BabyStore project the script element is <script src="/Scripts/jquery-1.10.2.js"> </script>. In the BabyStore project, this script element is generated by the line of code @Scripts.Render("~/bundles/jquery") located in the Views\Shared_Layout.cshtml file. This code uses a bundle in the same way that the CSS files are loaded, by referencing the following code in the App_Start\BundleConfig.cs file.

```
bundles.Add(new ScriptBundle("~/bundles/jquery").Include(
    "~/Scripts/jquery-{version}.js"));
```

jQuery Syntax

jQuery is based on JavaScript and therefore uses JavaScript syntax to allow you to write code. jQuery script works by checking that the page was first loaded to ensure that it can process any element within the page. To do this, all the jQuery is included in the surrounding code block:

```
$(document).ready(function() {
});
```

This code is known as the *document ready event* and tells jQuery to wait until the entire HTML document (the document variable) has loaded. Once this has occurred, it will then run any code within the function block. The code function(){} represents an anonymous function; this is a feature of JavaScript that allows functions to be declared without a name. The $ sign is prefixed to any code that is to be run from the jQuery library. Therefore, with the jQuery library included in the HTML source of the page, the code $(document).ready(function() {}); is recognized as jQuery.

There is also shorthand version of the document ready event as follows (although I prefer the longer version):

```
$(function(){
});
```

I've included jQuery along with CSS because it works on a similar premise to CSS; it uses selectors. We are only touching the tip of the jQuery iceberg in this book, but the basic format of all jQuery code is `$(selector).method` or `$(selector).attribute`. Methods and attributes can be chained together so, for example, you can write code in the format `$(selector).attribute.method`.

■ **Note**   The script that loads the jQuery library must be included in the HTML source before the document ready event code in order for the code to work. Otherwise, it will not be recognized as jQuery.

Using jQuery to Update the Main Image in the Product Details Page

We are now going to use jQuery to change the main image in the product details page when a user clicks on a thumbnail image. The HTML that generates the main image and the thumbnail image is as follows (this example shows the bibs product):

```
<dd>
    <img src="/Content/ProductImages/Bibs1.JPG">
</dd>
<dt></dt>
<dd>
    <a href="/Content/ProductImages/Bibs1.JPG">
        <img src="/Content/ProductImages/Thumbnails/Bibs1.JPG">
    </a>
    <a href="/Content/ProductImages/Bibs2.JPG">
        <img src="/Content/ProductImages/Thumbnails/Bibs2.JPG">
    </a>
</dd>
```

Based on this HTML, what we need to do in order to update the image is detect a click on any image within an a tag and then change the image that is the immediate child of a dd tag (the main image). We also want to ensure that the user stays on the page and is not redirected to the address of the link.

■ **Note**   There are no other images in the Product Details page that follow the pattern of the HTML above. If there were, then we would have to assign an ID to each element we wanted to use and then use each ID in the jQuery selectors.

To start the jQuery code to make this functionality work, update the Views\Products\Details.cshtml file to add a new document ready event as follows:

```
@model BabyStore.Models.Product


@{
    ViewBag.Title = "Product Details";
}

<h2>@ViewBag.Title</h2>

<div>
    <hr />
    <dl class="dl-horizontal">
        <dt>
            @Html.DisplayNameFor(model => model.Category.Name)
        </dt>

        <dd>
            @Html.DisplayFor(model => model.Category.Name)
        </dd>

        <dt>
            @Html.DisplayNameFor(model => model.Name)
        </dt>

        <dd>
            @Html.DisplayFor(model => model.Name)
        </dd>

        <dt>
            @Html.DisplayNameFor(model => model.Description)
        </dt>

        <dd>
            @Html.DisplayFor(model => model.Description)
        </dd>

        <dt>
            @Html.DisplayNameFor(model => model.Price)
        </dt>

        <dd>
            @Html.DisplayFor(model => model.Price)
        </dd>
```

```
    @if (Model.ProductImageMappings != null && Model.ProductImageMappings.Any())
    {
        <dt></dt>
        <dd>
            <img src="@(Url.Content(Constants.ProductImagePath) +
                Model.ProductImageMappings.OrderBy(pim =>
                pim.ImageNumber).ElementAt(0).ProductImage.FileName)">
        </dd>
        <dt></dt>
        <dd>
            @foreach (var item in Model.ProductImageMappings.OrderBy(pim =>
                pim.ImageNumber))
            {
                <a href="@(Url.Content(Constants.ProductImagePath) +
                    item.ProductImage.FileName)">
                    <img src="@(Url.Content(Constants.ProductThumbnailPath) +
                    item.ProductImage.FileName)">
                </a>
            }
        </dd>
    }
    <dt>
        Quantity:
    </dt>
    <dd>
        @using (Html.BeginForm("AddToBasket", "Basket"))
        {
            @Html.AntiForgeryToken()
            @Html.HiddenFor(model => model.ID)
            @Html.DropDownList("quantity", Enumerable.Range(1, 10).Select(i => new
                SelectListItem { Text = i.ToString(), Value = i.ToString() }), new { @class
                = "form-control" })
            <input type="submit" class="btn btn-primary btn-xs" value="Add to Basket">
        }
    </dd>
    </dl>
</div>
<p>
    @if (Request.IsAuthenticated && User.IsInRole("Admin"))
    {
        @Html.ActionLink("Edit", "Edit", new { id = Model.ID })
        @Html.Raw(" | ")
    }
    @Html.ActionLink("Back to List", "Index")
</p>

@section Scripts {
    <script>
        $(document).ready(function () {
        });
    </script>
}
```

The @Section Scripts code block ensures that this script is loaded after the jQuery library. If this was not used, then the script would load first and it would not function correctly.

First of all, add a new function that runs when a user clicks on a thumbnail image. Remember that in the HTML code listed previously, we identified a thumbnail image as an img tag within an a tag. To achieve this, add the following to the document ready event code:

```
@section Scripts {
    <script>
        $(document).ready(function () {
            $('a>img').click(function (evt) {

            });
        });
    </script>
}
```

This code first uses a jQuery selector to find any img tags that are direct descendants of a tag using the code $('a>img'). The jQuery click event is then called and, when this activates, a new anonymous function is going to run. This function is passed the click event as a parameter using the code function(evt).

Now update the script as follows to prevent the users following the link when they click on a thumbnail image:

```
@section Scripts {
    <script>
        $(document).ready(function () {
            $('a>img').click(function (evt) {
                evt.preventDefault();
            });
        });
    </script>
}
```

If you now click on a thumbnail, you will no longer be redirected to another page showing just the large version of the image. Next, add the following bold line of code to obtain the current address of the link that the thumbnail points to:

```
@section Scripts {
    <script>
        $(document).ready(function () {
            $('a>img').click(function (evt) {
                evt.preventDefault();
                var thumbnailAddress = $(this).parent().attr('href');
            });
        });
    </script>
}
```

This line of code is more complex than the others, but works on the same principle. It is simply a more complex selector. This selector first finds the parent of the selector we used to find the thumbnail image, which is referenced by using $(this). In this case, $(this) represents the img tag found by the a>img selector, so when we now find the parent we will find the a element. The code then finds the href element of the a tag by using the code $(this).parent().attr('href');.

Finally, add two new lines of code. The first line selects the main image (identified as being an `img` tag that is the direct descendant of a `dd` tag) to be replaced by using the `dd>img` selector. The second line finds the `src` attribute of this image and replaces it with the address of the thumbnail image that was clicked. This has the effect of replacing the main image with the large version of the thumbnail.

```
@section Scripts {
    <script>
        $(document).ready(function () {
            $('a>img').click(function (evt) {
                evt.preventDefault();
                var thumbnailAddress = $(this).parent().attr('href');
                var mainImage = $('dd > img');
                mainImage.attr('src', thumbnailAddress);
            });
        });
    </script>
}
```

To see the effect of this code, start the web site and view the details of any product. You should now be able to click on the thumbnail images and the larger version of the image will now become the main image for the product. Figure 17-19 shows the Pram and Pushchair System product with the main image updated by clicking on the middle thumbnail.

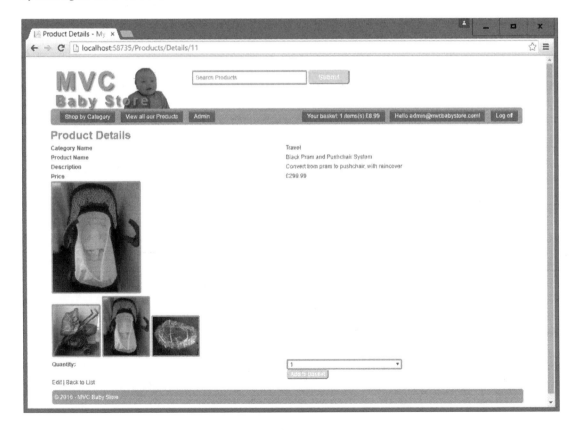

Figure 17-19. *Updating the main product image with jQuery*

■ **Caution**   It is possible to chain together lots of jQuery to make the code quite terse and complex looking. For example, we could have written the three lines after the line `evt.preventDefault();` as `$('dd > img').attr('src', $(this).parent().attr('href'));`. It is more compact, but it also becomes more difficult to understand, so when writing jQuery or indeed any JavaScript, try to find a balance between code length and ease of reading. It is also more efficient when using JavaScript to assign an HTML element to a variable if you are going to refer to it more than once.

■ **Note**   JQuery is a huge subject area within itself and has been expanded over the years to include other libraries for mobile and advanced UI features. For more information on jQuery, Apress has several other books available such as *Beginning jQuery* by Jack Franklin and *Pro jQuery 2.0* by Adam Freeman.

Summary

This chapter started by styling the navigation bar to appear horizontally. I then introduced how to use CSS positioning to move elements around the page and covered how to use scaling to make elements appear larger. The chapter closed with a brief introduction on to how use jQuery to update the main image of a product when a user clicks on a thumbnail image.

Responsive Web Sites: Styling for Mobile/Cell and Tablet Sized Devices

This chapter introduces responsive web design. Building a "responsive" web site basically means allowing the site to respond to the size of the screen it is being displayed on and reformat itself accordingly. The chapter will introduce CSS Media Queries to reformat the site for use on both mobile and tablet-sized devices and show you how to allow a development site running via Visual Studio to be viewed on another device on the same network.

▓ **Note** To complete this chapter, you must either have completed Chapter 17 or download the Chapter 17 source code from `www.apress.com` as a starting point.

Introducing Media Queries

CSS includes a concept called media queries, which let you assign styles to a page based on the browser's width and height. Using media queries, you can create custom styles for phones, tablets, and desktop browsers, to tailor your site's presentation so it looks its best on each type of device.

Media queries let you send different styles to browsers based on the screen widths, for example, less than 480 pixels, more than 480 pixels but less than 768 pixels, etc. These widths are known as breakpoints in responsive design. In the real world, a commonly used set of breakpoints are 480 pixels for a "mobile/cell" design, a screen between 481 and 768 gets "tablet" design, and anything over 768 gets a "desktop" design. We don't actually use these in the book simply to save some time and because we have a certain breakpoint at which we want to stop the navigation menu from wrapping around. There are several other more detailed standard breakpoints that target specific devices and these are constantly evolving.

© Lee Naylor 2016
L. Naylor, *ASP.NET MVC with Entity Framework and CSS*, DOI 10.1007/978-1-4842-2137-2_18

As an example, to write these media queries in CSS, you would add the following code to a stylesheet and then add the relevant styles inside each query:

```
/*write desktop styles here...*/

@media (min-width: 481px) and (max-width:768px) {
        /*write tablet styles here...*/
}

@media (max-width:480px) {
        /*write mobile/cell styles here...*/

}
```

Designing a Responsive Site

One thing to consider when designing a responsive site is which device you're designing for first. You should start with a default design, as we have done in the previous chapters, and then create media-query styles to override the default styles and reformat the page for your breakpoint screen widths. There are two main approaches to responsive design, known as *desktop first* and *mobile first*. In desktop first, you can add some styles with several columns and all the bell and whistles you want, and then tweak the site for other sized devices. Mobile first, on the other hand, creates a smaller page design as the default without several columns and then builds the site outward using media queries.

We've taken the desktop first approach in this book and as you see, for example with the shopping basket, everything can appear to be laid out fine in desktop but then can cause some small unexpected issues when you move to a mobile design.

Developing for Mobile/Cell Using Google Chrome

It might not seem very obvious at first, but the easiest place to start when developing for different sized devices is your desktop browser. Simply resizing the browser is one of the most useful tools you will find in your armory for getting started with developing for different screen sizes.

There is no substitute for actually testing your site in a physical device, but Google Chrome does offer an attempt to simulate behavior on popular devices, as shown in Figure 18-1. To use this simulation, you need to open the developer tools section of Chrome by pressing F12 and this will then allow you to use the *device mode* feature of Chrome. To use this, you press the *toggle device mode* button to the left of the Elements link in the developer tools menu. This is shown as the second button in from the left in the bottom menu in Figure 18-1. You can then choose a device to simulate by clicking on the menu at the top of the screen. Figure 18-1 shows how to select an iPhone6 device.

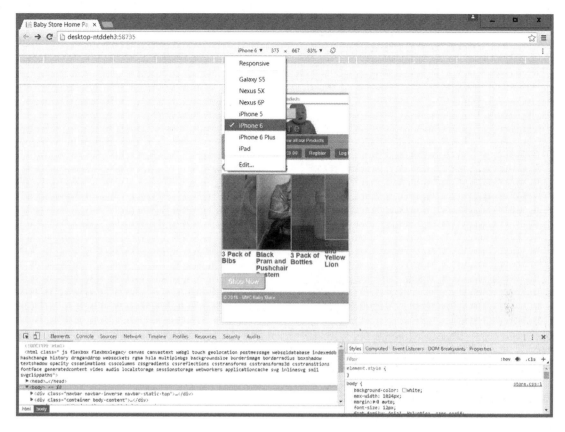

***Figure 18-1.** Using Chrome to simulate an iPhone6*

You can simulate events such as hover by inspecting an element and right-clicking on it in the elements pane. You then choose the event you want to simulate from the pop-up menu. My normal preference is to start with just resizing the browser at first and then use the device mode if I want to inspect a style in more detail using the developer tools.

Making the Home Page Responsive

We are going to start with changing the style of the home page. This actually covers a few topics in one page so is a good place to start. Figure 18-2 shows the home page when we resize the browser to be a cell/mobile phone size. Ignoring the navigation bar for now, let's focus on the bestseller images. They overlap one another due to the fact that they appear in columns.

Figure 18-2. The current home page on a smaller screen

As a reminder, the HTML that generates the bestseller images is shown here:

```
<h2>Our best sellers</h2>
    <div class="row">
        <div class="col-md-3">
            <a href="/Products/Details/6">
                <img src="/Content/ProductImages/Bibs1.JPG">
            </a>
            <p>
                <a class="large-bold-text" href="/Products/Details/6">3 Pack of Bibs</a>
            </p>
        </div>
        <div class="col-md-3">
            <a href="/Products/Details/11">
                <img src="/Content/ProductImages/Pram1.JPG">
            </a>
            <p>
                <a class="large-bold-text" href="/Products/Details/11">Black Pram and
                    Pushchair System</a>
            </p>
        </div>
        <div class="col-md-3">
            <a href="/Products/Details/5">
                <img src="/Content/ProductImages/Bottles1.JPG">
            </a>
            <p>
                <a class="large-bold-text" href="/Products/Details/5">3 Pack of Bottles</a>
            </p>
        </div>
        <div class="col-md-3">
            <a href="/Products/Details/3">
                <img src="/Content/ProductImages/Lion1.JPG">
            </a>
            <p>
                <a class="large-bold-text" href="/Products/Details/3">Orange and Yellow
                    Lion</a>
            </p>
        </div>
    </div>
```

You can see from this HTML that each image is contained inside a div element with the class col-md-3 assigned to each div. In the current Content\store.css file, this style is given a width of 25% and floated left with a padding of 5 pixels. We are going to add a media query to store.css but with a breakpoint at 900 pixels. I've chosen this breakpoint because below this, the navigation bar starts to wrap.

■ **Tip**   In Google Chrome, you can see the width and height of the current browser window in the top-right corner when using the developer tools.

To fix the issues with the home page images being squashed, we are only going to use columns in the site when the width is over 900 pixels (remember this is just an example and in reality you are likely to have more standard breakpoints). Add the following media query to the store.css file and cut and paste the column styles from store.css shown below into it:

```
@media (min-width:900px) {
    .col-md-1 { width: 8.333333333333332%; }
    .col-md-2 { width: 16.666666666666664%; }
    .col-md-3 { width: 25%; }
    .col-md-4 { width: 33.33333333333333%; }
    .col-md-5 { width: 41.66666666666667%; }
    .col-md-6 { width: 50%; }
    .col-md-7 { width: 58.333333333333336%; }
    .col-md-8 { width: 66.66666666666666%; }
    .col-md-9 { width: 75%; }
    .col-md-10 { width: 83.33333333333334%; }
    .col-md-11 { width: 91.66666666666666%; }
    .col-md-12 { width: 100%; }

    .col-md-1,
    .col-md-2,
    .col-md-3,
    .col-md-4,
    .col-md-5,
    .col-md-6,
    .col-md-7,
    .col-md-8,
    .col-md-9,
    .col-md-10,
    .col-md-11 {
        float: left;
        padding-right: 5px;
    }

    .col-md-offset-0 { margin-left: 0; }
    .col-md-offset-1 { margin-left: 8.333333333333332%; }
    .col-md-offset-2 { margin-left: 16.666666666666664%; }
    .col-md-offset-3 { margin-left: 25%; }
    .col-md-offset-4 { margin-left: 33.33333333333333%; }
    .col-md-offset-5 { margin-left: 41.66666666666667%; }
    .col-md-offset-6 { margin-left: 50%; }
    .col-md-offset-7 { margin-left: 58.333333333333336%; }
    .col-md-offset-8 { margin-left: 66.66666666666666%; }
    .col-md-offset-9 { margin-left: 75%; }
    .col-md-offset-10 { margin-left: 83.33333333333334%; }
    .col-md-offset-11 { margin-left: 91.66666666666666%; }
}
```

This means that the web site will now appear with a column layout only when it is wider than 900 pixels. Figure 18-3 shows how the home page now appears with the column widths and floats removed.

Figure 18-3. *The home page with columns removed on a smaller screen*

■ **Note**   As mentioned in Chapter 15, CSS now supports an alternative to working with floats known as Flexbox. This can be used as an alternative to the methods used here to produce a responsive page layout. You can learn more about Flexbox at http://www.w3schools.com/css/css3_flexbox.asp.

There are a couple more issue with the main content of the home page. The Shop Now button overlaps the content above it and the images for the bestsellers are stuck to the left edge of the window. To fix the issue with the button, add a new media query for when the page layout is less than 900 pixels and add a bottom margin to each div as follows:

```
@media (max-width: 899px) {
    div {
        margin-bottom: 20px;
    }
}
```

To fix the issue with the images being stuck against the left edge of the window, add a style above the first media query so that it always applies to the site as follows:

```
.body-content {
    margin: 0 10px;
}

@media (min-width:900px) {
    .col-md-1 { width: 8.333333333333332%; }
    .col-md-2 { width: 16.666666666666664%; }
    .col-md-3 { width: 25%; }
...
```

The effect of these two new styles is shown in Figure 18-4, which shows the bottom of the home page.

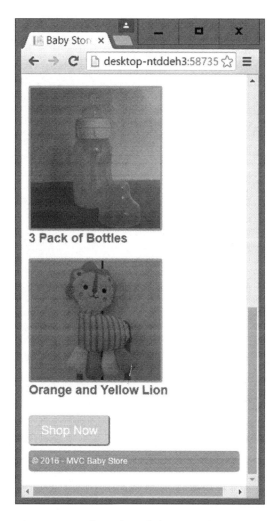

Figure 18-4. *The realigned Shop Now button and the images*

Although we have only focused on the home page, these changes have also had profound effects on the rest of the site; for example, all the forms in the site now have the labels above each input, which makes for a much better appearance on a small screen.

Styling the Navigation Bar for Mobile/Cell

We are now going to restyle the navigation bar and add a very simple example of displaying the menu when a user hovers over it so that it can be viewed easily on a mobile/cell phone. We are not going to use the bootstrap button for hiding/showing the menu, because it relies on the bootstrap JavaScript files to function.

We are going to make the navigation bar still appear blue with white text but we are also going to remove all the animations when someone views the site on a smaller device. To achieve this, simply cut and paste the styles from store.css file shown below into the min-width: 900px media query as follows:

```
@media (min-width:900px) {
    .col-md-1 { width: 8.333333333333332%; }
    ...code omitted...
    .col-md-offset-11 { margin-left: 91.66666666666666%; }

    .nav {
    float:left;
    }

    .navbar-left {
        float: left;
    }

    .nav li, .navbar-form .form-group {
        display: inline-block;
    }

    .nav li {
        padding: 5px;
    }

    .navbar-collapse {
    position: relative;
    }

    .navbar-form {
        position: absolute;
        bottom: 40px;
        left: 30%;
    }

    .navbar .form-control {
        padding: 5px;
        width: 250px;
    }

    .navbar-form button {
        padding: 5px 20px;
        font-size:1.2em;
    }

    .navbar-right{
        float: right;
    }
```

```
.nav li a{
    display: inline-block;
    background-color: rgb(14, 117, 204);
    border-radius: 2px;
    padding: 5px 10px;
    border: 1px solid rgb(14, 117, 204);
    max-width: 210px;
    -moz-box-shadow: inset 0px 1px 0px rgba(255,255,255,0.7);
    -webkit-box-shadow: inset 0px 1px 0px rgba(255,255,255,0.7);
    box-shadow: inset 0px 1px 0px rgba(255,255,255,0.7);
     -webkit-transition: ease-in .25s;
    transition: ease-in .25s;
}

.nav li a:hover {
    background-color: hotpink;
    border: 1px solid hotpink;
    transform: scale(1.1);
    text-decoration:none;
}
}
```

The navigation bar now only appears with animations when the browser is wider than 900 pixels. Figure 18-5 shows how the navigation bar appears in a smaller screen.

Figure 18-5. *The navigation bar on a smaller screen*

Showing/Hiding the Navigation Bar

We are now going to add some styles to initially hide and then show the navigation bar on smaller devices. First of all, add the Menu text to the top of the navigation bar and turn it white by updating the max-width: 899px media query as follows:

```
@media (max-width: 899px) {
    div {
        margin-bottom: 20px;
    }
```

```
.navbar-header:after{
    content: "Menu";
}

.navbar {
    color: white;
    }
}
```

This will change the navigation bar as shown in Figure 18-6.

Figure 18-6. *The navigation menu with some "Menu" text added to the beginning (zoomed in)*

Adding these styles has pushed the navbar-brand element down the screen slightly, so to correct this, add a new style to the max-width: 899px as follows:

```
@media (max-width: 899px) {
    div {
        margin-bottom: 20px;
    }

    .navbar-header:after{
        content: "Menu";
    }

    .navbar {
        color: white;
    }

    a.navbar-brand {
        bottom: 22px;
    }
}
```

After this, add a style to apply a Clearfix before the navbar-collapse element to push the rest of the menu underneath the menu text:

```
@media (max-width: 899px) {
    div {
        margin-bottom: 20px;
    }

    .navbar-header:after{
        content: "Menu";
    }

    .navbar {
        color: white;
    }

    a.navbar-brand {
        bottom: 22px;
    }

    .navbar-collapse:before {
      content: " ";
      display: table;
      clear: both;
    }
}
```

These two changes should now have formatted the navigation bar as shown in Figure 18-7.

Figure 18-7. The navigation bar with the "Menu" text and branding positioned above the navigation bar on a small screen (zoomed in)

Now, to hide the navigation bar apart from the menu text, add the following style. This also sets the size of the items in the bar to be slightly bigger:

```
@media (max-width: 899px) {
    div {
        margin-bottom: 20px;
    }

    .navbar-header:after{
        content: "Menu";
    }

    .navbar {
        color: white;
    }

    a.navbar-brand {
        bottom: 22px;
    }
```

```
.navbar-collapse:before {
  content: " ";
  display: table;
  clear: both;
}

.navbar-collapse {
    display : none;
    font-size: 1.2em;
  }
}
```

With the navbar-collapse element hidden, the navigation bar now appears as in Figure 18-8.

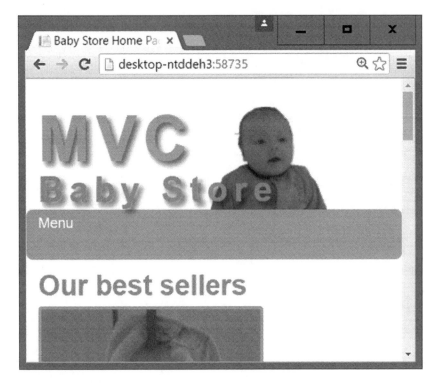

Figure 18-8. *The hidden navigation bar*

We are going to make the navigation bar display when a user hovers over the menu bar (not just the menu text). The reason I've done this is purely technical. You can only display a related element when hovering over an element. You cannot display something completely unrelated, so in this case I'm going to display the navbar-collapse element whenever the user hovers over the navbar element. This will also ensure the bar stays visible when the user hovers anywhere over it. To achieve this, add the following style to the max-width: 899px media query as follows:

```
@media (max-width: 899px) {
    div {
        margin-bottom: 20px;
    }

    .navbar-header:after{
        content: "Menu";
    }

    .navbar {
        color: white;
    }

    a.navbar-brand {
        bottom: 22px;
    }

    .navbar-collapse:before {
      content: " ";
      display: table;
      clear: both;
    }

    .navbar-collapse {
        display : none;
        font-size: 1.2em;
    }

    .navbar:hover .navbar-collapse{
        display: block;
    }
}
```

The navigation bar should now expand, as shown in Figure 18-9, whenever you hover over it.

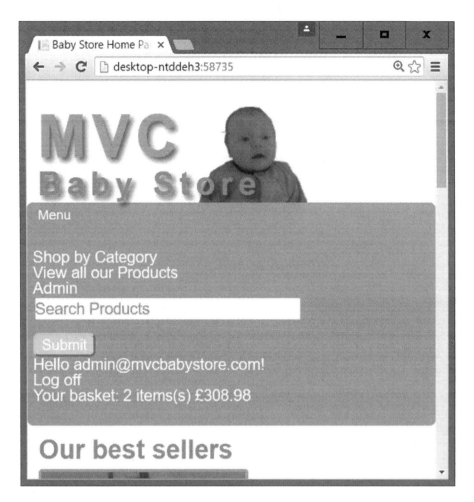

Figure 18-9. *The navigation bar as it now appears when hovered over (zoomed in)*

Selectively Adding Columns

The changes made in restyling the web site have had a big effect on the web site and most of the pages now look fine for displaying on a smaller screened device; however, some of the pages don't look right at all and still need some work.

The first page that doesn't look right is the basket index page. Figure 18-10 shows how the basket currently appears on a smaller screen.

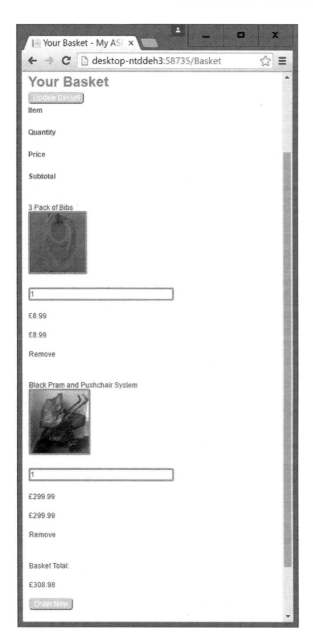

Figure 18-10. *The current basket appearance. Note that the headings are out of line with the rest of the page*

A quick inspection of the basket index page reveals that it uses HTML in the following format:

```
<div class="row">
    <div class="col-md-4"><label>Item</label></div>
    <div class="col-md-3"><label>Quantity</label></div>
    <div class="col-md-1"><label>Price</label></div>
    <div class="col-md-1"><label>Subtotal</label></div>
</div>
```

The page uses columns within rows to display data. This represents a problem because we've added a style to tell the columns only to display when the web site is greater than 900 pixels in width. To fix this, issue we've simply going to add another class to the row elements within the page and then add some styles for this class within store.css.

First of all, update the Views\Basket\Index.cshtml file as highlighted in bold to add a new class to each div with a row class assigned to it.

```
@model BabyStore.ViewModels.BasketViewModel

@{
    ViewBag.Title = "Your Basket";
}

<h2>@ViewBag.Title</h2>
@if (Model.BasketLines.Count() > 0)
{
    <div>
        @using (Html.BeginForm("UpdateBasket", "Basket"))
        {
            @Html.AntiForgeryToken();
            <input class="btn btn-sm btn-success" type="submit" value="Update Basket" />
            <hr />
            <div class="row floated-cols">
                <div class="col-md-4"><label>Item</label></div>
                <div class="col-md-3"><label>Quantity</label></div>
                <div class="col-md-1"><label>Price</label></div>
                <div class="col-md-1"><label>Subtotal</label></div>
            </div>
            <hr />
            for (int i = 0; i < Model.BasketLines.Count; i++)
            {
            <div class="row floated-cols">
                <div class="col-md-4">
                    @Html.ActionLink(Model.BasketLines[i].Product.Name, "Details",
                    "Products",
                      new { id = Model.BasketLines[i].ProductID }, null)<br />
                    @if (Model.BasketLines[i].Product.ProductImageMappings != null &&
                      Model.BasketLines[i].Product.ProductImageMappings.Any())
                    {
```

```
                <a href="@Url.Action("Details", "Products", new { id =
                  Model.BasketLines[i].ProductID })">
                    <img src="@(Url.Content(Constants.ProductThumbnailPath) +
                        Model.BasketLines[i].Product.ProductImageMappings.
                        OrderBy(pim
                        => pim.ImageNumber).ElementAt(0).ProductImage.FileName)">
                </a>
            }
        </div>
        <div class="col-md-3">
            @Html.HiddenFor(productID => Model.BasketLines[i].ProductID)
            @Html.TextBoxFor(quantity => Model.BasketLines[i].Quantity, new { @class =
              "form-control" })
            <p>
                @Html.ValidationMessageFor(quantity =>
                    Model.BasketLines[i].Quantity,"", new { @class = "text-danger" })
            </p>
        </div>
        <div class="col-md-1">
            @Html.DisplayFor(price => Model.BasketLines[i].Product.Price)
        </div>
        <div class="col-md-1">
            @((Model.BasketLines[i].Quantity *
              Model.BasketLines[i].Product.Price).ToString("c"))
        </div>
        <div class="col-md-1">
            @Html.ActionLink("Remove", "RemoveLine", "Basket", new { id =
              Model.BasketLines[i].Product.ID }, null)
        </div>
    </div>
    <hr />
    }
}
<div class="row floated-cols">
    <div class="col-md-8">
        @Html.DisplayNameFor(model => model.TotalCost)
    </div>
    <div class="col-md-1">
        @Html.DisplayFor(model => model.TotalCost)
    </div>
    <div class="col-md-1">
        @Html.ActionLink("Order Now", "Review", "Orders", null, new { @class = "btn
            btn-sm btn-success" })
    </div>
</div>
</div>
}
```

```
else
{
    <p>Your Basket is empty</p>
}
<div>
    @Html.ActionLink("Continue Shopping", "Index", "Products")
</div>

@section Scripts {
    @Scripts.Render("~/bundles/jqueryval")
}
```

Following these changes, add a new set of styles to the max-width 899 pixels media query to float any columns that appear inside the floated-cols class, as follows:

```
@media (max-width: 899px) {
    div {
        margin-bottom: 20px;
    }

    .navbar-header:after{
        content: "Menu";
    }

    .navbar {
        color: white;
    }

    a.navbar-brand {
        bottom: 22px;
    }

    .navbar-collapse:before {
      content: " ";
      display: table;
      clear: both;
    }

    .navbar-collapse {
        display : none;
        font-size: 1.2em;
    }

    .navbar:hover .navbar-collapse{
        display: block;
    }
```

```
.floated-cols .col-md-1 { width: 8.333333333333332%; }
.floated-cols .col-md-2 { width: 16.666666666666664%; }
.floated-cols .col-md-3 { width: 25%; }
.floated-cols .col-md-4 { width: 33.33333333333333%; }
.floated-cols .col-md-5 { width: 41.66666666666667%; }
.floated-cols .col-md-6 { width: 50%; }
.floated-cols .col-md-7 { width: 58.333333333333336%; }
.floated-cols .col-md-8 { width: 66.66666666666666%; }
.floated-cols .col-md-9 { width: 75%; }
.floated-cols .col-md-10 { width: 83.33333333333334%; }
.floated-cols .col-md-11 { width: 91.66666666666666%; }
.floated-cols .col-md-12 { width: 100%; }

.floated-cols .col-md-1,
.floated-cols .col-md-2,
.floated-cols .col-md-3,
.floated-cols .col-md-4,
.floated-cols .col-md-5,
.floated-cols .col-md-6,
.floated-cols .col-md-7,
.floated-cols .col-md-8,
.floated-cols .col-md-9,
.floated-cols .col-md-10,
.floated-cols .col-md-11 {
    float: left;
    padding-right: 5px;
}
}
```

The effect of these changes on the basket is shown in Figure 18-11. The columns now appear but need some work because the text is overlapping.

Figure 18-11. *The basket with columns on a small screen*

The issues with the text overlapping highlight that the some of the columns are a bit too wide and allocated too much space. Sometimes making a responsive layout is trial and error and what appears to be fine on a large screen can have issues when applied to a smaller screen. This situation is a good example. In this example, space can be taken away from the quantity column and given to the price and subtotal columns. To stop the overlapping issues, update the column widths in the Views\Basket\Index.cshtml file as follows:

```
@model BabyStore.ViewModels.BasketViewModel

@{
    ViewBag.Title = "Your Basket";
}

<h2>@ViewBag.Title</h2>
@if (Model.BasketLines.Count() > 0)
{
    <div>
        @using (Html.BeginForm("UpdateBasket", "Basket"))
        {
            @Html.AntiForgeryToken();
            <input class="btn btn-sm btn-success" type="submit" value="Update Basket" />
            <hr />
            <div class="row floated-cols">
                <div class="col-md-4"><label>Item</label></div>
                <div class="col-md-2"><label>Quantity</label></div>
                <div class="col-md-2"><label>Price</label></div>
                <div class="col-md-2"><label>Subtotal</label></div>
            </div>
            <hr />
            for (int i = 0; i < Model.BasketLines.Count; i++)
            {
            <div class="row floated-cols">
                <div class="col-md-4">
                    @Html.ActionLink(Model.BasketLines[i].Product.Name, "Details",
                    "Products",
                      new { id = Model.BasketLines[i].ProductID }, null)<br />
                    @if (Model.BasketLines[i].Product.ProductImageMappings != null &&
                      Model.BasketLines[i].Product.ProductImageMappings.Any())
                    {
                        <a href="@Url.Action("Details", "Products", new { id =
                          Model.BasketLines[i].ProductID })">
                            <img src="@(Url.Content(Constants.ProductThumbnailPath) +
                                Model.BasketLines[i].Product.ProductImageMappings.
                                OrderBy(pim
                                => pim.ImageNumber).ElementAt(0).ProductImage.FileName)">
                        </a>
                    }
                </div>
```

```
        <div class="col-md-2">
            @Html.HiddenFor(productID => Model.BasketLines[i].ProductID)
            @Html.TextBoxFor(quantity => Model.BasketLines[i].Quantity, new { @class =
                "form-control" })
            <p>
                @Html.ValidationMessageFor(quantity =>
                        Model.BasketLines[i].Quantity,"", new { @class = "text-danger" })
            </p>
        </div>
        <div class="col-md-2">
            @Html.DisplayFor(price => Model.BasketLines[i].Product.Price)
        </div>
        <div class="col-md-2">
            @((Model.BasketLines[i].Quantity *
                Model.BasketLines[i].Product.Price).ToString("c"))
        </div>
        <div class="col-md-1">
            @Html.ActionLink("Remove", "RemoveLine", "Basket", new { id =
                Model.BasketLines[i].Product.ID }, null)
        </div>
    </div>
    <hr />
    }
    }
    <div class="row floated-cols">
        <div class="col-md-6">
            @Html.DisplayNameFor(model => model.TotalCost)
        </div>
        <div class="col-md-2">
            @Html.DisplayFor(model => model.TotalCost)
        </div>
        <div class="col-md-2">
            @Html.ActionLink("Order Now", "Review", "Orders", null, new { @class = "btn
                btn-sm btn-success" })
        </div>
    </div>
</div>
}
else
{
    <p>Your Basket is empty</p>
}
<div>
    @Html.ActionLink("Continue Shopping", "Index", "Products")
</div>

@section Scripts {
    @Scripts.Render("~/bundles/jqueryval")
}
```

Figure 18-12 shows how this has now stopped the overlapping issues.

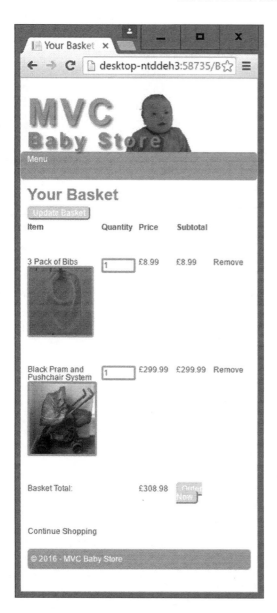

Figure 18-12. *The basket with adjusted column widths*

One issue still remains with this page. The *Order Now* button has been squashed and split in two because the text has wrapped. To fix this, update the style for a.btn and .btn to prevent text from wrapping as follows:

```
a.btn, .btn {
    border-radius: 5px;
    color: #ffffff;
    text-decoration: none;
    border: 2px outset buttonface;
    white-space: nowrap;
}
```

The *Order Now* button should now appear correctly, as shown in Figure 18-13.

Figure 18-13. *The basket with the Order Now button correctly displayed*

■ **Note** The Views\Order\Details.cshtml and Views\Orders\Review.cshtml files also have similar formatting issues. The source code for the chapter contains the updated HTML for these pages should you want to view it.

Displaying Tables on Smaller Screens

HTML tables do not display very well on smaller screens. If you try to shrink them, they become unreadable. If you leave them as they are, you end up with a wide table on a small screen, which means that the user has to scroll across the screen a lot. Figure 18-14 shows how the Products Index page currently appears on small screens. A lot of the information is off to the right side of the screen, out of view.

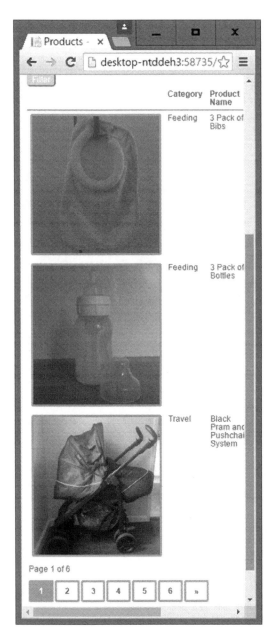

Figure 18-14. *Data displayed in a table forcing the user to scroll to the right to see it*

I am going to show you make the table appear from top to bottom rather than from side to side by using a combination of HTML data attributes and the before pseudo-selector.

A snippet of the HTML that generates the table used to display products follows. This shows how the headings are generated and how a product is listed, plus I've highlighted in bold the relevant elements we need to manipulate:

```
<table class="table">
    <tr>
        <th></th>
        <th>
            Category
        </th>
        <th>
            Product Name
        </th>
        <th>
            Description
        </th>
        <th>
            Price
        </th>
        <th></th>
    </tr>
    <tr>
        <td>
            <a href="/Products/Details/6">
                <img src="/Content/ProductImages/Bibs1.JPG">
            </a>
        </td>

        <td>
            Feeding
        </td>
        <td>
            3 Pack of Bibs
        </td>
        <td">
            Keep your baby dry when feeding
        </td>
        <td>
            &#163;8.99
        </td>
        <td>
            <a href="/Products/Edit/6">Edit</a> | <a href="/Products/Delete/6">Delete</a>
        </td>
    </tr>
```

Start by adding the following style to the `max-width` 899 pixels media query:

```
@media (max-width: 899px) {
    div {
        margin-bottom: 20px;
    }

    ...code omitted...

    td {
        width: 100%;
        display: inline-block;
        text-align:center;
    }
}
```

This has the effect of displaying each cell underneath one another rather than side to side, plus the style ensures they stretch the width of the screen and that the text appears in the center, as shown in Figure 18-15.

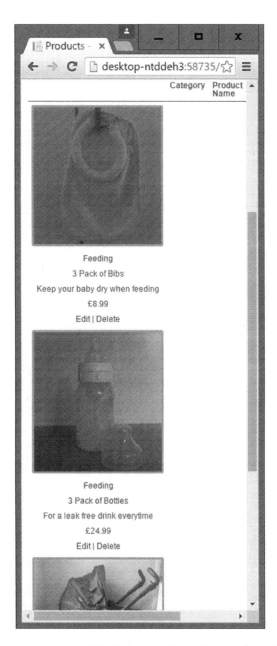

Figure 18-15. *Displaying a table's cells vertically rather than horizontally*

You can see in Figure 18-15 that this single style has had a big effect on the table. There are still some issues though. The headings are displayed at the top of the page and there are no headings associated with the data shown in the table.

Hide the headings at the top of the table add a style below the one you just added:

```
@media (max-width: 899px) {
    div {
        margin-bottom: 20px;
    }

    ...code omitted...

    td {
        width: 100%;
        display: inline-block;
        text-align:center;
    }

    th {
        display: none;
    }
}
```

Next we are going to use HTML5 data attributes to associate a table heading with the relevant table cell in each row.

■ **Note**　HTML5 introduced data attributes to allow storage of data associated with an application, where there is no other appropriate element for storing it. You can make up your own data attribute names, but they must always begin with data- and be lowercase.

To store the appropriate table heading with each table cell, update the Views\Products\Index.cshtml file as follows, with the changes highlighted in bold:

```
@model BabyStore.ViewModels.ProductIndexViewModel
@using PagedList.Mvc

@{
    ViewBag.Title = "Products";
}

<h2>@ViewBag.Title</h2>
@if (Request.IsAuthenticated && User.IsInRole("Admin"))
{
    @Html.ActionLink("Create New", "Create")
}
<p>
    @(String.IsNullOrWhiteSpace(Model.Search) ? "Showing all" : "You search for " +
        Model.Search + " found")  @Model.Products.TotalItemCount products
</p>
```

```
<p>
    @using (Html.BeginRouteForm("ProductsIndex", FormMethod.Get))
    {
        <label class="col-md-2"> Filter by category:</label>
        <div class="col-md-3">
            @Html.DropDownListFor(vm => vm.Category, Model.CatFilterItems, "All", new { @
            class
                = "form-control" })
        </div>
        <label class="col-md-2">Sort by:</label>
        <div class="col-md-3">
            @Html.DropDownListFor(vm => vm.SortBy, new SelectList(Model.Sorts, "Value",
                "Key"), "Default", new { @class = "form-control" })
        </div>
        <input type="submit" value="Filter" class="btn btn-default col-md1" />
        <input type="hidden" name="Search" id="Search" value="@Model.Search" />
    }
</p>
<table class="table">
    <tr>
        <th></th>
        <th>
            @Html.DisplayNameFor(model => model.Category)
        </th>
        <th>
            @Html.DisplayNameFor(model => model.Products.First().Name)
        </th>
        <th>
            @Html.DisplayNameFor(model => model.Products.First().Description)
        </th>
        <th>
            @Html.DisplayNameFor(model => model.Products.First().Price)
        </th>
        <th></th>
    </tr>

@foreach (var item in Model.Products) {
    <tr>
        <td>
            @if (item.ProductImageMappings != null && item.ProductImageMappings.Any())
            {
                <a href="@Url.Action("Details", new { id = item.ID})">
                    <img src="@(Url.Content(Constants.ProductImagePath) +
                        item.ProductImageMappings.OrderBy(pim =>
                        pim.ImageNumber).ElementAt(0).ProductImage.FileName)">
                </a>
            }
        </td>
```

```
    <td data-th="@Html.DisplayNameFor(model => model.Category)">
        @Html.DisplayFor(modelItem => item.Category.Name)
    </td>
    <td data-th="@Html.DisplayNameFor(model => model.Products.First().Name)">
        @Html.DisplayFor(modelItem => item.Name)
    </td>
    <td data-th="@Html.DisplayNameFor(model => model.Products.First().Description)">
        @Html.DisplayFor(modelItem => item.Description)
    </td>
    <td data-th="@Html.DisplayNameFor(model => model.Products.First().Price)">
        @Html.DisplayFor(modelItem => item.Price)
    </td>
    <td>
        @if (Request.IsAuthenticated && User.IsInRole("Admin"))
        {
            @Html.ActionLink("Edit", "Edit", new { id = item.ID })
            @Html.Raw(" | ")
            @Html.ActionLink("Delete", "Delete", new { id = item.ID })
        }
    </td>
    </tr>
}

</table>
<div>
    Page @(Model.Products.PageCount < Model.Products.PageNumber ? 0 : Model.Products.
PageNumber)
        of @Model.Products.PageCount
    @Html.PagedListPager(Model.Products, page => Url.Action("Index", new { category =
        @Model.Category, Search = @Model.Search, sortBy = @Model.SortBy, page}))
</div>
```

Now, we'll use the new data-th attributes add a style inside the max-width 899 pixels media query to display them before each td element, as follows:

```
@media (max-width: 899px) {
    div {
        margin-bottom: 20px;
    }

    ...code omitted...

    td {
        width: 100%;
        display: inline-block;
        text-align:center;
    }

    th {
        display: none;
    }
```

596

```
tbody td:before {
    content: attr(data-th);
    display: block;
    font-weight:bold;
}
}
```

This new style sets the content before a td element to the data in the data-th data attribute. Display: block ensures the content appears above each td element. Figure 18-16 shows the completed table in the Products Index page.

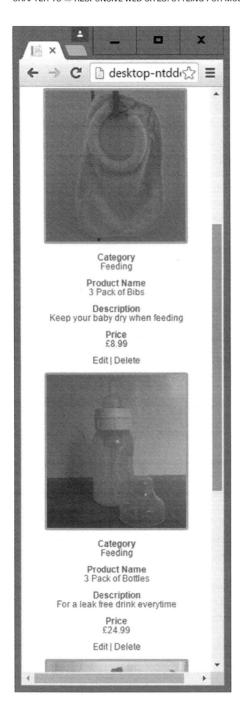

Figure 18-16. *The restyled table displayed on a smaller screen size*

■ **Note** The `Views\Order\Index.cshtml` file has similar formatting issues. The source code for the chapter contains the updated HTML for this page and some associated styles should you want to view it.

Viewing a Visual Studio Project on Another Device

So far in this book, we've always viewed the web page through a desktop browser. However, it is crucial for a commercial project that you test your site on as many physical devices as possible. There are also online simulators that can be used for testing purposes. When choosing one, always try to test it against a real device to ensure the emulator works. To allow physical device testing, it is possible to enable a site running in Visual Studio to be viewed on another device by taking a few simple steps as follows.

First of all, run a command prompt as an administrator and the run the following command `netsh http add urlacl url=http://computername:port/ user=everyone`. Replace `computername` with the name of your computer and `port` with the port number of the site. For example, I entered the `netsh http add urlacl url=http://desktop-ntddeh3:58735/ user=everyone` command.

Also run the `netsh http add urlacl url=http://localhost:port/ user=everyone` command at this point to allow the site to continue to run using `localhost`. This will ensure if you run the source code of any previous chapters, then IIS will still allow it to run. Replace `port` with the port number the site is running on.

Next open the `$(solutionDir)\.vs\config\applicationhost.config` file (this may be hidden by default) in Visual Studio and edit the `bindings` section for the port number of your project as follows:

Change this from:

```
<bindings>
    <binding protocol="http" bindingInformation="*:port:localhost" />
 </bindings>
```

To:

```
<bindings>
    <binding protocol="http" bindingInformation="*:port:computername" />
</bindings>
```

where `computername` is the name of your computer and `port` is the port number of the site. For example, I changed this setting:

```
<bindings>
    <binding protocol="http" bindingInformation="*:58735:localhost" />
 </bindings>
```

To:

```
<bindings>
    <binding protocol="http" bindingInformation="*:58735:desktop-ntddeh3" />
</bindings>
```

Next, right-click on the project in Solution Explorer in Visual Studio and view the project's properties. In the web section, update the Project Url setting so that it uses your computer name rather than `localhost`. Figure 18-17 shows the settings updated for my computer.

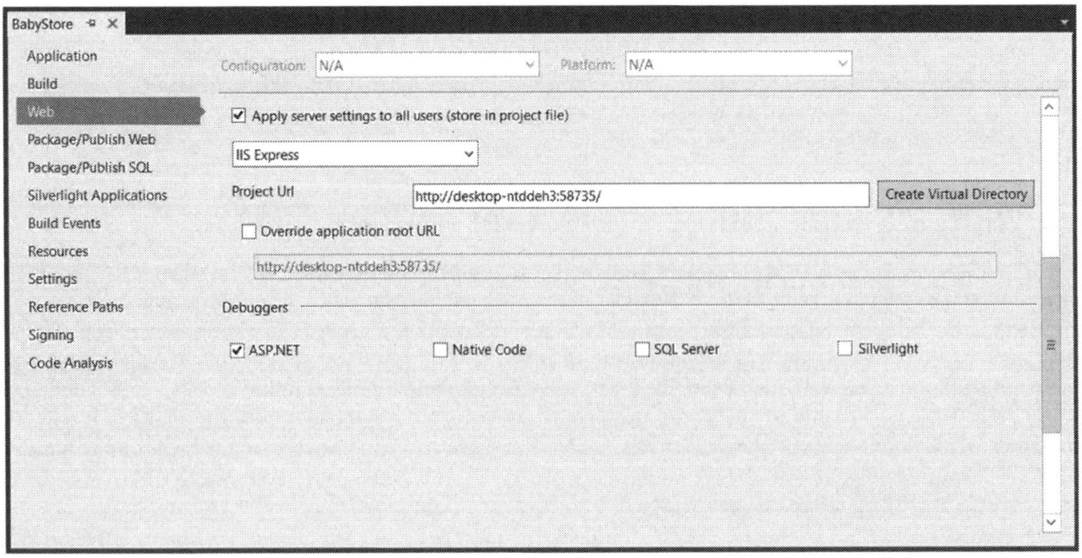

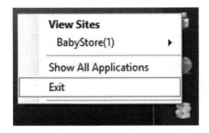

Figure 18-17. *Updating the Project Url setting*

Next, stop IIS Express if it is running by using the IIS Express Windows tray icon and choosing Exit (as shown in Figure 18-18). Alternatively, you can use Task Manager to stop IIS.

View Sites

BabyStore(1) ▶

Show All Applications

Exit

Figure 18-18. *Stopping IIS Express via the Windows tray icon*

Now start the site without debugging. It should open in your browser using your computer name in the address bar rather than localhost. Figure 18-19 shows how this local site now appears complete with an updated address.

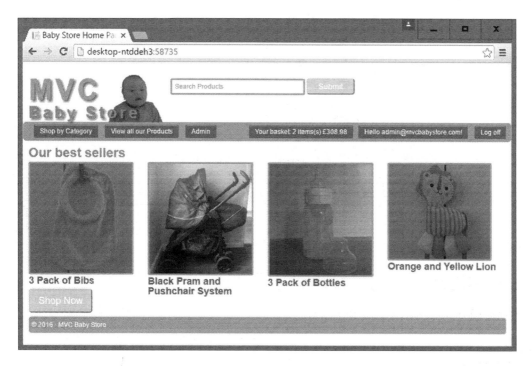

Figure 18-19. *The web site running using the computer name in the address bar*

Assuming this has worked as expected, one final step remains to allow another device to access the site. You need to add a firewall rule for incoming traffic. Open the application named *Windows Firewall with Advanced Security* and choose to add a new inbound rule for a port. To add a rule, right-click on the Inbound Rules icon and choose *New Rule* from the menu. Choose to create a rule based on Port and then choose the option TCP plus enter the Specific Local Port as the port your web site is running on. Next, choose the option *Allow the Connection* and apply the rule to your private network. Finally, give the rule a name. You should now be able to view the site from another device on your network, e.g., from a mobile/cell phone. Figure 18-20 shows the site running in Chrome on a Sony Experia Z2 phone.

Figure 18-20. *The site as viewed on a remote mobile/cell phone*

■ **Tip**   In order to get the web site to resize itself on a mobile/cell or tablet, you must include the code `<meta name="viewport" content="width=device-width, initial-scale=1.0">` in the HTML of every page.

Summary

This chapter covered how to make the site use a responsive design using CSS media queries, starting with tips on how to utilize Chrome's built-in developer support. We then moved on to restyling the home page, followed by how to add a simple hidden menu to replace the navigation bar. We also covered how to format tables for smaller devices and finished the chapter with instructions on how to view your local site on other devices. That concludes the book. I do hope it has been helpful to you and thanks for reading. If you wish to continue to enhance your knowledge of ASP.NET MVC then consider learning further topics, including unit testing and dependency injection, plus using Web API to allow web pages to be built in technologies such as knockout rather than Razor syntax and cshtml files.

Index

© Lee Naylor 2016
L. Naylor, *ASP.NET MVC with Entity Framework and CSS*, DOI 10.1007/978-1-4842-2137-2

Get the eBook for only $5!

Why limit yourself?

Now you can take the weightless companion with you wherever you go and access your content on your PC, phone, tablet, or reader.

Since you've purchased this print book, we're happy to offer you the eBook in all 3 formats for just $5.

Convenient and fully searchable, the PDF version enables you to easily find and copy code—or perform examples by quickly toggling between instructions and applications. The MOBI format is ideal for your Kindle, while the ePUB can be utilized on a variety of mobile devices.

To learn more, go to www.apress.com/companion or contact support@apress.com.

70259438R10353

Made in the USA
Middletown, DE
12 April 2018